Text and Tradition in South India

HEDGEHOG AND FOX

The fox knows many things, but the hedgehog knows one big thing

GENERAL EDITOR: RUDRANGSHU MUKHERJEE

Steven I. Wilkinson
ARMY AND NATION

Thomas R. Trautmann
ELEPHANTS AND KINGS

Partha Chatterjee, Sudipta Kaviraj, Nivedita Menon
THE INDIAN IDEOLOGY

Nayanjot Lahiri
ASHOKA IN ANCIENT INDIA

Nicholas B. Dirks
AUTOBIOGRAPHY OF AN ARCHIVE

Vasudha Dalmia
HINDU PASTS

Dipesh Chakrabarty
THE CALLING OF HISTORY

Mahesh Rangarajan
NATURE AND NATION

Bhavani Raman
DOCUMENT RAJ

Sumit Guha
BEYOND CASTE

Iqtidar Alam Khan
INDIA'S POLITY IN THE AGE OF AKBAR

Linda Hess
BODIES OF SONG

Charu Gupta
THE GENDER OF CASTE

VELCHERU NARAYANA RAO

Text and Tradition in South India

With an Introduction by

SANJAY SUBRAHMANYAM

in association with

Published by
PERMANENT BLACK
'Himalayana', Mall Road, Ranikhet Cantt,
Ranikhet 263645
perblack@gmail.com

in association with

Distributed by
ORIENT BLACKSWAN PRIVATE LTD
Bangalore Bhopal Bhubaneshwar Chandigarh Chennai
Ernakulam Guwahati Hyderabad Jaipur Kolkata
Lucknow Mumbai New Delhi Patna
www.orientblackswan.com

First paperback printing 2017
ISBN 978-81-7824-518-8

Typeset in Naurang
by Guru Typograph Technology, Crossings Republic,
Ghaziabad 201009
Printed and bound by Sapra Brothers, New Delhi 110092

for

Paruchuri Sreenivas

Stronger, even, than the bond
that comes from having the same mother
are the bonds we make
by sharing words.

Maḍiki Siṅgana, Sakala-nīti-sammatamu,
fifteenth century

Contents

Sources of First Publication

1 **Multiple Literary Cultures in Telugu: Court, Temple, and Public.** In Sheldon Pollock, ed., *Literary Cultures in History: Reconstructions from South Asia* (Berkeley: University of California Press, 2003).

2 **Notes on Political Thought in Medieval and Early Modern South India.** In *Modern Asian Studies*, 2008, pp. 1–36 (coauthored with Sanjay Subrahmanyam)

3 **Purāṇa as Brahminic Ideology**. In Wendy Doniger, ed., *Purana Perennis: Reciprocity and Transformation in Hindu and Jaina Texts* (NY: SUNNY Press, 1993).

4 **Coconut and Honey: Sanskrit and Telugu in Medieval Andhra**. In *Social Scientist*, vol. 23, no. 10/12 (Oct.–Dec., 1995), pp. 24–40

5 **Multiple Lives of a Text: The *Sumati Śatakamu* in Colonial Andhra**. In Michael Bergunder, Heiko Frese, and Ulrike Schrōder, eds, *Ritual, Caste and Religion in Colonial South India* (Halle: Verlag der Frankeschen Stiftungen, 2010).

6 **When Does Sita Cease to be Sita: Notes Toward a Cultural Grammar of Indian Narratives**. In Mandrakanta Bose, ed., *The Ramayana Revisited* (New York: Oxford University Press, 2004).

7 **A *Ramayana* of Their Own: Women's Oral Tradition in Telugu**. In Paula Richman, ed., *Many Ramayanas.*

The Diversity of a Narrative Tradition in South Asia (Berkeley: University of California Press, 1991).

8 **The Politics of Telugu Ramayanas: Colonialism, Print Culture, and Literary Movements**. In Paula Richman, ed., *Questioning Ramayanas: A South Asian Tradition* (Berkeley: University of California Press, 2001).

9 **Epics and Ideologies: Six Telugu Folk Epics**. In A.K. Ramanujan and Stuart Blackburn, eds., *Another Harmony: New Essays on the Folklore of India* (Berkeley: University of California Press, 1986).

10 **Texture and Authority: Telugu Riddles and Enigmas**. In G. Hasan-Rokem and D. Shulman, eds., *Untying the Knot: On Riddles and Other Enigmatic Modes* (New York: Oxford University Press, 1996).

11 **Buddhism in Modern Andhra: Literary Representations from Telugu**. In *The Journal of Hindu Studies*, vol. 1, 2008, pp. 93–119.

12 **The Indigenous Modernity of Gurajada Apparao and Fakir Mohan Senapati**. In Satya P. Mohanty, ed., *Colonialism, Modernity, and Literature: A View from India* (New Delhi: Orient Blackswan, 2011).

13 **Purāṇa**. In Sushil Mittal and Gene Thursby, ed., *The Hindu World* (London: Routledge, 2014).

14 **A Day in the Life of a Housewife: "Sīta Locked Out"**. Unpublished.

15 **Urmila Sleeps: A Rāmāyaṇa Song that Women in Andhra Sing**. Unpublished.

Preface and Acknowledgments

The essays in this book were written over a long period of time. The themes common to them relate to the concepts of author, text, reader, and the historicity of text cultures that have long exercised my mind. It took a while for me to see the quiet impact of colonial modernity on Indian text practices.

Concepts do not translate easily across cultures, yet give the false impression that they do. Orality and literacy, manuscript culture and print, especially the impact of print on fragile manuscripts stored in archives, and their use or misuse in creating critical editions, have been some of my concerns in these essays, most especially in Chapter 5, "Multiple Lives of a Text."

A number of essays in this book relate to the Ramayana theme. In them I discuss variations of the Ramayana narrative that emerge from the social location of the creators of the text, their gender, and their caste.

Almost all the essays relate to pre-nineteenth-century texts, except two (Chapters 11 and 12). Chapter 11 is about the literary representations of Buddhism in modern Andhra and Chapter 12 is about two modern writers, Gurajada Apparao in Telugu and Fakir Mohan Senapati in Oriya. They were contemporaries, and both were aware of the colonial impact on narratives—most significantly on economy and social formation in Andhra and Orissa.

Inevitably, there is some repetition and some overlap. The essays have in the main been reproduced straight, with the occasional editorial tweaking to eliminate errors and improve the odd phrase. Notes and

References have been updated and corrected. As much as possible, I have tried to make the system of diacritical marks consistent through the book, but at times I found the effort impossible.

Data for almost all the essays is drawn from Telugu sources. But my hope is that the ideas transcend the language and are applicable, *mutatis mutandis*, to Indian cultures generally.

This book would not have taken shape without the patience and forgiving nature of Rukun Advani. He suffered unconscionable delays on my part, at countless stages. In the course of our pleasant exchanges over the several years that it took to make this book I earned from him a valuable compliment—of being "the world's most relaxed author." I am still mulling over the precise nature of this nice euphemism.

I owe a deep debt of gratitude to Sanjay Subrahmanyam, friend and collaborator, who has written a glowing Introduction to this volume. To be bestowed with such an Introduction from a historian of his stature, one whom I have the honor of calling a friend, exceeds my wildest imagination. "Thank you" is a feeble expression of my gratitude—to both Rukun and Sanjay.

Paruchuri Sreenivas lies behind every word I have written over the past two decades. A walking bibliography, he has read the drafts of everything I wrote and constantly advised me of my shortcomings. To him I dedicate this book.

VNR

Atlanta, USA,

February 2016

VNR

Some Introductory Remarks

SANJAY SUBRAHMANYAM

> A great man once said to me
> write whatever you want to, but on the condition –
> it should be an improvement
> on the blank white page.
>
> —Nara, "White Paper"[1]

I

The intellectual history of pre-modern and modern India—and more largely modern South Asia—has so far been a sprawling but quite unsystematic enterprise, and has, moreover, been written in fits and starts. A certain sense of inertia dominates. Some figures from the nineteenth and twentieth centuries have received enormous attention and, in fact, have been the objects of such devotion that there are veritable little industries around them: here one thinks of pairings in the pantheon such as Rammohun Roy and Bankimchandra Chatterjee; or Rabindranath Tagore and Mahatma Gandhi; or Sayyid Ahmad Khan and Muhammad Iqbal; or Ramakrishna and Vivekananda; or, more recently, Sa'adat Hasan Manto and Faiz Ahmad Faiz. Attempts at moving away from the narrow study of the heroic individual's trajectory to a greater degree of generalization have often tended to cluster these figures under approximate headings such as "reformers," "cosmopolitans," "radicals," or "liberals," and again within these categories there are subdivisions to be made, rooted often on the basis of social origins and distinctions. In the category of "thinkers" or "intellectuals" one finds a distinct bias towards (male) persons with a political bent of mind, and only then to literary personages, with the odd mathematician, chemist, physicist, or historian bringing up the rear.[2] But the subject was not deemed important enough, or perhaps insufficiently researched, to deserve a volume (or more) in the twenty-three or so extant tomes of the *New Cambridge History of India* that appeared from the late 1980s on, though such questions have naturally been touched upon in the individual volumes when dealing with "socio-religious movements" or the "science and technology" of the colonial period, for example.[3] The contrast with the treatment of the history of Indian architecture, to offer one instance, is quite marked in this respect, perhaps because the latter can often content itself with merely describing and classifying.

Despite the inertia, the challenges facing the intellectual historian of India are many, some shared with other parts of the world, but others quite distinct and even truly unique to the region. The first of these is the absence of a largely shared canon of texts across the subcontinent, with some exceptions—usually the writings of the handful of authors mentioned above. A name considered virtually indispensable in Maharashtra such as Vishnushastri Chiplunkar may for all intents and purposes be unknown in Punjab; and the name and writings of Lakshminath Bezbaroa may not evoke a great deal south of the Vindhyas, or even west of Kolkata. This is in turn related to a second problem, namely that of polyglossia and heteroglossia, often embedded in a highly hierarchized environment of socio-linguistic interaction. The relationship of the regional languages to Sanskrit and Persian was already a complex and somewhat hierarchical one in the centuries preceding 1800, and in the period thereafter the particular place that English came to occupy in Indian intellectual life has rendered matters still more difficult to treat.[4] What passed for "intellectual history" in the colonial and immediate post-colonial period was thus often a more-or-less sophisticated form of reception history: that is, of how ideas first expressed in Europe passed through the medium of English into the public spheres of various Indian languages, while being modified or even sometimes contested in the process. In turn, this leads us to a third problem, namely the caesura that usually exists in studying the periods before and after roughly 1800. Either because of a simple assumption that colonial rule brought about a radical shift in the rules of the intellectual game, or because the forms of technical competence required to study the two periods are quite different, few historians venture to reflect at one and the same time on the pre-colonial as well as the colonial. This is even true when studying a transitional figure such as Rammohun Roy (*c.* 1772–1833), whose early education clearly bore marked traces of the sort of training given to the scribal class and landed elites of the later Mughal empire.[5]

As we shall see, these challenges have been addressed in some measure in the past quarter-century or so. This is in part because of the important interventions of a somewhat varied group of cultural and intellectual historians, located both in the subcontinent and outside it. Significant volumes, authored both by single individuals and by larger collectivities, have been published on the literary cultures of South Asia, and on the fraught relationship between print and manuscript cultures over the colonial period, and even increasingly on what may very broadly be termed a "history of political thought."[6] It is my contention that a major role in these changes has been played by the author of the essays collected in this volume, Velcheru Narayana Rao (usually known as VNR, or less frequently by his Telugu pen name "Nara"). However, because of his rather atypical trajectory, and his distance from the more recognizable (or stereotyped) positions and "schools," Narayana Rao's larger contribution has not been adequately recognized beyond an "insider group" of scholars, even though his contribution to the study of Telugu literature itself is broadly known to a public of enthusiasts as well as scholars.[7] In order to understand why this is the case, it may also be necessary to consider, even if briefly, the sociology of intellectual life in India, itself a subject in need of greater and deeper scholarly investment.

Two important works that appeared in 2011 sum up the state of the conventional wisdom with regard to Indian intellectual history. One by the (now late) Cambridge-based historian C.A. Bayly is entitled *Recovering Liberties* and purports in its subtitle to be a discussion of

"Indian Thought in the Age of Liberalism and Empire," running from the early nineteenth to the mid-twentieth century.[8] The other, by the prolific and versatile Indian historian of the environment, sports, and modern politics, Ramachandra Guha, is entitled *Makers of Modern India*, and is described as being "the first major anthology of Indian social and political thought." Both begin predictably enough with Rammohun Roy, whom Guha even describes as representing "the opening of the Indian mind," somewhat curiously disregarding the important interactions between Indian intellectuals and the wider world in the Mughal period and even earlier.[9] They then wend their way through a largely familiar list of names such as Gokhale, Tilak, Tagore, Jinnah, Gandhi, and Nehru, with each showing some original preferences nevertheless: Bayly for names such as M.G. Ranade, Dadabhai Naoroji, and Madan Mohan Malaviya; Guha for Tarabai Shinde, Kamaladevi Chattopadhyaya, C. Rajagopalachari, and so on. The intellectual centrality of English as the language of "thought" is naturally marked in both sets of selections, as is the centrality of political discussions, especially those having to do with nationalism and its variants.

Both Bayly and Guha would have surely agreed that others might have made up quite distinct lists of significant names while dealing with a history of "modern Indian thought." Some of these alternative lists would stem from different political preferences, though Guha does include within his purview the writings of right-wing ideologues like Golwalkar, and not merely "liberals" or those somewhat on the left of the political spectrum. Rigidly dogmatic Marxists might wonder at the relative absence of thinkers of that broad political stripe in Bayly's and Guha's conceptions. But the existence of very different genealogies of thought might also be the result of quite diverse forms of reasoning, having little to do with politics in the narrow sense. Given the long and powerful tradition of reflection on aesthetics in India, how curious it is to find the subject largely absent in these discussions of "Indian thought"! Nor do reflections on the nature of thought itself figure at all; David Shulman perspicaciously observes: "Surprisingly little has been written about the imagination in South Asia, both ancient and modern. But make no mistake: the topic is one of truly central importance to any understanding of the generative inner worlds of the subcontinent and to their development over time."[10] The time still seems far off when a sort of "history of concepts"—whether a *Begriffsgeschichte* in the Koselleckian manner or not—is attempted in South Asia.

Who then is the rightful object of intellectual history in South Asia? The celebrated phrase from the *Prison Notebooks* (Notebook 12, 1932) of Antonio Gramsci may be useful here: "All humans are intellectuals [. . .] but not all humans have the function of intellectuals in society" (*Tutti gli uomini sono intellettuali* [. . .] *ma non tutti gli uomini hanno, nella società, funzione di intellettuali*).[11] This phrase can be used to track a historical evolution, namely in the changing profile of those who have the "function of intellectuals" at different moments in the trajectory of a society. While once, in Western Europe, this function may have largely been held officially by churchmen and courtiers, the hold of these groups gradually loosened with time, and one remarks the emergence of ever newer institutional locations—universities, newspapers, publishing houses, television channels, and so on—for intellectual activity. But this implies in turn that different social histories are bound to produce different intellectual histories. If the Gramscian distinction between "traditional," "organic," and "universal" intellectuals appeared adequate in some contexts, it may be far less so in others. The possible spectrum of intellectuals may vary for a number of reasons, including the existence of significant variations in the sources of social and cultural power. Ignoring this may have rather grave consequences for analysis. Here, for example, is a sociological account of northern India, in which its intellectual history is laid out on the Procrustean bed of the received teleology of a form of modernization theory:

> [I]n ancient societies like India, along with English-speaking intellectuals there also existed [*sic*] "traditional" intellectuals who expressed themselves through the native languages. In the plains of north and central India, the role of the "traditional intelligentsia" was performed by those who wrote in Hindi or its various dialects. In the middle ages and the pre-British period of Indian history, the "traditional intelligentsia" espoused religious values, wrote devotional literature or erotic poetry, and provided entertaining works for the aristocracy and the masses. During the period of British rule in India,

> and with the development of Hindi prose, this group gradually acquired the attributes of a modern and secular intelligentsia. When India was seeking its independence, these intellectuals became one of the most important links between the English-speaking, westernized elite and the common man. This linkage was further strengthened with the rise of the Hindi press and the establishment of the mass media.[12]

At the same time, the process of "secularization" of the "traditional intellectual" is shown as accompanied by a considerable number of stresses and strains. Thus, "a majority of Hindi intellectuals come from traditional sectors of Indian society with lower economic status and predominantly rural origins. They appear to have developed an ambivalent attitude towards English-speaking intellectuals, criticizing their status within society . . ." This account, written in the late 1970s, already shows some greater sense of empirical nuance than that on display in the American sociologist Edward Shils' two-part essay from 1959, entitled "The Culture of the Indian Intellectual."[13] Shils, who lived for a period in India in the mid-1950s as part of a Chicago project on "tradition and modernity" defined by Robert Redfield, describes the Indian intellectuals whom he encounters as generally shallow, frequently wallowing in self-pity, with one of them quoting Wordsworth even while dressed like "a swami in saffron robes." This is a view that anticipates the tone and content of later critiques of Indian intellectual life by V.S. Naipaul and is constructed with much the same level of empirical rigor. The somewhat hollow thunder of Shils' own conclusion, written from the Olympian heights of Chicago's Hyde Park, is worth evoking at some length.

> The problems of the Indian intellectual will find their solution, to the extent that any problems are ever solved, by the emergence of traditions and institutions which foster individuality and creativity. If the Indian intellectual can come into a situation in which he perceives real tasks, then he will draw on whatever resources are within himself and his cultures, traditional and modern, to solve them. Then the synthesis, so much yearned for, will come forth.[14]

Shils' approbation was extended only to a relatively small handful of Indian intellectuals and writers, such as R.K. Narayan (with whom he apparently enjoyed fairly close relations), the Bengali modernist poet Sudhindranath Dutta (1901–60), and the novelist Attia Hosain (1913–98). Eventually, his approving gaze also embraced the young A.K. Ramanujan when he joined the faculty of Chicago in 1962. Since Ramanujan is often regarded as a paradigmatic figure, mediating between the literatures and cultures of South Asia and the Western academy, it may be worthwhile to present a brief consideration of his career and its significance here.[15] Though he received a PhD in Linguistics from Indiana University in 1963 for a dissertation entitled "A Generative Grammar of Kannada," he never really pursued the Chomskian line indicated there. Rather, he emerged by the late 1960s as a multilingual poet, an essayist, and a major translator into Kannada, but above all from Kannada and Tamil into English. The works he translated ranged from Tamil Sangam materials (as in the acclaimed work *The Interior Landscape* [1967]), to medieval Tamil and Kannada *bhakti* poems by Nammalvar and Basavanna, to modern works such as U.R. Anantha Murthy's Kannada novel *Samskāra* (1965/1976). In so doing, Ramanujan, we may say, far exceeded the role that had been assigned to him in the American academy of the 1960s, in which the dominant figures who were meant to speak for South Asia were either transplanted European Indologists or American anthropologists (and a few historians). It may also well be said that in the quarter-century between the publication of his first major translation from Tamil and his untimely death in 1993, his was the most powerful humanistic voice that spoke for and about South Asia in the United States.

Besides classical, medieval, and modern literature, Ramanujan had a considerable interest in the study of "folklore" and, more particularly, folk tales, which he analyzed using a mix of structural, formal, and psychoanalytical perspectives. His conception of a theoretical framework was eclectic and usually deployed with a light hand. He does not seem to have been much concerned with social context or even questions of performance in relation to his folk materials; equally, his ventures into literary translation are not marked by any great tendency to historicize. The effectiveness of his work, especially as a translator both of texts and cultures, lay therefore in his literary talents as a poet and prose craftsman of considerable attainment. As the linguist S.N. Sridhar wrote not long after his death: "Ramanujan's was poetry of subtlety and suggestion, not assertion, reflecting the author's own gentle nature. The simplicity was a product of self-discipline, an exquisitely refined sense of *aucitya* (propriety), a classical elegance delicately balanced between prose and poetry."[16] In a somewhat similar vein, David Shulman noted that Ramanujan's "translations—minimalist and musical—inevitably illumine the original with flashes of insight, the gift of a poet translating from his native language into a second language that has become paradoxically more than native, a consciously chosen second home."[17] It is therefore logical for his legacy to have remained strongest in the area of translation within Indian studies, more so than in the shape of particular analytical insights that have endured. Also, as translator, Ramanujan remains inseparable from the poet. The bilingual poet Arun Kolatkar has evoked this curious paradox, in a somewhat irreverent vein.

Will the real Ramanujan please stand up
There are several of them as you know

A.K. Ramanujan is a legion rather than an individual

There is a multitude of Ramanujans
the poet of course, the translator, the folklorist

There are any number of A.K. Ramanujans
I am personally acquainted/familiar with at least three of them
And love 'em all

I don't claim to know all of them

I wonder whether the Real Ramanujan expresses himself
Through his translations (rather than through his poems)

Ramanujan and his doubles.[18]

In reality, of course, there was only one Ramanujan, and his was scarcely a "formula" that could be replicated—as the two decades since his death have shown. Rather, let us now turn to an alternative trajectory from India, a complementary one in some ways perhaps, but no less singular in many respects.

II

The essays and reflections collected in *Text and Tradition in South India* bring together many—but by no means all—of the diverse contributions made by Velcheru Narayana Rao to the rewriting of India's cultural and literary history. However wide-ranging the contributions may be, they are still deeply rooted, to begin with, in a specific linguistic context, albeit a very ample one. As VNR himself wrote in 2003, not without a slight sense of irritation: "Every time I have written anything about Telugu for a non-Telugu audience, I have begun by saying that Telugu is the second most widely spoken language in India, spoken by about seventy million people in the southern state of Andhra Pradesh."[19] In early 1932, at the time he was (unofficially) born in the town of Pithapuram in coastal Andhra, the Telugu-speaking areas were divided between British-ruled Madras Presidency, and the interior Hyderabad state of the Nizam. Had he been born in the latter area, VNR might have received a quite different education. As it happened, he was born into a family of Golconda Vyaparis, this being a subcaste of the Niyogi Brahmins, to which the celebrated seventeenth-century Qutb Shahi ministers Akkanna and Madanna also allegedly belonged. His early life, however, was very much a coastal one, being largely spent in the village of Ambakhandi in the Srikakulam area, in the proximity of the Indian Ocean. Here VNR remained until the age of eleven under the tutelage of his father, Velcheru Buccinarasinga Rao, who trained him amongst other things to recite classical texts as a *paurānika*. It was both in this familial space, and in the village at large, that he acquired an early taste for poetry, as well as for songs, stories, and proverbs. But these were also difficult and uncertain years, on account of his mother's long illnesses and the family's circumstances, all of which are somewhat reflected in VNR's childhood nickname, "Pullayya," the sort of name given to vulnerable children to ward off the evil eye.

At the age of eleven VNR was sent off on a train to the town of Eluru in the recently formed West Godavari District, to enroll in high school, where he eventually completed his SSLC (Secondary School Leaving Certificate). He was the first in his rather indigent family to do so, essentially because of the largesse of an aunt, a type of arrangement which resonates with much I have heard from my own father's modest family in Tamilnadu. It is difficult today to imagine the intellectual ferment that was to be found in those years in Eluru, a town whose population barely exceeded thirty thousand at the turn of the twentieth century. But Eluru had had a rich and important past and could evoke not merely the nearby ruins of Vengi (where the eastern Chalukyas had once ruled)—there was also the time of the Golconda Sultanate, when a significant Persian community had settled here, helping to create an important center for carpet-making. In the early nineteenth century the celebrated Kavali brothers—who worked with Colin Mackenzie and the Survey of India—emerged from the town and mediated between the polyglot Indian world of the time and the newly formed colonial dispensation.[20] In the 1940s and 1950s Eluru was of far greater significance than its size and demography would suggest. Besides Eluru High School, it counted the Sir C. Ramalinga Reddy College, founded in 1945, where VNR completed first his Intermediate and then his BA (the latter in Politics and Economics, in 1954). A younger contemporary here was the Sanskritist and historian of science Sreeramula Rajeswara Sarma, who finished his BA from the same college in 1957. When they were in Eluru, the two won an elocution competition together, and the college rented a horse-drawn carriage to take them through the town in celebration. Sarma went on to study at Santiniketan and Marburg, in a classic institutional trajectory, before spending most of his career in the great center of medieval history at Aligarh.

VNR on the other hand remained far more rooted, we might say. As David Shulman has remarked, it is impossible to understand his intellectual trajectory without placing great significance on his Eluru years, which went on for almost a quarter-century from 1943 to the end of the 1960s, with only a few interruptions. This was a period of multiple immersions in several distinct and seemingly contradictory traditions. To understand these I will draw liberally here on the introductory text that Shulman wrote some two decades ago to a *festschrift* for VNR, but also on a special number of the online journal *Īmāta* (www.eemaata.com) from 2013, with a number of striking contributions from his friends and disciples.[21] It was in these years that VNR came to acquire the mastery over what can be termed the "classical" Telugu tradition, which remains one of his fundamental resources. This was the tradition which started with the eleventh-century figure of Nannaya, who began rendering the *Mahābhārata* into Telugu; he was followed by Tikkana in the thirteenth century, and Ĕrrana in the fourteenth. In the early sixteenth century, Allasani Pĕddana in his *Manucaritramu* would recognize this succession as a solid tradition.

> Nannaya made Vyāsa's Mahābhārata, as good as the Veda, into Telugu.
> He's praised for this all over the world.
> I think of him along with Tikkana,
> Who performed a sacrifice, and Ĕrrana, Śiva's servant.[22]

There were also the poets of the fifteenth century, a highly contested period politically, but where political fragmentation and the existence of a variety of court centers did not really impede cultural efflorescence. These were men such as Śrīnātha, Dhūrjaṭi, and Annamācārya, each of whom would be examined and substantively reinterpreted in great detail by VNR later in his career (often in collaborative work with David Shulman). This would lead in turn to the great sixteenth-century moment associated with Kṛṣṇadevarāya (r. 1509–29) at Vijayanagara, with poets such as Pĕddana (mentioned above), and the ruler himself, author of major works like the *Āmuktamālyada*. Though Vijayanagara's power waned in the late sixteenth century, its literary output continued to flourish—in the works of Piṅgaḷi Sūranna, and later Kṣetrayya and Sāraṅgapāṇi, as well as more generally in the tradition of *padam* songs which were meant to accompany stage performance. These are complex works, sometimes highly erotic in their charge, and often playfully referencing a world of commerce and political transaction where God himself (often Viṣṇu) is presented not only as a powerful entity but as a supplicant, even a "customer."

By the 1940s and 1950s, however, these works presented a problem, largely on account of the influence of two powerful figures, with both of whom VNR did not see eye to eye in their role as literary critics.[23] One was the important social reformer Kandukuri Viresalingam

(1848–1919), a prolific writer, journalist, and novelist also known for his investment in ideas of "reform" with regard to the status of women. The second, ironically enough, was Sir Cattamanchi Ramalinga Reddy (1880–1951), not only the founder of Andhra University but the man whose name VNR's own college was eventually to bear. Both men had cult followings within their lifetimes, and thereafter, and used them to shape the tastes and opinions of the reading public. Both broadly accepted the narrative according to which British rule was accompanied by a civilizing mission; as a recent analyst puts the matter, "English rule was a just and benevolent rule in Viresalingam's estimation. There were, of course, faults with that rule, just as with any other, and one had to work towards removing those faults." His lead was then followed by C.R. Reddy, who considered Viresalingam the "greatest Andhra of modern times," this greatness being such that he "towered above the distinction of Brahmin and non-Brahmin."[24]

The principal difficulty was that Viresalingam and Reddy had swallowed hook, line, and sinker what VNR has termed the "colonial high morality of the nineteenth and early twentieth century." They found many classical works immoral and therefore "unfit to read," producing as a consequence bowdlerized versions in order to protect the reading public. As VNR notes: "Reddy, in his *Kavitva-tattva-vicāramu*, went on to condemn some two hundred years of Telugu literature as decadent for its erotic themes [. . .] Backed by important officials in the colonial economy of education, both Viresalingam's and Reddy's views on literature held immense disciplinary power over literati of the colonial towns and cities."[25] This was certainly the case in Eluru, but the advantage was that theirs were not the only voices or influences heard in that particular context. The Bommakanti brothers, who were later to move to Chennai to work in the publishing business, held a sort of literary salon, welcoming great poets such as Visvanatha Satyanarayana (on whom more below). Other great scholars in the area were working on producing interesting works on the Telugu literary tradition, as well as commentaries on great texts like the *Manucaritramu*. Had Edward Shils visited Eluru, would he have even recognized these men as intellectuals? He would at any rate have found it difficult to miss the town's Marxist bookshop and its circle, including friends (like Suryanarayana Raju) through whom the writings of Sartre, Camus, Hemingway, James Baldwin, and others were brought into VNR's intellectual life.[26] These entered VNR's mental terrain not as writings requiring simple imitation or diffusion, but by creating a ferment that Shulman has termed "intoxicating, and unique to that place and moment."

Here then is the difficulty with our received sociological models of intellectual life in modern India, constrained as they are by the straitjacket of "trickle-down" knowledge transmission. These models are undecided as to whether they are meant to be merely descriptive, or normative and prescriptive. Certainly the seven decades since Indian independence have seen them increasingly playing the latter role, based on the largely unsaid assumption that a clear spatial hierarchy of educational institutions must exist in the national space. Knowledge here moves from center to periphery, while ambitious individuals would work their way up like fish swimming upstream from periphery to center. In turn, knowledge is assumed to be a substance that can be treated as homogeneous and indexable. It is meant to bear no traces of its origins and can pass smoothly from one place to another. Whether such a model can work for the natural sciences, or for the social sciences, is already debatable.[27] It is certainly fatally flawed when it comes to the humanities, especially in a country of the diversity of India, where one cannot conceive (as one might in some parts of the world) of a standard "liberal arts" curriculum that could move without friction from Santiniketan to Jamnagar, and take in Udipi and Eluru as well. This is a key insight that VNR's trajectory offers us: namely, the importance of rootedness in local and regional traditions for certain types of humanistic knowledge.

VNR himself proposes an interesting historical perspective on the matter. Despite the powerful top-down drives of Viresalingam, C.R. Reddy, and others, he sees a far more diverse intellectual landscape in late-colonial Andhra than many others have proposed for other parts of India. Three figures can be taken as representative in this respect. The first of these was Chellapilla Venkata Sastri (1870–1950), a Brahmin scholar of Telugu and Sanskrit, who became a popular performer and public reciter together with his companion Tirupati Sastri. Despite acquiring considerable fame through his compositions in a classicizing style, Venkata Sastri eventually became somewhat embittered on account of facing a cultural and institutional playing field tilted against him. One of his poems thus runs:

> They now read proofs at printing shops
> just to stay alive,
> or teach Telugu to white Huns,
> expound religion in the houses
> of those grocers who give them credit.
> Phenomenal scholars have been humbled.
> Times have changed.[28]

The second, whom VNR describes as possessing a "tricky nature," is Gurajada Apparao (1862–1915), whose play, *Kanyāśulkam*, VNR has translated with an important commentary. Apparao's characteristic device both in this play and in many of his poems is polyphony, so that "the surface meaning is quietly subverted by the silences of the poem or by oblique counterstatements." While accepting the growing reality of Western influence on Indian society, it appears that Apparao had his own notions of the proper direction of both social and literary change. In this regard Apparao, VNR suggests, believed "that the social reformist ideas that were being promoted by Viresalingam were shallow and misguided and would not really bring about a desirable difference in the life of the people." Perhaps the writer's somewhat ex-centric location in the princely state of Vizianagaram in northern Andhra had some relationship to his political, social, and literary positioning.

The third figure, perhaps the most controversial, is Visvanatha Satyanarayana (1895–1976), the only one in the trio with whom VNR had a personal relationship. A disciple of Chellapilla Venkata Sastri, Satyanarayana nevertheless developed a highly distinct style, which VNR has described as defying classification, and embodying "new sensibilities [that] make it difficult for anyone other than a modernist to appreciate . . ." Satyanarayana, in fact, presents two difficulties: first, his difficult and arcane style, which many have found impenetrable; and second, his social attitudes and extreme defence of Brahmanic ideology, which obviously did (and do) not resonate well with many readers. We learn from VNR that the tendency in Eluru (as elsewhere) was to draw a bald contrast between Satyanarayana, on the one hand, and the younger figure of the Marxisant poet Sri Sri (1910–83) on the other. One appeared wholly rooted in the past, and the other had seemingly turned his back on it. VNR writes: "Rarely did one poet talk to the other, and critics on each side convinced their readers that what the other group was reading was rubbish." Or, more poignantly: "It is almost as if they lived in two different countries, one alien to the other, and you needed a visa to cross the border."[29]

This is a familiar battle, it would seem, played out time and again in various regions of India, and can be seen as the barren conflict between "nativists" and "internationalists." It was certainly more interesting than many of the same genre, in the sense that it did not stifle or dampen the creativity of either "party." Still, the question was surely present of which side to choose in this quarrel. Like most intellectuals of his generation and milieu, VNR was heavily influenced by Marxism, a worldview that has left traces on his thinking and manner of formulating problems to the present day. Yet, he chose *not* to choose. Instead, he decided on a quite different strategy, namely to historicize. Such a perspective allowed him to see the literary strengths of both sides in the argument, as well as to build on them.

But this solution only came after a certain lapse of time. After a year in Chennai in the mid-1950s, working on the *Telugu Encyclopaedia* being compiled there, VNR returned to take up a position as a Telugu tutor in his college in Eluru, spent his spare time translating authors as diverse as Bertrand Russell and Thomas Jefferson into Telugu, and began publishing both poetry and short stories (an important collection of which appeared in 1965). Then, having passed through the near-obligatory rite of passage for the period of the study of structural linguistics—a trajectory not dissimilar to the one taken by Ramanujan—he began a dissertation at Andhra University under the formal supervision of Tumati Donappa, with a vast overarching and synthetic account of Telugu literary history, eventually entitled *Telugulo Kavitā Viplavāla Svarūpam* (The Structure of Literary Revolutions in Telugu; completed 1975, published 1978). In

Shulman's considered view, this is "arguably the most original book on any topic in Indian literary history, in any language, published in this generation," with a brilliant account of the long transition from *purāna* to *prabandha*, and thence to "the formation of modern literary forms in the nineteenth and early twentieth centuries."[30] The title's genuflection in the direction of Thomas Kuhn is no coincidence, as he and Roman Jakobson certainly were key influences of the moment. Though it went into a second edition in 1988, and a third revised edition in 2009, the book has never been translated.

By the time of the book's completion, VNR had begun the second phase of his career, an American one. The measure of this latter period is far more easily taken than of the earlier decades, because its public output is so visible both in terms of VNR's writings and that of other literary scholars and historians who have worked directly or indirectly under his guidance. In this phase, largely spent in the University of Wisconsin-Madison (where he first arrived in 1971), and then more recently in Emory University, it could be argued that the seeds sown in the first half of his career are being harvested with an astonishing and continuing level of productivity, the output having been sustained into VNR's ninth decade. Here is how the impact of his presence in the US was felt by one of his early students at Madison, Phillip Wagoner.

> Narayana Rao showed little interest in staying secluded in his office, working away in solitude like most of his colleagues. Instead, it seemed that he preferred to prowl the halls, always searching for the delight of conversation. Often, he would appear at the doorway of the graduate student lounge, eagerly joining in on whatever casual conversation was underway, and within minutes, the conversation would become both more serious and more excited in response to some provocative statement he would make, such as: "Authors don't 'write' texts; it's the text that 'writes' the author." It was in these impromptu conversations that I gained some of my most important and memorable insights in those days, and quite frankly, I suspect this may have been as true for Narayana Rao as it was for his graduate student interlocutors.[31]

Wagoner is equally right to stress that one of VNR's preferred modes in the second half of his career has been collaboration, notable in a highly fecund partnership with David Shulman, but also with others such as Ramanujan and myself. The works that have appeared in these years can be divided for purposes of convenience into several distinct categories (excluding some ventures into Sanskrit).

- Commented translations of texts from classical Telugu, beginning with *For the Lord of the Animals* (1987), and *Śiva's Warriors* (1990), with the most recent offering in the extended series being *The Story of Manu* (2015).
- Anthologies such as *Classical Telugu Poetry* (2002), and *Hibiscus on the Lake* (2003), usually with extensive Afterwords that serve to provide a historical context for the translated corpus.
- Commented translations of modern Telugu texts, such as Apparao's *Kanyāśulkam* (2007), and Chaso's *A Doll's Wedding and Other Stories* (2012).
- Interpretative works of cultural history, such as *Symbols of Substance* (1992), and *Textures of Time* (2001), as well as the monograph with David Shulman on *Śrīnātha* (2012).
- Various essays, singly or jointly authored, of which a selection appears in this volume.

The obvious point to be made is of the close and intricate link between the work of translation and that of interpretation, largely in a historicizing framework, of the literary materials. To command nearly a thousand years of a literary tradition is no small feat, but more important still is VNR's ability constantly to offer fresh readings and provocative frameworks for interpretation. Let us now turn, if only briefly, to what is possibly the small missing piece of the puzzle, which may help us understand how this whole body of work has been constructed.

III

My own first exposure to VNR as a scholar came through reading what I now realize was a rather uncharacteristic essay entitled "Banditry in Mughal India: Historical and Folk Perspectives."[32] Written jointly with the Mughal historian John F. Richards (also at that time in Madison), the article is made up of two quite discrete units, where the contributions of the two co-authors can be clearly seen; years later, Richards was to tell me that their communication was quite limited during the collaboration. Richards discusses the Mughal (and to some extent other contemporary) records for the career of a certain Pap Rai, who is portrayed as a troublesome element in the Deccan at the time of the Mughal conquest in the last decades of the seventeenth century. VNR then points to the sizeable collection of oral and "folk" materials concerning the same figure, known as Sarvayi Papadu; Papadu is shown to have both heroic and transgressive aspects, linked to the types of narratives in which he is celebrated as well as the groups that identify with him. The broad approach still owes much to the structural understanding of folk materials, while also taking elements from the well-known sociological model of Sanskritization.

A crucial aspect that must be mentioned is VNR's interest, visible already in this analysis, in the interplay between orally recorded and older written versions of the folk-epic, some of which date back to the nineteenth century. This is because of a long-standing preoccupation concerning what he usually terms the distinction between the "recorded" and the "received" versions of texts. Though a good part of his work actually concerns written texts, VNR is unusual for a scholar of the textual tradition in the extent of his interest in and devotion to orality. Many professional Indologists in fact have a hearty distaste for the oral sphere, perhaps because their own received models came from the study of what were thought of as "dead" languages (such as classical Greek), which by virtue of being dead afforded greater fixity and stability.[33] In turn, this is linked to VNR's constant desire to place texts in social contexts, which has over time become his main mode of argumentation. Here is how this line of thinking has been absorbed by a younger scholar influenced by VNR, a well-known specialist of Sri Lanka and Sinhala, Charles Hallisey.

> Narayana Rao's oral teaching in seminar rooms, in dining rooms, and in so many other places enriches his published scholarship in a way that is perhaps analogous to what he has said about the difference between a recorded text and a received text and the manner in which the received text adds to the richness of the recorded text: "What is recorded . . . on paper is not the entire text, it is only a part of it. It acquires its fullness

in performance."[34] Attending to the "received text" of Narayana Rao's scholarship will help us to take the measure better of the fullness of his contribution to scholarship about South Asia. Attending to the "received text" of his scholarship also helps us to appreciate better that what he has given us in his scholarship is not only to be discerned in terms of the evidence that he has made available to us, and his interpretations and analysis of that evidence, but also in the profound ways that he has helped us to appreciate the importance of reflecting on what we emphasize in our scholarship.[35]

Here is how VNR himself has set out the distinction between "recorded" and "received" text, drawing very clearly on his own experiences, but developing the necessary inferences:

> What is recorded on palm leaf, and later on paper, is not the entire text, it is only a part of it. It acquires its fullness in performance, at which time it is appropriately recreated by the *paurānika*, who is trained in reading the *Purāṇas* and interpreting them. His knowledge, which was not written down, would be crucial in determining the received text. The recorded *Purāṇa* text tells only part of the story. When the *paurānikas* who knew the received text disappeared, scholars were left with only the recorded text, which has become our sole text. Simply reading the recorded text in a linear order, without the training in performing it, scholars found a number of irresolvable contradictions and discontinuities, not to mention a plethora of scribal errors. But if the early scholars had actually studied the *Purāṇa* in performance and learned how the trained performer constructed and presented a *Purāṇa* in each performance, we would have an entirely different kind of *Purāṇa* scholarship today. Instead of suspecting the *panditas*, the agents of transmission of this tradition from generation to generation, if the early scholars had striven to understand the nature of this text culture, a whole different way of asking questions would have emerged.[36]

A fuller measure of this approach may be found in his work not on the *purāṇa* tradition, but on the Telugu folk-epic, which included a year of field research on performances of the *Kāṭamarāju kathā* in 1986. Included in this collection is his important essay entitled "Epics and Ideologies" (from that same year), in which he describes and contrasts six Telugu epics with quite different social moorings. The *Kāṭamarāju* epic, for example, is identified above all with the Gŏllas or Yadavas, a cattle-herding caste, and is shown by him to be a martial epic, rather like the well-known *Palnāṭi Vīrula Kathā*. These may be contrasted with other "sacrificial epics," where the central protagonists are women. But of particular importance for VNR's understanding is his deployment of the distinction between "right" and "left" hand castes, the former heavily invested in land and its control, and the latter more mobile people, whether pastoralists or traders. Concluding his essay, he insists once more that "the socioeconomic features of the community have influenced the nature of heroism, as well as the ideological process which the story has undergone."

It seems to me therefore that two elements combine to give VNR's body of work its particular strength and flavor. One is its longitudinal nature, that is the capacity to track the *longue durée* of a regional tradition in a way in which few others have done. This is the pandit's knowledge, bolstered moreover by his solid foundation in Sanskrit—in which he very much continues the tradition of Venkata Sastri and Satyanarayana. Rather than treating Sanskrit and the vernacular as opposed and warring traditions, as many have been ideologically predisposed to do in recent decades, he treats them—in his own evocative phrase—as akin to "coconut and honey." But the second is no less important, namely VNR's capacity to cut across latitudes, or the social spectrum of texts, and move fluidly between the world of orality and the script-bound. I would venture to suggest that this sensibility comes at least in part from the radicalism of the milieu in which he grew up, including its strong Marxist-style understanding of how literary traditions were formed and reformed. That attachment to orality can be seen equally in his devotion to the aphoristic form of expression, as any of his collaborators or students will be able to testify.

So I will conclude by citing a brief aphoristic text that he presented to a conference of Indologists in 1997, somewhat to their bemusement, it must be added.

> For two hundred years, we have been practicing a way of asking texts to give us something we can make sense of. This practice has created a sustained and solid text culture in which the text, as it appears on palm-leaf or beech-bark, and the scholars who work with it, are the only participants. We know texts deteriorate in time. Text, in its first appearance, was pure, free from

> blemish. Time has wrought [work] on it and we took as our most civilizing task to restore it to its original purity, as best we can. The project of critical editions has given us an enormous body of well-edited, carefully restored texts in practically all disciplines of learning. This is the Indological text.

But VNR then goes on to add that it is time to reflect on "a different kind of methodology of text reconstruction." Here are the reasons why.

> Texts have communities which use them, which have an active role in making and remaking them. Changes in texts are produced not only by scribal errors, which do occur and should be corrected, but more significantly, by community participation in using the text. If the community which uses the text is tight, unchanging and coherent, the text remains tight, unchanging and coherent. [. . .] However, when the communities which use the text are distributed over a wider area, are complex, and practice more than one kind of text culture, the text changes to suit the need of the community which uses it.
>
> Texts not only have histories, they have cultures and communities. Texts not only have births, they have *samskāra*, families, deaths and rebirths. Texts are not only isolated artefacts, they are members of societies. They also reflect and reproduce the practices of the society they belong to.[37]

Key Bibliographic Elements

- *Telugulo Kavitā Viplavāla Svarūpam* (The Structure of Literary Revolutions in Telugu), Vijayawada: Visalaandhra Publishing House, 1978; 2nd edition, Hyderabad Book Trust, 1988; 3rd revised edition, Tana Publications, 2009.
- *For the Lord of the Animals: Poems from the Telugu Kālahastīśvara Śatakamu of Dhūrjati*, with Hank Heifetz, Berkeley: University of California Press, 1987.
- *Śiva's Warriors: Basava Purāna of Pālkuriki Somanātha*, with Gene H. Roghair, Princeton: Princeton University Press, 1990.
- *Symbols of Substance: Court and State in Nayaka-Period Tamilnadu*, with David Shulman and Sanjay Subrahmanyam, Delhi: Oxford University Press, 1992.
- *When God is a Customer: Telugu Courtesan Songs by Ksetrayya and Others,* with A.K. Ramanujan and David Shulman, Berkeley: University of California Press, 1994.

- *A Poem at the Right Moment: Remembered Verses from Premodern South India*, with David Shulman, Berkeley: University of California Press, 1998.
- *Classical Telugu Poetry: An Anthology*, with David Shulman, Berkeley: University of California Press, Berkeley, 2002.
- *Twentieth Century Telugu Poetry: An Anthology*, Delhi: Oxford University Press, 2001; US edition: *Hibiscus on the Lake*, Madison: University of Wisconsin Press, 2003.
- *A Lover's Guide to Warrangal: Vallabharāya's Kridābhirāmamu*, with David Shulman and Phillip Wagoner, New Delhi: Permanent Black. 2002.
- *Textures of Time: Writing History in South India, 1500–1800*, with David Shulman and Sanjay Subrahmanyam, New Delhi: Permanent Black, 2001.
- *The Sound of the Kiss, or the Story that Must Never be Told* (translation of the *Kaḷāpūrṇodayamu* of Pingali Suranna), with David Shulman, New York: Columbia University Press, 2003.
- *God on the Hill: Temple Songs from Tirupati* (a selection of sixteenth-century Telugu poems by Annamacarya), with David Shulman, New York: Oxford University Press, 2005.
- *The Demon's Daughter: A Love Story* (translation of the *Prabhāvati-pradyumnamu* by Pingali Suranna), with David Shulman, New York: State University of New York Press, 2006.
- *Girls for Sale: Kanyāśulkam. A Play from Colonial India* (translation of the Telugu play by Gurajada Apparao), Bloomington: Indiana University Press, 2007; Indian edition, Penguin, 2011.
- *How Urvashi was Won* (translation of Kalidasa's *Vikramorvaśīya),* with David Shulman, New York: New York University Press, 2009; Clay Sanskrit Library.
- *A Doll's Wedding and Other Stories* (translation of short stories by Chaso), with David Shulman, New Delhi: Penguin India, 2012.
- *Śrīnātha: The Poet Who Made Gods and Kings*, with David Shulman, New York: Oxford University Press, 2012.
- *The Story of Manu* (translation of the *Manucaritramu* by Allasani Pĕddana), with David Shulman, Cambridge, Mass.: Harvard University Press, 2015; Murty Classical Library of India.

Notes

1. Nara, "White Paper," in Eunice de Souza and Melanie Silgardo, eds, *These My Words: The Penguin Book of Indian Poetry* (New Delhi: Penguin India, 2012).

2. For some recent and contrasting examples, see Ayesha Jalal, *The Pity of Partition: Manto's Life, Times and Work Across the India–Pakistan Divide* (Princeton : Princeton University Press, 2013); Dipesh Chakrabarty, *The Calling of History: Sir Jadunath Sarkar and his Empire of Truth* (Chicago: Chicago University Press, 2015); and Iqbal Singh Sevea, *The Political Philosophy of Muhammad Iqbal: Islam and Nationalism in Late Colonial India* (Cambridge: Cambridge University Press, 2012). Older examples include Sarvepalli Gopal, *Radhakrishnan: A Biography* (Delhi: Oxford University Press, 1989). For an interesting set of alternatives, see David Arnold and Stuart Blackburn, eds, *Telling Lives in India: Biography, Autobiography, and Life History* (New Delhi: Permanent Black, 2004).
3. A possibility would have been to focus on the institutional context for intellectual activity. Amongst a handful of works that have attempted this, see David Lelyveld, *Aligarh's First Generation: Muslim Solidarity in British India* (Princeton: Princeton University Press, 1978), and more recently Kavita Datla, *The Language of Secular Islam: Urdu Nationalism and Colonial India* (Honolulu: University of Hawai'i Press, 2013).
4. Partha Chatterjee, "Āmāder ādhunikatā," in Chatterjee, *Itihāser uttarādhikār* (Kolkata: Ananda Publishers, 2000), pp. 171–85; for an English version of this text, first delivered as a lecture in 1994, see Partha Chatterjee, "Talking about Our Modernity in Two Languages," in Chatterjee, *A Possible India: Essays in Political Criticism* (Delhi: Oxford University Press, 1997), pp. 263–85.
5. See Bruce Carlisle Robertson, *Raja Rammohan Ray: The Father of Modern India* (Delhi: Oxford University Press, 1995); also the classic statement in Sumit Sarkar, "Rammohun Roy and the Break with the Past," in V.C. Joshi, ed., *Rammohun Roy and the Process of Modernization in India* (Delhi: Vikas, 1975), pp. 46–68.
6. For some examples, see Susie Tharu and K. Lalita, eds, *Women Writing in India*, 2 vols (Delhi: Oxford University Press, 1991–93); Stuart Blackburn and Vasudha Dalmia, eds, *India's Literary History: Essays on the Nineteenth Century* (New Delhi: Permanent Black, 2003); and A.R. Venkatachalapathy, *The Province of the Book: Scholars, Scribes, and Scribblers in Colonial Tamilnadu* (Ranikhet: Permanent Black, 2012).
7. Thus, Narayana Rao in fact played an important initial role in the project that eventually became Sheldon Pollock, ed., *Literary Cultures*

in History: Reconstructions from South Asia (Berkeley: University of California Press, 2003). However, his own conception of the architecture of the volume was different from the more conventional one that was eventually adopted.

8. C.A. Bayly, *Recovering Liberties: Indian Thought in the Age of Liberalism and Empire* (Cambridge: Cambridge University Press, 2011); for a related project, see Shruti Kapila (with C.A. Bayly), ed., *An Intellectual History for India* (Cambridge: Cambridge University Press, 2010).
9. Ramachandra Guha, ed., *Makers of Modern India* (Cambridge, Mass.: Harvard University Press, 2011); compare the standard list in Adi H. Doctor, *Political Thinkers of Modern India* (New Delhi: Mittal Publications, 1997). I note that when Guha's book was released in Hyderabad in late 2011, Narayana Rao challenged him publicly about the relative absence of "vernacular" intellectuals in the volume.
10. David Shulman, *More than Real: A History of the Imagination in South India* (Cambridge, Mass.: Harvard University Press, 2012), pp. 3–4.
11. Antonio Gramsci, *Selections from the Prison Notebooks*, ed. and trans. Quintin Hoare and Geoffrey Nowell Smith (New York: International Publishers, 1971), pp. 3–5.
12. Yogendra K. Malik, "North Indian Intellectuals' Perceptions of their Role and Status," *Asian Survey*, vol. 17, no. 6, 1977, pp. 565–6. Contrast this with the essay by Narayana Rao, "Telugu Intellectuals' Role in the Process of Social Change," in Yogendra Malik, ed., *South Asian Intellectuals and Social Change: A Study of the Role of Vernacular-Speaking Intelligentsia* (New Delhi: Heritage Publishers, 1982), pp. 308–38.
13. Edward Shils, "The Culture of the Indian Intellectual" (in two parts), *The Sewanee Review*, vol. 67, nos 2 and 3, 1959, pp. 239–61, 401–21. On Shils' controversial role in relation to South Asian Studies in Chicago, also see Arjun Appadurai, "Knowledge, Circulation and Collective Biography," in Jackie Assayag and Véronique Bénéï, eds, *At Home in Diaspora: South Asian Scholars and the West* (Bloomington: Indiana University Press, 2003), pp. 30–3.
14. Shils, "The Culture of the Indian Intellectual" (Part 2), p. 421.
15. For Ramanujan's works other than his translations, see *The Collected Essays of A.K. Ramanujan*, ed. Vinay Dharwadker (Delhi: Oxford University Press, 2004).

16. S.N. Sridhar, "The Presence of the Past," *Deccan Herald*, July 24, 1993.
17. David Shulman, "Attipat Krishnaswami Ramanujan (1929–1993)," *Journal of Asian Studies*, vol. 53, no. 3, 1994, pp. 1048–50.
18. See "Making love to a poem," in Arun Kolatkar, *Collected Poems in English*, ed. Arvind Krishna Mehrotra (Tarset: Bloodaxe, 2010), pp. 354–5. For a discussion of this poem, see Laetitia Zecchini, *Arun Kolatkar and Literary Modernism in India* (London: Bloomsbury, 2014), pp. 193–4.
19. Velcheru Narayana Rao, "Preface," in *Hibiscus on the Lake: Twentieth-Century Telugu Poetry from India* (Madison: University of Wisconsin Press, 2003), p. xi.
20. On the Kavali brothers, see Rama Sundari Mantena, *The Origins of Modern Historiography in India: Antiquarianism and Philology, 1780–1880* (New York: Palgrave Macmillan, 2012).
21. David Shulman, "Towards a New Indian Poetics: Velcheru Narayana Rao and the Structure of Literary Revolutions," in David Shulman, ed., *Syllables of Sky: Studies in South Indian Civilization in Honour of Velcheru Narayana Rao* (Delhi: Oxford University Press, 1995), pp. 1–19.
22. Allasani Pĕddana, *The Story of Manu*, trans. Velcheru Narayana Rao and David Shulman (Cambridge, Mass.: Harvard University Press, 2015), p. 9.
23. For the perception of VNR as an iconoclast in relation to these consecrated figures, see Chekuri Rama Rao, "Mind Churning Experience in the City of Madison," in Rama Rao, *Crystallized Memories*, trans. M.V. Chalapathi Rao (New Delhi: Sahitya Akademi, 2005), pp. 34–7.
24. Vakulabharanam Rajagopal, "Fashioning Modernity in Telugu: Viresalingam and his Interventionist Strategy," *Studies in History*, N.S., vol. 21, no. 1, 2005, pp. 45–77 (quotations on pp. 69 and 75).
25. *Hibiscus on the Lake*, pp. 280–1.
26. American social scientists of that time seem already to have been fascinated by the phenomenon of Marxism in South India, but hardly took its intellectual aspects seriously; see Selig S. Harrison, "Caste and the Andhra Communists," *American Political Science Review*, vol. 50, no. 2, 1956, pp. 378–404.
27. See, for example, Partha Chatterjee, *et al., Social Science Research*

Capacity in South Asia (New York: Social Science Research Council, 2002).

28. *Hibiscus on the Lake*, p. 283.
29. Ibid., p. 303.
30. Shulman, "Towards a New Indian Poetics," pp. 8–9.
31. Phillip B. Wagoner, "Velcheru Narayana Rao, Collaborative Authorship, and Textures of Time," *Eemaata*, January 2013, consulted on 26 July 2015: http://eemaata.com/em/issues/201301/2037.html?fmtiast.
32. John Richards and V.N. Rao, "Banditry in Mughal India: Historical and Folk Perceptions," *Indian Economic and Social History Review*, vol. 17, no. 1, 1980, pp. 95–120.
33. See the discussion in Jan E.M. Houben, "Socio-linguistic Attitudes reflected in the Work of Bhartrhari and Later Grammarians," in Jan E.M. Houben, ed., *Ideology and Status of Sanskrit: Contributions to the History of the Sanskrit Language* (Leiden: E.J. Brill, 1996), pp. 157–93.
34. V. Narayana Rao, "Purāna," in Sushil Mittal and Gene Thursby, eds, *The Hindu World* (New York: Routledge, 2004), pp. 97–115 (citation on p. 114).
35. Charles Hallisey, "Narayana Rao on the Recorded Text and the Received Texts," *Eemaata,* January 2013, consulted on 26 July 2015: http://eemaata.com/em/issues/201301/2027.html?fmtiast.
36. Narayana Rao, "Purāna," pp. 114–15. These reflections also extend to his work on *kāvya*, in relation to Srinatha and others.
37. In François Grimal, ed., *Les sources et le temps/ Sources and Time: A Colloquium* (Pondicherry: Ecole Française d'Extrême-Orient, 2001), p. v.

1

Multiple Literary Cultures in Telugu

Court, Temple, and Public

History presupposes a narrative, a story of a process motivated by a causality. And as we have come to realize, such a story sometimes creates the object it purports to merely describe. There was no such thing as "Telugu literature" as we now understand it before literary historians produced its history in the early decades of the twentieth century for the purpose of teaching it in colleges, or to fill a perceived gap in knowledge. A history of Telugu literature required a beginning, dates for poets and their patrons, a geography of literary production, and a connected narrative, which scholars have worked hard to construct. In this essay I try to avoid such construction. I do not tell a story of events by narrating them chronologically. Instead I give a somewhat loosely connected but interrelated configuration of literary culture as it manifested itself in the geographical area of South India. The gaps that I leave are deliberate.

Linguistic and Geographical Boundaries of Telugu Literary Cultures

Modern political and linguistic boundaries can create confusion when we talk of literary cultures that pre-date them. It is therefore necessary to remind ourselves that during the premodern period, which is my primary focus in this essay, in many of the geographical locations discussed here Telugu was one of several languages in which literature was being produced. Poets who wrote in Telugu read and interacted with other languages widely used among scholars of their time. Among these languages, three had a direct impact on the making of literary texts in Telugu: Sanskrit, Tamil, and Kannada. Knowledge of Sanskrit was required for a person to be literary in Telugu—the Sanskrit of *purāṇa* and *kāvya*, if not the Sanskrit of *śāstra* and Veda. Tamil was a canonical language for Vaiṣṇava Telugu poets, just as Kannada was for those who were Vīraśaivas. Although its influence is not clearly visible on the surface, Persian did have an impact on Telugu literary culture, especially during the late sixteenth century.[1] However, with the significant exception of Pālkurīki Somanāthuḍu, who wrote in both Telugu and Kannada, every one of the poets I discuss here wrote only in Telugu.

Also, all poets seem to have been aware that they were participating in an enterprise of writing in Telugu. One of the earliest of these poets, Nannaya (eleventh century), expressly stated that he was writing "in Tĕnugu" for the welfare of the world (apparently meaning the Telugu world). Nannĕcoḍuḍu (twelfth century) spoke of the Cāḷukya kings who established "literature in Telugu." In the following generation, Tikkana (thirteenth century) had in view a people he called *āndhrāvaḷi* (Andhra people).[2] The poets who established literary traditions different from Nannaya's also expressed a clear awareness of belonging to the Telugu language, even as they were conscious of their own traditions with their own intertextual underpinnings and shared cultural discourse. Such an awareness made them participants in a common activity of writing in Telugu, even though their literary traditions varied. These disparate traditions were later reformulated as if they belonged to a linear and continuous story, and acquired the name Telugu literature.

The geography of these literary traditions is not as unified as the conceptual area of Telugu literature. Present-day Andhra gives the secure impression that the literary geography of Telugu is easily definable as the area we call Andhra Pradesh. The history of Telugu literary production gives the lie to this assumption, showing both that Andhra did not always correspond to Andhra Pradesh and that Telugu literature was produced in many areas that are not included in the Andhra Pradesh of today. Tikkana, writing from Nellore in the thirteenth century, had a concept of Andhra that included coastal Andhra and Rajahmundry, from where Nannaya had written a couple of centuries earlier. But Śrīnāthuḍu, writing in the late fourteenth century from the same Rajahmundry, had a much narrower concept of Andhra. For him, the center of the Andhra country was the Godāvarī delta.[3] During the reign of Kṛṣṇadevarāya, who called himself a Kannada king (*kannaḍarāya*), sixteenth-century Hampi, now located in the state of Karnataka, was the center of Telugu literary activity. Later, when the Telugu Nāyaka kings ruled the southern kingdoms of Madurai and Tañjāvūr, the center of Telugu literary production was located in the far south, where the predominant spoken language was Tamil. Telugu continued to be a language of literature in the Tamil-speaking south long after the decline of the Nāyakas. Even when Telugu literature was produced in areas that are now in Andhra Pradesh, Telugu was not always the only language of importance. For instance, during the reign of the sultans of Golconda, the language of administration was Persian, but Telugu poets flourished in the court and Telugu was accepted as a language of culture as well. The northwestern temple town of Śrīśailam, where Pālkuriki Somanāthuḍu wrote in the thirteenth century, was a multilingual center where Śaiva devotees spoke Telugu, Kannada, Tamil, and Marathi; and southeastern Tirupati, where Annamayya and his family members wrote in the fifteenth and sixteenth centuries, was a center for at least two major languages, Telugu and Tamil.

In contrast, the kings of the Kākatīya dynasty ruling from Warangal and the Rĕḍḍi kings ruling from Kondavidu, Rajahmundry, and Addanki—all of which were right in the thick of the Telugu-speaking area—did not evince much interest in encouraging Telugu poetry. They favored Sanskrit poetry instead. The Kākatīyas honored the Sanskrit poet Vidyānātha as their court poet, and the Rĕḍḍis celebrated Vāmana Bhaṭṭa Bāna as theirs. Meanwhile, the greatest Telugu poet of the time, Śrīnāthuḍu, was traveling from king to king and patron to patron all over the region including Kannada- and Tamil-speaking areas, receiving honors as well as audience for his poetry before finally being invited by

Vīrabhadrā Reḍḍi, the ruler of Rajahmundry, to dedicate his *Kāśīkhaṇḍamu* to him.

Clearly, language boundaries were much more porous in premodern south India than they are now, and literary production was not always associated with the majority language spoken in the area. Nor can we arrive at a neat, chronologically connected narrative of Telugu literary developments. We might love to imagine a definite, Aristotelian beginning, middle, and end for a narrative of literary history, such that this mass of events from Andhra would not frustrate us and appear wholly uncharted. But the search for chronology, the bulwark of positivist literary historians, frustrates even the most dedicated scholars as book after book turns up without a definite date of its composition or precise biographical details of its author.

Indeed, in this foggy chronological domain, finding a single author who gives a precise date for the composition of his book is cause for celebration. Appakavi, who we know decided to write one of his books on an evening in the year 1656 (Śaka 1578) in the village of Kāmepaḷḷi (probably in Guntur District), is just such an author.[4] I begin my essay with him—and not just because he gives us this precious bit of chronological information (which, as we will see, is immediately followed by a story of an altogether different historical order). Appakavi gives us a rich literary-cultural discourse and provides a vantage point from which to look back in time as well as forward.[5]

First, the story: One night the god Viṣṇu appeared to Appakavi in a dream, along with his insignia (the conch and the wheel) and his two wives, Lakṣmī and Bhūdevi. The god formally introduced himself and his wives, and he told Appakavi that he should write, in the Telugu language, the great grammar that Nannaya, the first poet, had composed in Sanskrit *sūtras*. These *sūtras* had been lost for centuries because Bhīmakavi, Nannaya's rival, threw the only copy into the Godāvarī river in retaliation for Nannaya's suppression of Bhīmakavi's own book on meter.

Fortunately, however, Nannaya's student, Sāraṅgadhara, had memorized every verse of the book before Bhīmakavi threw it away and thus had preserved it. This Sāraṅgadhara was none other than the son of

Rājarājanarendra, the patron king of Nannaya. According to a story well known in Appakavi's time, to which the poet refers, this king had married a young wife in his old age. The young wife fell in love with her stepson, Sāraṅgadhara, and enticed him to her palace. When Sāraṅgadhara refused to reciprocate her affection, the queen spoke false charges against him to the king, who hastily ordered his son's arms and legs to be cut off and the young man cast into the wilderness. But Sāraṅgadhara miraculously survived with the aid of a *siddha* (perfected being), Matsyendranātha, and he became a *siddha* himself, hence immortal. Having saved Nannaya's book from extinction, Sāraṅgadhara even gave a written copy of it to Bālasarasvati—a contemporary of Appakavi, who recorded this chain of transmission. Bālasarasvati had also written a gloss on the lost text.

Now the god was asking Appakavi to write an elaborate commentary on this first Telugu grammar of Nannaya's. But how would Appakavi get a copy of this book? This problem of the missing text was neatly solved by the god's promise that the next day a certain Brahmin from Mataṅga Hill (near Hampi) would personally deliver a copy to Appakavi.

There is more to the story. But let us pause to ask why anybody would even need this grammar, since for centuries poets had managed quite well without it. In the absence of the rules of an authoritative grammar, says the god, a certain *kavirākṣasuḍu*—a fierce and powerful poet—had made a rule that no poet could ever use a Telugu word unattested in Nannaya's Telugu retelling of the Sanskrit *Mahābhārata.* Because of the lack of a grammar, the earliest poet's text itself had come to serve as an empirical source for ordering the language. Now, however, Appakavi's new Telugu version of the absent grammar would open up the generative resources of the language and also confer authority.

An earlier grammar, *Āndhrabhāṣabhūṣaṇamu* by Ketana (thirteenth century), had no prescriptive authority. Ketana even modestly requests poets to bless his efforts and, if they find errors in his work, to kindly correct them.[6] He is far from assuming the authority of legislator of language, the title by which Appakavi recognizes Nannaya. Clearly, Appakavi found himself in a new situation, marked by an urgent need to establish the authority of grammar over poetry. And indeed, Appakavi exhibits a profound sense of confidence. He states that his book is as basic to Telugu as Pāṇini's *Śabdānuśāsana* is to Sanskrit. This is not just poetic license; he is relying on a tradition of several hundred years of linguistic creativity, during which Telugu literary culture had established for itself a certain social presence. Now Appakavi proceeds to give voice to an anthropology of poetry, to its power of producing political and social reality, and its role in ordering its own universe.

In Appakavi's words, a poem received by a patron brings him good luck or bad luck depending on its "marks," in the same way that a horse, a gem, or a woman acquired by him would. These things, if properly chosen for their lucky marks, could turn him into a rich man or, alternatively, leave him a beggar. In the case of poems, lucky marks are features of the correctness of the language and meter used by the poet. The power of the language used in a poem has a long prehistory, which has been ingrained in the minds of literate people. Building on this belief, Appakavi relates another belief, at least as old as the twelfth century, that a poem is one of the seven "children" a person could have.[7] A son, a water tank, a poem, an endowment, a temple, a grove, and a Brahmin settlement—these seven ensure life after death for the patron. Six of the seven fall into ruin in the course of time; poetry is the sole exception. So Appakavi recommends poetry as the most praiseworthy item for all patrons to acquire. But there is something even more valuable in poetry: However bad a patron's life might be, the poet can make him good. Just as drainage water from the city flows into the Godāvarī river and becomes pure, even a person who has lived a bad life can be rendered pure in the poet's depiction. The illustrations Appakavi presents as evidence for this image-building transform the Sanskrit poets Vālmīki and Vyāsa into court poets who served their patrons: Vālmīki made Rāma known, and Vyāsa made the Pāṇḍavas known, by writing their lives into poetry.

Underlying Appakavi's entire presentation, though left unmentioned, are the grammarian and the scholar-interpreter of grammar. The poet creates his poem within the rules set by the major grammar texts, which were written by ancient givers of laws of grammar. In this case, Nannaya is such a lawgiver and Appakavi is the commentator who interprets this old text. The commentator and the lawgiver form the world in which the poet works, so that it functions according to rules. The patron flourishes only if the poet executes the poem strictly within this rule-bound world.

The world of poetry that Appakavi imagines is remarkably analogous to the Brahminical social world. In the human world, the Veda and *śāstra* dictate the law; the Brahmin *purohita*, or ritual specialist, interprets the law; and the king administers it for the benefit of his subjects. In the literary world, similarly, the ancient texts on grammar and poetics give the law of language and poetic rules, the grammarian interprets the rules, and the poet executes the poem according to the rules for the enjoyment of cultivated readers. The following represents the homology:

	World of People (*laukikajagat*)	World of Poetry (*kāvyajagat*)
Law	Vedic texts (Veda and *śāstra*)	grammar (*lakṣaṇa*)
Interpreter	Brahmin (*purohita*)	grammarian (*lākṣaṇika*)
Executor	king (*rāja*)	poet (*kavi*)
Recipient	subjects (*prajā*)	readers (*sahṛdayas*)

However, the literary world did not behave according to Appakavi's imagination. That Appakavi had to visit the remote past of Nannaya's time and invent a whole grammar that had been lost until now, and that he needed the immortal Sāraṅgadhara and the god Viṣṇu to arrange for the delivery of that grammar, clearly suggest that he needed a power structure to confer the authority necessary to create a new literary world. To understand this more clearly, let us briefly take a look at the world of Telugu literary culture during Appakavi's time and in the centuries immediately preceding it.

In the century before Appakavi, a profound shift in the world of poetry had made the patron of poetry, the king, completely independent of the poet. He no longer needed the Brahmin as poet to elevate his status, to make him king. The king now assumed the position of the god himself. The most that a poet could do was to serve the king by celebrating his glory. I elaborate on this situation later, in the section on the Nāyaka courts; stated briefly, in preference to Brahmin men, courtesans and non-Brahmin men were now chosen as court poets. These poets did not feel superior to the king and therefore did not have any problem serving him. Not too long before Appakavi we find an unusual complaint in the words of Dhūrjaṭi, who lamented:

> Town after town
> every street singer becomes a poet.
> They go to these two-bit kings who cannot tell good from bad
> and praise them as the best connoisseurs of arts.
> Poetry is cheap.
> God of Kāḷahasti,
> where do good poets go?[8]

Clearly, Appakavi wished to restore a world he thought was lost or had degenerated, but he unwittingly presented a world of mean competition, personal jealousies, and unethical acts, like destroying a rival poet's work (almost as if it was a routine occurrence since the beginnings of Telugu literature). Nannaya himself, who was held in high reverence by Appakavi and was respected by the god, participated in such acts. However, this detail was lost on Appakavi, as well as on his readers, who were taken by the glory in which Appakavi presents Nannaya and his grammar. In a way, Appakavi was not inventing this glory. Nannaya was already recognized as the first poet, the inaugurator of Telugu poetry, by a number of poets previous to Appakavi. We find a Telugu literary world articulated as early as the sixteenth century. The following poem by Rāmarājabhūṣaṇuḍu, author of *Vasucaritramu*, addresses the Goddess of Speech, mentioning a "universe of Telugu words" (*āndhrôktimayaprapañcamu*)—in other words, Telugu literature.

> You are created by the Maker of Speech
> and nurtured by the Master of Words;
> The Moon and the Sun brighten you
> and the Lord of Wealth protects you;
> I celebrate your glory
> in the universe of Telugu words.[9]

Through a series of somewhat constrained puns, the verse invokes both a genealogy of poets and the major Hindu deities. References are to the Maker of Speech (Brahmā as well as Nannaya, who is credited with creating a literary language in Telugu), the Lord of the World (Śiva and also Ĕrrāpragaḍa, who is called the supreme master of poetic compositions, or *prabandhaparameśvaruḍu*), the Moon (Soma and also Nācana Somuḍu, who wrote *Harivaṃśamu*), the Sun (Bhāskara along with Huḷakki Bhāskaruḍu, who composed a Rāma story, popularly known as *Bhāskararāmāyaṇamu*, in Telugu), and the Lord of Wealth (Viṣṇu as well as Śrīnāthuḍu, the great poet of the fourteenth and fifteenth centuries). This is indeed an interesting list of poets, and the tone of the poem suggests an authoritative structure of the literary past, indeed, a canon of great poets.

However, what Appakavi seeks to express is not just the greatness of the poet as a creator of literary texts; he wants the poet to be subjected to the superior authority of the grammarian and the maker of the rules of meter—the poet should be only the executor of literary texts within the rules of grammar and metrical texts. To see Appakavi's worldview in perspective, we should pursue the main strands of competing literary cultures that preceded Appakavi and were in some ways still active during Appakavi's time.

The First Poet and the Production of a Brahminical/Puranic Literary Culture

Contrary to the conventional picture of the reader and the poet detailed earlier, and the ideological support articulated by Appakavi, Telugu did have multiple literary traditions and cultures, sometimes competing with each other but most of the time continuing in relative independence, each with its own poetics and aesthetics, and often with its own audience. I focus here on four of these, which I will call the Brahminical/Puranic, anti-Brahminical, courtly, and temple traditions. I discuss as the major poets of these literary cultures Nannaya (eleventh century) for the Brahminical tradition; Somanāthuḍu (thirteenth century) for the anti-Brahminical tradition; Nannĕcoḍuḍu (twelfth century), Śrīnāthuḍu (fourteenth century), Pĕddana, and Rāmarājabhūṣaṇuḍu (both sixteenth century) for the courtly tradition; and Potana (fourteenth century) and Annamayya (fifteenth century) for the temple tradition. Throughout my discussion, using both written texts and *cāṭu*s (oral verses circulated among literate people), I outline some of the main features of these traditions, which lead up to the popular perception of Telugu poetry and poets as reflected in seventeenth-century legends about them. Then I consider issues relevant to each of these literary cultures, such as choice of literary language, questions of translation and authenticity, and styles of orality and literacy. At the end of my account, I return to Appakavi.

I begin with Nannaya, since from at least the sixteenth century he has been repeatedly identified as the first poet in Telugu. The very idea that there should be one first poet in a language that has had more than one literary culture from early on is problematic and obviously stems from a homogenization of Telugu literature in the early-twentieth-century literary histories. In fact, only the poets of the Brahminical courtly tradition recognized Nannaya as the first poet; others, especially those who were aware of their literary culture as distinct and even opposed to the dominant traditions, did not mention his name.

The credit for creating a courtly literary culture, in fact, does clearly belong to Nannaya. Writing a *purāṇa* narrative in *campū* (a Sanskrit-based genre of metrical stanzas interspersed by prose), and the convention of addressing the poem to the patron by making him the listener to the entire narrative, are Nannaya's inventions. The patron's name is evoked at the beginning and the end of each of the chapters, and the context in which the patron commissioned the poem and the family history of the patron are described in some detail. The poet also takes the occasion to describe his own qualifications for composing such a poem. This style of contextualizing the narrative with the speaker and the listener embedded in the text found great favor with the courtly poets of the sixteenth century, who embellished and improved on Nannaya's invention. In the practice of the later courtly poets the patron is called the *kṛtipati*, the husband of the poem, and the poem itself is called the virgin poem, *kāvyakanyā*, who is married to the patron. Even the temple poet Potana adopts this style and addresses his *Bhāgavatamu* to his god, Rāma, calling him Rāmanṛpāla, King Rāma. The courtly poets used this style to accommodate the social and political aspirations not only of ruling kings but of a range of personalities including heads of the army and treasury, rich merchants, and landowners. The poets described the patron's extended family, including his grandfather, father, uncles, brothers, and their wives, in terms appropriate to the status to which the patron aspired.

Let us see in some detail how Nannaya, at the beginning of his *Mahābhāratamu*, gives a glorious description of the context leading to the composition of the work. The poet describes King Rājarājanarendruḍu, the Veṅgi Cāḷukya king of the eleventh century:

> Ravishing as the moon, he alone adorns the class of kings,
> outshines the splendor of other rulers; a true warrior,
> he illumines all worlds like pure moonlight on an autumn night.
> He, Rājanarendra, has put his enemies to rest
> with his indomitable arm—a honed sword—
> as a shower of rain settles dust.[10]

Nannaya also produces a complementary image of himself as a Brahmin family priest, devoted to the king and given to sacrifice and prayer. He is an expert on language (*vipulaśabdaśāsanuḍu*), he is learned in the *purāṇa*s, and, most significant of all, he never tells a lie.

Towards the end comes a description of the Sanskrit *Mahābhārata*, which the king loves dearly. It is one of the five things he never gets tired of (the other four are pleasing the Brahmins, worshiping Śiva, keeping the company of good people, and giving gifts). The king wants the *Mahābhārata* to be written in Telugu because, he says:

> My lineage begins with the moon, and then proceeds
> through Puru, Bharata, Kuru, and King Pāṇḍu.
> The stories of Pāṇḍu's famous sons, virtuous and beyond blame
> are ever close to my heart.[11]

We can see that the preamble by Nannaya has all the ingredients of a courtly poem: a noble king, a learned poet, and a great text. While it served as a major model in the formation of courtly patronage for literary compositions, Nannaya's text also responds to the way he saw the Sanskrit *Mahābhārata* of Vyāsa. Introducing Vyāsa's work to his Telugu listeners, Nannaya demonstrates a highly individual understanding of the Sanskrit text. Perceiving it as a work that falls under many descriptions, he writes in the preface to his own *Mahābhārata*:

> Those who understand the order of things
> think it is a book about order.
> Metaphysicians call it the Vedic system.
> Counselors read it as a book about conduct.
> Good poets treat it as a great poem.
> Grammarians find here usage for every rule.
> Narrators of the past see it as ancient record.
> Storytellers know it to be a rich collection of stories.
> Vyāsa, the first sage, who knew the meaning of all the Vedas,
> Paraśara's son, equal to Lord Viṣṇu, made the *Mahābhārata*
> a universal text.[12]

Obviously, Nannaya likewise designed his poem to be all things to his listeners. And the later tradition shows that Nannaya's Telugu text did answer most of the demands made on it. We know that Nannaya was seen as a great poet and that he was regarded as a sage—a combination of Vālmīki and Vyāsa for the Telugu literary tradition. His poem also served as an illustration for all the rules of a grammar which he was supposed to have composed, but which was lost, as noted earlier. In addition, Nannaya was appropriated by later *kāvya* poets as a *kāvya* writer, hence the tribute paid by Rāmarājabhūṣaṇa (a *kāvya* poet himself) in the poem already quoted. All this was possible because there was an organized literary cultural patronage, which continued over centuries, though with significant breaks, and which Appakavi sought to reinvent in his century.

The beginnings of traditions are always authorized as such after the event. That Telugu literature began with Nannaya's *Mahābhāratamu* in the eleventh century has been part of a well-established tradition for several centuries now. But by all the available evidence Nannaya's own intention was only to compose a Telugu work—not to begin anything, let alone a tradition. Even in the thirteenth century Nannaya was not called the first poet. Tikkana, who picked up the Telugu *Mahābhāratamu* almost where Nannaya had left it a century earlier, pays handsome tribute to his predecessor. He calls Nannaya the master of Telugu poetry (*āndhrakavitvaviśāradunḍu*), but stops short of calling him the first poet in Telugu.[13] Apparently, Tikkana knew other Telugu poets who wrote before Nannaya, and if he does not give us their names it could be because he was only interested in the man who had written the first part of the text he himself was to continue.

To Tikkana goes the credit of imagining a Telugu community (*āndhrāvaḷi*) and a strong Brahminical orientation for Telugu elite culture. Tikkana lived an active life. He wrote fifteen volumes to complete the Telugu version of the voluminous Sanskrit *Mahābhārata*; he was adviser and minister to the ruler of a small Telugu king, Manumasiddhi of Nellore; and he was mentor to other Telugu poets who looked up to him for advice and inspiration. Ketana, a student of Tikkana, wrote a grammar of Telugu (*Āndhrabhāṣābhūṣaṇamu*), a *dharmaśāstra* work in Telugu (*Vijñāneśvarīyamu*), and a book from the tale (*kathā*) tradition (*Daśakumāracaritramu*). The great kingdom of the Kākatīyas was not too far from where Tikkana worked. However, the Kākatīya kings were busy seeking elevation to the status of Kshatriyas, a service only Sanskrit poets could perform for them. It is not surprising, then, that the beginning of the Telugu canon of Brahminical poetry and the self-conscious orientation of an Andhra literary tradition should start in less powerful Nellore, rather than in the Sanskritized Kākatīya capital of Warangal.

Nannaya produced his *Mahābhāratamu* in the mixed prose-verse *campū* form—a narrative composition with poems in Sanskritic and indigenous meters interspersed with heightened prose (*gadya*). The meters themselves were already in use, as evidenced by the extant fragments in inscriptional and Sanskrit literary sources. What is striking, however, is the extraordinary brilliance shown in his use of the meters and the magical, almost *mantra*-like power achieved in his composition. One is compelled to say that it is Nannaya's talent as a great poet that alone accounts for the recognition he received from later generations; no political, social, or linguistic context could explain this achievement, which established for Telugu a level of poetic excellence it had never had before. The literary for Telugu was determined in favor of the *campū* primarily because Nannaya created a grand narrative in that genre. The varieties of meter that Nannaya chose—some from Sanskritic sources and others from regional sources—gave his text a dynamism no other texts in either Telugu or Sanskrit offered.

Furthermore, the *campū* was excellently suited for public exposition. In a typical *purāṇa* performance, a trained performer of the text selects an episode or a section of the narrative, makes an opening statement in his own words, prepares the audience by relating the narrative context, reads one verse or a cluster of verses from the text, and comments on them in his discourse. The *campū* genre, with its mixture of verse and prose, allows the performer to read the verses, then take a break and add his own prose exposition to the narrative, incorporating as he finds appropriate such topical references as would make the discourse interesting to his audience. The structure of the text, in fact, has a built-in role for the performer, without whose improvisation it sounds somewhat incomplete.[14]

In writing *campū*, Nannaya created a genre that presupposes a community of listeners who sit at a distance from the performer and who receive the text as it is delivered to them as part of a public discourse. The text is not immediately intelligible to all listeners. Even to those few people well educated in Sanskritized Telugu it fails to appeal if they try to read it for themselves. It needs an interpreting performer for its very literary existence. This was new in Telugu experience. Until then, there had been only two types of texts—those sung by a group and those sung by an individual. (Apparently all reading was reading aloud.)

Furthermore, Nannaya's style of adapting from Sanskrit established the practice not only of rendering Sanskrit texts into Telugu but making them aesthetically and even ideologically independent of the Sanskrit originals. In this last aspect lies the success of those literary cultures that are generally Sanskritic, that is, the Brahminical, puranic, and courtly cultures. In particular, Nannaya's way of handling meters became a model for all later poets who adopted Sanskritic meters and the *campū* genre. Unlike in a Sanskrit stanza, where words have to end at the end of the line and at the caesura within the line, in Telugu a word may extend beyond the line and across the caesura. This convention, which Nannaya established, made it possible for Telugu poets to borrow a four-line Sanskrit meter, such as *śārdūla* or *mattebha*, and play with it in a variety of intricate syntactic twists not allowable in Sanskrit.

To illustrate this point, let us look at a couple of verses from Nannaya's *Mahābhāratamu*, from the episode of the *rājasūya* (royal sacrifice) by Dharmarāja in the Book of the Assembly Hall. Śiśupāla, an enemy of Kṛṣṇa, was upset that Dharmarāja should honor this cowherd at such a glorious event in the presence of all the nobles and kings. Dharmarāja, the eldest of the Pāṇḍava brothers, tries to pacify Śiśupāla with gentle words:

Kṛṣṇa was the very source of the first born, Brahma;
all the ancient texts sing of him
and people in all three worlds worship him.
Bhīṣma knows this and that's why he advised
that Kṛṣṇa be honored here.
Listen to me—he is right.[15]

Dharmarāja's sentences, which contain a series of words with long vowels, are slow-moving and drawn out. Even the name he uses for Kṛṣṇa—Dāmōdara—has two long vowels in it. The total effect of the verse is one of thoughtful and non-confrontational explanation. But when all the gentle arguments offered by the senior Dharmarāja in favor of honoring Kṛṣṇa at the sacrifice fail to persuade Śiśupāla to allow the matter to be settled in peace, Sahadeva, the fourth of the five Pāṇḍava brothers, aggressively lifts his foot to crush his opponent and says:

"Yes, we honored Kṛṣṇa,
and we did so without
a trace of doubt in our minds.
You say you don't agree.
So be it. But if any one of you has a problem with it,
here is what you get."
And he furiously lifted his foot in the assembly.
Everyone fell silent in total fear.[16]

The original verse, in *campakamāla*, a four-line Sanskritic meter with twenty-one syllables on each line, fixed in a sequence of ˘˘˘–˘–˘˘˘–˘˘–˘˘–˘–˘–, goes like this in Nannaya's Telugu:

ĕḍapakan arghyam' acyutunak' i*ccitim' iccina dīnik' em' oḍam*
ba*ḍam'ani durjanatvamuna* pa*lkĕḍi vīrula mastakambupain*
iḍiyĕdan' añcu ta caraṇam' ĕṭṭĕ sabhan sahadevuḍ' aṭṭicon
uḍigi sabhāsadul palukak' uṇḍiri taddayu bhītacittulai.

Unlike in Sanskrit, the Telugu use of this meter includes the regulation that the consonant of the second syllable on each line—in this case the consonant *ḍ*, which is underscored—should be the same in all four lines. The caesura occurs at the thirteenth syllable on each line (represented here with syllables in roman font), which should agree with the first syllable on the line (also in roman font). Also, unlike in Sanskrit, the caesura is not a place for a new word to begin.

This four-line verse includes two full sentences spoken by Sahadeva and a sentence in the voice of the narrator. The first sentence ends in the middle of the first line of the stanza and the second sentence continues into the second line. The long narrative sentence that comes after runs through the last two lines. The metrical structure of the verse does little more than hold the composition in a general pattern, allowing for a rich syntactic and phonotactic drama to play itself out in the verse. In oral rendition the verse has breaks at the end of its semantic units, rather than at the end of its metrical units, as its Sanskrit cousin would. The following arrangement of lines graphically represents the way in which the verse is read:

ĕḍapaka
narghya
m' acyutuṇa
k' icciti
m' iccina
dīnik' emodambaḍamani
durjanatvamuna-palkĕḍi-vīrula-mastakambupain' iḍiyĕdan-añcu
ta
caraṇa
m' ĕttĕ-sabhan-sahadevu-
daṭṭicon-uḍigi-sabhāsadul-paluka k' uṇḍiri-taddayu-bhītacittulai.

The line breaks here indicate several short and snappy units. The dominant sound in the first unit is the retroflex *ḍ*, uttered with a plosive force. The next two units have the consonantal clusters *ghya* and *cyu* uttered one after the other, followed in the third and fourth units by identical clusters of *cci.* The short lines express an aggressive, attacking voice, while the long line that follows demonstrates with its breathless frenzy of words the threat that is delivered. The last line collapses into itself with a series of short vowels, almost as if it is afraid of expanding fully—suggesting the fear generated in the assembly by Sahadeva's show of aggression. This is a poem that is difficult to read slowly—every word chases the preceding word at a breathless speed—until the last line, which is too quiet to be fast. The meaning of the poem is captured in the contours of its sounds.[17]

By using Sanskrit meters in ways that Sanskrit does not use them, and so allowing a large variety of syntactic structures to be contained within the verse, Nannaya gave the Telugu poem a performative richness unparalleled in Sanskrit texts. Nearly every poet after Nannaya followed his style of crafting verses, making Telugu versification an independent art in itself. Furthermore, Nannaya, and more particularly Tikkana, brought to the Telugu *Mahābhāratamu* an atmosphere closer to Telugu domestic life. People in Andhra had long believed that the original Sanskrit text should not be read inside the home or from beginning to end in linear fashion, and that anyone who read it this way would die. The text was felt to generate a disturbing power (*ojas*) that needed to be brought under control through appropriate rituals of pacification.[18] In Nannaya's measured voice and disciplined diction, and later in Tikkana's representation of the epic events in Telugu native idiom, the Telugu *Mahābhāratamu* found a wholesome reception as a text that communicated peace and wisdom at home or in assembly or wherever people read it.

This vast transformation did not happen in a day, however. It wasn't until a hundred years after Nannaya that Tikkana addressed the fact that Nannaya left the Telugu *Mahābhāratamu* incomplete. Moreover, the evidence suggests that not all Telugu poets were ready to accept Nannaya's experiment in *caṃpū.* With intense vigor, Pālkuriki Somanāthuḍu, writing from Śrīśailam in northwestern Andhra in the thirteenth century, set about producing a text that presented an anti-Brahminical, anti-caste, militant Śaiva ideology.

The Literary Culture of Śaivabhakti

Śaivabhakti (devotion to Śiva), popularly known as Vīraśaivism or militant Śaivism, was a combative, egalitarian religious movement along the lines of Basaveśvara's twelfth-century teachings in Kannada.[19] Following Basaveśvara's philosophy, Paṇḍitārādhyuḍu and Pālkuriki Somanāthuḍu converted people to a religion devoted to Śiva in his form as the mobile *liṅga* (the non-iconic form of Śiva). The adherents to this religion believed that they were reborn when they were initiated to Śaivism. Once reborn, they denied their caste and their birth parents, and believed that every initiate belonged to the same high social status irrespective of previous identity. Vīraśaiva initiates rejected the god in the temple, the king who supported the temples, and the Brahmin priests who served the temples. They carried their own god, the personal Śiva in the *liṅga* form, around their neck.

Somanāthuḍu, who preached an uncompromising and militant form of Vīraśaivism, preferred to use the *dvipada* (lit. two lines) genre, which is composed in two-line metrical units that can continue without any change in meter for as long as the poet chooses. A competent poet using this meter can create a variety of moods with a choice of diction and a change of tone. A *dvipada* text allows a single reader to perform it for a group of listeners, or a group of readers to read it together for themselves; it does not require an interpreting performer. The experience that a *dvipada* reading gives its listeners is immediate, direct, and collective. The text does not create two distinct identities, a reader and a listener; it forces a merger of such identities and creates a community of singer-listeners. Obviously, Nannaya's *campū* form, which presupposes a hierarchy of performer and audience, was structurally unsuited to the egalitarian interests of the Vīraśaiva religion.

Somanāthuḍu knew full well that he was creating a counter-literary culture, one that was opposed to the *campū* both as aesthetic and ideological form. He did not mention Nannaya by name, and therefore we cannot be certain whether he was responding to Nannaya per se, or contesting a *campū* literary practice that might have been fairly well established by his time. In any case, Somanāthuḍu was determined to strike out on a different path.

In the two major works Somanāthuḍu composed in *dvipada*, the *Basavapurāṇamu* (The Story of Basava) and *Paṇḍitārādhyacaritramu* (Life History of Paṇḍitārādhyuḍu), he offers explanation for his choice of this genre and rejection of *campū*. In the *Basavapurāṇamu* he writes:

> Common Telugu is sweet
> and easier
> than those high-sounding compositions
> in prose and verse.
> I will compose *dvipada*s—please do not
> complain they are but
> Telugu. Treat them as the Veda.[20]

Again, in his *Paṇḍitārādhyacaritramu*, Somanāthuḍu expresses his opposition to *campū* texts:

> Texts written in prose and verse
> dense with Sanskrit
> are not suited for the people.
> Common Telugu is lucid.

But then he realizes that *campū* has already established its superiority in literature. He wants to compete with it and write *dvipada* that can stand comparison with it:

> I will compose *dvipada* equal in power
> to those texts in prose and verse.
> It is no less competent poetry.[21]

Somanāthuḍu not only aims at making a popular Vīraśaiva narrative in *dvipada*; a close look at the metapoetic statements in his *Paṇḍitārādhyacaritramu* gives us a picture of a poet who aims for an alternative poetics, one based on a combination of Daṇḍin's poetics and his own indigenous forms.[22] He intends his composition to function as a *kāvya* according to Daṇḍin's prescription for *mahākāvya*: with all eighteen descriptive sections, all thirty-six figures of speech, all seventy-two emotional states.

There is not enough historical data for us to ascertain whether Somanāthuḍu succeeded during his time in his attempt to give Telugu literature a new definition. All we know is that *dvipada* remained a parallel tradition to *campū*, and that rarely did the same poet write a *campū* as well as *dvipada* poem. We also know that no other poet controlled *dvipada* meter with the dynamism and vigor, variety and strength, that Somanāthuḍu demonstrated in his *Basavapurāṇamu*. In the hands of lesser poets it tended to be monotonous and repetitive.

As I discuss later, *dvipada* became a kind of second-class literature, practiced mostly by women and less learned, non-Brahmin authors. It gained some recognition at the time of the Nāyaka courts of the seventeenth century, possibly because non-Brahminical poetry re-emerged during this period. But the Brahminical tradition had rejected *dvipada* over the four-century period preceding the Nāyakas. An oft-quoted legend illustrates the Brahminical resistance to *dvipada*. As told by Piduparti Somanāthuḍu (a close follower of Pālkuriki Somanāthuḍu, who preferred to rewrite the *Basavapurāṇamu* in *campū*), King Pratāparudra, who ruled over Orugallu (present-day Warangal), noticed a group of Śaiva devotees reading the *Basavapurāṇamu* in a Śiva temple. When he wanted to know more about it, they told him that the sinner Pālkuriki Somanāthuḍu had written at length in *dvipada* with poor caesura. This was not standard and indeed had never been done before. Listening to their advice, the king left without paying attention to the reading. Other instances of Brahminical disrespect toward *dvipada* include a statement by an eighteenth-century poet who likened *dvipada* to an old whore (*mudilañja*).[23] Somanāthuḍu's elegant pun on *dvi-pada* (two feet; also, two locations)—it keeps one foot on the earth and the other in heaven, and therefore assures a good position for its readers in both places—was soon forgotten.

Why did *dvipada* lose its status? We might speculate on some of the reasons. Apart from the reported Brahminical opposition, which may indicate loss of royal patronage for *dvipada* but does not fully explain its loss of status, the Vīraśaivas failed to sustain themselves as a community in Andhra, and their message of a casteless, egalitarian society did not long endure. The structure of the caste order was more resilient than they imagined, and their revolution was too romantic to understand the social imperatives of endogamy and hierarchy that caste society comprised. Viewed from this perspective, the failure of Somanāthuḍu's literary invention was a failure of the community for which it was intended. His text needed an egalitarian, congregational community to use it, and when such a community disintegrated, the text fell into disuse. The work served as an effective rhetorical device to keep a community together, but such a text does not communicate effectively to an individual listener or reader.

Earlier we acquainted ourselves with the qualities and qualifications of a Brahminical *purāṇa* poet. The *purāṇa* poet borrowed his theme from a Sanskrit source, and he legitimized himself via the authority of Sanskrit texts. Somanāthuḍu did not indulge in any of these activities. His text was derived from the oral sources of his (Śaiva) community, the authority to compose the text was bestowed on him by his teachers, and his listeners were his friends—all of them were from his particular religious tradition, and not one of them participated in courtly culture. Under favorable conditions, the text would gain the acceptance of the community of devotees, who would elevate the poet to the status of a guru. It is clear that Somanāthuḍu had conceived of an entirely different literary culture in which he as a poet, and his text as literature, would survive.

Poetry for Pleasure: *Kāvya* Culture

Nannĕcoḍuḍu, who was perhaps a later contemporary of Nannaya, though we do not have hard evidence to determine his dates, represents the third strand, the *kāvya*, of early literary culture in Telugu. His *Kumārasambhavamu* is the earliest extant Telugu *kāvya.* But before examining *kāvya* as a genre in Telugu, let us follow what Nannĕcoḍuḍu has to say about Telugu literature itself. To Nannĕcoḍuḍu we owe the clearest statement concerning the origin of Telugu literature, which also introduces the major classificatory distinction of literary cultures into *mārga* (Sanskrit) and *deśi* (Telugu). To quote from his introduction to *Kumārasambhavamu:*

> Earlier, while there was the *mārga* poetry,
> the Cāḷukya king and many others caused *deśi* poetry to be born
> and fixed it in place in the Andhra land.[24]

A direct statement like this strongly suggests that the beginning of Telugu poetry can be marked with a specific date. Even though Nanněcoḍuḍu does not identify Nannaya or any other Telugu poet who preceded him, it is entirely possible that the Cāḷukya king he mentions is none other than Rājarājanarendra, Nannaya's patron. However, what is more important in this statement is that for Nanněcoḍuḍu all Sanskrit poetry is *mārga* and all Telugu poetry is *deśi.* In contrast, for Somanāthuḍu, Telugu poetry that follows the Sanskritized forms of *campū* is *mārga* and his *dvipada* is *deśi.* The two different ways of perceiving *deśi*, which I discuss later, are significant.

Nanněcoduḍu sees a distinct Telugu literary tradition, with its own *purāṇa*s and other genres—as opposed to the Sanskrit *purāṇa*s of Vyāsa and the *kāvya*s of Kālīdāsa, Bhavabhūti, Bhāravi, and others of that class.

Nanněcoḍuḍu sees himself as continuing that *deśi* literary culture by producing a *deśi kāvya.* He discusses his *kāvya* poetics in the *Kumārasambhavamu*; it is worth presenting them here in some detail:

> But when ideas come together smoothly in good Těnugu
> without any slack, and description achieves a style,
> and there are layers of meaning, and the syllables
> are soft and alive with sweetness, and the words
> sing to the ear and gently delight the mind,
> and what is finest brings joy, and certain flashes
> dazzle the eye, while the poem glows like moonlight,
> and the images are the very image of perfection,
> and there is a brilliant flow of flavor,
> and both *mārga* and *deśi* become the native idiom,
> and figures truly transfigure, so that people of taste
> love to listen and are enriched
> by the fullness of meaning—

that is how poetry works, when crafted
by all real poets.
Skilled words, charming movements,
ornaments, luminous feelings, elevated thoughts,
the taste of life—connoisseurs find all these
in poetry, as in women.

An arrow shot by an archer
or a poem made by a poet
should cut through your heart,
jolting the head.
If it doesn't, it's no arrow,
it's no poem.[25]

This is indeed the most complete treatise on Telugu *kāvya* poetics one can find for the period.[26] Nanněcoḍuḍu is clearly presenting a poetics different from the literary interests of Nannaya or Somanāthuḍu—both of whom had religious agendas. In contrast, Nanněcoḍuḍu's poetics are aimed at the aesthetic success of the poem. His theme in *Kumārasambhavamu* derives from religious sources, but the text is primarily aimed at working as a poem, free from religious preaching. For Nanněcoḍuḍu, poetry is an end in itself.

Again, for reasons that have still to be identified,[27] no full-fledged *kāvya* such as Nanněcoḍuḍu wrote appeared again in Telugu until Pĕddana in the sixteenth century. Śrīnāthuḍu made an attempt, two centuries after Nanněcoḍuḍu, with his Telugu rendering of Śrīharṣa's Sanskrit *Naiṣadhīyacarita* (The Life of Nala, Prince of Niṣadha). But as I discuss later in relation to problems of translation, he did not receive any recognition for this work. Or, to put it more bluntly, his attempt was not acceptable to the literary community or to the community of patrons on whom he depended for support. The group of upwardly mobile village heads and lesser chiefs in his vicinity were bent upon sponsoring religious *purāṇa* texts, which would elevate their status. Śrīnāthuḍu kept advertising himself as the maker of *Naiṣadhamu* in Telugu, but to no avail. The work was apparently too secular to be of interest to his patrons. He resorted to writings, the original versions of which could be traced to Vyāsa.

Court Poetry

Once *kāvya* found its mature expression in Telugu with Pĕddana's *Manucaritramu* (The Story of Manu), the literary culture reorganized itself to accommodate the aesthetics of pleasure rather than of religious merit.[28] *Manucaritramu* opened the way for an entirely new kind of poetry in Telugu. This is the poetry of refined composition, of a carefully worked texture of words chosen for their musical effect. Borrowed from the *Mārkaṇḍeyapurāṇa*, the story of the *Manucaritramu* is a long and somewhat complicated affair, taking many twists and turns. However, Pĕddana's interest is not in telling a story. The story exists for the sake of his style, which is a matter of language and the various ways of enhancing the pleasure a reader may find in language. Pĕddana in his exquisite composition creates a world of human pleasure so superior that the gods' women themselves desire it: for *Manucaritramu* includes the story of Varūthinī, a female *gandharva* (a class of divine dancing girls) who fell in love with a human, a Brahmin man named Pravaruḍu.

In this story, Pravaruḍu, who suffers from wanderlust, is given a magic ointment for his feet that allows him to fly to the Himalayas. When the ointment is washed off in the snow, Pravaruḍu finds himself stranded. In this unhappy predicament, Pravaruḍu encounters Varūthinī, who falls in love with him. Her attempt to attract Pravaruḍu's attention ends in frustration: Pravaruḍu is clearly aware of Varūthinī's charms, but, being committed to his life of rites and prayers, he rejects her advances and eventually makes his way home with the help of the god of fire, Agni.

The following verses describe Pravaruḍu's meeting with Varūthinī. Throughout this section Pĕddana makes the erotic feelings of Varūthinī explicit but deftly leaves Pravaruḍu's feelings to the reader's imagination, and even deliberately masks them. Pravaruḍu is first made aware that he is not alone in the remote mountain landscape by a characteristic fragrance:

One part musk enhanced by two parts camphor:
densely packed betel sent its fragrance,

masking all others, to announce
the presence of a woman.[29]

The fragrance is clearly indicative of a woman's presence, but, in the next verse Pravaruḍu apparently interprets it only as a sign of the presence of people. The neutral surface meaning of *janānvitamu* ("there are people here") allows Pravaruḍu the required cover not to exhibit his interest in women. But Pĕddana follows this with a relentlessly provocative description of Varūthinī.

He followed the fragrance
carried by the breeze, wave after wave,
thinking, "There are people here."
Then he saw her,

a body gleaming like lightning,
eyes unfolding like a flower,
long hair black as bees,
a face lit up with beauty,
proudly curved breasts,
a deep navel—

a woman, but from another world.

By now it is clear that Pĕddana's description of Varūthinī is what Pravaruḍu actually saw; the verse's enchanting words indicate that Pravaruḍu, after all, notices every detail to the last curve of Varūthinī's body. Pĕddana follows this beautifully refined verse—which moves with long lines, one metrical foot seamlessly flowing into the next—with a verse of short and quick lines, creating a dramatic staccato effect.

She saw him. Stood up
and walked toward him, the music
of her anklets marking the rhythm,
her breasts, her hair, her delicate waist
trembling. Stood by a smooth areca tree
as waves of light from her eyes
flooded the path that he was walking.

Rarely do we find in *purāṇa* poetry such a sensuous delineation of the internal feelings of a woman in love as in the following verses, which gently but surely follow the mental movements of Varūthinī:

First there was doubt,
a certain hesitation,
then a widening joy
as desires raced within her:
her mind was crying "Yes!"
her eyelids blinking,
for she was close to him now
and nearly paralyzed,
as her eyes, wide as the open lotus,
enfolded him in burning moonbeams.

Fluttering glances healed
her inability to blink,
and for the first time
she was sweating;
even her surpassing understanding
was healed by the new
confusion of desire.[30]
Like the beetle that, from concentrating
on the bee, *becomes* a bee,[31]
by taking in that human being
she achieved humanity
with her own body.

This remarkable passage suggests that being human is superior to the dull and unchanging state of the gods, who are forever young, do not blink or perspire, and of course do not die. In a later passage Varūthinī even regrets her inability to die and considers her immortality a punishment, and she envies human women who can kill themselves when they fail in love.[32] But, to continue with the present narrative: Varūthinī gives a playful description of her life by way of introducing herself, but Pravaruḍu is not impressed. His mind still set on his parents, wife, and rituals, he only asks her for directions to go home; he must return to see to his fire rites and sun worship. Varūthinī is desperate: she wants him in her embrace rather than in his village. Finally, Varūthinī unfolds her philosophy of life, love, and ultimate bliss. In one of Pĕddana's memorable verses, she states:

When the heart unfolds
in love, when it finds release from within

in undivided oneness, like a steady flame
glowing in a pot, when the senses attain
unwavering delight—

only that joy
is ultimately real.
Think about the ancient words:
ānando brahma, God
is joyfulness.[33]

Pĕddana's delightful treatment of this love story eclipses the rest of the long narrative, which tells of the birth of Manu, ostensibly the focus of the book; and ever since its composition, *Manucaritramu* has been read mainly for the story of Pravaruḍu and Varūthinī. Pĕddana's text was emulated as the greatest example of *kāvya* and served as a model for poets such as his near contemporary Rāmarājabhūṣaṇuḍu. Critics claim, however, that Rāmarājabhūṣaṇuḍu exceeded Pĕddana in the refinement and musical quality of his language.

After Rāmarājabhūṣaṇuḍu's *Vasucaritramu, kāvya* entered the realm of pure language, a world made of sounds and their meanings, independent of material reality. Creating a language that splits its meaning and envelops multiple meanings in one set of words in an elaborate, sustained pun is a special feature of a new kind of *kāvya*, called *śleṣa*, that developed during the late sixteenth century. Such a text can be read as two or even three different narratives. Piṅgaḷi Sūranna's *Rāghavapāṇḍavīyamu*, a *kāvya* that tells the story of the *Rāmāyaṇa* and the *Mahābhārata* simultaneously in one text, is the most famous of this genre.

We know that Nannaya and Tikkana professed religious purity: Nannaya described himself as one who never told a lie, and Tikkana is said to have performed a Vedic sacrifice to attain a level of personal perfection. But the *kāvya* poet is free from the burden of morality. All the legends of the *kāvya* poets show them as enjoying the pleasures of wealth, food, and women—especially women. These legends extol poets' sexual joy and even suggest that they were good poets because they were good lovers. For instance, the patron-king Kṛṣṇadevarāya of Vijayanagara (r. 1509–29) reputedly once asked in his court:

Why do Dhūrjaṭi's Telugu poems
overflow with sweetness incomparable?—

The court jester, Tenāli Rāmaliṅgaḍu, replied:

I know why. It comes from constant drinking
to quench his pain
at the honeyed lips of wild young courtesans
who drive the world insane.[34]

Respect for the poet in society was high, and he earned the right to enjoy a leisurely and comfortable life. In fact, he needed one. The following poem, attributed to Pĕddana, lists the comforts a poet needs to write a poem:

Without a quiet place, without a betel-nut flavored
with camphor sent by my lover through her
dear friend as messenger, without a good meal
that I find delicious, and a swinging cot,
and men of sensibility who can tell what
is good from what is bad, and the best of
scribes and performers who will understand the intent
of my work—unless I have all of these—
can anyone possibly ask me to compose poetry?[35]

Such images created a glorious impression of the court poet as a creator of pleasure and beauty, which also freed him from the normal rules of mundane life. His control of language gave him a power over the world equal only to the power of the creator god—if anything, the poet's creation was better than the god's because it was entirely pleasurable. The *kāvya* poet inherited from the *purāṇa* poet the power of the word to alter reality, which he used to protect and elevate the status of his patron. Yet he was not just a storyteller like the *purāṇa* poets who came before him; he was a story maker. He created with his words an edifice of extravagant grandeur that excited his listeners, who spent hours reflecting on each exquisitely crafted verse the poet produced. The *kāvya* poet was also realistic in his descriptions. Under the pretext of the eighteen different descriptions prescribed for a *kāvya*, the Telugu poet explored the life around him like an anthropologist giving a thick description of an event. By way of illustration, I quote a few verses from

Śrīnāthuḍu's *Śivarātrimāhātmyamu.* Here the poet describes the state of pregnancy:

Day by day, her pregnancy advanced,
to everyone's delight—though she was
getting tired. Yawn followed yawn,
her eyes grew languid and unsteady.
From time to time she was reminded
of the fatigue she used to get
from making love on top.

She moved slowly, heavy
with the child, like a raincloud
that has drunk the waters of the sea
just before the monsoon.

The description of the pregnancy is followed by the celebration of a rite to protect the pregnancy, a description of the childbirth, and then, a description of the delivery room in the household:

In the birth chamber, still impure from the birth,
the women were busy: putting a pot with white marks
at the head of the bed, drawing designs from white ashes,
sprinkling white mustard, preparing offerings,
mixing salt with neem leaves, setting up a fresh bed
out of rattan, burning buffalo horn,
blessing, applying sandal and oil,
cooking the *kāyamu* balls for the new mother,[36]
singing and making jokes.

One woman slapped on the wall a mixture of camphor and sandal.
Another held a frog upside down outside the birth chamber.
Wearing a yellow sari, a woman worshiped the goddess of poverty.[37]
With fresh paint of lime and turmeric, a lovely girl drew the sun and the moon on cloth.
Another draped an aging ram with a snakelike garland, a head on either end.
One sprinkled ghee. One set fire to a snake's discarded skin.[38]

Similarly, Pĕddana's description of the royal hunt in his *Manucaritramu* elaborately portrays the kinds, pedigrees, and names of dogs used in hunting; the hunting methods; and the style of cooking meat in the middle of the forest. With extraordinary realism in content and a meticulous formalism in style, *kāvya* produced a literary world simultaneously close to life and distanced from it. This *kāvya* world was suitable to create, authenticate, and sustain a glorified image of a real person. While *purāṇa* was essential to elevate the status of emerging chiefs, *kāvya* delighted the more established courts of the sixteenth and seventeenth centuries. *Kāvya*, however, continued the *purāṇa* style of addressing the patron and describing the patron's family in terms appropriate to their status. In fact, *kāvya* glorified the patron to such a degree that he became more than a sponsor or a supporter of the poet; he became an integral part of the poem.

Their sustained scholarly competence, grammatical and metrical skills, and especially their erudition in the Sanskrit texts gave the *kāvya* poets both a stature and a symbolic power that enabled them to attain the high status Sanskrit poets had enjoyed all along. Gradually, Telugu *kāvya* poetry replaced its Sanskrit equivalent and acquired a legitimizing power of its own. *Kāvya* became synonymous with poetry, and unless one composed a *kāvya* one was not a poet. *Purāṇa* poetry continued to be composed, but *kāvya* ruled the world of poetry to the extent that it became inseparable from the court. Even when there was no real court, *kāvya* created it in poetry. In fact, *kāvya* poetry elevated the small patron to the imagined status of a king. Perhaps this is a special feature of Telugu literary culture, not achieved to quite the same degree in other South Asian literatures, where *bhakti*, or devotional, poetry more often took and held center stage.

Poetry in the Temple

An entirely different literary culture began with Annamayya (1424–1503), a poet associated with the Veṅkaṭeśvara temple at Tirupati. Apparently patronized by a rich, stable god—perhaps richer and definitely more stable than any king of the period—Annamayya enjoyed a quiet, long life. According to the copperplates on which his songs were inscribed and preserved in the temple, Annamayya sang one song a day to his deity. The entire corpus of his *padam*s (songs) was grouped into two sections, *śṛṅgāra* (erotic) and *adhyātma* (spiritual). While it is very possible that the grouping reflects an editorial decision made by his son—who apparently paid for the expensive inscriptions of his father's songs—it still has an internal logic.

The literary culture surrounding the Annamayya tradition of song writing bears an entirely different ethos from courtly poetry, which created a patron in the process of its production. Located in the insulated atmosphere of the temple, Annamayya was unaffected by, if not uninterested in, the political atmosphere around him. He was not dependent on ascendant rulers and military leaders to support his literary work. He was also shielded from the courtly intrigues and personal politics of competing poets. His situation allowed him freedom in literary composition. For one thing, he sang in a meter of his own creation. His language was also free from the strict grammatical regulations of *kāvya* poetry (which were later made even stricter by Appakavi). Without a patron who sought social and political status from the act of sponsoring poetry, Annamayya was his own grammarian, his own literary theorist, and his own master. His legitimacy as a poet did not depend upon the mention of a great poet, grammarian, or guru of the past. In fact, a *śāstra* (a book of rules for later poets to follow while making *padams*) was later produced in Annamayya's name by his grandson, who along with other members of the Annamayya family helped institutionalize Annamayya as the master of the *padam* tradition in Telugu.[39]

Annamayya's family members—his son, grandson, and others—continued the *padam* genre, but due to its performative nature *padam* gradually came to be absorbed in the musical tradition of South India, rendering it unavailable for literature and literary theory. Not until recently, when modern scholars began to discuss Annamayya as a poet, has the literary world incorporated his work into its vision of Telugu poetry. Premodern literary culture considered Annamayya a singer-composer rather than a poet. However, the texts of Annamayya's large number of songs and his grandson's biography of him, written in *dvipada* meter, as well as Annamayya's own songs, strongly suggest that Annamayya and his followers were actually attempting to create a parallel literary culture based on the temple and not the court:

A story told about Annamayya clearly classifies him as a poet of a new tradition, which in retrospect we call the temple tradition. Sāḷuva Narasimharāya, a king of Vijayanagar (r. 1487–90), commanded Annamayya to compose a song for him similar to the ones he had sung for the god Veṅkaṭeśvara. When the poet refused, the king had him chained and thrown into prison. Annamayya, the legend says, appealed to the god in song, and the chains miraculously fell away.[40]

An opposition between courtly poets and temple poets finds a striking articulation by about the sixteenth century and continues unabated into the nineteenth century. Probably the best illustration of this opposition comes down to us in the legends about Potana. Legends are created about this poet who belonged to the fourteenth century to fit him into the discourse of temple versus court. Potana wrote in the *campū* genre, a style in which the court poets specialized. There is no hard evidence that he had antagonistic relations of any kind or that he was pressured by any king to dedicate his book to him. Nonetheless, legends about this poet represent him as one who steadfastly resisted a local king's request for the dedication of his *Bhāgavatamu.* When Potana refused the demand, legend has it, the king had the poet's manuscript buried in the ground. Later the manuscript was excavated; partly worm-eaten, it was completed by two of Potana's disciples. A verse in oral circulation states the popular esteem in which Potana was held for his moral strength in standing up to a king's power and insisting on dedicating his poetry to Hari, the god Viṣṇu:

Rather than giving his poems to lowly kings
and receiving money and mounts and dwellings,
then aging and dying and suffering
the hammer blows of the God of Death
this man, Bammĕra Potarāju, has, of his own will,
uttered his poem to be given to Śri Hari
for the sake of the welfare of the world.[41]

Yet another legend about Potana says that while he composed his *Bhāgavatamu,* Sarasvatī, the goddess of poetry, appeared before him with tears in her eyes, fearing that he might, like all other poets, sell her to kings. An oral verse describes how Potana reassured her:

Beloved daughter-in-law of Viṣṇu! Wife of Brahmā!
O my mother! Why do you weep so that the tears
fall to your breasts from your eyes dark with collyrium?
I will not, out of hunger, sell you, neither in thought
nor word nor action, to these meager kings of Karnataka
who are nothing but merchants. Trust me, Sarasvatī![42]

These stories also portray Śrīnāthuḍu, the prototypical court poet living in luxury, attempting to persuade Potana, who lives in poverty and tills the earth, to dedicate his poem to the king and get good rewards in return. To enhance the melodrama in these legends, Potana is represented as the husband of Śrīnāthuḍu's sister. Potana is said to have responded to Śrīnāthuḍu in perfect verse:

Instead of giving the virgin poem, tender as the fresh buds
of a young mango tree, to evil men, rather than eat
food earned through trade in women, what does it matter
if good poets become peasants, what does it matter if they
dig up roots in the depths of the forest so that they may
feed themselves and their wives and their children?[43]

In the tradition of temple poetry, the poet was not only pious and poor, but also modest. Unlike the court poet, who proudly announced his greatness in literary arts, the temple poet humbly presented himself as a servant of the god, not very learned, who prayed to the god to speak through him. A temple poet's poem was the god's work; it was blessed by the god. A legend about Potana says that when he was stuck in the middle of writing a poem, he took a break and went out for a walk. When he returned he found that the god himself had come, disguised as Potana, and completed the poem. A similar legend is told about Yathāvākkula Annamayya, the author of a Śaiva devotional text, *Sarveśvaraśatakamu* (Hundred Verses for the God of All). Yathāvākkula Annamayya wrote each verse on a palm leaf and threw it into the river; when a poem came back against the current, he understood it had been accepted by Śiva. Yathāvākkula Annamayya made a vow to himself that if any poem did not return from the current, he would kill himself. Inevitably, a palm leaf he threw into the water did not return. As he got ready to commit suicide, a shepherd boy came bearing a palm leaf and announced that it had just come floating in. The leaf did have a poem on it, but not the one Yathāvākkula Annamayya had written. The poet realized that the god was blessing his work by contributing a verse of his own to the collection.

Legends such as these elevate temple poets to a level of religious piety that is beyond human fault. The poets are revered as the chosen voices of the deity and their works are read for a devotional experience and not aesthetic pleasure alone. Temple poets typically even denied that they were making poetry; simile, metaphor, or other figure of speech, and aesthetic mood (*rasa*)—man-made as they are—are incapable of capturing the essence of the ultimate. For instance, Dhūrjaṭi says:

How can you be praised in elaborate language,
similes, conceits, overtones, secondary meanings,
or textures of sound? They cannot contain
your form. Enough of them!
More than enough. Can poetry hold out
before the face of truth?
Ah, but we poets,
O God of Kāḷahasti,
why don't we feel any shame?[44]

Potana even denied any respectability to poems unless they included praise of the deity:

A poem that praises god
is pleasant like the lake in heaven
with golden lotuses and geese.
A poem that does not praise god
is like a gutter in hell filled with dirty water—
never mind if it is written well.[45]

As we have observed in the case of Annamayya himself, in the culture of temple poetry the distinctions of patron, grammarian, and reader do not exist. The poem is the poet's direct communication to the deity; the poet sings to his god and to no one else. In this highly simplified mode, everything collapses into a devotional utterance. The narrative in such texts as Potana's *Bhāgavatamu* loses its story value; it is utilized as one more occasion to remember the name of the god and his deeds. All the characters of the story get reduced to two: the god and his devotee, the poet. The reader/listener enjoys the text only to the extent that he or she can identify with the poet's voice. In the *purāṇa* and *kāvya* cultures, by comparison, the reader/listener is associated with the patron, to whom the poem is addressed.

When the poet has the almighty god himself as his patron, he finds protection beyond what any earthly power can provide. This situation also allows the poet an opportunity for reflection and nourishes a subjectivity not available in a courtly narrative. The poet is now an individual looking deeply into himself and exploring himself, often in a confessional mode, with the god as listener. A genre that allows for such an expression of the self is the *śataka* (lit. one hundred), a loose collection of approximately one hundred verses in a single meter, tied together with a vocative, usually the name of the deity to whom the verses are addressed. *Śataka*s became popular after the sixteenth century, and we find countless poets composing them. In addition to providing a subjective space for introspection and self-criticism, this genre also gave poets a certain freedom to voice criticism of society, kings, and other politically powerful people. With his *Kāḷahastīśvaraśatakamu* (Hundred Verses for the God of Kāḷahasti), Dhūrjaṭi led the way with respect to both. The result is amazing: The poet emerges as a free individual, confessing his sins and censuring the sins of the society, playing alternately the sinner and the sage.

Temple poetry as a literary culture that gave rise to opposition to kings and other worldly patrons, to grammarians and court poets, each of which developed into a regular trope, has yet to be seriously studied. I briefly situate the broad features of these tropes in the larger context of a political culture in which the king who ruled the land was perceived as inseparable from the deity in the Viṣṇu temple of the area. Viṣṇu was viewed as the sovereign of the land, the ultimate *sārvabhauma*, or universal emperor. In opposition to this conceptualization stands the Brahminical king, the king according to the discourses in the Brahminical texts on moral order (*dharmaśāstra*). These texts say that the king only shares an aspect of Viṣṇu, that he belongs to the class of the Kshatriyas, who are a notch below the Brahmins in ritual status. The two modes of power, one stating that the king is the deity Viṣṇu and the other saying that the king embodies only an aspect of Viṣṇu, have important ramifications for the status of Brahmins. In a world where the king is Viṣṇu himself, the Brahmin becomes the servant of the king; whereas the Brahmin is ritually superior to the king if the latter is a human being viewed as an aspect of Viṣṇu. The differences between these two views of kingship, fundamentally unresolvable, occasionally surfaced in the court *kāvyas* during the reign of Kṛṣṇadevarāya but came into sharp focus in the seventeenth century, when warriors/traders from the Balija caste acquired kingship of the southern kingdoms of Madurai and Tañjāvūr.

Literature for the God-king in His Court-temple

During the height of the Nāyaka empire in Madurai and Tañjāvūr in the early seventeenth century, it was a common practice for the king's son to compose a *dvipada* poem equating his father with Viṣṇu.[46] Among these works were *Acyutâbhyudayamu* (The Victory of Acyuta), written by Raghunātha Nāyaka about the life of Acyuta Nāyaka; *Raghunāthanāyakâbhyudayamu*, by Vijayarāghava Nāyaka, Raghunātha's son; and *Vijayarāghavâbhyudayamu*, by Vijayarāghavā's son.[47] In describing the father/king as the god himself, the son was able to depict the king's love life, a topic that a son would never otherwise discuss. Once the king was equated with Viṣṇu, courtesans who served the king followed with their own compositions praising him. In a universe where king and god were assimilated into a single person, the poet's role was to devotedly serve him. This development opened up new possibilities for literary patronage. For one thing, a king could be both a ruler and a poet, writing about his own father who was also king; that is to say, the king could be both the patron and the hero of the poem. The hierarchy within the literary world was now:

god-king
poet as servant-devotee
readers who are also servant-devotees

Such a dramatic redefinition of the status of the king led to sweeping changes in the ideological order of social classes. To begin with, the poet as servant-devotee of the god-king no longer needed to be a Brahmin, or a man, either. The Brahmin male scholar-poet, who took pride in his learning in Sanskrit and who had earlier elevated the low-caste status of the king to the *varṇa* status of Kshatriya or its equivalent, that of a clean Shudra, by dedicating his *kāvya* text to the king, was now marginalized. In his place, accordingly, we find non-Brahmin male poets and courtesans elevated to the status of court poets. The dividing line between temple and court was erased, and so also the opposition between the temple poet and the court poet. The subject of the court poem was now the king himself, whose love-life was described in courtly *kāvya* style, except that it was now *kāvya* composed in the non-Brahmin *dvipada* meter rather than the grand, protean structures of the *campū* favored by the Brahmin poets of earlier courts.

The revolutionary reconceptualization of king as the god Viṣṇu gained even more significance because the Nāyaka king also happened to be a Balija, a left-hand caste of traders/warriors, according to the local South Indian social order. This caste, according to the Brahminical conceptualization of social order, is Shudra, the lowest of the four *varṇa* orders. This fusion of the god-king-warrior-merchant thus brought chaotic disturbance to the idealized Brahminical world of the four *varṇa*s—Brahmin, Kshatriya, Vaishya, and Shudra.

Literature in Public Space: The *Cāṭu* World

So far we have examined the roles of the poet, the patron, and the different genres of texts in different literary cultures in Telugu. But what can we say about the role of listeners and readers, those who enjoyed the texts? What was their image of the poet? What do we know about their understanding of poetry, their evaluation of various poets, and their criticism? A rare and valuable source for reader response to Telugu literature is offered by the *cāṭu,* the occasional verse independently circulated in oral tradition and quoted in conversations among literary communities. This new development began to crystallize around the seventeenth century. By this time, Sanskrit was accessible to literary communities not as a language of gods, *devabhāṣa,* but as one more language of poetry, in addition to Telugu. The *cāṭu* poems related to imagined stories around great kings and poets who adorned their courts in remembered history: Kṛṣṇadevarāya and Pĕddana for Telugu; King Bhoja and Kālidāsa for Sanskrit. Other Telugu and Sanskrit poets, such as Dhūrjaṭi and Bhavabhūti, parade across these poems along with other kings, courtesans, and ministers. The people who quoted these verses did not belong to the courts, nor were they superior scholars; they were ordinary educated people in cities, towns, and villages. They were intelligent, sensitive, and well-informed readers who reflected upon a rich literary body of texts. Verses in this tradition are available in the hundreds, many of them thematizing the popular understanding of a given poet's work. These verses best illustrate the role of poetry in what might be called a public space.

We considered earlier the scholar-poet as defined by Appakavi and described in the *kāvya* tradition. We are familiar now, too, with the *bhakti* poet as defined in the temple tradition. The *cāṭu* tradition built on both of these concepts of poets and created a distinctly different kind of poet who had the power to make and unmake reality, who was superior to both the king and the grammarian, and most of all who could see things no one else had seen. The following story about Bhīmakavi, popular in the *cāṭu* tradition, describes the *cāṭu* poet richly.[48]

Bhīmakavi's mother was a childless widow living at her parents' home. One day she went with a group of pilgrims to the Śivarātri festival at Dakṣārāma, the temple to Bhīmeśvara Śiva. She saw her fellow pilgrims praying to the god for boons. Skeptical, she said to the god, "If you give me a son like you, I will give you a tank of water as oil for your lamps and four tons of sand for your food." The god was pleased at this challenge and visited the widow that night; he slept with her and promised her a son, whom she was instructed to name after him.

She had a son and called the boy Bhīma. One day his playmates mocked him for being a bastard. He ran to his mother and threatened to hit her with a rock if she did not reveal the name of his father. She said,

"That rock in the temple [the *liṅga*] is your father; go ask him." So the boy went into the temple and threatened to hit the god with a rock. Bhīmeśvara Śiva, afraid, appeared before him in his true form and announced that he was, indeed, the boy's father. "In that case," said the boy, "from now on, whatever I say must come true." The god granted him that boon.

One day there was a Brahmin feast in the village, held behind locked doors. Bhīmakavi was not invited. He cursed the Brahmins in the following verse:

> Full of their own greatness, these lousy Brahmins
> insulted me and threw me out of their feast.
> I'll turn their fried cakes into frogs,
> their rice into lice, and all the side dishes
> into fishes.

When the Brahmins, witnessing these transformations, begged his forgiveness, Bhīmakavi sang a second verse:

> I'm Bhīmanna, son of Lord Bhīma himself,
> born into the great Vemulavāḍa clan.
> Now these Brahmins know me, and look at me with respect.
> I take back my curse: let their food
> become food.[49]

Famed in the *cāṭu* tradition as "capable of cursing and blessing" (*śapânugrahasamarthuḍu*), Bhīmakavi is said to have cursed kings and destroyed and restored thrones. He also made trees dry up and dry wood sprout. The word of the *cāṭu* poet is never empty of effect; it changes, or indeed creates, a reality in conformity with the vision implicit in the poet's speech.

The *cāṭu* world is also playful and funny, as is evident from the many stories told about Kṛṣṇadevarāya and his court poets. According to one story, Kṛṣṇadevarāya caught sight of his beloved queen Cinnādevi as she was drying her hair after a bath. Her beauty was irresistible to the king, who sneaked up from behind to kiss her. As he moved her hair to bring her face close to him her sari fell off and she shyly tried to cover herself with her hand, which was adorned with gem-studded bracelets and rings. Arriving late to the court, the king presented to his poets the following *samasya* (puzzle) in the form of one line in a possible four-line verse:

> *visphurita-phaṇā-maṇi-dyutula pŏlpagu nāga-kumāruḍo yanan*

> as a Cobra-Prince might spread his great gem-encrusted hood to guard a hidden trove

Mukku Timmana, the poet famed as having been sent as a wedding gift to the king by Cinnādevi's family, completed the verse and resolved the puzzle.

> *varuḍu ceraṅgu paṭṭinanu valv' aṭu vīḍina kānta sigguceṇ*
> *urutara-ratna-didhitulan ŏppĕḍu dāpali kela mūyagā*
> *karam' amaren karamb' ŏpuḍu kāmanidhānamu gāciyunna vi-*
> *sphurita-phaṇā-maṇi-dyutula pŏlp'agu nāga-kumāruḍo yanan.*

> When the lover pulled her sari
> and it came loose,
> in sudden shyness she moved to hide
> her treasure-house of love
> with her left hand, luminous with vivid stones—
> as a Cobra-Prince might spread
> his great gem-encrusted hood
> to guard a hidden trove.[50]

True to the *cāṭu* aphorism that a poet sees things that even the sun's rays cannot penetrate (*ravi gāñcanico kavi gañcune kadā*), the poet saw the events in the royal bedroom without being there and skillfully converted them into a universal love poem without mentioning names.

Another feature of the *cāṭu* world is that the poet defies authority and ridicules pomp and pride—especially if it is overbearing. According to one story, Pĕddana, who was Kṛṣṇadevarāya's court poet and proudly wore the victory anklet (*gandapĕnderamu*) given by the king himself in recognition of the poet's unparalleled excellence, asked Tenāli Rāmaliṅgaḍu:

> *vadalaka mroyun āndharakavi vāmapadambuna hemanūpuramb'*
> *uditamayūrakaṇṭhaninadôktulan ēmani palku palkurā.*

What does the golden anklet say that never stops jingling
on the left foot of the poet of Andhra and its voice is like
a lofty peacock? You! Tell me what does it say?

The king had a concubine, Gudiyala Sāni, to whom he gave lavish gifts for her skills—more lavish than he gave to any of his poets. Tenāli Rāmaliṅgaḍu answered Pĕddana in a verse that precisely captures the tone of the question:

gudiyalasāni nunnani trikoṇamun'andali bhāgyarekha nī-
nuduṭanu ledu led'anucu nuru vidhambula nŏkki palkurā.

It says in a hundred ways, that the line of fortune
which crosses the soft moans of Gudiyala the whore
isn't there for you on your forehead, it's not there![51]

The *cāṭu* culture paid close attention to the quality of language and the nuances of its uses and misuses even by the great poets of the time. Pĕddana, it is said, used a rather inelegant phrase, *amavasaniśi* (dark moonless night), instead of the usual *amāvasyāniśi*, apparently because the meter required a phrase with all short syllables. Tenāli Rāmaliṅgaḍu parodied the poet with the following verse:

ĕmi tini sĕpitivi kapitamu
bama paḍi vĕri puccakaya vaḍi tini sĕpito
umĕtah kaya tini sĕpito
amavasa niśi yanina māṭa alasani pĕdanā.

What did you have for breakfast,
Alasani Pĕdana,
before you made this verse?
Probably the squash
that makes your mind wander?
Or, you mistook that crazy berry
and ate it in a hurry.[52]

This verse comically removes long syllables and consonant clusters right through—including the poet's name at the end, which it changes from Allasāni Pĕddana to Alasani Pĕdana—to ridicule the poet for his use of one compound without its usual long vowels and consonant cluster.

Tenāli Rāmaliṅgaḍu is an imagined poet created by the *cāṭu* world. Modern literary scholars, unmindful of the nature of *cāṭu* tradition, mistakenly thought this poet really existed and began to identify him with the late-sixteenth-century poet Tenāli Ramakrṣṇuḍu. The stories told about Rāmaliṅgaḍu's outrageous literary pranks in Kṛṣṇadevarāya's court show that the *cāṭu* tradition was acutely aware of the vanity, verbosity, and greed of the court poets.

In the imagination of the *cāṭu* world, King Kṛṣṇadevarāya emerges as a fulltime literary patron with eight poets, the *aṣṭadiggaja*s (guardian-elephants of the eight directions), seated around him in his court. The *aṣṭadiggaja* legend has grown so strong that it even survived the critical eye of modern historians, who began listing the possible members of this group. Although the *aṣṭadiggaja*s did not exist in history, they are nonetheless real and enduring products of this literary culture.

In the *cāṭu* world, to sum up, the poet has a superhuman access to knowledge and the creative control to alter reality at will. The king in this world is a creation of the poet and remains in power only so long as he continues to respect, appreciate, and patronize the poets. The hierarchy of the literary universe is redrawn as follows:

poet
king
admiring readers

Because the poet rules this world as a *niraṅkuśa*—an elephant that no goad can restrain—the grand, controlling role of the grammarian, as Appakavi envisaged it, is thrown out. The poet sees everything, knows everything, and can envision past, present, and future. The poet does not suffer any opposition from the scholar, or even from the king.

The Question of Literary Language

Śaivabhakti poet Pālkuriki Somanāthuḍu had raised the question of the opposition of Telugu and Sanskrit—an issue in Telugu literary culture that continued for a long time. In the skillful hands of a court poet like Śrīnāthuḍu, Telugu comfortably accommodated a heavy input of Sanskrit words, even large Sanskrit compounds—larger than any commonly used by Sanskrit poets themselves. The sudden appearance of

Sanskrit and Sanskritic *purāṇa*s in Telugu during Śrīnāthuḍu's period (mid-fourteenth to mid-fifteenth century)—after a serious Teluguizing attempt by a major poet like Tikkana—is a phenomenon that is still to be explained. Part of the story may lie in the contemporary impact of the wars with the armies of the Delhi Sultanate and the fall of the Kākatīya empire in the mid fourteenth century. The Brahminical reaction to this historical dislocation was to return to the religious past and revive Sanskrit, in response to the Persian that was used by Śrīnāthuḍu's time as the court language of the Bahmani sultans in the Deccan, as well as the sultans of Delhi. This was perhaps less a confrontational stance than a sympathetic reaction to the emergence of Persian as the new elite's language of culture, irrespective of their religious affiliation. We know that at least one of the Brahmin patrons of Śrīnāthuḍu, Bĕṇḍapūḍi Annayamantri, was a competent scribe in Persian.[53]

The *kāvya* poets, especially Śrīnāthuḍu and Pĕddana, made the use of Sanskrit the hallmark of a learned poet. In this they were following a path laid down by Nannaya himself, but they extended the expressive range of Sanskrit beyond the limits of a narrative text. Given to the joy of composing and relishing each verse individually, extracted from narrative sequence, the *kāvya* poets constructed monumental compositions of skill and scholarship. Here, for example, is Pĕddana describing the Himalaya mountains in his *Manucaritramu.* The text in italics is Sanskrit; the Telugu is limited to the few words and suffixes in roman font.

> aṭa jani kāñce *bhūmisur*uḍ *ambara-cumbi-śiras-sarjjharī-*
> *paṭala-muhurmuhur-luṭhad-abhaṅga-taraṅga-mṛdaṅga-nisvana-*
> *sphuta-naṭanânurūpa-pariphulla-kalāpa-kalāpi-jālam*un
> *kaṭaka-carat-kareṇu-kara-kampita-sālam*u *śīta-śailam*un.[54]

The prose passages of *campū* compositions, among which the verses are interspersed, the poets packed densely with breathtaking, jaw-breaking Sanskrit words, unlimited as to length. Apparently the *kāvya* intended for scholars requires a demanding style.[55]

The old opposition to the Sanskritic *mārga*, inaugurated by Pālkuriki Somanatha, had lost its edge: now the question of Sanskrit versus Telugu was to be settled on the basis of style rather than the opposition between *deśi* and *mārga*. Poets who used *deśi* genres, like *dvipada* and *padam*, also used Sanskrit words extensively; and poets who adopted *mārga* genres, like the *campū*, began to reflect on the problems of using heavy Sanskrit words in their works. However, the perception remained that *deśi* is all Telugu and *mārga* is Sanskritic; and the styles are sometimes so different that one wonders if both were truly written in the same language. This example from Annamayya, written in the *deśi* genre of *padam*, is worth contrasting with the *campū* verse by his contemporary Pĕddana, just quoted:

kaḍal 'uḍipi nir'*āḍagā talacu vāralaku*
kaḍaleni manasu*ku kaḍama ĕkkaḍidi.*
dāham *'aṇagina vĕnuka*
taṭtvam'ĕrigĕdan anna
dāham*'el'aṇagu tā*
tattvam*'em'erugu.*

You say you want to bathe
when the waves subside.
Where is there an end
to the endless mind?

You say, "Let me quench my thirst,
and then I'll find the truth."
You cannot quench your thirst.
How can you know truth?
Is there an end?[56]

In this *padam* only seven words have a Sanskrit origin—four of which, *niru, manasu, dāhamu*, and *tattvamu*, are in the first stanza, which is quoted here—yet all five of them are so well known in Telugu that the average speaker thinks of them as Telugu words. The *padam* is accessible without commentary and without gloss, which makes its reception immediate. Annamayya wrote just a few *padams* in Sanskrit, but even these are not beyond the capacity of an educated Telugu audience. The opposition is not between Sanskrit and Telugu, as it is often perceived to be, but between arcane and accessible diction. Poets who enjoyed making their works available only to the very learned chose arcane diction, be it Sanskrit or Telugu, while other poets made their writings available to the average educated person by choosing well-known words of both Sanskrit and Telugu origin. The court poets, for instance, always tried to present themselves as scholars and wrote learned (*prauḍha*) poems, while the temple poets wrote unpretentious and accessible compositions.

The Politics of Translation

It is curious that in a language used to "translate" a large number of Sanskrit texts, there is no word equivalent to "translation." The Sanskrit-derived *anuvādamu*, now popular in modern Telugu, is itself a loan translation and was never used in this sense before the twentieth century. Nannaya, in rendering Vyāsa's *Mahābhārata* into Telugu, did not claim to be "translating" the Sanskrit text. The poet reports that his patron, the eastern Cāḷukya king Rājarājanarendruḍu, said to him:

> With all your learning, compose in Telugu
> a book that makes clear
> what Kṛṣṇa Dvaipāyana spoke—
> the proven meaning bound to the *Mahābhārata* text.[57]

Even a cursory comparison of the Sanskrit and Telugu texts will show that Nannaya did not follow the original in detail: he left out large sections and condensed others, and it is a matter of opinion whether or not he always captured the meaning of the original. From the internal perspective of the tradition, the question of translation, in the modern sense, never arises. Tikkana, who completed Nannaya's *Mahābhāratamu*, calls his predecessor the *creator* of Telugu poetry, not a translator of a Sanskrit text into Telugu:

> The one who produced, so skillfully,
> the first three books, starting at the beginning,
> was Nannaya Bhaṭṭu—the master of Telugu poetry,
> the Creator himself, great in spirit.[58]

As the tradition developed, poet after poet retold Sanskrit texts in Telugu. Styles changed, meters changed, genres changed, and narrative gave way to descriptive texts, but the presence of a Sanskrit source remained nearly constant, providing a legitimacy that a wholly new work might lack. (Perhaps here we have one definition of a tradition.) Rāmarājabhūṣaṇuḍu uses a fascinating analogy to reflect on the borrowing, embellishing, and reworking of Sanskrit:

> Invented stories are artificial diamonds.
> The old stories are precious stones
> straight from the mine.
> But ancient stories reworked by good poets
> with their irresistible imagination
> are precious gems perfectly cut.
> Make a poem like *that*
> for me.[59]

The idea that a theme of the poet's own making is not as valuable as one borrowed from an ancient source has an aesthetic justification. Old themes acquire a depth and fullness from their sustained life in the collective awareness of the community. Mythological and historical themes (*itihāsa* and *purāṇa*), and also tales and legends, have the advantage of having grown in the culture where the audience has invested its imagination for generations. While this advantage is common to any story of the past, the *mārga* literary culture in Telugu further stipulated that the source should be Sanskrit.

By the eleventh century, when literature in Telugu began to take shape, Sanskrit already had three well-established textual categories: Veda, *purāna* (which included *itihasa* and *śāstra*), and *kāvya.* Based on the binary division of sound, *śabda*, and meaning, *artha*, of the word, literary convention assigned these three categories to three different classes: Veda is classified as *śabdapradhāna*, a sound-primary text, that is, it is valued primarily for its phonic value. *Purāṇa* and *śāstra* are classified as *arthapradhana*, meaning-primary texts, valued for their meaning alone. In contrast, *kāvya* is classified as *śabdarthapradhāna*, a text that shows an inseparable union of sound and meaning, each critical in its own right.[60] The implications for translation are clear: Veda by definition cannot be translated or even retold, while *kāvya*, too, is completely resistant to translation. Only *śāstra, itihasa*, and *purāṇa* are available for translation; indeed, since their meaning can be constituted in different ways, they may be thought of as requiring repeated telling and reinterpretation. By the eleventh century, such an understanding of the textual world in Sanskrit was generally accepted and shared by elite scholars in Telugu.

It is in this context that we should understand the fact that a large number of *itihasa* and *purāṇa* retellings in Telugu have appeared since the eleventh century, while, with one major exception, no Sanskrit *kāvya* has been translated. The exception is Śrīnāthuḍu's *Śṛṅgāranaiṣadhamu* (The Prince of Niṣadha in Love). A translation of Śrīharṣa's Sanskrit *Naiṣadhīyacarita*, Śrīnāthuḍu's work is a magnificent accomplishment, in that it translates a poem considered in theory to be untranslatable. Śrīnāthuḍu appears to be aware of the difficulty. In a rare statement of his method of translation, unfortunately misread by recent literary scholars, Śrīnāthuḍu eloquently states his method of translating poetry. It is worth quoting in full:

> The erotic poem made by the great poet Bhaṭṭa Harṣa, the poet who traveled through paths unseen by other poets, is here rendered into Telugu in a way that makes use of the special features of the language to touch the hearts of great minds: following the sound (*śabda*) of the text, aiming at the poet's intention (*abhiprāya*), keeping the poetic feeling (*bhāva*) in view, supporting the mood (*rasa*), embellishing the figures of speech (*alaṅkāra*), taking care of propriety (*aucitya*) and eliminating impropriety (*anaucitya*), closely obeying the original.[61]

The most crucial words in the statement are "following the sound of the text." When the original words in the text are kept—that is, if the texture of the original is retained—problems crop up in translation. Sanskrit words, and even compounds, can be imported into Telugu with little change except for the final case endings, as we can see in Śrīnāthuḍu's large-scale incorporation of Śrīharṣa's phrases. For example:

Sanskrit: *vicitra-vākcitra-śikhaṇḍi-nandana*
Telugu: *vicitra-vākcitra-śikhaṇḍi-nandanuṇḍu*
Sanskrit: *suvarṇa-daṇḍaika-sitâtapatrita-jvalat-pratāpāvali-kīrti-maṇḍitaḥ*
Telugu: *tapanīya-daṇḍaika-dhavaḷātapatritôddaṇḍa-tejaḥ-kīrti-maṇḍaluṇḍu*

The first phrase is incorporated verbatim into Telugu with only a change in the final case suffix—*u* plus *ṇḍu*—to grammatically assimilate it. In the second example, the substitutions of the words *tapanīya* for *suvarna* and *dhavaḷa* for *sita*, as well as the rewriting of *jvalat-pratāpāvali* as *uddaṇḍa-tejaḥ*, are apparently intended to serve the metrical requirements of Telugu verse. Note, however, that the substituted words are close Sanskrit equivalents to the words in the original Sanskrit compound. It is this re-Sanskritization of the original Sanskrit text that makes Śrīnāthuḍu's translation subtle and deftly original. The replacement of one Sanskrit phrase for another makes the Telugu text different from the original and also close to it.

The sound sequences of one language may (and often do) produce unacceptable meanings when reused in another language. The alternative, restating the meaning of one language in the words of another language, has its problems too: whether the meaning "restated" was really the same as the one in the original language, or whether a different language "creates" a different meaning. Even in the case of such closely interacting languages as Sanskrit and Telugu, where a large body of Sanskrit vocabulary has been directly brought into Telugu, there are inevitable problems in reproducing words as they are. Telugu does allow into its fold many words from Sanskrit, in fact whole compounds directly. The impression one gets from this is that a Telugu poet could change the case ending to import an entire Sanskrit compound into Telugu. This is not actually true. Śrīnāthuḍu, who took upon himself to follow the "*sabda*" sound faithfully, knows the limitations. He took care in following only such sound sequences that sound poetic, and those that do not lead to undesirable meanings in Telugu.

Here is a random example from Śrīharṣa's original: Describing curd that is served in the wedding feast after Nala and Damayanti were married. Śrīharṣa writes:

> *vāhadviṣadbaṣkayaṇīpayaḥsrutam*
> *sudhāhradat paṅkam ivôdhṛtam dadhi.—Naiṣadhīya*, 16.92

Śrīnāthuḍu apparently saw that this compound with its phonetic sequence such as *vāhadviṣat*, "water-buffalo" and "*baṣkayaṇī*", "which gave birth a few months ago" with a *sandhi* that produces a harsh sound /*dbha*/, does not sound poetic in Telugu. The meanings of these words do not easily adopt to Telugu culture either. So he abandoned the whole verse. A further reason for rejecting the verse is the unpleasantness in the use of "*paṅkam*". In Telugu it means wet dirt, which does not sound right applied to curd lifted from the sediment from a lake, even if it is a take of ambrosia, whereas in Sanskrit it is perfectly acceptable.[62]

His vow that he would follow "*sabda*" (sound) of the original gives rise to problems and therefore he immediately explains the care he took in making sure that what he writes works as a poem in Telugu, with no flaws that arise if he had followed "*sabda*" in the Sanskrit original blindly.

Śrīnāthuḍu refers to his *Śṛṅgāranaiṣadhamu* as an original poem, not a translation. He calls himself the creator of the poem in Telugu and lists this work as the foremost of his achievements in literature. The modern literary critical establishment treats his work as a masterly creation of great scholarship and incomparable creative skill. However, legends in oral literary tradition tell us a different story. Although rejected by recent literary historians as historically unreliable, these legends, honored by tradition, have a value similar to literary criticism, and they are worth considering as serious representations of the collective wisdom of the literary community. One of these legends tells us that when Śrīnāthuḍu showed his translation to Sanskrit pandits, they laughed at him and said, "Take your *ḍu, mu, vu*, and *lu* [Telugu nominative case endings] and give our Sanskrit text back to us."

Why would the literary-critical tradition reject and ridicule such a brilliant text, written by one of the established masters of Telugu literature? Before we answer this question we should note that the oral legend about Śrīnāthuḍu was not, as is naively held in popular belief, contemporaneous with Śrīnāthuḍu but belongs to a seventeenth-century *cāṭu* tradition. We should also refer to the discussion earlier of the two conventional divisions of literature in Sanskrit and Telugu into *mārga* and *deśi* as presented by Nannĕcoḍuḍu and Pālkuriki Somanāthuḍu. Sanskrit pandits wanted to retain the special status of Sanskrit by maintaining, as Nannĕcoḍuḍu did some five hundred years earlier, that all Sanskrit literature is *mārga* and all Telugu literature is *deśi.* They would have had no problem if Telugu poets had followed Pālkuriki Somanāthuḍu and developed an internal hierarchy among themselves, elevating the Telugu poets who followed Sanskritic meters to *mārga* status. However, times had changed and the boundaries of *mārga* and *deśi* are not defined by language anymore. Up until this time Telugu poets had stayed within the Telugu tradition, borrowing from Sanskrit texts that were classified as meaning-primary; their claims to *mārga* status within the Telugu tradition had not been objectionable to Sanskrit pandits. But now Śrīnāthuḍu was presented as not only having violated a taboo and entered a realm of Sanskrit kept beyond the limits of regional language traditions, but also as having sought the approval of Sanskrit pandits for his audacity. This legend symbolizes a new conflict between Sanskrit and Telugu that emerged around the seventeenth century and an effort on the part of Telugu poets to break the language-based boundaries of *mārga* and *deśi.* It is this new claim to status—the claim that a Telugu text can be *mārga* in its own right, not just within a Telugu literary context—that is objected to in the oral legends about Śrīnāthuḍu's Telugu rendering of Śrīharṣa's *Naiṣadhīyacarita.*

However, texts that were translated were not limited to Sanskrit sources alone. In premodern South Asia, with its multiplicity of literary traditions and languages, multilingual scholarship, and contacts between poets of different regions and languages, texts moved across languages and poets borrowed from other poets in countless instances. Elsewhere I have suggested that the concept of a mother tongue is a foreign, post-nineteenth-century idea in India, and that the opposition between languages in premodern India was hierarchical rather than regional. All other languages were *deśabhāṣās* (languages of regions), and Sanskrit was *devabhāṣā* (language of the gods).[63] The nationalist identification of languages with regional populations, and the positing of language boundaries for regions, have produced the category of Telugu people, a category that ignores the fact that people living in the area now known as Andhra spoke and/or read other languages, such as Kannada, Tamil, Oriya, Persian, and Urdu as well. An extreme form of this language nationalism is reflected in the disappearance of multilingual literati. Very few scholars, if any, are literate in other regional languages, and it has become a common practice among regional scholars to take a nationalistic pride in the superiority and originality of the poets of their own literary tradition, even though a closer examination would reveal a lively mutual borrowing and translation from one regional language to the other.

Nowhere is the politics of language so clearly visible as in the area of translation. While a large number of premodern Telugu poets cited their source as one or another Sanskrit text, almost none acknowledged a non-Sanskrit source. We know, however, that many Telugu poets borrowed from Tamil, Kannada, and perhaps other regional language sources, as well as from other traditions within Telugu. Having a Sanskrit source elevated a regional language text and the borrowing poet to a higher status and therefore was invariably mentioned, while a regional language source never was. Illustrious examples are from Dhūrjaṭi, who used Tamil Śaiva narratives from *caṅkam* sources in his *Kāḷahastîśvaramāhātmyamu* (The Greatness of the God of Kāḷahasti), and Kṛṣṇadevarāya, who borrowed from Tamil Vaiṣṇava narratives for his *Āmuktamālyada* (The Girl Who Gave Her Garland to God). Neither of them ever mentioned their sources. It is the absence of identification of non-Sanskrit sources that led to the mistaken impression that Telugu literature was an independent island, uninfluenced by other regional languages, with only Sanskrit as its originating source.

The practice of not mentioning a non-Sanskritic source extends also to Telugu poets who borrowed from other Telugu sources. When Telugu poets who wrote in the *mārga* tradition translated from *deśi* Telugu poets, they did not mention their sources. For example, for his *mārga* text *Haravilāsamu* Śrīnāthuḍu translated Siriyala's story from Pālkuriki Somanāthuḍu's *deśi* text *Basavapurāṇamu* but did not mention his source. However, when Piḍuparti Somanāthuḍu translated Pālkuriki Somanāthuḍu's *Basavapurāṇamu* into a *mārga* text with the same title, because for him it was a sacred text he meticulously mentioned the name of the original author and paid respect to him, confirming the general practice that a poet mentions his source when the text he borrows from comes from a higher tradition. There are a few minor instances of a verse or two that Śrīnāthuḍu translated from famous Sanskrit authors without mentioning their names, but the question here is not about such minor instances.

There is another interesting instance that we might call masked translation. This is best illustrated by Śrīnāthuḍu's *Bhīmeśvarapurāṇamu*, which the poet claims to have retold from the "Godāvarīkhanda" of the Sanskrit *Skāndapurāṇa.* Recent scholarship has argued that the extant Sanskrit "Godāvarīkhaṇḍa" is in fact a translation of Śrīnāthuḍu's Telugu text, whether by Śrīnāthuḍu himself or by some other poet of his time. It is not possible to determine the truth of Śrīnāthuḍu's claim that this text is the original from which he had produced his own version. It is equally plausible that the Sanskrit text used by Śrīnāṭhuḍu was lost, and that some time later a new "original" was created that was based on Śrīnāthuḍu's Telugu text. Certainly such masked translations of other Telugu works into Sanskrit do exist, and they have invariably been claimed as the sources for the Telugu works. One can understand the motivation for such claims in the context of the legitimizing power of Sanskrit and the lack of status for regional-language works. Notably, this practice prevails only with texts that are held in reverence by one religious community or the other. The Śrīnāthuḍu text, for instance, is revered as the foundation story of the great Śiva temple known as Dakṣārāma, in the present-day East Godāvarī district of Andhra Pradesh. Apparently Śrīnāthuḍu's Telugu version of the story would not have attained the same status as a Sanskrit version attributed to Vyāsa.

The need to find a Sanskrit original for every Telugu literary work in the *mārga* tradition reached absurd proportions in premodern Andhra. We find in Vallabharāyaḍu's *Krīḍâbhirāmamu* (The Joy of Sex), a satirical play from the fifteenth century, that the author invents a Sanskrit play called *Premābhirāma* (The Joy of Love), attributes it to a second-rate poet (Rāvipāṭi Tripurāntaka), and claims that his *Krīḍâbhirāmamu* is a Telugu rendering of that Sanskrit original. The intention, obviously, is to ridicule the convention of finding a Sanskrit original for every Telugu literary creation.

Once a translation was made, however, the originals themselves ceased to be read as much as the Telugu renderings. Before the twentieth century, no literary critic compared the translation with the original in order to comment on the quality of the translation. Faithfulness to the original was never an issue. Sanskrit originals apparently provided legitimacy, while Telugu renderings were actually read. As Appakavi quotes from a Sanskrit text he attributes to Nannaya:

> Learned people love the language and dress of the region where they live; given to the pleasure of poetry, they enjoy poetry in their own language and do not care much for the other language.[64]

It seems an appropriate acknowledgment of the complex language situation that when Appakavi makes this statement, he needs the authority of the Sanskrit language and of Nannaya's name.

Two points emerge from this discussion: First, faithful rendering of a text is not a requirement for a good translation. It is the meaning of the text that is reconstructed, and no attempt is made to follow the original slavishly. A good poem, translation or not, is original by definition. The author (*kavi*) of the poem is the maker (*kartā*). Second, and closely related to the question of translation, is the accusation of plagiarism that has infested modern conceptions of premodern literary traditions in Telugu. In fact, in premodern traditions originality was never deemed to reside in the theme or the narrative outline of a text. Instead, it consisted in the skill exhibited in making a new variation on available material.

The Culture of Writing and the Propagation of Books

In a remarkable historical statement, Nannĕcoḍuḍu asserted that the Cāḷukya kings "caused [Telugu poetry] to be born [*puṭṭiñci*]" at a time when there was only Sanskrit poetry in the world. We know now that there was enough Telugu poetry around in the form of oral songs and metrical poems (recorded in inscriptions), but we have to conclude that Nannĕcoḍuḍu did not recognize any of this as literature. For him, only a composition by a poet made available in writing was literature, and he marked the beginning of Telugu literature with the Cāḷukya king (probably Rājarājanarendruḍu) because the court poet (probably Nannaya) wrote poems. In keeping with his values, he exhorts at the end of his *kāvya*:

Read my poem, listen to it, copy it;
god Śiva, goddess Parvati and their son Kumara
will grant your wishes.[65]

Pālkuriki Somanāthuḍu adds a similar request at the end of his *dvipada* poem *Paṇḍitārādhyacaritramu* (Biography of Paṇḍitārādhyuḍu), clearly suggesting that even a poem in *dvipada*, which was primarily meant to be sung, was written, preserved, and propagated as a book. So also epic narratives like *Bhāskararāmāyaṇamu*, which were meant to be read out before an audience, include, as acts meriting the god's grace (*phalaśruti*) the copying and saving of the work in book form, along with its reading. The reception of poetry still took place in the oral-aural mode, and a poet most often read out his poem in performance; but literary status was reserved only for a poet who was literate, and written compositions alone attained the status of literature.

A general diction of orality continued in literary discourse for a long time, until almost the twentieth century. The verb "to write" (*vrāyu*) meant to copy a text, and a scribe was called *vrāyasakāḍu*, writer. Poets made (*ceyu/onarcu*), spoke (*cĕppu*), constructed (*nirmiñcu*), built (*kaṭṭu*), and even wove (*allu*) texts, but only copyists "wrote" them. Chapters of books were called *ucchvāsa* or *āśvāsa*, after the word for breath, *śvāsa.* A well-read person was called a *bahuśruta*, one who listened (that is, learned) a lot. An illiterate person was derogatorily called a *nirakṣarakukṣi*, one who doesn't have syllables in his belly. Poets asked the goddess of speech, Sarasvatī, to stay on their tongue. Even the literary-critical terms belonged to an oral tradition, for example the emphasis on *dhārā*, a free-flowing style, which was in the first instance a value in oral composition.

Nannaya's written style was already one that required a reflective reading to appreciate the inner meaning of a tightly structured narrative, and not one that appealed to an immediate understanding, helped by repetitive lines, as oral-based styles did. But the surface texture of his verse appealed to the ear that was used to a flowing, harmonious style. His statement about his own poetry insightfully distinguishes and names these two levels: *prasannakathākalitârthayukti*, an expressive narrative embedded with meaning, and *akṣara-ramyatā*, harmony of syllables. The first of these, he said, appealed to learned people (*kavīndrulu*) of good mind (*sāramati*), and the second to the others (*itarulu*).

After Nannaya, the contest was not between orality and literacy, but between two kinds of orality—the orality of the literate, scholarly poet (*paṇḍita*), and the orality of the non-literate or barely literate poet (*pāmara*). We can see the contrast keenly in Tikkana, whose verses do not usually sing. In a way, he was a very different poet, with a strictly written style in which only an occasional verse really flows. Indeed, the tradition itself recognized and commented upon this feature. According to legend, Tikkana made a pact with his scribe, Gurunātha: the scribe would write without stopping or asking the poet to repeat what he had said, and the poet would dictate without pausing to think. If the scribe should fail, his hand would be cut off, and if the poet were to fail, his tongue would be cut off. The arrangement worked smoothly until a point in the text where the internal narrator, Sañjaya, was describing the epic battle of the Bharatas to Dhṛtarāṣṭra. Here Tikkana became stuck in the middle of a verse, unable to complete it. In despair, he cried out to his scribe, "What can I say, Gurunātha?" (*emi sĕppudun gurunātha*). The scribe kept writing without pause, as usual, and the poem worked: the poet's cry completed the verse precisely according to the meter and meaning. The nasal ending of the verb, *sĕppudun*, requires that *kurunāthā* (lord of the Kurus; i.e., Dhṛtarāṣṭra) become *gurunātha*—but only in *written* Telugu. Tikkana reached for his sword to cut off his tongue when the scribe explained to him that all was well with the verse.

This story, disarmingly simple in appearance, offers a powerful commentary on the further transition from oral to written that Tikkana represents. The narrative seeks, on the one hand, to rehabilitate him, making him look like an oral poet—since at this time poetry was still required to have a flowing quality (*dhārā*) to it. Tikkana's verses actually do not have this quality; on the contrary, he was extending the literariness (the stylistic feature of a written poem) beyond Nannaya. On the one hand, this story attempts to make Tikkana one of the oral poets, dictating his verses to a scribe without taking a break. Gurunātha's origins in the potters' caste reinforce this claim, since the potters are closely linked to the singing of texts. On the other hand, it also implies a recognition of the innovation that Tikkana had introduced into the tradition. The verse in question works only when sung; in writing, *kurunāthā* becomes *gurunātha*, the cry of despair to the scribe; in recitation, it remains *kurunāthā*, an address to the Kuru lord. One can see, in this vignette, the whole burden of the transition that Tikkana articulates for this tradition.[66]

But the transition did not stop with Tikkana. Poets through the centuries appear to have negotiated between oral performance and literate composition. The totally oral style of versification—in which the texture is loose and replete with filler words to accommodate metrical necessities—began to be rejected as bad composition. A legend from the *cāṭu* tradition tells how Brahmin scholar-poet Tenāli Rāmaliṅgaḍu dismissed Mŏlla, a potter woman, when she presented her poetry to him.

> You make poems as if weaving a basket to hold fish
> out of any old bamboo strips.
> Could any Brahmin put up with
> your howlers?[67]

Śrīnāthuḍu denounced oral poets by including them in the category of bad poets who are conventionally censured in the preface of *kāvyas*:

> Some poets become addicted: they write poems
> as if their tongue is a stylus,
> their mouth a blank palm leaf,
> and whatever they know
> is black ink stirred in the inkpot of their minds.[68]

Oral poetry still had its appeal, especially for its performance value in public. In a world of intense competition for the attention of the patron, oral versification was a powerful skill that gained fast recognition. Poets prided themselves on spontaneously composing for the occasion perfectly acceptable metrical verses, and a poet who could not come up with a verse at the moment often did not win the day. A long extemporaneous poem by Pĕddana in the court of Kṛṣṇadevarāya, which demonstrates how poetry should be composed in Telugu as well as in Sanskrit, is said to have earned for the poet a golden anklet from the king, symbolizing the poet's victory over all the rival poets. The entire *cāṭu* culture of poetry celebrated oral versification and even ridiculed scribes who claimed perfect writing skills. However, Appakavi strongly favored the written poem when he declared that a good poem requires well-thought-out words and meaning, which an oral composition does not have. His dictum, "a poem cannot be rushed" (*nilukaḍa valayu kṛtiki*),[69] drove the last nail into the coffin of orality.

An entirely non-oral poetry, which we might call concrete poetry, became popular as the literary culture swung toward graphic literacy, adoring the power of the inscribed syllable. Poems worked into interesting visual shapes, known as *citrakavitvamu,* acquired the favor of poets. Illustrations of verses shaped as a conch, a sword, a cow's tail, and other forms were elaborately described in texts on meter. This is the culmination of a scholarly trend that began as early as Nannĕcoḍuḍu, who wrote the first concrete poems in his *Kumāra-sambhavamu.* This trend encouraged poets to make verses with more than one meaning; verses that could be read as Telugu from beginning to end but would be Sanskrit if they were read backwards; verses that contained other verses in a different meter; and verses that were shaped like a coiled snake (*kuṇḍalināga*), sword (*khaḍga*), bracelet (*kaṅkaṇa*), a pair of drums (*mardala*), the marks made on the earth by a urinating cow (*gomutrikā*), and so on. Such skills were regarded as the hallmark of a competent poet. Appakavi included in his work a large number of examples of concrete poems. Fig. 1.1 is of a *kuṇḍalināgabandhamu*, a poem written in the form of a coiled snake. A prayer to Kṛṣṇa, the poem reads from the head of the snake to the tail, with the syllables separated by spaces. When written out, the poem contains eighty-four syllables, but in the figure we see only sixty-four, since twenty of them are where the snake crosses itself, and therefore are to be read twice.

dyu ti dha ra de va kī ta na ya to ya bha va stu ta bhū ra me śa sam
mi ta gu ṇa sā ra bhū ti da ya me ya bṛ ha jja na pū ru ṣā va nā
ji ta na ra kā pu rā ta na ya je ya su vi ṣki ra bhā ra vā ha śā
śva ta pu ru hu ta pi ta da va pā va ka śa sta pu rā ṇa ko vi dā[70]

Fig. 1.1: Poem-picture of a coiled snake (*kuṇḍalināgabandhamu*) by Appakavi. Reproduced from Appakavi [1962] 1966: 576.

We have come full circle. Appakavi made a valiant effort to establish a literary culture that he imagined was sanctioned by the first poet, Nannaya. Competing literary cultures of *śaivabhakti*, temple, *cāṭu*, and oral varieties were rejected in favor of constructing a canon of courtly poetry subjected to the strict standards of the texts on metrics and grammar. To be more exact, Appakavi did not reject those varieties of poetry totally—he accepted them if they conformed to the exacting standards of the grammar and meter.

Appakavi held sway for about two hundred years. His influence grew stronger as more and more prescriptive texts on metrics and grammar were written. The label "poet" now invariably implied the scholar and was rarely applied to a non-scholarly poet, as may be seen in the title *kavi* (poet) at the end of Appakavi's name. Grammars and books on meter were written with a view to establishing standards in the literary use, but not other uses, of language. How such a uniform, authoritarian literary standard sustained itself through the works of scholars emerging from small villages and towns, during a period when no major political formation exerted its influence and there were no royal patrons of literature, is one of the puzzles that remains to be solved. The fact remains, however, that modern Telugu literature, which began during the early decades of the nineteenth century, was able to establish itself only after successfully critiquing and denouncing Appakavi.

Notes

1. After Ponnikaṇṭi Tĕlaganārya wrote *Yayāti Caritramu* (*c*. 1574–1585) in an artificial Telugu known as *accatĕlugu* (pure Telugu, devoid of all words derived from Sanskrit), a number of poets followed him and wrote *accatĕlugu* poems. Tĕlaganārya and his followers were influenced by contemporary Persian poets who tried to eliminate all Arabic words from their works. But see also D.R. Nagaraj on the early-thirteenth-century Kannada poet, Āṇḍaiah, and his *Kabbigarakāva*. Pollock 2003: 366.
2. *Āndhramahābhāratamu*, 4.1.30 (Nannaya, Tikkana, and Errāpragaḍa [1901] 1989).
3. *Bhīmeśvarapurāṇamu* 3.50 (Śrīnāthuḍu 1958). Interpreting literary statements such as this in a strictly geographical way is problematic. The idea is presented here only to show variations in geographical conceptualizations of Andhra in premodern times.
4. This book, *Appakavīyamu*, popularly called after the author's name, does not have a title of its own. Appakavi intended this as a commentary to Nannaya's *Āndhraśabdacintāmaṇi*. The extant text covers only the first two chapters of Nannaya's work.
5. Though not as precise as Appakavi regarding dates, the poets who wrote prefaces to their works provide us with substantial descriptions of the cultures in which they and their patrons lived, the symbolic

statuses they and their predecessors attained in the society of their time, and interesting data about their own families, their patrons, and their families as well.

6. *Āndhrabhāṣabhūṣaṇamu* 9–11 (Ketana 1953).
7. Nanněcoḍuḍu (twelfth century) was the first poet to relate the indigenous belief of acquiring *saptasantāna*, seven kinds of "children," to ensure a secure place in heaven. In addition to a son, they are: *agrahāramu* (Brahmin colony), *devatālayamu* (temple), *udyānamu* (garden), *taṭākamu* (tank), *satkṛti* (poem), *nidhānamu* (source of money). This belief was restated in a number of poems over many centuries. *Kumārasambhavamu* 1.46 (Nanněcoḍuḍu 1968).
8. *Kāḷahastīśvaraśatakamu* 117 (Dhūrjaṭi 1925); translation, Heifetz and Narayana Rao 1987: 119.
9. *Vasucaritramu* 1.10 (Rāmarājabhūṣaṇuḍu [1967] 1995).
10. *Āndhramahābhāratamu,* Ādiparvamu 1.3 (Nannaya, Tikkana, and Ĕrrāpragaḍa [1901] 1989); translation, Narayana Rao and Shulman 2002: 57.
11. Ibid.: 59.
12. Ibid., Ādiparvamu 1.31: 61.
13. Ibid., Virāṭaparvamu 1.6.
14. For a comprehensive treatment of this point, see chapter 2, "Purāṇa Viplavam," in my *Tĕlugulo Kavitāviplavāla Svarūpam* (Narayana Rao 1978).
15. *Āndhramahābhāratamu,* Sabhāparvamu 2.18 (Nannaya, Tikkana, and Ĕrrāpragaḍa [1901] 1989).
16. Ibid., Sabhāparvamu 2.30.
17. I am indebted to the great Telugu poet Viswanatha Satyanarayana for his insight in reading this verse. My recollection is from a talk he gave in Eluru on Nannaya around 1960.
18. Modern literary scholars speculate that Nannaya might have died before he completed his Telugu rendering of the Sanskrit *Mahābhārata* because he broke the taboo: he began his translation from the beginning and wanted to reach the end. They also suggest that Tikkana, who wrote fifteen *parva*s (books), did not touch the small section of one half of the second book left incomplete by Nannaya because he feared the same fate. Finally, Ĕrrāpragaḍa (fourteenth century) completed the half of the second book left by Nannaya.
19. See Nagaraj 2003.

20. *Basavapurāṇamu* 1.83–85 (Somanāthuḍu [1926] 1952).
21. *Paṇḍitārādhyacaritramu* 5 (Somanāthuḍu 1990).
22. Ibid.: 5–6. Also see Pollock 2003.
23. *Vĕṇugopālaśatakamu* 55 (Śāraṅgapāṇī n.d.).
24. *Kumārasambhavamu* 1.23 (Nannĕcoḍuḍu 1968).
25. Ibid.: 1.35, 36, 41; Narayana Rao and Shulman 2002: 69–70.
26. Unfortunately, Nannĕcoḍuḍu was lost to Telugu scholars for a long period, until Manavalli Ramakṛṣṇa Kavi discovered him and brought the text to light in 1910. Discontinuity in scholarly tradition has resulted in loss of memory—many of the words Nannĕcoḍuḍu used fell into disuse, and their meanings are yet to be fully reconstructed.
27. One plausible reason is that during the fourteenth and fifteenth centuries an elite leisure class had not yet taken shape.
28. Modern Telugu critics call this courtly *kāvya* genre *prabandhamu.*
29. Women chewed betel-nut compounded with musk and camphor in these proportions.
30. Being a goddess, Varūthinī cannot blink, nor is she capable of sweating. Here she is transformed, in a movement seen as positive, from this divine state to a human mode of being.
31. A proverbial statement of transformation through mental obsession (*bhramarakīṭanyāya*).
32. On this theme and for a richer study of Pĕddana's text, see Shulman 1995a.
33. *Manucaritramu* 2.24, 25, 29, 30, 33, 62 (Pĕddana 1984); translation, Narayana Rao and Shulman 2002: 158–60, 164.
34. Narayana Rao and Shulman 1998: 22.
35. Heifetz and Narayana Rao 1987: 153.
36. A concoction of pepper and other ingredients that mothers who had recently delivered ate for several days after the birth.
37. The inauspicious and threatening Jyeṣthadevi, the goddess of poverty and the elder sister of Lakṣmī, was worshiped to avert her influence over the baby.
38. All of these acts were intended to protect the mother and child from evil. *Śivarātrimāhātmyamu* 2.50–51, 70–1 (Śrīnāthuḍu 1995); translation, Narayana Rao and Shulman 2002: 129, 132.
39. In his *Saṅkīrtanalakṣaṇamu,* Tāḷḷapāka Cinatirumalācāryulu, the grandson of Annamayya, claims that his work is a translation of a

Sanskrit original that Annamayya wrote. See *Saṅkīrtanalakṣaṇamu* 13–17 (Cinatirumalācāryulu 1935).

40. See the Afterword by Narayana Rao, in Heifetz and Narayana Rao 1987.
41. Ibid.: 146.
42. Ibid.
43. Ibid.: 151.
44. Ibid.: 63.
45. Potana 1964: 1.96.
46. For a more detailed study, see "Rhetoric of Kingship," in Narayana Rao, *et al*. 1992: 169–219.
47. Of these three, only the *Raghunāthanāyakâbhyudayamu* is available now.
48. See Narayana Rao and Shulman 1998.
49. Ibid.: 11–13.
50. Ibid.: 20–1.
51. Heifetz and Narayana Rao 1987: 154–5.
52. Narayana Rao and Shulman 1998: 123–4.
53. See Narayana Rao 1995: 35, 40, n.19. and Śrīnāthuḍu 1958: 1.74.
54. *Manucaritramu* 2.3 (Pĕddana 1984).
55. The *kāvya* poets in Telugu clearly followed Śrīharṣa, who states towards the end of the proverbially difficult *Naiṣadhīyacarita*: "Deliberately I placed/ tight knots in places/ so no fool enters here with a false pride/ to deny the worth of my work./ May it be a joy to float on the waves of comfort/ this poem provides/ for the good student for whom/ a well-served teacher unties the knots."
56. Annamayya 1998: 1: 226; translation, Narayana Rao and Shulman 2002: 148.
57. *Āndhramahābhāratamu*, Ādiparvamu 1.16 (Nannaya, Tikkana, and Errāpragaḍa [1901] 1989).
58. Ibid., Virāṭaparvamu 1.6.
59. *Vasucaritramu* 1.19 (Rāmarājabhūṣaṇuḍu [1967] 1995).
60. See Pollock 2003.
61. *Śṛṅgāranaiṣadhamu* 8.202 (Śrīnāthuḍu 1967).
62. In Andhra, the water buffalo does not hate horses. Curds from the milk of the *baṣkayaṇī* (water buffalo) that gave birth some six months before, is not particularly preferred in Andhra either. These are not culturally translatable concepts.

64. *Appakavīyamu* (Appakavi [1962] 1966: 1.6).
65. *Kumārasambhavamu* 12.225 (Nanněcoḍuḍu 1968).
66. Adapted from the Preface to Narayana Rao and Shulman 2002: 17–18.
67. Narayana Rao and Shulman 1998: 181–2.
68. *Bhīmeśvarapurāṇamu* 1.12 (Śrīnāthuḍu 1958); Narayana Rao and Shulman 2002: 120.
69. *Appakavīyamu* (Appakavi [1962] 1966: 1.60).
70. Ibid.: 4.576.

References

Histories of Literature and Biographies of Poets

Ārudra. 1990. *Samagra Āndhra Sāhityam*. Revised ed., 4 vols, 2002–4. Hyderabad: Telugu Akademi; Vijayavada: Prajasakti Book House.

Chenchayya, Pandipeddi, and M. Bhujanga Rao Bahadur. 1928. *A History of Telugu Literature*. London: Oxford University Press.

Krishnamurthi, Salva. 1994. *History of Telugu Literature from Early Times to 1100 AD*. Madras: Institute of Asian Studies.

Kulasekhara Rao, M. 1988. *A History of Telugu Literature*. Hyderabad: Published by the author.

Lakṣmīkāntam, Piṅgaḷi. 1974. *Āndhra Sāhitya Caritra*. Hyderabad: Andhra Pradesh Sahitya Akadami.

Lakṣmīkāntaśastri, Siṣṭa. n.d. *Vijayanagarāndhra Kavulu*. Vijayavada: Nirmala Publishers.

Lakṣmīkāntama, Uṭukuri. n.d. *Āndhra Kavayitrulu*. Secunderabad: n.p.

Lakṣmīrañjanam, Khaṇḍavalli. 1958. *Āndhra Sāhitya Caritra Saṅgrahamu*. Hyderabad: Venkataramana Publications.

Nāgayya, G. 1983. *Tělugu Sāhitya Samīkṣa*. 2 vols. Tirupati: Navyaparisodhaka Pracuranalu.

Rajanīkānta Rāvu, Bālāntrapu. 1975. *Āndhra Vāggeyakāra Caritramu*. 2d ed. Vijayavada: Viśālandhra Publishing House.

Śeṣayya, Cāganṭi. n.d. *Āndhrakavitaraṅgiṇi*. 14 vols. Kapilesvarapuramu: Hindu Dharmasastra Grantha Nilayamu.

Sītāpati, Giḍugu Veṅkaṭa. 1968. *History of Telugu Literature*. New Delhi: Sahitya Akademi.

Śrīnivāsacāryulu, Bǒmmakanṭi, and Bālāntrapu Naḷinīkānta Rao. 1983. *Tělugu Cāṭuvu, Puṭṭu Pūrvottarālu*. Madras: Kalyani Pracuranalu.

Śrīrāmamūrti, Gurujāḍa. 1913 (first ed. 1876). *Kavi Jīvitamulu.* 3rd. ed. Madras: Vavilla Ramaswamy Sastrulu and Sons.

Śrīrāmamūrti, Korlapāṭi. 1991. *Tĕlugu Sāhitya Caritra.* 4 vols. Visakhapatnam: Published by the author.

Telugu Akāḍemi. 1989. *Tĕlugu Sāhitya Kośamu: Prācīna Sāhityamu.* Hyderabad: Telugu Akademi.

Veṅkaṭa Rāvu, Niḍudavolu. 1978. *Dakṣinadeśīyāndhrāvaṅmayamu.* Madras: Madras University Press.

Veṅkaṭanārāyaṇa Rāvu, K. 1928. *Āndhravāṅmayacaritrasaṅgrahamu.* Madras: Vavilla Ramaswamy Sastrulu and Sons.

Vireśaliṅgam, Kandukūri. 1917. *Āndhra Kavula Caritramu.* Rajahmundry: Published by the author.

Primary Sources

[Names of Telugu authors appear with the Telugu nominative case endings.]

Annamayya [Annamācārya], Tāḷḷapāka. 1998. *Tāḷḷapāka Padasāhityamu.* 29 vols. Tirupati: Tirumala Tirupati Devasthanam.

Annamayya, Yathāvākkula. 1925. *Sarvēśvaraśatakamu.* Edited by Kāśināthuni Nāgeśvara Rāvu. Madras: Andhrapatrika Mudranalayamu.

Appakavi, Kakunūri. [1962] 1966. *Appakavīyamu* . Edited with a preface by Rāvuri Dorasāmi Śarma. Includes a critical introduction by Giḍugu Rāmamūrti Pantulu and Giḍugu Veṅkaṭa Sītāpati from a 1922 edition (edited by Giḍugu Rāmamūrti Pantulu and Utpala Veṅkaṭanarasiáhācārya). Madras: Vavilla Ramaswamy Sastrulu and Sons.

Cīnatirumalācāryulu, Tāḷḷapāka. 1935. *Saṅkirtanalakṣaṇamu.* In *The Minor Works of Annamacharya and his Sons*, edited by V. Vijayaraghavacharya and G. Adinarayana Naidu. Vol. 1. Madras: Tirumalai Tirupati Devasthanams Press.

Dhūrjaṭi. 1925. *Kāḷahastīśvaraśatakamu.* Edited by Kāśīnāthuni Nāgeśvara Rāvu. Madras: Andhra Patrika Mudranalayamu.

———. 1966. *Śri Kāḷahastīsvaramāhātymamu.* Edited with a commentary by Bulusu Veṅkaṭaramaṇayya. Madras: Vavilla Ramaswamy Sastrulu and Sons.

Ĕrrāpragaḍa. See Nannaya.

Huḷakki Bhāskaruḍu. 1953. *Bhāskararāmāyaṇamu.* Edited by Medepalli Veṅkaṭaramanacaryulu. Madras: Vavilla Ramaswamy Sastrulu and Sons.

Ketana, Mulaghaṭika. 1953. *Āndhrabhāṣābhūṣaṇamu.* Edited with a commentary by Devineni Sūrayya and introduction by Vaḍlamūḍi Gōpāla Kṛṣṇayya. Tenāli: Ajanta Art Press.

Kṛṣṇadevarāyalu. 1964. *Āmuktamālyada.* Edited by Vedam Veṅkaṭarāya Śāstri. Madras: Vēdam Vēṅkaṭarāya Śastri and Brothers.

Mārana. 1984. *Mārkaṇḍeyapurāṇamu.* Edited by G.V. Subrahmanyam. Hyderabad: Andhra Pradesh Sahitya Akadami.

Nannaya, Tikkana, and Ĕrrāpragaḍa. [1901] 1989. *Āndhramahābhāratamu.* 4 vols. Hyderabad: Telugu Visvavidyalayam.

Nannĕcoḍuḍu. 1968. *Kumārasambhavamu.* Edited by Korada Mahadeva Śāstri. Hyderabad: Telugu Visvavidyalaya.

Pĕddana, Allasāni. 1984. *Manucaritramu.* Edited by Timmavajjhala Kodaṇḍarāmayya. Hyderabad: Andhra Pradesh Sahitya Akadami.

Potana, Bammera. 1964. *Śrimadāndhramahābhāgavatamu* (known as *Bhāgavatamu*). 2 vols. Hyderabad: Andhra Pradesh Sahitya Akadami.

Ramakṛṣṇuḍu, Tĕnāli. 1968. *Pāṇḍuraṅgamāhātmyamu.* Edited by Bulusu Veṅkaṭaramaṇayya. Madras: Vavilla Ramaswamy Sastrulu and Sons.

Rāmarājabhūṣaṇuḍu. [1967] 1995. *Vasucaritramu.* Edited by K. Suprasannācārya. Hyderabad: Telugu University.

Śāraṅgapani. n.d. *Veṇugopālaśatakamu.* n.p.

Somana, Nācana. 1994–7. *Uttaraharivaṃśamu.* Edited with a commentary by Cadalavada Jayarama Sastri. Hyderabad: Telugu Goshti.

Somanāthuḍu, Pālkuriki. [1926] 1952. *Basavapurāṇamu.* Edited by Veṭūri Prabhākara Śāstri; reprint with a preface by Niḍudavolu Veṅkaṭa Rāvu. Madras: Andhra Granthamala.

———. 1990. *Mallikārjunapaṇḍitārādhya Caritramu* (known as *Paṇḍitārādhyacaritramu*). Edited by Cilukūri Nārāyaṇa Rāvu. Hyderabad: Telugu University.

Śrīnāthuḍu. n.d. *Haravilāsamu.* Edited by Veṭūri Prabhākara Śāstri. Madras: Vavilla Ramaswamy Sastrulu and Sons.

———. 1958. *Bhīmeśvarapurāṇamu.* Edited by Kambhampāṭi Rāmagōpālakṛṣṇamūrti. Vijayavada: Kalyani Grantha Mandali.

———. 1967. *Śṛṅgāranaiṣadhamu.* Edited by Vedamu Veṅkaṭarāya Śāstri Jr. Hyderabad: Telugu Vijnana Pitham.

———. 1992. *Kāśīkhaṇḍamu.* Edited by Mallampalli Śarabhēśvara Śarma. 2 vols. Hyderabad: Telugu Universit y.

———. 1995. *Śivarātrimāhātmyamu.* Edited by Jŏnnalagaḍḍa Mṛtyuñjaya Rāvu. Hyderabad: Telugu University.

Tikkana. See Nannaya.

Timmana, Mukku. 1968. *Parijātāpaharaṇamu.* Edited by Dūsi Rāmamūrti. Madras: Vavilla Ramaswamy Sastrulu and Sons.

Vallabharāyaḍu, Vinukonda. 1972. *Krīḍābhirāmamu.* Edited by Bŏmmakaṇṭi Veṅkaṭa Siṅgarācārya and Bālāntrapu Naḷnikāntarāvu. Machilipatnam: M. Seshachelam & Co.

Veṅkaṭakavi, Cemakūra. n.d. *Sāraṅgadhara Caritramu.* Madras: Vavilla Ramaswamy Sastrulu and Sons.

———. [1968] 1987. *Vijayavilāsamu.* Edited by Tāpī Dharmā Rāvu. Hyderabad: Visalandhra Publishing House.

Vijayarāghava Nāyakuḍu. 1951. *Raghunāthanāyakābhyudayamu.* Edited by N. Veṅkaṭaramaṇayya and M. Sōmaśēkhara ārma. Madras Government Oriental Series. Tanjore: TMSSM Library.

Secondary Sources

Heifetz, Hank, and Velcheru Narayana Rao. 1987. *For the Lord of the Animals: Poems from the Telugu, the Kāḷahastīśvara Śatakamu of Dhūrjaṭi.* Berkeley: University of California Press.

Nagaraj, D.R. 2003. "Tensions in Kannada Literary Culture." In Pollock 2003 (*vide infra*).

Narayana Rao, Velcheru. 1978. *Tĕlugulo Kavitāviplavāla Svarūpam.* Revised 3rd ed., 2008. Mundelein, Il.: Telugu Association of North America.

———. 1990. *Siva's Warriors: The Basava Purāṇa of Pālkuriki Somanātha.* Translation assisted by Gene Roghar. Princeton: Princeton University Press.

———. 1992. "Kings, Gods, and Poets: Ideologies of Patronage in Medieval Andhra." In *The Powers of Art: Patronage in Indian Culture*, edited by Barbara Stoler Miller. Delhi: Oxford University Press.

———. 1995. "Coconut and Honey: Sanskrit and Telugu in Medieval Andhra." *Social Scientist* 23: 24–40.

———. 2003. *Hibiscus on the Lake: Twentieth Century Telugu Poetry from India.* Madison: University of Wisconsin Press.

Narayana Rao, Velcheru, and David Shulman. 1998. *A Poem at the Right Moment: Remembered Verses from Premodern South India.* Berkeley: University of California Press.

———. 2002. *Classical Telugu Poetry: An Anthology.* Berkeley: University of California Press.

Narayana Rao, Velcheru, *et al.* 1992. *Symbols of Substance: Court and State in Nāyaka-Period Tamil Nadu.* Delhi: Oxford University Press.

Pollock, Sheldon. 2003. *Literary Cultures in History: Reconstructions from South Asia*. Berkeley: University of California Press.

Ramanujan A.K., *et al.* 1994. *When God Is a Customer: Telugu Courtesan Songs by Kshetrayya and Others.* Berkeley: University of California Press.

Shulman, David. 1995a. "First Man, Forest Mother: Telugu Humanism in the Age of Kṛṣṇadevaraya." In Shulman, 1995b.

———, ed. 1995b. *Syllables of Sky: Studies in South Indian Civilization in Honour of Velcheru Narayana Rao.* Delhi: Oxford University Press.

2

Notes on Political Thought in Medieval and Early Modern South India

In these days, when we don't have any kingdoms worth the name, texts on statecraft are of no use for ruling the state, and they are useful only for historians of *śāstra* texts. —*Veturi Prabhakara Sastri*

This country has seen the conflict between ecclesiastical law and secular law long before Europeans sought to challenge the authority of the Pope. Kautilya's *Arthaśāstra* lays down the foundation of secular law. In India unfortunately ecclesiastical law triumphed over secular law. In my opinion this was one of the greatest disasters in the country. —*B.R. Ambedkar*

Introduction

Past works on the nature and content of state-building in medieval South India have focused largely on the inscriptional corpus, and a limited set of narrative accounts, in order to support classic formulations of such ideas as the "segmentary state" and "ritual

This essay is written jointly by Velcheru Narayana Rao and Sanjay Subrahmanyam. It is a shorter version of a more extended analysis of *nīti* and *dharma* texts in medieval and early modern South India which may eventually take a monographic form. Early versions of this essay have been presented at St Antony's College (Oxford), the Haus der Kulturen der Welt (Berlin), the Centre for the Study of Social Sciences (Kolkata), the University of British Columbia, the EHESS kingship."[1] In this essay we return to some of the questions raised by our colleagues and predecessors in the field, but with a view to looking at ideological and ideational issues far more than concrete institutional arrangements. We should note at the outset that the specter of a perpetually receding horizon of universal concepts—those that can be used with equal confidence, say, for the analysis of pre-1800 societies in Europe, Asia, and Africa—has taken something of a beating in recent decades. Is it at all legitimate to assume that "money" existed in all or even most of these continents?[2] What of the "economy" itself, or even "society?" Is the notion of "art" applicable everywhere? Can "religion" be found in most societies?[3] It is well known by now that many postcolonial theorists wish to claim that "history" was certainly not present in any more than a tiny fraction of the societies they study, until European colonial rule apparently created the conditions for its worldwide spread as a hegemonic discourse. In other words, it is claimed often enough now that no fit whatsoever existed between these and other "etic" categories of the humanities and social sciences (with their uniquely Western origins and genealogy) and the highly varied "emic" notions that may be found in different locales and times in the world of the past, a claim that has become a source of anxiety for some, a source of indifference for others, and a ground for rejoicing for still others who see a positive virtue in "incommensurability," which they perhaps view as akin to a (necessarily virtuous) claim for species diversity.[4] Related to this is the recurrence of older formulae on the notoriously difficult subject of translation, both from those historians and from those social scientists who claim—on one extreme—that everything is translatable, and those who are eager to sustain equally extreme claims of "malostension" or "radical mistranslation" as a perpetual condition, rather than a contingent (and even potentially reversible) consequence of specific procedures and circumstances.[5]

(Paris), the Humanities Institute (Wisconsin-Madison) and the Center for India and South Asia (UCLA). For critical comments and suggestions we are particularly grateful to Partha Chatterjee, Don Davis, Carlo Ginzburg, Claude Guillot, Roland Lardinois, Patrick Olivelle, Anthony Pagden, and S.R. Sarma.

It is of interest that even in this welter of relativistic claims one category that few have sought to challenge in its universal applicability is that of "politics." Why has this been so, we may ask? Perhaps the reasons lie not only in an embarrassment with the charged, and patronizing, largely Marxist category of the "pre-political," but also in the fact that to deny the existence of "politics" would be tantamount to denying the existence somewhere in collective human existence of "power," a move that few if any in the academy today would wish to risk.[6] To be sure, we could follow Benedict Anderson, who in relativizing power argues that the "idea of power" in, say, Java, was not the same as that in the West; but this would be quite different to denying its very existence or utility as a concept for analysis.[7] In the case of India, almost any universal concept that one can mention has recently been challenged in its applicability to the present or past situation of that area, with the notable exception of "politics." Indeed, it is instructive in this regard to turn to an essay produced by a leading relativist amongst Indian social theorists, Ashis Nandy, who would argue that "politics" is practically the only category that one can use as a constant to speak of the past 2000 years in India.[8] Yet, this argument, first defended by him over three decades ago, came paired with an important caveat. For Nandy wished to argue that politics in twentieth-century India was in fact a split field. If on the one hand there were those who practiced politics in the "Western" mode, drawing upon concepts and notions that were all too familiar to Western political scientists and theorists, others continued to understand and practice politics through a deeply "emic" set of lenses, which is to say while using concepts that had no familiar equivalents in Western political vocabulary. To understand these concepts, and the working of this other field, Nandy went on to argue, it was necessary to return to a series of texts produced in the Sanskrit language in ancient India, which alone could explicate this deep-rooted and culturally specific vocabulary, involving (usually substantive and untranslatable) terms such as *dharma*, *karma*, *kāma*, *artha*, *sanyāsa*, and the like.

In making this argument Nandy was paradoxically drawing above all upon a claim that was first set out in colonial India, namely that the only source of "authentically indigenous" concepts could be found in ancient texts in Sanskrit. To his credit, however, it must be stated that he at least posed the problem of whether a possible field of political thought or political theory might have existed in India before colonial rule. Later writers, even those who were comfortable with the notion that concepts of "politics" could be applied to study moments in the precolonial Indian past, have rarely returned to this problem.[9] Those who have done so have usually drawn upon Persian language materials, and a learned tradition that has consistently maintained that, in Islamic societies at least, the idea of "politics" had long existed under such heads as *siyāsat*.[10] This view is lent credence by a genealogical claim, wherein the common Hellenic roots of Western and Islamic thinking on the issue can be pointed to; the problem then would arise with that part of India where Arabic and Persian never came to dominate as the languages of intellectual discourse.[11]

This is the heart of the issue that this essay seeks to address. We wish to argue that in reality a quite substantial and varied body of material can be found in South India between the fourteenth and the late eighteenth centuries that attempts to theorize politics, while doing so neither in Persian nor in Sanskrit, even if it may bear traces of contact with bodies of material in these two "classical" languages.[12] These materials may be found instead in the Indian vernacular languages, of which we shall focus on a particular body, that in Telugu (though a similar exercise could easily be attempted with materials in Kannada or Marathi).[13] Secondly, we suggest that most writers who have looked into the matter (and they are a mere handful, as noted above) have usually misidentified the location of such materials by seeking it solely in the corpus known as *dharmaśāstra*. Thirdly, we will attempt to show how the materials that we are fundamentally concerned with, and which usually term themselves texts on *nīti* rather than *dharma* (although there is some overlap in the two usages), changed over the centuries with which we are concerned. *Nīti* may be glossed here by such terms as "pragmatics," "politics," or "statecraft."[14] Finally, we shall briefly rehearse an argument on how the status of these materials was transformed in the nineteenth century, when British colonial rule reclassified them in ways that were at odds with their place in the universe of knowledge in India in earlier times.

We should begin perhaps with a rapid and schematic survey of the political history of the region with which we are concerned, namely the southeastern part of peninsular India, in which Telugu had emerged already by 1300 CE as a major literary language. A series of kingdoms can be found here, some of modest size and pretensions, others that can be classified as veritable imperial structures. To summarize, the early fourteenth century sees the demise of the rule of a fairly substantial regional polity, that of the Kākatīyas of Warangal, and the emergence of a set of far smaller kingdoms.[15] After a hiatus, the fifteenth century then sees the emergence of the great empire of Vijayanagara, which dominates the region (as indeed much of peninsular India) until the late sixteenth century.[16] The collapse of Vijayanagara power means in turn that the two centuries from 1600 to 1800 are marked by a complex period of contestation, without a single stable and hegemonic polity. The Mughals eventually come to play a substantial role in the region, but indirectly rather than as a centralized political structure.[17] In short, we can see an alternation, with two cycles of fragmented political formations sandwiching an extended central moment of a century and a half of imperial consolidation that is associated with Vijayanagara.

Although it was famously termed a "forgotten empire" by Robert Sewell in 1900, it is clear that the memory of Vijayanagara remained very alive in South India as late as the beginning of the nineteenth century.[18] However, the lack of adequate lines of communication between a society that already possessed a centuries' long set of continuous intellectual traditions, and a new political power that had assumed the role of "civilizing" a group of ostensibly uncivilized or partially civilized nations, was never more striking than at this early juncture of colonial Indian history. For the traditionally educated Indian intellectual of the early nineteenth century whom the East India Company might have consulted, India certainly had a sophisticated discipline termed *nīti*, beginning from early texts such as the *Arthaśāstra* and continuing until their time. There was a whole range of texts on *dharma*, beginning with Manu's *Dharmaśāstra* (and dating perhaps from the early centuries CE), and also continuing through the medieval period both in terms of a manuscript tradition and by way of extensive commentaries.[19] But the British administrators and their native assistants in early colonial South India were primarily looking for "moral instruction."[20] Of the two concepts in the Indian tradition that come close to the idea of morals—*dharma* and *nīti*—*dharma* was seen as somewhat unsuitable for moral instruction because it was too close to the religious world. Manu's celebrated *Dharmaśāstra* was also deeply embedded in the *varna* and *jāti* order, and discussed legal matters relating to marriages, property rights, and so on. Law courts needed these texts, to administer justice to Indians according to their indigenous laws. The story of Sir William Jones' efforts in this direction and Henry Thomas Colebrooke's translation of legal digests for use in the British courts is too well known to be repeated here.[21]

At the same time, it was also easy enough to argue that there was a direct line of ascent between the medieval regional language *nīti* texts and the *Arthaśāstra* of Kautilya, and thus to conclude that the regional language texts were derivative and, if anything, bad copies of an original (however elusive that original was in purely philological terms) and therefore not particularly interesting. Another problem was that since the authors of *nīti* texts invariably claimed to be poets, literary scholars of the late nineteenth and early-twentieth centuries, influenced by notions deriving from Western literary models, began by rejecting any formal literary merit in their texts and then showed no interest in analyzing them seriously for their content. Doubly neglected, the regional language *nīti* texts were relegated to a sort of intellectual no-man's land. Yet, as noted above, native schools still needed moral instruction, and in the absence of an Indian equivalent of the Ten Commandments, or similar codes of virtue, teachers often turned to *nīti* texts to fill the need.

The principal focus of this essay is the transformation and development of *nīti* discourse from classical Sanskrit texts to early-modern Telugu texts and their later use in the colonial period. Our interest is to show, first, that these texts demonstrate a lively change with time and context as guides to practical wisdom, and strategies of success; and second, that they are not concerned with religion and are therefore mostly "this-worldly" (*laukika*) or "secular" in character. A third point that is developed in the analysis is of how the late-nineteenth-century colonial interest in teaching morals in schools gave selective, and one might say distorted, attention to some *nīti* texts while ignoring the bulk of the others. The sources of the discussion are mainly from Telugu with a few examples from Sanskrit and Persian.

Some Ur-Texts

No Indian text from ancient times has arguably been as used and misused in the context of the twentieth century as the *Arthaśāstra* of Kautilya.[22] The first edition of this text, from 1909, was produced in Mysore by R. Shama Sastri from a single manuscript (with a commentary by a certain Bhattasvamin) originating in the Tanjavur region. It had already been preceded by a first translation (in the pages of the *Indian Antiquary*) from 1905 by the same scholar. The text quickly attracted massive attention, and a number of other manuscripts came to light, mostly in southern India (in Grantha and Malayalam characters), with one of the rare northern Indian manuscripts being from Patan, from a Jain collection. The confident initial assertion that the text's author was "the famous Brahmin Kautilya, also named Vishnugupta, and known from other sources by the patronymic Chanakya," and that the text was written at the time of the foundation of the Maurya dynasty, has of course been considerably eroded over the course of the twentieth century. Despite the relative rarity of manuscripts, it is clear that the text was known to the medieval tradition in various forms, and that its author was considered to be one of a series of important ancient authors of *nīti* texts. The Vijayanagara-period work, *Rāyavācakamu*, tells us that the king Vira Narasimha Raya in the early-sixteenth century was accustomed to hearing recitations from various texts, including Canura's *Nīti*, with "Canura" being a distortion of Canakya.[23]

The text of the *Arthaśāstra* in its modern critical edition, which was not necessarily the received version in the medieval tradition, is of course quite astonishing in its ambition and coverage.[24] It is a highly detailed text, and not one that simply contents itself to enunciate vague general principles. The text also quotes earlier authors, often pointing to the difference between its author's own opinions (in the third person, as "Kautilya") and those of others. A striking and oft-remarked aspect of the work is that a great deal of its content is markedly "secular." To be sure, in the initial part the text invokes Śukra and Bṛhaspati, and then the Vedas; but thereafter such location devices or references seem to disappear from the text. The first chapter discusses the overall contents, and Chapter 2 (*adhyakṣapracārah*) then begins by noting that there are normally four *vidyas*: philosophy; the three Vedas; agriculture, cattle rearing and trade (collectively *vārtā*), and law-and-order (*daṇḍa-nīti*). According to Kautilya there are, however, those who follow the Bṛhaspati's line of thinking, believing that there are only three disciplines (*vidyās*) and the Vedas are really a mere façade. We then get a version of the *āśrama* system of social ordering followed by a description of material life, with no reference thereafter in this extensive chapter to anything that might be understood as "religion." This is once again the case in later chapters on judicial and legal matters, criminals and how to deal with them, secret matters (*yogavṛttam*), and the manner of dealing with other kings and kingdoms (the themes of *maṇḍalayoniḥ* and *ṣāḍguṇyam*). The highly circumscribed place of *dharma* in the text has recently been summed up as follows by Charles Malamoud:

> The originality of the *Arthaśāstra* is that the science of government, the doctrine of royal conduct, is set out there in a perspective where *artha* appears in a highly limited form and not, as in the Epics or the Laws of Manu for example, where it is assimilated to the perspective of "duty" (*dharma*). The question in the *Arthaśāstra* is not that of knowing how, while obeying his "duty of state," the king contributes to order in the world and in society, or even how he guarantees it, but rather of what he should do to attain his ends: conquer territory and hold on to it. To be sure the two perspectives are not wholly incompatible, and many of the "Machiavellian" precepts of the *Arthaśāstra* also appear in texts that lay out the norms of *dharma*; and there are even some passages in the *Arthaśāstra* that recall some principles regarding the final ends which are *dharmic* in nature. But all in all, the *Arthaśāstra* does not justify the means by the ends: the means and the ends appear at the same level, and each means is a provisional end. The treatise sets itself the task of laying out in detail the modalities of royal action and to evaluate them in relation to its sole objective: to succeed.[25]

Unfortunately, we do not know a great deal about the history of the book's subsequent use until far later. The speculation of the past few decades is that it may date from the fourth century CE, but it is really quite difficult to make a definitive pronouncement on the matter. Buddhist sources seem to have been quite negatively disposed both to the text—on account of its alleged amorality—and to its author as a personage.[26] We may note that the *Kāmandaka* or *Nītisāra* also comes from broadly the same period, but slightly later, and that its author Kamanda states that he knows the *Arthaśāstra*, specifying that the text's author was Kautilya, also known as Vishnugupta. Kamanda also appears to be the source for the confusing claim that Kautilya was the one who broke the power of the Nandas. In a similar vein, the author of the *Mudrārākṣasa*, the Sanskrit play of Viśakhadatta from about 600 CE, seems to have known and used the *Arthaśāstra*.

Unlike later medieval texts that we will discuss below, the *Arthaśāstra* is not aphoristic in nature. Its literary quality is in fact rather interesting, the work having been written mostly in short prose sentences with some occasional *ślokas* in the middle, and one or sometimes more than one *śloka* at the end of each chapter; and yet it is composed in a way that does not lend itself to easy oral transmission in this form. It seems largely meant for readers of a written book, and once more demarcates itself from later texts in the fact that "Kautilya" himself, whoever he is, still poses and is regarded as an authoritative author. We shall have occasion to contrast this with the strategy of later texts, which seek legitimacy from their acceptability rather than invoking and using a notion of authority.

A second text from the early period that merits some mention, and seems to slightly postdate the *Arthaśāstra*, is Kamanda's *Nītisāra*, briefly noted above. This work is shorter and also far less detailed than that of Kautilya, but follows it largely in terms of tone and general content, being partly advisory and partly authoritative.[27] Again, this text is written in the form of Sanskrit *ślokas*, not particularly easy for memorization or oral transmission, but perhaps intended more for reading. This text survived far more clearly into the medieval tradition, appearing in a Telugu version in the later sixteenth century (about 1584) as the

Āndhra Kāmandaka, with some additional material that the Sanskrit "original" does not contain.

Nīti and its Opponents during the Medieval Period

A very active interest in creating *nīti* texts is found in Telugu from the Kakatiya period in Andhra, which is to say the period from about the twelfth to the mid-fourteenth centuries.[28] The emergence of a powerful dynasty of major rulers from the great center of Warangal and the conditions that existed for a general upward mobility among many communities in the Deccan apparently motivated many writers to produce such works in Telugu. Some of the authors of *nīti* books of this period were themselves kings or their ministers, and many were associated with people of power in some manner or the other. The *Sakala-nīti-sammatamu* (hereafter *SNS*), a major anthology of selections from a number of *nīti* texts in Telugu, is of particular interest to us because it demonstrates the popularity of *nīti* as a subject in medieval Andhra.[29] The compiler of this anthology, Maḍiki Siṅgana, was a poet in his own right. In his preface to the book he declares that *nīti* should have equal circulation everywhere like a coin with the stamp of the Sultan (*suratāṇi*), and appropriately enough he calls his book "*Nīti* acceptable to everyone."

Singana lived in a period when a number of *nīti* texts were already popular, perhaps each one in a different subregion or community. In his preface to the anthology he hence expresses a desire to produce a digest of *nīti*, and lists the names of books from which he has collected his selections. He notes that his compilation is of some 982 selections from 17 distinct *nīti* texts by known authors (many of the texts that were available to Singana are now lost), several verses from oral tradition, some verses by unknown authors, and his own verses as well. Among the known authors from whom Singana quotes, some are either kings themselves or ministers closely associated with kings. Rudradeva I (1150–95), who wrote *Nītisāramu*, was a king of the Kākatīya dynasty; Sivadevayya (1250–1300), who wrote the *Puruṣârthasāramu*, was the adviser and minister of the Kākatīya king Ganapatideva; and Badděna, also known as Bhadrabhupala, who wrote a particularly celebrated book called *Nīti-śāstra-muktâvaḷi*—better known as *Badděnīti*—is considered by modern Telugu scholarship to have been a king from the Telugu Cola family.[30] Not much is known about this last poet-savant who addresses himself in his verses with royal epithets, except that he lived sometime before Siṅgana (who himself flourished in about 1420), and that by the early fifteenth century his book had acquired considerable popularity, as is indicated by the short title which Singana uses when he quotes from it. The other *nīti* writers whom Singana quotes are mostly unknown, with the exception of Appamantri who wrote a Telugu version of Bhoja's *Cārucarya*, a book of advice about healthy habits for wealthy people to follow.

Siṅgana classifies his selections under 47 categories covering a range of topics related to kings as well as commoners—courtiers, physicians, pundits, and of course accountants and scribes (*karaṇams*). Two things stand out from Siṅgana's anthology. In the first place, it does not invoke an otherworldly authority in any place. The goal is mundane, this-worldly, and the only thing that counts is success in any profession. However, it is not an "amoral" text, as the desire for success is considered acceptable as part of a good human life, and it is implicit that success should be achieved within the framework of ethical conduct. The only concept that might suggest a Hindu "worldview" of some sort is that a certain number of the verses refer to the scheme of the four goals of life, the *caturvidha puruṣârthas* (that is *dharma*, *artha*, *kāma*, and *mokṣa*), of which *artha* and *kāma*—profit and pleasure—are the most significant areas upon which *nīti* texts focus. Even this reference, from the tone of its use, does not seem to be particularly religious in the context. While we do not have access to Śivadevayya's text in its entirety to see if it deals with the other two *puruṣârthas*, i.e. *dharma* and *mokṣa*, we know that no other extant *nīti* text deals with them, and in the use of later texts, for instance, the *Sumati-śatakamu*, the phrase *puruṣârtha-paruḍu* simply means a successful person.

It should also be noted that *SNS* for its part does not include even a single verse from the thirteenth-century *dharmaśāstra* work, Ketana's

Vijñāneśvaramu, a Telugu work based on the Sanskrit *mitakṣara* commentary of Vijnaneśvara to the *Yajñavalkyasmriti.* This, we suggest, emphasizes the conceptual separation that already operated in these authors' minds of *nīti* from *dharma.*[31] For Ketana's work, we should note, followed in the standard, rather Brahminic, *dharmaśāstra* tradition of normative texts. Its author was a close relative (probably the nephew) of the celebrated Tikkana, who seems to have instructed him and guided him in writing this text.[32] Ketana was also the author of two other texts, one the *Daśakumāracaritramu*, an entertaining book of stories, and a grammar of Telugu, *Āndhrabhāshābhūṣaṇamu.* He, like Tikkana, seems to have been creating an intellectual culture of a conservative and "revivalist" kind, as we see from a close reading of the huge *Mahābhārata* that Tikkana produced at much the same time in Telugu.

To gain a sense of Ketana's *Vijñāneśvaramu* it may be useful to turn to the *vyavahārakāṇḍa* section of his text, which—though a relatively short section of the whole—starkly brings out the contrast we wish to develop between *dharma* and *nīti* texts. Here is a passage where he sets out his conception of rulership:

> A king, without becoming greedy or angry,
> with *dharma* in his own heart,
> should decide issues of *dharma*,
> in the company of competent, well-known and scholarly Brahmins.
> In that group, he should have those
> learned in Veda, truthful,
> versed in the *dharmaśāstras*,
> and not given to love or hatred.
> Such Brahmins should be members of his council.
> In number, they should be seven,
> or five, or three,
> and if the king cannot attend,
> he should send a scholar of the *dharmaśāstra*,
> who is a good judge.
> And if the king does something unjust,
> and is supported by his council,
> they will be drowned in sin (*pāpambuna munuguduru*).[33]

So we see here the clear evocation of the idea of *pāpa* (sin) as the ultimate punishment for incorrect action even in the context of statecraft. At times, however, as noted by Malamoud in the classical context, the texts of *nīti* and *dharma* do converge, as when certain procedures are discussed (for example, on how to collect evidence in the context of a trial, or some other practical affairs). However, often enough, even the flavor of judicial considerations varies considerably, since texts like that of Ketana imply a strong caste variation in trials and punishments, and even seem directly to echo ideas from the Manu *Dharmaśāstra*. Thus, we have the following example:

If a Brahmin commits a crime
deserving capital punishment,
this is what should be done:
Shave his head,
Mark his forehead with the sign of a dog's paw,
Confiscate his money,
sit him on a donkey,
and drive him out of town.
This is as good as killing him.
But if a lower-caste person commits a crime
that deserves capital punishment,
taking his life
is quite appropriate.[34]

Where then, may we ask, do *dharma* and *nīti* texts in fact overlap without a great deal of tension? This is on those rare occasions when *dharma* texts deal with rather concrete commercial matters, such as the passage in Ketana dealing with how to write a promissory note (*patra*).

Mark the year, month, the fortnight,
the number and name of the day,
and the place.
Write the name of the lender,
Along with his father's name,
Then that of the borrower,
with his father's name too.
Then write the sum of the loan,
And the rate of interest,

And the witnesses must then write:
That they know and certify the facts.
The borrower should sign his name,
Saying that he has received the money,
and agrees to the conditions.
At last, the executor of the note must sign
to make what civilized people (*nāgarika*) call a trustworthy note.[35]

In general, however, Ketana's text is everywhere marked by a manner of thinking that reflects the *dharmaśāstras*, and is consequently anxious above all to protect and defend the caste hierarchy as the most important aspect of the functioning of the polity. Nowhere is this clearer than in the passages where he gives ways of testing the four *varṇas*, to see if they are telling the truth or not.

If it is a Brahmin,
first weigh him in scales
with a certain number of bricks.
Save the bricks,
and on the day of the test,
bring them back,
worship the scales,
invoke the lords (*dikpālas*) of the eight directions,
and have him sit facing east.
Put the same bricks back,
and call upon the gods (*daivambulāra*) saying:
If he speaks the truth, lift him up,
and if he lies, pull him down.
And when the judge says this, if the pan rises,
he does not lie.

In contrast to this somewhat soft treatment, Kshatriyas on the other hand are to be tested by fire, Vaishyas by water, and Shudras by poison. Thus, for Kshatriyas:

An iron ball of a certain weight
should be properly worshiped.
The person to be tested
should stand facing east.
In his palms, seven *pīpal* leaves should be placed,
and tied with seven twists.

The red hot iron ball should be brought with tongs,
and placed in his hands by a judge,
who all the while chants *mantras*.
If on account of the leaves,
his hands are not burnt,
the man is truthful.[36]

It is hence clear that different tests are to be administered to different castes, a feature that markedly does not appear in *nīti* texts. The division of property among children finds extensive mention in Ketana, as well as the circumstances in which it goes to other kin.

If someone wishes to dig a well,
or build a tank,
on someone else's land,
for the welfare of the people,
he still must ask the owner's permission,
and if the owner refuses,
he is obliged to stop.[37]

Thus, the difference between the *vyavahārakāṇḍa* of a *dharma* text like that of Ketana, and sections dealing with similar matters in a typical *nīti* text, are rather clear. Divine intervention (*daivas*) is constantly invoked in the former, the notion of sin (*pāpa*) is brought in, and punishments are explicitly hierarchized by caste. Even judgment is a ritual, requiring the chanting of *mantras*. In general, we may note that in this vision of things, punishments suggested with regard to castes lower down in the hierarchy (including scribal groups) are very heavy, and most of the discussions, including even those on how murders should be investigated, wind up having a strongly *dharmic* flavor about them. The example below demonstrates this amply:

If a person of a low caste
forces himself on the wife
of a man of higher caste
he should be killed for it.
That is the *dharma* of a king.
If a man forces himself
on a housewife of his own caste
fine him a thousand *paṇas*.

But if a man of high caste
makes love to a woman of lower caste
fine him five hundred *panas*.
If a lower-caste man
makes love to a higher-caste virgin
he should be killed.
But if he is a higher-caste man
and the virgin loves him,
the two should be married.[38]

The role of the king is clear enough; he is, in large measure, the guarantor of the caste hierarchy and the protector of upper-caste males, but also the defender of their virtue—even against themselves. The examples below make this perfectly clear, and reinforce our notion that we are dealing with a socially conservative text.

If a Brahmin makes love to an untouchable (*caṇḍāla*) woman,
the drawing of a vagina should be inscribed on his body,
he should be fined,
and driven out of the country.
That's appropriate for a king to do.[39]

The text does occasionally adopt a mildly humorous—or if one prefers, "realistic"—tone, but this is far more an exception than the rule. One example of this appears in the same section.

If a woman is found with an illegitimate lover,
and tries to claim that he is a burglar,
he should still be fined five hundred
as an illegitimate lover.[40]

At the same time, Ketana is a strong defender of royal authority, which he sees as requiring defense with an iron hand and the most severe of deterrent punishments. Hence:

If someone insults the king,
Or reveals the royal secrets,
His tongue should be cut out
And he should be driven out of town.[41]

All in all, then, this is a text that is remarkable for its censorious tone, and marked desire to regulate the moral life of society, rather than the harmonious combination of its parts in some form of social equilibrium. Virtue, for Ketana, must be produced, and if that production requires pain—whether physical or financial—so be it. Even gossips and malicious speech are seen by him as requiring regulation in some form, and that too by the king.

If a person lacks one limb,
or if he has a deformed limb,
or if one limb is badly diseased,
one should not talk ill of them.
And those who ridicule them by saying:
"How well formed he is,"
"No one compares to him,"
should pay a fine of three *rūkas*.[42]

In a similar vein, ethnic slurs, or insults based on caste, are not to be allowed, in this most "politically correct" of utopias.

If someone says that people from Murikinadu are stupid,
that the Arava [Tamil] people are quarrelsome (*penaparulu*,)
or that Brahmins are greedy,
and abuses people by country, language or caste,
such a person should be fined a hundred *paṇas*.[43]

In other sections, notably the *ācāra-kāṇḍa*, many passages seem to bear a close resemblance to Manu's *Dharmaśāstra*, at times literally and at other times in spirit. A great preoccupation of the author, Ketana, is with the mixing of castes and the potentially negative effects of this phenomenon. Further, gender roles are distinctly asymmetrical in this vision of things, all the more so in the context of intercaste relations. Thus:

If a high-caste woman
Makes love to a *shudra* man,
She may become pure again
by ritual punishment (*prāyaścitta*).
But if she becomes pregnant,
her husband should leave her.

Further, unlike what we would find in *nīti* texts, it is understood that the rights of women are far more limited, and that they can be unilaterally disciplined for a number of faults, often merely on the basis of accusation. A last verse from Ketana below demonstrates how thoroughgoing and consistent a vision he embodies.

If a woman drinks,
and has a sharp tongue,
if she wastes all the money,
if she hates men,
or if she is barren,
or if she only has female children,
if she is sick,
if she is a termagant,
then the man can leave her, and marry again.
There is nothing wrong in that.[44]

To develop the contrast, and the opposed visions that we have suggested inhering in the different genres, we should now turn to the *nīti* tradition of roughly the same period. In the *nīti* texts that were written during the Kākatīya period, by such writers as Śivadevayya and Rudradeva, the localized nature of the king and his kingship is quite evident. Even though the king they address is portrayed as a strong monarch, he is not an emperor ruling over multiple regions or extensive domains. The advice given relating to the protection of *durgas* (fortresses), for dealing with spies, and for invading the enemy's territory, the conduct of battle, and so on, is not on a scale anywhere suggesting a large empire. Yet, the advice is practical and clearly derived from real experience of the administration of a kingdom. We may take, for instance, the following excerpts from Siṅgana:

- A king who does not command, is like a king in a painting (good only for looks). If a king doesn't punish anyone who defies his command—even if the wrongdoer is his own son—he does not rule long.
- To allow merchants to take as much as they want is to ruin your people.
- If you don't make scales and measures uniform, it means you effectively permit thieves to go scot-free.
- If a king increases taxes, that effectively prevents (foreign) goods from entering his country.

- Wherever a letter might come from, a king should never disregard it. It is only through letters that a king knows everything—from alliances to enmities.
- Not killing a criminal amounts to killing a host of gentle people. All that you need to do in order to kill cows is to spare a tiger.

Some of the quotations in the *SNS* are clearly influenced by a traditional Sanskrit model of kingship, for example when the king is equated with god, quoting Manu's *Dharmaśāstra*:

- The king is godly, and that is what Manu says, and he should be treated as such, and wise people should not treat him otherwise.
- Even if he is a boy, a king should not be treated like an ordinary mortal. He is god, and that's how he should be treated.
- The king may be bad, but the servant should serve his interests.
- If he [the servant] should leave his master for another to make a better living, the new master will never respect him for his loyalty.

However, in the same anthology we find some advice regarding bad kings. It is interesting to note that this advice comes from writers who perhaps served kings themselves in various capacities such as scribes (*karaṇams*), or soldiers.

- If anyone has caused you harm, go and complain to the king. But if the king himself harms you, who can you complain to?
- If serving a ruler causes incessant pain to the servant, the servant should leave such a master right away.
- He may be rich, born in a good caste, a strong warrior beyond comparison, but if a king is an ignoramus, his servants will no doubt leave him.
- If a king does not distinguish between the right hand and the left, a precious diamond and a piece of glass, it is humiliating to serve such a king—no matter how great a warrior you are.
- A bad king surrounded by good people turns out to be good. But even a good king is difficult to serve if his advisers are bad.
- A king who enjoys hearing stories of others' faults, who enjoys putting people through trouble, and steals other men's wives, brings calamity to his people.

The authoritative figure of Baddĕna is generously quoted in the *SNS*, and has some fascinating instructions to a king in his *Nīti-śāstra-muktâvaḷi*. Contrary to the later importance *karaṇams* acquired in managing the affairs of the kingdom as ministers and scribes, Badděna strikes a note of caution against too much dependence on the minister. In his words:

- A king should not direct his people and his servants to his minister for all their needs. The king should be his own minister and treat the minister as an assistant.

The major writers on *nīti* whom Siṅgana quotes in his *SNS* are already aware of the whole *nīti* tradition before them, including the Sanskrit *Arthaśāstra* text. Besides, closer to hand, we find medieval texts from the Deccan, such as the *Mānasollāsa* of the twelfth-century Cāḷukya king, Someśvara III.[45] Such works as these can certainly be seen to participate in a culture of political realism, and thus give the lie to those who have argued that pre-colonial politics in India was conceived along purely idealist lines. At the same time, the genre of the "Mirror for Princes" is well known in the Indo-Islamic context, where a number of such texts exist both from the time of the Sultanate of Delhi, under the later Mughals, and from the regional sultanates such as those of the Deccan.[46] Such texts, often written in Persian, are themselves at times influenced by Indic models such as the *Pañcatantra*, known in the Islamic world through its translation as the *Kalīla wa Dimna*. Yet, they also bear the clear imprint of the non-theological perspective on kingship that had emerged in the Islamic lands in the aftermath of the Mongol conquests, when Muslim advisers and *wazīrs* struggled with the problem of how to advise *kāfir* rulers and princes on the matter of government, without taking them into murky and controversial theological waters.[47] The "Mirror for Princes" genre ranges wide, and attempts to do everything—from forming the prince's musical tastes, to refining his table manners—but the core of the matter is usually politics, both in the sense of diplomatic relations between states, and relations between a prince and his companions, or between different elements in a courtly setting.[48]

The authors included in the *SNS* appear to be aware of these different traditions, and even draw upon them quite explicitly.[49] Yet, in contrast to the typical "Mirrors for Princes," these authors offer a top-down, hands-on vision, partly rooted in pragmatic experience, partly creatively adapting the existing literature of *nīti* statecraft. This is no armchair pontificating but a largely practical synthesis reflecting the political, economic, and institutional changes of the fifteenth century. Still, highly individualized statements that can be attributed directly to the book's author Singana, do alternate with verses that seem to be lifted from standard *nīti* texts about politics and kingship. Nonetheless, we are left with a total impression of a unique concoction of pragmatic wisdom, specific constraints, an inherited normative politics.

An Imperial Interlude: Kṛṣṇadevarāya

Singana wrote in the fifteenth century, and the immediate textual heritage he had available to him came from the period of the Kākatīyas. These were rulers who had dominated a relatively well-defined regional space in the eastern Deccan, and their preoccupations reflected that fact. In the case of Singana, we may suspect that the political landscape had fragmented even further, and that the kings he referred to were ruling over domains that would qualify a few centuries later as no more than *zamīndārīs*. But this was certainly not the case by the latter half of the fifteenth century, when a new, diverse, and complex polity had emerged to control much of peninsular India south of the Tungabhadra river, namely the state that is normally known as Vijayanagara (from the name of its capital city).

Normative texts on kingship, or statecraft, are hard to come by for fifteenth-century Vijayanagara. But we are far better served for the sixteenth century, and the times of the Third (Tuluva) and Fourth (Aravidu) Dynasties that ruled over Vijayanagara. A particular high point in terms of literary production, including that within the *nīti* genre, is the reign of the Tuluva monarch Kṛṣṇadevarāya (d. 1529).[50] When Kṛṣṇadevarāya ascended the throne in 1509 it is clear that a number of crucial problems regarding political management still remained to be resolved.[51] One major concern in the mind of the king was to make himself generally acceptable, and secure an area that encompassed more than one region, one language, and one religion. The king's self-perception given to us eloquently in his major work, *Āmuktamālyada*, suggests that he sees himself as a Kannada Raya, a Kannada king, while the god to whom he had dedicated his book was a Telugu Raya, a Telugu king. Without anachronistically invoking regional nationalisms and language loyalties in the context of the sixteenth-century Deccan, we can still see local polities conflicting with each other, wary of dominance by someone from the outside.

Another way to formulate the dilemma that this king confronted is in terms of an enduring tension between local and translocal forces. There is a consistent effort to conceptualize some basis for a translocal polity that could extricate the state from its constant re-submergence in diffuse local contexts. A striking element in this conceptual effort lies in the king's own dynastic origins in one of the most marginal and recently conquered localities—the western coastal plain of Tulunad. A kind of upstart, whose own family inheritance dictated that he prove himself outside the family context, finds himself articulating, at times somewhat inchoately, a vision of trans-regional, highly personalized loyalties. Once a trans-regional state system is conceivable, its ruler runs up against its external boundaries. The *manyam* forest regions (especially the northern and north-eastern frontiers, but also implicitly to the south-west in Kodagu, or Coorg, and the Western Ghats) thus figure prominently in the *Āmuktamālyada*'s section on *rāja-nīti* and require special treatment. External boundaries, however, coexist with the internal wilderness, as we see in a verse about a farmer marking off his field and then slowly making it free of stones and other impediments. But the text is also marked by a consistent suspicion, at times bordering on hostility or even contempt, for peoples like the Boyas and the Bhils, who could be found both at the border regions of the empire (in the north-east) and at the internal frontier. A prose passage within the *nīti* section thus advises the listener: "Allay the fears of the hill-folk, and bring them into your army. Since they are a small people, their loyalty or faithlessness, their enmity or friendship, their favor or disfavor, can all easily be managed." Another passage, this one in verse, runs as follows:

> Trying to clean up the forest folk
> is like trying to wash a mud wall.
> There's no end to it. No point in getting angry.
> Make promises that you can keep and win them over.

They'll be useful for invasions, or plundering an enemy land.
It's irrational for a ruler to punish a thousand
When a hundred are at fault.

This then is *rāja-nīti* for building an empire, composed by a rather introspective, yet by now quite experienced king, who has been on the throne for perhaps a decade. In certain key respects, the author departs from conventional wisdom. For example, he recommends posting Brahmins as commanders of forts (*durga*), and the fact that this was practical advice is shown by the prosopography of the empire in that time.[52]

Make trustworthy Brahmins
The commanders of your forts
And give them just enough troops,
to protect these strongholds,
lest they become too threatening.

Brahmins, in this view, have certain clear advantages over non-Brahmins, even though this caste is theoretically at least not to be associated with warrior functions (though numerous exceptions, both in the epics and earlier historical instances, could be found):

The king will often benefit by putting a Brahmin in charge,
for he knows both the laws of Manu and his own *dharma*.
And from fear of being mocked
by Kshatriyas and Shudras,
he will stand up to all difficulties.

Beyond this, however, lies the Brahmin's relative freedom from local attachments. At the same time, these Brahmins are clearly trained by now in military ways and engaged in worldly activities.

The potential for conflict between kings and ministers, that would be a staple of the histories and treatises produced by the *karaṇams*, the class from which the ministers themselves came, is also ever-present here, though its resolution is rather more to the king's advantage. The following extended passage makes this clear enough:

Employ Brahmins who are learned in statecraft,
who fear the unethical, and accept the king's authority,
who are between fifty and seventy,

from healthy families,
not too proud, willing to be ministers,
capable of discharging their duties well.
A king with such Brahmins for just a day
can strengthen the kingdom in all its departments.
If such ministers are not available,
a king must act on his own,
and do whatever he can.
If not, a bad minister can become
like a pearl as large as a pumpkin—
an ornament impossible to wear.
The minister will be out of control,
and the king will live under his thumb.

Early Modern Variations

The post-Kṛṣṇadevarāya period in Vijayanagara changes the context of such writings, in particular once we enter the period of the dominance of the Aravidu family. The growing role of Aravidu ("Aliya") Rāmarāya's relatives and his extended family spread out in smaller kingdoms all over the Deccan already marks a significant shift in this respect. The *nīti* of the empire, articulated by Kṛṣṇadevarāya, again gives way to the *nīti* of small kingdoms, most of which survive with the help of kinship relations and support from the extended family. While this also creates the usual family intrigues, rivalries, and battles, the new political conditions also give rise to opportunities for upward mobility. The emergence of the Nayakas from the flexible and uncertain political conditions in the post-Kṛṣṇadevarāya period is reflected in the *nīti* texts of this time.[53]

The *Āndhra Kāmandakamu* by Jakkarāju Veṅkaṭakavi was written in 1584, and is of crucial interest to us in this context. Veṅkaṭakavi was employed in the court of Kŏṇḍarāju Veṅkaṭarāju, himself a small king from the Aravidu family. The personal history of this Veṅkaṭarāju is interesting, especially because he is reputed to have renovated the Ahobilam temple, when it had been ruined by the Turks (*turakalu*). Even so, the *nīti* book Veṅkaṭakavi has authored does not have any mention of Muslims, either disapproving or approving. What is instead noteworthy for us now is the regional and "secular" (in the sense of non-sectarian) nature of *nīti* in the *Āndhra Kāmandakamu*. Even though the author states that his work is a translation of the earlier Sanskrit *Kāmandakiya* or *Nītisāra*, the later work in fact includes a number of *nīti* statements that are not to be found in the original, making it more an early modern *nīti* text rather than a simple restatement of a classical *nīti* vision. For instance, here is a passage concerning the treatment of relatives and other political allies.

> Sons of your maternal uncle and aunt, and your nephews and your maternal uncle himself, sons of your mother's sister's sons—these people are allies by blood (*aurasa-mitrulu*).
>
> Your sons-in-law, brothers-in-law, your wife's brothers and sisters, are allies by marriage (*sambandha-mitrulu*).
>
> Kings of the lands on the other side of the country with which you share a border are allies from a related foreign land (*deśakramāgatulu*). Kings who seek your protection in time of need are protected allies (*rakṣitamitrulu*). A king should take note of these four kinds of allies and nurture their friendship.[54]

We have already noted that the relationship between kings and their ministers had been a matter of concern for both Badděna and Kṛṣṇadevarāya, both of whom have some words of caution to the king regarding the choice of his ministers. Veṅkaṭakavi goes a step further and describes the corrupt practices that bad ministers could adopt in order to enrich themselves. The verse below gives several kinds of bribes a minister could take:

> If the minister comes to a festival, what he gets is called *kānuka*. What he receives by way of things he appropriates from people is called *porabaḍi*.
>
> If he gets kickback in cash it is called *paṭṭubaḍi*. The money he gets privately in return for taking care of their business is called *lañcam*.
>
> A king should make sure that his minister does not take any of the above, and such a person should work for the king and receive his livelihood only from the king.[55]

Nīti and *Karaṇam* Culture

The political landscape we have described changes again from the seventeenth century onwards. A new group of people who made writing their profession emerged as a politically and culturally important group. In Andhra, Karnataka, and Orissa these people were often called *karaṇams* and were considered the counterparts of *munshīs* in northern India.[56] Often seeing themselves as *mantris* or ministers of kings, the *karaṇams* perceived themselves broadly as managers of public affairs. Most members of this group were not connected with major empires or powerful kings, but they nevertheless had an enormous influence in running small kingdoms, *zamīndāris*, and petty principalities. They were also successful managers of properties, accountants, poets, and historians. They prided themselves in their multiple language skills, their ability to read scripts of many languages, and above all their skill in calligraphy. They were also at the same time accomplished at writing a highly unintelligible cursive script, which could be read only by other *karaṇams*. They came mostly from Brahmin castes, and in Andhra they were mostly Niyogi Brahmins—as opposed to the Vaidikis.[57] The former managed public affairs while the latter specialized in ritual texts and ritual performances, even though both wrote poetry. *Karaṇams* used the pen for their power and prestige. They were writers in the true sense of the word as we understand it today.

The self-image of the *karaṇams* is fascinating. They have left behind a large body of writings about themselves, their code of conduct and training, in addition to a number of historical texts. Here is what some of the verses tell us about a *karaṇam*:

> By good fortune a person becomes intelligent.
> By his intelligence, he receives the king's respect.
> When the king respects him, he becomes his adviser,
> and begins to manage public affairs.
> And when he becomes his chief adviser, he runs the kingdom.
>
> He writes, reads and speaks intelligently.
> He listens to what people say.
> He interprets foreign languages to the king, and
> calms the assembly when it is out of control.
> He says the right words at the right time, and brings people together,
> and sees, right away, honesty from trickery.
> He is capable of bringing people together and separating them too.

Or favoring enemies and offering them the throne.
He is humble, dignified, skilled and giving.
That's what a good *mantri* should be.

When the king is against you,
You need to make friends with the scribe.
When the god of death, Yama, was angry and declared a person dead, *gatāyu*,
didn't Citragupta, his scribe, make him live a hundred years, a *śatāyu*, by changing *ga* to *śa*?

Included in a list of thirty-two legendary ministers is a certain Rāyani Bhāskaruḍu, who appears most frequently in manuscript sources. Here are a few poems about him from tradition.[58]

There should be twelve *bhāskaras* (suns) in the sky, Why do I see only eleven?
One of them is now serving as a minister on earth.
You mean the famous minister Bhāskara? I don't see a thousand hands (rays) on him.
You see them when he gives to people, when he kills enemies, and when he writes.

When Rāyani Bācaḍu writes,
sitting in front of his king Kāṭaya Vema,
the sound of his pen gives
chills to his enemies
and shivers of joy to the poets.

Even when he was learning his alphabet,
Rāyani Bācaḍu did not join *la* and its e-curve
or write *da* and make a loop on its side.
The letters together would make, *ledu*, which means "no."
That was how generous he was to those who asked him for help.[59]

We also find a verse concerning a minister inscribed on the front gate of the Gopinathasvami temple in Kondavidu.

He built the town of Gopinathapuram
with incomparable walls on all sides.
Compelling in gentle power, he conquered
the Yavanas and all their armies.

He installed the deity, Gopikā-vallabha, and
organized his worship in a regular order.
He ruled over the Andhra *mandala* area
with a name for law and justice.
He is the one who is praised among
the best of *mantris* of the best of kings,
who worked for the honor and good of Acyutadevarāya
He is Rāmayabhāskara, brilliant as the mid-day sun.

We can see that a number of developments led to the growing importance of *karaṇams* in the affairs of the state. The increased use of Persian as a language of administration, and the presence of multiple languages in which smaller kings had to correspond with their political allies and neighbours, the availability of pen and paper, and the elaborate new accounting responsibilities made the position of scribes far more important in society than what it had been before. Now scribes were employed in jobs of higher status and power than simply serving as persons who could take down dictation or copy manuscripts. Reality is now what was written down, and not, as earlier, what was uttered. We can see a corresponding change even in the popular mythology and Hindu iconography. The goddess of language and arts, Sarasvatī was now endowed with a book in one of her hands, in addition to a *vīṇa*, the stringed musical instrument. Yama, the god of death, acquires an assistant, Citragupta, who keeps accounts of living beings in separate files, and as in the poem that was quoted earlier, can even become more powerful than Yama himself.

The people who called themselves ministers (*mantris*) were not always ministers of a ruling king. *Mantri* was in a sense more an honorific caste title rather than a fixed position or office. Often these "ministers" were themselves independent chiefs of a locality or even a village. However, in keeping with the convention that a king should be a warrior, the minister who has taken independent control of an area also describes himself in military terms. But by the seventeenth century there was a significant shift in the values of peninsular Indian society. Greater importance was given to *dāna* (charity), rather than *vīra* (valour) in battle. The possibility of acquiring wealth in the form of cash created conditions of upward mobility, different from those created by simple military conquest. The emergence of the left-hand caste of Balijas as trader-warrior-kings, as evidenced in the Nayaka period, is a consequence of such conditions of new wealth. This produces a collapsing of two *varṇas*, Kshatriya and Vaishya, into one. Acquired wealth, rather than status by birth in a family now leads to an entirely new value system where money talks. The *Sumati Śatakamu* records this change rather cynically:

> Never mind if he is born in a low caste,
> never mind if he is timid,
> never mind if he is son of a whore.
> If he has money, he is king.

The presence of cash also generates charity. Members of the nobility are now constantly advised to excel in charity. In keeping with the changes in the social values, *nīti* is no longer regarded as a matter that simply concerns kings and courtiers. It is for everyone, and in particular for anyone who desires status and social recognition. *Nīti* is now told in the form of stories rather than aphorisms and *śāstric* statements. Kucirāju Ĕrrana's *Sakala-nīti-kathā-nidhānam*, a book of stories that teaches *nīti*, indicates an early recognition of this change.[60] Ĕrrana adopts a number of stories from *Betāla-pañca-vimśati* and other *kathā* sources, both from Sanskrit and from Telugu. The main thrust of the stories is to teach the individual wise and tactful ways of handling oneself, and thus maximizing one's chances of success.

One book that codifies the conduct of *karaṇams* is the *Sumati Śatakamu*.[61] Written by an unknown author, probably in the eighteenth century, this book is variously attributed to Badděna and to an even more ancient Bhīmana. Perhaps both authorships were ascribed by *karaṇams* to make the text serve two different purpose. Badděna's authorship serves the interests of the *karaṇams* in claiming political legitimacy among kings and other aspirants to rule an area, and the Bhīmana authorship makes the text speak with a voice of the authority of an ancient, godlike poet to serve the interests of the same community when they desire legitimacy among the people in general. The *Sumati Śatakamu* elevates the role of the minister (*karaṇamu*) and treats it as more crucial for the maintenance of the order of the kingdom than that of the king himself.

A kingdom with a minister runs smoothly with its strategy intact.
And a kingdom without a minister breaks down like a machine with a critical part missing.
A king without a minister is like an elephant without a trunk.

It also gives practical wisdom for ordinary people such as the following:

Don't live in a village where you don't have a moneylender, a doctor, and a river that does not dry up.

If you don't spend the money you earn for your pleasures,
part of it goes to the king and the other part is lost into the earth.
That's very much like the honey that bees gather in the forest— part of it goes to people who collect honey and part of it falls to earth.

The lord of wealth Kubera is his friend, but Śiva still begs for his living.
What you have is your wealth, not what your friends or relatives have.

Don't ever trust the tax-collector, the gambler,
the goldsmith or the whore. Don't trust a merchant
or a left-handed person, that is not good for you.

Listen to everyone, but wait to think through what they say.
Only one who accepts things after ascertaining truth or falsehood, is a wise man.

A wise man is stronger than a man who is only physically strong.
A slim rider controls an elephant big as a mountain.

A snake has poison in its head.
A scorpion has poison in its tail.
An evil person has poison all over his body, head to toe.

Despite such practical advice, the *Sumati Śatakamu* is at bottom a cynical (rather than simply an amoral) text, which believes women are not trustworthy, that kings never keep their word, and friends last only as long as you have money. In the hard world it depicts, you have to take care of yourself—no one else helps.

Conclusion

When the British government and its native employees wanted "morals" to be taught in the early nineteenth century, the Telugu equivalent that their pundit informants could find was *nīti*. This was based on a rather curious misunderstanding: for even if there are some ethical teachings and moral statements in these texts, they are not exactly the kind of moral code that one would apply to all people. Vennelakanti Subbarao (1784–1839), translator for the *Sadr 'adālat* of the Madras Presidency, a Telugu Niyogi Brahmin who rose to the highest post a native could aspire to in the East India Company administration at the time, and who commanded competence in about half a dozen Indian languages in addition to English, was one of the more prominent of the Company's interlocutors from an early time. When he was appointed member of the Madras School Book Society, he submitted a report in 1820 on the state of teaching in schools, in which he wrote that children in schools were taught neither adequate grammar nor morals. So they came out of their schools with no real ability in using the language and they were not trained to become upright members of their society either. Therefore, he recommended—addressing the need for teaching morals—that "tales extracted from different books composed chiefly of morals written in modern languages" be prescribed for study.[62]

In this context, Ravipati Gurumurti Sastri also put the *Pañcatantra* stories into Telugu prose and taught them at the College of Fort St. George in Madras. This was soon followed by another translation of the *Pañcatantra* by the very influential Paravastu Cinnaya Suri.[63] Now the *Pañcatantra* was not in fact a "Book of Morals;" rather, it was statecraft taught by means of animal fables. When the first generation of colonial schoolboys needed a textbook, Puduri Sitarama Sastri, a pundit in Madras wrote a text called *Pĕdda Bāla Siksa* (The Big Book of Lessons for Children), which was published in 1847. This work contains a number of items such as basic arithmetic, the names of the weekdays, months, and years according to the traditional lunar calendar, and many items of conventional wisdom, a few stories, and aphorisms modelled after the statements from *nīti* texts, to teach "*nīti*" (now translated in an unproblematized way as "morals") to schoolboys. To be sure, in every *nīti* text, there were occasional statements that looked like teachings of virtue, which were carefully selected and included in school textbooks. Verses from Bhartṛhari, which were translated into Telugu by several poets during the medieval period, came in handy. Even the *Sumati Śatakamu*, which, as we have seen, is actually a handbook for *karaṇams*, yielded some nice and acceptable moral statements.[64] Because of the simple language in which the *Sumati Śatakamu* was written, it came to be particularly popular in school moral curricula. Soon enough, lines from these verses came to adorn classroom walls and copybooks. Thus, in the end, books on statecraft and worldly wisdom could serve as acceptable substitutes for the Ten Commandments.

Our central purpose here has been to widen the rather narrow conception within which "political thought" has hitherto been studied in an Indian context. We would only caricature very slightly if we were to say that the usual strategies espoused by analysts are two: either they assume that modern politics in India was a pure product of the interaction with colonialism and colonial modernity, or at best they leap over the intervening centuries to classical India and its materials. In this context, we welcome the development of interest in recent times in the Indo-Persian corpus, and what it might tell us about both institutional arrangements and political thought at the time of the Sultanaṭe and the Mughals. The problem does remain however of that part of India where Persian was not the principal language in which such thought was expressed. The example of the Maratha polity in the seventeenth and eighteenth centuries brings this home, even though the Marathi used by them was heavily inflected by Persian. It is clear from the researches of Hiroyuki Kotani and Narendra Wagle, however, that the eighteenth-century Maratha Deccan continued to witness a struggle between precisely the forces we have set out in this essay, that is, between the proponents of *nīti* (who no doubt drew on the Indo-Persian corpus as well) and those who remained fiercely attached to the highly *dharmaśāstra*-oriented vision of social ordering and political functioning. The continued presence of terms such as *doṣa* and *prāyaścitta* in the vocabulary of the Maratha polity possibly testify to the waning influence of the *nīti* tradition in that system.[65]

A celebrated reflection on the "history of concepts" written some thirty-five years ago proposed to historians of Europe that they needed to go beyond their preoccupation with social (and political) history to look at both individual concepts, and groups of concepts, to clarify that which underlay the functioning of the political and social systems in the societies they studied. In that context, Reinhart Koselleck wrote:

> The relationship between the history of concepts (*Begriffsgeschichte*) and social history (*Sozialgeschichte*) appears at first sight to be very loose, or at least difficult to determine, because the first of these disciplines primarily uses texts and words whereas the latter only uses texts to deduce facts and movements which are not contained in the texts themselves. It is thus that social history analyses social movements and constitutional structures, the relations between groups, social strata and classes; beyond the complex of events, it tries to come to terms with medium or long-term structures and their changes . . . The methods of the history of concepts are very different.[66]

We would hardly wish to be so immodest as to claim to be introducing the history of concepts (*Begriffsgeschichte*) into the study of the Indian past. However, we hope to have opened a window into a neglected and yet highly significant, corpus.

We began with two quotations, one by a scholar and editor of forgotten texts lamenting the loss of importance suffered by the *nīti* tradition, the other by one of the most important political figures in twentieth-century India. B.R. Ambedkar was, we are aware, a keen student of the Indian past, and had even studied with R.P. Kangle, an authority on the *Arthaśāstra*. The remark by him that we quote refers precisely to the tension between the *nīti*- and *dharma*-oriented traditions that have lain at the heart of this essay. He glossed these respectively as "secular law" and "ecclesiastical law," and there are many—especially among the growing number of "anti-secularist" intellectuals in India—who would immediately object to these translations.[67] But perhaps Ambedkar was not so wrong after all in his use of the term secular (however problematic the word "ecclesiastical" might be). Not as cavalier in his disregard of the Indian past—or dismissive of history—as writers such as T.N. Madan and Ashis Nandy have usually been, it may well be that his view of a struggle between different conceptions of political and social arrangements in pre-colonial India might shed light on the deeper roots and more profound purchase that "Indian secularism" has, than that of a mere transplant from distant climes. To explore that line of inquiry would take us, however, beyond the confines of this essay.

Notes

1. Burton Stein, "All the King's *Mana*: Perspectives on Kingship in Medieval South India," in J.F. Richards (ed.), *Kingship and Authority in South Asia* (Delhi, 1998), pp. 133–88 (with a brief mention of some Jaina *nīti* texts on pp. 144–5). For a succinct critique of Stein's formulations on the period under consideration here, see Sanjay Subrahmanyam, "Agreeing to Disagree: Burton Stein on Vijayanagara," in *South Asia Research*, vol. 17, no. 2 (1997), pp. 127–39.
2. For anthropological perspectives, see Jonathan Parry and Maurice Bloch (eds), *Money and the Morality of Exchange* (Cambridge, 1989); C.A. Gregory, *Savage Money: The Anthropology and Politics of Commodity Exchange* (Amsterdam, 1997); Stéphane Breton, "Social Body and Icon of the Person: A Symbolic Analysis of Shell Money among the Wodani, Western Highlands of Irian Jaya," in *American Ethnologist*, vol. 26, no. 3 (1999), pp. 558–82.
3. On the problem of religion, see Talal Asad, "The Construction of Religion as an Anthropological Category," in Talal Asad, *Genealogies of Religion: Discipline and Reasons of Power in Christianity and Islam* (Baltimore, 1993), pp. 27–54; drawing on the earlier work by Wilfred Cantwell Smith, *The Meaning and End of Religion: A New Approach to the Religious Traditions of Mankind* (New York, 1964).
4. Thomas N. Headland, Kenneth L. Pike, and Marvin Harris (eds), *Emics and Etics: The Insider/Outsider Debate* (Newbury Park, 1990).
5. See the useful discussion in Ian Hacking, *Historical Ontology* (Cambridge, MA, 2002), pp. 152–8.
6. The category of the "pre-political" appears most famously in Eric Hobsbawm, *Primitive Rebels: Studies in Archaic Forms of Social Movement in the 19th and 20th Centuries* (Manchester, 1959).
7. Benedict Anderson, "The Idea of Power in Javanese Culture," in Claire Holt, Benedict R. Anderson, and James T. Siegel (eds), *Culture and Politics in Indonesia* (Ithaca, NY, 1972), pp. 1–69; also the

earlier essay by Anderson, "The Languages of Indonesian Politics," in *Indonesia*, no. 1 (April 1966), pp. 89–116.

8. Ashis Nandy, "The Culture of Indian Politics: A Stocktaking," in the *Journal of Asian Studies*, vol. 30, no. 1 (1970), pp. 57–79. Also see Nandy, "The Political Culture of the Indian State," in *Daedalus*, vol. 118, no. 4 (1989), pp. 1–26.
9. For example, see V.R. Mehta and Thomas Pantham (eds), *Political Ideas in Modern India: Thematic Explorations* (New Delhi, 2006).
10. Patricia Crone, *Medieval Islamic Political Thought, c. 650–1250* (Edinburgh, 2004). The most important recent exercise on Indo-Islamic polities, and exploring the genre termed *akhlāq*, is that of Muzaffar Alam, *The Languages of Political Islam: India 1200–1800* (Chicago, 2004).
11. Our problem thus parallels in some measure that faced by historians of political thought in China. For some examples, see Roger T. Ames, *The Art of Rulership: A Study in Ancient Chinese Political Thought* (Honolulu, 1983), and Hsiao Kung-chüan, *A History of Chinese Political Thought. Volume 1, From the Beginnings to the Sixth Century A.D.*, trans. F.W. Mote (Princeton, 1979).
12. By focusing on the vernacular traditions, we seek to distinguish ourselves from a few earlier attempts which remain focused on Sanskrit; see, for example, Upendra Nath Ghoshal, *A History of Indian Political Ideas: The Ancient Period and the Period of Transition to the Middle Ages* (Bombay, 1959); and more recently the disappointing essay (again deriving from a secondary literature, but referring to Sanskrit materials) by Bhikhu Parekh, "Some Reflections on the Hindu Tradition of Political Thought," in Thomas Pantham and Kenneth L. Deutsch (eds), *Political Thought in Modern India* (New Delhi, 1986).
13. See, for example, Ramacandra Pant Amatya, *Ajñapatra*, ed. Vilas Khole (Pune, 1988).
14. We should note in passing that the word *nīti* is etymologically related to *netā*, the most common North Indian word in use today for "politician."
15. For a recent examination of this period, see Cynthia Talbot, *Precolonial India in Practice: Society, Region, and Identity in Medieval Andhra* (Delhi, 2001).

16. For Vijayanagara's relationship to (and memory of) earlier polities in the region, see Hermann Kulke, "Maharajas, Mahants and Historians: Reflections on the Historiography of early Vijayanagara and Sringeri," in A.L. Dallapiccola and S. Zingel-Avé Lallemant (eds), *Vijayanagara—City and Empire: New Currents of Research*, 2 vols (Stuttgart, 1985), vol. I, pp. 120–43.
17. On Mughal involvement in the region, see Sanjay Subrahmanyam, *Penumbral Visions: Making Polities in Early Modern South India* (Delhi/Ann Arbor, 2001).
18. Robert Sewell, *A Forgotten Empire—Vijayanagar: A Contribution to the History of India* (London, 1900; reprint, Delhi, 1962).
19. Patrick Olivelle, *The Law Code of Manu* (Oxford, 2004), p. xxiii: "the composition of the *MDh* may be placed closer to the second century CE."
20. On this early interaction, also see the essay by Phillip Wagoner, "Precolonial Intellectuals and the Production of Colonial Knowledge," in *Comparative Studies in Society and History*, vol. 45, no. 4 (2003), pp. 783–814, which however appears to us far too influenced by the model of "dialogic interaction" put forward in Eugene F. Irschick, *Dialogue and History: Constructing South India, 1795–1895* (Berkeley, 1994).
21. The classic study remains J.D.M. Derrett, *Religion, Law and the State in India* (New York, 1968). Also see, more recently, Richard W. Lariviere, "Dharmaśāstra, Custom, 'Real Law' and 'Apocryphal' Smrtis," in B. Koelver, ed., *Recht, Staat und Verwaltung in klassischen Indien* (Wiesbaden, 1997), pp. 97–110.
22. The standard work is R.P. Kangle, ed. and trans., *Kautilya's Arthaśāstra*, 3 vols (Bombay, 1965–72), but there is a vast secondary literature.
23. Phillip B. Wagoner, *Tidings of the King: A Translation and Ethnohistorical Analysis of the "Rāyavācakamu"* (Honolulu, 1993), pp. 182, 197. This Telugu text bears a close and interesting resemblance to a Kannada text of the same period, *Śrīkṛṣṇadevarāya dinacari*, ed. V.S. Sampatkumara Acarya (Bangalore, 1983).
24. We have used Kautilya, *Arthaśāstram*, ed. Pullela Sriramacandrudu (Hyderabad, 2004) with Balanandini's commentary, in the Telugu script.

25. Charles Malamoud, "Croyance, crédulité, calcul politique: Présentation et traduction commentée de l'Arthaçāstra de Kautilya, livre XIII, chapitres I et III," in *Multitudes*, 1997 (http://multitudes.samizdat.net/Croyance-credulite-calcul.html).
26. Thomas Trautmann has in particular attempted to date the text from linguistic evidence. See Thomas R. Trautmann, *Kautilya and the Arthaśāstra: A Statistical Investigation of the Authorship and Evolution of the Text* (Leiden, 1971). Also see K.J. Shah, "Of Artha and the *Arthaśāstra*," in *Contributions to Indian Sociology*, N.S., 15 (1982), pp. 55–73, and H. Scharfe, *Investigations in Kautilya's Manual of Political Science* (Wiesbaden, 1993).
27. Kāmanda, *Nīti-sāra*, ed. with a Telugu translation by Tadakamalla Venkata Krishna Rao (Madras, 1860).
28. See Talbot, *Precolonial India in Practice*.
29. Maḍiki Siṅgana, *Sakala-nīti-sammatamu* (eds), Nidudavolu Venkataravu, and P.S.R. Apparao (Hyderabad, 1970) (this includes a facsimile of the 1923 edition by M. Ramakrishna Kavi).
30. Baddĕna, *Nīti-śāstra-muktâvaḷi*, ed. M. Ramakrishna Kavi (Tanuku, 1962).
31. Ketana, *Vijñāneśvaramu*, ed. C.V. Ramachandra Rao (Nellore, 1977). Ramachandra Rao in his preface to the work already notes that Singana does not include Ketana's work in his anthology, but assumes that this is due to the lack of "popularity" of the latter during his time. Also see Ketana, *Vijñāneśvaramu*, ed. C. Vasundhara (Nellore, 1989).
32. On Tikkana, see V. Narayana Rao and David Shulman, *Classical Telugu Poetry: An Anthology* (Delhi, 2002).
33. Ketana, *Vijñāneśvaramu*, ed. Ramachandra Rao, p. 25, verses 1–4.
34. Ibid., p. 27, verse 42.
35. Ibid., p. 32, verse 109.
36. Ibid., pp. 33–4, verses 113–20.
37. Ibid., p. 36, verse 149.
38. Ibid., pp. 21–2, verses 107, 108, and 110.
39. Ibid., p. 23, verse 126.
40. Ibid., p. 23, verse 129.
41. Ibid., p. 23, verse 134.
42. Ibid., p. 6, verse 42.
43. Ibid., p. 17, verse 56.

44. Ibid., p. 10, verse 113.
45. See Someśvara, *Mānasollāsa*, 3 vols, ed. Gajanan K. Shrigondekar (Baroda, 1925–61).
46. Linda T. Darling, "'Do Justice, Do Justice, for That is Paradise': Middle Eastern Advice for Indian Muslim Rulers", in *Comparative Studies of South Asia, Africa, and the Middle East*, vol. XXIII, nos 1–2 (2002), pp. 3–19. Also see Wagoner, *Tidings of the King*, pp. 182, 197; and especially his "Iqta and Nayankara: Military Service Tenures and Political Theory from Saljuq Iran to Vijayanagara South India," unpublished paper presented at the 25th Annual Conference on South Asia, Madison, WI, October 18–20, 1996. In this latter essay, Wagoner presents convincing evidence for the influence of Persian-Islamic political thought on Baddena.
47. On this thorny issue, see Jean Aubin, *Emirs mongols et vizirs persans dans les remous de l'acculturation* (Paris, 1995).
48. For a recent, and stimulating, reconsideration of the genre, see Jocelyne Dakhlia, "Les Miroirs des princes islamiques: Une modernité sourde?," in *Annales HSS*, vol. 57, no. 5 (2002), pp. 1191–1206.
49. For an earlier translation, see A. Rangasvami Sarasvati, "Political Maxims of the Emperor-Poet Krishnadeva Raya," in *Journal of Indian History*, vol. IV, no. 3 (1926), pp. 61–88; also the later rendition (with the Telugu text of the *rāja-nīti* section) in K.A. Nilakantha Sastri and N. Venkataramanayya (eds), *Further Sources of Vijayanagara History*, 3 vols (Madras, 1946). We have already dealt at length with this text in V. Narayana Rao, David Shulman, and Sanjay Subrahmanyam, "A New Imperial Idiom in the Sixteenth Century: Krishnadeva Raya and his Political Theory of Vijayanagara," in Jean-Luc Chevillard and Eva Wilden (eds), *South Indian Horizons: Felicitation Volume for François Gros on the Occasion of his 70th birthday* (Pondicherry, 2004), pp. 597–625.
50. There is, unfortunately, no recent biography of this monarch. See, however, the works of Oruganti Ramachandraiya, *Studies on Krsnadevaraya of Vijayanagara* (Waltair, 1953), and N. Venkataramanayya, *Kṛṣṇadevarāyalu* (Hyderabad, 1972).
51. For the succession dates of Krishnadevaraya and his coronation, see P. Sree Rama Sarma, *A History of Vijayanagar Empire* (Hyderabad, 1992), p. 133.

52. Cynthia Talbot, "The Nayakas of Vijayanagara Andhra: A Preliminary Prosopography," in Kenneth R. Hall (ed.), *Structure and Society in Early South India: Essays in Honour of Noboru Karashima* (Delhi, 2001), pp. 251–75.
53. On the emergence of the Nayaka polities, see Velcheru Narayana Rao, David Shulman, and Sanjay Subrahmanyam, *Symbols of Substance: Court and State in Nayaka-Period Tamilnadu* (Delhi, 1992); and for a study based on the inscriptional record, Noboru Karashima, *A Concordance of Nayakas: The Vijayanagar Inscriptions in South India* (Delhi, 2002).
54. Jakkarāju Veṅkaṭakavi, *Āndhra Kāmandakamu*, ed. Veturi Prabhakara Sastri (Tanjore, 1950), verse 2.112.
55. Ibid., verse 2.82.
56. We return here to a set of themes treated in Velcheru Narayana Rao, David Shulman, and Sanjay Subrahmanyam, *Textures of Time: Writing History in South India, 1600–1800* (New York, 2003).
57. Komarraju Venkata Lakshmana Rao, "Āndhra brāhmaṇulaloni niyogi-vaidikabheda-kāla-nirṇayamu," in *Lakṣmaṇarāya vyāsāvaḷī*, 2nd edition (Vijayawada, 1965), pp. 1–17.
58. Veturi Prabhakara Sastri (ed.), *Cāṭu-padya-maṇi-mañjari*, vol. II (Hyderabad, 1988) (including the 1913 edition), section entitled *Mantrulu*, pp. 251–308. Also see the section on *Sabhāpati-vacanamu*, in *Cāṭu-padya-maṇi-mañjari*, vol. I, pp. 283–9.
59. Prabhakara Sastri (ed.), *Cāṭu-padya-maṇi-mañjari*, vol. II, p. 257. The combinations of vowels and consonants are now described in their graphic terms such as *etvamu, kŏmmu*, rather than as phonological terms such as *ĕkāra*, and *ukāra*.
60. Ĕrrayya, *Sakala-nīti-kathā-nidhānamu*, ed. T. Chandrasekharan (Madras, 1951). The exact date of Errayya (or Errana) is not known and the suggestion by the editor Chandrasekharan that he belongs to the late-fifteenth century seems to be too early.
61. The text of the *Sumati Śatakamu* has been printed many times with a number of variations, some of them indicating that the text itself changed with time, including a bowdlerized edition by Vavilla Ramasvami Shastrulu & Sons (Madras), and reprinted it many times. The edition we have used is dated 1962. But also see Macca Haridasu, *Tathyamu Sumati* (Hyderabad, 1984). In the nineteenth century, C.P. Brown collated a number of verses from manuscripts and translated

them, for which see C.P. Brown, *Sumati śatakam*, ed. C.R. Sarma (Hyderabad, 1973).

62. Vennelakanti Subbarao, *The Life of Vennelacunty Soobarow (Native of Ongole) as Written by Himself* (Madras, 1873), pp. 65–75.

63. On Cinnaya Suri, see Velcheru Narayana Rao, "Print and Prose: Pandits, *Karanams*, and the East India Company in the Making of Modern Telugu," in Stuart Blackburn and Vasudha Dalmia (eds), *India's Literary History: Essays on the Nineteenth Century* (New Delhi, 2004), pp. 146–66.

64. For instance, the following verse:
A good deed in return for another—
That's nothing special.
Doing good in return for harm—
Think about it: that's really good strategy.

This verse, actually stated as a form of political strategy, is now interpreted as an altruistic moral statement.

65 Hiroyuki Kotani, "*Doṣa* (sin)-*Prāyaścitta* (penance): The Predominating Ideology in the Later Medieval Deccan," in Kotani (ed.), *Western India in Historical Transition: Seventeenth to Early Twentieth Centuries* (New Delhi, 2002); N.K. Wagle, "The Government, the Jāti, and the Individual: Rights, Discipline and Control in the Pune Kotwal Papers, 1766—94," in *Contributions to Indian Sociology*, N.S., vol. 34 (2000), pp. 321–60. Cf. the earlier pioneering work of V.T. Gune, *The Judicial System of the Marathas* (Pune, 1953). Also of interest to this discussion is Sumit Guha, "An Indian Penal Régime: Maharashtra in the Eighteenth Century," in *Past and Present*, no. 147 (1995), pp. 101–26.

66. "Begriffsgeschichte und Sozialgeschichte," in *Kölner Zeitschrift für Sociologie*, no. 16 (1972), translated in Reinhart Koselleck, *Le Futur Passé: Contribution a la sémantique des temps historiques*, trans. Jochen Hoock and Marie-Claire Hoock (Paris, 1990), p. 99.

67. Most notable amongst these are Ashis Nandy, "An Anti-Secularist Manifesto," in *Seminar*, no. 314 (1985), pp. 14–24; T.N.Madan, "Secularism in its Place," in *Journal of Asian Studies*, vol. 46, no. 4 (1987), pp. 747–59. The debate is summed up in Rajeev Bhargava (ed.), *Secularism and Its Critics* (Delhi, 1998).

3

Purāṇa as Brahminic Ideology

During Labor Day weekend in 1985 I attended a meeting of Telugu people in the United States held at Los Angeles, where a singer of *harikathā* ("Tales of Viṣṇu") gave a performance. *Harikathā* singing is relatively new in Andhra; evidence suggests that Ajjada Adibhatla Narayana Dasu (1864–1945) was the originator of this tradition. A learned Sanskrit scholar and a wonderful musician, Narayana Dasu brought a new popularity to the recitation of Purāṇic stories, which he had composed in a musical style, interspersed with entertaining prose commentaries. This new genre acquired wide popularity and has been adopted by hundreds of learned singers. Along with its popularity came a respectable history of the genre. At the beginning of every *harikathā* performance, the singer spoke, as a part of his performance, about the antiquity of his profession. The singer whom I heard in Los Angeles did the same. To paraphrase his statement, he said:

> The first *harikathā* singer was Nārada, the celestial singer who sang for the god Viṣṇu. Then came Kusa and Lava, the twin sons of Rāma, who sang the *Rāmāyaṇa* for him. (He abridged the list and stopped with only two because he was singing in Los Angeles and not in India.) And then in the Kali Age (the last of the four Ages) the great guru Narayana Dasu was born to popularize *harikathā* on the earth.

Let me narrate another anecdote concerning similar connections to mythology. On October 31, 1854, a Brahmin village landowner, Maciraju Venkatrayudu, sent an appeal to the British governor of Bengal. His land was occupied by the local Kāpu, a non-Brahmin peasant. His complaints to the lower officers of the administration did not help. The Brahmin felt that the lower officers were working hand in glove with the Kāpu peasant. Therefore he thought that the highest authority of the land should be informed of this injustice. Venkatrayudu wrote: "During the time of the kings who ruled this country in the past, King Srīrāma, the sixteen great emperors beginning with Hariścandra, King Bali and King Vikramārka, Brahmins suffered no poverty. In your government, however, you treat all human beings equally and you are not respecting the code of *varṇa* and *āśrama* (class and stage of life)." Then the Brahmin went on to quote from a Sanskrit text showing how King Nala treated the Brahmins. Finally he appealed to the governor general to restore his land to him.[1]

Going a few centuries back to the period of King Kṛṣṇadevarāya (sixteenth century), I would like to quote one more illustration of the use of mythology. This relates to the genealogy that Pĕddana, the court poet, provides for his royal patron. Pĕddana writes in his *Manucaritra:*

> First there was the moon. His son was Budha.
> To him was born Purūrava, and he, in turn,
> generated Ayuvu, and to Ayuvu,
> Yayāti the king was born.
>
> Yadu and Turvasu were born as his sons
> killers of the enemies and connoisseurs of the arts
> and of these two, Turvasu, a vessel
> of virtue, acquired illustrious fame.
>
> His family became the dynasty of Tuluvas
> to which many kings were born, filling the world
> in its entirety with their surging and eternal
> fame. Then in that family, Timma was born.[2]

Yadu and Turvasu, as is well known, are mythical descendants of Budha, who was the son of the moon god, whereas the Tuluvas are historical, as is Timma of this dynasty.

What is common to all the three cases I have mentioned above is that all of them begin with what we call "myth" and move into what we call "history," with no dividing line between them, as if it is one continuous line of events. I intend to show here that this continuity is what the Purāṇic worldview promotes, and that it results from the ideological frame of the Purāṇas. Further down I shall attempt to explore the nature of the Purāṇas as conceptually organized texts whose meanings are best perceived by what they say about themselves as well as by what they do not say.

The Five Distinguishing Marks

Again and again we are told that the Purāṇas have five *lakṣaṇa*s, or distinguishing marks.[3] These components of a Purāṇa are: primary creation or cosmogony (*sarga*); secondary creation or the destruction and renovation of worlds, including chronology (*pratisarga*); the genealogy of gods and patriarchs (*vaṃśa*); the reigns of the Manus (*manvantarāṇi*); and history, "or such particulars as have been preserved of the princes of the solar and lunar races, and of their descendants to modern times (*vaṃśānucarita*)."[4]

Earlier scholars who discussed the five *lakṣaṇa*s accepted them as constituting the definition of a Purāṇa. But many Purāṇas do not conform to this definition. Therefore the conclusion was that the Purāṇas that now exist are not the old versions of the Purāṇas and that much of the older version has been lost.

Scholars also thought that the five features constituted the subjects or the contents of the Purāṇas. Again there was a problem, because the information regarding the five *lakṣaṇa*s was very minimal in most of the Purāṇas. To quote Vans Kennedy, "Though these topics are certainly treated of at greater or less length in most of the Purāṇas, they still by no means form the principal subject of the study."[5] As Ludo Rocher has stated, "The fact that the *Purāṇa*s contain relatively little *pañca-lakṣaṇa* materials has been noticed repeatedly in the scholarly literature."[6] According to Kane's calculation, the five topics occupy less than 3 per cent of the extant Mahāpurāṇas.[7]

Then why does *pañcalakṣaṇa* continue to be considered important for distinguishing a Purāṇa from other genres? Setting aside suggestions that *pañcalakṣaṇa* is a literary myth,[8] or explanations that our understanding of this compound word is erroneous and that it means something else,[9] I would like to suggest and try to demonstrate that *pañcalakṣaṇa* is the ideological frame that transforms whatever content is incorporated into that frame. Since the ideas of *pañcalakṣaṇa* are tacitly assumed in the Brahminic worldview, they do not even appear in every Purāṇa and do not constitute a sizeable length of the text even when they appear.

I shall not concern myself with the texts that describe the *pañcalakṣaṇa* for identifying the oldest strata of the Purāṇas. My interest is not text-historical. I am interested, rather, in the nature of text as an ideological product. The strategy here is to listen to what the texts say and what they do not say. It is analogous to the question Nietzsche asked: What is man saying? What is he hiding when he says what he says? By asking these questions, I believe, one can see the ideology of text production, which, in the words of Macherey is "silently inscribed" within the text.[10]

All civilizations make their own past to make sense of the present, to control the present. When a new power emerges, the first thing it does is to reject the old past and create a new one in its place. This is done not just by altering the "facts" of the past but by creating a new way of perceiving the "facts." An extreme instance of creating a new way of perceiving facts is evidenced when the very concepts of time and space in which events take place are changed.

Such a change in the concepts of time and space was made when Western civilization via the British colonial power came to dominate India. An earlier concept of time and space is that of Brahminic civilization, which coexists with what might be called, for want of a better name, a "folk concept" of time and space. Thus, India has had three different ways of conceptualizing time and space, all of which are still at work in the lives of Indian people. The low-caste, nonliterate people have a folk concept of time/space, upper-caste Sanskrit-educated Brahmins have a Purāṇic concept of time/space, and Westernized educated Indians have a modern concept of time/space. My low-caste milkmaid has great difficulty in understanding how I calculate the first day of the month (according to the Gregorian calendar, when I get my salary and she gets paid for the milk she had supplied to me all the month) without the aid of the moon. I have a similar difficulty in reckoning without the aid of my family priest the death anniversary of my father, which is to be observed according to the Brahminic *pañcāngam* calendar.

Folk time is repetitive and regenerative. It shares some of the features of a cyclic view of time, such as the return of similar events like seasons, phases of the moon, and so on; but it does not deteriorate and therefore does not spiral downward. Folk time is analogous with agricultural seasons: the rainy season, which brings growing crops, then a season of harvesting, and then summer, when the earth dries up, followed by rains and new life.

Purāṇic time, however, deteriorates. Each of the four Ages (*yugas*) is inferior to the previous one until the final dissolution (*praḷaya*) completes the cycle and starts a new one. Thus it spirals downward until a new cycle begins. In keeping with this view, the Purāṇas say that the texts themselves deteriorate. The *Matsya Purāṇa* says that originally the Purāṇas were one Purāṇa, which belonged to the world of the gods (*devaloka*) and was a billion verses long (*śatakoṭipravistara*). For the benefit of human beings, who have an inferior intellect, Hari took the form of Vyāsa and reduced the huge text into eighteen texts with a total of four hundred thousand *śloka*s. This story repeats itself. Vyāsa is born in every third *yuga.* Kṛṣnadvaipāyana is the Vyāsa in the twenty-eighth third *yuga* of the eon of the White Boar.

It is in this context that I propose to examine the *pañcalakṣaṇa* of the Purāṇas. *Lakṣaṇa* is not a definition; nor do the five *lakṣaṇa*s inform us of the contents of a Purāṇa. *Lakṣaṇa,* as the dictionary tells us, is a distinguishing mark. Furthermore, *lakṣaṇa*s are not necessarily objective, empirically observed facts; they could be perceived "facts." If Brahmin scholars say that Purāṇas have the five *lakṣaṇa*s, they have them. The question, for me, is not locating, textually, where they exist and then examining their relative length in words as determinants of their importance or antiquity. The question rather is why Brahmin scholars call them distinguishing marks. There is plenty of evidence that a Purāṇa is viewed as having the five *lakṣaṇa*s. Not only does an early text like *Nāmalingānusāsana* identify the Purāṇas with *pañcalakṣaṇa,* and a number of Purāṇas themselves speak of the five distinguishing marks, but as late a text as *Śukranīti* says, describing a Paurāṇika (a Purāṇa performer/scholar), "One who is a scholar of literary theory, who is knowledgeable in music, has a good voice, and knows the five *lakṣaṇa*s, creation and the others, such a man is known as a Paurāṇika."[11]

The five *lakṣaṇa*s order the events of the Purāṇas. They provide the listeners with a view of time and space in which the events narrated in the Purāṇas occur. In other words, the *pañcalakṣaṇa*s create a world and a worldview.

Purāṇizing the Folk Tradition

Any event placed in the frame of the *lakṣaṇa*s will have a specific meaning for anyone who lives in this particular world. If I say that I wrote my paper on July 25, 1985 of the common era, in Visakhapatnam, South India, that date and place constitute only a small part of the text of my paper. For all of us who participate in the ideology of dating things on the linear scale of time, it does not even appear to be significant. But then, it is not the same thing as saying that I wrote my paper in the first quarter (*prathama pāda*) of the fourth Age (the Kali Age) of the reign (*manvantara*) of Manu Vaivasvata, in the eon (*kalpa*) of the White Boar (*svetavarāha*), sitting in a place located in the southern part of the land (*daksina digbhāga*) with reference to Mount Meru. Locating an event in time and place appears nominal if you participate in the specific ideology that gives you those concepts of time and space. The contrast is striking if you do not participate in that ideology. For example, questions regarding when Vyāsa was born and when the Purāṇas were composed would have two completely different answers in these two different systems of belief.

To illustrate the nature of ideological change that a folk story undergoes when it is Purāṇized, let me cite a story of the Komaṭi caste of Andhra. Komaṭis are a caste of merchants who were at one time considered a left-hand caste. Now their status has moved up and they are included in the Vaishya class, the third class in the four-*varṇa* system. The story of the Komaṭis centers on their caste goddess Kanyakā, whose name means "a virgin." The story is set in Penugonda, the city of the Komaṭis in West Godavari district. There the wealthy Komaṭi leader Kusumaśreṣṭi lives with his daughter Kanyakā, the most beautiful woman in the world. One day, the king of the area visits the city and the Komaṭis receive him with honor; Kanyakā welcomes him with a flame offering. When the king sees her, he desires her and sends word to her father that he wishes to marry her; if the father refuses, he will invade the city and abduct her.

For the Komaṭis this is a serious problem. It would be loss of caste purity to give a woman from their caste to a non-Komaṭi man. And not to be able to protect themselves when they are forced to surrender would be humiliating. The Komaṭi elders meet to discuss the crisis but cannot find any solution. They conclude that they are powerless to fight and some even suggest a surrender so that they can gain favors from the king.

Kanyakā evaluates the situation. She sends word to the king that her father agrees to the marriage but needs time to prepare for it. The king is to wait outside the city, behind the hills surrounding it. Meanwhile, Kanyakā assembles the elders and informs them of her intention to immolate herself. She asks which caste families will be willing to die with her; among the 102 families (*gotras*) who agree to die with her, she selects only the wives and husbands, leaving the yet unmarried young men and women to continue the caste line. All other families are ordered out of the caste.

She then orders a deep pit to be dug and a fire kindled in it. When the king sends some soldiers to see what is causing the delay, they learn of Kanyakā's plans and decide to serve her instead of the king. When the soldiers do not return, the king grows suspicious and invades the city, but it is too late; Kanyakā and the others have died in the fire. Before that, however, Kanyakā has sanctioned a code of conduct for the caste. Cross-cousin marriage is never to be avoided, even when the boy or girl is poor, sick, or deformed; all Komaṭi girls are to be given her name. All Komaṭi girls, moreover, are to be born ugly so that no man will desire them. She also ordains that the king who caused this calamity will die instantly when he enters the city. Penugonda is to become a pilgrimage center for Komaṭis with Kanyakā as its goddess, and an annual ritual is to be celebrated there in her honor.

This is the summary of the folk version of the story, which I gathered in Andhra Pradesh from interviews with the folk singers called "Mailārlu."

In the *Vāsava Kanyakā Purāṇa*, a Sanskrit text that claims to be a part of the *Sanatsujātīya Khaṇḍa* of the *Skanda Purāṇa*, the story remains faithful to the outlines given above, but becomes Purāṇized.

First, the story is set in the Naimiṣa Forest. Sūta is the narrator. Śaunaka and other sages ask him to tell them a story of the Vaishyas. This story is narrated to Dharmanandana (Yudhiṣṭhira) by Ādiśeṣa, the ancient snake. Being set in a Purāṇic context, the story elaborately narrates how it first takes place in the world of gods (*devaloka*). A *gandharva* (demigod) there falls in love with a Vaishya girl, but the Vaishya elders reject his proposal to marry her. The *gandharva* curses the Vaishyas to fall from the world of gods onto the earth, where they will all burn in fire and perish. In return, the Vaiśyas curse the *gandharva* to take a miserable human birth and die a horrible death. The Vaishyas are reluctant to go to the earthly world of sin, but the gods insist that they are needed there to restore order and trade and to uplift the human beings. And in the end they will return to the world of Śiva through their death by fire. After the *gandharva* is born as the king and the girl as Kanyakā, the story is re-enacted on earth.[12]

It is obvious that these changes in the story are not neutral. Placing the story in the Purāṇic context transforms the nature of the events. To make a quick note of such transformations, the merchant-caste Komaṭis are now Vaishyas with a status in the four-class system. They are here in the human world for a purpose; they are no ordinary profit seekers. The events of the story are re-enactments of a predetermined script, and the Vaishyas are part of a divine scheme. In the folk version, Kanyakā is the chief player, who makes decisions for herself as well as for the caste. In the Sanskrit version the decision-making role is played by the Brahmin priest Bhāskarācārya, who is obeyed by all the Vaishyas. Kanyakā, in this version, is a chaste woman, obeying the commands of the family and the priest.

Vast bodies of folk/regional stories, events, legends, and histories have been incorporated into the Purāṇas along with prescriptive codes of behavior appropriate to people of different stations of life. Such incorporation has made a Brahminic interpretation of the material possible without necessarily erasing local color and regional flavor.

The ideological import of the Purāṇas is not limited to the *pañca-lakṣaṇa* frame; it is inscribed in the concepts that surround the Purāṇa texts. We have a tendency to look at the Purāṇas as disparate texts, each neatly bound in identifiable volumes. But the texts do not work in isolation; they are part of a totality of a text tradition with intertextual relationships and commentorial contexts. One could make sense of any of these texts only by listening to the texts as a part of this tradition.

Purāṇa: What it is and What it is Not

One way to conceptualize the Purāṇas is to compare them with texts that are not Purāṇas. Such a contrast is made by means of two variables, sound (*śabda*) and meaning (*artha*), the two technically inseparable components of a word. Mammaṭa, the twelfth-century writer on poetics, tells us that the Veda is sound-primary (*śabdapradhāna*), and Purāṇa is meaning-primary *(arthapradhāna*), while ornate poetry (*kāvya*) accords equal importance to sound and meaning (*śabdārthapradhāna*). This aphorism is worth exploring. If the Veda is important for its sound, it is unalterable. Every nuance of this sound has to be reproduced without change. It cannot be written down, because a graphic representation of the sound does not guarantee its accurate reproduction; nor can it be translated into another language, paraphrased, or summarized, because any such effort changes its sound. If, then, the sound is fixed, its context is also fixed and unalterable. The fact that it is orally reproduced does not make it an oral text. It is more fixed than any written text; it is inscribed in sound.

We know that, in practice, many who recite the Veda do not even know its meaning, nor are they expected to know. On the other hand, those who know the meaning may not often chant the Veda; they have not learned the chanting well enough to reproduce the sound correctly. Vedic sound-text is preserved in complex chanting styles with terrible taboos invoked against any mispronunciation.

An unalterable, fixed text by itself is incapable of serving as an active vehicle of ideology. For that you need a text flexible in content but fixed in its ideological apparatus. *Purāṇa* and *itihāsa*, which are often combined to make one compound word, are such texts, which serve as correlates to the Veda. Vatsyayana says in the *Nyāyabhāṣya*: the subject matter of *itihāsapurāṇa* is the events of the world.[13] It is also stated that the Veda speaks like a king, a Purāṇa like a friend, and a *kāvya* like a loving woman (*prabhusammita, mitrasammita,* and *kāntāsammita*).[14] The contrast, the tradition wants us to believe, is not in the essential meaning but only in the style. And there is a difference not only in style but also in status.

Elsewhere I have argued that authorship of a text, in the Indian tradition, is not intended to inform us about the actual producer of the text, to offer biographical data about him, but has a semiotic function of conveying the status of the text.[15] The texts of the highest authority are above human authorship. The Veda comes under this classification. Texts of the next level of authority are composed by a superhuman, and therefore infallible, person, Vyāsa. The texts of the next level of authority are the *kāvyas*, made by human poets, who have creative abilities given by Sarasvatī, the goddess of the arts, but who are still human and therefore fallible. You could find errors in a Kālidāsa, but not in a Vyāsa, and certainly not in the Veda.

If the Purāna is valued for its meaning, it is also stated that it is not the meaning we get from its words; it is the meaning known to the *ṛṣi,* the one who sees. A popular statement about Śrīdhara, who wrote a commentary on the *Bhāgavata Purāṇa,* says, "Vyāsa knows, Śuka knows; whether the king [Parikṣit] knows or not, Śrīdhara knows everything, because of the blessing of the Man-lion god."[16]

The person who knows the meaning of the Purāṇa is in a class by himself; he belongs to the status of Vyāsa, Śuka, and the commentator Śrīdhara. This is knowledge beyond logic (*na hantavyāni hetubhiḥ*). It is recognized that Purāṇas differ in status among themselves.[17] But those differences do not lead to a contradiction in meaning. A *Mahābhārata* aphorism reconciles the apparent problem:

> The revealed texts conflict with each other as
> the remembered texts do.
> And there is no seer whose words are not the authority.
> The essence of *dharma* lies hidden from view.
> So, follow the path of great men.[18]

The great men, *mahājana,* are the commentators, the knowers of the meaning.

The Author/Speaker of the Purāṇas

Like that of the Veda, the origin of the Purāṇa is beyond humans. Brahmā spoke the Purāṇas, from all four of his mouths According to the *Mārkaṇḍeya Purāṇa,* the Puranas came first and then the Veda.[19] The *Mārkaṇḍeya Purāṇa* says that as soon as Brahmā was born, both the Purāṇa and the Veda came out of his mouth; the seven *ṛṣis* took the Veda and the *munis* took the Purāṇa.[20] Vyāsa, as we have seen, was only the compiler and editor of the texts in an abridged form.

Then there are different speakers of the Purāṇas for different listeners. Each Purāṇa has a specific speaker. However, it is important to note that no speaker ever directly narrates. All the Purāṇa narratives are reported narratives. Each speaker has an earlier speaker. Each listener has an earlier listener. They look inward and backward, drawing us into an ideologically closed environment. But if the Purāṇas are ideologically closed texts, they are functionally open texts: they have accepted into their fold events, stories, legends, and occurrences of many regions and communities, transforming them to conform to a fixed ideology.

Purāṇa and Orality

Purāṇas are available as written texts, and we know that as such they cause the worst possible headaches to scholars who work on critical editions. One reason suggested for the state of Purāṇic texts is that they were originally oral and were later put into writing. Continuing our position of looking into the text for what it says and for what it does not say, we find that inside the text the Purāṇas do not furnish evidence that they were written texts, except for the story of Gaṇeśa as Vyāsa's scribe, which occurs in the *Mahābhārata.* In fact, in Purāṇic literature the Sanskrit verb *likh,* "to write," was never used to mean "to compose." Purāṇa texts are spoken. Writing was known in India from a very early period, at least the third century BCE, but its use was limited to preserving a text rather than producing it or communicating it. Scribes were a different group of people in India, who, like modern-day typists, specialized in a technical skill. There are many instances, even as late as the nineteenth century, of scholars who could not "write." They composed the texts mentally and recited them orally, and then the scribe wrote them down. But the Purāṇa scholar who did not write was not illiterate. Sanskrit has a syllabic organization independent of the graphic form of the letters. The *varṇa,* the basic unit of Sanskrit syllabary, is a sound unit roughly equivalent to a phoneme. Sanskrit grammarians syllabified the language and developed a sophisticated morphological analysis but felt no compelling need to write it down. This situation is different from that of the Western languages, where "letter" indicates a graphic form, with a name of its own, distinct from the several phonemic values that it represents. In the West, to be literate in a language inevitably means to be able to write, but in India there is also a kind of oral literacy, as it were. The Purāṇa scholar had all the sophistication of the language scholar, with a complete awareness of grammatical organization. Therefore, he set himself apart from the illiterate oral poet who not only could not write but also lacked any awareness of the grammar of his language.

Thus, while the internal evidence in the texts of the Purāṇas shows that they were originally oral, it is important for us to note that their orality is different from the orality of the folk narratives. The orality of the Purāṇas is literate orality. These are scholars who are oral in performing the Purāṇas, and probably even in composing some of them, but who are very proud of their knowledge of grammar and their ability to possess a written text of what they perform orally. Therefore we meet with an interesting contradiction. The texts say they were oral, Brahmā uttered them, Vyāsa spoke them, and a number of his disciples narrated them. But outside the text you can see that every Paurāṇika values the written tradition by carrying a book with him. An oral narrative of the illiterate low castes is derisively called in Telugu a *pukkiṭi-purāṇa*, an "oral Purāṇa," referring to the fact that it does not have a written text to authenticate it. In summary, a Purāṇa without a written text that says in writing that it is not a written text but a text spoken by a great God is not an authentic Purāṇa.

What the Purāṇas Say

At this point it will be useful to summarize what the Purāṇas say about themselves so that we can go on to the next step, to examine what they do not say.

1. Brahmā originally uttered the Purāṇas; in their original form they are one hundred million.
2. Vyāsa in every *manvantara* organizes the Purāṇas into eighteen texts by abridging them for the benefit of the inferior humans, whose intelligence, over the course of generations, gradually deteriorates until the end of the Kali Age.
3. A Purāṇa has five features, features that are valued as definitive marks of the genre. Together these five features provide a concept of time and space to the audience of the Purāṇa.
4. Purāṇas speak like a friend, whereas the Veda speaks like a master, but they say the same thing.
5. Purāṇas are oral.
6. In the Purāṇa tradition, the earlier and mythical narrators are more authoritative than the later human narratives.
7. A Purāṇa is valued for its meaning, a meaning that is known only to the sage or sage-like commentator.

What the Purāṇas do not Say

Texts come into writing when someone records what he has heard earlier or when he composes the text himself. The vast body of written materials of the Purāṇas obviously came into existence because a host of scholars wrote them. But the Purāṇas do not say who wrote them. A large body like the Purāṇa literature, which clearly received materials from different sources, including folk sources, contains a host of self-contradictions. But the Purāṇas maintain that such contradictions are only apparent and that, underneath, they are all one, with a unified meaning that is in conformity with *śruti,* the Veda. Purāṇas do not inform us where the different narratives and other received elements were borrowed from, nor do they give us any understanding of how such materials are transformed by being incorporated into the Purāṇas. Finally, the Purāṇas do not inform us why it is said that there are eighteen Mahāpurāṇas and eighteen Upapurāṇas, while the textual evidence shows that the actual number is greater. Nor are we told what precise reasons generated the difference between the Upa- and Mahāpurāṇas.

Anyone acquainted with Hindu society with its hierarchy and differences in status, religious oppositions, and divisions of caste knows that it presents an intense scene of conflicts and tensions. At the same time the dominant ideology of the society presents a homogeneous view of a well-ordered society. But despite the best efforts of the dominant ideology to present a homogeneous picture, we can still detect the ideological tensions both within the texts and outside the texts. I shall present some evidence to show that such tensions exist between the Vaidikas and the Paurāṇikas, between the Paurāṇikas and the Ālankārikas (scholars of ornate poetry), between one group of Purāṇas and another group, and finally between the literate Paurāṇikas and the illiterate low-caste oral-epic singers.

The great respect that a reciter of the Veda receives in Hindu society is well known. But what is less well known is that he is also slighted as a *vedajada,* a moron whose mind is dulled by constant repetition of the Veda. *Chandas* in Sanskrit means a "Veda verse." A *chāndasa* therefore means one who is well versed in the Veda. But in popular Sanskrit, *chāndasa* is a disrespectful term that refers to a stupid ritualist, who does not understand the way of the world as a Paurāṇika or a *kāvya* poet does. Connoisseurs of *kāvya* give Vyāsa the nickname *cakārakukṣi,* "one who has *ca* syllables in his belly." A *śloka* in Purāṇic Sanskrit contains a number of filler syllables, *cas,* as in *sargas ca pratisargaś ca vaṃśo manvantarāṇi ca.* For a *kāvya* poet who values a tightly composed style, this is poor Sanskrit. The statement by Cornelia Dimmitt and J.A.B. van Buitenen that the Purāṇas are "composed in Sanskrit of a mediocre quality" reflects a *kāvya* bias.[21] There is also another bias, often heard from grammarians and other *śāstra* experts, that the Purāṇas are popular literature, meant for the ordinary folk. The implication is that they are not good *śāstra.*

It is well known that the Purāṇas are classified according to the system of three *guṇas,* or strands that together constitute matter: lucidity, or goodness (*sattva*); energy, or passion (*rajas*); and torpor, or darkness (*tamas*). Thus there are Purāṇas characterized by lucidity (*sāttvika*), Purāṇas characterized by energy (*rājasika*), and Purāṇas characterized by torpor (*tāmasika*). The *Parāśarya Upapurāṇa* even states that the Purāṇas of torpor are unworthy of reading. The dispute as to whether a particular Purāṇa is a Mahapurāṇa or an Upapurāṇa also belongs in this category. The *Brahmavaivarta Purāṇa* states that the five *lakṣaṇas* apply only to Upapurāṇas and that Purāṇas that have more than ten *lakṣaṇas* are known as Mahāpurāṇas. If one were to pursue this logic further the *Matsya, Vāyu,* and *Brahma Purāṇas* would have to lose their status and be classified as Upapurāṇas.

The Change in the Nature of the Purāṇas

Like all the aspects of Brahminic Hinduism, Purāṇas have also undergone a major shift as a result of *bhakti.* The devotional mode of relationship between the deity and the devotee, and between one devotee and other devotees, has a profound influence on the Purāṇas. The mode of Purāṇa composition has changed significantly; the *Bhāgavata Purāṇa* marks that shift more definitively than any other Purāṇa.

While it is not easy to demonstrate the shift in any detail here, I shall refer to one prominent feature of the *Bhāgavata Purāṇa*. Let me quote from the Telugu version of this Purāṇa, where Parīkṣit asks Śuka for the story of Kṛṣṇa's birth.[22]

> He is the form of Time and Being. He is inside and outside
> of people in this world. He gives life and death, bondage
> and liberation. Pray, narrate his story in full.
> You said that (Bala) Rāma was the son of Rohini. Then why
> was he in the womb of Devakī? How did the lotus-eyed
> lord leave his parents to live with the cowherds? Where did
> he live? What did he do, and why did he kill his uncle
> Kaṃsa? How long did he live as a man on earth? How many
> wives did he take? And what else did he do? Tell me
> everything of the life of Mādhava.

> And further he said: The more I hear you, the more I drink
> the nectar of Kṛṣṇa's stories that flows from your mouth,
> my body grows livelier; my grief is gone; I feel neither
> hunger nor thirst, my heart is pleased.

When Parikṣit had said this, the son of Vyāsa replied to him:
Viṣṇu's stories purify the man who enjoys them and the man who asks for them, like water from the river which flows from Viṣṇu's foot.

Parikṣit's request is to be informed of the story of Kṛṣṇa's birth; but a closer look will reveal that he actually asks to listen to a story he already knows, for the joy of listening to Kṛṣṇa's story another time, for the mere joy of hearing. The earlier Purāṇas have informed their listeners about creation, mythology, history, and a host of other subjects, instructed them in the essential religious modes of behavior, sermonized on codes of conduct, and legitimized local gods and goddesses. The *bhakti* Purāṇas now essentially create an atmosphere of participation in religious ecstasy. The emphasis is not on information but rather on a renewed opportunity to experience the divine. It is not communication but communion.

While this shift in the aesthetics of the Purāṇa sets the *bhakti* Purāṇas in a class by themselves, the Paurāṇika tradition indicates this by a change in the number of *lakṣaṇas* that this Purāṇa contains: instead of the usual five *lakṣaṇas,* the *Bhāgavata Purāṇa* has ten. This numerical adjustment is an effort on the part of the Brahminic ideology to signify two things: one, the incorporation of *bhakti* into its fold, and, two, Purāṇic approval of *bhakti.* But still the enhancement in the number of *lakṣaṇas* leads to a small-scale controversy regarding the relative status of Purāṇa texts. *Bhakti* Purāṇas now claim far higher status than pre-*bhakti* Purāṇas. But in Hindu society, this is no more problematic than a caste that is normally classed low but claims a higher status in society and justifies its claim to an enhanced self-image because of a greater devotion to a deity than other castes or because of some such merit.

Sociologists study texts as models for societies; they study societies as texts. I am suggesting the reverse. We should look at texts in India as a society. Sanskrit texts are organized just as Brahminic society is organized, in four *varṇas*: Brāhmaṇas, Kṣatriyas, Vaiśyas, and Śūdras. We know that, in reality, we find hundreds of different castes, and we do not find the neat classification of the four Purāṇas. I am afraid that we in Purāṇa Studies are like the early empirical anthropologists who found a bewildering variety of *jātis* and were at a loss to understand why Brahmins spoke of only four. They later knew that the *varṇa* is an ideological system that organizes the *jātis* into a Sanskritic conceptual scheme. I suggest that, if we are to understand the Purāṇas, their status in Brahminic textual traditions, and their role in Brahminic culture, we get little help from a empirical study of the Purāṇic texts themselves. We have to listen to what the tradition says and what it does not say, to consider the totality of the Brahminic textual tradition as an ideological system.

Notes

1. Ganti Jogi Somayaji, ed., *Telugu Documents: Being Petitions Etc. in Telugu Preserved in the Oriental Collections in the National Archives of India* (Waltair: Andhra University Press, 1957), pp. 63–9.
2. Allasani Pĕddana, *The Story of Manu*, trans. V. Narayana Rao and D. Shulman (Cambridge, MA: Harvard University Press, 2015).
3. Ludo Rocher, *Purāṇas,* vol. 2, fasc. 3 of *A History of Indian Literature*, ed. Jan Gonda (Wiesbaden: Otto Harrassowitz, 1986), pp. 24–30.
4. The verse reads: *sargaś ca pratisargaś ca vaṃśo manvantarāṇi ca/vaṃśānucaritaṃ ceti purāṇaṃ pañcalakṣaṇam*. My translation follows the paradigmatic one given by Horace Hayman Wilson in his introduction to his translation of the *Viṣṇu Purāṇa* (1840), pp. iv–v.
5. Vans Kennedy, *Researches into the Affinity of Ancient and Hindu Mythology* (London: Longman, 1831), p. 153n.
6. Rocher, *Purāṇas*, p. 29.
7. Pandurang Vaman Kane, *History of Dharmaśāstra*, vol. 5.2 (Poona: Bhandarkar Oriental Research Institute, 1962), p. 841.
8. Rocher, *Purāṇas*, p. 30.
9. Ibid.
10. Pierre Macherey, *A Theory of Literary Production* (London: Routledge and Kegan Paul, 1978), pp. 85–9.
11. *Śukranīti* (Varanasi: Chowkhamba Sanskrit Series, 1968), 2.180. The verse reads: *sāhitya śāstra nipuṇaḥ saṅgītajñaś ca susvaraḥ/sargādi pañcakajñātā ca sa vai paurāṇikaḥ smṛtaḥ.*
12. For a more detailed study of this story in its folk and Purāṇa versions, see Velcheru Narayana Rao, "Epics and Ideologies," in *Another Harmony*, ed. Stuart Blackburn and A.K. Ramanujan (Berkeley and Los Angeles: University of California Press, 1986).

13. Vātsyāyana's commentary on Gautama's *Nyāydarśana* (ed. Swami Dwarakadasa Sastri; Varanasi: Bharatiya Vidya Prakasan, 1966), 4.1.62.
14. This statement is often made in books on Sanskrit poetics, including Vidyanatha's *Prataparudrīya.*
15. Velcheru Narayana Rao, "Texts Without Authors and Authors Without Texts" (Paper presented at the Annual Conference on South Asia, University of Wisconsin-Madison, 1985).
16. Quoted by Elūripati Anantarāmayya, Introduction to *Viṣnupurāṇam* (Gunturu: Anantasahiti, 1979), p. 45. The verse reads: *vyāso vetti śuko vetti rājā na vetti vā/śrīdharaḥ sakalam vetti sakalam vetti śrīnṛsiṃha-prasādataḥ.*
17. The saying goes: *itihāsapurāṇāni bhidyante lokagauravāt.*
18. A slightly different version of this oft-cited verse appears in *The Mahābhārata* (Poona: Bhandarkar Oriental Research Institute, 1942), 3, Appendix 1, # 32, lines 65–70.
19. *Nāradīya Purāṇa* 1.60–1: *purāṇam sarvaśāstrāṇāṃ prathamaṃ brahmaṇā smṛtaṃ/anantaraṃ ca vaktrebhyo vedās tasya viniśrutāḥ.*
20. *Mārkaṇḍeya Purāṇa*, ed. Satyavarata Simha (Sitapuri, 1984), 45.20.
21. Cornelia Dimmit and J.A.B. van Buitenen, *Classical Hindu Mythology: A Reader in the Sanskrit Purāṇas* (Philadelphia: Temple University Press, 1978), p. 5.
22. Bammera Potana, *Śrimahābhāgavatamu* (Hyderabad: Andhra Pradesh Sahitya Akademi, 1964), 10.8–13.

4

Coconut and Honey

Sanskrit and Telugu in Medieval Andhra

It was January 15, 1517.[1] Kṛṣṇadevarāya, the Vijayanagara king, who was on his way to invade the Kaliṅga country, stopped at the temple of the god Āndhramahāviṣṇu in Śrīkākuḷam on the bank of the Krishna river. That night the god appeared in his dreams. As reported by Kṛṣṇadevarāya himself in his *Āmuktamālyada,* the god said:

You told the *Story of Madālasā,* exciting connoisseurs of poetry
with skillful similes and metaphors and the trope of true description.
You sang of Satyabhāmā, a poem resonant with rich feeling.
You made a collection of superb stories culled from all ancient books.
You composed the *Gem of Wisdom.* an eloquent work
that dispels residues of darkness in those who hear it.
You astounded us with honeyed poems in the language of the gods,
The Pleasures of Poetry and other essays.
Is Telugu beyond you? Make a book in Telugu
now, for my delight.

Why Telugu? You might ask.
This is the Telugu land.
I am the lord of Telugu.
There is nothing sweeter.

You speak many languages
with kings who come to serve you.

Don't you know?
Among all the languages of the land,
Telugu is best. (*Āmuktamālyada* 1–13, 15)[2]

The final statement—*deśabhāṣal' andu tĕlugu lĕssa,* "among all the languages of the land, Telugu is best"—has acquired new meaning in the context of post-nineteenth-century linguistic nationalism, as a slogan of superiority for Telugu people. It even appears on a postal stamp released by the government as a recognition of Telugu pride.

However, there is no evidence of language serving as symbol of "national" identity before the nineteenth century. There were Telugu-speaking people, Telugu land, and even love of one's own language—but no Telugu people whose identity was formed by a "mother-tongue." Indeed, there is no such a word as "mother tongue" in medieval Telugu.[3] The modern *mātṛbhāṣā* is a loan translation from English. Nor was there any opposition between one regional language and the other; the distinction drawn was always between *devabhāṣā* (the language of the gods, Sanskrit), and *deśabhāṣās* (the languages of people). It is necessary to steer clear of the language nationalism which has fueled a major political movement in contemporary Andhra and led to a redrawing of the map of India along linguistic lines in the post-Independence period. Care in distancing premodern language sense from twentieth-century nationalist formations is especially necessary because modern Telugu intellectuals have read into their literary history a sustaining love of language as a means of establishing national identity and have at the same time erased all existing relationships with neighboring languages.

Going back to the words of the god to Kṛṣṇadevarāya makes this point clear. The king had already achieved the status of a poet in Sanskrit by virtue of his having authored several books in that language. Being a master of the language of the gods, controlling a language of humans should be easy for him. But then, while there exist a number of human languages, why choose Telugu?

It should be remembered that Kṛṣṇadevarāya was not born in the Telugu area. He was a Tuluva, from an area of south-western Karnataka. As the god himself says, he is a Kannada *rāya*—a Karnataka king, though a Telugu speaker all the same. Apparently he spoke more than one language and found that speaking Telugu made it easier for him to rule what was largely a Telugu area.

The politics of the empire were crucial here to the choice of language. Sanskrit is the language of pride and power. It is already enshrined in the hearts of the scholarly world as a language of great glory. All the great books—*vedas, śāstras, itihāsas*, and *kāvyas*—are in that language. What is more, it is the only language that can confer on Kṛṣṇadevarāya the status of a Kshatriya in the four-*varṇa* ideology of the Brahminic/Hindu world. In his own locality, Kṛṣṇadevarāya was only a peasant and, if legends are to be believed, a low-caste peasant at that. But he was a peasant warrior with aspirations to kingship. Outside his language area, his status did not translate into anything intelligible or respectable. One would not know where to place a Tuḷu Nāyaka in the regional hierarchy of an area outside Karnataka. On the other hand, the pan-Indian categories of status are well established in the four classes: Brahmin, Kshatriya, Vaishya, and Shudra. Brahmins obsessively carried the learning of Sanskrit books over generations, created a wider viability to Sanskrit and the Brahminic ideology.[4] It would thus be possible for Kṛṣṇadevarāya to adopt Kshatriya status, which in turn can be conferred upon him by the Brahmins. This dialectic of mutual construction—Brahmins conferring the status of Kshatriyahood on kings and the Kshatriyas making Brahmins powerful by their patronage—is predominantly the story of Brahmin ideology in premodern India.[5]

We should pause briefly to observe the nature of this Brahmin class, without understanding which we cannot get an idea of the power of ideology in premodern India. Here is a class of people, unlike any other class, who are unusually mobile, in a sense uninterested in acquiring roots in any locality, and therefore no threat to any local peasant or land-owner. What they carried with them is an obsessive dedication to the Vedic chants—which they preserved in oral tradition with phenomenal patience—to the *śāstra* texts, especially grammar, to the great epics of *Mahābhārata* and the *Rāmāyaṇa,* and to a host of literary texts of poets like Kālidāsa. The power of Sanskrit is partly derived from the wide distribution of Brahmins all over the Indian subcontinent and the cultural influence they wielded, in working with the local religious and political groups—in some sense "converting" them and their deities to what we now call, for lack of a more suitable word, Hinduism. While preserving their Sanskrit intact, the Brahmins were also proficient in learning the local languages, sometimes more than one, and composing poetry in them. Images of a cultural militia, or of an ideological army, would not be too far-fetched to apply to the Brahmins of premodern India, when one sees the scale of their operation and the constancy of their ideological message. Kṛṣṇadevarāya thus showed profound pragmatism in demonstrating his expertise in Sanskrit and his patronage of Brahmins both as political allies and religious leaders. There was considerable evidence of history before him to show the wisdom of this move. Nearly every family that has aspired to royal status on a scale larger than their limited native locality—Coḷas, Cāḷukyas, and Kākatīyas—sought the support of Sanskrit-chanting Brahmins to elevate themselves to the status of Kshatriyas. Elite and wealthy establishments such as the Śrīvaiṣṇava *maṭhs* (monasteries) patronized and expounded in Sanskrit. Moreover, Brahmins and their Sanskrit texts were predominant in imaging a pan-Indian empire, an empire "encircled by four oceans," which includes a wide geographical/mythological area—an area that could be as large as South Asia.

In a curious way, the distance and the aura that Sanskrit had acquired were related to its unintelligibility. The Vedas and all the prescriptive texts of Sanskrit, including its venerated grammar, derived their power precisely from their being distanced from the ordinary person. However, their ideological impact would not be felt if they were not made somehow accessible. In fact a number of Sanskrit texts, like the Vedas, were considered too pure to be made accessible to the uninitiated, that is, the non-Brahmins. It was in this context that the *mārga* poet—the elevated Sanskritized author—came in. He wrote and commented, interpreted retellings of such texts that could be brought closer to the people, without defiling their purity. Massive retellings of *purāṇa* texts, among which the *Mahābhārata* was the first, were undertaken by a host of Brahmin poets between the eleventh and fourteenth centuries, an activity that has gone on virtually unabated right into the twentieth century. The *purāṇas* were not just translated, they were performed in temples and other religious establishments for public hearing, thus bringing the retold Telugu texts closer to the audience for whom they were intended. Thus, the distance between the unintelligible Sanskrit texts and the audience was systematically bridged—without compromising the pure status of Sanskrit texts. It was an ideal situation where you could have your cake and eat it too. The Sanskrit texts retained their high status and at the same time were made available to the audience through their retellings.[6]

The retellings are not just "translations," as is sometimes supposed. To take the Telugu example, what Nannaya or Tikkana did in retelling the *Mahābhārata* in Telugu was to create a domestic *Mahābhārata,* transformed to a regional story of medieval South India, that could happen in any South Indian kingdom or, for that matter, any large joint family. These retellings reinterpreted the Sanskrit texts and at the same time created an elevated and regional discourse and values. This explains why Kṛṣṇadevarāya chose to represent himself as a scholar of Sanskrit and also a creator of an elevated Telugu text. Something more can be learnt from Kṛṣṇadevarāya's own statements regarding his choice of Telugu. The following passage in *Āmuktamālyada* reflects a complex ambivalence that marked his relationship with the landed lords of his kingdom, whose language was Telugu. Here Kṛṣṇadevarāya recommends a course of action for a successful king. He clearly trusts the Brahmins but is a little wary of non-Brahmin (Telugu-speaking) lords:

> The king should never go to battle himself. He should elevate
> someone else to the level of a lord, and send him. It has to be
> someone strong, equipped with money, land,
> elephants, and horses. Give him fortified lands.
> But if such a person is a non-Brahmin, he will soon become
> a rival. Still, you need him too.[7]

Kṛṣṇadevarāya's choice of Telugu was a political one. He wanted to please the local speakers of Telugu by calling their language "sweet." He needed their support, as well as the support of Sanskrit. His praise for Telugu is carefully nuanced: the comparison is only between Telugu and other regional languages. As for Sanskrit, it is on a different plane. As the language of the gods, it is not in opposition with Telugu or with any other language of the land.

The Śaiva Protest

We have to go back a few centuries to detect anything like a hint of conflict between Telugu and Sanskrit—indeed, not just centuries, we also have to cross the boundaries of religion, into the militant Śaiva religion of Basaveśvara of twelfth-century Karnataka, who advocated a creed without caste barriers and gender discriminations. His thirteenth-century follower Pālkuriki Somanātha is the first to find Sanskrit alienating. He reasons that Sanskrit and books composed in Sanskritic meters are not accessible to ordinary people. He says in his *Basavapurāṇa*:

> Telugu is simple, beautiful to hear.
> It reaches all, unlike these big words of verse and prose.
> I will therefore sing in *dvipada* couplets. A good poet makes
> great meaning with small words.[8]

By "big words of verse and prose," Somanātha means the *Mahābhārata* composed in a genre called *campū,* a genre of verse interspersed with rhythmic prose, by Nannaya (eleventh century), who later came to be revered as the first poet of the Telugu literary canon. The genre and style created by Nannaya became the standard for *mārga* poets. Nannaya was a Brahmin and a respected Sanskrit scholar of his time in the court of King Rājarājanarendra, who ruled the central Andhra deltaic region. In all probability he was not local to Rājamahendravaramu (modern-day Rajahmundry on the east coast of Andhra), but migrated with his Tamil-speaking king of the Eastern Cāḷukya dynasty as his family priest. The king himself was not very strong and stable in his empire, and his rule was rather short-lived. This was the underlying cultural context for Somanātha's thirteenth-century rebellion against Sanskrit forms of literature and Brahmin superiority.

Somanātha composed in meters close to Telugu women's songs, deploying *dvipada* "couplets." Somanātha's movement had all the potential of blossoming into conflict not just on linguistic lines, but also on caste and religious lines. Considering the fact that Somanātha was leading a militant anti-Brahminic Śaiva movement, Sanskrit now could become synonymous with Brahmin superiority and Brahmin religion. The potential battle lines are clear:

Bhavis (non-Śaivas)	vs.	Śaivas
Mārga (Sanskritic)	vs.	Deśi (Indigenous)
Brahmin	vs.	Low-caste

However, matters were not that simple. For one thing, Somanātha himself did not maintain a consistently anti-Sanskrit stance. His position against Sanskritic meters and the *campū* genre is based on the rationale of easy accessibility. It was in the interest of reaching common readers, especially the "left-hand" groups of artisans and petty traders, that he chose the indigenous *dvipada* couplet meter. Further, there is an unmistakable sense of inferiority he feels in using Telugu:

tĕlugu māṭalananga valadu; vedamula
kŏladiyakā jūḍuḍu. . . .

Don't just say
these words are only Telugu; look at them
as Veda.

The communities of people for whom Somanātha intended his poetry remained on the periphery of the political system in Andhra (although in Karnataka, to the west, they briefly captured the political center at Kalyan). Moreover, the militant Śaiva message of the *Basavapurāṇa* presented no program for the acquisition of political power. It offered no role for a king, and no ideology of kingship. In this sense it makes a striking contrast to the role of Sanskrit and Sanskrit poetry in the construction of political roles for the "right-hand," land-based communities.

Mārga and *Deśi*

By the time Somanātha was writing, Telugu as a language had hardly begun its literary career. To have any status as a literary language, it needed the support of Sanskrit. If Sanskrit is the *mārga,* the "path," Telugu could only hope to be *deśi*, "local" or "regional," if it did its job right. Unlike Tamil, which had a secure and respectable past and sat by the side of Sanskrit as an equal, Telugu had to claim maturity by incorporating from the language of the gods and, by extension, of Brahmins, the gods on earth.

We have on the authority of Nanněcoḍa (a twelfth-century poet) that Telugu poetry began as *deśi* under the patronage of the Cāḷukyas, who ruled central Andhra during the tenth and eleventh centuries.[9] But in contrast with Pālkuriki Somanātha, who developed a more distinctly indigenous style, the courtly poetry of Nannaya became *mārga* itself. From then on *mārga* and *deśi* come to mark a distinction in Telugu styles, one more Sanskritic and the other more indigenous. We can see, in the centuries that follow, *mārga* poetry receiving more and more patronage from kings and patrons assuming kingly status—which include even deities of temples—while *deśi* poetry was left more or less as its poor cousin. Though cultivated by poets of high family status like Gona Budhārĕḍḍi, who composed *Raṅganātha Rāmāyaṇa* in *dvipada,* and Kaṭṭā Varadarāju, who composed another *Rāmāyaṇa* in *dvipada* (more about this later), this meter has an unmistakably low status in the eyes of scholars. An oft-quoted segment of a poem from a forgotten source even condemns *dvipada* by grouping it with an old whore, a backyard sewer, and a patron who does not pay.[10]

According to legends recorded some three hundred years after Somanātha, *dvipada* seems to have faced severe opposition even during the time of the militant author of the *Basavapurāṇa*:

> Some Śaiva devotees were reading the *Basavapurāṇa* in the Śiva temple at Orugallu [Warangal]. The Kākatīya King Pratāparudra, who happened to go to the temple at that time, inquired what was going on there. Brahmins who were with the king said that some Śaiva devotees were listening to a reading of *Basavapurāṇa.* When the king wanted to know more about it, an evil Brahmin told him that it was a recent work composed by the sinner Pālkuriki Sōmanātha, who had made it in extended *dvipada* couplets with-poor caesura (*madhyavaḷḷu pĕṭṭi pĕnacĕ dvipada*); it was substandard and did not deserve the king's respect. The king left without paying any more attention to the text.[11]

With Tikkana, another thirteenth-century Brahmin poet who retold large parts of the *Mahābhārata,* the militant Śaiva non-Brahmin protest against Sanskrit had been effectively diffused. Tikkana called himself *ubhaya-kavi-mitra,* a friend of both schools of poets—the Śaiva-Telugu and the Brahminic-Sanskrit. He used a predominantly Telugu style in a text composed in Sanskritic meters. His influence on later generations of poets was enormous, He was not just a poet but also a politician: as the minister of Manumasiddhi, he negotiated and gained the military support of the mighty Kākatīya king in behalf of his (Tikkana's) patron. Legends also tell us that Tikkana was effective in having the Kākatīya king annihilate the Jaina temples.[12]

Meanwhile, as we have seen, Somanātha's *dvipada* meter itself had lost some of its non-Brahminic Śaiva identity when it was borrowed by authors like Budhārĕḍḍi (fourteenth century) for telling the *Rāmāyaṇa* story, hardly a non-Brahminic narrative. The *deśi* style of literature continued to thrive, but as a quiet complement to the dominant *mārga* style, which flourished in the courts of royal patrons and even rich temples. So much so that when Annamayya (1408–1503) sang for the god on Tirupati hill in southern Andhra, he had no difficulty in using *deśi* meters for his Telugu songs while composing songs in Sanskrit in the same vein.

Separation of Styles

Thus *deśi* and *mārga* became complements to each other rather than contestants, as Somanātha might have intended them to be. But the awareness that Sanskrit and Telugu represent two distinctly different styles even within the *mārga* category persisted. This is demonstrated with great expressive power in a long metapoetic poem attributed to Pĕddana, the court poet of Kṛṣṇadevarāya, which highlights the distinct separation of Telugu and Sanskrit styles. According to legend, Kṛṣṇadevarāya offered a golden anklet (*gaṇḍapĕṇḍeramu*) to any poet who could excel in composing verses in Sanskrit and Telugu with equal ease. Pĕddana accepted the challenge and came up with this extempore verse in *utpala-mālikā.* The king, stunned by the extraordinary performance, personally honored the poet by himself putting the golden anklet on the poet's feet. Here is the poem:

> *pūta mĕruṅgulun basaru pūpa bĕdangulu jūpunaṭṭi'vā*
> *kaitalu jaggu niggu nena gāvale gammuna gammananvalĕn*
> *rāitiriyun baval marapurāni hoyal cĕli yārajampu nid-*
> *dātaritīpuloyanaga dārasilanvalĕ lo dalañcinan*

bātiga baikonanvalĕnu baidali kuttukaloni pallaṭī
kūtalananvalen sogasu korkulu rāvale nālakiñcinan
jetikolandi kaugiṭanu jercina kanniya cinni ponni mēl
mūtala cannudoyivale muccata gāvalĕ baṭṭi cūcinan
dātoḍan' unna minnula miṭārapu muddula gumma kamman' au
vātera donḍapanḍuvale vācavigāvale banta nūdinan
gātala dammicūlidora kaivasapun javarāli sibbĕpun
meteli yabburampu jigi nibbarap' ubbagu gabbigubba pon-
būtala nunna kāvāsari poḍimi kinnera melubanti san-
gātapu sannatanti bayakārapu kannaḍa gauḷa pantukā
sātata tāna tānala pasandivuṭāḍeḍu goṭa mīṭu bal
mrotalununbalen haruvu mollamu gāvalenaccatengu lī
rītiga saṃskṛtamb'upacariñceḍu paṭṭuna bhāratīvadhū-
ṭītapanīyagarbhanikaṭībhavadānanaparvasāhitī-
bhautikanāṭakaprakarabhāratabhāratasammata
prabhāśitanagātmajāgiriśasekharasītamayūkharekhikapātasudhā-
prapūrabahubhaṅgaghumaṃghumārbhaṭī-
jātakatāḷayugmalayasaṅgaticuñucuvipañcikāmrdan-
gātatehitattahitahādhitadhimdhanudhānudhimdhimi
vrātanayānukūlapadavārakhūdvadhahārikiṅkinī
nūtanaghalacaraṇanūpurajhatājhāḷīmarandasaṅ-
ghātaviyaddhunīcakacakadvikacotpalasarasaṅgrahā-
yātakumārgandhavahahārisugandhavilāsayuktamai
cetamu jallajeyavale jillana jalla valen manohara
dyotakagostanīphalamadhudravagōghṛutapāyasaprasā-
dātirasaprasāraruciraprasarambuga sāre sarekun.

Is poetry a surface sheen,
the green delusion of unfolded buds?
It must be real inside
and out, exploding fragrance,
an aching touch your body can't forget
by day or night, like of your woman,
whenever you think about it.
It should come over you, it should murmur
deep in the throat, as your lover in her dove-like moaning,
and as you listen, yearning comes in all its beauty.
If you take hold of it, your fingers tingle
as if you were tracing the still-hidden breasts
of a young girl, wholly embraced.

If you sink your teeth into it, it should be succulent
as the full lips of a ripe woman from another world,
sitting on your knees. It should ring
as when godly Sound strokes with her fingernails
the strings of her vīṇa, with its golden bulbs resting
on her proud, white, pointed breasts,
so that the *rāga*-notes resound.
That is the pure Telugu mode.

If you use Sanskrit, then a rushing, gushing
overflow of moonlight waves, luminous and cool,
from Śiva's crest, the mountain-born goddess beside him,
enveloping actors and their works, the dramas
spoken by Speech herself in the presence of the Golden Seed,
pounding out the powerful rhythms, the beat
of being, through drums and strings
and chiming bells and thousands of ringing anklets
dancing, drawing out the words, the fragrant and subtle
winds wafting essence of unfolding lotus
from the Ganges streaming in the sky should
comfort your mind. You should shiver
in pleasure again and again, each time
you hear it, as rivulets of honeyed juices and butter
and sweet milk flow together
and mix their goodness more and more
and more.

What we offer here in translation does not reflect the exuberant texture of the poem, which dramatically demonstrates the variation in Telugu and Sanskrit styles, the first with soft, lyrical, and intimately murmuring syllables; the second with its high-sounding Sanskrit phrases, infused with the energy of repeated aspirates in an increasingly dense compound. This second style retains the attention and marvel of listeners, even though they are almost certainly unable to follow the precise meaning of this intricately woven and immensely long Sanskrit compound, the like of which one rarely sees even in Sanskrit texts.

Both the marked separation and the close proximity of Sanskrit and Telugu are well-established features in all Telugu literary texts of the *mārga* class, right from Tikkana onwards. Each poet paid respects to the poets before him (*pūrva-kavi-stuti*) in the preface to his work. As a matter of convention, respect was always offered to the Sanskrit poets first—Vyāsa, Kālidāsa, Bhavabhūti, Bāṇa, and so on—followed by the great poets of Telugu: Nannaya, Tikkana, Errāpragaḍa and others. The choice of poets is fairly constant through a period of about eight hundred years, indicating a firmly established canon, always including an equally well-established respect for Sanskrit.

Along with this awareness of separation between Sanskrit and Telugu, there was also a certain sensitivity to the problem of going too far one way or the other. Śrīnātha, the great fifteenth-century poet, is fully aware of the problem of being too Sanskritic in his style. Legend has it that his translation of Śrīharṣa's *Naiṣadhīyacarita* was severely criticized for being too Sanskritic. According to a popular joke, Sanskrit scholars approached Śrīnātha and said: "Take your Telugu case suffixes (*ḍu, mu, vu* and *lu)* and give us our Sanskrit text back." Śrīnātha used long Sanskrit compounds as they appear in the original Sanskrit text verbatim, with only a Telugu suffix added to them. He seems to have anticipated such criticism:

Śrīharṣa's learned poem
is juicy and meaty as a ripe coconut.
You have to break it open
to taste it.
Lazy readers can't appreciate it.
That's how it is.
When a young woman strokes the cheek of a little boy
With her fingernail,
does his heart start pounding
with love?[13]

Again, in his later work *Bhīmeśvara-purāṇamu,* Śrīnātha states:

Seeing its erudition, some say it's tough as Sanskrit.
Hearing the idiom, others say it's nothing but simple Telugu.
Let them say whatever they want. I couldn't care less.
My poetry is the true language of this land.

The problem of style does not get resolved. Poet after poet returns to this problem and attempts to resolve it, each in his/her own way. Potana, of about the same time as Śrīnātha, tries to be gentle and friendly to both the camps, Sanskrit and Telugu:

> Some like Telugu, others like Sanskrit
> and yet others like both languages.
> I will try to please all of them,
> with varying styles in different places.

And Kŏravi Goparāju (*ca.* sixteenth century) even complains:

> If I write lucidly in Telugu, they say
> the poem is not tight, it is too soft, lacks strength.
> If I use Sanskrit with some force,
> they complain it is thorny as *darbha* grass
>
> and don't listen to it.
>
> So, I will make a judicious mix
> of Telugu and Sanskrit words.[14]

Mŏlla, a poetess who produced a version of the *Rāmāyaṇa,* tells us in her Introduction:

> When a drop of honey touches the tongue,
> your whole mouth is filled with sweetness.
> The whole sense of a poem
> should fill you all at once.
> A poem composed with arcane words
> is a dialogue
> of the deaf and the dumb.

Gūḍha-śabdamulanu gūrcina kāvyamu, "a poem composed with arcane words," must indicate that a high proportion of obscure Sanskrit words are woven into the Telugu text, as is frequent in Telugu court poetry.

Nearly every major Telugu poet, especially those who aspired to recognition in royal courts, has declared his competence in Sanskrit *śāstras.* Poets like Śrīnātha professed profound knowledge in all branches of learning as well as their skill in making poetry in both Sanskrit and Telugu. By convention, scholarship meant scholarship in Sanskrit texts, and poetic skills meant competence in Telugu poetry. This distinction between creativity and scholarship often implied that if a poet were not also a scholar, he or she was a poor poet. Such a poet rarely entered a king's court where Sanskrit scholarship reigned supreme. Proud challenges were issued by pandits to other pandit-poets, and there are reports of public disputations and great royal honors. The famous disputation between the Telugu poet Srīnātha and the Orissa poet Ḍiṇḍima in the court of the Vijayanagar king Prauḍhadevarāya is one such instance celebrated in Telugu literary texts. Ḍiṇḍima had a bronze drum made as a demonstration of his undisputed superiority among scholars. Śrīnātha defeated Ḍiṇḍima and had his bronze drum broken into pieces. However, excessive superiority of Sanskrit scholarship was met with opposition, as is reflected in the following popular legend:

> Once, a Sanskrit scholar came to the court of Kṛṣṇadevarāya and saw all the poetry in Telugu being read there. Impatient with the position Telugu acquired in the court, the Sanskrit pandit blurted out:
>
> *āndhrabhāṣāmayaṃ kāvyam ayomayavibhūṣaṇam*
>
> A poem in Telugu is like an ornament made of iron—
>
> Tenāli Rāmaliṅga, the scholar-poet and court jester, immediately retorted:
>
> *saṃskṛtāraṇyasañcārividvanmattebhaśṛṅkhalam*
>
> a perfect chain to restrain
> pandits prowling like wild elephants
> through the Sanskrit jungle trails.

Another, again parodic, formulation of this tension comes from Vallabharāya's *Krīḍābhirāmamu* (early fifteenth century). Vallabharāya refers to Sanskrit's alleged status as the mother of all languages, and to the choice of Telugu for practical purposes.

> *janani saṃskṛtambu sakalabhāṣalakunu deśabhāṣal' andu dĕnugu lĕssa*
> *jagati dalli kaṇṭĕ saubhāgya-sampada-mĕccuṭ' āḍubiḍḍa melu gade*
>
> They say "Sanskrit is the mother of all languages,
> But among the languages of the land
> Telugu is best." Of course.
> Between the aged mother
> and the ravishing young daughter,
> I'll take the daughter any day![15]

The satirist is apparently quoting popular statements, including one we have already seen in Kṛṣṇadēvarāya's sixteenth-century text (*desa-bhāṣal' andu dĕnugu lĕssa).* The identification of Sanskrit as the mother of tongues is also found in Ketana's *Āndhra-bhāṣā-bhūṣaṇamu* (thirteenth century).[16] In any case, the satire drives home the point that Telugu is to be preferred—again for entirely mundane reasons!

The position of other regional languages in the medieval period is also worth investigating. We know that poets knew more than one regional language and often were influenced by poets and texts from various languages of the region. Śrīnātha makes a proud declaration of his competence in Sanskrit, Prakrit, Sauraśeni, and other languages. By other languages he means the rest of the *aṣṭa-bhāṣās,* eight languages: Māgadhi, Paiśāci, Cūlika, Apabhraṃśa, and Telugu. Poets prided themselves as being capable of composing in these eight languages: *aṣṭa-bhāṣā-kavīśvara.*[17] We know from Śrīnātha's descriptions that the ministers of his time were veritable polyglots.[18] They knew a number of languages, including Arabic, Persian and Turkish, Kannada, Gujarati, and Malayalam.[19] An interesting tidbit that might be noted here is that people who ridiculed other languages were to be punished by the king with a fine of one hundred *paṇas,* and that *arava* is cited as a derogatory word for Tamil![20]

The Late-Medieval Crystallization

There seems to be a significant shift in the status of Telugu and Sanskrit in works composed during the late-medieval period (especially the seventeenth century). During this time, when Telugu-speaking Nāyakas ruled a predominantly Tamil-speaking area of South India, Telugu acquired a status almost similar to that of Sanskrit in the preceding centuries. Now Telugu assumes a position in the court as an intellectual language. *Purāṇas* and *śāstras,* grammars and books on poetics, were written in Telugu. Sanskrit was still used, but it was not necessarily the only means of elevating one's status. Telugu was good enough for that purpose. The contrast between Sanskrit and Telugu styles came to occupy less of the poets' attention, as did the contrast between *mārga* and *deśi.* In a way, the distinction between these styles became less clear, and the court itself began patronizing *deśi* or *deśi*-like texts. The Nāyaka kings themselves wrote *yakṣagānas,* a genre of musical play derived from the *deśi* tradition. More important still, non-Brahmin poets became prominent. The court was full of them. While there was no great effort to reduce the importance of Sanskrit or to oppose it, and no visible attempt to oppose the Brahmins, there was an unmistakable importance given to Telugu poets—non-Brahmins at that.

This important change expresses the self-confidence acquired by the non-Brahmin king and a new class of merchant-warriors who initiated far-reaching changes in the political and social order. We argued in our *Symbols of Substance: Court and State in Nāyaka-Period Tamilnāḍu* (Narayana Rao, *et al.* 1992) that the new order reflects a new set of values in poetry, historiography, and political and cultural institutions. One important change that this touches on is the status of the king in relation to the Brahmin. The king no longer needed the Brahmin to legitimize his status. The king was god himself, and thus the Brahmin became the god-king's servant rather than his superior. This shift, only briefly stated here, is also reflected in the relative status of Sanskrit and Telugu. In the new royal court, Telugu was the language of the king. However, despite the fact that the king was equated with God, Telugu had not been elevated to the level of the language of the gods.

At roughly the same time, but further north, in the village of Kamepalli in the interior of Guntur District, there emerged a very influential scholar-poet, Appakavi. His book, a grammar principally of metrics, popularly known as *Appakavīyamu,* held sway over the literary tradition for about three hundred years, right until the rise of modern movements in Telugu poetry in the early decades of the twentieth century. In the Introduction to his book, Appakavi tells us a powerful tale as narrated to him—by God himself in a dream—about the allegedly "original" grammar of Telugu, composed in Sanskrit (by the great Nannaya, the first poet himself) and then nearly lost. This story, perhaps more than any other text, reveals the crystallizing structure of the late-medieval tradition at the stage which perhaps marks its intellectual acme.

The power of Sanskrit in medieval Andhra rested on the respect it had acquired as the language of the gods, a position sustained because of the supreme awe in which its grammar had been held. Pāṇini, the great grammarian of Sanskrit, his commentator Patañjali, the author of the *Mahābhāṣya,* and Kātyāyana, who contributed the *vārttika* rules—all three were revered as divine beings. Grammar, in this culture, was not merely a set of rules that describe the language; it was the knowledge given by god to create a sanctified language—the very essence of ultimate reality.

Telugu had never had a grammar of that power—not until Appakavi "revealed" it. Appakavi tells us (through the mouth of the god in his dream) that Nannaya composed such a grammar in Sanskrit *sūtras,* which were suppressed by his jealous rival Bhīmakavi, who threw the only copy into the Godavari river. Fortunately, a student of Nannaya's (Sāraṅgadhara) had memorized the whole text. We know Sāraṅgadhara's story from a Telugu *kāvya* composed in seventeenth-century Tanjavur by Cemakūra Venkaṭakavi, as well as from other sources (Gaurana's *Nava-nātha-caritra,* late-fifteenth century). In these texts, Sāraṅgadhara is the object of his stepmother's sexual advances, which he resists; she then slanders him to his father, the king Rājarājanarendra, who orders his hands and legs cut off. Sāraṅgadhara survives the unjust punishment and eventually joins the Siddhas, spiritually powerful healers who live forever. Appakavi hints at this story (without mentioning the seduction episode); he identifies Sāraṅgadhara as a Siddha, himself magically healed by Matsyendranātha, as a long-lived Siddha, Sāraṅgadhara can thus preserve Nannaya's grammar over the hundreds of years that divide Nannaya from Appakavi. As Appakavi tells the story, Sāraṅgadhara transmits the grammar both to Bālasarasvati, a learned Brahmin from Matanga Hill (at Hampi/Vijayanagara?) who will eventually compose a Telugu *ṭīkā* on it, and to another text which purports to be a Telugu commentary on the *sūtras* of Nannaya's lost and restored grammar (although in fact we have only Appakavi's metrical analysis in full).

This fascinating and complicated story achieves two things: It produces a grammar of great antiquity, written by the very first poet of Telugu, one who has been regarded for centuries as the creator-deity *(vāg-anuśāsana)* of Telugu poetry. And it also gives Appakavi god-given authority to comment on Nannaya's rules. Now, Telugu has a Pāṇini. The language is on its way to being as sanctified as Sanskrit.

Incidentally, the foundational Telugu grammar is also brought into line with the standard view of all major texts—beginning with the Veda itself—as having been lost or fragmented and then at least partially restored.

It is also striking that, according to Appakavi, during the long centuries when Nannaya's grammar was lost, poets used only such words as were attested in Nannaya's surviving works:

> Later a mighty poet, *Kavi-rākṣasa,* in Dakṣavati made a rule:
> Telugu poets must never use a single word unless it is attested
> in the *Bhārata* of Nannaya, the law-maker of language,
> since no rules of grammar survived.[21]

From that time on, the great poets of the past, Tikkana and the rest, composed their works following the words and ways of Nannaya, in his three volumes.

Such is the medieval tradition's ultimate view of itself, its prehistory, and its structures of authority. It is in this context that we can also observe the mature tradition's vision of the peculiar merits of Telugu. Appakavi cites the following Sanskrit *sūtra* attributed to Nannaya:

> *svasthānaveṣabhāṣâbhimatāḥ santo rasapralubdhadhiyaḥ*
> *loke bahumanyante vaikṛtakāvyāni cānyad apahāya* (2)

> Learned scholars love the language and dress of their region, and have a weakness for aesthetic joy. Therefore they respect poetry in their language, rather than Sanskrit.

Now Appakavi adds, in his commentary (first reformulating the Sanskrit *sūtra*): Intelligent scholars love the language and dress of their own region, and have a weakness for aesthetic joy. They always take as their own what belongs to their region and have no liking for the poetry of other places, because it is not immediately evocative. The poetry of each region is good for that region, but not appropriate for other areas, whereas poetry in the language of the gods (*amarôktulu*) is good for all lands. Sanskrit books give all four benefits for human beings,[22] even if their meaning is not always clear. Although they refer to the stories of Viṣṇu, the beautiful texts of another regional language cannot bring release if you don't experience their flavor or their meaning.[23] Poetry *in the language of your own region* gives the same benefits as Sanskrit to its readers. Women and Shudras who know no Sanskrit will need to have texts retold to them in their own language. The language of the barbarians *(mlecchabhāṣā)* is despised by the Veda, but still should not be rejected in disgust, because without it daily life will be affected *(Appakavīyamu* 1.60–7).

Here the linguistic map is fully worked out and arranged in accordance with its new hierarchies and the values of the late-medieval system. Sanskrit gives benefit no matter what—whether it is intelligible or not. Tamil poetry for Viṣṇu would perhaps count as useful, if only it could be understood. Telugu—the obvious paradigm for a regional language—is equal to Sanskrit, autonomous, worthy of complete respect. Poetry in the regional language has its own necessity—it communicates Sanskrit texts to women and non-Brahmins. Finally, even barbaric tongues such as Arabic and Persian have a utilitarian value and should not be left out.

Still, complaints against difficult Sanskrit continue right into the modern period. Let me conclude with a poem parodying Viśvanātha Satyanārāyaṇa, who is known for his hard-to-follow Sanskritic style:

Torture us, please,
impossible poet,
with your exuberance of stunning words
and delicious feeling slightly mixed
with bitter dryness. We need jaws of stone
to grind the elevated phrases you utter with ease
as you tease us through your labyrinths,
books cooked to the texture of rock.[24]

Notes

1. The date is suggested by Cāgaṇṭi Śeṣayya. See his note in his grandfather Vedam Veṅkaṭarāya Śāstri's edition of *Āmuktamālyada* (1964: 21).
2. I am deeply indebted to David Shulman, whose insights and scholarship have greatly enriched this paper. All translations are done in collaboration with him.

3. An undated medieval Tamil verse ascribed to the poetess Auvaiyār does use the Tamil term *tāymoli,* "mother tongue":

aimporuḷum nārporuḷum mupporuḷum peyt' amaitta
cemporuḷai emmaraikkum cetporuḷait taṇkurukūrc
ceymoliya t'enpar cilariyan ivvulakil
taymoliya t'enpen takaintu

Five, four, three,
and the one, beyond all knowledge,
that flows through them all—
it belongs
in a distant tongue
in this temple of Kurukūr,
or so they say,
but as for me, it's all there
in my mother tongue.

[Five elements, four goals of human life, the three great gods—Śiva, Viṣṇu, Brahmā—all these are externalizations of true being (*poruḷ*) identified as the god at the temple of Tirukkurukūr. When the poetess Auvaiyār arrived there, she was drawn into a discussion as to the relative merits of Sanskrit and Tamil in the liturgy. This verse is her response.]

4. By Brahmins, I intend the *varṇa* category, and not the many endogamous groups generally known by the cover word Brahmin. Just as only a few of the many endogamous groups of peasants acquired the *varṇa* status of the Kshatriya, only a small number of the endogamous groups of Brahmins acquired the *varṇa* status of the Brahmin in premodern India.
5. See Rao and Heifetz 1987: 131–6 for another discussion of the relationship between the king and his court poet in medieval Andhra.
6. For the ideological nature of Sanskrit *purāṇas*, see Rao 1993: 85–100.
7. *dharṇipuḍ' ĕndune dagadu tā janan ūraṭak' ŏkkanin dagun*
dŏran ŏnariñci pampan ari durbaluce jĕḍaḍ ātad' artha-bhū-
kari-turagārddhi leka koragād' aṭu seya dvijānyuḍ' alkakun
nerav' agun' ātaḍun valayu niṇḍina durga-balorvi yī dagun.
(*Āmuktamālyada* 4.155).

8. *urutara-gadya-padyôktula kaṇṭĕ*
sarasamai paragina jānudĕnuṅgu
carcimpagā sarva-sāmānyam' aguṭa
gūrcĕda dvipadalu gorki daivāra . . .
alpāksaramulan analpārtharacana
kalpiñcṭuaya kādĕ kavi vivekambu
(Pālkuriki Somanātha, *Basavapurāṇa* 1.165–74.)

9. "While *mārga* poetry flourished in the world from times long ago, the Cāḷukya king and many others made *deśi* poetry in Telugu stand firm in the Andhra area" (Nannecoda, *Kumārasambhavamu* 1.23).

10. *yambu mudilañja diḍḍikanta*
iyyanerani raṇḍa nālg' ekājāti.

From a verse in *Veṇugopāla Śatakamu* attributed to Sāraṅgapāṇi (early-eighteenth century), but probably written by a later poet at the Kārveṭinagaram court, Polipeddi Veṅkatarāyakavi.

11. Pidaparti Somanātha, a devoted follower of Pālkuriki Somanātha, records this legend in his retelling of the *Basavapurāṇa* in *campū,* a genre from the *mārga* tradition current from the time of Nannaya's *Mahābhārata,* but opposed by Pālkuriki Somanātha. For further discussion of *mārga* and *deśi,* see Rao and Roghair 1990: 3–31.

12. See *Siddheśvaracaritramu* of Kāsĕ Sarvappa (early-seventeenth century).

13. *panivaḍi nārikela-phala-pakamunan javiyaina bhaṭṭaha-*
rṣuni kavitānugumbhamulu somari-potulu kŏndar' ayyal' au-
n'ani ani kŏniyāḍa nerar' adi yattida le-javarālu cĕkku gī-
ṭina vasa valcu bālakuḍu ḍĕndamunan galaganga nĕrcunĕ
(Śrīnātha, *Śṛṅgāranaiṣadhamu* 1.17.)

14. *kondaraku denugu guṇamagu*
gondarikini saṃskṛtambu gunamagu renḍun
gondariki guṇamul' agu nē
nandari meppintu gṛtulan ayyai' yeḍalan
(*Śrīmahābhāgavatamu,* 1.16.)

15. *tĕnuguna teṭagā kathalu tĕlpina kāvyamu ponduledu niti-*
tana pasacāladaṇḍru viśadambuga saṃskṛtaśabdam' ūda jĕp-
pinan avi darbhamuṇḍl' anucu bĕṭṭaru vīnula gāvunan rucul
danara dĕnuṅgu desiyunu dadbhavamun galayanga jĕppĕdan.
(*Sihāsanadvātriṃśika,* 1.32.)

16. *Krīḍābhirāmamu,* 37. My reading differs from the conventional reading by Telugu scholars, who fail to see the parodic tone of the verse.
17. Ketana, *Āndhra-bhāsā-bhūṣaṇamu* 14, cited in Arudra 1990, 2: 158.
18. This is how, for instance, Śrīnātha describes the polyglot capabilities of his patron Areti Annaya, a minister of king Allāḍarĕḍḍi:

    arabī bhāṣa turuṣka bhāṣa gaja karṇāṭā' ndhra gandhāra ghūrjara bhāṣa malayāḷa bhāṣa śakabhāṣa sindhu sauvīra barbarbarabhāṣal karahāṭabhāṣa mariyun bhāṣaviśeṣambul acceruvai vaccun areeṭi yannaniki gosṭhīsamprayogambulan. (*Bhīmesvarapurāṇamu* 1.73.)

    "Arabic, Turkish, the languages of Gaja, Kaṃāta, Āndhra, and Gandhāra, Gujarati, Malayalam, the Śaka language, the barbarian languages of Sindhu and Sauvira, Konkani, and many others—Areṭi Anna can use them all in royal assemblies." Another verse also speaks of his beautiful calligraphy in Persian (*pārasi-bhāṣā*) on paper (*kākitam*).
19. The regions where the eight languages are spoken are: Sanskrit in heaven, Prakrit in the Maharashtra region, Sauraśeni in the Surasena region, Māgadhi in Magadha, Paiśāci [the demons' language] in the Pāndya, Kekaya, Sālva, Bāhlika, Anūpa, Gandhāra, Nepāḷa, Kuntala, Sudeṣṇa, Bhoja and Kanoja areas, Paiśācika-Cūlikā and Apabhraṃśa in the Ābhīra region, and Telugu in the Āndhra area *(Appakavīyamu,* 1.81).
20. *murikināṭivāru morakulu penaparu*
    l'aravavāru dvijulak' āsa pĕdda
    anucu deśabhāṣalanu kulambunu dittun'
    ataḍu daṇḍuvaccu śata phaṇamulu.

    Ketana, *Vijñāneśvarīyamu* 2.56 (thirteenth century), as quoted by Arudra 1990, 2: 163.
21. *Appakavīyamu pīṭhika,* 46–7.
22. All four benefits: *dharma* (religious merit), *artha* (wealth), *kāma* (desire), and *mokṣa* (release).
23. Here Appakavi seems to be referring to the Tamil Vaiśnava texts (the *Divyaprabandham*).

24. *kiṃcit-tikta-kaṣāya-ṣāḍaba-rasa-kṣepātirekātivāk-*
samcāra-pracayāvakāśamulalo kav'yudgha gandāśmamul
cañcal-līlan' udātta-vāg-garimato sādhinci vedhincumā
pañcāriñci pravahlikā-kṛta-kṛtin pāṣāṇa-pāka-prabhū

This verse was composed by Jalasutram Rukmininadha Sastri ("Jaruk" Sastri) in ironic praise of the great Viswanatha Satyanarayana, whom he regarded as his guru. The texture of rock (*pāṣana-pāka)* is a parodic addition to the well-known three textures (*pāka),* literally "cooking to a certain consistency"): *drākṣa-pāka,* "the grape," as in a poem savored without effort; *kadalī-pāka,* "the banana," which requires peeling before tasting; and *nārikeḷa-pāka,* "the coconut," where the thick fibrous exterior has to be removed and then the hard nut broken open.

References

Arudra, *Samagra Āndhra Sāhityam,* vol. 2, Vijayavada: Prajasakti Book House.

Rao, Velcheru Narayana. 1993. "Purāṇa as Brahminic Ideology." In Wendy Doniger, ed. *Purana Perennis: Reciprocity and Transformation in Hindu and Jaina Texts.* Albany, NY: SUNY Press, pp. 85–100.

———, and Hank Heifetz, trans, 1987. *For the Lord of the Animals: Poems from the Telugu: The Kāḷahastīśvara Śatakamu of Dhūrjaṭi.* Berkeley: University of California Press.

———, trans., assisted by Gene Roghair. 1990. *Śiva's Warriors: Basavapurāṇa of Pālkuriki Somanātha.* Princeton: Princeton University Press.

———, David Shulman, and Sanjay Subrahmanyam. 1992. *Symbols of Substance: Court and State in Nāyaka-Period Tamil Nadu,* Delhi: Oxford University Press.

Sarma, Gadiyaram Ramakrishna, ed. 1982. *Siṃhāsanadvātriṃśika* (of Koravi Goparaju). Hyderabad: Andhra Pradesh Sahitya Akademi.

Venkaṭarāya Śastri, Vedam, ed. 1964. *Āmuktamālyada* [of Kṛṣṇadevarāya]. Madras: Vedamu Venkataraya Sastri Brothers (first edition, 1924).

5

Multiple Lives of a Text

The *Sumati Śatakamu* in Colonial Andhra

The nineteenth century was undoubtedly a particularly eventful period in Indian history. This was the century when British rule in India consolidated itself and—after the turbulence of 1857–8—eventually emerged confidently, not just as the inheritor of the fortunes of a trading company that had "accidentally" found India falling into its lap, but as an agency that had accepted responsibility for bringing India from barbarity to civilization. Interactions between Britain and India—the former at the peak of its civilizational achievements and the latter in a perceived state of decline—produced monumental results that are open to varieties of interpretation. India received from British rule the mixed benefits of industrialization, English education, print culture, the ideas of the Enlightenment, Victorian sensibilities, Christian morality, and a number of other features which add up to a phenomenon that may be called colonial modernity. And these ideas led in turn to a momentous paradigm shift in Indian thought and a worldview resulting in the formation of what we call modern India.

I want to focus on two features among the many that are said to have ushered in modernity: one is print, and the other is public education. Here I examine the impact of both these new developments on Indian text-culture. The Gutenberg revolution and its influence on India is too large a subject for me to cover in a mere essay, so I want to be modest in studying the fortunes of one text, the *Sumati Śatakamu,*[1] a Telugu work, through the nineteenth and twentieth centuries. By means of examining this one text and its use in public education, I will present the epistemological shifts that colonial modernity brought about in Indian text-culture. I have called this "colonial modernity" to distinguish it from another modernity India had experienced before the colonial version, a subject about which I have written elsewhere.[2]

One of the responsibilities that the East India Company undertook was to open schools to teach natives so they might grow up to be upright subjects. The responsibilities of public instruction gave new powers to the government—of deciding what to teach. By that time, those Indian intellectuals who were trained in English and were enjoying the benefits of their education by landing lucrative jobs in the service of the English East India Company were already convinced of the superiority of British culture. There was a general agreement in their minds that Indians lacked morals. Vennelakanti Subbarao (1784–1839), translator for the *Sadr adālat* of the Madras Presidency, a Telugu Niyogi Brahmin who rose to the highest post a native could aspire to in the East India Company administration at the time, felt that Indian children should be taught two things: namely, grammar and morals. When he was appointed to the Madras School Book Society, he submitted a report in 1820 on the state of teaching in schools. Addressing the need for teaching morals he recommended that " tales extracted from different books composed chiefly of morals written in modern languages" should be prescribed for study.[3]

From *Nīti* to Morals

Scholars in the service of the East India Company began to scramble for suitable books in Telugu to teach morals to schoolchildren. The closest word they found to "morals" in Telugu and Sanskrit was *nīti,* which had some overlap with the English word in colloquial usage. Assuming that the semantic range of *nīti* and morals was similar, they looked for available texts that could be used to teach *nīti* to schoolchildren. The pandits who were associated with the East India Company were competent in Sanskrit and classical Telugu. Based on the general consensus among them that *Pañcatantra* stories were best suited to children, Ravipati Gurumurti Sastri retold them in Telugu in 1834 for classroom use. In 1853 Cinnaya Suri rewrote them, in what he considered grammatically proper Telugu, under the title *Nīti-candrika*.[4] The *Pañcatantra* is a well-known book of fables in Sanskrit. Viṣṇuśarman, its author, had vowed to educate the three idiot sons of a king to make them expert at government in six months and wrote this book for that purpose, and not exactly to teach them morals.[5] Problems of cultural translation are already apparent in the choice. *Nīti* is a concept for which as Arthur W. Ryder—the translator of the *Pañcatantra* into English—perceptively notes, there is no equivalent in European languages: "The word *nīti* means roughly 'the wise conduct of life.' Western civilization must endure a certain shame in realizing that no precise equivalent of the term is found in English, French, Latin, or Greek. Many words are necessary to explain what *nīti* is, though the idea, once grasped, is clear, important and satisfying."[6]

The concept of *nīti* in these stories relates to political policy and strategies suitable for worldly success. It is not in any way related to moral instruction as understood by colonial administrators and Christian intellectuals. But this did not deter scholars from teaching these stories for that purpose.

A Telugu Book on *Nīti*

In 1846 Puduri Sitarama Sastri (Tel. *pudūri sitārāma śāstrī*) compiled his famous *Pĕdda Bāla Śikṣa* (or the "big book to teach small children"). This book, reprinted again and again for decades, contains moral sayings composed by the author. *Nīti* now acquired a new meaning as a code of morals. Some of the moral sayings Sitarama Sastri included in his book appear as though paraphrased from a book called *Sumati Śatakamu* (hereafter *SS*).[7] A version of the *SS* was first published in 1870 by Adi Sarasvati Mudranalayamu,[8] a family firm which later became a well-known publishing house, Vavilla Ramaswami Sastrulu and Sons. This edition (hereafter *PSS*) became popular and was printed by a number of publishers again and again, mostly with no publication dates.

In course of time a number of verses from this book began to appear in textbooks prescribed to school students. *Ānanda Vācakamu,* a Telugu textbook for the third grade, compiled in 1930,[9] and approved for school use by the director of public instruction, contains ten verses from the *PSS* under the heading *nīti padyamulu* (moral verses).[10] Some publishers issued the *PSS* with a subtitle: "Morals suitable to be taught for boys and girls," but there is an awareness on the part of at least some editors that *PSS* is not actually a book of morals, and that many of its verses are unsuited as teachings for young children. One of the volumes of the *PSS*, printed in 1922,[11] carried instructions to teachers on how to teach the verses, and it separated the verses that should be taught from those that should not be taught—but a glossary and notes were provided for all the verses anyway.[12]

A Guide to Success

To put the matter simply, the *Sumati Śatakamu* is a guide to success in worldly life, in the same class as the Sanskrit *Pañcatantra, Hitopadeśa,* and *Nītisāra,* but without their high profile. It is a humble text by an unknown author, more applicable to real life in villages, written in simple verses easy to memorize.

Beginning from the thirteenth century, a number of books on *nīti* were written in Telugu. Verses from these books often served as authoritative sources to provide strategies for success in life for upper-caste men who aspired to be kings. While most *nīti* books concern the conduct of kings, ministers, armies, spies, etc., the *SS* differs somewhat from such books in its content. Despite occasional references to kings, the focus of the *SS* is the typical Andhra village with its local landlord, a few Brahmins, people of other upper castes, and courtesans. The *SS* is not the product of a king's court, nor was it intended for people in the court.

The *SS* is in sum a manual for success in life for upper-caste men. It is characterized by its proposal for the uninhibited enjoyment of wealth and pleasure. In particular, the *SS* is concerned with sexual pleasure. A number of verses extol sexual enjoyment and belittle those who do not enjoy sex. Women are classified as wives or as courtesans. A courtesan never loves any man, no matter how handsome and skilled in the art of love he may be. Even wives do not care for a husband who does not earn money. As a general rule, the *SS* tells you that a woman should never be trusted, and a man should never confide in her. Without her husband's surveillance, a wife will certainly turn to prostitution. While a housewife is neither trusted nor loved, she is, paradoxically, respected as a goddess, as the magical source of all riches. The goddess of riches refuses to stay in a house where women cry. The man who causes grief to his wife risks losing the family's wealth. Although housewives are treated as goddesses, widows are treated as unworthy of respect. A household should be managed by a wife, not a widow, who is considered to be dangerous.

Socially, the *SS* presents a world of interdependence and tensions, of cooperation and mistrust. Considerable attention is given to the king, but it is likely the book is not dealing with any major rulers. Pompous words like *bhūpāluḍu,* "ruler of the earth," and *maṇḍalapati,* "lord of the country," are used to describe them. Men from literate castes served as their scribes and ministers. A number of verses in the *SS* relate to them. For instance, a kingdom without a competent minister is like an elephant without its trunk. Scribes are advised not to serve a king who is himself literate. A scribe should never trust another scribe. He should be strong and never appear harmless. In the world of the *SS* each caste has its inherent defects, and a person's qualities are determined by birth. A *kṣatriya* is difficult to please, a *vělama* is undependable, a goldsmith is not trustworthy, a *komaṭi* is a liar. Even Brahmins are censured; a *vaidiki* lacks worldly wisdom, and a *karaṇam* is too full of stratagems to be trusted. Literary skills are extolled; to be able to write good poetry is valued highly but teaching the beauty of poetry to an idiot is like blowing a conch before a deaf person.

Low castes, in particular, are denounced. A low-caste person is variously referred to as *durjāti* ("bad caste person"), *nīcuḍu* ("low person"), *aviveki* ("unwise man"), *pāmaruḍu* ("ignorant person"), and *mūrkhuḍu* ("fool"). By nature, they are dishonest. Friendship with them is foolish. If a low-caste person happens to be literate, he should be avoided like an elephant in rut. Low-caste people are specifically discouraged from saving money; their savings are always confiscated by kings, just as honey saved by bees is taken by people passing by. As a general principle, money exists for enjoyment or for charity. If a fool saves money without enjoying it himself or donating it to deserving people, then it is confiscated by kings, stolen by thieves, or lost in the bowels of the earth.

Although the message of the *SS* is largely amoral, it does contain what appear to be moral sayings. For instance, desiring sex with another man's wife is wrong, stealing others' wealth is bad, anger is a person's worst enemy, and so on. In general, the *SS* conforms to the traditional scheme of Hindu life in which the four goals of *dharma, artha, kāma,* and *mokṣa* are evenly balanced. Everything thus has its place.

A man receives rewards or punishments according to his actions in previous lives. If he performed charitable deeds in his previous life, he is rich in this life, whether or not he works. If he was not generous in his previous life, he is poor in this life, no matter what he does to escape from poverty. In general, everything spoils: love ends in enmity, growth leads to destruction, low prices are replaced by high prices, and happiness is transformed into grief.

Probable Readership of the *SS*

By the seventeenth century a considerably large section of Brahmins known as *karaṇams* took to political occupations and jobs that required worldly skills instead of their usual profession of studying religious texts and conducting religious rituals. All of them were literate, some were scholars, who composed superior poetry in Telugu. They were good diplomats proud of their scribal skills and their competence in multiple languages and scripts. They were not always associated with a king's court but an imagined royal court served as a model for their behavior. They composed a substantial body of poetry during this period. To attest to their writing skills, they made copies of their works and promoted them without much support from royal patrons. They were respectfully called *mantris* (ministers of kings), even when they did not actually serve a king. This seems to be the community that produced the *Sumati*

Śatakamu. True to their nature of not appearing important, but always managing affairs from behind the scenes, the *karaṇam* author of the *Sumati Śatakamu* did not sign his name.

Despite their humble appearance, the self image of *karaṇams* is quite interesting. One of the verses about a *karaṇam* says:

> He writes and reads and speaks intelligently.
> He listens to what people say inside and out.
> He interprets foreign languages to the king,
> and controls the assembly if it goes out of line.
> He says the right words and makes hearts unite,
> and sees right away, honesty from trickery.
> He can bring people together and separate them again
> or favor enemies and offer them the throne.
> He is humble, dignified, skilled and giving.
> That's what a good *mantri* should be.

Karaṇams are portrayed as confident of their skill in manipulating matters to turn any situation favorable. They can make impossible things possible with their diplomatic skills:

> If the king is against you, you need to be friends with the scribe.
> When the god of death Yama was angry and declared a person
> dead, "gatāyu," didn't Chitragupta, his scribe, change the "ga" into a "śa"
> and make him live a hundred years, a "śatāyu"?

The *SS* devotes a number of verses to *karanams*. However, the *karaṇams* the *SS* talks about seem to refer to the small group of persons employed in the hereditary position of a village revenue accountant—rather than the broad class mentioned above. *SS* also has several verses against goldsmiths *(agasālĕ* caste). A legend that has acquired some acceptance, told by the noted intellectual Arudra,[13] is that in 1145 CE a certain Rama Pradhani removed goldsmiths from *karaṇam* positions in some 6000 villages and employed Brahmin *niyogis* in their place. Reading this legend and the negative representation of goldsmiths in the *SS*, Arudra suspects a certain opposition between *karaṇams* and goldsmiths, whereas Macca Haridasu suggests that the author of the *SS* was most certainly a *karaṇam* revenue accountant from the *niyogi* subcaste of Brahmins.[14] An earlier scholar, Vanguri Subbarao (1924), also thought that the author of the *SS* was perhaps from the caste of *karaṇams* (*mantri kulam*), though he does not categorically say that the author of the *SS* was a *karaṇam* revenue accountant himself.[15]

Whatever the historical truth value of Arudra's reading of this legend, there is a prominent group of *niyogis* called *āruvela vāru,* the six thousand. We don't know the real origin of this name, but in Andhra most village revenue accountants belonged to this group, which was known for its pride and self-confidence. The poet Kaṅkaṇṭi Pāparāju (mid-eighteenth century), who came from this group, writes in praise of them:

> They steal the hearts of the members of the courts
> of any king with their learning.
> They give like the wishing tree, the ocean of milk, the legendary Karṇa and Bali.
> They are known for doing good deeds with no ulterior motive.
> They make the impossible possible to help the master they serve.
> They break the pride of any enemy that stands up to them—
> such are the qualities of the six thousand.[16]

However, a close reading of the verses of the *SS* does not seem to support the idea that the author is a *karaṇam* revenue accountant. The book is critical of the *karaṇam* accountants, just as it is critical of all other castes. Its negative representation of goldsmiths reflects the general mistrust of this community prevalent in Andhra and does not reflect any conflict between the Brahmins and goldsmiths. In fact, the *SS* does not seem to carry any personal views of the author, whoever he might be. The text only represents the general perceptions of upper-caste men, their prejudices included. All we can say is that this text is the product of a larger community of upper-caste scribes—whom we may call *karaṇams.* Later I will discuss the different versions of the *SS* that circulated among different groups of people.

Śataka Genre

The *SS* is called *śataka,* which is a genre containing a notional 100 verses (*śata*). Conventionally it has 108 verses, the first of which begins with the syllable *śrī,* a feature that makes the *śataka* auspicious. Verses in the *śataka* genre are unrelated to each other in terms of a narrative sequence but they are all composed in one kind of meter and carry a common word or phrase at the end of each verse. This is always a vocative, addressing a person or a deity, sometimes the author of the *śataka* himself, and is called *makuṭa,* or crown. The *makuṭa* is the only unifying feature that binds the disparate verses in a *śataka* into one single text. A *śataka* often gets its title from the *makuṭa,* thus the present text is called *Sumati Śatakamu* because each of its verses ends in the vocative *sumatī. Śatakas* were usually composed by one poet but were almost never read from beginning to end as one unit. Modern scholars classify *śatakas* by their theme—such as *bhakti śatakas* (which contain verses of devotion to one Hindu god or the other), *nīti śatakas* (which speak of *nīti*), *śṛṅgāra śatakas* (with erotic verses), and so on.[17] The independent nature of the verses in a *śataka* and their readability make them easy to memorize and recite. Some verses may become more popular than others, and their oral communication from person to person introduces a number of structural and lexical changes in the process. I will have more to say about these changes later.[18] People who recite the verses of a *śataka* sometimes tell legends about the author and his life; later we will learn a few legends about a supposed author of the *SS*. The available manuscripts of the *SS* are fragmentary. There is no single manuscript that contains all the verses—we don't even know how many there were to begin with.[19]

C.P. Brown and the *SS*

Charles Philip Brown (1798–1884), an employee of the English East India Company, who took a great interest in the study of Telugu language and literature, had an enormous influence on Telugu scholars. Born to evangelical parents in Calcutta, he spent a total of thirty-four years in two equal periods of seventeen years each in India, during which time he served the East India Company in several administrative capacities. He devoted most of his energies to learning Telugu and trying to "revive" Telugu literature. Brown's understanding of a literary text was grounded in the nineteenth-century European concept of a fixed, unified text. A text found in fragments or otherwise corrupted had in his view to be carefully copied from several manuscripts, collated, and corrected for inaccuracies and scribal errors. It could then be printed and made available to readers. Print was new to Andhra and Brown himself was largely instrumental in making Telugu texts available in print. Most texts in Telugu literature, which had some nine hundred years of continuous literary production, did not appear in manuscripts that were "clean" enough for Brown to accept them as authentic. Furthermore, manuscripts were not easily available to Brown when he sought to collect them. Had he lived among Telugu people and tried to gain a proper understanding of the literary culture of this language, he would have had some sense of their textual practices.[20] However, Brown did not pause to think if the text-culture in Telugu was different from his own. The absence of the kind of texts he had expected assured him that Telugu literature was in a state of decline. His limited knowledge of Telugu coupled with his confidence in the superiority of Western culture made him comfortably assume responsibility to save the literature.

Brown's interest in the *SS* developed neither because he was attracted to its *nīti* sayings nor because he thought it was an important text, but because it was written in a simple language that was easy for him to learn.[21] His interest in the text as a useful tool for a beginner like him to learn Telugu as a foreign language prompted him to have a pandit produce a version with a glossary so he could understand the text easily. As he read the text he began to translate it into English, apparently as part of his exercise to learn Telugu. He collected the *SS* verses in 1832 from some ten manuscripts. Following the methods employed by European philologists in restoring Greek and Latin texts, he had different manuscripts collated by eliminating spurious, blemished, or corrupted readings. Thus he created a version of 150 verses and printed it in 1842 with his English translation of 85 of them. No information is available as to how many copies were printed, but scholars have not been able to trace even one copy of this initial edition. The only evidence that Brown printed this edition comes from an advertisement for the book in 1842 reported by Macca Haridasu.[22] In 1973 the Andhra Pradesh Sahitya Akademi eventually published Brown's version, again from his manuscript. I refer to this text hereafter as the *BSS*.

While we know about the manuscript sources of the *BSS,* we do not know anything about the manuscript sources of the *PSS*. If Adisaraswati based its 1870 edition on a manuscript, it is nowhere reported. The two major changes in the Adisaraswati edition are that the verses are ordered alphabetically and the spelling conforms to what is by then accepted as the literary standard, with features such as silent nasal marks (*ardhānusvāras*). None of the manuscripts of the *SS* carries these features. Later reprints of the *PSS* either clearly followed the 1870 edition, or, more likely, later editions of Adisaraswati, which appeared under the imprint of Vavilla Ramaswami Sastrulu and Sons. The 1870 edition of the *PSS* contains 105 verses, but at some point of time after that the *PSS* acquired a few more verses, the most important of which is a prayer verse at the very beginning, *śrīrāmuni daya cetanu* (by the kindness of god Rama), which includes the customary auspicious syllable *śrī* and a colophon verse attributing the authorship to Bhīmana (Ṫel. *bhīmana*). Some editions carry a word-by-word explanation following each verse (*ṭīka*) and a prose summary of the verse *(tātparya)*.[23]

Alphabetizing is not common in Telugu; in fact only two more *śatakas,* both of which are printed much later than the *PSS,* are alphabetized.[24] As is well known, even dictionaries were not alphabetized until the nineteenth century. One suggestion is that this is based on *Akṣarâṅkagadya,* ritual verses composed for Siva, where the verses are alphabetized. Another suggestion is that alphabetization is a Jaina influence and that a Jaina monk called Sumati is the author of the *SS*. These suggestions are tantalizing at best and have no real basis to follow through.[25] It is also interesting to note that no manuscripts of the *SS,* nor the edition created by C.P. Brown, are alphabetized, nor do they carry the standard spelling, as the *PSS* does.

The name *SS* and the *makuṭa* refrain at the end of each verse were a strong enough indication that all these free-floating verses were generally perceived as belonging to a single text. However, it is the *PSS* that gave it a concrete unity, by making it a book, and truly a *śataka,* with the generic requirement of 108 verses, and with the auspicious syllable of beginning the first poem and a colophon attributing the authorship of the text to Bhīmana.[26] The text is further enhanced by the arrangement of the verses in alphabetical order. I located on the internet scanned fragments of a palm-leaf manuscript from the Theosophical Society Library at Adyar.[27] This manuscript contains among its early verses, but not as its first verse, the prayer poem to Rama that begins with the words *śrīrāmuni daya cetanu*, "by the kindness of god Rama," which, as we have noted, is printed as the first verse in the *PSS* sometime after 1870. Arudra and Haridasu report that they did not find this poem in any of the manuscripts they had seen. The Adyar manuscript looks interesting because it is the only one that contains the prayer verse, and because it seems to record verses that are closest in style to the *PSS*. However, the verses in the Adyar manuscript are not ordered alphabetically, nor does the spelling conform to the standard given to them by Adisaraswati. Unfortunately, the scanned fragments of the Adyar manuscript are not legible enough for me to make definitive comments.

Features of Oral Transmission

All the *PSS* verses show features of oral transmission compared to the *BSS* which contains a large number of verses in a literary style. One might say that all Telugu literature before the twentieth century is oral in the sense that all verses were recited or sung, but I am making a distinction here between texts that were passed from person to person in a written form and those that were transmitted orally. The verses of the *PSS* were circulated orally, whereas most of the verses in the *BSS* were circulated through writing. In effect, there were two different kinds of transmission—oral and written. Inevitably the verses that entered the oral transmission process spread among a larger community than the ones that remained written. Both communities were literate, and both were upper caste. The community amongst whom the verses of the *BSS* were circulated included scribes who had a penchant for preserving written knowledge. The other community among whom verses of the *PSS* were orally circulated was more accustomed to orality and was much larger. These verses were good conversation pieces and were often quoted to legitimize a viewpoint. Upper-caste men in village circles quoted verses in imitation of scholars who quoted from Sastras (Skt. *śāstra*). It was customary to learn the verses orally from a person who had memorized them, and an orally quoted verse had a much higher authority than one written down.

Such oral transmission brings about significant structural changes in the text, which I call organization. Every single verse of the *PSS* carries features of oralization, which I will elaborate on below. If one person in the chain of oral transmission happened to be a scribe and wanted to have a written copy of an oralized verse, he wrote it as he had heard it, but the verse continued in oral circulation. In fact, one can find several oralized verses in the *BSS*, which, as we know, is a collated version from many manuscripts. For convenience I use the *BSS* to illustrate literary features of oralizaion.[28]

The Metrics of *Kandamu*

In order to discuss the features of oralization in the *PSS* verses, and contrast them with the literary features in the *BSS,* let me briefly present the metrics of *kandamu,* the meter in which all the *SS* verses were composed.[29] This is a meter of four lines where a long syllable has a value of two *mātras* while a short syllable has a value of one. A *gaṇa* (cluster of syllables) used in *kandamu* could consist of two long syllables, or one long syllable and two short syllables, or four short syllables. The first and third lines are composed with three such *gaṇas* while the second and fourth lines are composed of five. The second syllable of each of the four lines should use the same consonant or consonant cluster. This is called *prāsa.* In the second line and the fourth line, the first syllable of the first *gaṇa* and the first syllable of the fourth *gaṇa* should be euphonically similar. This is called *yati.* A list of syllables that are euphonically similar to each other is given in books on meter. The metrics of *kandamu* are presented below as an abstract diagram, where X represents the *yati* and the asterisk represents the *prāsa* and each length of straight line represents a *gaṇa.*

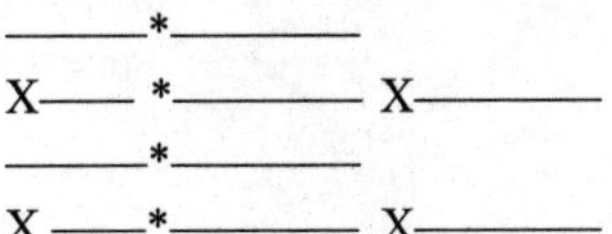

The following is a *kandamu* verse in roman transcription with each syllable separated with spaces. Here, the consonant cluster in the second syllable of each line, /ll/ is the *prāsa*. The first syllable of the first and the fourth *gaṇas* in lines two, /gō/ and /ko/, and five, /te/, are the *yati*.

a *llu* ni man ci ta nam bu nu
gŏ lla ni sā hi tya vi dya—*ko* ma li ni ja mun
pŏ *llu* na dañ ci na bi yya mu
*tĕ ll*a ni kā ku lu nu le vu—*tĕ* li yu ra su ma tī

Features of the *PSS*

An important feature of the *PSS* is the absence of enjambment; there are no run-on lines in its verses. In recitation each short line is one segment, while each long line, broken at the *yati,* makes two segments. Each segment begins with a new word. Rarely does a word extend over two segments. In recitation, it is customary to pause at the end of each segment before picking up the next segment. Since the syntactic structure of the poem corresponds to the pauses at the end of each segment, the meter in the *PSS* reinforces the meaning, and the meaning reinforces the meter. Reading *PSS* verses breaking at every segment has given rise to a style of reading *kandamu* now considered by literary people as schoolboyish. Another feature of the *PSS* is its simplistic observance of *yati,* using simple euphony as a guiding principle.

A significant feature of the style of the *PSS* is its extensive use of filler words. A filler word does not make a specific semantic contribution to the verse; it only helps to fulfill the meter. Filler words almost always occur where the metrical restrictions of *prāsa* and *yati* must be observed. For example, of the 108 verses in the *PSS,* 71 verses use a filler word; 52 use fillers in *yati* places, while 19 use filler words in *prāsa* places. The following is a list of words that occur in the *yati* place:

ilalo	"on the earth"
bhuvilo	,,
mahilo	,,
medini	,,
vasudhanu	,,

ĕrugumu	"know" (imperative)
tĕliyura	,,
nayam'idi	"this is right"
mari	"and"
nikkamu	"it is true"
tathyamu	,,
siddhamu	"that's how it is"
sahajamu	"it is natural"
gadarā	"is it not?"

Filler words are viewed by scholars as *vyartha padas,* "useless words." However, in the oral tradition they have great value; they are predictable and make the verse easy to memorize. They reduce the semantic burden while preserving the euphonic beauty and the metrical structure of the poem.

A number of the *PSS* verses are built on a repetitive formulaic syntax, which helps memorization beyond the devices of *prāsa* and *yati.* For example, a string of negative imperatives followed by a declarative sentence is very common in the *PSS.* The following verse is an example (the *yati* is shown in italics and the *prāsa* is shown in capitals):

naVVakumī sabhalopala
*na*VVakumī talli daṇḍri—*nā*thula toḍan
naVVakumī parasatito
*na*VVakumī vipravarula—*na*yam'idi sumatī

Do not laugh in the assembly.
Do not laugh with your father, mother or master.
Do not laugh with another man's wife.
Do not laugh at a sacred Brahmin.
Sumati, that's the right thing to do.

Also note the final segment begins with a filler word, *nayam'idi,* thus saving the poet from having to choose a meaningful word that begins with a /na/.

Features of Literary Style

In contrast with the oralized style of the *PSS*, the literary style is compact: it does not use filler words. Complex combinations of *yati* and *prāsa* as well as long and involved sentences are normal features of the literary style. Complexity rather than spontaneity, and manipulation rather than fluidity of phrases, are the predominant qualities of a literary style. A literary stylist works at a slower pace than an oral versifier and therefore has the time to choose his words with an aim to build a tightly composed verse. For an oral versifier, meter and syntax fuse into a structure that organizes both his language and the verse at the same lime. For the literate poet, meter structures the verse but not always his language. Therefore, in a literary composition syntax tends to be relatively free from meter. To illustrate this point, I will present a verse, in the same meter, *kandam,* in which all the *SS* verses are composed, written by a literary poet of the first order, the thirteenth-century Tikkana. This poem doesn't need to be translated; just a look at the complex structure of long Sanskrit compounds running into the next line, with *yati* and *prāsa* syllables embedded in them, shown here with strings of syllables with no spaces, visually demonstrates the point (the *yati* is shown in italics and the *prāsa* is shown in capitals):

triBHuvanaśukadṛḍhapañjara-
*vi*BHavamahitunaku tri*vi*ṣṭapanirmo-
kaBHujaṅgapatiki sakala jagad-
*a*BHinnarūpunaku bhāvan*ā*tītunakum.[30]

None of the *SS* verses, the *PSS*, or the *BSS* have this kind of high literary style. At no time did the *SS* include verses of great literary complexity. But we can see a literary style in many of the *BSS* verses, though it is much simpler than Tikkana's verse shown above. Let me take the following verse from the *BSS* as an example (the *yati* is shown in capitals):

trāSUnu veśyayun' ŏka samam
au SAndehimpavalavad *a*vanīsthailo
vīSAm badhikamb'ĕccaṭan
o SArigāk andu mŏgguc '*u*ṇḍunu sumatī

Listen Sumati, a courtesan is like a balance. She tilts to the side which has a little more gold.

The syntax of this verse camouflages the metrical structure. A detailed breakdown of the metrical units and syntactical units of the verse would facilitate examination of this feature.

Metrical Units	Syntactical Units
1. trāsunu veśyayun'ŏka sama	1. trāsunu veśyayun'ŏka samam'au "A courtesan and a balance are one kind"
2. m'au sandehimpavalava	2. sandehimpavalavad' "There's no doubt about it"
3. d'avanīsthalilo	3. avanītsthalilo "on this earth" (filler word)
4. vīsamb' adhikab 'ĕccaṭa	4. vīsamb' adhikamb'ĕccaṭano "wherever there is a little more (gold)"
5. no sarigāk 'andu mŏggu	5. sarigāk' "without being level"
6. c'uṇḍunu sumatī	6. andu mŏgguc' uṇḍunu "to that side (she) tilts"
	7. sumatī "wise man" (vocative)

On the metrical side of the chart, the four lines of the poem are divided into six segments to reflect the way it is recited. On the syntactical side, one can see the first clause extends by one syllable beyond the first segment of the verse into the second segment where a new clause begins with the *prāsa* syllable /sa/. If a pause is made at the end of the clause to complete the meaning, the euphony of *prāsa* is affected. If, on the other hand, no pause is made so the euphony of *prāsa* is preserved, the clarity of the meaning is compromised. A similar situation occurs at the end of the fourth segment and at the beginning of the fifth segment. The last word, *ĕccaṭano,* extends into the fifth segment where a new clause begins with the *prāsa* syllable. Clearly, this verse cannot be read adopting the same style of recitation as a *PSS* verse.

The only oral feature of this verse is its use of the filler word *avanīsthalilo*, "on this earth," which, however, is a less easily understood Sanskrit phrase, compared to similar filler words in the *PSS*. We don't find this verse in the *PSS*. It did not enter the oral transmission process, apparently because the metrical structure was not amenable to easy alterations to suit oralization.

Let me take a verse found in the *BSS* and show how it changes in the *PSS* to suit an oralized style. First, the verse from the *BSS* (*yati* marked in italics):

dānamb'ivvani kuḍuvani
vāni dhanamu rājacora*va*hnula jerun
gānala nīgalu gūrcina
*te*niya tĕravarula jeru *tī*runa sumatī

Listen Sumati, a person who does not enjoy or share his wealth will lose it to the king, thieves, or fire, like honey which bees gather in the forest is taken by passersby.

This verse has a long Sanskrit compound, *rājacoravahnulu,* "kings, thieves, or fire," extending across the two segments of the second line and absorbing the identity of the *yati* syllable /*va*/, which would have been clearly demarcated in an oralized verse. Furthermore, the verse is tightly constructed in one long, somewhat complex sentence, which never happens in the *PSS*.

Let us see how this verse is transformed in oral transmission though the meaning remains the same. Here is its *PSS* counterpart (*yati* marked in italics):

tānu bhujimpani yarthamu
*mā*navapati jeru gŏnta *mari* bhūgata mau
gānala nigalu gūrcina
*te*niya yŏru jerunaṭlu *ti*ramuga sumatī

Listen Sumati, if you do not enjoy your wealth, some of it goes to the king, and the rest is lost into the earth, as the honey the bees gather in the forest is taken by others, sure and certain.

Two advantages result from this change. First, the long Sanskrit compound *rājacoravahnula* with the *yati* hidden in it is eliminated. It is inconvenient for a reciter to remember a long compound which sweeps through two segments of a line particularly if it hides the *yati* syllable. He uses the *yati* as a memory landmark for the segment of the verse that begins with it. Therefore, the long compound is replaced by a line which is broken into two parts which are synchronous with the two segments they cover:

*mā*navapati jeru kŏnta *ma*ri bhūgata mau.

The use of the filler word *mari* makes it easy to remember the *yati.* The second change is made in the fourth line. In the *BSS jeru tīruna* is one word that extends across two segments. In the *PSS* the segments are clearly broken, facilitating oralized recitation.

teniya tĕravarula jeru tīruna sumatī (*BSS*)
teniya yŏru jerunaṭlu tiramuga sumatī (*PSS*)

In the *PSS* text a filler word, *tiramuga* ("surely"), begins the sixth segment. The *BSS* version of the line has a more complex arrangement in which the clause *tĕravarula jeru tīruna,* " like (honey) goes to passersby," extends across two segments of the line across the *yati* place. Also, the lexical choice of *tĕravarulu ,* "passersby," is indicative of the interest of the literary stylist who wants three similar "t" sounds repeated in the same line for alliteration, which does not interest the oral reciter, who would prefer regularity and symmetry in a verse.

However, the stylistic gap between these two poems is too wide to permit a precise mapping of the process of transition of literary style into an oralized style. A better opportunity for observing this transition is provided by examination of the following two verses in the *BSS* and the *PSS*. Here are verses with the lines numbered for reference (*yati* syllables are in italics):

BSS:

1. mantri gala vāni rājyamu
2. *ta*ntrambula jĕḍaka śāsva*ta*mbai nilucun
3. mantri vihīnuni rājyamu
4. *ja*ntrapu kīl'ūḍinaṭlu *ja*rugadu sumatī

PSS:

1. mantri gala vāni rājyamu
2. *ta*ntramu cĕdak'uṇḍa nilucu *ta*racuga dharalo
3. mantri vihīnuni rājyamu
4. *ja*ntrapu kīl'ūḍinaṭlu *ja*rugadu sumatī

The variations in these two texts are limited to lines 2 and 4. The variations in line 2 are of two kinds. One is stylistic while the other is syntactic. The word *śāśvatamb'ai* ("permanently") in the *BSS* text extends across two segments of the line. The first segment of the line ends at *śāśva* and the next segment begins with *tambai.* A customary pause in oral recitation at the end of each segment would break the word unnaturally and awkwardly into two parts: *śāśva* and *tamb'ai.* If, on the other hand, the line is recited as one unit, the euphony between the initial *ta-* and the *ta-* in the *yati* place in the middle of *śāśvatamb'ai* loses its emphasis. Furthermore, it is inconvenient to memorize a line that does not have the usual break at the end of each segment.

A reciter resolves these problems by making appropriate changes in the text. A rephrasing of the text with the filler word *taracuga dharalo* ("frequently in the world") restores the break at the end of the first segment. The change makes the poem easy to memorize and recite.

As may be seen from the discussion above, the preferences of the literary style are very different from those of the oral style. A literary poet considers it more artful to compose a tight verse in which *yati* places are filled with meaningful words, not fillers. He avoids breaking at the end of each segment and aims at more complex line movements; his *yati* and *prāsa* places are usually hidden in long words. A literary stylist considers it artless to compose verses that break at every joint. Such composition is compared to the weaving of a fish basket, *cepala buṭṭa,* loose with a lot of holes in it. The use of filler words to satisfy *yati* and *prāsa* is especially undesirable because they show that the poet does not have a mastery over meter, and is rather led by it. The literary features discussed above were greatly admired by learned poets who scorned oral poetry.

The other variation in line 2, which is syntactic, is the result of a change in dialects. The *BSS* has *tantrambula jĕḍaka,* whereas the *PSS* has *tantramu cĕḍa'kuṇḍa,* both meaning "without losing strategic efficiency." Old Telugu uses both negatives freely while modern Telugu retains the non-progressive non-finite negative (the *-aka* form) for the specialized use of indicating a condition for an inevitable consequence; the progressive non-finite negative (the *-akuṇḍa* form) is used in all other situations. The following sentences are acceptable both in Old Telugu and modern Telugu since the clause ending with the *-aka* form marks a condition, an inevitable consequence which is revealed in the principal clause. Here are a few examples to illustrate this point:

Modern Telugu:
vānalu *leka* pantalu poyayi
"The crops failed for lack of rain."
tiṇḍi *leka* parajalu bādhapaḍutunnāru
"People are suffering for lack of food."
nidra *cālaka* kaḷḷu baruv'ĕkkāyi
"The eyes are heavy because of lack of sleep."

Old Telugu:
vānalu *leka* panṭalu poyināvi
"The crops failed for lack of rain."
tiṇḍi *leka* prajalu bādhapaḍucunnāru
"People are suffering for lack of food."
nidra *cālaka* kaḷḷu baruv'ĕkkinavi
"The eyes are heavy because of lack of sleep."

The following sentences, which use *aka* forms, acceptable in Old Telugu, are not acceptable in modern Telugu because the event indicated by the finite verb is not an inevitable consequence of the event indicated by the non-finite.

Old Telugu:

atanu nāto *cĕppaka* vĕdalipoyĕnu
"He left without informing me."
Ī pustakamu *caduvaka* māṭlāḍakuḍu
"Do not talk without reading this book."
Ī goḍa *padipoka* nilucunā?
"Does this wall stand without falling?"

Consequently, these sentences have to be rephrased with the *-akuṇḍā* form in modern Telugu:

Modern Telugu:

stanu nāto *cĕppakuṇḍā* veḷḷipoyāḍu
"He left without informing me."
pustakam *cadavakuṇḍā* māṭlāḍakaṇḍi

"Do not talk without reading this book."
goḍa *paḍipokuṇḍā* nilustundā?
"Does this wall stand without falling?"

Preference for the *-akuṇḍā* form in the *PSS* indicates the influence of modern syntax on the reciter. The *-aka* form is syntactically obsolete and is consequently rejected in favor of the modern *-akuṇḍā* form . The process is perhaps not deliberate but a natural propensity of the reciter to adopt a modern syntax. This brings into focus an important change that enters into an orally transmitted text: its syntax gets updated with time.

A comparison of verses in the *BSS* and the *PSS* suggests that most variations fall into the two categories discussed above: (1) stylistic variations introduced to render the verse easier to memorize and recite, and (2) dialectical variations to update the grammar of the verse.

Occasionally, a line or two in a verse composed in an especially intricate literary style becomes unintelligible to the oral reciter. In such instances, the line is altered to make it more intelligible, even if it results in a change in meaning. The following verse exemplifies this:

BSS:

kāraṇamunu leka navvunu
preraṇamunu leni prema priyaratikeḷul
pūraṇamu leni būrĕlu
vīraṇamunu leni peṇḍli vṛtharā sumatī

Listen Sumati, a laugh without a reason, love play with a woman who is not aroused, dumplings without (sweet) stuffing, and a wedding without music—these are futile.

The second line of the verse is difficult for the oral reciter not only because of the Sanskrit compound *priyaratikeḷul* ("love play with / of the beloved") but also because of the number of *pra* sounds. The *PSS* alters the line:

peraṇammunu leni lema pṛithvīsthalilo

The oralized style brings in the filler words *prithvīsthalilo* ("in the earth") to replace the difficult compound *priyaratikeḷul* in the second segment of the line. This change also makes it easy to remember the segment, because it begins with the *yati* syllable. But now the line means "a woman who does not have a blouse." This change works perfectly for the oral reciter because it reflects a new style of wearing stitched clothes that came into vogue around the seventeenth century because of the cultural influence of Persianized Islam. Upper-caste women began to wear blouses, which the lower castes did not adopt.[31] A woman without a blouse is therefore low caste and not desirable.

Popularity of the *SS*

In economics, Fisher's Equation in relation to the Quantity Theory of Money states that the velocity of the circulation of money should be factored in while measuring the quantity of money in use.[32] A million dollars kept in a safe for one year has a value of zero, while a dollar bill that changes hands a million times in one year does the work of a million dollars exchanged just once. A similar measure applies to the social impact of literature. A poem by a scholar-poet which is read by an elite group has less influence on popular ideas than a poem by a minor poet which is read, remembered, and recited by a large community. In the world of ideas, the *PSS* was like a dollar bill that changed hands a million times while the verses of great poets were like a million dollars kept in a safe, or perhaps transacted just once in a while. The popularity of a book is usual1y established by the number of press runs and copies sold. This standard, of course, is not valid in the oral tradition. The *PSS*'s popularity indicates the general acceptability of its ideas to the community in which they circulated. Some verses of the *PSS* appear to be metrical restatements of well-known proverbs, and accepted prejudices, while other verses seem to carry the wisdom imparted by the poet. The epigrammatic nature of the text, the simplicity of the language, the prescriptive tone of the verses, and above all their immense quotability imbued the *PSS* with the power of a *śāstra* in the popular mind.

Critical Editions of the *SS* and Authorship of the *SS*

Another concept that became acceptable to Indian literary scholars during the colonial period is that every text must have a unique and historically identifiable author. It is true that in our own experience a text comes into existence because an author writes it. The sequence is as follows:

author > text > reader

In pre-colonial India, with its oral tradition and written culture operating in tandem, the situation was somewhat different. Here the author does not neessarily write the text. Rather it may well be the other way round: the text writes the author. For instance, a text received by its listeners / readers as an epic / *itihāsa,* generates an author of superhuman powers like the sage Vālmīki for the Ramayana. If the same text is read as a bhakti / devotional text, a text that gives religious merit to its readers, the author is given a different "biography." This Vālmīki is a bandit who turns into a sage by repeating Rama's name. In effect, if a text changes its function, the author changes along with it.[33] A number of legends are told about authors of texts in the oral tradition. Such legends about an author mark an important shift in the meaning of the text, or indicate a new status to which the text is elevated. Legends about authors are in effect parts of the text. But the new concepts of an original author and an Ur-text led to such questions as who the author of the *Sumati Śatakamu* was and where and when he lived. The next task would be to establish the Ur-text by the original author, free from interpolations and spurious verses. Legends told about authors were of no use for new scholars of literature, because they were unhistorical. C.P. Brown trained a number of scholars who worked under him in the methods of collating texts, and creating "authentic editions." Following Brown's ideas, the search for "authentic editions" and reliable information about the real "authors" became a major occupation for scholars of literature. It is striking that these scholars rejected concepts of author and text from their own culture. As late as 2002, Arudra, the influential poet and historian of Telugu literature, writes in his magnum opus *Samagra Āndhra Sāhityam* (Comprehensive History of Telugu Literature): "We need to produce a critical edition (*samśodhita-prati*) of the *Sumati Śatakamu* to find out what interpolations the scribes indulged in, and this in turn would also resolve the question of authorship." From the early decades of the twentieth century, scholars began to argue whether Baddĕna or Bhīmana was the author of the *SS*. Those who argued in favor of Bhīmana based their belief on a poem found in some manuscript copies of the *SS*.[34] Furthermore, Kūcimañci Timmakavi (mid-eighteenth century) identifies Bhīmana as the author of the *SS*, in his *Sarvalakṣaṇsārasaṅgrahamu,* a book on meter. The following is the poem:

srī karamuga bhīmana munu
lokamunaku bōgaḍagā vilokinci madin
brākaṭamuga sumatiki mati
cekūḍaga sumatinīti cĕppadŏḍangĕn

Auspiciously Bhīmana,while the people admired him, thought well in his mind to teach good sense to Sumati and began to tell *Sumati-nīti.*

Note that here the text is not called *Sumati Śatakamu* but *Sumati-nīti,* a name that brings to mind *Baddĕ-nīti,* a text scholars agree was written by Baddĕna. Interestingly, the same poem also appears at the end of several printed *PSS* texts.

However, Manavalli Ramakrishna Kavi, Vanguri Subbarao, N. Venkata Rao, and other scholars argued that Baddĕna composed the *SS.* They base their arguments on the following verse from Baddĕna's *Nītiśāstra-muktâvaḷi*, a book of *nīti* verses:

śrīvibhuḍa garvitāri
kṣmāvaradaḷanopalabhajayalaksmīsam
bhāvituḍa sumatiśatakamu
gāviñcina proḍa gāvyakamalāsanuḍan

I am the lord of the goddess of wealth, honored by the goddess of victory for destroying the proud enemy kings, and I am the expert composer of *Sumati Śatakamu* and the creator of many other poems.

Bhīmana *vs.* Baddĕna

However, not much is reliably known about Baddĕna. Scholars such as Vedam Venkataraya Sastri and Manavalli Ramakrishna Kavi suggest that he was a king of a principality in Andhra during the 11th–12th century. His book, *Niti-śastra-muktâvaḷi,* is also known as *Baddĕ-nīti,* In this small book of 162 verses, he follows the tradition of such Sanskrit books as *Kāmandaka,* which prescribe the code of conduct for kings and courtiers. He was clearly a scholar competent in writing a well-turned verse, and a person with considerable understanding and perhaps experience in the political strategies of running a kingdom. His book seems to have been popular among the class of people who aspired to kingship or worked for kings. In any case, we know that Madiki Singana (fourteenth century), the editor /compiler of the *Sakala-nīti-sammatamu,* included in his volume as many as 38 verses from *Baddĕ-nīti,* which indicates Baddĕna's popularity among the class of people who were politically minded.[35]

Not much is known about Bhīmana either, if such a person ever existed. Legends told about him say that he lived in the village of Vemulavāḍa. His mother was a Brahmin widow who conceived him after the death of her husband. She went to the Bhīmeśvaraśiva temple in Daksharama along with a group of women who had husbands. When they all asked the god for a son, she naively followed their example and asked for a son as well. The God Bhimesvara (Skt. *bhīmeśvara*) blessed her and gave her a son. But because of his suspected illegitimacy, the young boy was badly treated by people in the temple town. One day he demanded that his mother tell him who his father was. She told him that the god Bhimesvara in the temple was his father. Angry that the god Bhimesvara had never showed up to admit his paternity nor ever taken care of him, the boy rushed into the temple with a big rock in his hands, He stood before the god and yelled, "Are you my father? If so, speak or I am going to hit you with this rock." The god Bhimesvara, who was himself a big rock *liṅga,* spoke: "Son, I am your father. From now on, no one shall ever call you a bastard. If anyone does, you may teach them a lesson. I give you the power to curse or bless. Whatever you utter will come true. You will be known as *śāpānugraha-samartha,* 'one who can curse and bless as well.'"

From then on, everything Bhīmana uttered came true because his power derived from god. Once, the young boy was expelled from a feast by Brahmana who objected to the presence of a bastard in their company. Bhīmana angrily said:

annam'antā sunnam'avāli.
appāl 'annī kappal'avāli.
ayyal'andarū kŏyyal'avāli.

The rice should become lime.
The sweet cakes should become frogs.
All the men should turn into wood.

Instantly his words came true, and all the rice turned into a heap of lime and frogs began to jump across the dinner plates, and the offending Brahmanas turned to wood. Others in the room fell at the feet of the young boy asking for forgiveness. Bhīmana then uttered a reversal of the curse and everything turned to normal. Other legends about Bhīmana tell of how kings who ignored him lost their kingdoms and regained them only after repenting.[36] Śrināthuḍu (in the fifteenth century) includes Bhīmana at the head of a chronologically ordered list of several great Telugu poets who preceded him.[37] Piṅgaḷi Sūranna, of the late sixteenth century, refers to Bhīmana as one who reportedly wrote a bi-textual narrative poem, *Rāghava-pāṇḍavīyamu*, a single text that can be read as the *Ramāyaṇa* and the *Mahābhārata* as well, the like of which he (Sūranna) was commissioned to write.[38] Appakavi (seventeenth century) mentions Bhīmana's name in the context of telling a legend about Bhīmana's rivalry with Nannaya (eleventh century).[39] None of the above authors who invoke Bhīmana's name give any verifiable information about him.[40] Their knowledge of Bhīmana was probably based on legends and not necessarily on any hard facts. However, the fact that they mention his name clearly indicates that Bhīmana's name was revered as early as the fifteenth century, that he was respected as a legendary poet, feared and honored as a poet of superhuman powers.

Rival claims of authorship become meaningful when they are related to the mode of transmission and to the clientele of the *SS*. For *karaṇams* who wanted this text to be treated as the authoritative guide to success, an author like Baddĕna would be preferable because he has the stature of a wise ruler. However, for the oralized *PSS,* which became popular among a larger readership and acquired the status of a Śāstra, an author with superhuman powers like Bhīmana would be preferable. All *śāstras* in Sanskrit were written by people who were known only from legends. One important point that needs to be noted here is that a real person called Bhīmana need not actually exist for a legend to be generated about him. Historical evidence one way or the other does not make any difference for those who believe that he existed. Legends of his birth and his superhuman powers make him the right kind of person to authorize a *śāstra*. Such an author allows for a consistency in legends about him and the possibility for him to live over many centuries.[41]

Nor was *SS* the only text attributed to Bhīmana to elevate the status of the text. A book on meter of unknown date, *Kavijanâśrayamu,* perhaps written by a certain Malliya Recana, is popularly known as Bhīmana's work. Appakavi clearly says *Kavijanāśrayamu* is Bhīmana's work. However, one of the manuscripts carries several prefatory verses where Bhīmana says that he wrote the book for Recana and made it look like Recana himself wrote it. Recana is said to be a Jaina that belongs to a merchant (*vaiśya*) caste. Scholars went to town with the problem of authorship, when Jayanti Ramayya Pantulu edited *Kavijanâśrayamu* and published it with his preface defending Bhīmana's authorship.[42] Other scholars that entered the debate and defended Recana's authorship include such famous names as Kandukuri Viresalingam and Arudra. The fact is that during pre-colonial times this work was consistently called *Bhīmana-chandamu,* the metrics of Bhīmana. Arudra picked up on the caste status of Recana and strongly argued that attributing the text to Bhīmana was a Brahmin conspiracy against merchant castes and Jainas. Now the debate included caste and religion in addition to nineteenth-century ideas of text and author. It would be more logical to argue that *Kavijanâśrayamu* needed an elevated status as the first infallible prescriptive book, i.e. a *śāstra* on meter and the name of Bhīmana provided such a status to the work.

I would imagine that the community of Niyogis, who initially made the *SS* their own, apparently found it very comforting to see that it had acquired such a high status, and they found no reason to interfere with Bhīmana's authorship, while they themselves believed the text was authored by Baddĕna. It is interesting to note that the verse that attributes authorship of the *SS* to Baddĕna is in a high literary style, whereas the verse that claims Bhīmana as the author has the features of the oral style, with filler words and segment breaks.

Conclusion

The *Sumati Śatakamu* has traveled a long way from *nīti* to morals. Most people in Andhra today do not even remember that the *SS* was a guide to *nīti*, as a policy for success for upper-caste men. The epistemological shift that colonial thinking has brought about was more or less thorough in this regard. *Nīti* in Telugu usage now only means morals.

I have tried here to demonstrate the effects of the epistemological shifts that colonial education brought about in the concepts of texts and authors in India. Using the *Sumati Śatakamu* as an example, I indicated that such Western ideas are unsuited to understand the nature of Indian texts. I have also suggested that legends about authors and texts cannot be dismissed as unhistorical, and that they are valuable sources to understand the nature of indigenous text-culture. During the past several decades, especially under the influence of the postmodern ideas of Foucault and Derrida, a new way of thinking has effectively dismantled most of the nineteenth- and early-twentieth-century concepts of texts and authors. Scholars have used postmodern ideas effectively to revise our understanding of Indian texts as well. I have tried to argue here that indigenous concepts of text and author in India are, in themselves, already very sophisticated and can be efficiently employed for a better understanding of Indian text-culture.

Notes

1. Sreenivas Paruchuri and V.S.T. Sayee found and made accessible in record time a number of printed texts of *Sumati Śatakamu* dating from the early decades of the twentieth century, as well as many obscure secondary sources. Macca Haridasu gave me a copy of his notes about the manuscripts of the *Sumati Śatakamu.* I am deeply grateful to them for their assistance. The manuscripts of the *SS* were inaccessible to me when I wrote this article. My conclusions should therefore be considered tentative and subject to revision after further research. Parts of this essay draw upon Narayana Rao and Subrahmanyam 2008: 25–65.

2. See my Afterword to Apparao 2007.
3. Subbarao 1976: 65–75.
4. The circumstances that led the *Pañcatantra* fables to be taught to schoolchildren are not clear. We, however, know that Cinnaya Suri, who worked as Telugu Headmaster in the Madras University, wrote these fables in a grammatically acceptable high-flown Telugu. He gave his book a title in English, *Neeti Chandrika or Moral Stories,* which he "Respectfully Dedicated as a Mark of Respect" to A.J. Arbuthnot, Esq., Secretary to the Madras University, and College of Fort Saint George. Virabhadra Rao 1986: 239–40.
5. Olivelle 1997.
6. Ryder 1962: 5.
7. See Sitarama Sastri 1916: 46–7. In their Preface, the publishers of this book say that they reprinted the 1847 edition free from the errors and alterations that crept into many of its reprints and published it exactly as it was in 1847 "with only minor changes."
8. Nidadavolu Venkata Rao, in his Preface to the *Sumati Śatakamu* (Venkata Rao 1966: 62), reports that the first edition of the *PSS* was published by Adisarasvati on April 20, 1868. Such precise information with the date and month of publication is an unusual piece of knowledge about any book in Telugu, more so about a book published almost a hundred years earlier, and Venkata Rao does not say how he acquired this information. The year of publication is repeated by Macca Haridasu in his *Tathyamu Sumati: Parisodhana Vyāsālu* (Haridasu 1984: 67) and Aruda in his *Samagra Āndhra Sāhityam* (Aruda 2002: vol. 1, 224.) I have not found the 1868 edition in any library, nor have I been able to ascertain from any scholar that this edition actually exists. I take the 1870 edition of the *PSS* to be its first edition, until the reported 1868 edition is located.
9. This book was actually compiled in 1920 by Kuchi Narasimham and Panuganti Lakshmi Narasimha Rao, even though the edition I have is dated 1930. I was not able to find any older elementary school readers, but it is possible that *SS* verses appeared in them as well.
10. Schoolbooks do not give their sources, but the verses included in them are identical with verses in the *PSS*.
11. *Sumati Śatakamu* 1922. Several editions of the *PSS*, from 1913 on, are spelled *Sumatī Śatakamu*, with /ī/, which is how the title the *PSS* is pronounced in popular Telugu. Scholars insistent on grammatically

correct Telugu, who probably edited the first edition of the *PSS*, spelled it with a short /i/.

12. During the early decades of the twentieth century a large number of books were written for schoolchildren teaching them *nīti* (morals). Over the years 1916–30, a cursory search yielded ninety-two books on *nīti* such as *Nīti Padyamulu* (moral verses), and *Nīti Kathalu* (moral tales), and so on. I thank Sreenivas Paruchuri for this information.
13. Arudra 2002: vol. 1, 227–8.
14. Haridasu 1954: 52–4.
15. Subbarao 1924.
16. Pāparāju 1970: 5.
17. For instance, see Gopalakrishna Rao 1976.
18. In several cases, only a small number of verses survived from which scholars inferred the rest of the *śataka*. It is hard to say if the author wrote only a few, or if only a few survived from a complete text.
19. Haridasu 1984 and Arudra 2002 inform us of ten manuscripts of the *SS*, each of which has a different number of verses, in the Oriental Manuscript Library in Madras. Haridasu reports another four manuscripts in the Saraswati Mahal Library at Tanjavur. An additional fifty verses are reported in the *Āndhra Sāhitya Pariṣat Patrika*, August–September 1938.
20. Brown wrote in his autobiography: "I never mixed with Hindu society, feasts or celebrations, and except those who worked with me I had few Hindu acquaintances. Indeed I was rarely visited by natives; and I was considered a deliberate enemy of the Hindu idolatry." Brown and Reddy 1978: 68–9. Peter Schmitthenner describes in some detail the problems Brown faced in acquiring Telugu manuscripts: Schmitthenner 2001: 94–100.
21. It is apparent that Brown assumed *nīti* meant morals, since he included the *SS* among texts that he thought were written "principally on morals." See Brown 1827: 9. But later he lost interest in the *SS* and concentrated on Vemana's verses, which were equally easy for him to read and appealed to him for their attack on Brāhmaṇas and practices of Hindu society. Schmitthenner 2001: 72–8.
22. Haridasu 1984: 67.
23. The prayer verse appears in *PSS* 1913, and the colophon verse appears in *PSS* 1962, though I think these verses must have been included much earlier.

24. The two are: *Bhāskara Śatakamu,* attributed to Mādayyagāri Vĕṅkanna in collaboration with his younger brother. Sarma 1987, and Venkatarayakavi 1982: 76–123.
25. Venkata Rao 1966: 64, suggests the influence of the Śaivite *Akṣarâṅka-gadya.* Kolavennu Malayavaisini (oral communication) suggests Jain influence; and *Sumati Śatakamu* 1962 suggests a Jain monk, Sumati, as a probable author of the *PSS.*
26. According to Arudra 2002, this colophon verse is in the palm-leaf manuscript of 1810 in the Oriental Manuscript Library at Madras.
27. http:/www.gutenberg.e.org/kam01/adyarṣumati/ This is palm-leaf manuscript no. 74882, placed on the internet probably by Michael Katten.
28. Brown collected every manuscript available to him without regard to the style of the verse and collated them all into the *BSS.* Therefore the *BSS* includes some verses which look like the *PSS* verses.
29. The metrics of *kandamu* are minimally presented here, leaving out details which are not relevant to this discussion.
30. Tikkana, *Srīmadāndhra-mahā-bhāratamu* 4.1.33.
31. New styles from a foreign, likely Persian, influence in the sixteenth century made sewn clothes popular among the upper castes in Andhra. Brahmin men, however, did not wear stitched clothes when they performed religious rituals.
32. Fisher's equation, used in the quantity theory of money is: MV = PT, where M represents the money supply, V represents the velocity of money, P represents the average price level, and T represents the volume of transactions in the economy.
33. This idea, presented all too briefly here, needs a longer essay, which I am writing.
34. Haridasu 1984 identifies this verse in manuscript No. 1810 from the Oriental Manuscript Library, Madras (now Chennai). Unconfirmed reports say that all Telugu manuscripts from this library were moved to the Oriental Manuscript Library, Tirupati.
35. See Narayana Rao and Subrahmanyam 2008: 26–65.
36. A good source for legends about Bhīmana is Seshayya 1959–71: vol. 1, 208–65.
37. Śrīnāthuḍu 1969.
38. Sūranna 1968: Pīṭhika, verse 11.
39. Appakavi 1962: Pīṭhika, 44.

40. Arudra identifies nine different Bhīmanas and complicates this matter even further.
41. The Telugu literary tradition speaks of at least one other invented person: Tenali Ramaliṅgaḍu, who is said to have been active in the court of Kṛṣṇadevaraya, the emperor of Vijayanagara, and about whom a number of stories are popularly told. For more about this poet, see Narayana Rao and Shulman 1998.
42. Nidadavolu Venkata Rao adds another wrinkle to the already tangled question of authorship of this text on metrics. Citing the fact that one of the many titles Badděna uses to refer to himself in his *Nīti-śāstra-muktâvali* is Komaru Bhīma, Venkata Rao argues that people may have called Badděna by his title Bhīma(na) when they identified him as the author of *Kavijanâśrayamu.* This argument does not explain why his particular title, among many titles of Badděna, came to be chosen. See Bhimakavi 1959.

References

Anantāmātyuḍu. 1962. *Bhojarājīyamu.* Madras: Vavil1a Ramaswamy Sastruluu & Sons.

Appakavi, Kākunūri. 1962. *Appakavīyamu.* Gidugu Ramamurti, Utpala Venkata Narasimhacharyulu, and Ravuri Dorasami Sarma, eds. Madras: Vavilla Ramaswamy Sastrulu & Sons.

Apparao, Gurajada. 2007. *Girls for Sale: Kanyāśulakam, A Play from Colonial India.* Translated from the Telugu by Velcheru Narayana Rao. Bloomington: Indiana University Press.

Aquil, Raziuddin and Partha Chatterjee. 2008. *History in the Vernacular.* Ranikhet: Permanent Black.

Arudra. 2002. *Samagra Āndhra Sāhityam.* 2002. 4 vols. Hyderabad: Telugu Akadami.

Badděna. 1962. *Nītisastramuktāvaḷi.* Ramakrishna Kavi, Manavalli, ed. Tanuku. Narendranatha Sahitya Mandali.

Bhīmakavi, Vemulavāḍa. 1959. *Kavijanāśrayamu* (1917). Jayanti Ramayya, ed. Kakinada: Andhra Sahitya Perishattu.

Brown, C.P. 1827. *Āndhragīrvāṇacchandamu: The Prosody of the Telugu and Sanskrit Languages Explained.* Madras: The College Press.

——— (ed. and trans.). 1973. *Sumati Śatakam.* C.R. Sarma, ed. Hyderabad: Andhra Pradesh Sahitya Akademi.

Brown, C.P. and G.N. Reddy, ed. 1978. *Literary Autobiography of C.P. Brown.* Tirupati: Sri Venkateswara University.

Gopalakrishna Rao, K. 1976. *Āndhra Śataka Sāhitya Vikāsamu.* Hyderabad: Published by the author.

Haridasu, Macca. 1984. *Tathaymu Sumatī: Pariśodhana Vyāsālu* (2002). Karimnagar: Indu Pracuranalu.

Narayana Rao, Velcheru and David Shulman. 1998. *A Poem at the Right Moment: Remembered Verses from Premodern South India.* Berkeley: University of California Press.

Narayana Rao, Velcheru and Sanjay Subrahmanyam. 2008. "History and Politics in the Vernacular: Reflections on Medieval and Early Modern South India," in Raziuddin Aquil and Partha Chatterjee, eds, *History in the Vernacular.* Ranikhet: Permanent Black.

Olivelle, Patrick (trans.). 1997. *Pañcatantra.* New York: Oxford University Press.

Pāparaju, Kaṅkaṇṭi. 1970. *Uttara Rāmāyaṇamu.* Madras: C.V. Krishna Book Depot.

Ryder, Arthur W., trans. 1962. *The Panchatantra* (1956). Chicago: University of Chicago Press.

Schmitthenner, Peter. 2001. *Telugu Resurgence: C.P. Brown and Cultural Consolidation in Nineteenth-century South India.* Delhi: Manohar.

Seshayya, Caganti. 1959–1971. *Āndhra Kavitaraṅgiṇi.* 14 vols. Kapilesvarapuramu: Hindu Dharmasastragranthanilayamu.

Sitārāma Śāstri, Pudūri. 1916. *Pĕddabālaśikṣa.* Madras: Vavilla Ramaswami Sastrulu & Sons.

Srīnāthudu. 1969. *Kāsīkhaṇḍamu.* Madras: Vavilla Ramaswami Sastrulu & Sons.

Subbarao, Vanguri. 1924. *Śataka Kavula Caritramu.* Narasapuram: Kamalkutir Press and Publishers.

Subbarao, Vennelakhanti. 1976. *The Life of Vennelacunty Soobarow (Native of Ongole) as Written by Himself* (1873). Sikindrabadu: Sri Bharati Pracuraṇalu.

Sumati Śatakamu. Madras: Adi Sarasvati Mudranalayamu, 1870.

Sumati Śatakamu. Ed. by Scholars. Kakinada: Karra Accayya, 1913.

Sumati Śatakamu. With a commentary by Gundu Raghava Diskshitulu. Bezawada: Marutiram and Company, 1922.

Sumati Śatakamu. Rajahmundri: Madeti Sanyasayya. 1923.

Sumati Śatakamu. Madras: Vavilla Ramaswami Sastrulu & Sons. 1962.

Sūranna, Piṅgali. 1968. *Rāghavapāṇḍavīyamu.* Madras: Vavilla Ramaswamy Sastrulu & Sons.

Venkata Krishna Sarma, Chennubhatla, ed. 1987. *Bhāskara Śatakamu.* Kurnool: Balasaraswati Book Depot.

Venkata Rao, Nidadavolu. 1966. *Śatakasampuṭamu,* Part I. Hyderabad: Andhra Pradesh Sahitya Akadami.

Veṅkaṭarāyakavi, Polipěddi. 1982. "Veṇugopala Śatakamu," in K. Gopalakrishna Rao, ed., *Adhikṣepa Śatakamulu.* Hyderabad: Andhra Pradesh Sahitya Akadami, pp. 76–123.

Virabhadra Rao, Kottapalli. 1986. *Tělugu Sāhityamupai Inglīshu Prabhāvamu.* 2nd revised edition. Secunderabad: Published by the author.

Viresalingam, Kandukuri. 2005. *Āndhra Kavula Caritramu.* Hyderabad: Visalandhra Publishing House.

6

When Does Sītā Cease to be Sītā?

Notes toward a Cultural Grammar of Indian Narratives

"Of all the *Rāmāyaṇas* that have been told so far, is there anyone in which Sītā does not go to the forest with Rāma?" asks Sītā when Rāma discourages her from following him to the forest in one of the versions A.K. Ramanujan reports.

Anachronistic and even postmodern as it might sound, this question raises the more general issue—when does Sītā cease to be Sītā? Clearly, Ramanujan's Sītā knows that she must go to the forest because every Sītā in every version of the *Rāmāyaṇa* goes to the forest. If Sītā does not go to the forest, she is not Sītā, nor is the story a *Rāmāyaṇa* story. My question in this essay is simple: How many changes in the narrative does a Sītā character comfortably accept and at what point does a change trigger another character that is no longer Sītā? To use a linguistic analogy, the phoneme /*p*/ in English is a cluster of features of a particular sound value within which you may vary, but by the time you shift from the feature of voiced to unvoiced, you are no longer saying /*p*/. Now it is /*b*/. Is there a similar boundary for the features that make up the "phoneme" Sītā in the "language" of the *Rāmāyaṇa*?

Using Vālmīki's text for *Sundarakāṇḍa,* and several versions of the events of *Uttarakāṇḍa*, where Sītā's personality is on full display, I discuss this question, drawing upon several non-Vālmīki versions of the *Rāmāyaṇa* and some more recent "anti-*Rāmāyaṇa*" texts to illustrate this point further. Making a broad classification of narratives based on a tripartite cultural ideology of land, trade, and pastoralism, I suggest that the Sītā in Vālmīki and Vālmīki-based texts is a heroine of a land narrative, in contrast to the heroines of the trade and pastoral narratives. In conclusion, I suggest that the prominence of Sītā as a role model of Indian womanhood is the result both of the political dominance of the landed ideology at the expense of the other two and of a recent impulse to imagine the *Rāmāyaṇa* as a national epic. I will begin with a reading of Sītā in Vālmīki.

Vālmīki's name, if not his actual narrative, provides the infallible basis for all *Rāmāyaṇa* texts. What I intend to do here is something unconventional: I want to suspend all the religious and devotional layers tradition has invested in Vālmīki's name, which transform his text into a sacred utterance. I want to read Vālmīki's text for its human drama. Since my intention is to discuss gender and power relations in *Rāmāyaṇa* narratives, I hope to be forgiven for this somewhat literalist project.

Sītā in *Sundarakāṇḍa*

Let us begin with Sītā as Vālmīki presents her in *Sundarakāṇḍa.* Vālmīki gives a woman extraordinary passive power as long as she stays within the limits of the house, trusts in the strength of her husband to save her from all troubles, and does not sleep with any other man. A chaste woman, a *pativratā,* has a social and moral power that she can manipulate to her advantage. This is what Sītā does more intelligently than *bhakti* readers of Vālmīki's text usually realize. *Sundarakāṇḍa* provides strong evidence of her manipulative skills.

In captivity Sītā is utterly helpless, with no apparent strategy to protect herself. Her total helplessness and her unshaken confidence in Rāma's ability to save her are the two inseparable qualities that endear her to her readers. In the face of death threats from the *rākṣasa* women who guard her, Sītā defiantly says she is ready for any physical suffering, including death, because life without her husband is worse than death.[1] She continues to reject the advances of Rāvaṇa, saying she would not touch such a despicable creature even with her left foot. Immediately after this, she goes into a soliloquy about Rāma's invincible strength. She wonders how this puny demon Rāvaṇa is able to imprison her while she has a mighty husband who can easily kill him in battle. However, she has one worry: perhaps Rāma has neglected her, forgotten her? Otherwise, why would he not come to save her? She consoles herself with the one comforting thought available to her: Rāma does not know that she is on this godforsaken island. To keep her sanity, she continues to remain confident that Rāma will come and save her. She imagines in graphic detail how totally and completely Rāma will destroy Laṅkā—and more particularly, how the women in Laṅkā will suffer widowhood when Rāma, along with Lakṣmaṇa, comes and kills their husbands in battle!

As is well known to every reader of *Sundarakāṇḍa*—in almost any telling—Hanumān offers to take her away from Laṅkā and solve the problem once and for all. Sītā can reunite with her husband, put an end to her own and everyone else's suffering, and the story can end happily ever after. The arguments that Sītā gives against this solution demonstrate her manipulative intelligence at its perfect pitch. First, she compliments Hanumān for his strength and agrees he is capable of rescuing her.

> I know your strength and courage.
> You are the greatest among monkeys.
> You have the speed of wind and the strength of fire
> astonishingly blended in you.[2]
>
> I know you are able to return home
> and take me with you, too.
> And the swift accomplishment of Rāma's mission
> is to be the goal in all our plans.[3]

Then a host of reasons follow why it would not be correct for Hanumān to rescue her. She could fall off Hanumān's shoulders and die. Or the demons could chase after Hanumān, and Hanumān could find the responsibility of protecting her an additional burden. Sītā could also fall out of fear, or even from an accidental push when Hanumān is involved in a fight. The demons would then get a second chance to imprison her, and this time they would hide her in a secret place, impossible for anyone, even Hanumān, to find. They might even kill her. And then Rāma, Lakṣmaṇa, even Sugrīva and Aṅgada would die of grief. The inclusion in this list of Sugrīva and Aṅgada—total strangers to her until Hanumān tells her of them—is clearly to discourage Hanumān from any further interest in pressing his offer. Finally, the last argument is the real clincher: Hanumān himself might be killed; after all, success or failure in battle is never sure.

At this point, Sītā realizes that she is probably humiliating Hanumān by so graphically depicting his defeat in this imaginary battle with the demons. She quickly corrects herself by adding that she knows Hanumān could kill all the demons and more. But then, if Hanumān takes care of all those who deserve to be killed, what is left for Rāma to do? Rāma's fame as an incomparable warrior would be deflated. Hanumān should not show off his strength now; it would be a disservice to Rāma.

Sītā then offers a final argument that cannot fail. She, as a *pativratā,* will not touch another man and for this reason she cannot sit on Hanumān's shoulder. She immediately remembers that the demon Rāvaṇa did actually touch her; he lifted her with his hands on her buttocks and placed her on his chariot when he took her away to Laṅkā. But she excuses herself this lapse because she was helpless. She was utterly weak, unprotected, and was not in a position to resist or fight with Rāvaṇa. Touching Rāvaṇa was not her doing, whereas touching Hanumān would be her choice, and therefore very compromising.

This argument makes Hanumān feel guilty for having suggested that he take her on his shoulders, and he offers an apologetic explanation. Sītā now concludes her presentation with a request: She wants Hanumān to persuade Rāma to come and save her. She is absolutely confident of the invincible power of Rāma:

> If Rāma kills Rāvaṇa, his family and his relatives,
> takes me in pride and returns home, that's an action that befits him.
> I know his strength and I have seen him fight.
> He is powerful, a killer in battle.
> Gods, demigods, dragons or demons—
> no one equals him if he decides to fight.

Who can stand up to him in an open battle?
He holds no ordinary bow.
In his strength he equals the king of the gods.
Coupled with his brother, Rāma is invincible.
He is like fire ablaze, quickened by wind.

He is like the burning sun at the end of the world.
He is like an elephant guarding space.
He is a killer in battle. Who can stand up to him
if he comes with his brother, swift as an arrow?

So bring him here and make me happy
with his army, his commanders and his powerful brother.
I grieve without him, alone in this island.
Great monkey, do this for me.[4]

What Sītā wants is to make Rāma destroy Rāvaṇa, his family, his entire clan, and the city. Not until then is she willing to leave Laṅkā. She is willing to extend her personal suffering until that moment, until Hanumān convinces Rāma to go to Laṅkā to battle with Rāvaṇa.

Sītā relates an incident from her life to Hanumān that only she and Rāma know of. This would serve as proof to Rāma that Hanumān did actually find Sītā herself. The story she chooses is carefully calculated to appeal to Rāma's male pride by reminding him how he was provoked to valor when someone tried to molest his wife. When a demon in the form of a crow attacked Sītā in the forest, tearing at her breasts, Rāma took a blade of grass and infused it with the power of *Brahmāstra,* the ultimate weapon of destruction, and sent it against the crow. Sītā concludes, addressing Rāma:

You know your weapons; they are the best.
You are strong and truthful, for certain, but
why not use these weapons on this demon.
if you really care for me? (36.36)

And why doesn't that brother of yours
take orders from you?
That scourge of his enemies doesn't help me.
What could the reason be? (36.39)

The two of you, strong as tigers
and equal to wind and fire.

Even gods can't face you, let alone demons.
Why are you so passive about me? (36.40)

You used the deadliest of your weapons
on a mere crow that hurt me.
Why do you then forgive the demon
who stole me away from you? (36.43)[5]

She continues her message to Rāma, complaining about his tardiness in rescuing her and questioning why his brother has not been helping him in this task. Sītā's competence as a skillful diplomat is not complete without her compliments to Lakṣmaṇa as part of her final message to the brothers. She praises Lakṣmaṇa's physical strength as a warrior with broad shoulders and long arms, and compliments him on his good heart. She acknowledges that Lakṣmaṇa respects his brother as a father and—what's more critical here—loves Sītā as his mother. She concludes by saying she is very fond of Lakṣmaṇa and knows he will skillfully complete any task given by his brother, no matter how difficult.[6] These words about Lakṣmaṇa appear on the surface to be good wishes sent by a sister-in-law to her brother-in-law. But they have a crucial significance for Lakṣmaṇa, who knows that Sītā had accused him of harboring a secret desire for her. Lakṣmaṇa had left Sītā alone against his brother's command precisely because of this terrible accusation. It was her adamant demand that Lakṣmaṇa leave her alone in the forest and go to help Rāma who had gone after the magic deer that precipitated matters in the first place and brought her to her present captivity. She remembers very poignantly that Lakṣmaṇa might feel justified in letting her suffer her fate for her willfulness and abusive temper. But now she needs Lakṣmaṇa's support to encourage his brother to invade Laṅkā. This message is carefully worded as a veiled apology for her past behavior and is a poignant appeal for help.

The Sītā of *Sundarakāṇḍa* is weak, unable to help herself, and by the very same token very skillful in prodding her man to become the hero he has to be in order to protect her. It is this Sītā that makes Rāma the warrior and punisher of demons. In other words, the hero we know Rāma to be is a male response to a weak and dependent Sītā, generated by the power relations in the gendered world of the Vālmīki *Rāmāyaṇa*.

Problematics of *Uttarakāṇḍa*

Now let us turn to *Uttarakāṇḍa,* the "later" *Rāmāyaṇa*, the more complicated part of the Rāma story that describes his abandoning the pregnant Sītā in the forest without even warning her. The details of the narrative are too well known to need repetition here. The narrative is beset with difficult and troubling events that have challenged the imagination of *Rāmāyaṇa* poets for ages. Some of them, such as Kampan in Tamil and Viswanatha Satyanarayana in Telugu, have even rejected the entire late *Rāmāyaṇa* as an interpolation and saved themselves the trouble of answering uncomfortable questions. If Vālmīki did not write it, it has no validity. The easiest way of devaluing a text is to divest it of its original source of authority, its author. But then there are great writers such as Kālidāsa, Bhavabhūti, and Diṅnāga who took the narrative and presented it in brilliantly creative ways, interpreting Vālmīki without apologies. I will begin with a close reading of Vālmīki's text to argue that the Rāma created by the first part of the *Rāmāyaṇa* is obligated, in the second part, to behave the way he does toward Sītā, and that Sītā has no choice other than to accept Rāma's decision.

In *Uttarakāṇḍa*, Rāma is happy that his wife is pregnant, that she is going to give him a child, and so he lovingly asks her what she desires and what he may do to please her. She requests to see the forests on the shore of the river Ganges where sages practice their austerities. She even wants to spend one night there eating roots and berries among the trees. Eager to satisfy the craving of his pregnant wife, her loving husband Rāma is willing to give that gift to her. "You will definitely go to the forest tomorrow," he says, "trust me."[7] Rāma spends time with his friends, who banter and joke with him, when he casually asks one of them, "What are people saying about me and my wife and my brothers?"[8] Evidently, the friends come from among the ordinary folk of the city and have access to people in all walks of life. The friend who was asked this question responds in the same friendly and intimate tone, "They say a lot of things about you, both good and bad (*śubhāśubham*)."[9] He describes how people praise Rāma for his extraordinary achievements, such as building a bridge across the ocean, something unheard of before, and killing the powerful demon Rāvaṇa, making friends with monkeys, bears, and even demons. They also say that Rāma has put his anger behind him, has brought Sītā back and taken her into his inner chamber. Now comes the criticism. His friend reports that people say:

> He [Rāma] must really love the sexual pleasure she gives to him (*sambhogajam sukham*). He is not disgusted that she sat in Rāvaṇa's lap when he dragged her to Laṅkā and later kept her in the Aśoka garden. That whole time she was under Rāvaṇa's control (*vaśam*). How could he take her back? From now on this behavior will be the law of the land because whatever the king does, the people also do (*yathā hi kurute rājā prajā tam anuvartate*). This is what people have been saying in the city and the countryside, all over.[10]

It is clear that Rāma does not suspect his wife himself, but feels he has to be a good king to his people, a role model for them all. Clearly, the conflict is between his personal feelings and kingly responsibilities. He discusses the matter with his brothers Lakṣmaṇa, Bharata, Śatrughna, and tells them with tears in his eyes the problem that he faces. He describes how this slandering of Sītā pains him. He reminds them that Sītā was born into a noble family and points out that Lakṣmaṇa witnessed the events in the forest when Sītā was taken by force. Then he confesses that he did have questions in his mind about bringing Sītā back to Ayodhyā. Would his people accept her? He describes how Sītā entered the fire to prove her chastity and how, while Lakṣmaṇa and everyone else was looking on, the god of fire and the god of wind both testified that Sītā was pure. Even the sun and the moon gave the same testimony to a group of gods and sages. Sītā was unblemished.[11] He agonizes. "I know in my own mind that Sītā is unblemished. But people still speak ill of her. The good name (*kīrti*) of the royal family is important."[12] He therefore decides that he has no alternative but to banish Sītā.

A question arises from his decision: Could he not convince the people by properly informing them and educating them? Apparently he could not, because it would be self-serving to speak in favor of his own wife. Anything he does to prove her chastity would be suspect. But, more important, the social norm that makes women responsible for showing evidence of their chastity and constantly suspects them is the very bedrock of this culture. It cannot be changed. It is this conviction that makes

Rāma choose to behave like the king he is in preference to the husband he is—at the expense of his and Sītā's personal feelings.

What is significant is that Sītā understands this too. She does not fight against the cultural values that cause this suspicion to begin with. She does not question the value of chastity. She is not even angry with Rāma for what he has done to her. She approves of his decision to discard her for fear of scandal and takes the responsibility upon herself to clear Rāma's name. She even rejects the idea of suicide because that would kill Rāma's children that she is carrying in her womb. If she blames anyone at all, she blames her own fate, the sins she may have committed in a past life. In effect, Sītā wants to continue to be a respected *pativratā* in this culture, and accepts all the pain and suffering that it brings, hoping that in the end she will be rewarded with the absolute approval of being a chaste wife.

Here Vālmīki enters the story to rescue Sītā. He does not suspect her because he has seen everything with his divine vision and therefore knows the truth. Toward the end of *Uttarakāṇḍa* we are reintroduced to the context that was first narrated in the beginning of the text, when Sītā's sons Kuśa and Lava sing the *Rāmāyaṇa* story as composed by Vālmīki to King Rāma. Realizing that Sītā is still alive and that Kuśa and Lava are none other than his sons, Rāma wants to know who is the author of the story and wants Sītā to be brought back to him. After being informed that Vālmīki, who incidentally is visiting the city, is the author, Rāma tells Vālmīki that he would accept Sītā back if she performs an act of truth (*śapatha*) to prove that she is chaste. By performing such an act of truth, Rāma hopes that her name will finally be cleared and with it his name as well (*śodhanârtham mamaiva ca*). Vālmīki approves of the idea and promises that Sītā will do as required. Rāma is happy that he will get his wife back because she will now have an occasion to prove her chastity in front of all the sages, citizens, and anybody else who wants to witness it. Sītā arrives with her head bent, walking behind Vālmīki. Putting his own reputation as a sage and the merit of all his austerities on the line, Vālmīki declares in the presence of everyone gathered that Sītā is pure, and that the twins are Rāma's sons. Sītā does perform an act of truth, asserting her absolute fidelity to Rāma, but not in a way Rāma would have expected, Sītā declares:

> I have never set my mind on any man other than Rāma, so may the goddess of the earth open up for me. I have served only Rāma in thought, word and deed, so may the goddess of the earth open up for me. If all that I have spoken is true, and if I do not know any man other than Rama, may the goddess of the earth open up for me.[13]

At that moment, the earth breaks open and a golden throne rises from below with the goddess Earth seated on it. The goddess invites Sītā into her lap, and the throne disappears into the underworld as gods rain flowers from the sky. An amazed Rāma realizes what has happened and gets angry at Earth for taking his wife away from him. He demands the goddess return his wife to him or else he will destroy the entire earth with its mountains, forests, and all. He wants her back badly (*matta*). He is even willing to go and live in the underworld or anywhere else as long as he can have Sītā back. Once the good name of Sītā is re-established to the satisfaction of his people, he is free to admit that he loves her and wants her back. But it is too late; Sītā is gone forever.

This is the most intriguing part of Vālmīki's text and one that is difficult to interpret definitively. Based on her behavior as an obedient and chaste wife, one would expect Sītā to ask Earth or some other god or goddess to clear her name for everyone to hear, so she could be taken back by her husband. In choosing to return to the earth, she has accomplished two things: she has proven her chastity and demonstrated her independence, as well. It is both a declaration of her integrity and a powerful indictment against a culture that suspects women. It is difficult not to interpret this as Sītā protesting against the way she was treated by her people and by her husband. She probably concluded that the people would never believe in her chastity, and Rāma would never be allowed to take her back with love and affection. The only course left for her was to leave the scene once and for all. Even with this, Sītā has not done anything that would compromise her status as a faithful wife. An expression of such independence is apparently acceptable as long as she has not touched another man.

Diṅnāga in his *Kundamālā* and Bhavabhūti in his *Uttararāmacarita* revisit the story of Sītā's abandonment in the forest. Apparently, there is something ideologically unacceptable and emotionally unsatisfying for them when Sītā demonstrates her independence in rejecting Rāma as well as the people, albeit within her bounds. Both playwrights have expressed an intense need to reunite Rāma and Sītā as husband and wife separated by a third, inevitable force, whatever that might be. Both Diṅnāga and Bhavabhūti repeat what we know from Vālmīki: that Rāma abandoned Sītā not because he suspects her but because the people in his kingdom suspect her. Lakṣmaṇa says to Sītā in the forest where he has taken her to be abandoned on his brother's orders: "The sages saw, as did the rulers of the world. Rāma himself was there and I watched too. You came out pure from the fire. The people still blame you and the people are beyond control (*loko niraṅkuśaḥ*)."[14]

Both Bhavabhūti and Diṅnāga take us through an elaborate and complex psychology, drawing a distinction between Rāma as a private person and Rāma as a player in the larger theater of the world. Both authors distinguish between being for oneself and being for others—the inevitable existential tragedy of a king's life. Diṅnāga does this with great sensitivity to Sītā. In his play, Sītā is intensely aware of the painful distinction between her role as a mother and carrier of the seed of the Raghu dynasty and her place in Rāma's heart as his beloved companion.

In a poignant scene, Vālmīki encounters the pregnant Sītā in the forest yet unaware of her identity. Vālmīki asks her if she has been exiled by King Rāma. When Sītā answers affirmatively, Vālmīki says: "If you are driven out by the king who is dedicated to establishing the rule of *varṇâśrama* social order, good luck to you, I am going (*yadi tvam varṇâśramavyavasthābhutena mahārājena nirvāsitâsi tat svasti bhavatyai gacchāmy aham*)." Sītā repeats her appeal for help—this time in a different tone: "If you cannot show compassion to me because Rāma threw me out, you should at least rescue me because I carry the seed of the family of Raghu, Dilīpa, Daśaratha and others in my womb." A curious Vālmīki asks if she is the daughter-in-law of Daśaratha and the daughter of Janaka. Sītā answers, "Yes." Vālmīki pursues further, "Are you then Sītā?" And Sītā says, "Not Sītā. I'm an unfortunate woman."[15]

It is very significant that Sītā disowns her own identity as Sītā when her faithfulness to Rāma is in question. She ceases to be Sītā when she is suspected of not being a faithful wife of Rāma. The distinction is important. Sītā as suspected wife has no status in this world. But as a mother she has all the power she would want to command, provided she uses it powerlessly, so to speak. She shows her personal anger against Rāma, but in a very controlled manner. When Lakṣmaṇa takes her to the forest to abandon her there on Rāma's orders, he asks if she has a message for Rāma. Sītā says: "If I am giving a message to that cruel man, it is because you asked and I can't say no to you. Tell him to take care of the kingdom and the rule of law, not to disregard his duties as a king worrying about me. Ask him to take care of his health." The sarcasm is obvious. Then she collects herself and asks Lakṣmaṇa: "Am I being too harsh to the king?" To which Lakṣmaṇa responds, "You have the right to be, don't you?"[16] Sītā is acutely aware of her public status as a wife when she says: "People always mention—when they talk about ideal couples—Śiva and Pārvatī in heaven, and Sītā and Rāma on earth."[17] Despite all her anger, she is aware of her place in Rāma's heart—and does understand the difference between Rāma's action in his kingly role and his feelings toward her as loving husband.

Even after convincing herself that Rāma abandoned her to save the kingship from being tarnished, in her own mind Sītā continues to doubt if Rāma really loves her. In her conversation with her sons in Vālmīki's hermitage, she always refers to Rāma as "that merciless man," *niranukrośa* (giving the impression to the boys that that is actually their father's name).[18] Sītā never expresses her doubts to anyone, even her intimate friends. The conversation between Vedavatī and Sītā illustrates Sītā's public posture. Vedavatī asks, "Why do you suffer for him? You are growing thin like the waning moon. He has no love for you. He doesn't want you back." Sītā immediately objects, and insists that Rāma loves her and has not really left her. He has only left her physically; not in his heart. She confidently says, "His heart is never far from me."[19]

The question still persists: *Loko niraṅkuśaḥ*, the people are beyond anyone's control. Neither Diṅnāga nor Bhavabhūti accept this as inevitable and refuse to live within the dictates of the people. They believe that people can be educated to examine the evidence and change their minds, and, unlike Vālmīki, both authors want Sītā to reunite with Rāma.

Both show in some detail that Rāma suffers for Sītā in her absence, as much as Sītā suffers the separation, clearly suggesting that he had to abandon her as king, but as husband her absence was unbearable for him. In the *Kundamālā*, the poet devises a strategy to make this happen. Through his ascetic power Vālmīki arranges it such that women become invisible to men when they walk around the river, so their freedom is not curtailed when Rāma and his retinue visit the hermitage on the invitation of the sage. This allows Sītā to walk invisibly close to Rāma, whom she can see but who in turn is unable to see her. Thus, an invisible Sītā overhears Rāma speaking to himself, expressing his feelings for her. A similar but more elaborate strategy is adopted by Bhavabhūti to let his audience know that Rāma has suffered quietly in agony because of Sītā's absence.[20] Clearly, both Diṅnāga and Bhavabhūti show that in order for her to return to Rāma, Sītā needs the personal reassurance that Rāma really loves her, just about as much as Rāma needs public testimony that Sītā has been faithful to him, so his people would be convinced of her chastity. There are incidents in both plays when Rāma is directly condemned by one of the characters; for instance, in *Kundamālā,* Vālmīki publicly rebukes Rāma for not respecting the testimony of Fire and for choosing to obey the slander of uneducated people. One wonders, listening to the harsh tone of the sage addressing Rāma, if Diṅnāga is condemning Rāma much like an anti-*Rāmāyaṇa* author of modern times. Listen to Vālmīki's words in the play:

> Hey King, you think of yourself as a kind-hearted man, a person of noble birth, wise and just. Is it proper for you to abandon your wife Sītā—a woman given by King Janaka, received by your father Daśaratha, recognized as auspicious by Arundhatī, declared chaste by sage Vālmīki, accepted as pure by Vibhāvasu, daughter of the goddess Earth, and mother of your sons, Kuśa and Lava—just because you happened to hear some people slander her?[21]

The interrogation continues, "After you killed the ten-headed antigod Rāvaṇa, when you took Sītā back, who vouched for her chastity?" Rāma meekly responds, "The god of Fire." Then Vālmīki asks, "What then made you disregard his testimony?" At this point, Sītā feels that she is to blame for the public condemnation her husband is being subjected to by Vālmīki. She covers her ears so as not to hear Vālmīki railing against her husband, calling him a dictator (*niraṅkuśa*). Soon the goddess Earth appears with great fanfare and declares to all assembled there that Sītā is chaste, totally above blame. The people accept this declaration with approval and celebration. Rāma accepts Sītā, acknowledging her chastity.[22] On closely reading this section of the play, we realize that Vālmīki's angry words are not really aimed at Rāma but at the people who are assembled there and who have slandered Sītā unjustly. This is the education that Diṅnāga believes the people in the story require, and which he provides through this incident. In the end, Rāma remains justified in his act of abandoning Sītā, as Sītā is honored in willingly going through the suffering without blaming Rāma.

To summarize, in the world of Vālmīki and his followers, women have to carry the seed of the family in its purity and therefore not only are they bound to be chaste, they also bear the responsibility of proving their chastity. A *pativratā* has to accept the burden of proof that she is a *pativratā.* In other words, she is guilty until proven innocent. Once the *pativratā* creates herself, she also creates her protector who by definition has to turn into her tormentor. If this man has to live up to what is expected of a *pativrtā* husband, he has no alternative except to abandon her when her *pātivratya* is suspected, giving her the opportunity to prove her innocence in public. In effect, Sītā creates Rāma, and Rāma creates Sītā. They mutually construct each other. You cannot have one without the other.

Sītā in Selected Non-Vālmīki Versions

Long before modern revisionist readings of the Rāma/Sītā relationship, there were several radical readings during the premodern period, some of which are well known, such as the Jaina versions of the *Rāmāyaṇa* and the version popularized by Kṛttivāsa in Bengal. Among them, the versions told by women in Telugu are quite striking. Telugu women's *Rāmāyaṇa* songs include a song entitled *Kuśalava-kuccala-kathā*.[23] In this story, Rāma's sons kill him without knowing who he is. The story begins when Rāma leaves a horse to roam the world unchecked as a part of the horse sacrifice he is performing, a ritual that allows him to declare himself king of the whole world. Anyone who objects to this declaration would have to stop the horse from crossing their land. Rāma would then fight and defeat them and get the horse released. If he fails to do so, he would lose the title of king of the world. When Lava and Kuśa notice the horse where they live, they catch it as an expression of their strength. The guards following the horse go and report to Rāma that two young boys have captured the horse. Rāma sends his army to fight the boys, but the boys defeat the army. Puzzled and bewildered, Rāma sends Lakṣmaṇa to take care of the problem, but the boys kill Lakṣmaṇa as well. Left with no other choice, Rāma himself goes to battle the boys. The boys kill Rāma too, and quietly go to tell their mother that they have killed a couple of men who were pretending to be the kings of the world. Sītā wonders who they could be and goes to the battlefield to discover the dead heroes are Rāma and Lakṣmaṇa. A saddened Sītā tells the boys they have killed their father and uncle, and runs to Vālmīki for help. Vālmīki recognizes the tragedy and with his spiritual power brings the dead heroes and their army back to life. Rāma realizes that the heroic boys are his own sons and that Sītā is still alive. He wants the boys and Sītā to be reunited with him, but the boys adamantly refuse and declare that Sītā is not going either. They demand that Rāma apologize for his treatment of Sītā and bow down to them seeking forgiveness. Sītā and Vālmīki, and all those gathered, advise the boys to show respect for their father, but the boys do not listen. They reject the advice even of Vālmīki because, after all, he wrote the *Rāmāyaṇa* favoring Rāma. The point of the story is clear. Sītā as a wife has no proper way of opposing her husband, whereas her sons can fight for her and can be as critical as necessary to condemn their father for all his faults while protecting their mother from being victimized. Sītā retains her status as a good wife by standing outside the conflict while her sons fight for her and say all the harsh words against Rāma—which Sītā may have wished to say herself but could not as a proper wife.

Another story that comes from women's songs and represents Sītā in a different light is "Śūrpanakhā's Revenge."[24] Śūrpaṇakhā, angry that her brother Rāvaṇa died at Rāma's hands, wants to avenge his death. She goes to Sītā dressed as a religious mendicant and asks her to draw Rāvaṇa's picture. Sītā protests that she has never set eyes on that man's face; she has only seen his toes. Sūrpanakhā persuades Sītā to draw a picture of Rāvaṇa's big toe. Sūrpanakhā then completes the picture herself and gives life to the picture. She leaves the picture in Sītā's possession and abruptly leaves. Sītā, who is stuck with the picture, tries to get rid of it by throwing it into the well behind her house, but the picture returns to her. She tries to destroy the picture, tear it, burn it, bury it. No matter what she does, the picture comes back to her. It just won't leave her. Desperate, Sītā hides the picture under her bed and lies on top of it. Rāma, who comes to bed at night, feels the pressure of the picture from under his side of the bed. Even before he begins to wonder what is pushing him, the picture pushes Rāma off the bed. Rāma is furious with Sītā for pushing him off, but when he sees the picture, he is firmly convinced that Sītā is in love with Rāvaṇa. This is the most innovative reason women's songs find for the banishment of Sītā to the forest. These songs mention neither the people's suspicion of Sītā's chastity due to her living in Rāvaṇa's Laṅkā nor the people's disapproval of Rāma's decision to accept her as his loyal wife. Such an emphasis on Rāma's suspicion of his wife rather than his sense of duty to his people clearly isolates Rāma as the person to be blamed. If the men's version saw Rāma as a tragic character, torn between his duties as king and his desires as a husband, this women's song views him as a suspicious husband and therefore a flawed man. Significantly, the song does not make any effort to hide the eroticism in the narration of the story. The big toe, the bed, lying right on top of Rāvaṇa's picture—the entire narrative texture of the song is quietly permeated with erotic suggestions that subvert the narrative structure, which ostensibly defends Sītā's *pātivratya.* The images of the story playfully suggest a hidden sexual desire on the part of Sītā for Rāvaṇa, which, very much like the hidden picture under the bed, is never out in the open. The traditional representations of Sītā are rarely erotic—we hear of her chastity, nobility, her suffering, and her motherly love, but we usually do not hear much about her sexuality. The erotic descriptions in this song are mild, too, and that is as far as the singers of the song can go, while carefully protecting Sītā's honor as a chaste wife. Anything more radical would cause Sītā to lose her status as a *pativratā,* and as I suggest, her identity as Sītā.

There is a tradition at weddings in Andhra whereby the family of the bride praises the virtues of their daughter while putting down the groom. This discourse, popularized in women's wedding songs, takes the *Rāmāyaṇa* theme as a metaphor. In these songs, Rāma is depicted as a hard-hearted, tricky, and deceptive husband, while Sītā is extolled as an innocent, trusting, and virtuous woman. During weddings, the bride's family often sings songs with this theme to celebrate the good qualities of the bride's family while playfully denigrating the negative qualities of the groom's family. The bride's family may even claim that whatever good fortune the groom has acquired is due to his luck in choosing their daughter as his wife. A popular song by Tyāgarāja uses this theme and suggests that Rāma would not have been so great a king, nor would he have been famous if he had not married Sītā:

> You chose our Sītā for your wife, and now you are king of kings
> And on top of that you have the fame of slaying the demon Rāvaṇa.
> Because you chose our Sītā for your wife
> She obediently followed you to the forest,
> took a false form, stayed by the fire for real,
> followed the demon, lived under the Aśoka tree in his garden.
> She was furious at his words, but did not kill him right away.
> She wanted *you* to get the fame of killing the mighty Rāvaṇa.
> Lord of Tyāgarāja,
> Because you chose our Sītā for your wife.[25]

Sītā in the Twentieth Century

The narrative changes even more radically in the hands of the authors of modern anti-*Rāmāyaṇas.* Gudipati Venkatachalam, popularly known as Chalam, is a great writer to whom Telugu literature owes a whole new language of sexuality, especially female sexuality. Among the several plays he wrote questioning religious/mythological narratives that preach female chastity, his *Sīta Agnipraveśam* (Sītā enters fire), is the best known.[26] The play presents Rāma and Sītā for the first time as human beings similar to us, rather than as distant and divine characters beyond ordinary human accessibility. They speak ordinary spoken Telugu as opposed to the Sanskritized high literary style of classical texts. Hearing Rāma and Sītā speak like man and wife, like our nextdoor neighbors, brings them into an emotional world we all inhabit. The play focuses on the events in Laṅkā immediately after Rāvaṇa's defeat and death. A rejoicing Sītā welcomes Rāma and invites him to embrace her, but Rāma expresses his unwillingness to accept Sītā because she has lived in another man's house for many years. Sītā responds sharply that it was not her choice; she was in captivity. Rāma argues that it does not make a difference, and that as a heroic descendant of the Raghu family he fought to protect his honor and destroyed Rāvaṇa; he cannot bring dishonor to it by accepting a woman who was touched by another man. Sītā protests:

> Let me speak. Ravana loved me. Even your sharp arrows could not kill his love for me. Your love, it was gone the moment you suspected that another man might have loved me . . . Did I love him in return? That's what you fear, don't you? If I had loved him, I would have covered his body with mine as a shield against your arrows. Did he molest me? No, he was too noble a person for that. He loved me, even when he knew I would never love him in return . . . I feel sorry I did not return his love. I shall pay the price for it now. I shall purify my body, which was soiled when I uttered your wretched name, by the flames of fire which touched his blood-stained limbs. You, Rama, reject me because you fear that my body was defiled by his touch, though you know my heart is pure. This antigod wanted my heart, even though he knew my body was taken by you. Some day, intelligent people will know who was a nobler lover.[27]

Sītā then throws herself into the funeral pyre burning Rāvaṇa's body instead of walking through the fire Rāma has set for her to prove her chastity. The passage could be interpreted in two ways: Sītā performs a type of *satī* by throwing herself into Rāvaṇa's funeral pyre, which simultaneously marks her as his wife in death. Or, she regrets not having loved Rāvaṇa in return and wants to purify herself of that flaw by throwing herself into his funeral pyre.[28] In either case, the limits clearly are crossed. This character is not the chaste wife of Rāma anymore. The story of the *Rāmāyaṇa* is stretched beyond recognition.

The following poem by the Telugu modern poet Pathabhi, a contemporary of Chalam, and a rebel in modern poetry, is in the same vein.

Sita was my classmate.
She and I pored over
that great new poem the *Ramayana*
of Satyanarayana.

When we were finished I asked her,
looking at her thoughtful eyes:

"You listened to the whole story.
We followed Rama
with the swiftness of poetry
into the wilderness of ancient time.
We met him, went to the forest with him; we saw him
kill Vali from behind the tree
and test his wife by fire.
Now tell me, do you really want to
live like Sita, the wife of the hero
Rama?"

When she heard me, she said:
"Hey, Pathabhi,
Sita is the very epitome of
Indian womanhood.
It's a dream, having
the good fortune
to live like her.

"But even if I should want to be Sita,
I would never want to be Rama's wife.
Tell me, would you ever want to be Rama
yourself?"

"Why would I, when you don't want
to be Rama's wife?
My desire, rather,
is to become Ravana.

"With all my ten mouths
I will kiss your lips, your face. I will bind you

with the gaze of my twenty eyes.
I will press you to my chest
with twenty strong arms
and make you one with me
in one embrace."

Now,
Sita is my wife.[29]

Breaking all notions about Sītā being forever devoted to Rāma, the poem introduces new nuances in the imagined relationship between Sītā and Rāvaṇa. Sītā, in this poem, wants to be like the Sītā of the *Rāmāyaṇa* because of the latter's honesty and love for her husband. But the husband she wants is not Rāma. And the man in the poem also vehemently rejects identifying with Rāma, and chooses to be Rāvaṇa instead, with all the erotic excitement that comes with that choice. Both characters in this poem reject Rāma and, in effect, reject Sītā too, and create a new Sītā outside the parameters of Vālmīki's narrative. The new Sītā says:

Sita is the very epitome of
Indian womanhood.
It's a dream, having
the good fortune
to live like her.

Clearly, she is choosing the good name of Sītā and the honor that comes with the status of a *pativratā.* She follows this with a rejection of Rāma, meaning that she only wants the honor and not the suffering that goes with this choice. By definition, Sītā is Rāma's wife. She has no existence without Rāma in Vālmīki's world. Once Rāma is rejected, there can be no Sītā. Therefore, the new Sītā who marries Rāvaṇa is not a *pativratā,* even assuming that she is faithful to Rāvaṇa.

Chalam and Pathabhi were writing at a time when a modernist trend in Telugu literature created an atmosphere of a critical rejection of religion and tradition. This trend was, however, limited to the English-educated middle class, which enjoyed a certain degree of latitude and therefore freely exercised its liberal ideas in literature. At present, a conservative and revivalist movement is growing strong, with a goal to reverse the trend started in the early decades of the twentieth century of modernist anti-*Rāmāyaṇas*.

In January 2000, *Andhra Jyoti,* a popular Telugu weekly magazine, received a long story, *Rāvaṇa Josyam* (Rāvaṇa's prophesy) by D.R. Indra, a relatively unknown writer, and the journal decided to publish it in three parts. The first part of the story apparently angered some people. The magazine received a letter that threatened dire consequences should it continue publishing the story. Namini Subramanyam Naidu, the editor of the weekly magazine, refused to be intimidated, and went ahead with the publication of the second part of the story. In response, nearly a hundred men and women, all self-proclaimed members of the Rashtriya Swayamsevak Sangh (RSS), forced their way into Namini's office on the afternoon of January 25, showered him with obscenities, rampaged through his office, and threatened him with physical harm. A staff member who came to his rescue was reported to have been physically assaulted. Cowed by the threats and vandalism, the editorial management of *Andhra Jyoti* withdrew the publication of the third part of the story, and published an apology for "unintentionally hurting (readers') sentiments."

I will not discuss the issues related to the freedom of the press and civil liberties that arise from this incident, which should be obvious and which in fact led to a wide-scale protest by intellectuals, poets, and writers against the perpetrators of this incident and against the magazine management, which had yielded to the pressure of conservative thugs. My interest here is to focus on the representation of Sītā and Rāma in the story. To summarize the relevant portion of the story:

> Sītā and Rāvaṇa take long strolls in the Aśoka garden. They enjoy talking to each other; Sītā admits that while she was rattled when she was first kidnapped, she does not find Rāvaṇa half as demonic as people say he is. She listens to him boast of how he has seduced or raped hundreds of the most beautiful women of the gods. But in the case of Sītā, he has fallen in love and will patiently wait until she herself loves him in return. Sītā rejects him and spurns his vanity, but she also realizes that Rāma is no better; he is just as vain, boastful, and cruel, and is as lustful a womanizer as Rāvaṇa is. She finds no great choice between them. The only benefit she finds in

her captivity is that ever since she has been brought to the Aśoka garden, she finds new freedom and peace—away from the pressures of the palace and the forest, released from the tensions of being a wife and the burden of having to be a *pativratā*. She finds this freedom to be herself more enjoyable than any glory or greatness in the world. Meanwhile, Rāma attacks Rāvaṇa. Mortally wounded in the battle, Rāvaṇa comes to Sītā with his last wish—to hear from Sītā's lips that she loves him. Sītā consoles him in her lap, and assures him that she loves him as her son. Rāvaṇa dies in her lap. Soon, Rāma arrives and expresses his suspicion of her chastity. Rāma asks her to prove herself by walking through fire. In front of her is a blazing fire ignited by Lakṣmaṇa for her to walk through to prove she is chaste. She approaches the fire, takes off her wedding necklace, *māngalya,* throws it into the fire and walks away.

A couple of decades ago, this story would probably have received critical acclaim from the modernist critics of the traditional *Rāmāyaṇa* narrative, and quiet disdain from the devotees of Rāma, as Chalam's play and Pathabhi's poem received in the 1930s. That it generated a more violent protest in 2000 is due to the activist nature of militant Hindu groups and the general deterioration of political discourse. The point, however, is clear. The Sītā represented in this story as well as in Chalam's play and in Pathabhi's poem is not the same character as is presented in Vālmīki's text and that of his followers. She is a distorted Sītā, an anti-Sītā. The crucial boundary that makes her Sītā is her loyalty to Rāma and the moral power that comes from it. Once she has crossed that boundary, even with the symbolic act of throwing her wedding necklace into the fire, she is no longer Sītā.

Why, then, have authors in the twentieth century deliberately changed the well-understood traits of a character so deeply embedded in the popular mind? Why do these authors feel the need to rewrite the *Rāmāyaṇa* by violating its narrative grammar? Part of the answer is in the obvious modernist artistic impulse of reworking classical themes with individual imagination unfettered by conventions. The answer to these questions perhaps also lies in the unprecedented importance the *Rāmāyaṇa* has received in the nationalistic imagination. The Gandhian use of *Rāmāyaṇa* metaphors such as Ramrajya for the ideal of independent India and the nationalist fervor of presenting Indian women as the symbol of purity and passive resistance, suffering for a noble cause, presented Sītā as the supreme role model for all Indian womanhood. Due to its vast popularity, the *Rāmāyaṇa* is mistaken for an epic that represents the entire range of value systems in India. An attempt to make the *Rāmāyaṇa* and its heroine Sītā stand for a variety of cultural role models apparently has not led to a uniformity of national values; on the contrary, it has led to a masking of complexity. We now have a superficial uniformity that hides the contours of this complexity. Sītā now appears in a variety of roles not available to her as the heroine of Vālmīki's text. In effect, a number of heroines are now called Sītā, while retaining at the same time the special features the heroines portray in the narratives of their particular culture. This, I would believe, partly explains the multiplicity of *Rāmāyaṇa* narratives that differ from the Vālmīki narrative among the modern *Rāmāyaṇa*s and the variety of comments on the role of Rāma and Sītā, such as the ones we encounter in Madhu Kishwar's study.[30]

An Ecology of Indian Narratives

This would lead us into a survey of the types of heroines in Indian narratives, a task too big to attempt in the space of this essay. I would still ask if there are compelling and significant representations of women other than Sītā, depicted positively in literature. At the expense of being simplistic, I want to place the major Sanskrit narratives in the context of the broad cultural systems of India: agricultural, pastoral, and mercantile. In this classification, the *Rāmāyaṇa* belongs to the agricultural, the *Mahābhārata* to the pastoral, and the narratives of the *kathā* tradition to the mercantile cultures. I would suggest that each of these narratives reflects distinctly different types of value systems and different types of heroes and heroines.

Land is significantly different from other forms of property that are movable, such as gold, material goods, or marketable skills. In times of crisis, other kinds of property can be taken to a safer place. Land is immobile; you cannot put it in your pocket and walk away with it. The only way of protecting it is to fight for it. A hero in this value system is one who fights to protect the land and dies fighting. He does not negotiate a settlement, a compromise, or a politically acceptable deal; he wants all or nothing. Castes that primarily share in the landed culture equate women with their land; own them as they own their land; restrict their movements; control their sexuality; and deny them remarriage. Loyalty to one man (*pātivratya*), which is generally perceived as a value for all women in India, is primarily a landed-caste value. Landed culture values certain qualities in men, such as the willingness to protect their women. A woman herself is not allowed to fight for her own safety. She should wail for her man to save her. Indian history, literature, and folklore relating to the landed castes are littered with stories of women who die voluntarily when their men are unable to save them. Death is preferable to falling into the hands of the enemy. A woman who falls into captivity is considered truly "fallen." A permanent stigma attaches to her character because people assume she may, either willingly or by force, have had sexual relations with her captor. The biological and therefore uncontrollable condition of life that women become pregnant and give birth to children makes them vulnerable to conquest, just like the land, and for that reason it makes their constancy a matter of anxiety and suspicion. Chaste women are given miraculous powers in legends and myths: men who threaten their chastity can be cursed to death by chaste women. The same women, however, cannot curse men who threaten their lives. Chastity for a woman in this culture is more important than life itself. In the culture of the landed, the inheritance of land is strictly limited to the authentic male heirs of the owner, and the legitimacy of children is assured only by strictly controlling women's sexuality. As might be seen in Diṅnāga's narrative, Rāma declares his son Lava king as soon as it is made publicly clear that Sītā is chaste. The *Rāmāyaṇa* is a narrative that reflects the ideals and cultural ideologies of landed communities, but not all Indian communities.

Communities that live on trade and manufacturing skills, on the other hand, are not tied to the land and are generally mobile. People with such skills are capable of migration and of finding themselves a new livelihood in a new place. Manufacturing is also very different from growing food. Craftsmen create a new reality different from the reality of nature. Food growers, who have a sense of dependence on nature to produce their world, often marvel at the skill of the "makers." At the same time, they are also suspicious of their craft, which they see as crafty, untrustworthy. The stories and epics of trading communities stand in sharp contrast to landed-caste stories. In Sanskrit there is a huge body of *kathā* literature, from the legendary *Bṛhat-kathā-śloka-saṁgraha.* The hundreds of such stories, generally interpreted as collections of erotic stories, reflect the cultural ideology of mercantile communities.

Women in these stories are intelligent, capable of protecting themselves, and can control their lives without total dependence on their men. They are clever, cunning, and are celebrated not so much for their chastity as for their skill in having affairs without being caught. The theme of the clever adulteress in the narratives of the *kathā* tradition, such as *Śuka-saptatī,* is too well known to need repetition. The ideal woman in this culture is the heroine of "The Red Lotus of Chastity," who cleverly protects herself from the mischievous advances of men in the absence of her husband while at the same time safeguarding her husband from the allure of other women. Chastity and fidelity to the husband are still important for a woman in this culture, but she is not bound to depend on her husband to save her; nor is she bound to prove that she is a *pativratā.* The heroine in this story takes the initiative, plans her future, and manages to achieve a triumphant end for her plans. Furthermore, heroes in the narratives of the mercantile classes use cunning and trickery to achieve their goal—as against the heroes in the narratives of landed culture, for whom battle is the first choice. Heroism in the narratives of mercantile classes consists of gaining success and living happily afterward, rather than a foolhardy rush into battle and death in order to gain *vīrasvarga*—the hero's heaven. A mercantile hero is intelligent, just, and capable of judiciously resolving conflicts, as is King Vikramāṅka in the *Vetāla-pañcaviṁśati* stories.[31]

A similar value system is found in the literatures of other Indian languages, which have a number of epic narratives that reflect the values of pastoral culture. Pastoral communities have a functional interest in land, which they need to graze their cattle. They do seek to control the land, but do not care who actually owns it. Pastoral stories celebrate heroism but do not value death on the battlefield as superior to success in gaining power over the enemy by cunning. The heroes and heroines of pastoral epics reflect characteristics very different from the epics of the landowning class. To represent the *Mahābhārata* as a pastoral epic would drastically reduce its complexity, but it should be clear that none of the women in the *Mahābhārata* resembles Sītā in her relentless pursuit of fidelity to and dependence on her husband. Apart from the well-known Draupadī, who has five husbands and is an extremely strong woman who takes control of any situation she is in, women such as Damayantī and Sāvitrī demonstrate a characteristic agency, an ability to take the initiative to resolve a problem rather than wait for their husbands to come and save them. They are no less *pativratās* for the strength and independence they demonstrate, but they are not Sītā. It is easier to see the features of a pastoral culture in oral epics such as *Cāndāinī, Devnārāyan*, and *Kāṭamarāju kathā*.[32]

Since landed culture is socially dominant to the extent of projecting itself as the only culture of the country, non-landed values get short shrift as low castes are treated as less respectable. Modern scholars tend to class these narratives as folklore, while in the Sanskrit literary tradition themes borrowed from the *Kathā-sarit-sāgara* do not have the same high status as those borrowed from the *itihāsa.* Pressured by the dominant landed culture, non-landed communities tend to borrow cultural practices from landed communities in order to present themselves as respectable. In South India, a large number of castes of non-landed cultures are classified as left-hand castes, among whom women follow a lifestyle more relaxed than the landed culture would sanction. Women of these communities remarry and maintain a certain degree of economic and personal independence. Such groups tend to be socially invisible, and their stories and cultural traditions are lost to scholarship.[33]

One significant feature of Indian narrative is retelling. Stories and themes from major narrative traditions have been told—again and again—for centuries. As a result, characters of these narratives take on a life of their own, away from authorial controls and become as familiar as your next-door neighbors. Poets and writers and tellers and performers enjoy a wide degree of freedom in depicting these well-known characters. At the same time, there are restrictions to this freedom. We know a lot about the variations in the telling of these stories, and the freedom the tellers take. What is not well understood is that there are limits to this freedom. The limits, I suggest, are best understood by exploring the underlying cultural grammar of these narrative traditions.

Notes

1. *bhidyatām bhakṣyatām vāpi śarīram visṛjāmyaham /*
na câpyaham ciram duḥkham sahyeyam priyavarjitā //
caraṇenāpi savyena na spṛseyam niśācaram /
rāvaṇam kiṃ punar aham kāmayeyam vigarhitam //
chinnā bhinnā vibhaktā vā dīptevagnau pradīpitā /
rāvaṇam nôpatiṣṭeyam kiṃ pralāpena vaś ciram //
(*Sundarakāṇḍa*, 24.8.9.11)
2. *tato nihatanāthānāṃ rākṣasīnāṃ gṛhe gṛhe /*
yathâhamevaṃ rudatī tathā bhuyo na saṃśayaḥ /
anviṣya rakṣasām laṅkām kuryād rāmaḥ salakṣmaṇaḥ /
anviṣya rakṣasām laṅkām kuryād rāmaḥ salakṣmaṇaḥ //
(Ibid., 24.23)
3. *tava sattvaṃ balaṃcaiva vijāmi mahākape /*
vāyoriva gatimapi tejaścâgnerivâdbhutam // (Ibid., 35.42)
jānāmi gamane śaktiṃ nayane câpi te mama /
avaśyaṃ sampradharyāśu kāryasiddhir ihâtmanaḥ //
(Ibid., 35.42.44)
4. Ibid., 35.64–8.
5. *Sundarakāṇḍa,* 36.36, 39, 40, 43.
6. Ibid., 36.45–6, 48.
7. *Uttarakāṇḍa*, 41.26.
8. Ibid., 42.4–6.
9. Ibid., 42.13.
10. Ibid., 42.17–19.
11. Ibid., 44.5–9.
12. Ibid., 44 .11–12.
13. Ibid., 88.10.
14. *Kundamālā,* Act 1.
15. Ibid., Act 2.
16. Ibid., Act 1.

17. Ibid., Act 2.
18. Ibid., Act 5.
19. Ibid., Act 2.
20. Bhavabhūti, *Uttarāmacarita,* Act 7. Bhavabhūti devises a play produced by Vālmīki within the play. Vālmīki invites all gods, antigods, animals, serpents, and all classes of human beings to his play, which presents Sītā's story following her abandonment, as follows. A distressed Sītā tries to kill herself by drowning in the Ganges river. The goddesses Gaṅgā and Earth dramatically rescue her and present her with the twins she has given birth to in the water. Following their birth, the Jṛmbhaka weapons manifest themselves to serve the boys. Earlier, when Sītā was pregnant and was still with Rāma in Ayodhyā, Rāma had declared that these weapons would one day belong to his sons. True to his utterance, the weapons promptly appear upon their birth. This act serves as a divine DNA test which proves that the twins are Rāma's legitimate sons. Toward the end of the play, Arundhatī testifies to the purity of Sītā in front of all the people assembled, and ṭhus Rāma and Sītā are reunited.
21. *Kundamālā,* Act 6.
22. Ibid.
23. See Gopalakrishnamurti 1955, pp. 256–62. I discussed this story in my essay "*Rāmāyaṇa* of Their Own: Women's Oral Tradition in Telugu" (1991). Here I extensively adapt that discussion.
24. Narayana Rao 1991, pp. 126, 130. See chapter 7 in this volume.
25. Tyāgarāja, *Mā jānaki cețța bațțaga mahrājuvaitivi*, Rāga Kāmbhoji, *Ādi tāla.* Madhu Kishwar argues in "Yes to Sita. No to Ram" (2001) that people believe Rāma was wrong to abandon Sītā in the forest while she was pregnant, whereas Sītā lived up to the expectations of Indian womanhood, suffering silently without saying one harsh word against Rāma. She presents evidence from her fieldwork among a number of people from different classes, castes, and occupations in favor of this position. But the value system of the *Rāmāyaṇa* is not that simple.
26. Venkata, Chalam (1934J 1976).
27. Ibid. Following Telugu usage, diacritical marks have been omitted. The discussion here is adopted from my essay "The Politics of Telugu *Rāmāyaṇas*" (2001).
28. I am indebted to Paula Richman for this interpretation.

29. Pathabhi 2002.
30. See note 25.
31. J.A.B. van Buitenen drew attention to these stories as early as 1959 in his introduction to *Tales of Ancient India*. See chapter 8 in this volume.
32. For summaries of these epics, see Blackburn, *et al.* 1989, and for a study of the Cāndānī epic, see Flueckiger 1989.
33. See my "Tricking the Goddess" (1989), and "Epics and Ideologies (1986), where I discuss the narratives of left-hand castes.

References

Bhavabhūti. 1990. *Uttararāmacarita.* Edited by R.S. Tripathi. Varanasi: Krishnadas Academy.

Blackburn, Stuart, *et al.* 1989. *Oral Epics in India.* Berkeley and Los Angeles: University of California Press.

Diṅnāga. 1983. *Kundamālā.* Edited by Jagdish Lal Shastri. Delhi: Motilal Banarsidass.

Flueckiger, Joyce Burkhalter. 1989. "Caste and Regional Variants in an Oral Epic Tradition." In *Oral Epics in India,* ed. Stuart Blackburn, *et al.* Berkeley and Los Angeles: University of California Press.

Gopalakrishnamurti, Sripada ("Krishna Sri), ed. 1955. *Strīla Rāmāyaṇapu Pātalu.* Hyderabad: Andhra Sarsvata Parishartu.

Kishwar, Madhu. 2001. "Yes to Sita, No to Ram." In *Questioning Rāmāyaṇas: A South Asian Tradition,* ed. Paula Richman. Berkeley and Los Angeles: University of California Press.

Narayana Rao, Velcheru. 1986. "Epics and Ideologies: Six Telugu Folk Epics." In *Another Harmony: New Essays in the Folklore of India,* ed. Stuart Blackburn, *et al.* Berkeley and Los Angeles: University of California Press.

———. 1989. "Tricking the Goddess: Cowherd Katamaraju and Goddess Ganga in the Telugu Folk Epic." In *Criminal Gods and Demon Devotees: Essays on the Guardians of Popular Hinduism,* ed. Alf Hiltebeitel. Albany: State University of New York Press.

———. 1991. "A *Rāmāyaṇa* of Their Own: Women's Oral Tradition in Telugu." In *Many Ramayanas: The Diversity of a Narrative Tradition* in *South Asia,* ed. Paula Richman. Berkeley and Los Angeles: University of Califomia Press.

———. 2001. "The Politics of Telugu *Rāmāyaṇas:* Colonialism, Print Culture, and Literary Movements." In *Questioning Rāmāyaṇas: A South Asian Tradition,* ed. Paula Richman. Berkeley and Los Angeles: University of California Press.

Pathabhi. 2002. "Sita." In *Twentieth Century Telugu Poetry: An Anthology,* ed. Velcheru Narayana Rao. Delhi: Oxford University Press.

Richman, Paula, ed. 1991. *Many Ramayanas: The Diversity of a Narrative Tradition in South Asia.* Berkeley and Los Angeles: University of California Press.

———. 2001. *Questioning Rāmāyaṇas: A South Asian Tradition.* Berkeley and Los Angeles: University of California Press.

Vālmīki Rāmāyaṇa. 1960. Ed. J.M. Mehta, *et al.* Baroda: Oriental Institute.

Van Buitenen, J.A.B. 1959. *Tales of Ancient India.* Chicago: University of Chicago Press.

Venkata Chalam, Gudipati. 1976. *Sīta Agnipraveśam.* 3rd ed. Vijayawada: Aruna Publishing House.

7

A *Rāmāyaṇa* of Their Own

Women's Oral Tradition in Telugu

As a boy growing up in a Brahmin family in the northeastern district of Srikakulam in Andhra Pradesh, I used to hear my mother humming in the mornings:

leve sītammā māyammā muddulagumma leve bangāru bŏmma leve
leci rāmuni lepave vegamu leḍikannuladāna leve
tĕllavāravaccĕnū

Wake up Sīta, my mother, my dear, you are my golden doll
Wake up yourself and wake up Rāma, you have the eyes of a doe
It is morning!

She had a notebook in which she had written down a number of songs, many of them on the *Rāmāyaṇa* theme, which she would sing on occasions when women gathered at our house. The notebook my mother carried is lost now, but those songs and many others like them are still sung by women in Andhra Pradesh. They tell a *Rāmāyaṇa* story very different from the familiar one attributed to Vālmīki.[1]

The *Rāmāyaṇa* in India is not just a story with a variety of retellings; it is a language with which a host of statements may be made. Women in Andhra Pradesh have long used this language to say what they wish to say as women.[2] I shall discuss two separate groups of songs, those sung by upper-caste Brahmin women and those sung by lower-caste women, although my major focus will be on the former. I shall demonstrate that while the two groups of songs represent a distinctly female way of using the *Rāmāyaṇa* to subvert authority, they are still very different from each other, both in the narratives they use and in the specific authority they seek to subvert.

Some Background

While upper-caste men in Andhra associate the *Rāmāyaṇa* with the Sanskrit text attributed to the legendary Vālmīki, Andhra Brahmin women do not view Vālmīki as authoritative. Vālmīki appears in their songs as a person who was involved in the events of Sītā and Rāma's lives and who composed an account of those events—but not necessarily the correct account. Like most of the participants in the tradition, these women believe the *Rāmāyaṇa* to be fact and not fiction, and its many different versions are precisely in keeping with this belief. Contrary to the usual opinion, it is fiction that has only one version; a factual event will inevitably have various versions, depending on the attitude, point of view, intent, and social position of the teller.

The events of the *Rāmāyaṇa* are contained in separate songs, some long and some short. These are sung at private gatherings, usually in the backyards of Brahmin households or by small groups of older women singing for themselves while doing household chores. Altogether, about twenty-five of them are especially popular, which together constitute a fairly connected story of the epic.[3] Most of these songs, especially the longer ones, are also available in printed "sidewalk" editions, although the oral versions vary in small details from the printed versions.[4]

Since it is difficult for a man to be present at women's events, I could not record all the songs myself. With the help of two female colleagues, however—Kolavennu Malayavasini of Andhra University, Waltair, and Anipindi Jaya Prabha of the University of Wisconsin-Madison, both of whom are Brahmins—I was able to acquire a number of *Rāmāyaṇa* songs on tape. The few songs I was able to record were sung by Malayavasini and Jaya Prabha, who demonstrated singing styles to me while reading the words from a printed book. My information about the context of singing, the singers, and their audience comes partly from my childhood experience and partly from Malayavasini and Jaya Prabha.

Brahmins are perhaps the most widely studied community in India, with the result that South Asian anthropological literature offers considerable ethnographic information about Brahmins in general. However, the Brahmins of Andhra Pradesh have not been that well studied, and, in particular, little is known about the Brahmin women of Andhra. Unfortunately, the following brief sketch cannot be a full ethnographic study of Brahmin women, but it will at least provide the background for my conclusions here.

Brahmins (Telugu: *brāhmaṇulu* or, more colloquially, *brāmmalu*) is a cover word indicating a cluster of endogamous groups in Andhra. These groups have independent names,[5] but in terms of the fourfold hierarchical order of Hindu society they are all placed in the highest category, namely, the *brāhmaṇa.* Vegetarian and considered ritually pure by virtue of their birth, Brahmins have held the highest level of social respect in Hindu society for centuries. Brahmin families have a very high percentage of literacy, and the men have traditionally been scholars, poets, and preservers of learning both religious and worldly. Brahmins have thus set the standards of Sanskritic culture, and their dialect is considered correct speech. Other castes imitate this dialect in order to be recognized as educated.

In Andhra, women of Brahmin families are segregated from men, though they are not veiled— as are women of North India; nor are they kept from appearing before men in public, as are women of the landed castes. But they are encouraged to live a sheltered life. In premodern Andhra, before the social-reform movements and legislation of the late-nineteenth and early-twentieth centuries, Brahmin girls were married before puberty to a bridegroom arranged by their parents. He was often much older than the bride, and the Brahmin wife was not allowed to remarry if her husband died. Even today widows are considered inauspicious and undesirable; they cannot, for instance, bless young brides at weddings. They are also denied access to ornaments, colored clothes, bangles, turmeric, and the red dot on the forehead, which are symbols of auspiciousness. In some families, especially those belonging to the Vaidiki subdivision of the caste, widows have to shave their heads. However, older widows are respected for their age, especially if they have raised a family, and the younger women look up to them for guidance and help. They are repositories of caste lore and often good at singing songs. Auspicious women, in contrast to widows, are treated with affection. They are looked upon by their men as sources of family prosperity, and their rituals are considered sacred and valuable. Men are expected to facilitate such rituals by staying away from them but providing all the necessary resources. Until recently, a woman was not allowed to own property, except gold given to her as a gift by her parents or husband.

Proper behavior on the part of a wife requires that she obey her husband and parents-in-law, as well as her husband's older brothers and older sisters. Any disobedience is severely punished, and defiant women are disciplined, often by the mother-in-law. In a conflict between mother and wife, the son is expected to take his mother's side and punish his wife. In fact, a man is often ridiculed as effeminate if he does not discipline his wife into obedience. Female sexuality is severely repressed; a proper Brahmin woman has sex only to bear children, who should preferably be male. The pursuit of sexual pleasure is offensive to good taste, and a woman is severely punished for any deviance in word or deed. Women should be modest; an interest in personal appearance or a desire to be recognized for physical beauty is discouraged. Women should not even look into a mirror except to make sure that they have placed their forehead dot correctly. According to a belief popular in Brahmin families, a woman who looks into a mirror after dusk will be reborn as a prostitute. However, women often guide their husbands from behind the scenes in decisions that have a bearing on family wealth and female security, which suggests that this code of obedience, if creatively manipulated, can be a source of power.

Brahmin women who sing the *Rāmāyaṇa* songs discussed in this essay generally come from families relatively less exposed to English education and urbanized styles of life, in which singing such songs is going out of fashion. They are literate in Telugu, but most of them are not formally educated. Their audience consists of women from similar backgrounds, usually relatives and neighbors, and may also include children, unmarried young women, or newly married brides visiting their mother's house for a festival. Often a marriage or similar event provides the occasion for a number of women to gather. The audience does not generally include women of other castes. While adult men are not supposed to be present at such gatherings, young boys stick around. Nonetheless, men do hear these songs, or more precisely overhear them, even though they tend to pay no attention to them, as it is "women's stuff," not worth their time.

Not every singer knows all of the approximately twenty-five popular *Rāmāyaṇa* songs. There is a general recognition, however, that a certain person knows the songs; such a person is often called upon to sing. Some singers have learnt certain songs well, but when a singer does not know a song adequately, she uses a notebook in which she has recorded the text. Singers do not need special training, nor do they consider themselves experts. No musical instruments accompany the singing of these songs, and the tunes are simple, often monotonous. At least one song has refrains, *govindā* at the end of one line and *govindā rāma* at the end of every other line, suggesting that it may be used as a work song.[6] Some of these songs only take about twenty minutes to half an hour to sing, but others are very long, taking several hours to sing.[7]

The precise age of the *Rāmāyaṇa* songs is not easy to determine. While they are accepted as traditional, and therefore must be fairly old, there is no reliable way of dating them since oral tradition has a tendency to renew the diction while keeping the structure intact. It is also difficult to determine to what extent the songs are truly oral compositions. All are orally performed, but at least some were written by a single individual. Several songs contain a statement of *phalaśruti* (the merit which accrues from listening to the song), some of which include the author's name, and a few even mention an author in the colophon.[8] That the singers as well as the authors of the songs are acquainted with literary texts is beyond doubt: many songs have references to writing and written texts. However, the singing styles are passed down from person to person, and the performance is often from memory—though, as we noted, a singer does not mind also using a book. In short, we do not know whether these songs were composed orally and then preserved in writing, or were originally written compositions.

Nearly every scholar who has studied these songs has either assumed or concluded that their authors were men. Only Gopalakrishnamurti has suggested that many of these songs were composed by women, and I am convinced he is right.[9] Judging from the feelings, perceptions, cultural information, and the general attitudes revealed in the songs, it seems likely that all of them—except one minor song, a waking-up song for Sītā, which happens to mention a male author—were women's works. Certainly, the songs are intended for women: many of the songs mention the merit women receive from singing or listening to them.

Even a cursory look at the subject matter of the songs indicates that female interests predominate among the themes. Together they comprise a very different *Rāmāyaṇa* than that told by Vālmīki or other poets of literary versions.

1. *Rāmāyaṇa* in summary, narrated with Śāntā (Rāma's elder sister) as the central character
2. Kausalyā's pregnancy, describing her morning sickness
3. Rāma's birth
4. A lullaby to Rāma
5. Bathing the child Rāma
6. Sītā's wedding
7. Entrusting the bride Sītā to the care of her parents-in-law
8. Sītā's journey to her mother-in-law's house
9. Sītā's puberty
10. Several songs describing the games Rāma and Sītā played
11. Sītā locked out
12. Sītā's describing her life with Rāma to Hanumān in Lanka
13. Incidents in Lanka
14. Sītā's fire ordeal
15. Rāma's coronation
16. Urmilā's sleep
17. Sītā's pregnancy
18. The story of Lava and Kuśa, Sītā's twin sons
19. Lava and Kuśa's battle with Rāma
20. Lakṣmaṇa's laugh
21. Śūrpaṇakhā's revenge

Significantly, these songs do not mention many of the familiar *Rāmāyaṇa* events—Daśaratha's glory, the rituals he performed in order to obtain children, Viśvāmitra's role in training Rāma as a warrior, the Ahalyā story, the events in the forest leading to the killing of demons, Rāma's grief over Sītā's loss, Rāma's friendship with Sugrīva, the killing of Vālin, the search for Sītā, the exploits of Hanumān, and the glories of the battle in Lanka—none of these incidents receive much attention in these songs. On the other hand, events of interest to women are prominently portrayed and receive detailed attention: pregnancy, morning sickness, childbirth, the tender love of a husband, the affections of parents-in-law, games played by brides and grooms in wedding rituals. Moreover, significant attention is given to the last book of the *Rāmāyaṇa*, the *Uttarakāṇḍa*; some of the longer songs in my recorded collection as well as in the printed book relate to the events of the *Uttarakāṇḍa*, especially Sītā's abandonment and Lava and Kuśa's battle with Rāma.

The Songs

As the saying goes among men in Andhra, "The news of the birth of a son is pleasant but not the process of the birth." Men are not very interested in the details of pain women undergo in childbirth. Perhaps not surprisingly, then, literary *Rāmāyaṇas* in Telugu describe Rāma's birth in glorious terms. They relate how the king and his kingdom were delighted by the news, and describe in eloquent phrases the festivities celebrated all over the city of Ayodhya and the gifts given to Brahmins. Only in the women's song versions of the *Rāmāyaṇa* do we find a description of Kausalyā in labor, graphically depicting the pain associated with it. The song describes how the child is delivered while the pregnant woman stands upright, holding on to a pair of ropes hung from the ceiling.[10]

Now call the midwife, go send for her.
The midwife came in royal dignity.
She saw the woman in labor, patted her on her back.
Don't be afraid, Kausalya, don't be afraid, woman!
In an hour you will give birth to a son.
The women there took away the gold ornaments,
They removed the heavy jewels from her body.

They hung ropes of gold and silk from the ceiling.
They tied them to the beams, with great joy
They made Kausalya hold the ropes.
Mother, mother, I cannot bear this pain,
A minute feels like a hundred years.

Attention to ritual is common in many *Rāmāyaṇas,* but the rituals are the grand Vedic rituals, in which Brahmin priests play the leading part. Rituals in the women's songs pertain to more domestic matters in which women are prominent. The only man present is usually the bridegroom Rāma, and as the bridegroom in women-dominated rituals, he is controlled by and subservient to the demands of the women surrounding him. In addition to the rituals, the songs describe various games Sītā and Rāma play during the wedding and in the course of their married life in the joint family. In all such games Sītā comes out the winner. Rāma even tries to cheat and cleverly escape defeat, making false promises of surrender.

Another point repeatedly stressed in the songs is the auspicious role women have in Brahmin households as the protectors of family prosperity. Women are personifications of the goddess Lakṣmī, the goddess of wealth, and it is a well-known belief that the women of a household bring prosperity to the family by their proper behavior and ruin it by improper behavior. In these songs the bride enters the house of her new husband, always with her auspicious right foot first. It is the women who perform all the appropriate actions to remove the evil eye from the newborn baby. Women, again, serve a delicious feast to the Brahmins and the sages who come to bless the newborn. The ceremonies described in these songs—the naming ceremony and the ceremony of placing the boys in new cribs (especially made for the occasion, their designs and decorations described in detail)—show how important women are on all those occasions. Even the humor is feminine: when Kausalyā gives the women boiled and spiced *sĕnagalu* (split peas) as a part of a ritual gift, they complain among themselves that the *sĕnagalu* were not properly salted.

A song about Sītā's wedding presents a reason—not found in the Sanskrit text of Vālmīki—why Sītā's father Janaka decides on an eligibility test for Sītā's future husband. In her childhood, Sītā casually lifted Śiva's bow, which was lying in her father's house. Janaka was amazed at her strength and decided that only a man who could string that bow would be eligible to marry her. Only a hero can be a match for a hero. Several literary *Rāmāyaṇa* texts, including Tulsīdas's *Rāmcaritmānas*, also give this explanation, which is therefore not unique to women's *Rāmāyaṇa* songs. But this event gains a special significance in the context of women's hopes for a husband who is properly matched to them. In an arranged marriage, where the personal qualities of the future husband are often left to chance, women dream of having a husband who loves them and whom they love. Significantly, therefore, the song describes Sītā's feelings for Rāma, whose charms have been described to her by her friends. Sītā falls in love with him and suffers the pangs of separation (*viraha*) from him. Closely following the conventional modes of love in separation, the song delicately presents Sītā's fears that Rāma might not succeed in stringing the bow. She prays to all the gods to help him string it.

The song then describes how Rāma falls in love with Sītā. He arrives and sees the bow. He has no doubt that he can easily break it. But he wants to make sure that Sītā is really beautiful. He asks his brother Lakṣmaṇa to go and see Sītā first. In his words:

> If a meal is not agreeable, a day is wasted
> But if the wife is not agreeable, life is wasted.

He asks Lakṣmaṇa to make sure that Sītā has a thin waist, that her skin is not too dark, that her hair is black and her feet small. The breaking of the bow itself, which is prominently and powerfully described in literary *Rāmāyaṇas,* is presented in an almost perfunctory manner in the women's songs: it is the mutual love between Rāma and Sītā that is prominent in the song. All too often, women in this community find that there is little real love between them and the husband who has been chosen for them. An elaborate description of the mutual love and desire of Rāma and Sītā thus serves as a wish fulfillment. The wedding festivities that follow are seen through women's eyes—every detail relating to women's roles in the wedding ceremony is carefully described, even the saris the women wear. Toward the end, an incident that portrays Sītā as an innocent girl is narrated. Rāma shows her a mirror. Seeing her image in the mirror, Sītā thinks that it is a different woman, to whom Rāma has already been married. Why did Rāma marry her if he has a wife already? Has he not vowed to live with one wife and no other? Rāma quietly moves closer to the mirror and stands by her side. Sītā, seeing Rāma's reflection also in the mirror, recognizes her innocence and shyly bends her head down.

A song entitled "Sītā Locked Out" describes a delicate event in which Sītā is delayed in coming to bed because she has work to finish in the house. Rāma waits for her, but, growing impatient, closes the bedroom door and locks it from inside. Sītā arrives and pleads with him to open the door. He stubbornly refuses.[11] Sītā quietly informs Kausalyā, who has already left for Daśaratha's bedroom. Kausalyā comes out, knocks on Rāma's door, and admonishes him for locking Sītā out. Rāma has to obey his mother: Sītā knows how to manipulate the situation in her favor by enlisting Kausalyā's help. Kausalyā is represented here as the ideal mother-in-law every daughter-in-law dreams of in a joint family, a mother-in-law who shows warmth and support for her daughter-in-law and who helps bring her closer to her husband.[12]

Men's *Rāmāyaṇas* have no great use for Śāntā, who is sometimes nominally mentioned as Daśaratha's foster-daughter and who is married to Ṛśyaśṛṅga. But for women she is a very important person in the *Rāmāyaṇa* story. In Brahmin families, an elder sister is allowed to command, criticize, and admonish her younger brother. As Rāma's elder sister, Śāntā often intervenes on behalf of Sītā in these songs.

Śāntā's importance in women's *Rāmāyaṇa* is best represented by a long song called "Śāntagovindanāmālu," which describes Śāntā's marriage. A striking feature of this song, which narrates most of the early part of the *Rāmāyaṇa,* is the importance women have in all the events: at every important juncture women either take the initiative themselves and act, or advise their husbands to take a specific step. Men's position is presented as titular; the real power rests with the women.

The story tells how Lakṣmī, Viṣṇu's consort, decides to be born on earth to help Viṣṇu, who will be born as Rāma. She descends to earth and is born as Sītā on a lotus flower in Lanka. Rāvaṇa finds her and gives her to Maṇḍodarī. When Sītā is twelve years old, he wants to marry her as his second wife. The Brahmins, however, advise Rāvaṇa that Sītā will destroy Lanka and that therefore she should be cast into the sea. The song then moves on to narrate other events leading to Rāma's birth.

The two most significant stories in the early books of Vālmīki's *Rāmāyaṇa* are the birth of Daśaratha's sons and Kaikeyī's evil plot to send Rāma away to the forest. In the first story women have no role to play except as passive bearers of children; in the second, the evil nature of women is highlighted in the descriptions of Kaikeyī's adamant demands to have her son Bharata invested as the heir to the kingdom and to banish Rāma to the forest for fourteen years.

The narrative in "Śāntagovindanāmālu" ingeniously transforms both these events so that women acquire the credit for the birth of sons and the evil nature of Kaikeyī's demand is eliminated. First, according to this song, Kausalyā advises Daśaratha that they should adopt Śāntā as their daughter. This daughter will bring good luck to the family and they will have sons. This is a powerful change indeed. The usual Brahmin family belief is that the firstborn should be a son. A firstborn daughter is greeted with disappointment, though it is not always openly expressed. This story suggests that a firstborn daughter is actually preferable because she, as a form of the goddess Lakṣmī, blesses the family with prosperity, which then leads to the birth of sons. Moreover, it is significant that the whole strategy is planned by a woman—whereas in the Vālmīki *Rāmāyaṇa,* for example, the sage Ṛśyaśṛṅga performs a sacrifice for Daśaratha which leads to the birth of sons. What is interesting here is that Daśaratha listens to his senior queen's advice. Kaikeyī, however, initially refuses to go along because she will gain nothing from the plan. But Sumitrā convinces Kaikeyī, who finally accepts the plan on the condition that Bharata, her son, will inherit the kingdom. Śāntā is duly adopted and brought to Ayodhya with great honors, where she is received as the very goddess of wealth. When she grows of age she is married to Ṛśyaśṛṅga, again on the advice of Kausalyā. The song then describes in fine detail the festivities of the wedding and the harmonious atmosphere of the palace, where the women are in control.

The innocence, fun, love, and gentle humor of the songs come to an end and serious problems in Sītā's life begin with the events of the later portion of the *Rāmāyaṇa*—events that take place after Sītā is brought back from her captivity in Lanka. But the women described in these songs are far from meek and helpless: they are portrayed as strong, quite capable of protecting their position against the unfair treatment meted out to them by Rāma.

One song depicts how, after abandoning the pregnant Sītā, Rāma decides to perform a sacrifice. Since ritual prescribes that he have a wife present, he has a golden image of Sītā made, to be placed by his side at the ritual. The image has to be bathed, and the person doing the bathing must be Rāma's sister, Śāntā. However, when Śāntā is called to perform the bathing, she refuses because she was not consulted before Sītā was abandoned.

A more serious situation develops when Rāma's sacrificial horse is captured by his sons, Lava and Kuśa. He does not know that Sītā is still alive and being taken care of by the sage Vālmīki in his forest hermitage, nor does he know that Lava and Kuśa are his sons. Appeals by Lakṣmaṇa and Rāma to the young boys fail to convince them to surrender the horse. In fact, they will not even reveal their identities. In the inevitable battle that ensues, all of Rāma's best fighters, including Hanumān and Lakṣmaṇa, are killed. Finally, Rāma himself goes to battle, and even he is killed. When Sītā comes to know of this, she grieves and chastises her sons for killing their father and their uncle. Vālmīki, of course, comes to the rescue and brings everybody back to life.[13]

Even then, the boys insist that Rāma bow to their feet before he gets his horse back. Is he not the cruel husband who banished his pregnant wife? Rāma, realizing now that Sītā is alive and that these boys are his sons, wants to see her, and so Vālmīki arranges for Sītā to be brought before him. Sītā dresses in her best jewelry to meet Rāma, but Lava and Kuśa run into the hermitage to prevent their mother from meeting him. How can she go to a husband who has treated her so cruelly? To resolve the problem, all the gods appear on the scene, Brahmā, Śiva, and Indra in the company of their wives. The gods take Rāma's side, while their wives support the boys. Śiva's wife, Pārvatī, advises the boys not to surrender, while Brahmā's wife, Sarasvatī, makes the boys insist that Rāma should bow to them first. The gods advise the boys to accept the arbitration of the Sun god, but the boys reject that idea: Rāma belongs to the solar dynasty, so the Sun will not be impartial. How about the Moon god? No, Viṣṇu saved the Moon when Rāhu and Ketu swallowed him. Therefore, the Moon's arbitration cannot be trusted. Nor is Indra an acceptable arbiter because he owes favors to Viṣṇu, who cheated the demons out of their share of ambrosia and gave it all to him. Vālmīki's name is suggested, but even he is not impartial, since he wrote the *Rāmāyaṇa* in praise of Rāma. Brahmā, Śiva, and Ṛśyaśṛṅga—all are rejected one after the other. Rāma has no choice. He decides to fight the boys. Pārvatī opposes this idea, suggesting instead that Rāma bequeath Ayodhya to the boys and go to the forest. Ultimately, a compromise is reached: Rāma should bow to the boys, intending thereby to honor his parents. So Rāma bows to his sons' feet, uttering Kausalyā's name, and thus the dispute is resolved.

Finally the family is reunited, and Rāma embraces Lava and Kuśa. But even then the boys refuse to go to Ayodhya, for they feel they cannot trust a father who planned to kill his sons while they were in the womb. Only after much pleading do the boys agree to go with their father. Soon after they reach Ayodhya they demand to see the "grandmother" (Kaikeyī) who banished Sītā to the forest! They announce that Sītā is under their protection now and nobody can harm her anymore.

Among the male characters, Lakṣmaṇa receives very affectionate treatment in these songs. He is closer to Sītā, understands her problems, supports her, and even protects her in her time of troubles. In Vālmīki, Rāma banishes Sītā to the forest under the pretext of fulfilling her desire to see the hermitages, instructing Lakṣmaṇa to leave her in the woods and return. According to the women's version, Rāma orders Lakṣmaṇa to kill her. Lakṣmaṇa takes her to the forest but, realizing she is pregnant, decides not to kill her. He kills a hare instead and shows its blood to Rāma as evidence. Rāma then prepares for her funeral and asks Lakṣmaṇa to go to the hermitages and invite the sages' wives to the ceremonies. When Lakṣmaṇa goes to the forest, Sītā asks him if Rāma is preparing for her funeral. To spare her further pain, Lakṣmaṇa tells the lie that they are performing a special ritual to rid the palace of evil influences. Lakṣmaṇa's wife, Urmilā, protests against her husband's cruelty in killing Sītā. She demands that she be killed too, as does Śāntā.

Unable to stand their anger and their determination, Lakṣmaṇa tells them the truth: Sītā is alive, pregnant, and will deliver soon. Lakṣmaṇa goes to the forest to visit her after she has delivered.

Another song in this collection concerns Urmilā, whom Vālmīki barely mentions. What happens to Urmilā when Lakṣmaṇa leaves for fourteen years to accompany his brother to the forest? According to the women's version, Urmilā and Lakṣmaṇa make a pact: they trade their sleeping and waking hours. Urmilā will sleep for the entire fourteen years while Lakṣmaṇa will stay awake so that he can serve his brother without interruption. Fourteen years later, when Rāma has been successfully reinstated on the throne and Lakṣmaṇa is serving him at the court, Sīta reminds Rāma that Lakṣmaṇa should be advised to go visit his wife, who is still sleeping. Lakṣmaṇa goes to Urmilā's bedroom and gently wakes her up. Urmilā does not recognize him, however, and thinks that a stranger has entered her bedchamber. She questions him, warning him about the sin of desiring another man's wife.

> If my father Janaka comes to know about this,
> he will punish you and will not let you get away.
> My elder sister and brother-in-law
> will not let you escape with your life.

As a proper wife she does not even mention the name of her husband. Instead, she refers to him indirectly:

> My elder sister's younger brother-in-law
> will not let you live on the earth.

Then she tells him how, in the past, men who coveted others' wives suffered for their sin.

> Did not Indra suffer a disfigured body
> because he coveted another man's wife?
> Was not Rāvaṇa destroyed along with his city
> because he desired another man's wife?

That the sleeping Urmilā could not possibly have known about Rāvaṇa kidnapping Sītā and his eventual death at Rāma's hands is immaterial.

Lakṣmaṇa gently identifies himself, whereupon Urmilā realizes that he is none other than her husband. The rest of the song relates in loving detail how affectionately they embrace each other. Kausalyā receives them, prepares a bath for them, and feeds them a delicious meal. Lakṣmaṇa and Urmilā sit side by side—as husband and wife rarely do in conventional Brahmin families—and the members of the family tease them. When they are sent to the bedroom Lakṣmaṇa combs and skillfully braids Urmilā's hair while Urmilā asks him about all the events of the past fourteen years. How could Rāvaṇa kidnap Sītā when a man like Lakṣmaṇa, courageous as a lion, was present? Lakṣmaṇa relates the story of the golden deer, telling her how Sītā spoke harsh words to him and forced him to leave her alone and look after Rāma instead. All the major events of the epic have now been narrated briefly, and the song ends wishing all the listeners and singers a place in heaven.

A related song also takes as its starting point Lakṣmaṇa and Urmilā's pact. When the goddess of sleep visits Lakṣmaṇa in the forest, he asks her to leave him alone for fourteen years and go to his wife instead. She can come back to him exactly fourteen years later, when he returns to Ayodhya. Sure enough, as Lakṣmaṇa is serving Rāma in the court hall after their return from Lanka, the goddess of sleep visits him. Amused at her punctual return, Lakṣmaṇa laughs. Lakṣmaṇa's sudden laugh amidst the serious atmosphere of the court makes everybody wonder. The song describes how each person in the hall thinks that Lakṣmaṇa laughed at him or her. Thus Śiva, who is present in the court, thinks that Lakṣmaṇa laughed at him because he brought a low-caste fisherwoman (Gaṅgā, actually the river Ganges) and put her on his head, while Śeṣa, the ancient snake, thinks that Lakṣmaṇa was ridiculing him because he served Viṣṇu for a long time but is now serving Viṣṇu's enemy, Śiva. Aṅgada assumes that Lakṣmaṇa was laughing at him for joining the service of his own father's killer, Rāma. Sugrīva has his insecurities too: he had his brother killed unfairly and stole his brother's wife. Vibhīṣaṇa revealed the secrets of his brother's kingdom to Rāma and thus caused the ruin of Lanka. Hanumān is bothered by the fact that he, a mighty warrior, was once caught by a young soldier, Indrajit. Bharata and

Śatrughna, too, have something to be ashamed of: they were given the empire as a result of their mother Kaikeyī's cunning plot, which deprived Rāma of his position as future king. Even Rāma thinks that Lakṣmaṇa laughed at him because he, Rāma, has taken back a wife who has lived in another man's house—while Sītā thinks that Lakṣmaṇa laughed at her for having lived away from her husband. Furthermore, she was the one who suspected Lakṣmaṇa's intentions when he insisted on staying with her to protect her in the forest. She spoke harshly to him, forcing him to leave her alone and go help Rāma, who appeared to be in danger from the golden deer—thus causing the chain of events that led to the battle of Lanka. Everyone in the court has a secret shame, and Lakṣmaṇa's laugh brings their insecurities to the surface. In this skillful way the song suggests that no character in the *Rāmāyaṇa* is free of blemishes.

Angry at Lakṣmaṇa for his improper act of laughing in court, Rāma draws his sword to cut off his brother's head, at which point Pārvatī and Śiva intervene. They suggest that Lakṣmaṇa should be asked to explain his reasons for such irreverent behavior: he is young and should not be punished harshly. When Lakṣmaṇa explains, Rāma is embarrassed at his rash and uncontrolled anger. He asks Vasiṣṭha how he, as a proper king, should expiate his sin of attempting to kill his innocent brother. Vasiṣṭha advises Rāma to massage Lakṣmaṇa's feet. So a bed is made for Lakṣmaṇa, and, like a dutiful servant, Rāma massages his feet as Lakṣmaṇa sleeps comfortably. When Lakṣmaṇa wakes up and sees what Rāma is doing, he dutifully dissuades his glorious elder brother, the very incarnation of the god Viṣṇu, from serving him.[14]

Rāvaṇa's sister Śūrpaṇakhā's role in the women's *Rāmāyaṇa* songs is especially noteworthy. Rāma and his brothers are living happily in Ayodhya when Śūrpaṇakhā happens to see them. She desires to avenge her brother Rāvaṇa's death, but she is a woman. If only she were a man, she could have fought against Rāma and killed him—but as a woman, she can only disrupt his happiness. So she decides to plant suspicions in Rāma's mind about Sītā's fidelity. Taking the form of a female hermit, Śūrpaṇakhā goes to the palace and asks to see Sītā. Although Sītā hesitates, surprised that a forest hermit has come to see her, after some persuasion she consents to see her. The hermit asks Sītā to paint a picture of Rāvaṇa, but she replies that she never set eyes on the demon's face; she looked only at his feet. So the hermit asks Sītā to paint the feet, and Sītā draws a picture of Rāvaṇa's big toe.

Śūrpaṇakhā takes the drawing and completes the rest of the picture herself—strong ankles, thighs, and the rest. She then asks Brahmā, the creator god, to give life to the image so she can see her dead brother again. When Brahmā does so, Śūrpaṇakhā brings the picture back to Sītā, drops it in front of her, and runs away saying, "Do what you want with this picture." When the image of Rāvaṇa starts pulling at Sītā, asking her to go to Lanka with him, Sītā grows perturbed. Urmilā, Śāntā, and all the other women in the palace try to get rid of the picture. They make a big fire and throw the picture in, but it does not burn. Then they throw the picture into a deep well, but it comes back up. By no means can they destroy it. Finally Sītā utters Rāma's name, which temporarily subdues the image.

Suddenly Rāma enters the house. Not knowing what to do with the picture, Sītā hides it under her mattress. Rāma approaches Sītā and embraces her, wishing to make love to her. He unties her blouse, but Sītā is distracted. Puzzled, Rāma tries to show his affection by describing in many words how he loves her. When he takes her to bed, however, Rāvaṇa's picture under the mattress throws him off the bed. Thinking that Sītā threw him off, Rāma is angered. He turns around and sees Rāvaṇa's picture. This convinces him that Sītā is really in love with another man and that women are unreliable. He decides to banish Sītā to the forest along with her picture, but all the women of the palace protest. They explain to Rāma how a certain hermit made Sītā draw Rāvaṇa's picture; they tell him that Sītā is pure, but Rāma does not listen. In his anger, he speaks rudely to his mother, Kausalyā, who pleads in favor of Sītā. When Sumitrā, Lakṣmaṇa's mother, intervenes, he tells her that she could have Sītā as her daughter-in-law, suggesting thereby that Sītā could be Lakṣmaṇa's wife. Ordering that Sītā be killed in the forest, he leaves the house for the royal court. Urmilā, Māṇḍavī, and Śrutakīrtī, the wives of Rāma's three brothers, go to Rāma to protest his unfair punishment of Sītā. One after another they assure Rāma that Sītā was not at fault. Finally, Śrutakīrtī tells him:

We are all born in one family,
married into one family.
Our sister is not the only one
who loves Rāvaṇa now.
We all love him together
so kill us together.
Because we are women
who stay within the palace,
your actions pass without check.

This united front only makes Rāma more angry. He commands Lakṣmaṇa to take Sītā away to the forest, cut off her head, and bring the sword back (thus setting the stage for the events described above).

The Structure of the Songs

The structure of these songs, which open with praise of Rāma before moving on to the story at hand, might appear somewhat commonplace, but becomes significant in relation to the time and place of their performance. The songs are usually sung in the late afternoon, after the midday meal, when the men of the family have all retired to the front part of the house to take a nap or chat on the porch, the younger among them perhaps playing cards. Having been served a good meal, they now want to be left alone, to relax and rest, until evening. Their daily chores completed, the women are now free from marital and family obligations, at least for the moment. This is their own time, during which they can do what they please—provided, of course, that they don't violate the norms of good behavior. Very much like the place in the house where the songs are sung, then, this time period is largely insulated from the demands of the men, for whom women must otherwise play their dutiful roles.

A Brahmin house is divided into three areas. The front is where the men sit, conduct business, receive guests, or chat among themselves. Except when they are called for meals or when they retire for the evening, men do not usually go into the interior of the house, and when they do, they indicate their arrival by coughing or calling to one of the women from outside, who then comes into the middle part of the house to receive them. The middle part of the house is a relatively neutral area, where men and women meet together. In the back of the house are located a kitchen and a verandah opening into the backyard, often with a well in it. It is here that women gather. Women visitors, servants, and low-caste men use the back entrance of the house to converse with the women.

At the front of the house, the conventional male-dominated values reign supreme, but the back part of the house, and to a somewhat lesser extent the interior, are primarily the women's domain. Women are relatively free here from the censuring gaze of their men, and thus enjoy some measure of control over their own lives. Men are even ridiculed for lingering in the back of the house, although male relatives of the wife's family may enter, as can the husband's younger brothers if they are much younger than the wife.

The structure of the songs precisely replicates the structure of the house. Each song begins with a respectful tribute to Rāma, the king. Rāma in these songs is not only God, as in *bhakti Rāmāyaṇas,* but also the *yajamāni*, the master of the house—albeit a master who is not entirely in control. This opening dutifully made, the song moves toward the interior—and the people who inhabit the interior of the songs are mostly women. Much like certain male relatives, however, some men are allowed to enter this area: Lakṣmaṇa, the younger brother-in-law; and Lava and Kuśa, the young twins.

Sītāyana

Women in these songs never openly defy propriety: they behave properly, even giving themselves advice that the male masters of the household would accept and appreciate. The tone of the songs is innocently gentle, homely, and sweet—no harsh or provocative language, no aggressive opposition to male domination. Daughters-in-law thus take great care to observe the conventions in addressing mother-in-law Kausalyā and sister-in-law Śāntā. Likewise, on several occasions proper behavior is preached to young brides, as when Sītā is told to

> Be more patient than even the earth goddess.
> Never transgress the words of your father-in-law and mother-in-law.
> Do not ever look at other men.
> Do not ever speak openly.

Do not reveal the words your husband says in the interior palace,
even to the best of your friends.
If your husband is angry, never talk back to him.
A husband is god to all women: never disobey your husband.

While proper respect is always paid to authority, what follows on the heels of that respect can seem strikingly different. There are polite but quite strongly made statements that question Rāma's wisdom, propriety, honesty, and integrity. However, Sītā herself never opposes Rāma or her other superiors: as a new bride, Sītā is coy, innocent, and very obedient to her husband and the elders of the family. Rather, criticism against Rāma is leveled only by women who have the authority to do so, like Rāma's mother, Kausalyā, or his elder sister, Śāntā, a mother surrogate. Rāma's brothers' wives question Rāma, too, but in order to do so, they need the support of Śāntā. Rāma's young sons, Lava and Kuśa, are also permitted to criticize their father, provided they are acting in their mother's defense.

The affections and tensions of a joint family both come out clearly through these songs. Beneath the apparent calm of the house, joint-family women often suffer severe internal stress. The songs reveal a similar atmosphere in their use of language. The general style of the language is deceptively gentle. Very few Sanskrit words are used, the choice of relatively more mellifluous Dravidian words lending to the texture of the songs an idyllic atmosphere of calm and contentment. However, the underlying meanings reveal an atmosphere of subdued tensions, hidden sexuality, and frustrated emotions. On occasion, even the gentle words acquire the sharpness of darts, hitting their targets with precise aim. Under the pretext of family members teasing each other, every character is lampooned. No one's character is untainted; no person loves another unconditionally. Even Sītā's chastity is open to doubt: the picture episode suggests that Sītā harbors a hidden desire to sleep with Rāvaṇa, her drawing of Rāvaṇa's big toe making veiled reference to his sex organ. The final picture that emerges is not that of the *bhakti Rāmāyaṇa,* with an ideal husband, an ideal wife, and ideal brothers, but of a complcx joint family where life is filled with tension and fear, frustration and suspicion, as well as with love, affection, and tenderness.

The *Rāmāyaṇa* songs also make a statement against the public *Rāmāyaṇas,* the *bhakti Rāmāyaṇas,* which glorify the accepted values of a male-dominated world. In the songs, it is the minor or lowly characters who come out as winners. Urmilā, Lakṣmaṇa, Lava and Kuśa, Śāntā, and even Śūrpaṇakhā have a chance to take their revenge. Sītā does not fight her own battle alone: others fight it for her. She even enjoys the freedom she acquires by the (false) report of her death; for once, she can exist without living for Rāma. As Rāma prepares for her death ceremonies, burdened by the guilt of having her killed unjustly, Sītā gives birth to twins and awaits her final victory over Rāma, won through her agents, her sons. In the final analysis, this is her *Rāmāyaṇa*, a *Sītāyana.*

Non-Brahmin Songs

A similar strategy of subverting authority while outwardly respecting it is found in the *Rāmāyaṇa* songs sung by non-Brahmin women. These are not as long as the Brahmin women's songs, nor are they as prominent in the non-Brahmin women's repertoire as they are in Brahmin women's. Although the *Rāmāyaṇa* is often alleged to be universally popular in India, closer examination will, I believe, reveal that the epic's popularity increases with the status of the caste. At any rate the number of *Rāmāyaṇa* songs sung by non-Brahmin women that are available in published collections is relatively small, though the songs are by no means less interesting. My information regarding these songs comes almost entirely from these published collections, and as such my use of thc data is rather constrained.

The label "non-Brahmin" masks more than it reveals. Unfortunately, the published information about these songs does not record the precise caste of the singer. As Gangappa informs us, the songs are sung by women when they are working in the fields, grinding flour, or playing *kolāṭam* (a play of music and dance in which the players move in circles as they hit wooden sticks held in each other's hands). Female agricultural labor in Andhra largely comes from Mālas, a caste of Untouchables, and other castes of very low status. Women of these castes work in the fields with men, make their own money, and thus live relatively less sheltered and controlled lives. Separation of the sexes is not practiced to the same extent as among the upper castes, although women are seen as inferior to men, paid lower wages, and given work which is supposed to require less skill, like weeding and transplanting, as opposed to plowing, seeding, and harvesting. Women also work in groups, which are often supervised by a man. The household chores that these women perform are also distinct from those of the men, but the separation is not as clear-cut as it is among the upper castes. Lower-caste men, for example, do not consider it demeaning to feed children and take care of them.

Women of these low castes have the same kinds of family responsibilities as Brahmin women do: raising a family, bearing (male) children, being sexually faithful to their husbands, and obeying their husbands and mothers-in-law. But the low-caste women are not as dependent on their husbands as are Brahmin women. Widows are not treated as inauspicious, nor are their heads shaved; and they are not removed from family ritual life. Among some non-Brahmin castes widows even remarry.[15]

The *Rāmāyaṇa* songs sung by non-Brahmin women reflect this difference. These songs also concentrate on women's themes: Sītā's life in the forest. Urmilā's sleep, Sītā's request that Rāma capture the golden deer, Rāvaṇa's kidnapping of Sītā, and the battle between Rāma and his sons, Kuśa and Lava. But there is little interest in descriptions of women's role in ritual, in their wish for importance in family decisions, or in saris and ornaments, nor is there much allusion to the inner conflicts of a joint family. Also significantly absent are hidden sexuality, feminine modesty, and descriptions of games played by husband and wife.

Interestingly, there is a song describing how Rāma grieves when Lakṣmaṇa swoons in battle and how Hanumān brings the mountain with the life-giving herb *saṃjīvini*. Another song describes how Vibhīṣaṇa advises his brother Rāvaṇa in vain to surrender Sītā and how he deserts Rāvaṇa to join Rāma. Their mother advises Vibhīṣaṇa to take half of Lanka and stay. Describing the glory of Lanka she says:

> The god of wind sweeps the floor here in Lanka.
> The rain god sprinkles cow-dung water to keep it clean.
> The fire god himself cooks in our kitchen,
>   cooks in our kitchen.

Three hundred thirty-three million gods take
shovels and crowbars and work for us as slaves
all the time, work for us as slaves.

It is fascinating to see how the song reverses the hierarchy and relishes the description of gods working as slaves, for in truth it is the low-caste women and men who must work as slaves for their masters, the "gods on earth." The chores of sprinkling cow-dung water in the front yards and cooking are women's work, while digging earth for the landed masters is the work of low-caste men. The song thus refers jointly to the tasks of both men and women of the low castes, opposing their situation to that of the upper castes.

Another short song in this collection describes the glory of houses in Lanka where Rāvaṇa and his brothers live.

Steel beams and steel pillars, whose palace is this?
Lovely Srīrāma [Sītā], this is Kumbhakarṇa's palace.
Teak beams and teak pillars, whose palace is this?
Lovely Srīrāma, this is Indrajit's palace.

Silver beams and silver pillars, whose palace is this?
Lovely Srīrāma, this is Rāvaṇa's palace.[16]

Sung during *kolāṭam* play, this group song, its lines repeated again and again, enchants the listeners with its play on words and sound, the increase in value of the house keeping pace with the increase in the tempo of singing. Here, it is Rāvaṇa, not Rāma, who is described in glorious terms befitting a king. We hear of Rāma more as a name in the devotional refrain than as the hero of the epic story.

Among the other male characters Lakṣmaṇa again receives affectionate treatment as Sītā's younger brother-in-law. As surrogate father he takes care of Sītā's sons. He puts oil on their scalps, feeds them milk, and they urinate on his clothes. Lakṣmaṇa loves it; his face glows like the full moon.

The joint family does merit a favorable description in a song depicting Sītā's answer to the demon women guarding her in Lanka.

Cool lemon trees and fine *pŏnna* trees all around
have you seen, Sītā, Rāvaṇa's Lanka.
Time and again you think of Rāma,

who is this Rāma, Sītā of Rāgavas?
Rāma is my man, Lakṣmaṇa, my *maridi.*
Barta and Śatrīka are my younger *maridis.*
Kausalya is my real mother-in-law,
Kaika, the older one and Sumitri, the younger.
Ūrmiḷa and I are daughters-in-law.
All the world knows, Janaka is my father.
All the directions know, Daśaratha is my father-in-law.
All the earth knows, the earth goddess is my mother.[17]

So Sītā is neither alone nor unprotected. When threatened by an alien power, she can count on all members of her extended family to come to her support.

An incident that makes Sītā look somewhat childish in the upper-caste *Rāmāyaṇas* is her demand for the golden deer, even though Rāma tells her that the animal is a demon in magical disguise. In the *Rāmāyaṇa* of the low-caste women, though, Sītā does not insist on getting the animal like a spoiled child; she says instead:

You give me your bows and arrows
I will go right now and get the animal.

His ego hurt, Rāma rushes forth to capture the golden deer.

These songs are sung in rice fields and play areas—not in the private backyards of houses, as the Brahmin songs are. Interestingly, songs collected from the fields where women sing as they work begin with a straightforward narration but end almost abruptly; they seem rather unfinished. One wonders if the open structure of the work songs does not reflect the low-caste women's lack of interest in finishing what really does not belong to them. Rather than indicating an inability to produce a finished song, the songs' structure is thus an expression of rejection: like the open fields where they work, the story of the *Rāmāyaṇa,* with its regal settings and brahminical value, really belongs to others. The same women can, moreover, sing beautifully finished songs when the theme interests them, as, for example, the *kolāṭam* play song describing the glory of the houses Rāvaṇa and his brothers live in. And there is that devotional mention of Rāma's name, perhaps a thin façade covering the actual lack of interest in Rāma's stature as a hero.

Conclusion

Why do women sing these songs? Edwin Ardener has proposed a theory of muted groups, who are silenced by the dominant structures of expression.[18] India's lower castes and women fall in this category. However, muted groups, according to Ardener, are not silent groups. They do express themselves, but under cover of the dominant ideology.

The contents of the women's *Rāmāyaṇa* songs do not make their singers or listeners feminists. If anything, the Brahmin women to whom I talked consider singing these songs an act of devotion, a proper womanly thing to do in the house. Nor have men who have listened to these songs or read them in print objected to their use by the women of their households. None of the scholars (of both sexes) who have written on the Brahmin *Rāmāyaṇa* songs perceive in them a tone of opposition to the public *Rāmāyaṇas*, the "male" versions.[19]

Do the women consciously follow the meaning of the songs when they sing them for themselves? They have so routinized their singing that they seem to receive the meaning subliminally, rather than self-consciously. Furthermore, the very same women who sing these songs also participate in the public, male *Rāmāyaṇa* with all the devotion appropriate to the occasion. Does the contrast between what they sing at home and what they hear outside the home receive their attention? Do they discuss these issues among themselves? The texts women sing are not esoteric. Their language is simple, their message clear; they protest against male domination. I believe it is the controlled context of their performance that makes their use properly "feminine." Perhaps the value of the songs consists precisely in the absence of conscious protest. The women who sing these songs have not sought to overthrow the male-dominated family structure; they would rather work within it. They have no interest in direct confrontation with authority; their interest rather is in making room for themselves to move. It is this internal freedom that these songs seem to cherish. Only when such freedom is threatened by an overbearing power exercised by the head of the household do the women speak up against him, even then subverting his authority rather than fighting openly against him. These songs are a part of the education

Brahmin women receive, a part of brahminic ideology which constructs women's consciousness in a way suitable to life in a world ultimately controlled by men.

In sharp contrast to the Brahmin women's songs, the songs sung by the low-caste women seem to reflect their disaffection with the dominant upper-caste masters for whom they work rather than with the men of their own families. No low-caste women, these singers are doubly oppressed. As women, they share some of the feelings of the upper-caste women, and to that extent they understand Sītā's troubles. Perhaps more intriguing, however, is the lack of interest in Rāma and the attention shown instead to Rāvaṇa and Lanka, in an apparent rejection of Rāma. But again, as in the Brahmin women's songs, the rejection is not open and confrontational, but subtle and subversive.

Notes

Sanskrit loan words in Telugu shorten the long vowel at the end of feminine nouns: Sīta, Urmiḷa. In the passages quoted from the songs these names appear without the final long vowel and with Telugu diacritics.

I am grateful to Kolavennu Malayavasini for collecting these *Rāmāyaṇa* songs for me. Her cultural insights and her knowledge of the *Rāmāyaṇa* song tradition have been very useful to me. Thanks are also due to Jaya Prabha, who collected several songs from her mother. Peter Claus and Robert Goldman read and commented on an earlier version of this paper when it was presented at the 40th annual meeting of the Association for Asian Studies in San Francisco, March 1988. Joyce Flueckiger, A.K. Ramanujan, Joe Elder, Kirin Narayan, and Paula Richman read a later draft and made a number of suggestions for improvement. I am grateful to all of them. Responsibility for the interpretation (and misinterpretation) is entirely mine.

1. The songs women sing on the *Rāmāyaṇa* theme have received extensive attention from Telugu scholars for some time. The earliest collections of these songs were made by Nandiraju Chelapati Rao, *Strīla Pāṭalu* (Eluru: Manjuvani Press, 1899), and Mangu Ranganatha Rao, *Nūru Hindū Strīla Pāṭalu* (*c*. 1905). The existence of these early collections is reported in Sripada Gopalakrishnamurti's

introduction to another collection, *Strīla Rāmāyaṇapu Pāṭalu,* ed. "Krishnasri" (Hyderabad: Andhrasarasvata-parishattu, 1955), but they were unavailable to me. A more recent collection of folksongs, which includes several shorter women's *Rāmāyaṇa* songs, is that of Nedunuri Gangadharam, *Minneru* (Rajahmundry: Sarasvathi Power Press, 1968). A small but extremely interesting collection, which includes *Rāmāyaṇa* songs collected from low-caste women, is found in Siramappagari Gangappa, ed., *Jānapadageyarāmāyaṇamu* (Gunturu: By the author, 1983). Another collection, also by Gangappa, is *Jānapadageyālu* (Vijayawada: Jayanti Publications, 1985), which includes a number of the *Rāmāyaṇa* songs already published in his 1983 collection.

Earlier studies of these songs include: Hari Adiseshuvu, *Jānapadageyavāṅmayaparicayamu* (Gunturu: Navyavijnanpracuranalu, 1954; repr. 1967), pp. 245–50; Birudaraju Ramaraju, *Tĕlugujānapadageyasāhityamu* (Hyderabad: Janapadavijnanapracuranalu, 1958; 2nd ed. 1978), pp. 78–126; Tumati Donappa, *Jānapadakaḷāsampada* (Hyderabad: Abhinandanasamiti, Acarya Tumati Donappa Mudu Arvaila Pandaga, 1972; repr. 1987); Panda Samantakamani, *Tĕlugusāhityamulo Rāmakatha* (Hyderabad: Andhrasarasvataparishattu, 1972), pp. 248–69; T. Gopalakrishna Rao, *Folk Rāmāyaṇa in Telugu and Kannada* (Nellore: Saroja Publications, 1984); and Kolavennu Malayavasini, *Āndhra Jānapada Sāhityamu: Rāmāyaṇamu* (Visakhapatnam: By the author, 1986). Donappa includes several *Rāmāyaṇa* songs from the Rayalaseema region of Andhra Pradesh, unavailable in any other published collections. In addition, Gopalakrishna Rao mentions K. Srilakshmi's " Female Characters in Folk Songs Based on Ramayana" (M. Phil. thesis, Osmania University, Hyderabad, 1980), but unfortunately I was not able to consult it.

2. To continue the language metaphor, it may be said that there are *Rāmāyaṇas* whose grammar is less conventional, such as the DK (Dravida Khazagam) version popular in Tamilnadu. There are also several such *Rāmāyaṇas* in Telugu, most notably a recent feminist, Marxist version by Ranganayakamma entitled *Rāmāyaṇa Viṣvṛkṣam* (The Rāmāyaṇa: A Poison Tree), 3 vols (Hyderabad: Sweet Home Publications, 1974–6).

3. It should be noted that the popularity of these songs is waning: most young Brahmin women who attend college or university no longer sing these songs.
4. In 1955 Andhrasarasvataparishattu, a literary service organization in Hyderabad, assembled forty-two of these songs into one volume entitled *Strīla Rāmāyaṇapu Pāṭalu,* with a critical introduction by Sripada Gopalakrishnamurti, but no information is given about the methods of collection, the singers, or the context of singing. Absent also is information regarding the tunes to which these songs were sung. It is possible that the book drew chiefly or entirely on earlier printed sources. Gopalakrishnamurti's otherwise valuable introduction is silent about these matters. Even though the title page of the book says that it is edited by "Krishnasri"—presumably a pseudonym—the introduction indicates that Gopalakrishnamurti was not directly involved in the collection of these songs.
5. For example, Vaidikis, Niyogis, Madhavas Drāviḍas, etc., each group boasting numerous subdivisions.
6. In a work song, the lead singer sings the main text, while the refrain is repeated by the group of women working along with her. On my tape, however, one singer sings both the text and the refrain.
7. I was not able to acquire sung versions of several of the long songs, but they are available in print.
8. The author of "Kuśalavula Yuddhamu" says that the song was composed "following" (*tarapuna*) the *Rāmāyaṇa* of Vālmīki, referring to himself/herself in the third person but without giving a name: *varusaga idi vālmīki rāmāyaṇamu tarapuna vrāsenu ī kavi tanu.* "Kavi" in Tamil and folk Telugu means "poem." In another song, " Kuśalavakuccalakatha," the author refers to herself as *sati,* "auspicious woman," again without mentioning her name. Quite possibly women poets preferred not to give their names because to do so would be immodest. Only one song, " Sīta Melukŏlupu," mentions its author's name: Kurumaddali Venkatadasu, a man. Gopalakrishnamurti thinks that two other songs, "Laṅkāyāgamu" and "Laṅkāsārathi," were also composed by men, because men as well as women sing them.
9. See Gopalakrishnamurti's introduction to *Strīla Rāmāyaṇapu Pāṭalu,* pp. ix–x.

10. Apparently this was the practice in premodern Andhra; it is attested to in carvings on temple carts and *kalamkāri* cloth paintings.
11. In another song, also with a "locked out" theme, it is Rāma's turn to be locked out and Sītā refuses to open the door for him. See M.N. Srinivas, "Some Telugu Folk Songs," *Journal of the University of Bombay* 13, no. 1 (July 1944): 65–86, and no. 4 (January 1945): 15–29. See David Shulman, "Battle as Metaphor in Tamil Folk and Classical Traditions," in *Another Harmony: New Essays on the Folklore of India*, ed. Stuart H. Blackburn and A.K. Ramanujan (Berkeley and Los Angeles: University of California Press, 1986), pp. 105–30, for a study of this song in a different perspective.
12. In reality, the mother-in-law is often a hindrance to the union of wife and husband. Women's folksongs make many references to quarrels between mother-in-law and daughter-in-law.
13. Again, this motif is not unknown in literary *Rāmāyaṇas*: for example, the Bengali *Rāmāyaṇa* of Kṛttivāsa tells a similar one to those found in Jaina versions. It is possible that the Jaina versions were popular with Telugu Brahmin women, or, alternatively, that the Jain *Rāmāyaṇa* authors borrowed from the women's versions—or both. At this stage of our research, it is difficult to tell for sure.
14. In another version, Rāma suggests that he will serve Lakṣmaṇa in another birth; for now, it would be improper for an older brother to serve a younger one. Thus, in the next avatar, Rāma (i.e., Viṣṇu) is born as Kṛṣṇa and Lakṣmaṇa as Balarāma, Kṛṣṇa's older brother—so Lakṣmaṇa now receives Rāma's services. (I am grateful to Jaya Prabha for this information.)
15. For information on castes among whom widow remarriage is permitted, see V. Narayana Rao, "Epics and Ideologies: Six Telugu Folk Epics," in *Another Harmony*, ed. Blackbum and Ramanujan, pp. 131–64. Chapter 9 in this volume.
16. The reason why Srīrāma here stands for Sītā is unknown to me.
17. In Sanskrit the name is Rāghava; Bharta and Śatrīka are Bharata and Śatrughna; Kaika is Kaikeyī; and Sumitri is Sumitrā. (Such adaptations of Sanskrit names are common in the dialects or the castes described here.) *Maridi* is a Telugu kinship term for a husband's younger brother.
18. Edwin Ardener, "Belief and the Problem of Women" and "The Problem Revisited," both in *Perceiving Women*, ed. Shirley Ardener (London: Dent, 1975), pp. 1–17 and pp. 19–27, respectively.

19. Ramaraju, however, comments that the events in the later part of the song "Kuśalavula Yuddhamu" are "blemished by impropriety" *(anaucitīdoṣaduṣitamulu)*, apparently referring to the harsh words Lava and Kuśa speak against their father. Rāma: *Tĕlugujānapadageyasāhityamu*, 117.

8

The Politics of Telugu Ramayanas

Colonialism, Print Culture, and Literary Movements

When the play *Śambuka Vadha* (Śambuka Murdered) was published in 1920, it caused a considerable stir.[1] The play is based on a story from the Rāmāyaṇa but was presented in a manner that repelled its readers, who had been used to reading devotional stories of Rāma. The author of the play, Tripuraneni Ramasvami Chaudari (1887–1943), whom I will introduce more fully later, depicts the killing of the Dravidian Śambuka as a murder committed by the Aryan Kshatriya king Rāma at the behest of his Aryan Brahmin advisers. All traditional readers of the Rāmāyaṇa in Telugu know that Śambuka is the Shudra who violates the law of hierarchically ordered social classes—Brahmin, Kshatriya, Vaishya, and Shudra—which determines a person's status by birth (*varṇadharma*). Śambuka performs asceticism, a practice reserved for Brahmins, according to the dharma. As a consequence of this violation, a young Brahmin boy dies, and the father brings the corpse to Rāma to seek explanation for this unprecedented happening. It is the king's duty to protect the dharma, and when he performs this duty no misfortune befalls anyone in his kingdom; no one dies young, and certainly no young Brahmin dies. Rāma accepts the blame and goes out to see if a violation of dharma has occurred within his kingdom. He finds Śambuka behaving like a Brahmin and kills him as punishment. When dharma is thus restored, the

Brahmin boy comes back to life. However, in Ramasvami Chaudari's version, Śambuka is a Dravidian performing religious austerities in his region. Vasiṣṭha and other Aryan Brahmin ministers of Rāma see his austerities as a threat to their superiority and direct Rāma to kill him in order to punish what they interpret as the violation of dharma. In order to make it look like a serious offense against gods and cosmic harmony, Vasiṣṭha conspires with the Aśvins, the divine physicians, to cause the temporary death of the young Brahmin boy. Thus Rāma is forced to act and kill an innocent Dravidian.

Conventional Rāmāyaṇa readers were deeply disturbed at this violently unconventional reading of the Rāmāyaṇa. Bringing to prominence this troubling story from the later part of the Rāmāyaṇa, which many would rather overlook, proved disconcerting to many Rāmāyaṇa devotees.[2] Even supposing that such a focus were necessary, plenty of traditionally acceptable options for treating the story were available. For example Kālidāsa, in his *Raghuvaṃśa*, gives the incident a flavor of heroic elegance befitting a ruling king. In this version Rāma does kill the erring Shudra, but the culprit goes to heaven—far more easily, because the king punished him, than he would have if he had pursued his path of asceticism.[3] Bhavabhūti, the great eighth-century Sanskrit dramatist, presents this story in his *Uttararāmacarita* (The Later Story of Rāma). This playwright highlights Rāma's compassion and unwillingness to hand down cruel punishment to a Shudra for his violation of dharma. Bhavabhūti depicts the tragic element in the life of a king who must sacrifice his personal feelings of love and compassion in order to perform the harsh duties of kingship. In Bhavabhuti's version the Shudra attains an immortal form, thanks Rāma for traveling a long distance to the forest to see him, and becomes a friend of Rāma.[4]

According to Chaudari, however, Śambuka was murdered entirely because of a Brahmin conspiracy. Brahmins, who feared a Dravidian rebellion against their Aryan authority, advise Rāma to kill the Dravidian sage. In a skillfully developed plot, Chaudari depicts Śambuka as a social activist who organizes Dravidian opinion in favor of fighting for their religious rights of performing asceticism according to Vedic instructions. Rāma initially shows reluctance to punish a gentle ascetic, and determines that his guilt or innocence has to be established before he can be punished. Vasiṣṭha, the royal priest, gets impatient at Rāma's vacillation and demands that the sinner be instantly beheaded. Rāma invites Śambuka to a debate with the Brahmin priests, but Śambuka refuses this debate unless the king assures him that the standard of judgment will be based on the Veda, the revealed texts, and not *smṛti*, the texts written by Brahmin sages. Rāma pays a visit to Śambuka and finds conversation with him very convincing and satisfying. He then returns, wishing Śambuka well, but upon his arrival Vasiṣṭha warns him that weak policies will eventually destroy his empire. He cleverly explains to Rāma that the mutually supportive relationship between Brahmins and Kshatriyas has maintained the state from time immemorial. Dravidians will destabilize the Brahmin–Kshatriya bond and eventually ruin both Brahmins and Kshatriyas. For political expediency Rāma must kill Śambuka. Rāma is convinced, even though he feels unhappy at having to kill an innocent Dravidian. With tragic resolve, admitting that kingly duty allows no room for personal feeling, he reminds himself of the cruel act he has recently committed in banishing innocent Sītā to the forest to fulfill his kingly duty, He then solemnly cuts off Śambuka's head. Śambuka ascends to heaven in the form of a flash of light.

Chaudari's presentation of this story ran counter to the basic trust that the Telugu people had built in the Rāmāyaṇa narrative. Reading Aryan/Dravidian divisions into this story proved repulsive for many Brahmin readers and traditional scholars condemned Chaudari for concocting a false tale. For almost ten years this unconventional presentation faced stiff resistance. The author persisted, arguing in favor of his position in town after town. Gradually Chaudari's reading gained attention, especially with a large educated readership from the non-Brahmin castes and a modern cultural movement that questioned Brahminism and its religious sanctions.

There were serious discussions in town halls, clubs, and restaurants bar-rooms of district courts, the press, and most importantly within literary gatherings. Did Rāma really rule with compassion, as depicted in the images of Rāmrāj, the kingdom of god? Did he act only to preserve the interests of the Brahmins? Why can't Śambuka perform austerities for his own spiritual liberation? Why should such practices be protected as the exclusive right of Brahmins? Was the Rāmāyaṇa really a sacred text which was meant to liberate all its readers? Might Brahmins have distorted the text to perpetuate their control over the lower castes? Disturbing questions all—about the truth value of the Rāmāyaṇa. Educated readers were split into two camps, those that supported the traditional Rāmāyaṇa interpretations and those that demanded a critical reading.

During the next fifty years Telugu authors rewrote many Rāmāyaṇa themes, reflecting the new trend of interrogating the conventional Rāmāyaṇa: they produced plays, poems, essays, books, and at least two full-length retellings of the Rāmāyaṇa. Together these constitute what can be seen as an anti-Rāmāyaṇa discourse. The general features of this discourse take two directions. Some assume that there was one *Rāmāyaṇa*, the one written by Vālmīki and followed by regional language writers, and that it has one uniform ideology— supporting the Brahmins. Others assume that there was an original Rāmāyaṇa written by Vālmīki in which the Brahmins interpolated sections in support of their superiority. In either case, the common core of the anti-Rāmāyaṇa discourse remains its anti-Brahminism.

In this essay I present a brief study of this anti-Brahmin discourse which contests the Rāmāyaṇa's claim to truth by questioning the Vālmīki text and by rewriting his version to correct his pro-Brahminic biases. But first I shall outline the historical and social conditions which led to the production of such a discourse.

The Rāmāyaṇa Tradition and Vālmīki

When we talk of the Rāmāyaṇa, we begin with the version attributed to Vālmīki. Well known to Western Indologists, this version has received academic attention for more than a century. The recent Rāmāyaṇa translation project, which includes a team of eminent Sanskritists headed by Robert Goldman, has brought the Vālmīki text once again to the center. The Rāmāyaṇa received more compelling attention when Ramanand Sagar's television version made news with its unprecedented mass appeal;

the violent destruction of the Babri mosque by Hindu fundamentalists followed soon after. Decades of Western scholarly attention as well as the Indian television event strengthened a homogeneous Rāmāyaṇa discourse. However, with the burgeoning studies of oral epics and other folk-narrative genres in India, culminating in the publication of *Many Rāmāyaṇas* (1991), scholarly understanding of the Rāmāyaṇa tradition has been radically diversified. Yet the perception remains that the Rāmāyaṇa originates with Vālmīki. As Sheldon Pollock puts it:

> One may readily concur that the Rāmāyaṇa can interestingly be viewed not as a fixed text but as a "multivoiced entity, encompassing tellings of the Rāma story that vary according to historical period, regional literary tradition, religious affiliation, genre, and political context (Richman 1991: 16). But these tellings are always *re-tellings of a text everyone knows*. . . . In short, the foundational version, the version everyone knows in AD 1000–1400 and for the whole millennium preceding this period, is that of Vālmīki and his epigones . . . (emphasis in the original)[5]

The position that traces the origin of the Rāmāyaṇa narrative to Vālmīki stands at the very center of the Rāmāyaṇa problematic. Both traditional Rāmāyaṇa readers and the leaders of the anti-Rāmāyaṇa discourse see Vālmīki as the author of the *Rāmāyaṇa.* Yet there is a difference: the leaders of the anti-Rāmāyaṇa discourse state this in a factual mode; they base their arguments on nineteenth-century Western textual scholarship and assume that the Vālmīki version is empirically verifiable. For traditional readers and listeners, however, Vālmīki's authorship is ideological; they do not base their statement on empirical textual evidence. They believe that Vālmīki wrote *the* Rāmāyaṇa, *any* Rāmāyaṇa, and *every* Rāmāyaṇa. Given all this, the question of Vālmīki's association with the Rāmāyaṇa narrative needs to be restated with some conceptual clarity.

For one thing, there is no version of the Rāmāyaṇa that follows the Vālmīki narrative in any significant detail. But then there is rarely a Rāmāyaṇa author who does not state that he/she is retelling the narrative as Vālmīki told it. Vālmīki's name and authorship are venerated, even if his narrative is not followed. We can resolve this apparent contradiction when we separate the legendary author from his narrative. Perhaps because we have locked ourselves into a position that claims for every narrative an author who precedes it, we seem unable to dissociate Vālmīki from the narrative named after him. And because we believe that every narrative begins as a single original version, to which every other telling can be traced as its retelling, we authorize the Vālmīki version as the primary narrative.

We would arrive at a better understanding if we conceive of a situation where a number of Rāmāyaṇa narratives are composed, based on a story popular in oral tradition, and one specific version becomes linked with the name of Vālmīki. Such an association functions to construct an ideological coherence and a status for the narrative. The story of Vālmīki and the killing of the *krauñca* birds, included in the Sanskrit text, serves to elevate Vālmīki to the position of the first poet, one who has access to Nārada, Brahmā, and other celestial beings. Associating such a venerated poet with a text in turn elevates the narrative. I thus see Vālmīki as a signifier of the status of the narrative rather than as the producer of a particular text.

This view could also explain why there are several Vālmīkis. First we have Vālmīki the sage who felt compassion toward the *krauñca* bird hunted down by a Niṣadha hunter, and who uttered the first verse, thus inventing poetry. This is the Vālmīki we know in the epic text. Tradition also tells of another Vālmīki, the bandit who turned devotee by chanting Rāma's name. Brahmins gave him the syllables *rāma* inverted as *marā* because he was ineligible to receive this gift directly; he repeats it as a mantra, and via a process of repetition it turns into the sacred name of Rāma. The bandit turns into a sage, around whom an anthill, *valmīka*, grows as he meditates in total devotion; he emerges from this shell when Rāma himself comes to see him and asks him to compose his (Rāma's) story. Born out of a *valmīka*, he is known as Vālmīki. This is the Vālmīki of the bhakti Rāmāyaṇas.[6] In women's Rāmāyaṇas we find Vālmīki as the biased biographer of Rāma, the author who denied Sītā her legitimate place in the epic. During the course of this essay I shall also meet Vālmīki the composer of a smaller, original Rāmāyaṇa, which was later tampered with by Brahmins, and yet another Vālmīki who served the interests of male upper-caste feudal masters to enslave the masses. Finally, there is no *author* called Vālmīki: he simply appears, in non-literary Rāmāyaṇas, as a character in the narrative. Each Rāmāyaṇa narrative thus constructed a Vālmīki suitable to its needs of authorship—or left him out if no author was needed.

The Rāmāyaṇa tradition allows for considerable flexibility. Some Rāmāyaṇas have earned recognition as superior works of literature, especially those written by great poets such as Kamban or Tulsidas; others, such as those produced by Telugu poets from the thirteenth to nineteenth centuries, have not acquired such acclaim; yet other Rāmāyaṇas remain authorless although they are accepted as Rāmāyaṇas all the same. This multiplicity suggests that the basic Rāma story itself is treated as a kind of a text-field out of which poets, including the authors responsible for the Vālmīki version, constructed a Rāmāyaṇa suitable to the needs of their time and their community of listeners. Elsewhere, I have likened the Rāmāyaṇa to a language, a language which enables the user to say many very different things.[7] The Rāmāyaṇa text named after Vālmīki is a literary epic, an *itihāsa*. By an epic I mean a text perceived as history that is ideologically influential, in forming a set of new values, its institutions, and new ideals of good behavior. In the introduction to his translation of *Ayodhyākāṇḍa*, Pollock identifies the new values Vālmīki's epic has established for the society of its time. According to Pollock the Rāmāyaṇa's integral problem is kingship itself and its attendant problems: the acquisition, maintenance, and execution of royal power, the legitimacy of succession, the predicament of transferring hereditary power within a royal dynasty. We are naturally led to wonder why this acquisition should assume such importance for the Indian epic. One explanation may be that the problems of kingship addressed so insistently by the epic texts were new ones and, in their very nature, urgent.[8]

Regional-language Rāmāyaṇas are not epics, however—at least not the kind the Vālmīki text represents. They differ in the quality of the narration and they function as bhakti texts rather than epics. I use the term bhakti to indicate that their authors composed them in the spirit of devotion to Rāma as God.

The central issue of the bhakti Rāmāyaṇas is neither kingship nor the maintenance of dynastic power, but a personal relationship of the reader-listener with the deity. Rāma reigns as the supreme lord, and the reader-listener enjoys every telling and retelling of his story for the sheer ecstasy of participating in the experience. The intent of the bhakti Rāmāyaṇas is not so much to tell a story but to allow the listener to experience Rāma one more time in a slightly different way. The listeners already know the story. They have heard it many times, but they want the opportunity to savor their participation in the play of God. Elsewhere I have called this transformation a movement from communication to communion.[9]

However, the transition from communication to communion occurred gradually and unevenly. Many medieval Rāmāyaṇas continued to focus on the epic quality of the Rāmāyaṇa narrative, so they could formulate a new social and political meaning, and a new ideology, through their text. Over the centuries the Rāma story has served as a vehicle for many meanings—social, political, theological, familial, and personal. Telugu poets of the Rāmāyaṇa theme, as well as poets in other regional languages, present an infinite variety of modes in speaking about Rāma and an endless playfulness in depicting his story. The number of Telugu literary Rāmāyaṇas alone is enormous. No theme in Telugu was retold as many times, and in as many ways, as the Rāmāyaṇa theme.

For over five hundred years, from about the thirteenth to the eighteenth centuries, Telugu poets from Brahmin families composed literary texts which they dedicated to the heads of upwardly mobile peasant-warrior clans, to traders, and to local rulers. Such dedications helped elevate the patrons to the varṇa status of Kshatriyas. Elevating the patron families to a varṇa status raised these Brahmin poets in turn to a varṇa status of what one might call a high-status Brahmin. Thus we find a symbiotic relationship between ordinary Brahmin families and peasant leaders, aspiring together to fill the Sanskritic slots of Brahmin and Kshatriya as approved by the *dharmaśāstra* texts.

A few examples will illustrate this process. Tikkana (thirteenth century) dedicated his *Uttara Rāmāyaṇa* (Later Story of Rāma) to Manumasiddhi, a small ruler of Nellūru (Nellore in southern Andhra). Ĕrrāprĕgaḍa (fourteenth century) dedicated his Rāmāyaṇa to Prolaya Vēma Rĕḍḍi of the Reddi dynasty. Huḷakki Bhāskara (fourteenth century) dedicated his Rāmāyaṇa to Sāhiṇi Mara, a head of cavalry. Ayyalarāju Rāmabhadruḍu (mid-sixteenth century) composed the *Rāmābhyudayamu* in the *kāvya* mode, with erotic descriptions of the love between Rāma and

Sītā, and offered it to Gŏbbūri Narasarāju, nephew of the famous Aliya Rāmarāya; here the choice of text, and hero, resonates with the name of Rāmarāya, the king and founder of the new Aravīḍu dynasty.

Sometimes rulers from non-Brahmin families sought to enhance their status by composing a Rāmāyaṇa themselves. They hoped, by producing a devotional text on Rāma, to win respect from their people as good kings. In a way this process bypasses Brahmin intervention to acquire status, though it does not reject Brahmin values. For example, we have the case of a son who composes a Rāmāyaṇa and dedicates it to his father, whom he describes as a man of great religious merit, a gentle and pious ruler. This text, popularly known as *Raṅganātha Rāmāyaṇamu*, was composed in the non-Sanskritic *dvipada* meter by the non-Brahmin poet Gona Buddharāju (fourteenth century?). Raghunāthanāyaka, a Balija who ruled Tanjavur during the early seventeenth century, also wrote a Rāmāyaṇa. Yet another was composed, again in Tanjavur, by Katta Varada Rāju (*c.* 1630), another Balija who claims descent from Karikāḷa Coḷa. The Maharashtra king of Tanjavur, Ekoji (late seventeenth century), wrote an *Ekojī-Rāmāyaṇa* in *dvipada* and, following the custom of the Nayaka kings who preceded him, dedicated it to his father. In fact, the Rāmāyaṇa seems to be the favorite narrative of ambitious non-Brahmin kings. However, no evidence exists of any anti-Brahminic impulse in any Rāmāyaṇa composition before the nineteenth cenrury.[10]

Thus a huge Rāmāyaṇa literature in Telugu came into existence in the early modern centuries as the creation of Brahmin poets, non-Brahmin warriors and rulers, and also other devotees—including a famous poetess, Mŏlla (sixteenth century?), from the potter caste (Kummari). All of these texts reflect the contexts that generated them and the major patterns of social mobility, from medieval through Nayaka and post-Nayaka times—until the entry of the colonial power into the scene. But the politics and aesthetics of using the Rāmāyaṇa theme have significantly changed since the later decades of the nineteenth century. I wish to explore the reasons for this dramatic shift; to do so, we need to examine the changing social dynamics of this period.

The most important shift may be traced to the rupture of political ideology at the hands of a foreign power. The British, who controlled political power, in effect took over the Kshatriya position. However, their position was anomalous since they did not need the varṇa status of a Kshatriya to maintain themselves in power, nor the active role of a Brahmin to legitimize them in that position. This anomaly brutally disturbed the ideological order. Brahmins lost their usual roles as kingmakers, advisers, ministers. Occasionally, they tried to accord the British the status of Kshatriya in the hope of regaining their earlier Brahmin status, but this strategy was not very successful. The British did not need Brahmins to elevate them to a varṇa status. However, they needed indigenous support in maintaining their administration, and the Brahmins were their best choice. In other words, the British told the Brahmins that they needed them as servants, not as superiors. In this context there were three choices left for Brahmins. Those families that desired to keep the old ways of chanting Vedic texts, learning Sanskrit *śāstras*, and fostering traditional Sanskrit or Telugu poetry, sought the patronage of the remaining small kings, the zamindars—who, while they had no real political power, still needed the trappings of kshatriyahood and therefore actively patronized the varnahood of Brahmins. A history of late-eighteenth/early-nineteenth-century Andhra would reveal that the zamindars strongly supported Vedic and Sanskrit scholars. On the other hand, people who desired to pursue English education and move away from the lifestyle of the varṇa Brahmin went to live in modern towns and cities such as Madras. A third choice was to keep working in the old scholarly modes, maintaining traditional values while living in a modern city. Scholars who chose the third option often worked for private publishers, or, if they were enterprising enough, started printing presses. Brahmins of the nineteenth and early-twentieth centuries practiced all these options in varying degrees. But changes in political ideology, and the consequent change in their condition, have been powerful enough to transform their imagination of their past and mythology.

Bhakti-ization and Iconization of Rāma's Story

The Rāmāyaṇas of the nineteenth and twentieth century reflect these changes. I would like to present these practices as representing two modes: Bhakti-ization and Iconization. The Bhakti-ization of Rāmāyaṇas is not new to Telugu. We have already observed the transition in the use of Rāmāyaṇa themes from a complex narrative focusing on the inner world of its characters—as kings and queens, fathers and mothers, husbands and wives—to a song celebrating the experience of a devotee toward God. What is new during this period in Andhra is the intensity of the Bhakti-ization of Rāmāyaṇas, which now begin to depict a heightened state of surrender to God. This move requires reducing the complexity of the Rāmāyaṇa narrative to a relatively straightforward, unproblematic story, where Rama becomes the absolute, flawless, all-powerful God. Even the enemy, Rāvaṇa, is depicted in some of these bhakti Rāmāyaṇas as Rāma's devotee in disguise, too impatient to reach him by the slower route of service; instead, he chose the shorter route of conflict—*vairabhakti*, devotion through enmity. In the larger frame of the Rāmāyaṇa performance, the performer and the listeners now all become merged into one category, that of *dāsas*, servants.

As an example, I cite a mid-twentieth-century Rāmāyaṇa, Sripada Krishnamurti Sastri's *Śrī Kṛṣṇa Rāmāyaṇamu.* Perhaps the most bowdlerized of all Telugu bhakti Rāmāyaṇas, it was written in full acceptance of non-Brahmin criticism from reformers like Tripuraneni Ramasvami Chaudari. Sripada told Rāma's story in a way that sanitized all the major problematic incidents: Āhalyā, in this Rāmāyaṇa, is a chaste woman; her association with Indra was nothing more than a handshake. Kaikeyī has no idea why she asked to send Rāma off to the forest; she does so under the influence of Brahmā, who possesses her at that time. Later, she wonders why Rāma had to go away and weeps at his departure to the forest. Most striking of all, Rāma refuses to abandon Sītā in the forest. He does hear from his spies that a certain washerman scandalized the name of Sītā. But on inquiry he finds that the washerman is insane and ignores his words. Finally, Śambuka is not killed; he is only asked to refrain from his ascetic practices.[11]

A simplistic reductionist narrative of this kind, devoid of the drama and conflicting motivations of an epic, is bound to be boring. But popular bhakti Rāmāyaṇa narratives compensate for the loss of complexity of meaning by musical and verbal power. Music of the congregational *bhajan*, as well as the refined musical compositions of composers like Tyāgarāja and Rāmadāsu (Kañcarla Gopanna), elevate the fragmented individual consciousness beyond thinking to a realm of oneness, a state of highly satisfying integrity. A popular form of Rāmāyaṇa performance during this period was the singing, to melodious instrumental music, of a set of songs from the *Adhyātma Rāmāyaṇa*—incidentally the text which informs Tulsī's *Rāmacaritmānas* narrative. Composed by the fine lyricist Munipalle Subrahmanya Kavi (*c.* 1760–1820), these songs were performed with interspersed prose commentaries by competent performers, engrossing hundreds of people.

A widespread public performance tradition of *harikatha*, invented and popularized by the great singer Ajjada Adibhatla Narayandasu (1864–1945), was another mode through which bhakti Rāmāyaṇa narratives spread across the Telugu area. Each year almost every town and village in Andhra celebrated the nine-day festival of Ramanavami, culminating on the ninth day of the lunar month of Caitra, which was believed to be Rāma's birthday as well as his wedding anniversary. Rāma temples and bands singing Rāma chants proliferated in the countryside. During this period there was a veritable explosion of devotional expressions for Rāma. Songs, rhymes, street plays, chants, and poems that occupied the public and private space of Telugu life make a huge inventory. It became a convention for people to write Rāma's name first on the page, before writing anything else at all, even a laundry list!

Most noteworthy of all was the tradition of copying Rāma's name ten million times, *rāmakoṭi*, as a means of liberation. These performances and practices reinforced Rāma's position as the supreme deity and encouraged devotion and surrender. Rāma is called the favorite god of the Telugu people (*Tĕlugu-vāri āradhya-daivamu*). So pervasive was this wave of devotionalism for Rāma that even a traditionalist poet like the great Viswanatha Satyanarayana sensed its shallowness and parodied it in the following verse:

Everyone is jumping around like crazy,
yelling, "Telugu, Telugu!"
The whole nation is confused. And you
are part of it, our Telugu god.

So let me praise you in Telugu,
until I have let it all out,
all night long, until darkness ends,
O Rāma, lord of Bhadradri Hill.[12]

To the extent that Brahmins saw their loss of political power as total, their submission to their god became total. Loss of power now becomes a source of power over the god who is imagined as the most powerful of all. In a very paradoxical way, that very god is powerless to disobey the wishes of his devotees, because their devotion to him is greater than he himself. This theme is best illustrated in a newly popular play, *Rāmāñjaneya Yuddham*, "the Battle of Rāma and Hanumān," which depicts Hanumān as stronger than Rāma—because Hanumān is armed with unfailing devotion to Rāma![13]

By the end of the nineteenth century, bhakti Rāmāyaṇas occupied the public space in Andhra so completely that they excluded other versions of the story. The change is striking when we compare the use of the Rāmāyaṇa themes by premodern poets with the usage of the new bhakti poets. Premodern poets in Telugu used Rāmāyaṇa themes in nearly all genres of Telugu literature. More importantly, they allowed their texts to breathe. They joked with Rāma and even ridiculed him. Here is a verse from Kāsula Puruṣottama Kavi (eighteenth century), referring to Rāma's departure for the forest, dressed as an ascetic, renouncing his kingdom:

You gave up the kingdom because your father said so,
but have you ever given up power?
You took off your ornaments because you wanted to,
but you always kept your bow.
You rejected royal robes, of course,
but you have the muscles of a warrior.
We know you denied wealth;
but you never let go of your pride.
All this is a game you played to kill
your enemies. Would anyone believe you were a sage?[14]

Parallel to bhakti-ization of the Rāmāyaṇa is iconization. Earlier I said that while Vālmīki was revered as a great poet, the Sanskrit version of the Rāmāyaṇa attributed to Vālmīki was not well known. Except for a few scholars who knew Sanskrit, most of whom were Brahmins who possessed a manuscript copy of the text, the Vālmīki version was not even widely available. However, by the beginning of the twentieth century Vālmīki's text achieved unprecedented prominence. This was due to a complex set of reasons. While the Rāmāyaṇa became the holiest of all themes, no Telugu literary Rāmāyaṇa stands out as a sacred text. No author of Telugu Rāmāyaṇas was viewed as a saint. There were poets from the past who attained such respect—Potana, for instance, the author of the *Bhāgavata Purāṇa*—but alas, no one of this class wrote a Rāmāyaṇa.

To make up for this lack, verbatim translations of Vālmīki's text began to appear. In fact, such a project was first completed under the patronage of the zamindar of Gadvala in the later part of the seventeenth century.[15] The most prominent of such projects was the Rāmāyaṇa completed by Vavilikolanu Subbarao (1863–1939), appropriately called the Vālmīki of Andhra. After his retirement as Telugu pandit at Presidency College, Madras, Subbarao lived the pious life of a devotee, translating Vālmīki's text into Telugu, verse by verse. Like the Gadvala version, he thinks of his text as a *yathā-vālmīka-rāmāyaṇamu*—a Rāmāyaṇa strictly according to Vālmīki. In keeping with the belief that Vālmīki's text has powerful mantric syllables embedded in it, Subbarao attempted to bring similar syllables into his Telugu text. He supplemented his translation with an elaborate multi-volume commentary. However, this was not quite enough for people who looked up to Vālmīki's text as essentially untranslatable. This view is best illustrated by a late-eighteenth-century text, the *Tattva-saṅgraha-rāmāyaṇa,* which says:

> That idiot
> who rejects the Sanskrit text
> and reads the Rāma story in another language
> desires to drink water
> from a mirage.[16]

Religious leaders began to claim that the Sanskrit Rāmāyaṇa has the powerful syllables of the *gāyatrī* mantra embedded in it; thereore its power does not carry over into a translation. Devotees were encouraged to keep on reciting the Sanskrit Rāmāyaṇa for the efficacy of the sound, an activity which was called *pārāyaṇa*. The *Sundarakāṇḍa* was identified as especially powerful, and devotees were told to chant it to overcome troubles in life and to achieve success. Publishers released the *Sundarakāṇḍa* in separate volumes with special instructions for chanting. Such books carried specific directions as to what particular section of the *Sundarakāṇḍa* one should chant for such common personal problems as finding a good job, a promotion, a good husband/wife, success in examinations, and so on.[17]

The second reason for the new interest in Vālmīki was the popularity of the printing press. If earlier even educated people had depended on a public oral performance of the Rāmāyaṇa by a pandit performer (*paurāṇika*), now more and more people could buy a copy of their own for private use. In the absence of a highly revered Telugu literary rendering, Vālmīki's Sanskrit text became the holy book. It was even available with a verbatim Telugu prose paraphrase printed under each stanza of the original Sanskrit. However, this did not necessarily mean that readers were ready to explore the Sanskrit version to compare the differences between the epic and the bhakti versions. There were two reasons for this. One was the indoctrination of the bhakti Rāmāyaṇas, which had generated a general acceptance of the Rāmāyaṇa as a holy text; the very printed book was worshiped as an icon. The second was the role of publishing houses in the production of classical works. Major publishing houses which produced classical Telugu and Sanskrit books were controlled by Brahmin pandits. Vavilla Ramasvami Sastrulu, an enterprising Brahmin scholar, founded what soon grew to be the foremost publishing house of literary and scholarly works in Telugu and Sanskrit. The influence of this publishing house in the production of the Rāmāyaṇa may be best illustrated by an incident which reportedly happened when the Vālmīki text was printed by the Adisaraswati press in Madras in 1856. The Brahmin managers of the press were not willing to have the text typeset by non-Brahmin compositors—who usually did all the typesetting jobs in the press. (These were the days of the letterpress, where lead type was set by hand.) So, they trained Brahmin boys in typesetting specially to typeset the Rāmāyaṇa. The text was too sacred to be touched by non-Brahmins even during the printing process!

Change in the Status of Non-Brahmins

Meanwhile the role of the peasant castes of Andhra had been changing too. In premodern Andhra, as stated earlier, the Shudra king acquired Kshatriya status, legitimized by the Brahmin poet. When the British occupied the role of the king, the non-Brahmin castes were left with no hope of becoming Kshatriyas. In parallel with the ideology of the bhakti Rāmāyaṇas, they progressively became the servants of Brahmins.

However, the younger generation of landed castes—Kammas, Reddis, and Kapus—went to Western schools, as the Brahmins had done, receiving an education suitable for jobs in the colonial administration. The new jobs these non-Brahmin young men were seeking placed them in competition with the Brahmins, their erstwhile gurus, and their former collaborators and legitimizers in the pursuit of kshatriyahood. For the first time in the history of Andhra culture, upwardly mobile non-Brahmin castes saw Brahmins as their enemies. Among the newly educated non-Brahmin young men, Tripuraneni Ramasvami Chaudari from the Kamma caste (already mentioned) and Cattamanci Ramalinga Reddi (1880–1951) from the Reddi caste, stand out. Ramasvami Chaudari, trained as a barrister in Ireland, founded a center for his followers in Tenali, a small town in Guntur district, which he called Sūta-āśramam, after the non-Brahmin bard of the Mahābhārata epic. Ramasvami Chaudari undertook an active campaign of rewriting the Purāṇas, criticizing the existing texts as Brahmin constructions to enslave Shudras. His most important contribution to the anti-Rāmāyaṇa discourse, however, is his play, *Śambuka Vadha,* which I mentioned earlier.

At this time the protocols of reading were undergoing a revolutionary change as well. Texts that were orally recited and commented upon in a public performance appeared in print, available for silent reading. Bringing palm-leaf texts into print was not an innocent act of making multiple copies available to readers. Before the advent of the printed text, the manuscript served as the recorded text, from which the performer/

interpreter created a new text for his/her audience. This was the received text, which actually lived in the minds of the listeners. Reading the recorded text was a specialist's job and required a certain training in using it. Printing the recorded text, and making it available to readers untrained to using the text, generated new and unprecedented modes of reading. Western education prepared the minds of young scholars to receive the printed text as a univalent artifact, with every page and every word consciously produced by a single putative author.

Assumptions of textual integrity led to complementary propositions such as interpolations and textual corruption. Western textual theories such as Jacobi's claim that the first and last books of the Rāmāyaṇa were later additions to an original Rāmāyaṇa became influential among English-educated Telugu intellectuals. Taking advantage of the easy availability of Vālmīki's text in verbatim translation, modern scholars began to focus on other deviations from Vālmīki in regional-language Rāmāyaṇa texts. These scholars subjected Vālmīki's text to a new type of reading—never practiced before the advent of the printing press. In this new reading, a number of internal inconsistencies and problematic repetitions began to emerge. These were viewed as serious flaws by their author, or irresponsible interpolations by mischievous outsiders.

While the modern Rāmāyaṇa scholars of this time began to question Vālmīki's text, which was now perceived as the authoritative text of the narrative, some of these very same people adopted the freedom available to the Rāmāyaṇa poets all through the centuries to tell the story in any manner they chose. But they invariably wrote a preface to their literary work questioning the textual authenticity of the Vālmīki version as it had been handed down to the present generation. Nearly every writer accepted the textual critical studies of Western scholars. They attempted to find an "Ur-Rāmāyaṇa," written by Vālmīki, and to treat all unacceptable and contradictory parts of his text as Brahminic forgeries, or condemn Vālmīki himself for his Brahminic bias.

Ramasvami Chaudari did this with a new confidence by using the race theories of colonial anthropologists who claimed to have identified Aryan and Dravidian races in the Indian subcontinent. For Ramasvami Chaudari, all Brahmins were Aryan intruders; regional landed castes like Kammas and Reddis were Dravidians. In his major work *Sūta Purāṇamu* (1924) Ramasvami Chaudari wrote the Rāma story as he wanted it to happen. According to him, Rāvaṇa is born in the Dravidian tribe of Koyas;[18] when he ascends the throne, he rules as a peace-loving king who prohibits animal sacrifice in his kingdom. He is also a great scholar of the Vedas, a great grammarian, physically handsome, and a noble ruler.

Then the Brahmins of the north come down south and begin their fire rituals, which include killing cows, a practice prohibited in Rāvaṇa's kingdom. When the Brahmin sage Viśvāmitra announces a fire sacrifice, Rāvaṇa sends Tāṭaka to gently persuade the sage to refrain from killing cows, as it breaks the law of the land. The sage does not listen and Tāṭaka's assistants release the cows from their bonds and put out the fires as a punishment. The Brahmin sage regrets that his attempts to convert the Dravidians have not succeeded. He says:

> I tried my best, but it did not work.
> They just refuse to eat beef,
> nor would they taste liquor.
> That's the cause of all this trouble.[19]

So he goes to the Saketa king Daśaratha and gets his sons Rāma and Lakṣmaṇa to kill Tāṭaka.

In Chaudari's retelling, Rāvaṇa's sister Surpanakha is an old woman; instigated by Brahmin sages, Lakṣmaṇa kills her son Jambukumara. Grieving about the loss of her son, she goes to Rāma to find out why her son was killed. Angered by his irresponsible reply that her son was an enemy of sages, she attacks Rāma with her knife. Rāma overreacts, holds the old woman down and orders Lakṣmaṇa to cut off her nose and ears. Rāvaṇa decides to capture Sītā only to teach Rāma a lesson; he treats Sītā with honor and—most significant of all—entertains no erotic feeling for her.

With his *Sūta Purāṇamu*, Ramasvami Chaudari set the agenda for the anti-Rāmāyaṇa discourse, and for anti-purāṇa discourse in general. He characterized the Brahmin texts as obscene, immoral, cruel and—of course—Aryan. He had no doubt that all the Sanskrit purāṇas, and especially the Rāmāyaṇa, were written to subjugate the independent and highly civilized Dravidians. Sanskrit, Brahmins, and North India represented Aryan civilization; and South India, South Indian languages, and non-Brahmins represented Dravidian civilization. In this scheme of things, Brahmins were perceived as colonizers of the south and all Sanskrit texts, especially the Rāmāyaṇa, were seen as imperialist. Rāma acted as the chief agent of Brahminic imperialism of North India, whereas Rāvaṇa reigned as a noble king of the Dravidian south.

All this will sound very familiar to South India scholars. E.V. Ramasami's reading of the Rāmāyaṇa, analyzed in detail by Paula Richman, bears close resemblance to Ramasvami Chaudari's reading.[20] There is, however, an important difference, in addition to the fact that Chaudari's reading appeared several years earlier than E.V. Ramasami's work.[21] Unlike E.V. Ramasami, Chaudari presents a fully worked out Dravidian anthropology. According to him the classification of different castes and their occupations in South India before the Aryan occupation conformed to the following hierarchical order:

1. Land-owning castes like Kammas, Reddis, Velamas: warriors/ kings, analogous to the Kshatriyas of Aryan society.
2. Golla, Palli, Kummari and such other castes: priests analogous to Brahmins of Aryan society.
3. Balijas, Komati, Sali and such other castes: trading castes analogous to Vaishyas of Aryan society
4. Kasa, Boya, Cakali and other similar service castes: servants analogous to Shudras of Aryan Society.[22]

This is a sophisticated scheme indeed. In this classification, the Brahmin occupation ranks below that of the Kshatriya. Chaudari's observation that lower castes conduct priestly activities in village-goddess temples in Andhra is accurate. According to Chaudari the Aryan invasion of the south placed Sanskritic Brahmin priests over and above the kings, while simultaneously downgrading castes like Kammas and Reddis, who enjoyed the status of kings, as Shudras.

Chaudari built his anti-Rāmāyaṇa argument on a larger anti-Aryan argument. For him, the Aryans, wherever they went, suppressed the other races and their civilizations. He extends his anti-Aryan position to the white race of the United States where they suppressed Blacks. Dravidians are faultless, showing love for their family and neighbors. He even suggests that Vibhīṣaṇa betrayed his brother Rāvaṇa not because he was evil, but because Vibhīṣaṇa's wife Saramā, who is part Aryan (Gandharva), influenced his thinking in favor of Rāma. Their daughter Trijaṭā, who has Aryan blood in her, turns out to be a betrayer, too; she supports Sītā and hates Rāvaṇa.

As may be seen from the later anti-Rāmāyaṇa works, Chaudari's general agenda of denouncing the purāṇas as Brahminic, obscene, immoral, and superstitious found an enthusiastic following, whereas his racial theme—dividing Telugu people into Aryan versus Dravidian—was quietly rejected. Despite general acceptance among university linguistics departments of the existence of the Dravidian family of languages, among which Telugu is included, literary scholars did not evince interest in discussing Telugu literature in terms of Dravidian versus Aryan cultures.

While Ramasvami Chaudari was openly anti-Aryan and pro-Dravidian, Ramalinga Reddi was a "modernist," advocating a "progressive" culture in an industrialized, egalitarian, capitalist society. Educated in Cambridge, where he studied economics, his main interest was Telugu literature. From the time he returned from England, he devoted his energies to modernizing Telugu literary history and criticism. As regards the Rāmāyaṇa, Ramalinga Reddi conducted a somewhat subtler form of resistance than Chaudari. As vice chancellor of Andhra University, he sponsored a critical edition of the *Raṅganātha Rāmāyaṇa*. He conducted a well-documented polemic arguing that, contrary to current belief, the non-Brahmin Buddhā Rĕḍḍi was its real author. He coupled his rejection of the Brahminic culture with a call for modernism, which soon drew a large number of secularized Brahmin young men into its fold.

Modernity and its Respondents

Meanwhile, English schools and colleges included in their syllabus powerful new kinds of learning: history and geography, as well as the natural and physical sciences. Students trained in the new schools were asking difficult questions such as: Where was Lanka in relation to the Daṇḍaka forest? How wide was the ocean that Hanumān was supposed to have crossed? How could monkeys have a civilization complex enough to have a society, a kingdom, and a king, and if so, why describe them as animals? In this social and political context non-Brahmin poets and intellectuals, and later modernist writers including Brahmins, turned against the conventional Rāmāyaṇas and began rewriting Rāma's story. Invariably these anti-Rāmāyaṇas focused on problem areas of the Vālmīki narrative, showing that Ram was not as great as he was depicted to be, and that his image was exaggerated to serve Brahminic, feudal, or patriarchal interests.

Modernity in Andhra expressed itself primarily as a literary movement, which came to be known as Bhāva-kavitvam, somewhat similar to the Romantic movement in English poetry. Rejection of the Brahmin past proved easier under the new ideology of modernity and the younger generation of poets and writers undertook the task of questioning the authenticity of the Rāmāyaṇa narrative as given in the Vālmīki telling.

While Ramasvami Chaudari contended with Brahmin scholars, he also used their style and idiom in his endeavors. Although ideologically opposed to them, he wrote his *Śambuka Vadha,* as well as his other works, in a classical style of Telugu, strictly in accordance with the regulations of prescriptive grammars followed by Brahminic poets. He took care to follow Brahminic literary style, meters, and conventions with considerable skill. Hence, he received the acceptance and praise of his Brahmin contemporaries, who called him the King of Poets (*Kavirāju*), in admiration. By contrast, the modern literary movement of Bhāva-kavitvam, which began in opposition to the classical worldview, adopted literary conventions that encouraged poets to write in defiance of pandit-made rules. Protest-Rāmāyaṇa themes adopted by Bhāva-kavitvam poets now appeared in a modern literary idiom.

One such play is Muddu Krishna's *Aśokam* (1930), which presents Rāma, Sītā, and Rāvaṇa speaking conversational Telugu, looking like your nextdoor neighbors. Tradition so far had dictated that all mythological characters speak a dialect removed from modern speech, filled with Sanskritic and archaic forms of Telugu. This strategy elevated the characters above the human level and provided them with an aura of distance and divinity. Even demons spoke such a dialect if they were high-caste characters like Rāvaṇa. This convention underwent a radical transformation in the works of Chalam (see below), who made gods speak like ordinary people in his works and whose lead Muddu Krishna followed.

The theme of *Aśokam* is briefly this: Rāvaṇa stops by at Sītā's house to express his love for her, even before her wedding to Rāma. Sītā listens to his declaration of love but answers that she has chosen to leave the final decision of marriage to fate and to her father. Then Rāma arrives and declares his love to Sītā. Sītā gives the same answer, but feels attracted to Rāma and falls in love with him. Rāma meets Rāvaṇa and realizes that Rāvaṇa too is in love with Sītā but, instead of being jealous, he nobly admits that Rāvaṇa's love for Sītā could be as "pure" as his, so he decides to let Sītā choose between them.

Next we meet Sītā in the forest. Rāma regrets experiencing such hardship in the forest but feels grateful to her for choosing to accompany him there. Then Rāvaṇa shows up and invites both of them to his palace in Lanka. He offers to relinquish Lanka for Sītā and her husband, and depart to a faraway place. His love for Sītā is so great that he offers to sacrifice his empire for her. Next, we meet Sītā in the Aśoka grove in Lanka, reprimanding Rāvaṇa for being so rash as to bring her there. Rāvaṇa admits that he had been wrong, but says he could not resist his love for her; he worships her and could not live without seeing her. Sītā tells him how much she understands his feelings for her, but explains that she cannot give herself to him. We finally see Rāma telling Sītā how deeply Rāvaṇa had loved her, and how he spoke of her even at the time of his death. Sītā understands, and Rāma does too, that Rāvaṇa had a pure heart. He was a noble lover. But Sītā still goes through the fire ordeal to satisfy the fears of the people!

Retold in this form, the story may look sentimental and silly. Yet in the atmosphere of the Bhāva-kavitvam movement of the 1930s, Telugu literature was raging with poems on platonic love; in keeping with the trend of the times, writers wrote about men who fell in love with women only to sacrifice their lives for their love, never even thinking of a physical relationship. This play depicts Rāvaṇa professing his "pure love," *pavitra prema,* to Sītā. The writer makes no effort to depict Rāma in a poor light, but then he is not the center of the play either.

Muddu Krishna did not stand out as one of the major writers of the period. Remembered mostly for his anthology of Bhāva-kavitvam poems, he is one of the few non-Brahmin poets of this modern poetry movement. However, the new ideology of modernity seemed to defy the claims of caste hierarchies, at least in poetry, and a number of Brahmin writers themselves wrote anti-Brahminic poems.

With Gudipati Venkata Chalam (1894–1979), one of those rebel Brahmins, the "feminist" anti-Rāmāyaṇa narratives begin. Chalam believed that women should be freed from the sexual bondage of marriage; he wrote of sexual liberation of women in his novels and short stories. Although they might look mild by present-day standards, such works were revolutionary in Chalam's time. A writer who handled Telugu prose with masterly subtlety and power, he wrote with a sensitive understanding of female sexuality and a passionate desire to affirm female sexual pleasure as the celebration of human life. Sharply critical of Brahminic moral standards, Chalam relished shocking the conservative minds of his time. In one novel (*Maid Anam*), he relentlessly describes the sexual adventures, with two Muslim lovers, of a married Brahmin woman from a conservative family. He wrote a number of plays reinterpreting puranic themes from his rebellious point of view. Among them, the one that concerns us here is *Sīta Agnipraveśam* (Sītā Enters Fire, 1935?). Despite his unconventional interest in depicting uninhibited sexuality, Chalam shares the romantic attitudes of love prevalent in the literature of his time.

In his *Agnipraveśam*, Chalam rewrites the well-known Rāmāyaṇa incident where Sītā has to walk through fire to prove her fidelity to Rāma. The play begins after the war with Rāvaṇa ends, with Sītā inviting Rāma, with words of great longing and love, to embrace her. But soon she finds out that Rāma has doubts about her because she has lived in the enemy's house for an extended time. Rāvaṇa had loved her. "Is it my fault?" asks Sītā. But realizing that Rāma sees her only as an object to be possessed as long as it gives him pride, which he is willing to abandon the moment he sees it might be polluted, she declares:

> Let me speak. Rāvaṇa loved me. Even your sharp arrows could not kill his love for me. Your love, it was gone the moment you suspected that another man might have loved me . . . Did I love him in return? That's what you fear, don't you? If I had loved him, I would have covered his body with mine as a shield against your arrows. Did he molest me? No, he was too noble a person for that. He loved me, even when he knew I would never love him in return . . . I feel sorry I did not return his love. I shall pay a price for it now. I shall purify my body, which was soiled when I uttered your wretched name, by the flames of fire which touched his blood-stained limbs. You, Rāma, rejected me because you fear that my body was defiled by his touch, though you know my heart was pure. This anti-god wanted my heart, even though he knew my body was taken by you. Some day, intelligent people will know who was a nobler lover.[23]

And even before she finishes her sentence, Sītā jumps into Rāvaṇa's funeral pyre, performing a sort of suttee for him!

While an influential anti-Brahminic discourse was spreading through the middle class, especially after the new trend beginning with the Bhāvakavitvam movement during the early decades of the twentieth century, a totally unprecedented Rāmāyaṇa took the literary world by storm: Viswanatha Satyanarayana's *Rāmāyaṇa Kalpavṛkṣamu* (Rāmāyaṇa, the Giving Tree). As soon as the first volume of this remarkable book was published, the literary world realized its power and beauty.[24] However, there was a problem. Satyanarayana took a vehemently conservative position and spoke unapologetically in support of Brahmins. It was trendy among the educated middle class during those days to be anti-traditional, which also meant being anti-Brahmin. Even Brahmins adopted a vigorous anti-traditional position. The modern English-educated person agreed that the Vedas, purāṇas, and similar old texts kept the country in ignorance; they agreed that the caste system, child marriages, the proscription of widow remarriage, and all the Hindu practices relating to purity were features of backwardness. India had to change, and nearly everything traditional should be abandoned for a modern, Western model. In this context, Satyanarayana came out in support of traditional customs and values, including the caste system and child marriages. He advocated a society based on the rules of the *Mānavadharmaśāstra*.

It would probably have mattered little had Satyanarayana not been a powerful poet; there were plenty of old pandits who argued like him. They were all eventually marginalized as outdated and fossilized minds (*chāndasulu*), with nothing intelligent to say, even if they controlled the knowledge from some old books, for which skill they sometimes needed to be consulted. But Satyanarayana was different. Breathtakingly brilliant, well-educated in English, he was on top of all this a dazzling poet. When he read his Rāmāyaṇa verses in public, hundreds of people listened in rapture. Satyanarayana's literary presence and his energetic scholarly and poetic personality made his audience pay renewed attention to the Rāmāyaṇa. While his Rāmāyaṇa was admittedly devotional, his depiction of character and his narration of the story were anything but flat. To an audience tired of reading insipid retellings of the Rāma story just because Rāma was God, Satyanarayana offered a lively and exciting option.

He pre-empted questions about his choice of theme in the opening verses of his six-volume magnum opus:

> If you ask, "Why yet another Rāmāyaṇa?"
> my answer is: In this world,
> everyone eats the same rice every day,
> but the taste of your life is your own.
> People make love, over and over, but only you
> know how it feels. I write about the same Rāma
> everyone else has known, but my feelings of love
> are mine. Ninety percent of what makes a poem
> is the genius of the poet. Poets in India know
> that the way you tell the tale
> weighs a thousand times more
> than some facile, novel theme.[25]

Such a renewal of the Rāmāyaṇa with a strong Brahminic message quickly elicited an equally strong non-Brahmin reaction. Modern secularists, and Marxists, all ideologically anti-Brahmin, found Satyanarayana a threat. They felt repelled by Satyanarayana's conservative arguments, which, to them, sounded like a call to turn their backs on a century of progress toward Enlightenment, rational thinking, and scientific understanding. Public criticism against Satyanarayana was vehement and relentless. He was attacked as a blind revivalist and a difficult writer to understand. (He used archaic Sanskrit words and compounds, testing even the most learned scholar's control of Sanskrit.) Satyanarayana himself took a vehement anti-colonial stand, advocating that the evil of English education had destroyed the dharmic genius of Indian culture and enslaved Indian minds to a foreign ideology. In addition to his *Rāmāyaṇa Kalpavṛkṣamu*, his other publications, too, fueled the anti-Rāmāyaṇa discourse of the past five decades. Among the leaders of this new anti-Rāmāyaṇa discourse two writers stand out: Narla Venkateswara Rao (1908–85) and Muppala Ranganayakamma.

Narla Venkateswara Rao, a younger contemporary of the major modern writers in Telugu, earned a greater reputation for his leadership role in Telugu journalism than as a writer. But he wrote two Rāmāyaṇa plays, *Jābāli* (1974) and *Sīta Josyam* (Sītā's Prophesy, 1979). As the editor of the most widely circulated Telugu daily newspaper, *Andhra Prabha,* he played an influential role in molding public opinion. He stood up for freedom of the press and fearlessly advocated liberal ideas. He wrote his editorials in a vigorous style and they remained the talk of the town day after day. For Venkateswara Rao, Sanskrit and Brahmanic ideas represented a dead past which only blocked the path to progress. He looked to Western scholarship for wisdom; ideas of Enlightenment served as his guide to the future. In his *Jābāli,* Venkateswara Rao depicts an atheist character who appears in the *Ayodhyākāṇḍa* of Vālmīki's *Rāmāyaṇa.* Jābāli, in Venkateswara Rao's play, is a weak character, too scared to face the powerful Vasiṣṭha, the Brahmin minister. After trying in vain to dissuade Rāma from going to the forest, by giving him his atheist advice, Jābāli sees Vasiṣṭha approaching and escapes with the excuse that he was only testing Rāma's resolve. Jābāli's conversation with Rāma reveals the intrigues, jealousies, and pettiness of the Brahmin sages at the court.

The second play, *Sīta Josyam,* is more interesting, and also more skillfully written. In a long Introduction to this play, Venkateswara Rao says:

> The Rāmāyaṇa, the Mahābhārata, the eighteen purāṇas—the major aim of all these texts is to protect the caste system; the feudal order. If they continue to be propagated in the way they are now, progress toward a new social order will remain an empty slogan. For about fifteen hundred years, these texts have stood as severe obstacles to our intellectual development and social progress. If we do not remove these obstacles even now, we cannot enter the modern age, nor can we move forward on a progressive path.[26]

In this play Venkateswara Rao depicts the conflict between sages and demons in the Daṇḍaka forest as a conflict between food gatherers and food producers. Rāma, depicted as a vain character, kills the demons when the sages flatter him as the greatest warrior of the Raghu clan. Sītā, on the other hand, understands that the demons are innocent food gatherers whose livelihood is being destroyed by sages who burn their forests to clear land for their cultivation. The demons fight back. Sītā wants Rāma to leave them alone. The sages, she advises, are seeking expansion into the south to occupy more and more land, but Rāma refuses to listen. He has vowed to protect the Brahmins, whatever the price. The play ends with Sītā prophesying that one day he will leave her—to please the Brahmins!

One of the most recent, most complete and also highly controversial of the anti-Rāmāyaṇas is Muppala Ranganayakamma's *Rāmāyaṇa Viṣavṛkṣam* (*Rāmāyaṇa, The Poison Tree*). By the 1960s the novel had become the major mode of Telugu literature. For about a decade women writers dominated prose fiction and their novels sold in larger quantities than any other works. Serialized in weekly magazines, novels written by women significantly increased magazine circulation. Ranganayakamma is one of the new group of women writers who came into the literary world through her novels. Sometime in the early 1970s Ranganayakamma discovered Marxism, and since then she has stopped writing novels and begun writing Marxist works.

Fiercely polemical in its style, *The Poison Tree* vehemently rejects all Brahminic as well as non-Brahminic interpretations of the Rāmāyaṇa and proposes that Vālmīki's text was written with the sole intention of keeping all low castes and women in feudal bondage. Partly a critical commentary on Vālmīki's text and partly a retelling of the story as Ranganayakamma thought it had happened, *The Poison Tree* is a rambling text in a style that spares neither innuendo nor invective against feudalism and Brahmins. Ranganayakamma's belief in Marxism gives her enormous confidence in rejecting Vālmīki as an unskilled poet who was writing at a stage in civilization when the art of telling stories and composing books was still in its infancy. Her Marxist knowledge has an answer for everything; there are no uncertainties or questions in her mind about the absolute accuracy of her theory that human civilization progresses in clearly defined stages based on the means of production, and that the Rāmāyaṇa reflects the feudal stage. She rewrites the story to unmask the mystique which kept the true intention of the narrative hidden from readers. Summarizing her three-volume retelling of the Rāmāyaṇa, Ranganayakamma declares: "The Rāmāyaṇa favors men; favors the rich, favors the upper castes, and the ruling class. It supports exploitation; it was never a progressive text, not even at the time it was written."[27]

Conclusion

What is the impact of these anti-Rāmāyaṇas on the Telugu public? None of them achieved recognition as outstanding works of literature, except perhaps *Sīta Josyam,* which received the Sahitya Akademi award in 1981. Each one of them remained controversial for a time. Educated readers argued about them. Ranganayakamma's *The Poison Tree* even sold well. It generated violent disagreements; some responded to it as a liberating reading, and others genuinely hated it. Ranganayakamma, a writer not particularly gentle in her responses to criticism, added fire to the acrimonious nature of the debate. The official position of the Marxist parties themselves was somewhat lukewarm: they did not oppose the book but they did not enthusiastically embrace it either. With all the excitement the anti-Rāmāyaṇa authors generated, they missed out on something that makes a literary text literary. They uniformly failed to understand that the literary consciousness of Telugu culture was deeply embedded in myth, a valorized narrative from a sacred past. They failed to create anything even remotely satisfying to sustain a counter-myth.

However, author after author wrote a lengthy polemical essay as a preface to their literary work. Their ideas were intellectually provocative, even if their artistic skill was not satisfying. Literary scholars wrote books discussing the value of the Rāmāyaṇa in the light of new knowledge of anthropology, history, and science.[28] The essays and books led to serious discussions, charges, and counter-charges.

As a result of the long and sustained discourse of the anti-Rāmāyaṇas, a level of cultural openness was achieved, at least among intellectuals. The religious impact of the bhakti Rāmāyaṇas on the public mind was not greatly diminished, but educated middle-class readers became familiar with critical discourse on what is believed to be a sacred text. If in earlier times premodern literary Rāmāyaṇas and folk Rāmāyaṇas kept the multivocality of the Rāmāyaṇa alive, the modernist anti-Rāmāyaṇas have played a major role in keeping the diverse interpretations alive in the face of the homogenization and production of what, one sometimes fears, could become a fascist Rāmāyaṇa discourse.

Notes

1. Tripuraneni Ramasvami Chaudari, *Śambuka Vadha,* 1920, rept. in vol. 2 of *Kavirāju Sāhitya Sarvasvaṁ* (Complete Works of Ramasvami Chaudari), 2 vols (Gunturu: Kaviraju Sahiti Samiti, 1996), pp. 1–79. Each text in these volumes is independently numbered.
2. For the Vālmīki telling, see 7.73–5 and 76.1–16: *Rāmāyaṇa of Vālmīki,* ed. Katti Srinivāsa Sāstri (Delhi: Parimal Publications, 1983).
3. *Raghuvaṁśa,* 15.42–53, esp. verse 53.
4. *Uttarāmacarita,* 2.10–13, ed. S.K. Belvalkar (Poona: Oriental Book Supplying Agency, 1921).
5. Sheldon Pollock, "*Rāmāyaṇa* and Political Imagination in India," *Journal of Asian Studies* 52. 2 (May 1993): 263.
6. This is the story told by King Raghunāthanāyaka of Tanjore in his *Vālmīki Caritramu* 1919, 1940. Third edn, ed. B. Ramaraju (Hyderabad: Potti Sriramulu Telugu University, 2008),
7. Narayana Rao, "A *Rāmāyaṇa* of One's Own: Women's Oral Tradition in Telugu," in Chapter 7, this volume.
8. Sheldon I. Pollock, *The Rāmāyaṇa of Vālmīki: An Epic of Ancient India,* vol. 2, *Ayodhyākāṇḍa* (Princeton, NJ: Princeton University Press, 1986), p. 10.

9. Velcheru Naryana Rao, unpublished remarks at panel on "Audiences and Indian Literature," presented at the Association for Asian Studies, 1982.
10. There was, however, no lack of Rāmāyaṇas that presented events from the perspective of Sītā. For example, a number of women's songs and tales did so as discussed in detail in the present volume.
11. Rāvūri Dorasāmi Śarma, *Telugu Sāhityamu: Rāma-kathā* (Machilipatnam: Triveni Publishers, 1972), pp. 71–6.
12. From *Visvanātha Madhyākkaralu,* cited by Śarma, *Tĕlugu Sāhityamu,* 247. Bhadradri, or Bhadracalam, is a famous Rāma shrine in West Godavari District.
13. Tāṇḍra Subrahmanyam, *Śrī Rāmājaneya Yuddham* (Tenali: Śrī Venkaṭaramaṇa Book Depot, 1979). This play, which does not have a source in any purāṇa, has been performed widely in Andhra Pradesh and was also produced for radio. A phonograph album of this play sold well; a movie was also made.
14. Kāsula Puruṣottamakavi, *Āndhranāyaka Śatakamu,* ed. Yārlagaḍḍa Bālagāngādhara Rāvu (Visakhapatnam: Nirmala Publications, 1975), verse 88.
15. Professor Ravvā Śrīhari says Kāmasamudram Appalācāryulu led a five-scholar team for this project, including Kānādam Pĕddana Somayāji, a great Sanskrit scholar of his time: Preface to Kānādam Pĕddana Somayāji, *Mukundavilāsamu* (Hyderabad: Tĕlugu Vijñāna Pītham, 1985), pp. 9–10.
16. *saṁskṛtaṁ rāmacaritaṁ parityajya narādhamah*
paṭhan bhāṣāntara-kṛtam mṛgatṛṣṇā jalam pibet.
17. Two such books, for instance, are: *Sakala-kārya-siddhiki Śrīmadrāmāyaṇa-pārāyaṇamu* (Reading Rāmāyana for Success in All Efforts: (Madras: Little Flower Company, 1967), reprinted several times, and *Sundara-hanumadvaibhavamu* (*Sundara-kāṇḍa* with rules for reading) by Śiṣtlā Candramauli Śāstri (Pedapadu, Andhra Pradesh: Author, n.d.).
18. Chaudari presents "linguistic evidence" to suggest that Rāvaṇa's name was derived from the Koya language. See *Sūta Purāṇamu,* 2 vols (Gunturu: Kaviraju Sahiti Samiti, 1996), vol. 1, pp. 224–5.
19. *Sūta Purāṇamu,* 3.210, 210.
20. Richman, "E.V. Ramasami's Reading of the Rāmāyaṇa," in idem, ed., *Many Ramayanas: The Diversity of a Narrative Tradition in*

South Asia (Berkeley: University of California Press, 1991), pp. 175–201.

21. Chaudari clearly anticipates E.V. Ramasami of Tamil Nadu. The chronology of their ideas has not received attention since Ramasvami Chaudari is not as well known as E.V. Ramasami in the West. Ramasvami Chaudari wrote *Śambuka Vadha* during 1914–17; however, he published it, along with a long preface, only in 1920. His *Sūta Purāṇamu,* with several detailed prefatory essays for each of its chapters, was published in 1924, whereas E.V. Ramasami's anti-Rāmāyaṇa pamphlet *Irāmāyaṇappāttiraṅkaḷ* made its first appearance in 1930, a full decade after Chaudari's *Śambuka Vadha.* Their ideas bear very close resemblance, yet significant differences as well. No work has yet been done to determine whether there were any contacts between the two leaders.
22. Introduction to *Śambuka Vadha*, pp. 17–18.
23. Guḍipāṭi Veṅkaṭa, Calam, *Sīta Agnipraveśam* (Vijayawada: Aruna Publishing House, 3rd edn., 1976), p. 45.
24. Satyanārāyaṇa began writing the first volume of his six-volume *Śrīmad Rāmāyaṇa Kalpavṛkṣamu,* popularly known as *Rāmāyaṇa Kalpavṛkṣamu*, in 1934 and concluded the sixth volume in 1962. The first volume was not published until 1944.The other volumes were published during the following years, ending with the sixth volume in 1963. Satyanārāyaṇa gave readings from his book long before the first volume was published. The six volumes have been reprinted several times.
25. Viśvanātha Satyanārāyaṇa, *Rāmāyaṇa Kalpavṛkṣamu* (Vijayawada: Viśvanātha Publications, 1992; 1st edn., 1944), 1.5. Translation in collaboration with David Shulman.
26. Nārla Venkateśvara Rao, *Sīta Jōsyam* (Vijayawada: Navodaya Publishers, 1979), p. 131.
27. Muppāḷa Raṅganāyakamma. *Rāmāyaṇaviṣavṛkṣam*, 3 vols (Hyderabad: Sweet Home Publications, 1974–6). The title parodies *Rāmayaṇa Kalpavṛkṣamu* (Rāmāyaṇa, The Giving Tree), written a few years earlier by Viśvanātha Satyanārāyaṇa (see n. 24).
28. Two such books are Suravaram Pratāpa Reḍḍi, *Rāmāyaṇa Viśeṣamulu* (Hyderabad: Āndhra Racayitala Saṅgham, 1957), and Kotta Satyanārāyaṇa Chaudari, *Rāmāyaṇa Rahasyālu* (Nidubrolu: Bhaśapōṣakagranthamaṇḍali, 1968).

9

Epics and Ideologies

Six Telugu Folk Epics

The existence of oral epics in India has been known for some time, but only in the past few years have folklorists paid them serious attention. In particular, two recent full-length studies of individual epics—Roghair 1982, and Beck 1982—have opened up this new world of folklore study in India. This essay is intended as a continuation of these studies and others on the oral epic in India. Though the data are taken exclusively from Telugu, the analysis might have applications in other areas of India, or of the world.

Despite the wide popularity of oral epics, Telugu has no specific word for them, nor does any other Indian language, though the Sanskrit *itihāsa* (which is applied to the *Mahābhārata*) comes closest. The Telugu word for a narrative is *katha*, which in itself does not distinguish narratives which have epic qualities from those which do not. However, one distinction that is clearly made by Telugu audiences is based on the truth value of the narrative: some stories are perceived as real events, some are not. A common statement about "real" stories made to me during fieldwork was "This really happened" (*idi nijamgā jarigindi*). Other stories, folktales for example, were called *kaṭṭukathalu*, "a fabricated story." Tales which I heard told in prose always ended with a colophon: *katha Kāñciki, manam iṇṭiki*, "The tale goes to Kanci and we go home." I have no special information about the relevance of Kanci, the famous South Indian temple town, in this statement, but I suspect that the colophon signifies the fictional nature of the tale. "True stories," by contrast, do not go away; they live with their audiences.

If folktales are generally perceived as fictive, there is no general agreement about the truth value of other, sung narratives among participating communities. Communities which tend to adopt a narrative as "their story" give it a historical status, whereas communities that do not regard it as fiction. For example, *Bālanāgamma Katha*, a sung narrative about a young prince who wins his bride by heroic adventure from a demonic character in a dangerous land, was perceived as historically true by a group of women who listened as I was recording it in Virabhdarapuram, Srikakulam district, Andhra Pradesh. The same story was called *kaṭṭu katha* by men among the same group of listeners; from their point of view, it is a fictional story. These differences in perception regarding the truth value of the story, I suggest, are related to the level of identification with the story. For the audiences who see a model of behavior in the story, it is real; for those who do not, it is fiction.

The mere presence of identifiable historical elements, therefore, does not cause a narrative to be accepted as a "true story"; it must also represent a worldview for a caste or a social group. An example is the story of Sarvāyi Pāpaḍu, a narrative song celebrating the adventures of a low-caste bandit; it has all the formal elements of an epic, and it is historical in the sense that there are documented facts in Mughal records about the bandit, and the narrative has identifiable place names.[1] The birth, life, and death of the bandit also have similarities with those of other folk heroes. Yet the story is not accorded the status of a "true story" by its listeners. Many singers whom I interviewed stated that they sing this story for the pleasure of their listeners, as entertainment only. Though no caste or group, to my knowledge, identifies this narrative as their own, there are several highly educated literary people who show great interest in interpreting and re-creating the story in an effort to represent Sarvāyi Pāpaḍu as a model Hindu warrior against the Muslim tyrants. If their view gains wider acceptance, it is possible that the story will acquire epic-like proportions and status as a "true" story.

Whereas investing a narrative with truth value is significant in the making of an epic, the converse also appears to be true: to unmake an epic one must deny its historical validity. A question constantly debated in India is whether the *Mahābhārata* and the *Rāmāyaṇa* have any historical truth. From the point of view of English-educated scholars, history is based on evidence from archeological, numismatic, inscriptional, or other recorded sources. With this bias, scholars of ancient history argue for or against the date of the Battle of Kurukṣetra in the *Mahābhārata* or the geographical location of Lanka in the *Rāmāyaṇa*.[2] Such efforts are not always seen in the context of historical research, however. Newspapers in India frequently report the results of archeological research about the *Mahābhārata* and *Rāmāyaṇa* with an unmistakable interest in the status of these epics. The new research in archeology is perceived as crucial because it could preserve or destroy the stature of an epic by confirming or disproving its factual basis.

Modern poets and opinion makers who hold non-traditional views, rejecting the religious values and the brahminic message of the epics, have vehemently asserted their fictional status. A well-known poem of Śrī Śrī, a modern Telugu poet, restates the *Bhāgavata Purāṇa* episode of the fight between the elephant Gajendra and the crocodile, declaring it to be a tale fabricated by conservative leaders of the community to deprive ordinary people of their strength and self-confidence.[3] For thousands of his readers, then, the *Bhāgavata Purāṇa* is not a reliable document, whereas in the minds of traditional Hindus it is a text of undisputed fact. The point worth noting is that the status of an epic is dependent on the perception of its truth value.

For this reason, epics in India serve as vehicles of ideology. This is especially true for folk epics, such as those in Telugu, because they are associated with specific communities which tend to claim them as their epics. Several of these Telugu folk epics have rituals related to them, in which the story is re-enacted annually. There are also authorized singers who claim authority to perform the epic for participants in the ritual. An epic perceived as a real event and commemorated in a ritual acquires deep meaning for the participating community and organizes its worldview. It defines the community's role in the larger society, legitimizes its limits, strengthens its internal relationships, and conditions its behavior.

The events of the epic are believed to be true and their characters real, yet both undergo transformations over time. Such transformations are not merely accretions or improvements made by imaginative singers. Many of them are closely related to the ideology of the community which identifies itself with the epic. In India epics are still being made in this way, and perhaps also unmade. This is true for both literary and folk epics and, to an extent, breaks down the separation between them: folk narratives are transformed into literary narratives and literary epics give rise to local variants.

To examine this epic process, I first discuss six Telugu folk epics and the communities that participate in their performances. Later I examine their transformations in order to reflect on the ideological nature of the epic process. The six Telugu epics are: *Palnāṭi Katha, Bŏbbili Katha, Kāṭamarāju Katha, Kanyakā Ammavāri Katha, Sanyāsamma Katha*, and *Kāmamma Katha*.

The Epic Stories

Based on certain narrative features, these epics fall under two types, which I call "martial" and "sacrificial" epics. As will be clear later, the martial epics center on male warriors who die a heroic death in battle, and the sacrificial epics center on women who immolate themselves. Before I discuss these types in detail, let me provide brief outlines of the epics—first three martial epics, then three sacrificial epics.

Palnāṭi Katha is a long, complex narrative describing the struggle between two factions of half-brothers—one led by the widow Nāyakurālu, and another led by the warrior Brahmanāyuḍu. Alugu Rāju, who has three sons by one wife and five sons by another, at the point of death, calls his minister, Brahmanāyuḍu, and entrusts all his sons to him.[4]

The eldest of Alugu Rāju's sons, Nalagāmarāju, is made king. Soon the widow Nāyakurālu gains influence over Nalagāmarāju and estranges him and his half-brother Pĕdda Malideva Rāju. Brahmanāyuḍu divides the kingdom between them and takes Pĕdda Malideva Rāju under his protection, ruling his portion of the kingdom, since the boy is still young. The opposition between the widow Nāyakurālu and the minister

Brahmanāyuḍu culminates in a cockfight between their two factions. The Brahmanāyuḍu faction loses and goes into exile for seven years, but in the end Nalagāmarāju (on the advice of Nāyakurālu) refuses to return half of the kingdom to Malideva Rāju, and war ensues.

As the armies of the rival forces are preparing to go to war, Nāyakurālu sends a message saying that Nalagāmarāju is ready to give his share of the kingdom to his half-brother. But the attempt at peace fails when Bālacandruḍu, the son of Brahmanāyuḍu, insists on avenging the death of a friend and begins the battle. Nāyakurālu flees, and many heroes die in the battle, including Bālacandruḍu.

Kāṭamarāju Katha, another long and complex narrative, is told about the Yādavas, a caste of cattle herders also known as Gŏllas. "Yādava" is a Sanskrit name indicating the prestigious ancestral relationship of the caste with the god Kṛṣṇa.[5] The story traces the lineage of the Yādavas from Kṛṣṇa through Yadu of the *Mahābhārata*. The protagonist is Kāṭamarāju, who owns a large herd of cattle and enters into an agreement with Nallasiddhi, a king of the Coḷa dynasty: in return for all the male calves, the king will let Kāṭamarāju's cattle graze on Nallasiddhi's land. The actual words of the contract are these: "All the grass that is born out of the water is yours, and all the male calves that are born from the cattle are ours." When a drought afflicts the area and there is not enough grass for the cattle, Kāṭamarāju takes his contract literally and grazes his cattle on the rice crop, since it is also a kind of grass which grows from water. The result is a disastrous battle, resulting in the tragic death of many Yādava heroes.

A woman (and mistress of Nallasiddhi), Kundavā Devi, figures as a source of conflict between Kāṭamarāju and Nallasiddhi. Her pet parrot is accidentally killed by Yādavas who are shooting arrows at animals which threaten their cattle; in retaliation, Kundavā incites the hunters of the area, who harbor a grudge toward the Yādavas because the latter kill wild animals to protect their cows, to kill the cattle of the Yādavas. Kāṭamarāju argues with Nallasiddhi and refuses to pay rent.

The martial theme of warriors dying in battle to protect their land is also prominent in *Bŏbbili Katha*.[6] This story concerns the valor of the Velama caste heroes of Bobbili, a small zamindari of northeastern

Andhra Pradesh in the eighteenth century. Military activities by the French commander, Bussy, intensify the local rivalries between Bobbili and Vijayanagar, two local chiefdoms with a long-standing enmity. The Vijayanagar king is a Kshatriya and an enemy of Ranga Rao's Velama family, the rulers of Bobbili. When the French commander, Bussy, visits the locality, the king of Vijayanagar seeks his help to settle a grudge against Bobbili. Bussy's local interpreters, bribed by the Vijayanagar king, manipulate Bussy into ordering Ranga Rao to surrender Bobbili fort and to relocate himself further south. The zamindar of Bobbili, for whom it is an insufferable insult to be ordered out of his fort, refuses to obey. The Vijayanagar king attacks the fort with assistance from the French armies. In the end, the Velama warriors of Bobbili die defending their fort, and all their women commit suicide by jumping into a fire.

In contrast with the above three martial epics, the next three are sacrificial epics. In them, the lead character is a woman who immolates herself at the end and is deified as a goddess.

The *Kanyaka Ammavāri Katha* is set in Penugonda, the city of the Komaṭis in West Godavari district. There the wealthy Komaṭi leader Kusumaśreṣṭi lives with his daughter Kanyaka, the most beautiful woman in the world. One day, the king of the area visits the city, and the Komaṭis receive him with honors, including Kanyaka's welcoming him with a flame offering. When the king sees her, he desires her and sends word to her father that he wishes to marry her. If the father refuses, he will invade the city and abduct her.

The Komaṭi elders meet to discuss the crisis but cannot find any solution. They conclude that they are powerless to fight, and some even suggest a surrender so that they can gain favors from the king. Kanyaka evaluates the situation and has word sent to the king that her father agrees to the marriage, but needs time to prepare for it. The king is to wait outside the city, behind the hills surrounding it.

Meanwhile, Kanyaka assembles the elders and informs them of her intention to immolate herself. She asks which caste families will be willing to die with her; among the 102 families (*gotras*) who agree to die with her, she selects only the wives and husbands, leaving the young men and women to continue the caste line. All other families are ordered out of the caste.

Now Kanyaka has a deep pit dug and a fire kindled in it. When the king sends soldiers to see what is causing the delay, they learn of Kanyaka's plans and decide to serve her instead of the king. When the soldiers do not return, the king grows suspicious and invades the city, but it is too late: Kanyaka and the others have perished in the fire. Before that, however, Kanyaka has sanctioned a code of conduct for the caste. She states that cross-cousin marriage is never to be avoided, even when the boy or girl is poor, sick, or deformed, and that Komaṭi girls are to be given her name. All Komaṭi girls, moreover, are to be born ugly so that no man will desire them. She also ordains that the king, who caused this calamity, is to die instantly when he enters the city. Penugonda is to become a pilgrimage center for Komaṭis with Kanyaka as its goddess, and an annual ritual is to be celebrated there in her honor.

The *Sanyāsamma Katha* begins when Sanyāsamma is born in a family of Gazula Kāpus, a caste of bangle sellers. When her mother dies and her father, Dālnāyuḍu, leaves her to marry another woman, she is raised by Rāmināyuḍu, her older brother. She is then married to Cĕncanna, her paternal aunt Dālamma's son. Following the marriage, Sanyāsamma stays in Rāmināyuḍu's house because she has not yet matured. Rāmināyuḍu raises Sanyāsamma with great love and care. When he leaves his village to attend to his lands in a distant place, he asks his wife, Pāpamma, to take care of his sister in his absence.

One day, after Rāmināyuḍu has left, Sanyāsamma goes out to watch a show of dancing bulls and takes along her young stepbrother. Suddenly, her stepmother rushes up to her, accuses her of taking the child without her permission, and hits her with a broomstick. Sanyāsamma tells her stepmother that if she is in the right and the stepmother in the wrong, the pain of the blows will revert to her stepmother. Soon the stepmother's body shows the pain of the blows and starts to bleed.

Then Sanyāsamma goes to her mother-in-law's house to live, but her husband, Cĕncanna (who has been educated in English), leaves home in search of a job with the British East India Company. Sanyāsamma suffers at the hands of her scheming sisters-in-law and cruel mother-in-law. She is given difficult chores to perform, and completes them all through her superior powers as a *satyavatī*, a "woman of truth." Her husband's younger brother, Appanna, soon realizes that she is being starved and offers her a glass of milk. She hesitates to accept it, because if her mother-in-law sees her, she will accuse her of illicit sexual contact with Appanna. But Appanna insists that Sanyāsamma drink the milk, and she drinks half of it. When the mother-in-law sees Appanna leaving Sanyāsamma's room, she shouts that Sanyāsamma is living like a prostitute.

Sanyāsamma shuts herself up in her room, lies on her bed, and sends her soul out of her body in search of her husband. Her disembodied soul miraculously locates her husband in Madras, tells him of her misery, and asks him to come home. When Cĕncanna arrives home, Sanyāsamma relates to him in detail the suffering that she has been subjected to by her mother-in-law. Cĕncanna takes pity on her and assures her that he will seek to separate himself from the family so they can live together happily. Cĕncanna asks his older brother for his share of the family property, but his older brother refuses. He goes so far as to insult Cĕncanna, as a result of which the younger man, who feels he has been humiliated, kills himself.

The news of her husband's death is quickly brought to Sanyāsamma, who decides to die along with her husband by performing *satī*. Accompanied by Appanna, she goes to Madras to the officers of the East India Company to get permission to perform *satī*. The English officer tries to discourage her from dying and puts her in prison. But Sanyāsamma miraculously escapes and then performs several miracles which persuade the English officer to grant her permission. After giving gifts of turmeric and *kumkum* to Appanna, she disappears into the flames.

The *Kāmamma Katha* is about Kāmamma, born in the Besta caste. When her father and mother die in a famine, her uncle raises her with affection. Later, she is married to a cross-cousin, Mārayya, who leaves for Madras, where he finds employment as a soldier in the British East India Company. After seven years of service, he takes his salary and starts for home, but falls sick and dies. Kāmamma informs her caste members that she wants to perform *satī*, puts the dead body of her husband in a room, and locks the door. She then goes to see the District Collector in Kakinada, to seek his permission for *satī*. On her way she has to cross a canal, but the water is too deep for her to cross. Since she was born in a fisherman's family and Ganga (the river) is her own sister, the waters become shallow when she orders the canal to give way. But the men following her are not able to cross the canal, so Kāmamma creates two boats for them.

When Kāmamma meets the English officer and asks his permission to die on the funeral pyre of her husband, he says that women in the Besta caste may have a second marriage and advises her to marry again. Kāmamma then accuses the officer of insulting her caste and curses his head to break if he continues. The officer puts Kāmamma in prison and, in order to prove that she is a woman of truth, demands that she starve and yet suffer no pain. While Kāmamma remains in prison without food for seven days, the officer orders the dead body of Mārayya to be cremated. Kāmamma, who knows all of this, leaves her body in prison and sends her soul to Madras to appear in a superior officer's dream. The superior officer asks to be shown supernatural powers before he can be convinced that Kāmamma is truthful. Kāmamma shows all the miracles asked for, gets his permission, and returns to the District Collector, who arranges for the funeral pyre, where Kāmamma dies, having invited all her relatives and friends to watch.

Let me mention here some of the central differences between the three martial epics and the three sacrificial epics. The protagonists of the martial epics are men, whereas those of the sacrificial epics are women. The crisis in martial epics results from conflict with a member of the same caste or a caste of similar status; in sacrificial epics it results from the aggressive interference of an alien authority. The cause of conflict in the martial epics centers on the control of territory, whereas protecting caste integrity or elevating the caste status is the central problem in sacrificial epics. The martial epics employ the physical strength of male warriors as the chief mode of power; the sacrificial epics, on the other hand, stress the internal resources of women: their determination, their powers of mind, and the magical powers of ritual sacrifice. Warriors in the martial epics kill and get killed in battle; characters in the sacrificial epics die of self-immolation or from curses. Martial epics end in tragedy: the warriors die, and often the survivors mourn their death. Sacrificial epics end in the defeat of the enemy and achieve security and prosperity for the caste and/or elevate its social status.

These contrasts between the two types of epics are summarized in Table 9.1.

Epic Communities

Each of the epics described above is patronized by a caste or a cluster of castes who identify with it, to varying degrees. Most of the epics also have annual ritual performances and "authorized" singers. The rituals are attended almost exclusively by the caste or castes associated with the epic. The ritual performance of the Palnāḍu story, for example, is sung by the *Vīravidyāvantulu* ("those who are skilled in the heroic tradition"), and the participants are called *ācāravantulu* ("those of the tradition"). The singers are mostly untouchable Mālas, and the participants come from the Telaga, Kamma, and Velama landowning castes. Another martial epic, the *Kāṭamarāju Katha*, is associated with the Gōllas, who hire untouchable Mādiga singers (called *Kõmmulavāḷḷu*) to perform the epic at a festival (*Gaṅga Jātara*).

Among the castes who participate in the rituals, there is a tendency to call the epics their "own." When I interviewed singers and participants

Table 9.1: Two Types of Epics

	Martial Epics	Sacrificial Epics
Protagonist	Male warrior	Female leader
Antagonist	Member of the same (or similar status) caste	Member of an alien, authoritarian caste
Central Theme	Control of territory	Protection of caste integrity
Sources of Power	Physical strength/courage	Mental strength, cunning, and/or magic
	Warrior; outer-directed power	Saint; inner-directed power
Mode of Action	Kill others	Kill self
End Result	Heroic death of warriors; tragedy	Victory over the enemy, prosperity; comedy

at the Palnāḍu ritual, one sentiment expressed repeatedly was: "These heroes belong to our Palnāḍu soil where they fought and died." A similar, but different, association between the heroes and the land is found in Bobbili, where the *Bŏbbili Katha* is known. There the heroes are identified with the Velama caste as well as with the land. The story was spoken of as "the story of our Bobbili Velama heroes." And the phrase *Bŏbbili puli* ("tiger of Bobbili") is often used to describe a Velama from the area.

By contrast, identification with the Kāṭamarāju and Kanyaka stories is by caste only. This is particularly clear for the Kanyaka story and the Komaṭis, who have taken the deity Kanyaka and her story with them wherever they have migrated. Thus, all along the east coast of South India there are Kanyaka temples patronized by Komaṭis. All publications of the story have also been sponsored by Komaṭis, and a number have been written by them. Penugonda, a town with a sizeable Komaṭi population, is also (following the epic story) a pilgrimage center for the caste, where an annual ritual is celebrated to the goddess Kanyaka. In the absence of an annual ritual and authorized performers, the Sanyāsamma and Kāmamma stories are less clearly perceived as associated with any caste; several persons of upper-caste families in the area where these stories are known could not identify them with any specific caste.

It is worth exploring the ethnographic data to see if any connections can be made between the themes of the story and their participating communities. Since ethnographic information on castes which identify themselves with the epics has not yet been systematically collected, the most important source is still Edgar Thurston's *Castes and Tribes of Southern India.* Drawing from Thurston, as well as from my own field notes, I present here a brief note on the castes connected with the six epics. The castes fall into two broad categories: landowners and traders, a division related to the "right hand/left hand" division among lower castes in South India (see Beck 1972). Although Telugu does not have the neat classification in local terminology which Tamil does, caste behavior, rituals, ideologies, and aspirations all indicate that Telugu lower castes are divided in a similar scheme. Landowners are right-hand castes, and traders are left-hand castes.

Landowners in premodern Andhra society were the dominant political power; as the chief producers of food, they controlled the day-to-day productive activity of society. These landowning castes were the Jajmān, who claimed status in the Kshatriya, king-like role. Their superiority was recognized by those castes that served on their land and earned their living from agricultural operations. Lower castes accepted the superiority of such families; they and the Brahmins served the Jajmān landowner. Priestly functions were distributed among certain Mālas who sang the epics and certain Gŏllas who performed the worship of goddesses like Ankālamma. Brahmin families functioned as priests in the temples of Sanskritic deities, but they were not the exclusive priests of the community, nor were their functions limited to priestly activities alone; they served also as scribes, messengers, and advisers. It is important to note that the worship of folk deities which required animal sacrifice was conducted by lower-caste priests.

In this scheme, the landowner was at the top of the hierarchy, with all other castes, including Brahmins, below him. The landowner held such titles as Nāyuḍu, from *nāyakuḍu,* "leader," or Rāju, from *rāja,* "king." The self-image of the dominant landowners in these communities incorporated the ideology of warriors who protected the community and the territory: an ethic of men who preferred heroic death on the battlefield to the humiliation of survival in defeat. Physical strength and readiness to fight in protecting one's honor were idealized as superior male virtues. Women, on the other hand, were objects to be protected, like land or family honor.

Inasmuch as this was the ideology of the dominant landowner, it was accepted as the value system of society at large. Lower castes which served the landowner adopted militaristic virtues as befitting men, and chastity, as appropriate to women. The most despised characters were women who assumed leadership and men who did not show courage. In special circumstances, a man or a woman was exempt from these general expectations. Examples would be Brahmin men who were scholars and scribes rather than warriors, and women from courtesan castes for whom chastity was not a possible virtue. However, the exemption granted these persons also diminished their social stature. Outside the dominant ideology also were traders who did not compete for landownership. Their relative independence from land afforded them a certain degree of social space through which they maintained a separate ideology.

Now let us look at the various castes associated with our epics. Those associated with the *Palnāṭi Katha* are Telaga, Velamas, and Kammas—all traditionally landowning castes. The strong emotional ties which these castes feel with the land and martial values are evidenced by numerous proverbs and beliefs. In order to distinguish themselves clearly from women, the men grow a prominent moustache, cultivate a specific manner of speech and body movements, and occupy an exclusive area in front of the house. The worst insult that can be hurled against a man is to call him effeminate. Verbal insults which suggest that a man has bangles on his wrists, or that he does not have a moustache, or that he follows the advice of his wife, invariably provoke him to violent action.

Women in these castes are equated with the land. It is the duty of the men to protect the women in order to preserve both the honor and the identity of the caste. Women are not permitted to remarry and are often married before puberty. According to a prevalent belief, their chastity is associated with the fertility of the soil. A woman's place of honor is in the house and not in public life. Unwed women and widows are a dishonor to the family if they appear in public. A widow is equated with a prostitute; one word, *muṇḍa*, indicates both.

The caste closely identified with *Kāṭamarāju Katha* are the Gŏllas, who call themselves Yādavas when they claim the status of Kshatriyas. They are traditionally cattle-owners who live by grazing and breeding cattle, and are therefore relatively more mobile than the landowning castes. However, while the landowning castes have emotional ties with the land they own, Gŏllas have only a functional interest in the land which they rent for grazing. Instead, their emotional ties are with water, indicated by their caste deity Gangamma, a water goddess. The *Kāṭamarāju Katha* epic reflects this value placed on water in the drought which leads to Kāṭamarāju's fight with Nallasiddhi. Yet Gŏllas still have a predominantly martial ideology.

Gŏlla women are not permitted to remarry. However, unwed women and widows, the available evidence suggests, are not treated with disrespect. Thurston reports that Gŏlla women do not remove or break their glass bangles (symbolic of removing a woman from the auspicious status which she enjoyed during the life of her husband) when their husbands die.

The *Sanyāsamma Katha* is closely associated with the Gazula Kāpus. Traders by profession, Gazulas retain their specific caste name for internal uses (marriage and other rituals), but adopt Kāpu for public purposes. Gazula men sell bangles, visiting the back of the house, which is traditionally the part occupied by women. Men of the caste, as well as men of other castes which have adopted Kāpu as their name, show little concern for a clearly defined set of male activities and styles of behavior. Men among these families take care of children, cook, and clean the household with no concern to separate man's work from woman's. In some Kāpu communities, Thurston reports,

> women play an important part, except in matters connected with agriculture. This is accounted for by a story to the effect that when they came from Ayodhyā, the Kāpus brought no women with them. and sought the assistance of the gods in providing them with wives. They are told to marry women who were the illegitimate issue of Pāndavas. And the women consented on the understanding that they were to be given the upper hand, and that menial service, such as husking paddy (rice), cleaning vessels, and carrying water, should be done for them.[7]

Associated with the *Kāmamma Katha* are Bestas, a group of fishermen who trade in fish; they also undertook the professions of palanquin bearers and mercenary soldiers during the administration of the East India Company. Thurston reports that wealthy families become farmers, but that none hire themselves out as agricultural laborers. He also states that they employ Brahmins and Sātānis, non-Brahmin Vaiṣṇava priests, for their domestic ceremonies and imitate Brahmin customs, such as prohibiting widow remarriage. This would suggest that, prior to brahminization, widows were allowed to remarry.

The best example of a trader caste associated with a sacrificial epic is the Komaṭis and the Kanyaka epic. Komaṭis were viewed as timid, miserly, cunning, untrustworthy, secretive, and even physically ugly. They cared for profit rather than honor. Proverbs, legends, folk tales, and folk aphorisms confirm the humiliating position of Komaṭis in premodern Andhra. "If you hit a Komaṭi," says a proverb, "he would say 'Try hitting my neighbor, then we will see how strong you are.'" The point is that a Komaṭi is too timid to fight by himself; he would rather see his assailant punished by his stronger neighbor than risk fighting himself. *Komaṭi sākṣyam*, a Komaṭi's testimony, is proverbially indecisive and unreliable. A Komaṭi is believed to be unwilling to take sides in a dispute for fear of reprisal from the faction which is displeased. Many folk stories indicate that a Komaṭi cleverly attempts to please both factions by using vague, indecisive terms which prevent his evidence from being used one way or the other. A Komaṭi's voice is perceived to be hoarse; he is ugly, dark, and lethargic and has a fat belly. The stereotype of Komaṭi women is similarly unflattering. As among the Gŏllas, widow remarriage was not permitted, but Komaṭi women enjoy higher status and respect than women in landowning castes.

In the context of such social humiliation, Komaṭis strived to adopt an ideology which converted this weakness into strength. In contrast to the aggressive warrior which was the model for the landowner, the Komaṭis preferred the saint model—associated with self-sacrifice. These are the two power strategies in Hindu society: one gained control over the outside world by force; the other turned the aggression inward, resulting in self-immolation, and thus magical power over the outside world. The other trading castes described here have not shown as clearly as the Komaṭis a tendency toward the saint paradigm; however, in times of trouble, the resource they drew on was inner strength, represented by their women who sacrificed themselves,

The information presented thus far is summarized in Table 9.2.[8]

Sex-Role Reversals

As we have noted, the strengths of the landowning castes and the trading castes are different: men of the landowning castes aspire to heroic warrior status and keep their women under strict control of the men, whereas in the trading castes women represent an inner strength, and the men remain largely passive. These different types of power are reflected in the roles of male and female characters in the two types of epics.

Table 9.2: Epic Type and Caste Type Correlated

Name of epic	Castes	Traditional occupation	Self-image of men	Position of women	Hero of epic	Central theme	Epic type
1. *Palnāṭi Katha*	Velama Telaga Kamma	Landowning peasants	Warriors	Controlled by men; widow remarriage not permitted	Male warriors	Kin conflict over land	Martal
2. *Bŏbbili Katha*	Velama	Landowning peasants	Warriors	Controlled by men; widow remarriage not permitted	Male warriors	Conflict due to injured pride	Martial
3. *Kāṭamarāju Katha*	Gŏlla	Cattle-owners and grazers	Warriors	Relatively high; widow remarriage not permitted	Male warriors	Battle with landowning king over land use	Martial
4. *Kanyaka Katha*	Komaṭi	Trade and commerce	Non-warriors	Relatively high; widow remarriage not permitted	Women	Self-immolation of woman to protect caste honor and identity	Sacrificial

Table 9.2 (*contd.*)

Table 9.2 (*contd.*)

Name of epic	Castes	Traditional occupation	Self-image of men	Position of women	Hero of epic	Central theme	Epic type
5. *Sanyāṣamma Katha*	Gazula Kāpu	Trade, effort to gain landowning peasant status	Mercenary soldiers	Relatively high; widow remarriage permitted	Woman	Self-immolation of woman to elevate caste status	Sacrificial
6. *Kāmamma Katha*	Besta	Trade; fishermen	Mercenary soldiers	Relatively high; widow remarriage permitted	Woman	Self-immolation of woman to elevate caste status	Sacrificial

In *Palnāṭi Katha*, Brahmanāyuḍu, the Velama chief, is described as a warrior of great power and divine virtue. But the most admired hero of the epic is his son Bālacandruḍu, the boy warrior who defies even his father, to prove his abilities. In pursuance of the standard virtues of the society, males of the subordinated castes who served the king also emulated the virtues of their master. Examples are the Māla warrior Kannamadāsu of *Palnāṭi Katha* and the Brahmin Tikkana of *Kāṭamarāju Katha*. Such behavior is not expected of them, but it is the only way of entering the realm of heroes.

The least respected male character in the martial epics is the one who loses his male qualities of heroic leadership and submits to the power of a woman. Nalagāmarāju in *Palnāṭi Katha* represents this type in his total acceptance of the control of the widow Nāyakurālu over the affairs of his kingdom. Another example is Tikkana, a curious Brahmin soldier in the *Kāṭamarāju Katha*. He goes to war, but when he sees the enemy his courage fails him. He returns home from the battleground and is ridiculed by the people for his cowardice. When he reaches his house, his wife treats him as if he were a woman by arranging a hot-water bath behind a cot-screen. She also sets out a ball of turmeric, a symbol of femininity, as an insult to him. Even Tikkana's mother humiliates him: she gives him curdled milk in his dinner. Just as he broke under the pressure of battle, she explains, the cows which saw him return from the battlefield gave curdled ("broken") milk. Tikkana cannot stand the insults, goes to the battlefield, and dies a heroic death; later, his wife enters the funeral fire alongside his body.

Following this pattern, the most valued female characters in the martial epics are faithful wives and devoted mothers who stay in the background and encourage their husbands or sons to gain heroism through fighting and dying in battle. In the end, they die on the funeral pyres of their dead husbands. Any woman who takes the lead and acts like a man is despised. Nāyakurālu, the chief opponent of the hero Brahmanāyuḍu in *Palnāṭi Katha*, is a prominent example. She is a childless widow, in itself an indication of her dangerous power, whose treachery and cunning eventually lead to the destruction of the whole family.

By contrast, the roles of the male and female characters in the sacrificial epics indicate a complete reversal from those in the martial epics.

This is easily illustrated by the *Sanyāsamma Katha*. The male characters in the epic are Dālnāyuḍu, the father; Rāmināyuḍu, the elder brother; Cĕncanna, the husband; and Appanna, the young brother-in-law. Of these men, the father, Dālnāyuḍu, never says a word or does anything; he watches passively even when his daughter is ill-treated. The husband, Cĕncanna, is equally "inactive"; all he does is leave home, return after seven years, and kill himself. In the landowner-martial ideology, killing oneself when humiliated is viewed as a feminine trait.

As for the older brother, Rāmināyuḍu, he is also, from the martial view, not very manly. The words of the narrator describing Rāmināyuḍu suggest that he acts as a surrogate "mother" of Sanyāsamma rather than as a father figure. Rāmināyuḍu raises his orphaned sister, doing all that a mother would do for her: he braids her hair, he puts *kāṭika* (mascara) on her eyes, he bathes her and feeds her, whereas Pāpamma, his wife, does none of these tasks. He even cries like a woman when he has to leave Sanyāsamma for a few days.

While Rāmināyuḍu seems more like a woman, his wife behaves quite unlike one. When he asks her to take care of the child in his absence, she flatly refuses, saying she is busy managing the servants and might forget to do what the child needs. This reversal of roles, a woman who refuses to care for a child, and a man who attends to the child, is narrated by the singer as if it were normal, worth no special attention.

The role played by Appanna, the young brother-in-law, is even more interesting. One incident is symbolic of the "feminine" nature of his role. Appanna takes a glass of milk to Sanyāsamma when he finds out that she is being starved by his mother. Sanyāsamma drinks half and Appanna drinks the other half of the now polluted milk. Normally, the saliva-polluted food, *yĕngili*, of a man is taken only by his wife as a symbolic recognition of his superiority; in upper-caste Telugu marriage rites, the bride takes the *yĕngili* of her husband. In the case of deities, the *prasāda* is the *yĕngili* of the deity, which all devotees accept with pleasure. It is significant that when Sanyāsamma was about to burn herself, she gives turmeric and *kumkum* to Appanna as her auspicious gifts. These items are especially feminine, and men never receive them. In the worldview of the martial epics, giving them to a man is a serious insult, but the event is narrated by the singer with no special comment.

Secondary Epic Formations

Scholars have long been aware of an active social mobility in the seemingly rigid social structure of India. Models like Sanskritization and Westernization have been used to explain the mechanism of caste mobility. These models involve some kind of emulation of the symbols of the dominant caste group in a locality. The castes which have identified themselves with the epics discussed in this essay have all, in different ways, sought social mobility. While the oral texts themselves indicate that the epics are inseparably associated with the statuses of caste, the subsequent changes in the status are reflected in later developments of the epic texts. These epics are literary/written versions, which I call secondary epics. In this section I discuss the process of secondary epic formation, associated with four features: (1) identifying the epic text with the name of a legitimizing author; (2) renaming the epic in a sanskritic style; (3) rejecting the folk ritual singers in preference for a literate author/performer; and (4) changing the role of women in the epic.

All six stories discussed here are primarily oral, but all have written/printed versions; in some cases, an author/poet's name is associated with the written version. Folk versions are still available and continue to be performed for five of the six epics: the Kanyaka story is found now in written versions only.

Ever since Akkirāju Umākāntam edited and published a chapter of the *Palnāṭi Katha* from palm-leaf manuscripts and supported its attribution to Śrīnātha, a famous Brahmin scholar-poet of the fifteenth century, Telugu scholarly interest has focused on the authorship of the epic.[9] However, the ascription was much older and had been known to folk singers as well. The *Kāṭamarāju Katha* has also been attributed to Śrīnātha; Tangirāla Venkata Subbā Rao, who collected and edited palm-leaf and paper manuscripts, reports that the singers say that Śrīnātha was the original author of the text.[10] For the *Bŏbbili Katha* there are two printed versions, one based on a paper manuscript bearing the name of Pěddāḍa Malleśam, and another with no author's name.[11]

The case of the Kanyaka story is different. The printed versions include two Sanskrit texts said to be parts of the *Skandapurāṇa*, and a Telugu literary version attributed to the legendary author Bhāskarācārya.[12] Several later Telugu literary verse versions were composed by poets, all of whom belong to the twentieth century.[13] Most Komaṭis, especially literate groups, consider the literary texts of Kanyaka to be the authentic versions; and the Telugu literary retellings, mostly by Komaṭi scholars, of the Sanskrit texts confirm their authority with some innovative changes which I shall discuss later. There is also oral evidence (from the Mailāru, a caste of singers who traditionally served as priests of the Komaṭi caste) that there was a folk version of the Kanyaka story.[14] Since the Mailāru are no longer used as priests, this version has fallen into disuse and I have not been able to record it. The singers said they adopted a Telugu literary version in its place.

In the absence of definite information, the conditions under which folk versions were transformed into literary texts can only be speculated. If we disregard the view that Śrīnātha or some other poet "wrote" the texts first and that they later were corrupted by illiterate singers, it would still be interesting to examine the motivation for recording these texts, for attributing them to a legendary poet in the case of the Palnāḍu and Kāṭamarāju stories, and for the near extinction of folk text and the emergence of Sanskrit texts in the case of the Kanyaka story. One would also want to know why the *Bŏbbili Katha* has only one palm-leaf text attributed to a lesser-known poet, whereas the Sanyāsamma and Kāmamma stories have no palm-leaf texts, only substandard sidewalk printed texts with no ascription to a poet.

What interests me here is the ideological underpinnings of the written texts and their ascription to authors. In an attempt to investigate this, I interviewed singers about their knowledge of the written texts and, in relevant instances, about the authors who have been associated with them. We should note here that some of the authorized singers of the *Palnāṭi Katha* and the *Kāṭamarāju Katha* are literate and do possess palm-leaf texts. Both Arādhyula Piccayya and Subbā Rao similarly report that several of the *Kāṭamarāju Katha* texts were collected from the singers themselves. One singer of the *Bŏbbili Katha* whom I contacted is literate but does not possess any written texts; he is, however, aware of printed texts. The singer from whom I recorded the Sanyāsamma and

Kāmamma stories is illiterate and does not know that printed versions of his songs exist.

For the *Palnāṭi Katha*, Roghair reports that the style of the performance bears little resemblance to the printed version;[15] and even a cursory examination of the tape-recorded versions of the *Kāṭamarāju Katha* and *Bŏbbili Katha* indicates that the performed texts are very different from the written texts. Exceptions, however, are the *Kanyakā Ammavāri Katha*, whose written texts are the only ones performed, and (surprisingly) the Sanyāsamma and Kāmamma stories, whose sidewalk editions very closely resemble the performed text.

Writing and the materials of writing, like palm leaves, have an almost magical, authoritative significance in oral societies (which corresponds to the mystique of the oral singer in print cultures). In India, traditional people worship books as deities. People in Andhra Pradesh pick up books or paper which they have accidentally hit with their feet and bring them close to their eyes to ask the goddess of knowledge (Sarasvatī) to forgive them for the sin of disrespecting her. For a folk singer, accordingly, the palm-leaf text is worthy of worship. It is also a means of legitimizing his oral text.

The Telugu epic singer has two roles: as a priest in the context of a ritual and as a professional performer outside the ritual. As a priest, the folk singer is his own authority, representing the voice of the goddess (Ankālamma, in the case of the *Palnāṭi Katha* ritual). As a performer outside the ritual, the singer is in a different environment, under the pressure of the more dominant, literary, and upper-caste performers of the Sanskritic epics. Outside the ritual, his authority is not insulated from competition nor is his knowledge self-validating. The Sanskritic epic tradition is already well established; the status of the text is a function of its author, and Vyāsa and Vālmīki (authors of the Sanskrit epics) are sages possessing infallible knowledge of events. A performance not based on a text, nor authored by a great sage, is a *pukkiṭi purāṇam*, a merely oral story.

The palm-leaf texts of the *Palnāṭi Katha* and *Kāṭamarāju Katha* have two categories of authors: the legendary author Śrīnātha, and non-legendary authors, whose names appear in the prefaces or colophons.[16]

The latter are, most probably, singers themselves or members of the singing communities who learned the style of literate composition. In any case, they are ordinary poets with no superior learning or sage-like wisdom; no biographical legends of extraordinary birth or other events are told about them.

Śrīnātha, however, is distinguished from ordinary poets as a legendary person of superior powers. In Brahminical literary tradition he is one of the great poets, but in folk tradition he is credited also with magical powers. Discussing Śrīnātha's authorship of the *Kāṭamarāju Katha*, Subbā Rao reports the following story, narrated to him by a singer:

> When the Yādavas learned that Śrīnātha composed *Palnāṭi Vīrabhāgavatamu* in a style useful for singing, they went to the poet and said: "Lord, we shall give you a *tūmu* (a large measuring vessel) full of *varahās* (gold coins); write for us *Kāṭamarāju Caritra*." Śrīnātha worked hard and completed the entire *Yādava Bharatamu*. But the Yādavas had played a trick on him. Since the hole of an axe-head is also called tūmu, they gave him gold coins that filled the tiny hole of the axe-head. Śrīnātha was angered by this breach of trust and threw the palm-leaf text in the river. Yādavas swam down the river and collected whatever leaves they could gather: some found the middle part of the text, some the last part, and some the earlier part. The poet had not numbered the pages nor did he indicate the tune for singing the text, so the Yādavas ran after the poet, who was walking away in indignation, and requested him to indicate the page numbers or at least tell them the tune. The poet would not listen, but the Yādavas still followed him. Nearby, a tribal woman slapped a child who was not behaving. When the child began to weep, Śrīnātha snapped, "Go sing your epic in the weeping tune." The innocent Yādavas followed the command literally.[17]

A similar story, reported by Umākāntam, is discussed by Roghair in his study of the Palnāḍu epic.

> Śrīnātha lost his health because of his sexual excesses and moved to Palanāḍu where god Cennakēśava, appearing in his dream, told him to write the story of the heroes of Palnādu. Since he did not have the physical strength to write, he employed seven scribes to whom he dictated the story in two months. When the work was completed, Śrīnātha regained his health, but fell into bad ways once again. The god, angry with the poet, appeared in his dream and cursed him saying that his work would fall into the possession

> of the untouchables, Mālas and Mādigas. Śrīnātha, who was saddened by the curse of the god, threw the text in the river. The Mālas and Mādigas found pieces of the text.[18]

Roghair reports that he heard "virtually the same story" from a singer of the Palnāḍu tradition; the only change, Roghair says, was that the scribes were Lambadis, a tribal group.[19]

These legends connect the text to the superior powers of the sage Brahmin poet, but at the same time retain a non-Brahmin origin for the epic, since the tune and the singing of the text come from mostly Untouchables. It is also interesting to note that the author-sage, like the hero of folk stories, has to commit a great error to elevate himself to superhuman status. Something very low has to be associated with the sage's life to make him great: Vālmīki, according to folk legends, was a bandit before he turned into a great poet; Vyāsa was born out of wedlock to a fisherwoman. Śrīnātha follows this pattern by his immoral behavior, before Cĕnnakeśava saves him. The sage-poet also loses control of the epic by his own fault: according to the Palnāḍu legend, Śrīnātha resorts to immoral behavior once he regains health; in the Kāṭamarāju legend he fails to see the verbal trick the Gŏllas play upon him.[20]

The motif, in both legends, of the text thrown into the river and later retrieved, accomplishes a number of symbolic functions. Sacred knowledge has to be lost and then regained. The Vedas, too, were stolen and brought back by Viṣṇu from under the earth, where the demon Somaka had hidden them; according to some Tamil sources, the Vedas even had to purify themselves by going to a temple.[21] Furthermore, the sacred texts are not available in their entirety—only fragments came down to the human beings, The rivers into which the epic texts are thrown represent both the sacred waters and the flowing of oral tradition. The motif explains the fragmented nature of the available epics, and also presents the singers, who swam the river, as saviors of the text.

Another important change in written secondary texts concerns narrative sequence. No palm-leaf manuscript contains the entire story; both Subbā Rao and Lakṣmīkāntam report that each palm-leaf version is limited to one or two episodes of the whole story.[22] Roghair reports that the oral performance of the Palnāḍu epic is episodic, too. The singers segment the story into episodes measured by the time taken to perform them: "one-night story," "two-night story," and so on—each episode is called a *katha*, the term for the whole narrative.

What is important to note is that the editors of the published texts arrange the stories, with or without internal alterations from the palm leaf, in an order which makes it "read" as a connected narrative, with a beginning and an end.[24] When the editors string the episodes together, an oral structure of the narrative is changed into a written structure. Such a structural change has a far more significant role in the development of a secondary-epic text than the textual alterations that inevitably occur in any graphic recording of an oral text.

This structural change is not an invention of modern editors; it can be seen even in the palm-leaf manuscripts. In performance, each episode is complete; the singer gives a short summary of the elements of the previous story and jogs the memory of the audience to provide a context for the current episode. The background of the story is thus brought forward to make the episode a self-contained performance. But episodes in the manuscript versions lack this dimension; instead, they have a prefatory statement by the "poet," which includes his biography and his intent in composing the text, and a concluding statement. These statements added as substitutes for the oral singer's opening and concluding statements transform an oral text into a written text. The modern editors of the manuscripts are only participating in (and completing?) a process, which began centuries ago, of converting an oral text to a written form. Unwittingly, they are changing not just the language but the very structure of the narrative.

The secondary epic also acquires a new name. Although the story of Palnāḍu is referred to by the singers as *Palnāṭi Katha*, Subbā Rao reports that manuscripts bear the title *Palnāṭi Vīra Bhāgavatamu*. An author of one of the manuscripts of the *Kāṭamarāju Katha*, who explicitly refers to Śrīnātha as his model, calls his text *Yadu Śāstramu*.[25] The case of the Kanyaka story is even clearer: the texts in Sanskrit and Telugu literary verse ascribed to Bhāskarācārya are called *Śri Vāsavi Kanyakā Purāṇamu*, whereas the folk singers refer to the story as *Kanyakā Ammavāri Katha*.

These two features, a new name and a new author, signify the conceptual beginning of the secondary epic. The text itself changes only later and only gradually with appropriate literary polishing of the recorded text and/or with the modifications required for the status of the new name and the superior author. This process is complete in the Kanyaka story, partial and fragmentary in the Palnāḍu and Kāṭamarāju stories, hardly begun in the Bobbili, and not yet evident in the Sanyāsamma and Kāmamma stories.

Komaṭis who patronized the Kanyaka story aspired to Vaishya status (the third of the four *varṇas* in the Sanskritic pan-Indian scheme), and the ideological needs of that status required that they have Brahmin legitimization. This need was fulfilled by Bhāskarācārya, who ranks among the sages. Understandably, the Mailāru folk priests who had served the Komaṭi community could not confer this new status of Vaishya. Hence the Komaṭis adopted a new Sanskrit text, and the Mailāru folk priests were rejected.[26] This transformation was so complete that the primary folk text fell into disuse and was replaced by a secondary epic.

This secondary Sanskrit text of the Kanyaka story transforms the epic in several major ways. The first is in the time frame of the story. Folk time is linear and periodic, with seasons which come one after the other in sequence. Time in folk narrative does not deteriorate; it changes from birth to death and again to a new birth. In contrast, puranic time is a spiral that gradually but inevitably deteriorates, going down to the Kaliyuga. The Kanyaka story is placed in this puranic time scheme with its five features: *sṛṣṭi*, the primary creation; *pratisṛṣṭi*, secondary creation; *manvantara*, the specific age in which events are located; *vamśa*, the family; and *vaṃśânucarita*, the story of the family.

In this time frame, the family of Kanyaka is located in a particular *manvantara*, and the story setting is shifted to *devaloka*, the world of gods. A *gandharva* man there falls in love with a Vaishya girl, but the Vaiśyas reject his proposal to marry her. The *gandharva* curses the Vaishyas, saying they will fall from the world of gods onto the earth where they will all burn in fire and perish. In return, the Vaishyas curse the *gandharva* that he will have a misery-filled human birth and die a horrible death. The Vaishyas are reluctant to go to the human world of sin, but the gods insist that they are needed there to restore order and trade in the human world. And in the end they will return to the world of Śiva through their death by fire. The *gandharva* is born as king and the girl as Kanyaka and the story is re-enacted on earth (as summarized above).

The second major change in the Sanskrit, secondary epic occurs in the role of Kanyaka herself. In the folk version, Kanyaka was the leader, an initiator of action. She decided to kill herself and organized the men of her caste to die with her; she sanctioned a code of conduct for future generations and declared that the families who were too timid to die with her were to be sent out of the caste; she planned the strategy to keep the king away from the city.

In the secondary epic, Kanyaka is still the supreme power, Ādiśakti, but she is also identified with Pārvatī, the wife of Śiva. Consequently her role as caste leader is diminished and the role of the Brahmin Bhāskarācārya gains prominence; as the wise seer who knew the past and future and who could guide the Vaishyas in distress, he plans the strategy to stall the king while the Komaṭis are preparing for self-immolation.

Deified Virgin and Chaste Wife

This change in Kanyaka's role is part of a larger transformational pattern effected by the secondary epic. In this pattern, the role of a virgin goddess, the distinguishing feature of sacrificial epics, is minimized so as to conform to the dominant landowning ideology. Kanyaka's name, in fact, means "virgin" in Sanskrit. The folk singers also describe Sanyāsamma as *satyavatī*, "woman of truth," a word used only to denote powerful virgins. The general Telugu term for deified virgins is *peranṭālu.* It is these women who dominate the sacrificial epics.

In these stories the crisis centers on the heroine's virginity; though constantly under attack, she never loses her virgin status, even after she marries. Her transition from the status of a virgin to that of a deified virgin, a goddess, takes place at the death of her husband, the only man who could "take" her virginity and, in the face of a crisis, demand that she surrender to another man. Having preserved the power of her virginity, the goddess now possesses the ability to mete out punishment to those who stood against her and to reward those who supported her.

Male concepts of feminine sexuality, evidenced in male-oriented literature, indicate fear, mistrust, and anxiety about female sexuality. Women need twice as much food and six times as much sex as men, observes a Sanskrit aphorism. In copulation, men lose semen while women gain it. *Sumatī Śatakamu*, a popular book on successful conduct, notes that men and horses age when they copulate, whereas women grow old if they abstain from sex. Moreover, women are conceptualized as non-men; thus eunuchs are equated with women. But folk narratives about virgin wives indicate a different conception of women. In this view, women have a power of their own which they lose by copulation with men. Virginity is crucial for a woman's status as a powerful goddess capable of cursing and blessing.

The *pativrāta*, the faithful wife, is very different from the powerful virgin. She is strong because of her total devotion to her husband; whether he is sick or healthy, stupid or intelligent, evil or saintly, she lives for him in thought, word, and deed. One aphorism states that a wife should act like a slave when she serves her husband, like a minister when she is consulted for advice, like a mother when she feeds him, and like a courtesan when he takes her to bed. Well-known mythic *pativratas*, like Sītā, Sāvitrī, Damayantī, and Anasūyā, each underwent an ordeal to prove her fidelity: Sītā's fire ordeal; Damayantī's troubles after her husband lost his kingdom in a game of dice; Sāvitrī's struggle to bring her husband back from the world of the dead; and Anasūyā's ability to transform gods into infants when they asked her to serve them food naked.

The Nala episode in the *Mahābhārata* demonstrates the special powers of the *pativratā*. When a python attempts to swallow Damayantī and she cries for help, a hunter rescues her. Seeing that she is a beautiful young woman, he asks her to marry him; but when he tries to force himself upon her, she curses him with death. One wonders why Damayantī could not curse the python itself. But *pativratās* only have special powers when their chastity (not their life) is threatened; otherwise, they are helpless women, with nothing to do but suffer and wait for direction from their men.

These differences between the deified virgin and the chaste wife are summarized in Table 9.3.

Shifting the categories and equating the *perantālu* character with a *pativratā* marks the subtle beginning of an ideological change in the sacrificial epics. A shift in the Kanyaka ritual is pertinent here. I was told that the image of Kanyaka was ritually married to Nāgareśvara Svāmi, a Śiva image in Penugonda; a marriage badge (*mangalasūtram*) was tied around her neck to signify the change of status to a married woman. Now Kanyaka, it was stated, is only another form of Pārvatī (the wife of Śiva), a *pativratā*.

Ideological changes have gone one step further in the case of the Kanyaka story. During the last two decades, the Komaṭis of Andhra Pradesh found themselves in opposition to Brahmins when learned Komaṭis began to aspire to the status of poets, scholars, and priests. Doma Venkaṭasvāmi Gupta was one such Komaṭi scholar, who wrote poetry, calculated *pañcāṅgam* (the almanac which determines auspicious and inauspicious times), and advised his caste people in matters for which Brahminic priests were usually consulted. He and several others like him saw the need to re-examine the superior role of Brahmins written into the available texts of *Kanyakāpurāṇamu*. Gupta reports that the Brahmin priests who conducted worship in the temples of Kanyaka would not

Table 9.3: Two Types of Epic Heroines

Perantālu, the deified virgin	Pativratā, the chaste wife
Virgin, even though married	Married, totally submissive to husband
Becomes goddess when she refuses to surrender to the man who poses a threat to her virginity	Becomes a goddess by being sexually faithful to her husband, and by dying before he dies
Has power to dispense both boons and curses	Power available only to curse, and that only when her chastity is threatened
Makes new rules for her caste people to follow and presides over their future	Is ruled by the code of the caste, which she helps to maintain

utter the deity's name, but would rename her Rājarājeśvari. The Brahmin priests do not themselves eat the *prasāda* of the deity, because it is not pure enough for them; they only distribute it to the devotees present. Further, Brahmins do not chant Vedic texts in the temple, nor do they teach the *gāyatrī* (the sacred text taught to the twice-born castes at the time of initiation) to Komaṭis, even though they are called a twice-born caste and Brahmins perform the ritual of initiation for them. The Brahmins, Gupta complained, did not participate and apparently did not like it when a group of Komaṭi devotees once chanted *puruṣaśūktam* (a Vedic text) in the temple.[27]

Several Komaṭi scholars also investigated the status of Kanyaka and determined that she was not married to Śiva. She was a virgin and therefore to be seen as *Ādiśakti*, the supreme power. These scholars also utilized historical data to insist that the role of the Brahmin Bhāskarācārya was a later addition to the secondary Kanyaka text. Komaṭi scholars objected also to the portions of the *Kanyakāpurāṇamu* in which it was stated that Kanyaka issued a curse that henceforth no woman in her caste would be beautiful. Another serious objection concerned Kanyaka's order that a girl shall be given to her cross-cousin, whether he is rich or poor, handsome or ugly, sick or healthy, potent or impotent. The Komaṭi scholars argued that inbreeding is unhealthy for the caste, and that a goddess would never utter curses and give laws that would make their caste women ugly.[28]

For the Palnāḍu and Kāṭamarāju stories, neither the ascription of authorship to Śrīnātha nor the development of secondary epics has resulted in new versions for the primary epic or in new singers. The partially successful upward mobility of the landowning castes associated with these epics has brought only a partial development of secondary epics. That this process is under way in the case of the *Kāṭamarāju Katha* may be seen from the activities of Gŏlla caste leaders. Prominent among such leaders is Ārādhyula Piccayya, who exhorts his castemen to emulate Vedic rituals. He was also instrumental in publishing several episodes of the *Kāṭamarāju Katha*. He argues, in the prefaces to the books he published, that the illiterate Kommulavāḷḷu who sing the text corrupted it. It was originally composed by *pūrvakavis* ("ancient poets"), he says, and therefore flawless.[29]

Of the two manuscript versions of *Bŏbbili Katha*, one is less elaborate than the sung version, and the other more elaborate. The first was not known until the text was edited and published by Mallampalli Somasekhara Śarma in 1956. The other (called *Pĕdda Bŏbbilirāju Katha*, The Big Story of the Bobbili King) is available in a cheap sidewalk edition. This version includes an episode of a cockfight between the Bobbili and Vijayanagar kings, a clear case of diffusion from the Palnāṭi story. It is a perfect example of the process in which epic elaboration occurs through intertextual contact between several epics of a region. This second version, however, is not ideologically different from either the sung version or the first written version.

The chiefs of the house of Bobbili apparently did not take much interest in the folk versions, in either their oral or written forms. Under the overlordship of the British colonial rulers, they aspired for a Kshatriya-like status as well as a Westernized lifestyle. Several literary versions of the story were sponsored, and one of them, *Rangarāyacaritramu* by Diṭṭakavi Nārāyaṇa Kavi (an eighteenth-century scholar-poet), did receive the attention of literary scholars. Velama families tend to respect the literary versions even though the folk version is still very popular today.

The castes which identify with the Sanyāsamma and Kāmamma stories have not made much economic progress, and their aspirations to a high status, expressed in the stories, have not materialized. It would appear that the absence of literary versions of these stories represents this relatively weak economic position. We should note also that the Bobbili, Sanyāsamma, and Kāmamma stories relate events which took place in the eighteenth and nineteenth centuries and that the Palnāḍu, Kāṭamarāju, and Kanyaka stories are much older, dating back to medieval times. Epic transformations take a long time.

Conclusion

Each of the six epics examined have "heroes" who defied death. The manner of defiance, however, is what makes it possible to classify the epics into martial and sacrificial types. That each of the epics has its own audience/participants makes it necessary for us to relate the narrative to the life and culture of the patron community. It appears, from the evidence, that the socioeconomic features of the community have influenced the nature of heroism, as well as the ideological process which the story has undergone. The stories are considered epics not simply because of the formal features of length, performance style, and poetic quality, but because the narratives have ordered the worldview of the communities that identify with them. The participating communities, for their part, see the epic as recording true events. The transformations of such a narrative thus follow the ideological trajectory of the community that participates in its truth value.

Notes

Fieldwork for this paper was done during several trips to India between 1979 and 1982. Parts of the paper were presented at the Conference on Oral Epics (Madison, 1982) and at the Meeting of the Association for Asian Studies (San Francisco, 1983). I am grateful to Stuart Blackburn, Peter Claus, David Shulman, and Abbie Ziffren, who read drafts of the papers and made valuable suggestions for revisions.

1. For further discussion of this story, see John Richards and V. Narayana Rao 1980.
2. Prominent among the archeologists and historians who have discussed the historicity of the Sanskrit epics is B.B. Lal (1981: 27): "the archeological evidence obtained from the sites associated respectively with the Mahābhārata and the Rāmāyaṇa stories, however incomplete, indicates that there is a kernel of truth at the base of both these epics, though poetic imagination and literary embellishment have often rendered the descriptions of places and persons highly exaggerated and consequently unacceptable from a strictly historical point of view." See also Lal 1976; Sankalia 1973.
3. See Śrīraṅgam Śrīnivāsarāo (Śrī Śrī) 1970, especially the stanza on page 60: *idi jarigina katha kādani/ĕvaro kalpiñcindani/iñcuka yociñcagalā/ḍeva ḍaina grahistāḍu.* "This is not a story. which really happened;/ It is made up by somebody./ Anyone who can think a little/ will know that" (trans. mine).
4. Roghair 1982: 216, 239, n. 1.

5. See Tangirāla Venkaṭa Subbā Rao (1976–8) who has collected the written texts of the epic and added elaborate and informative introductions.
6. The summary is based on one version of the story which I tape-recorded; other printed and tape-recorded versions do not differ from the essential outline presented here. Unless noted, all other references to oral epic texts are from my field recordings.
7. Thurston 1909, vol. 3: 245.
8. Despite the neat typology suggested here, the *Kāṭamarāju Katha* appears to be anomalous, not quite fully "martial." The Gŏllas are probably a trading caste who have adopted a landowning-martial ideology. For them, land is a grazing facility rather than an area to be protected; yet they are not landowning peasants like the Kammas, Reddis, and Velamas. Also, the women in Gŏlla society appears to be relatively free.
9. For information regarding the written versions of the Palnāḍu epic, see Roghair 1982: 10–19.
10. Subbā Rao 1976–8: cxxxxv.
11. Mallampalli Somaśekhara Śarma, who edited *Bŏbbili Yuddha Katha,* says in his Preface that he used two almost identical paper manuscripts and one printed text with no date and no publisher's name (1956: xxiv).
12. The Sanskrit text, part of the *Skandapurāṇa*, was published at Penugonda in 1950 as *Śri Vāsavakanyakāpurāṇamu*. The Telugu text attributed to Bhāskarācārya is entitled *Vaiśyapurāṇamu* and is not available to me.
13. Prominent among them are Venkaṭasvāmi Gupta 1968 and Satyanārāyaṇa Gupta 1956, which contain elaborate critical Introductions and Afterwords.
14. The story summary given earlier is taken from a prose telling which the singers gave me. Satyanārāyaṇa Gupta (1956: 17) also attests to the existence of a folk text and even quotes several lines from it.
15. See Roghair 1982: 68. 11.14.
16. According to Subbā Rao (1976–8: xxxviii), the manuscript texts relating one or more incidents of the *Kāṭamarāju Katha* bear the names of Gaṅgula Pina Yĕllayya, Madduleṭi Kavi, Kanakabaṇḍi Ghaṭṭayya, Kaṭṭĕboyina Mārayya, Kadirimangalamu Venkaṭādri, and Jarugupallĕ Cĕnnayya.

17. Subbā Rāo 1976–8: cxxxxv–vi.
18. Roghair 1982: 10.
19. Ibid.: 17, n. 8.
20. The Brahmin Śrīnātha would know only the standard meaning of *tūmu*, "a measure of grain." The second meaning, "the hole of an axe-head," is specific to an occupational dialect and would not be known to him. One can note also that another verbal trick is used in the Kāṭamarāju story when the Gŏllas interpret the contract made with the king to suit the theme—that the rice, born of water, is part of their rights.
21. The theme af lost sacred knowledge and its retrieval appears again and again in Sanskrit texts. The story of the theft of the Vedas by demons appears in the *Mahābhārata* (12.334.21–65), the *Viṣṇu Purāṇa* (5.17.11), and the *Bhāgavata Purāṇa* (5.181.6) where the demons Madhu and Kaiṭabha steal the Vedas, and Viṣṇu rescues them by assuming the form of the horse-headed Hayagrīva (see O'Flaherty 1976: 100). In the Tamil text of *Tirumayilaittalapurānam* (8.1: 26), Somaka steals the Vedas and enters the ocean. Śiva sends Viṣṇu as a fish to kill the demon and bring back the texts. Viṣṇu becomes a huge fish, goes to the shore of the ocean, and drinks it up; when Somaka appears, Viṣṇu springs on him and kills him. The Vedas, relieved of the fault of being hidden, sing Śiva's praises: "We have become weak from being kept captive by that evil creature." Then they take the forms of men and go to Mayilais (Mylapore), where they install the *liṅga* called Mi<u>n</u>eśvara. Śiva appears to them and they become pure; then Śiva enters the *liṅga*, and the Vedas return to their former place. Similarly, in the *Tiruvā<u>n</u>miyūrtalapurāṇavacaṇam* (8:27) the Vedas complain that they have been reduced to a low state (*eḷumai*) by the touch of the demon's hand and by being hidden in evil-smelling mud. Also, in the *Tiruvo<u>rr</u>iyūrpuraṇam* (5:1–28) and the *Kāñcipurāṇam* (55: 3–9) the demons, seeing that the gods used Vedic mantras to fight against them, decide to steal the Vedas. Madhu and Kaiṭabha together with Maya, steal them, chop them into pieces, and hide them in the sand at the bottom of the sea. Viṣṇu, with the help of Śiva's Śakti, searches for them in Pātāḷa, but cannot find them; he calls out to them, and they answer from the sea bottom. Viṣṇu then takes the form of a *makara*, recovers them and brings them to the lord of Tiruvo<u>rr</u>iyūr (Śiva), who reunites them and makes them pure. Śiva then sends Viṣṇu to catch up on his sleep, since he has been fighting

the demons for many years. (I am indebted to David Shulman for his finding and translating these selections from Tamil texts.)

22. Subbā Rao, 1976–8: 31–4; Lakṣmīkāntam 1961, Preface, 29. Subbā Rao calls the Kāṭamarāju texts a "ballad cycle."
23. Roghair 1982: 62ff.
24. Ibid.: 62.
25. The use of the Sanskritic words *śāstramu* and *caritramu* is significant here. Gangulla Pina Yĕllayya, a poet who wrote several episodes of the Kāṭamarāju story, calls his work *Yadu Śāstra Caritramu*. Gurramukoṇḍa Bhaktavatsalakavi, who wrote several episodes of the epic in *campu*, a well-established meter in Telugu literary tradition, called his work *Kariyāvula Kāṭamarāju Caritra*. Mudigoṇḍa Virabhadrakavi called his versions of the Palnāḍu story, written in the same *campu* form, *Palnāṭi Vīrula Bhāgavatamu*. Similar titles calling the epic *bhāratamu* or *caritra* are popular among literates.
26. The rejection of the Mailāru priests, however, is not complete. Even though they do not perform the role of priests in the chief ritual to the goddess Kanyaka at Penugonda, they still bring an image of Kanyaka for worship to Komaṭi households, where they are received in the back of the house by the women.
27. Venkaṭasvāmi Gupta 1968: 35–59.
28. Satyanārāyaṇa Gupta 1956: 116–26. He argues that the marriage between Kanyaka and Nāgareśvara was an invention of Bhāskarācārya "some 500 years after" the life of Kanyaka.
29. Madduleṭikavi 1976: 3.

References

Beck, B.E.F. 1972. *Peasant Society in Koṅku: A Study of Right and Left Hand Subcastes in South India*. Vancouver: University of British Columbia Press.

———. 1982. *The Three Twins: The Telling of a South Indian Folk Epic*. Bloomington: Indiana University Press.

Ghaṭṭayya, Kanakabaṇḍi. 1970. *Polurāju Caritra*, ed. Ārādhyula Piccayya. Eḍvūru, India: The Editor.

Lakṣmīkāntam, Pingaḷi, ed. 1961. *Palnāṭivīracaritra*. Vījayavāḍa: Viśālāndhra Pracuraṇālayam.

Lal, B.B. 1976. "Mahābhārata and Archaeology." In S.P. Gupta and K.S. Ramacandran, eds, *Mahābhārata: Myth and Reality*. New Delhi: Agam Prakashan, pp. 52–72.

———. 1981. "The Two Indian Epics *vis-à-vis* Archaeology." *Antiquity* 55: 27–34.

Madduleṭikavi. 1976. *Valurāju Caritra*, ed. Ārādhyula Picayya. Eḍvūru (India): The Editor.

O'Flaherty, Wendy D. 1976. *The Origins of Evil in Hindu Mythology*. Berkeley: University of California Press.

Richards, John, and V. Narayana Rao. 1980. "Banditry in Moghul India: Historical and Folk Perspectives." *Indian Economic and Social History Review* 17: 95–120.

Roghair, Gene H. 1982. *The Epic of Palnāḍu: A Study and Translation of Palnāṭi Vīrula Katha, a Telugu Oral Tradition from Andhra Pradesh, India*. New York: Oxford University Press.

Sankalia, H.D. 1973. *Rāmāyaṇa: Myth or Reality?* New Delhi: People's Publishing House.

Sanyāsammakatha. 1976. Madras: N.V. Gopal.

Satyanārāyaṇa Gupta, Garrĕ. 1956. *Kanyakāpurāṇamu*, Vijayavāḍa: The Author.

Somaśekhara Śarma, Mallampalli, ed. 1956. *Bŏbbili Yuddha Katha*. Madras Government Oriental Manuscripts Library.

Śrinivāsarao, Śrīraṅgam (Śrī Śrī). 1970. Sadasatśamsayam. In K.V. Ramana Reddy, ed., *Śrī Śrī Sāhityam*, vol. 3. Visakhapatnam: Śrī Śrī Ṣaṣṭipūrtisanmānasangham, pp. 54–63.

Śrī Vāsavakanyakāpurāṇamu. 1950. Penugonda: Āravaiśyayuvajanasanghamu.

Subbā Rao, Tangirāla Venkaṭa, ed. 1976–8. *Kāṭamarāju Kathalu*. 2 vols. Hyderabad: Andhra Pradesh Sahitya Akademi.

Thurston, Edgar. 1909. *Castes and Tribes of Southern India*. 7 vols. Madras: Government Press.

Tirumayilaittalapurāṇam of Amurtaliṅkatampurāṉ. 1893. Madras.

Tiruvānmiyūrtalapurāṇavacaṉam of Ra. Vicvanātan. 1966. Madras.

Tiruvoṟṟiyūrpurāṇam of Tiruvoṟṟiyūr Nāṇappirakācar. 1869. Madras.

Venkaṭasvāmi Gupta, Doma. 1968. *Kanyakāpurāṇamu*. Guntur: Jamili Nammāḷvāru.

10

Texture and Authority

Telugu Riddles and Enigmas

Familiarity with the language becomes more important the higher the stylization of a folklore genre.—Elli Köngäs-Maranda

Pŏḍupukatha

This essay is about Telugu riddles; the data comes from Telugu sources. In Telugu there are several native forms that correspond to the riddle. One of them—the closest to what folklorists call a true riddle—is *pŏḍupukatha.*[1] As in other cultures, it is used in a contest between two individuals. You hit (*pŏḍucu*) your opponent with a riddle which he/she has to resolve (*vippu,* "untie"). The participants are often young, aged ten to twelve, and the riddling sessions, if so they can be called (since they are not consciously organized), are almost exclusively theirs; no adults participate. Adults do have an interest in riddles, but they do not actively show it in a competitive context for fear of being considered childish. Adult interest in riddles of a different kind will be discussed later.

Here is a riddle I heard, or rather overheard, from a young boy at a friend's family that I was visiting in Hyderabad:

vĕṅkayya pantulu gāḍu
vāḍi muḍḍiki mūrĕḍu tāḍu

vāḍu lepote vūrĕlla pāḍu[2]

This fellow Veṅkayya
has a cubit of string on his ass.
The village is dirty without him.

Some of the young kids giggle. The riddle respectfully gives Veṅkayya a title, *pantulu*—Brahmin/teacher/respectable person—but adds an irreverent, insulting suffix, *gāḍu.* And the rhyme includes the mildly obscene term *muḍḍi,* "ass." The texture brings a certain sense of covert satisfaction at the liberty of using objectionable words with impunity. But apparently the riddle is not new. Some of the young people have already heard it. One of them yells, mischievously: "I know," and he offers an answer: "the scavenger." No, the answer is not acceptable. Why not? The scavenger has a string on his loins, which resembles a G-string, and he is the one who cleans all the dirt from the village. Another child says: "the crow." That is not acceptable either. The crow does have a tail and does eat refuse and thus, one might say, makes the village clean. But the real answer is "broom," a bunch of stalks of straw tied with a string. The boy accepts this solution: he had not known the answer before and was just trying to bluff his way.

You wonder if the accepted answer is logical. It is and it isn't. It is logical because "broom" fulfills the conditions of the riddle; but the other, equally logical, answers are rejected. The only way you can resolve the riddle correctly is by being informed in advance what the accepted answer is. In other words, you cannot logically arrive at the answer, though the accepted answer does make sense.

The riddlers know the rules of the game; when they do not know the answer, they may try a clever solution—but they are willing to accept defeat. Akundy Anand, today a trained folklorist, reports that as a child in the eighth grade he was posed the following (rather lyrical) riddle:

nallaṭi ceṭlalo tĕllaṭi dāri
ā dārilo nallaṭi dĕyyam vĕḷṭondi

A white path through dark trees,
a dark ghost is walking through it.

The accepted answer was "head-lice." When Anand suggested "comb," his answer was rejected.

Here are some more riddles of this kind:

tokaleni piṭṭa tombhai āmaḍa potundi[3]

A bird without tail flies ninety miles.—(letter)

kiṭakiṭa talupulu
kiṭāri talupulu
ĕppuḍu mūsinā
cappuḍu kāvu[4]

Tight doors
Cute doors
Close them any time
They make no noise.—(eyelids)

According to Wittgenstein, the riddle does not exist.[5] If a question can be framed at all, it is also possible to answer it. For Telugu people, too, a riddle has an answer. But that in itself does not prevent it from being a riddle. What makes it a riddle is that among the potential answers, the correct one is not known to you unless you are initiated into the community of riddlers. Much effort has been devoted to studying the structure of the riddle and the logic of its answer. It is even argued that the riddle sharpens the logical skills of young people. Thus, Elias Lönnrot wrote: "As mathematics is in the school of the learned, so is the riddle in the home school of the folk. Both exercise the mind to understand the unknown, starting with the known conditions."[6] We might agree that riddles do, perhaps, exercise the mind—though some forms of riddles do so better than others, especially scholarly riddles. These are not, however, *pŏḍupukathalu.* There are other names for them: trick questions (*cikku praśnalu*), problem questions (*samasyalu*), hidden questions (*prahelikalu*), and so on. What folklorists call "true riddles" do more than offer mental exercise; they present a situation where there are several logically correct answers, only one of which can be accepted. As E. Köngäs-Maranda says, "The relationship between the riddle question and the acceptable or accepted answers has not been studied enough."[7]

Most studies of this question focus on semantic analysis, as in the case of Ben-Amos: "The diverse answers to a riddle, unrelated as they might appear, constitute the semantic set of a riddle."[8] Though this may be true, we still have no dependable way of determining which one of several possible answers is the accepted one. The Telugu example suggests that it is the accepted answer that makes the riddle a riddle. An outsider to the cultural knowledge which produced the riddle will have no way of knowing it. Sometimes, it is true, contesting groups may argue about the correct answer. I have witnessed several riddle sessions where disputes about a contested answer were not resolved logically but ended either with the co-option of the contesting individual by the group that held the "correct" answer or with a complete parting of the ways.

Riddles make communities of people who share common knowledge. In this they resemble conversion through initiation. The age group of ten- to twelve-year-olds constitutes such a community, which shares a special body of knowledge exclusive to its members.

An examination of a large corpus of riddles published by several collectors in Telugu brings out additional features. Most riddles have a poetic quality to them. They are structured metrically, often with some kind of rhyme. The style of the riddles, the language used, is irreverent and often obscene. Even when they are not explicitly pornographic, their texture and diction have a coarse and disrespectful tone. I am referring not only to the overtly obscene meanings found in many riddles, which vanish like fog the moment the correct answer is given. Even when the surface meaning is not obscene, the choice of words tends to be crude, as in the riddle about the broom given above. Here are several examples of overt obscenity:

ŏttŏtti pĕṭṭaṅga
ŏyi ŏyi anaṅga
cālu cālu anaṅga
santoṣa paḍaṅga

Pressing pressing pushing
saying *oyi oyi*
saying enough enough
feeling very happy.[9]

The diction, the style, and the tone of the riddle point to sexual intercourse, while the answer is fixing bangles on a woman's hand. This was a common sight in premodern Andhra: a male bangle seller brought bangles to the house; he sized up a woman's hand by holding it, chose the right-size bangles, and pressed her hand tightly to slide the bangle onto her wrist. The woman often felt the pain of squeezing as he slid the bangle on. This rather painful experience led to a happy ending, with the woman pleased with her new bangles.

Similarly:

Kāllu paṅgabĕṭṭi kāma cetula paṭṭi
pŏkka sūṭi cūci poṭu pŏḍici
potuk'ŏkka pilla nīṭugā dīyarā
dīni bhāvamemi tirumaleśa?[10]

Widen [your] thighs and hold the shaft
aim at the hole and hit it
take out a child each time you hit
What does this mean, Lord of the Tirumala hill?

The answer to the riddle is the potter, who works on his wheel by rotating it with a stick. Again the texture of the riddle, its diction and style, indicate a pornographic surface meaning. The riddle is composed in a meter used in literary texts, with the last line borrowed from literary riddle verses.

Handelman, commenting on a suggestion by Ramanujan, says, "Riddles are not indexical, for their structures are directed to answers and not to meaning . . . [They] are concerned primarily with effect (i.e. answers) rather than affect (i.e., meaning)."[11] However, a look at the texture of adolescent riddles, as well as some adult riddles, in Telugu suggests that they may also have an affective role to play. After examining a large corpus of Telugu riddles, I conclude that riddle as a genre is irreverent in style and culturally defiant in attitude. Scholarly riddle collectors in early twentieth-century India either cleaned up some of the obscenities or simply excluded whatever was too objectionable.[12] A recent study of Telugu riddles by Kasirĕḍḍi Veṅkaṭa Rĕḍḍi includes a number of overtly pornographic riddles, but avoids commenting on their texture by giving them the respectable aesthetic label *śṛṅgāra* (erotic), one of the nine *rasas* or sentiments of classical Sanskrit aesthetics. Literary riddles—a different genre—generally have a less objectionable texture, though even a little obscenity often appears there as well (especially in the literary *samasyas*).

Adolescents as a group are located on the boundary between adulthood and childhood. Adults treat them as children, while they think of themselves as adults. As children they are discouraged from using proverbs, which are clearly demarcated as an adult genre. Proverbs are strictly hierarchical in use. Even among adults, persons of lower status do not generally use proverbs, unless the one chosen reinforces humility before persons of higher status. Boys and girls are discouraged from using proverbs. By and large, proverbs maintain the status quo.[13] Riddles, by way of contrast, question the established cognitive order.[14]

There seems to be a certain pride these young people take in being free to violate family conventions in the context of a riddle. This process appears to have two aspects. The adolescents are defeating the adults and their rules. Often an adult may not even be able to answer the riddle if confronted with a group of adolescents playing with this form. Adults are visibly embarrassed because they see only the surface obscenity of the riddle. By the time the answer is supplied, the adult's embarrassment is doubled because of his inability to answer the riddle himself. This gives the adolescents an opportunity to make their own communities distinct from, and in some sense superior to, those of the adults. If there is a sufficiently large group of adolescents who know the answers to the riddles, they form a riddle gang ready for battle with other adolescents uninitiated into the world of correct responses. Perhaps riddles offer adolescents a particular kind of opportunity in a world that does not entirely accept them as individuals.

Riddles are generally thought to be the property of the young, as has been repeatedly stated by editors of riddle collections. But Kasirĕḍḍi Veṅkaṭa Rĕḍḍi reports several intriguing instances where riddles are used in villages by adult men and women both at work and at leisure. His ethnography is often unclear, inadequate, and faulty. It is difficult to see from his book whether he is recording a riddle performance from a real occurrence, remembering it from his past experience, or just imagining a possible event and writing it up. Despite these defects, the riddle texts he presents are compelling even if we discount the contexts he describes. Here is an example. An old man sitting at the public place at the center of the village is accosted by a younger man who "hits" him with a riddle:

tātā tātā tai bŏmmalāṭa
bāṭalunnādi baṅgāru mūṭa
mūṭa muṭṭicci mūḍigaṭṭu tāta
tātā tai bŏmmalāṭa[15]

Grandpa, grandpa, play of dolls
A heap of gold lies on the path
touch it, pick it, tuck it into your bag
O grandpa, grandpa, play of dolls.

The old man misidentifies the answer as a bag village men carry, containing a flint stone, a piece of steel, and a piece of cotton rope for making fire to light up their cigars. The young man ridicules the old man for his inability to resolve the riddle and supplies the answer: feces—a valuable manure. Farmers gather them, pack them in a bag, and put them in their fields. (The first line and the last line of this rhyming riddle are formulaic.) The old man laughs it off: "Every farmer does that, doesn't he?"

Kasirĕḍḍi Veṅkaṭa Rĕḍḍi also offers the following, from adult use:

siṭuku siṭuku maṭṭĕlu vĕṭṭuka
mañciniḷḷa bāyikostĕ
kŏṇṭĕmuṇḍakŏḍukŏcci
kŏṅgu vaṭṭi guñjĕ[16]

Rings jingling on my toes
I was going to the water well
A naughty bastard came
and pulled the end of my sari.

Answer: thorny *regu* bush (that grows on the edges of farmland).

And one more:

ḍĕbbhai rūpayilu vĕṭṭi
ḍibbila raika dĕstĕ
ennu vagili
sannu gānoccĕ[17]

I spent seventy rupees and
bought this blouse of beads
It ripped on the back
and the breast is exposed

Answer: *sītāphalam,* a fruit which cracks open when it is ripe to reveal its meaty interior.

According to Kasirĕḍḍi Veṅkaṭa Rĕḍḍi, the above two riddles are used exclusively by village women working in the field.

Other Riddle Forms

Other forms of riddles have separate names: they are not *pŏḍupukathalu.* One such genre is a trick question that tests a person's intelligence. These questions occur in folktales and legends. Often there is a king in search of a minister, or a beautiful maid looking for a suitable husband. Here is a legend about Timmarusu, minister of King Krishnadevarāya. The king took a piece of paper with a line drawn across it and sent it around his kingdom with an announcement that anyone who could make the line shorter without erasing any part of it would be chosen as his minister. No one thought it was possible, until a young boy took the paper into his hands and drew a longer line next to it.

There is the story of a young and beautiful woman who made a vow that she would not marry any young man unless he could make three statements about her which she could not controvert. Many tried, but she denied every statement they made about her. Finally a young man came and said:

Your mother is not a barren woman.
You are not ugly.
You are a chaste woman.[18]

Unable to deny any of these statements, the woman married the young man.

Literary Riddles

Often listed in the category of riddles, literary riddles test the intellectual skills of adults, their wit and wisdom, and, above all, their ability to play with language. Used in royal courts of medieval Andhra as demonstrations of cultural excellence, there is a variety of forms of literary riddles: they include *śleṣa padyamulu* (punning verses), *citra kavitvamu* (picturesque verses), *garbha kavitvamu* (verses including other verses within them), *camatkāra cāṭuvulu* (riddling verses), and *samasyalu* (tricky statements). Among them, *camatkāra cāṭuvulu* look most like *pŏḍupukathalu.* These are verse-riddles composed by known poets and circulated among educated adults as a scholarly pastime. Hundreds of these verses are often included in riddle anthologies. They are always in proper verse form, in chaste literary style, with no crude obscenity or irreverence. These riddles require no more than common sense and a good knowledge of mythology to answer them. In structure, they look like the riddles adolescents use, but they differ from the latter in that they can be solved logically. As Dan Pagis suggests, "The text of the literary riddle, in order to fulfill its social role, must pose a challenge which can be met through reasoning alone and does not require extraneous or esoteric information."[19] Often the riddle itself includes clues to its answer, which is always singular. Here is an example:

It moves in the sky; but it is not a bird.
It has a tail, but it is not a goat.
It has a rope, but it is not a bull.
What is this, Lord of Tirumala Hill?

Despite being in a verse form and literary in style, this riddle is almost similar to a *pŏḍupukatha*. However, there are literary riddles that play complex language games.

rāmuḍĕvvari gūdi rāvaṇu mardiñcĕ	(*to ka mū ka to*)
paravāsudevuni paṭṇam' edi	(*ran ga na ga ram*)
rājamannāruce rañjillu śaram' edi	(*la ko ri ko la*)
velaya gānuga vaṇti vitt'adedi	(*jam bi ra bi jam*)
sītanu cekona cĕracina dhanuvedi	(*pañ cā stru cā pam*)
sabhavāri navviñcu jāṇa ĕvaḍu	(*vi ka ṭa ka vi*)
ala rambha kŏppulon alaru mālika edi	(*man dā ra dā mam*)
śrīkṛṣṇuḍ' eyinṭa cĕlagucunḍĕ	(*nan da sa da nam*)

anniṭiki jūḍan aidesi yakṣaramulu
onaran iru desa cadivinan ŏkka tīre

cĕppa galgina nen ittu cinni mada
cĕppalekunna nagdu ne cinni nagavu

Who helped Rāma kill Rāvaṇa?
What's the name of Krishna's city?
What is the weapon held by Vishnu?
What is the seed that looks like *kānuga* seed?
Which bow was broken to win Sītā?
Who makes people laugh in the court of the king?
Which is the flower-garland in Rambhā's hair?
Where did Krishna grow up?

All these answers have five syllables each.
You can read them backwards, they will be the same.
If you can tell them, I will give you money.
If not, I will give myself a little smile.

The answers given in parentheses next to each line of the verse indicate that all of them are palindromes carefully crafted to fit the conditions of the answer.

A different kind of literary riddle is *samasya,* which is presented to a poet who wishes to be tested in his skills of extempore versification. *Samasyas* of this kind are presented as a line of an unfinished verse; the poet is supposed to use the line and compose a verse around it, thereby making the verse meaningful. The following *samasya* was often used to test the skills of poets in *śatāvadhāna* (a mnemo-technic) performances. The famous twin poets and extempore versifiers, Tirupati Veṅkaṭakavulu, known for their wit and phenomenal skills of memory, completed scores of *samasyas* like this one:

sati sati gavayaṅga putra santati galigĕn

A woman slept with another woman and gave birth to a son.

On the face of it, the *samasya* is nonsense. The poet's trick is to let the third line of the improvised verse end in a *va-*. Read together, the first word *sati* (woman/wife) of the *samasya* now changes to *vasati* (house). The nonsense *samasya* is rendered sensible by this change and is contextualized by the rest of the verse: a certain young man who had no male children had a new house built in harmony with his astrological signs; he slept with his wife in this new house and she gave birth to a son. *Samasyas* like this are a favorite pastime of poets, who enjoyed being tested for their versifying and problem-solving skills. Often mildly obscene overtones of the *samasya* line disappear when the rest of the verse is elaborated around it.

Literary riddles play with language. It is as if language itself becomes an area of endless playfulness, replete with enigmatic modes, opening up labyrinthine possibilities to explore. Where the answer is logical and undisputable, the process of finding it becomes a game. For the true riddle, the *pŏḍupukatha* of adolescents and of adults of nonliterate low castes, where the process of finding the answer is not logical, the answer itself is enigmatic. Here the play is with meaning, not with the language.

Forms similar to the literary riddle are reported from non-literate traditions, too. One such form is sung in groups of playing or working men and women. The examples I have found are overtly erotic and lead to only one logical answer, which is predictably nonerotic. Here is a woman singing:

I am going, I am going, on my way to *cārkamān*
I gave my feet to one and my hands to another
and now I am going for yet another.

I gave my feet to the goldsmith, my hands to the banglesmith,
and now I am going for money to pay them.

I am going, I am going
I have one guy on top of me and another under me
and I am going for yet another.

I have bŏṭṭu *on my forehead, betel in my mouth,*
and I am going to find a mirror.

I am going I am going
I hid one and killed the other
and one more I have fanned with my sari.

I covered the pot and put out the fire
I blew out the lamp with the breeze from my sari[20]

The first part of each of the segments describes what appears to be the behavior of a brazen and promiscuous woman. The answer reveals a very ordinary woman busy with her household work. There are several variations on this theme, suggesting that this type of song is a genre by itself, though there is no native name for it.

Riddles with Stories

Sanskrit has a name for riddles with stories: *prahelikā.* Literary Telugu borrows the word, but folk Telugu has no name for this genre, and the available reports suggest that this is also called *pŏḍupukatha.* However, each of these riddles has a long story to explain it. Here is an example given by Kasirĕḍḍi Veṅkaṭa Rĕḍḍi:

katalanni ĕtalāyĕ
kāpural rĕṇḍ'āye
āḍu sacci ar'nell'āyĕ
ad'esina kundelu iyyala mapati kūr'āyĕ
saccina magaḍu saṇḍlamīda
manunna magaḍu mañcammīda[21]

Stories are sad
Two lives, two men
He died six months ago
The rabbit he killed
Is dinner tonight
The husband who died is on my breast
The husband I married is in my bed.

A certain woman loved a man. Her parents did not approve of him and got her married to another man. The broken-hearted lover hung himself on a tree in the nearby forest. The woman visited the tree every day and poured water on the feet of the dead body. Gradually a thick shrub of grass grew under his feet, and a rabbit lived in it. In course of time, the rope holding the body—now only a skeleton—fell on the rabbit and killed it. The woman collected the rabbit, made dinner, and served it to her husband.

An extended version of the story adds that the woman skinned the dead body of her lover and made a blouse from it and wore it. A variation on this theme says the husband suspected his wife's relationship with her lover, killed him by hanging him to a tree, had his body skinned, and hung the skin on a peg in his home. The wife, who knew all this, quietly collected the skin and made a blouse from it.

Another instance is built around a Sanskrit verse, not different in tone from any other verse advising good conduct. The story associated with it makes it an enigmatic projection of events that happen later. A certain rich Sanskrit scholar had two sons. At the time of his death, the scholar called his sons and asked them to choose either his texts or his wealth. The elder one chose the wealth, while the younger one chose the texts. One day a prince visited the young man and bought, for a vast sum, "a single stanza" from his texts. The king was furious with the prince for wasting his money on a stupid Sanskrit stanza. Here is the verse:

bhojanaṃ bali-bhuktam ca
śayane hasta-mārjanam
paradeśe ca jāgaram
prathamakopanivāraṇam

Eat after feeding animals.
Sleep after tidying the bed with your hand.
Be watchful in a foreign country.
Avoid impetuous anger.

The king drove his son out of his kingdom; the prince wandered into a nearby city. A courtesan saw him, was taken by his princely appearance, and invited him into her house. But he was not attracted by her, and the rejected courtesan tried to poison him. The prince remembered the verse he had bought and gave the first morsel of his food to a cat passing by. The cat died at once. The prince, realizing the danger he was in, went away without showing anger. Soon another courtesan found him and invited him to her house. The prince was not attracted by this courtesan either. Angered by his rejection, the courtesan made a bed for him over a deep well, carefully covered up. The prince remembered his verse and tidied the bed, firmly pressing it with his hands; it sank into the well. Realizing the treachery of these courtesans, the prince went off to another country—again without showing anger.

The princess of that land suffered from a strange curse: anyone who married her died on the nuptial night. One after another, many princes married her and died; no one knew why. The prince decided he would find the secret of these mysterious deaths. He married her, and on the first night was duly shown into her bedroom. He found his bride deep in sleep. Unable to understand this strange behavior, the prince waited for a while. The room looked rather inhospitable. He remembered he was in a foreign country; the verse he had bought prescribed wakefulness, so he kept awake. Right at the stroke of midnight, two snakes came out of the two nostrils of the princess. The prince swiftly hacked them with his sword. Soon there was a demon who stood before him, about to throttle his neck. The prince cut off the demon's hands. The handless demon ran out of the room and disappeared.

When the princess woke and saw the dead snakes and arms on the floor, her bridegroom consoled her and told her what had happened while she slept. She was relieved to discover that she had been freed from the demon who possessed her. And the prince ruled the kingdom and lived happily with the princess.

Here a seemingly straightforward Sanskrit verse turns out to be proleptically potent, capable of offering protection from unforeseen dangers, hence well worth the enormous investment in acquiring it.

There are ritual parallels to this kind of story. Riddles and riddle-like forms employing tricky or enigmatic language are often used in weddings. The Telugu wedding ritual includes an expressive moment when the new couple enters the bridegroom's home: at the doorway, the young man is asked (mostly by members of his own family) to divulge his bride's name. The bride is similarly asked to state her husband's name. Normally, husbands and wives do not mention the name of their spouse; it is considered immodest to do so. (Originally, perhaps, naming was felt to expose the person to the dangers of black magic.) Here, the bridegroom either boldly mentions his new bride's name or he makes an intriguing, riddle-like statement, the answer to which would be her name. Thus P. Nāgarāju, a Hyderabad folklorist, reports that he composed the following riddle at his wedding to encode his wife's name—Veṅkaṭa Nāgarāmarājyalakṣmī: "The political slogan of the Bharatiya Janata Party (= *Ramarājya*) has entered my name (= *Nāgarāju*). The deities of our houses (= *Veṅkaṭa*) united and began the story. At the end I found the goddess of wealth (= *Lakṣmī*)."[22]

The Enigma of the Future: A Telugu Nostradamus

There is a genre of songs extensively used by mendicant singers in Andhra called *tattvālu* (philosophical songs), authored by the prophet-poet Potulūri Vīra Brahmam. Telugu classification does not see these songs as riddles, but it does consider their language secretive (*mārmika bhāṣa*). That there is something riddle-like in these songs is clearly perceived by both the singers and the listeners. But first let me present the context of these songs.

A group of men, dressed in soiled ochre robes stuck to their perspiring bodies, sit in an open space on the street corner on a hot summer evening. One of them has a beard and matted hair. He holds a lute with one string; several others have cymbals. A pipe of ganja is being passed around, and as each one of them takes a deep puff, the group becomes quieter. A few passers-by watch them from a distance. The man with the lute starts tuning it, and his humming explodes into a song in his loud and clear voice. The people with cymbals follow the last line. They are singing a song popularly known as a Brahmam song.

> Don't say, I didn't tell you.
> Listen, if you reach the guru and bow to him
> you will live.
> The guru's word never fails.
> The spirits will chew up all those who go the wrong way.
> In youth you fail to know.
> In pride you fail to see.
> You can't say when—now or tomorrow.
> Someday, sometime no one knows but
> you will clearly hear the sounds of his horse's hoofs.
> Don't say I didn't tell you.
>
> Your mind is filled with foul thoughts
> but you will learn to see if proof is shown.
> Mothers and children will be separated,
> walk in the wilderness eating roots and berries,

cry like crows and die alone.
They scream for help and give up their life-breath,
cry as if an army of demons had attacked them.
The sky turns red.
Six religions are mixed up.
People of the world die by fire and water.

Don't say I didn't tell you.

They see smoke bellowing from the earth,
stars in the middle of day.
The sky makes frightening sounds,
and people fly like helpless birds.
Sinners die, but those with merit are saved.
Those who do not chant "Rāma Rāma"
will drop dead, watch out.
You do not see what will come to pass.
The guards of Yama will force you to the city of death.

Don't say I didn't tell you.

After these strange events
the golden age of truth will begin.
Vīrabhogavasantarāyalu will rule with pleasure
the seven islands, with a single wheel.
Don't say I didn't tell you.[23]

Potulūri Vīra Brahmam, believed to be an incarnation of Viṣṇu, foretold the future and promised rebirth of the golden age. Probably belonging to the late eighteenth century, this guru, worshiped by artisan castes in Andhra Pradesh, composed a number of songs (*kīrtanas*) sung by mendicants. These songs present, in enigmatic language, a picture of a deteriorating world and its ultimate doom. According to the chapbooks describing his biography, Vīra Brahmam is the ultimate *brahman,* who came to teach the world that the present Brahmins are impostors usurping the position that truly belongs to the Viśvabrāhmaṇas, or artisan castes. Here is a brief summary of his story.

When the wheel of time moves on, and the age of Kali begins—the fourth in the ages of progressive deterioration—human beings fall into bad ways. Dharma grows weak, and people lose their knowledge. Chaste women become rare. The goddess Earth goes to Brahmā and cries: "I cannot bear this burden. Even one sinner is heavier than all the cardinal mountains. Save me." Brahmā asks her to be patient. "The Kali age has hardly begun," he says. "There is still a long way to go. The Mahābhārata war has only recently ended."

King Parīkṣit comes to rule. Even during his rule, the cow of dharma loses three of her legs and is left standing on one. The evil Kali, taking a low-caste Shudra form, kicks her leg. Three thousand years go by. Harihararāya of the Vijayanagar dynasty rules the earth. His dynasty ends, and then come the Muslims. Viṣṇu decides it is time to help the human world: he calls for all the gods, asks Śiva to take birth in a Kshatriya family in Benares with a human name, Ānandabhairavayogi. Śiva sends Brahmā to be born in a Viśvabrāhmaṇa (goldsmith) family as Ānanda, while he (Viṣṇu) himself decides to be born in another goldsmith family as Vīra Brahmam.

In the Nandikōṇḍa monastery, sage Vīrabhojayāchāryulu has no male children. One day, when he is absent from home, a hermit comes to his house. His wife Vīrapāpamāmba receives the hermit, but he refuses the honors because she has no children. When she begs for a blessing, the hermit says that she will not have a child of her own but will receive a male child from a sage. The boy will be no ordinary child, for he is the very avatar of God. She should go on pilgrimage to look for that child. The couple set off on pilgrimage. Meanwhile another goldsmith couple, Paripūrṇācāryasvāmi and his wife Prakṛtimāmba, have no children. In response to their prayers, God appears in the wife's dream and says: "I will be born as your child: but your husband will die soon after that." That night, a light enters her womb, and soon she is pregnant. Nine months later she gives birth to Vīra Brahmam. Just before his birth, a star appears on the sky. Ordinary people fear that the star indicates calamities, but sages know that God has been born on the earth to save the world. Soon after, Paripūrṇācāryasvāmi dies. Prakṛtimāmba then finds a sage to whom she entrusts the child, and she leaves the world in peace. The sage gives the boy to Vīrabhojayācāryulu and Vīrapāpamāmba, who come to see him on their pilgrimage.

Vīra Brahmam grows up in their house; one day he teaches divine knowledge to his mother. He shows her his cosmic form and informs her how the goldsmiths lost their ancient status of priesthood to the Brahmins. This is how it has happened.

Vyāsa Deceives His Teacher Viśvakarma

The great author of sacred texts, Vyāsa, serves Viśvakarma, the divine architect, who is born out of Maya, the Viśva-brahma. He studies with him for twelve years with great devotion and learns from him all the *Vedas, Vedāṅgas, Purāṇas,* and *Itihāsas.* He writes them all down, with one change. He substitutes the word "Brahmins" wherever the word "Viśvabrāhmaṇas" occurs in the original texts. He writes that only Brahmins shall be worshiped, only they shall have the right to perform rituals, and so on. Then he performs penance for long years. When his guru appears and offers to give him his wish, Vyāsa asks that the books he has written, the *Vedas,* the *Vedāṅgas* and all the *Purāṇas,* be regarded as authoritative in the Kali age. The guru, having given his word, realizes his error, but says that is how it shall be for five thousand years of the Kali age during which time the caste order will deteriorate.

Vīra Brahmam Announces that he will Come as the Savior

At the appropriate time, Vīra Brahmam will come as Vīrabhoga-vasantarāyalu to protect the good people and punish the sinners. Assuring his mother of the future, Vīra Brahmam leaves for the village called Hariharapuram, where he performs penance under a tree. Ānandabhairava-yogi, the incarnation of Śiva, comes that way hunting animals. He sees a tiger about to kill a cow. Aiming to kill the tiger and save the cow, Ānanda-bhairavayogi shoots an arrow, which misses its aim and hits the cow instead. Ānanda is distressed that he has unwittingly committed an evil act. He approaches Vīra Brahmam, asking for help to get rid of his sin. Vīra Brahmam reminds Ānanda that he (Ānanda) is Śiva himself who has taken human birth. But since human life has to be lived, he will suffer the consequences of the sin he committed. For this reason, Ānanda will be reborn in a Muslim family. However, that should not matter: even as a Muslim, Ānanda will retain knowledge of the *brahman* and will rule his people justly.

Vīra Brahmam himself goes to another village and serves a woman called Accamma. Every day he takes her cattle out into the field, draws a line around the herd and sits at a distance, writing a book. That book is the famous *Kālajñānam*, the knowledge of time, in which all that is going to happen is foretold.

Kālajñānam is a folk genre; several texts of this genre are reported in Telugu folklore. A Sanskrit *Kālajñānam* is attributed to the sage Vidyāraṇya, the royal guru of the Vijayanagar dynasty.[24] Typically, *Kālajñānam* books describe the events of the past in future tense, including statements that look like predictions.

Every day while Vīra Brahmam writes his book, the cattle stay inside the line and yet get enough grass to graze on. Every day Accamma gives him lunch, but Vīra Brahmam puts it in a ditch. He also puts the pages of the book he has written in a ditch near Accamma's house, covering them up with a huge rock. One day some cattle thieves see the herd of well-fed cattle standing alone with no herder around, and try to steal them. When the thieves enter the area inside the line, they become blind. Frightened, they run outside the line, and their eyesight returns. The thieves go to Accamma, confess their dishonest intent, and pray to her for forgiveness. Accamma realizes that Vīra Brahmam is no ordinary cattle herder and seeks his blessing when he returns home.

Vīra Brahmam has by now completed his book. He tells Accamma who he is and describes the contents of his book:

> Eight thousand eight hundred and eight years after the beginning of the Kali age, dharma perishes. The goddess survives only in sacred places. Untruth flourishes. People lose knowledge. They commit all the five deadly sins. Nations fight among themselves. Planets miss their given path. The Ganges loses its purity. Shudras pretend that they are Brahmins. People steal each other's wives. Women marry more than once. Gods lose their power. Mantras lose their efficacy. Brahmins cross oceans and eat meat. Castes get mixed up. Epidemics increase. A widow rules over the people. Sexual desire in women increases, and they mate with any man-father, brother, or son. A woman nine cubits tall will be born on Indrakīlādri mountain; she

> will behead all sinners. A *śakti* arises from Palnāḍu and ruins all the towns and villages. A strange thing will happen in Bangalore: on the second day after the new moon, lightning will hit the city. Following the lightning, huge persons will descend onto the earth. They will have feet seven times as big as ours. Three hundred and sixty different new diseases grow. No drugs can cure those diseases. New gurus emerge, a dime a dozen. Atheists flourish. Untouchables become kings. The village Kandimallayyapalli grows to be a city six miles long. The Krishna river in Vijayawada swells and submerges the goddess Kanakadurga's temple on the hill: water reaches up to the nose ring of the goddess. A pathway will be built to Tirupati hill. Thieves enter the temple and steal temple property. Mlecchas study Vedas. New theories appear teaching that all men are equal. It will be argued that the only distinction between humans is that of sex. Temple worship will be taken over by low castes. Kings will have to follow people, instead of the other way around. Brahmins sell Vedic learning for money. Vehicles move without the help of cattle. People grow physically so small that they will need a ladder to climb a *vempali* bush.

After revealing these prophecies, Vīra Brahmam performs a number of miracles. He takes the Muslim Siddhayya as his chief disciple and teaches him his predictions. Finally he enters *samādhi*, his final resting place, and, promising to return at the right time, directs that his burial place should be sealed with a rock.

Just before he enters his *samādhi,* Vīra Brahmam sends Siddhayya away. When Siddhayya returns to find that his guru has entered his final resting place, he mourns the loss and asks his guru to come back to talk to him. Vīra Brahmam returns from his *samādhi* and briefly speaks to him. His disciples still believe that he will return as Vīrabhogavasantarāyalu to save the world. It is predicted that he will come wielding a sword and riding a horse.

Predictions and prophecies are not uncommon in religious literature. One might view them as riddles—in Vīra Brahmam's case, riddles in reverse order. As predictions of events that have not yet happened, they are riddles with answers yet unborn. When Indira Gandhi became prime minister of India, Vīra Brahmam's followers found one of his prediction riddles that a widow will rule the country, confirmed.

Riddling of this variety is similar to finding familiar shapes in clouds. As children we found the entire *Mahābhārata* battle in the clouds on the evening sky. It is a certain willingness to see things realized that brings the event to happen. You find what you already have in your mind. But there is a difference. Riddling needs a community. A shared acceptance of a world—a world of letters that look like birds without tails, eyelids that appear like doors that do not make any noise, and so on; a world believed to have a prior existence, but actually created in the process of riddling—performs a creative trick. It brings a community into existence, while allowing the members of this community to believe that it existed prior to their creating it. A world which the community has not created is not *its* world; and a world which does not exist prior to the community's creation of it is also not a world, for it lacks substance. Riddling performs both tricks: it allows you the freedom to create a reality without interfering with your belief that you have not created it.

Riddling with the future performs a similar task. A feature of all belief in predictions is the conviction that the future exists, already made, only to be revealed in due course. Such a future is actually a "past" veiled by time.

Such a belief needs the authority of a guru who has seen that future before ordinary people have the chance to do so. A firm belief in such an authority requires that the guru perform miracles to prove that he has the power to "see" the future, has lived in the future as well as in the past. Vīra Brahmam's biography does just that. Here is a guru who is beyond time and who therefore "knows" time. Vīra Brahmam's biography is thus a part of the whole story, an integral part of the riddle he and his community have created.

Conclusion

We have seen that riddles use irreverent and often obscene language, enigmatizing the world of secure meanings; or, if they are literary riddles, they disturb the comforting solidity of ordinary language and open it up as a world of endless double meanings and miraculous rearrangements of syllables which playfully present themselves to our consciousness. The world of everyday experience, the world ordered by rules and rituals, hierarchies, and authority is ingeniously disturbed and mysteriously reordered. All riddles, and especially true riddles, are open-ended. Their answers are not immediately seen; they are *adṛṣṭārthas*, having a resolution beyond our control. This quality of the riddles underlies their location in problem situations in folk tales, such as weddings and funerals.

Proverbs, by way of contrast, establish an order, respect authority, and confirm convention. They are perceived as wisdom of the many, the knowledge of the ancients.[25] In usage, too, proverbs belong only to the elders, who have the authority to use them. They therefore come to be cited in dispute settlements, or folk courts, where order as perceived by the elders of the community prevails. Riddles are the playful tools of the young, of the illiterate, and of those who test and question one's claims to be eligible. Proverbs establish the order; riddles question it. Proverbs are at the center of community life, in the central space of the village, where adults gather. They flow in one direction from above to below. Riddles are situated at the peripheries, among adolescents or uneducated men and women, and in the boundary spaces of ritual situations such as choosing a bridegroom or a minister. Riddles operate among equals to form a community, often opposed to communities of a higher status. Gurus employ riddles to test the readiness of their disciples or to couch truth in a language accessible only to initiates.

Notes

1. Other words for *pŏḍupukatha* are: *ŏḍḍu katha, aḍḍu katha, māru katha, taṭṭu katha*, and *viḍupu katha.*
2. Recorded from Tarani Teja (age nine years).
3. Reddy: 90. There are a number of printed anthologies of riddles in Telugu. Most of them list the riddles in alphabetical order and give the answers at the end of the book or at the bottom of each page. Almost all these books are poorly printed and full of errors. They are circulated among barely literate people, suggesting that *pŏḍupukatha* is not a genre of educated adults. Scholarly interest in riddles appears to be an early-twentieth-century phenomenon. Many literary magazines at that time began publishing riddles, especially literary riddles and trick questions. A very early anthology, probably the earliest in Telugu, was compiled by Nandiraju Chelapati Rao (1910?). Andra Seshagiri Rao, a pioneer in the collection and study

of oral texts, listed the following riddle collections in Seshagiri Rao 1984: (1) *Camatkāra Pŏḍupukathalu*, Madras, 1936; (2) *Camatkāra Pŏḍupukathalu anu 200 Tĕlugu Sāmĕtalu*, Rajahmundry, 1951; (3) *Camatkāra Pŏḍukathalu*, Vijayawada, 1954; (4) *Camatkāra Pŏḍupukathalu*, Tenali, 1955. Nedunūri Gaṅgādharam, a pioneering collector of folk materials, published an anthology, *Pasiḍi Palukulu*, in which he included 135 riddles. A recent study on Telugu riddles is Kasirĕḍḍi Vĕṅkaṭa Rĕḍḍi 1990, which includes a number of riddles not published anywhere before.

4. Reddy: 50.
5. Wittgenstein 1961: 148–9.
6. Quoted by Köngäs-Maranda 1976: 127.
7. Ibid.: 129. See also Köngäs-Maranda 1971: 193, observing that both parts of the riddle, image and answer, are coded. In this respect, the semantics of Telugu *vippu*, often used for riddles, are similar to the connotations of the corresponding English and Finnish terms. *Vippu* connotes "untying a knot, opening, revealing"; cf. Finnish *arvoitus* < *arpa*, "dice, instrument used in divination"; "riddle," German *Rätsel*, connoting "advise, counsel, guess, divine."
8. Ben-Amos 1976: 254.
9. Vĕṅkaṭa Rĕḍḍi 1990: 423.
10. Ibid.: 416.
11. See Handelman.
12. Seshagiri Rao 1984: 37 even admits to having censored objectionable riddle-texts.
13. See Narayana Rao 1981.
14. See Köngäs-Maranda 1976: 136, and also Michael Lieber's critique of Maranda in the same issue, Lieber 1976: 255–65.
15. Vĕṅkaṭa Rĕḍḍi 1990: 153.
16. Ibid.: 159.
17. Ibid.: 160.
18. This incident has been used in a 1959 Telugu movie-song: *o rūpavatī nen' avun' annadi nuvvu kād' anagalavā? / ne kād' annadi nuvv' avun' anagalavā? nīvu kurūpivi kādu / / kori ninu ganna talli gŏḍrālu gādu,* Thanks to P. Subbachari, folklorist from Hyderabad, for informing me of this song.
19. See Pagis.
20. Vĕṅkaṭa Rĕḍḍi 1990: 155. For a similar song, see ibid.: 148.
21. Ibid.: 289–92.

22. My thanks to Nagaraju for this recollection.
23. From *Kāla-jñāna-tattvamulu*, songs of Potulūri Vīra Brahmam, chapbook, no date.
24. See Wagoner 1993: 165–9.
25. See Mieder and Dundes 1981. See especially Taylor 1981, in that volume. In Telugu proverbs are called *śāstras*, equating them with great prescriptive knowledge handed down by sages in Sanskrit.

References

Ben-Amos, Dan. 1976. "Solution to Riddles." *Journal of American Folklore* 89: 249–54.

Köngäs-Maranda, Elli. 1971. "The Logic of Riddles." In Pierre Maranda and Elli Köngäs-Maranda, eds, *Structural Analysis of Oral Tradition.* Philadelphia: University of Pennsylvania Press, 189–232.

———. 1976. "Riddles and Riddling: An Introduction." *Journal of American Folklore* 89: 127–37.

Lieber, Michael D. 1976. "Riddles, Cultural Categories, and World View." *Journal of American Folklore* 89: 255–65.

Mieder, Wolfgang, and Alan Dundes, eds. 1981. *The Wisdom of the Many: Essays on the Proverb.* New York: Garland.

Narayana Rao, Velcheru. 1981. "Proverbs and Riddles." In D.P. Pattnayak and P.J. Claus, eds, *Indian Folklore* I. Mysore: Central Institute of Indian Languages.

Reddy, G.N. n.d. *Pŏḍupukathalu:* Tirupati: Śaṣtipūrti-sanmāna-sangham.

Seshagiri Rao, Andra. 1984. *Āndhra Jānapada Sāhityam.* Waltair: The Author.

Taylor, Archer. 1981. "Wisdom of the Many and the Wit of One." In W. Mieder and A. Dundes, eds, *The Wisdom of the Many: Essays on the Proverb.* New York: Garland,

Vĕṅkaṭa Reḍḍi, Kasireḍḍi. 1990. *Telugu Pŏḍupukathalu.* Hyderabad: The Author.

Wagoner, Philip B. 1993. *Tidings of the King: A Translation and Ethnohistorical Analysis of the Rāyavācakamu.* Honolulu: University of Hawaii Press.

Wittgenstein, L. 1961. *Tractatus Logico-Philosophicus.* London: Routledge.

11

Buddhism in Modern Andhra

Literary Representations from Telugu

On 30 January 1948, the news that Gandhi had been assassinated by a Hindu fanatic named Nathuram Vinayak Godse was broadcast through the All India Radio station. Within minutes, along with the details of the news, the well-known excerpt from the *Bhagavadgita* could be heard on the airwaves:

yadā yadā hi dharmasya glānir bhavati bhārata,
abhyuttānam adharmasya tadātmānam sṛjāmy aham
paritrāṇāya sādhūnām vināśāya ca duṣkṛtām
dharmasamsthāpanarthāya sambhavāmi yuge yuge[1]

Son of Bharata,
whenever there is
a decline
in *dharma*,
and the absence
of *dharma*
increases,
I create myself.
I come into being
from age to age
with the purpose
of fixing *dharma*—
as a refuge

for those who do good
and as a doom
for those who do evil.

The idea is clear: The Mahatma is seen as an incarnation of the god Viṣṇu born to free India from the non-*dharmic* rule of the English. But when oleographs of Gandhi's images started to appear in the market the choice of equating Viṣṇu with Gandhi did not work. The painters of Gandhi's images were unable to come up with any avatar of Viṣṇu that was non-violent, and they invariably painted Buddha in the background with Gandhi in the foreground, both blessing the people of India from up above in the sky.

A year earlier, when India's new government chose the symbols of the nation, the Ashoka chakra on the national flag and the lion capital as the seal, no one objected. Using clear Hindu symbols, on the other hand, would have been objectionable to the Muslims, Christians, Sikhs, and a number of secular-minded people. One way of avoiding religion in national symbols was to adopt Buddhist images almost as if they represented not a religion but a culture.[2] Long before these Buddhist symbols came to be acceptable as national symbols, Buddhist themes became popular in literature. Andhra is known for its Buddhist monuments, which take the memory of Buddhism back to the second century before the common era. Modern Telugu people are constantly reminded of their Buddhist past by the great monuments at Nagarjunakonda, Amaravati, and a large number of other sites. However, nothing by way of the written word from this past has survived.[3] In the early twentieth century, during the colonial period, Buddhism was (re)introduced to Telugu literature via Britain, through English. Here I want to explore the hermeneutics of these new writings on Buddhist themes in Telugu literature during the course of the twentieth century, and how poets and writers shaped the modern understanding of Buddhism among Telugu people.

There are two striking facts related to Buddhism in the history of twentieth-century Telugu literature. One: an unusually large number of poets and writers wrote on Buddhist themes. Two: none of them were Buddhists. Nor did their works lead to anything like a revival of Buddhism in Andhra. I wish to examine four literary texts—three poems and a play—written by major poets and writers in the twentieth century and ask two questions of each of them: What were the reasons that led the authors to choose the Buddhist theme, and what was the meaning their readers derived from their work? I will introduce the writers briefly with some biographical information, locating their place in modern Telugu literary history, and discuss in detail the Buddhist-themed texts they wrote and their impact on readers of the time.

Colonial Backdrop: *Buddhacaritramu* by the Twin Poets

Buddhacaritramu is the result of collaboration between Venkata Sastri (1870–1950) and Tirupati Sastri (1872–1920).[4] Together they called themselves Tirupati-Venkata poets (hereafter, Twin Poets). As a team they were a powerful influence on Telugu literature during the first half of the twentieth century. They developed a genre called *śatāvadhānam.* The two of them would stand before a hundred scholars and poets and respond orally to their requests in verses created on the spot. The requests included riddles to be solved, verses to be composed in a particular meter describing some theme, person, or event, using specially chosen words which often were not easy to weave into the verse. The poets were to take up each request and give their responses in verse. They composed the verse together, i.e. if one poet composed the first line, the other would compose the next. By the end of the event, they would both recite all the verses in the order in which they had been requested. This new performance genre—called *śatāvadhānam*, because it demanded *avadhāna*, attention, to *śata*, a hundred [people]—became famous. They were received by scholars and poets all over the state and zamindars awarded them their choicest honors. The Twin Poets were not just collaborators; they were friends who behaved as if they were one person living in two bodies. Their friendship was such that after the death of Tirupati Sastri, Venkata Sastri continued to publish his own work under their collective name: Tirupati–Venkata poets.

Neither Venkata Sastri nor his collaborator Tirupati Sastri knew much English; their strength was in their Telugu and Sanskrit, in which they were great scholars. Their extemporaneous poems were so popular that they were memorized and quoted by educated people in conversation. Verses from their plays based on the *Mahābhārata* theme were remembered and sung even by peasants and farmhands in villages.[5]

For most of their lives, Venkata Sastri and Tirupati Sastri did not have stable jobs. Their major patrons were Telugu zamindars scattered all over Andhra. One such zamindar was Krishna Rao of the Koccerlakota family. A Brahmin, he was educated in English and even had a BA degree, which was considered a very high degree in those days. He read English literature and developed a taste for it. During this time, the early 1900s, Edwin Arnold's biography of Buddha, *Light of Asia*, was enjoying an unusual degree of popularity among English-educated Indians. If you did not appreciate *Light of Asia*, you were not considered a person of good taste. Indians were coming to recognize the greatness of their culture through the eyes of European and British scholars and savants who had developed a deep interest and admiration in things Indian. Those who had earlier accepted the colonial message that India was a decadent and downtrodden country that needed the help of the British to be civilized began to see a new respect and admiration for their own culture in Western writings about India. Edwin Arnold's *Light of Asia* came at exactly the right time to appeal to this clientele.

Krishna Rao wanted the Twin Poets to translate *Light of Asia*[6] into Telugu for him.[7] The Twin Poets were rigorous Smārta Brahmins who lived by the traditions and ritual conventions that their families had practiced for generations. They grew up in an atmosphere where "Buddhist" was the harshest term fathers could hurl against their sons when young boys deviated from strict Brahminic practices. Furthermore, the poets were scholars who had studied Śankara's Advaita Vedānta and knew that Buddha was unacceptable to Brahmins because he rejected the authority of the Veda. This was the background in which the Twin Poets wrote the *Buddhacaritramu*—the Life of Buddha.

It is interesting to speculate why the Twin Poets should have agreed to create a Telugu version of the *Buddhacaritramu*, and that too using an English source, a language they did not control as well as Sanskrit, when Aśvaghoṣa's poem about Buddha's life, *Buddhacarita*, was easily accessible to them.

One obvious reason for not following Aśvaghoṣa is that he was not popular among Telugu scholars of Sanskrit. His *Buddhacarita* was not considered much of a *kāvya* by pandits who favored Kālidāsa, Bhavabhūti, Murāri, and such illustrious *kāvya* poets. For more substantial reasons, one has to look into the contemporary political situation, with its historical and cultural components.

English, the New Language of Power

It is well known that the British Raj wisely distanced itself from Christian missionary activities. It shrewdly left the Brahmins free to practice their religion without governmental interference, and even patronized Hindu temples. Most Brahmins found no difficulty in allowing the British to take over the symbolic role of the Kshatriya in the Sanskritic four-varna order, as long as they, the British, let the Brahmins be Brahmins without question. In the early days of the Raj, Brahmins were very supportive of the government and even enjoyed munificent administrative positions under the Raj. They quickly learned English and played courtier to the new kings.

The Brahmin poets under the patronage of zamindars found no contradiction in accepting Queen Victoria and, later, King George V as their monarchs and praising them in the traditional style reserved for great Hindu emperors of the past. The zamindars provided a comfortable space for traditional Brahmin pandits and poets who continued to live in the imagined world of the glorious patron–king relationship familiar from the remembered history of South India. Long ago, in the sixteenth century, Emperor Kṛṣṇadevarāya held court in his assembly hall called *Bhuvana-vijayamu*—"Conquest of the World"—with his eight poets called *aṣta diggajas*, after the eight mythological cardinal elephants that kept the earth stable. The symbol suggests that the poets supported the empire through poetry, with their emperor enthroned in the centre. This symbol endured historical scrutiny and was firmly implanted in the minds of educated Telugu people. For Brahmin poets who were supported by one of these zamindars, their imagined world continued undisturbed.

Following the trend of the times, the Twin Poets traveled from one zamindar to another seeking support. They imagined themselves in the role of great poets like Śrīnātha of the fourteenth century who traveled from king to king, patron to patron, reciting his poems for them and receiving honors, including *gajārohaṇa*, being paraded through the town on an elephant. As was conventional with poets of the past, the Twin Poets also generated for their zamindari patrons an imagined status as great kings. For instance, the language which the Twin Poets use to describe their patron Krishna Rao unmistakably announces the glory they imagine for him. They call him Kṛṣṇarātprabhu, Lord Kṛṣṇa Rao, and Kṛṣṇarāḍbiḍauja, Krishna Rao who is like Indra the king of gods, and so on. Furthermore, taking advantage of the similarity in name between the zamindar Krishna Rao and the sixteenth century monarch Kṛṣṇadevarāya, the Twin Poets wrote: "Though the victorious Kṛṣṇarāya ruled his kingdom on the shores of the river Tungabhadra and supported a number of great poets, he was not happy because he was born as the son of a servant maid—so he was born again in a Brahmin family, as Krishna Rao, to rule his kingdom from the shores of the river Godavari." There is a folk legend that Kṛṣṇadevarāya was born to a maidservant. His father was told by a sage to make love to his wife at a certain auspicious moment so a great warrior would be born. When his wife delayed coming to bed, he made love to a nearby maid so as not to let the auspicious moment pass.

Despite the glorious images the Twin Poets imagined for the zamindars, and in turn for themselves the zamindars were hardly more than tax farmers, and the poets hardly more than everyday supplicants. Zamindars leased land from the British government and paid a fixed amount of money agreed upon at the time of lease. They enjoyed the trappings of kings sporting titles such as "Raja" or, if the British government permitted, even more glorious titles such as Maharaja (as in the case of the Maharaja of Vizianagaram). They had no real political power and their crowns, if they wore them, were "hollow," to borrow from Dirks (1987). These zamindars came in all shapes and sizes. Some of them were very learned in the two trans-regional languages of high culture, Sanskrit and Persian, and had a good English education as well. But most of them had a smattering of Sanskrit and Telugu and an English education from one of the newly established British-style colleges. Most zamindars came from landowning castes such as Velama and Kamma, but there were a few from traditionally non-landowning castes such as Brahmin and Vaishya. Not all zamindars were of the same status. Some, like the Maharaja of Vizianagaram, had their own kingdoms before the British took away their troops and reduced them to tax farmers. They had relatively richer properties in addition to recognition as "kings" of their area. Other newer zamindars, like Krishna Rao, were upwardly mobile wealthy people who acquired their position by courting the favors of local British officers.

No matter what the origin, caste, or source of wealth of these zamindars, they were all uniformly loyal to the British Raj. They were obedient servants of the British royalty, whose authority and glory they obeyed and celebrated. They invariably hung royal portraits in their court halls and made sure they paid appropriate tributes on every important occasion, such as birthdays. During the coronation of King George V, these zamindars had their court poets write poems for the king and the queen, wishing them a long and healthy life. Poems written in ornate Telugu with high-flown Sanskrit vocabulary, applying to the British royals the same epithets that were once used to celebrate great Hindu emperors such as Kṛṣṇadevarāya, would of course make no sense to an English-speaking Christian monarch sitting in Buckingham Palace in London, even assuming that the poems reached His Majesty, which they did not. Some of the best poets of the time, including the Twin Poets, wrote such poems.

While playing loyal courtier to the British king, some of these zamindars felt a faint sense of pride in their own culture. Politically, they were loyal to the British, and culturally they were getting closer to Western styles of living. They were pleased when Sanskrit scholars and Telugu poets addressed them with Sanskritic titles and praised them as if they were kings wearing a crown, while they themselves were dressed in suits, played cricket, spoke English, and enjoyed the company of white men and women. Thus they lived in two worlds, with a deep respect for Hindu/Indian culture and a sense of pride in it, and a fascination for the West. At this juncture, when Orientalist British and German scholars themselves came to admire India's great culture, these zamindars hailed them enthusiastically. For instance, publication of Max Müller's translation of the Ṛig Veda was underwritten by the Maharaja of Vizianagaram.

A new elite generation was coming up, one learning about the greatness of India through English. Edwin Arnold's *Light of Asia*, and later Ananda Coomaraswamy's *Dance of Siva* were welcomed with open arms by the new elite. They did not know Sanskrit well enough, nor were they interested in reading the English texts with enough care to notice the Orientalist slant (in the Saidian sense) and defend the integrity of the Sanskrit texts and their meaning and message. The power of English was so overwhelming that the very fact that these texts were written in English was enough to elevate them to a status far higher than that of Sanskrit. English names themselves—London, Her Majesty Queen Victoria, or King George V—resounded in their ears with the ring of power. The court poets, who owed their lives to these patrons, followed their example. The following verse by the Twin Poets from the preface to *Buddhacaritramu*, invoking the Supreme Goddess, illustrates the atmosphere clearly:

> The three gods, Śiva, Viṣṇu and Brahmā are like the Governors,
> The minor gods are the lower level officials,
> The great island Maṇidīpa is like London,
> And she herself is Her Majesty the Queen,
> May she, the Great Goddess who rules the world,
> Protect Krishna Rao with compassion.

For the Twin Poets, the location of London and the titles Queen and Governor enhance even the position of the goddess of the universe and of the gods that surround her. This is the background to the Twin Poets' acceptance of Arnold's *Light of Asia* in preference to Aśvaghoṣa's *Buddhacarita* in writing their *Buddhacaritramu*.

As I will show later, Arnold's poem, once the Twin Poets began to translate it, transformed them, as it did many of its readers at the time.[8] But before we see how the English poem transformed the Twin Poets' ideas, let me outline the features of the Telugu *prabandha* genre, which the Twin Poets chose for their translation of Arnold's *Light of Asia*, and the main problems they faced in conforming to the conventions of that genre.

The *Prabandha* Genre in Telugu

The *prabandha* is an ornate, descriptive, and elaborately stylized form that became popular from the sixteenth century onwards. The goal of the poet who chooses this genre should be to give aesthetic pleasure to the readers rather than to inform or instruct, as older texts such as the *puranas* or *itihasa* do. The *prabandha* poets demonstrate their skill in the use of language, in describing various things such as sunrise, sunset, moonrise, seasons, a walk in a garden, hunting, battle, and so on. They try to exceed each other in their descriptions of the heroine's beauty from head to toe, the hero and heroine falling in love, their love when they are separated from each other, and their eventual coming together. Most *prabandhas* are erotic in focus. In choosing the *prabandha* genre for their translation of Arnold's book, the Twin Poets already faced a huge problem in transforming Arnold's Victorian style of subdued sexuality into a *prabandha* style of excessive eroticism. The Twin Poets' work is replete with mellifluous descriptions of the glory of the royal palaces, pleasure gardens, and voluptuous women eager to offer their erotic services to provoke the young Siddhartha to play. Thematically, Arnold's text does have similar scenes, but the descriptions in the Twin Poets' work are far more erotic than the Victorian Arnold could have imagined. However, the Twin Poets were careful not to go beyond the propriety of the occasion. The scene where Prince Siddhartha offers gifts to the princesses of the neighboring royal houses is described with heightened eroticism, but by way of contrast the prince is presented in carefully chosen words that indicate his dispassionate aloofness. The prince gives gifts to each of the women without even looking at them until he sees the last one to come: Yaśodhara. She is dazzlingly beautiful. As she stands before him, the prince sees:

a young woman,
graceful as a golden goose,
eyes like petals of a fresh lotus blossom,
breasts towering and round,

body fragrant as *campak* flowers,
her face veiled by shyness,
Yaśodhara—
with a lovely lower lip.

She stands before him and, as if she knew him well, asks with an intimate tone,

Where are my gifts—give them and I've got to go.[9]

Siddhartha smiles and sees that all the gifts are gone, and says:

"Woman with beautiful eyes!
The gifts are given away,
but here is one that no one else deserves."
He was speaking in a special way.
As everyone looked on, he took
a chain of emeralds from his neck
and placed it around hers
with his own hands.[10]

Despite the *prabandha* requirements, the Twin Poets handle *śṛṅgāra*, the erotic mood, minimally so as not to compromise the main theme of the book, which depends on *śānta*, the mood of peace.

There is another area where the Twin Poets made a major change. While they follow Arnold's narrative fairly faithfully, they do not even mention Arnold's name. Instead they mention Aśvaghoṣa's *Buddhacarita* as their source. To a modern reader it is clear plagiarism not to acknowledge Arnold, and a lie to give the credit to Aśvaghoṣa. This is where we should take a careful look at the conventions of *prabandha*.

The template of a *prabandha* requires that it should begin with a prayer to the gods, blessings to the patron of the work for whom it is recited in court, detailed praise to the great Sanskrit and Telugu poets of the past (*pūrva-kavi-stuti*), and a censure of bad poets (*kukavi-ninda*). This is followed by a full description of the family of the patron. The poet then narrates in detail the occasion in which the patron has requested a specific poem to be written for him by giving the poet betel leaves (and gold) and thus sealing the commission. The *prabandha* is courtly poetry, and its conventions require that the patron be described as a king. This template has been in place for at least nine hundred years, from the time

Rājarājanarendra, the Cāḷukya king of Veṅgi, requested his court poet Nannaya to compose in Telugu the *Mahābhārata* "spoken" in Sanskrit by Vyāsa. Such a time-honored template requires that the patron ask his poet to take a Sanskrit text as his original in order to compose his Telugu poem. Because the convention was so rigid, a Sanskrit book was always presented as the original even when it was not really followed. Clearly this tradition would not allow an English poem to be brought into the picture. That would be unacceptable and literarily jarring. Everyone in the literary community knew for a fact that the Twin Poets were commissioned by their patron Krishna Rao to compose a Telugu poem based on Edwin Arnold's *The Light of Asia.*[11] Venkata Sastri himself says in his autobiography (which he wrote in verse in third person as if someone else wrote it)

ātaḍ' inglīṣu bhāsalon āranāḍu
kavi raciñcina buddhuni katanu dĕlgu
jesi kṛti tanak immani vāsiy alara
gorĕ tirpati venkaṭa dhīra kavula.

"Make into Telugu the story of the Buddha written by Aranālḍu [Arnold] in the English language and dedicate it to me." That's what zamindar Krishna Rao asked of the Tirupati–Venkata poets.[12]

The mention of Aśvaghoṣa in the preface to the Telugu poem is, as they say in Telugu, *śastrāniki*, to respect the convention.[13] The Twin Poets leave themselves room to bring Arnold in when they say that Krishna Rao commissioned them to "write the life story of Buddha following Aśvaghoṣa and others." The tag "and others" allows the Twin Poets to bring in Arnold without a problem.

Brahmin Acceptance of Buddhist Non-violence

One tricky point the poets faced relates to the ideal of Buddhist non-violence. One day, Bimbisāra orders a large number of goats to be slaughtered for a Vedic ritual. When Buddha sees the shepherds driving their goats from the pasture into the city earlier than their usual time, he asks why they are rushing back so soon and finds out that King Bimbisāra has ordered them to bring the goats for the ritual. Buddha, who is himself carrying a wounded goat on his shoulders in order to nurture it back to health, asks to go with them. He arrives at the ritual place where the Vedic priest is chanting the mantras and is about to raise his knife to cut off the head of a goat. Buddha dramatically stops him from bringing the knife down on the goat's neck and lectures Bimbisāra on the virtues of non-violence. Convinced that violence is wrong, Bimbisāra announces by way of an inscription that people thereafter should avoid killing animals, eating meat, and so on.

The Twin Poets adopt Arnold's description of the sacrifice very faithfully. However, powerful as this description is, it poses two problems. First, from a Brahminic perspective, ritual killing is not violence; and second, this is not the way an animal is killed at a Vedic sacrifice. What Arnold describes is the way an animal is killed for a village goddess. It is very likely that Arnold had seen such ritual sacrifices at village goddess shrines during his time in India. Technically speaking, no animal is killed with a knife in a Vedic sacrifice. It is smothered to death, spilling no blood. As David Knipe says in his seminal essays on Vedic practices in the Konasima area of Andhra Pradesh, *paśubandha* is practiced even today by Vedic Brahmins in their *śrauta* rituals such as Pauṇḍarika or Agnicayana.[14]

One might ask how these nuances were lost on the Twin Poets who were traditional Brahmins. They were the least Westernized among the Telugu poets of the twentieth century. They dressed in the most conventional Brahmin way, without a shirt and with a *śāluva* (shawl) on their shoulders. They wore their sacred thread visibly across their chest, strictly observed restrictions on food, and meticulously followed their daily ritual observations. They were the most Brahmin of the Brahmin poets of the time. Given their lifestyle, religious learning, and knowledge about the ritual killing of animals, one might wonder why the Twin Poets found no difficulty in translating Arnold verbatim, representing all killing as violence and furthermore overlooking the technical difference between *eṭa*—the killing of an animal at a village goddess shrine—and *paśubandha*—the killing of an animal at a Vedic ritual.

In an essay published in 1944, some forty-two years after the publication of the *Buddhacaritramu*, Chellapilla Venkata Sastri, the senior of the Twin Poets who survived his partner by several decades, writes thoughtfully on the concept of violence. He quotes from the *Mahābhārata* to show that killing animals at Vedic rituals was not acceptable to some great sages of the past. He admits that Manu says in his *Dharmaśāstra* that eating meat is not wrong (*na māmsabhakṣaṇe doṣam*) but interprets it as a statement for the times "because everyone was eating meat at that time." After reflecting on the pros and cons of the issue, he finally declares that animal-killing is cruel even if it is accepted by the Vedas. He unequivocally concludes that following the teaching of Buddha in this matter is the right thing to do.[15]

Traditionally, Brahmins in South India are strict vegetarians. They do not kill animals for food, nor do they eat the meat of animals killed by others, as Buddhists do. Their vegetarianism is so strict that they do not even go near a place where meat is being cooked, nor do they sit by the side of a person eating meat. In this sense, South Indian Brahmins are stricter vegetarians than Buddhists. Any suggestion that Vedic Brahmins ate meat and had cows killed to feed honored guests would be repulsive to a South Indian Brahmin even if it were factually correct.[16] That the ritual killing of animals was practiced by a few Vedic Brahmin families in the secluded area of Konasima, as discussed by Knipe, was not common knowledge among all Brahmins. While the Vedas and Vedic rituals are generally glorified in Sanskrit and Telugu literary texts, the practice of killing animals at one of those rituals does not find detailed description in any of them.[17] For all practical purposes, the vegetarian Brahmins who chanted the Veda had virtually erased from their minds the idea that animals were killed at Vedic rituals and would not even know what method of killing was adopted. The only killing they would be aware of was the one low-caste people practiced at a village goddess shrine.

It would therefore make sense to assume that the Twin Poets did not find it difficult to describe killing at Vedic rituals as violence and, since they apparently were not mindful of the technical difference between the Vedic *paśubandha* and village *eṭa*, went along with Arnold's description of animal sacrifice. In their mind non-violence was a Brahminic virtue as well. Generations of vegetarianism in their families easily confirmed this conclusion.

In his autobiography, Venkata Sastri describes his meeting in Madras with Annie Besant, the Irish leader of the Theosophical movement, who was hugely popular for her lectures on Hinduism among the English-educated elite. Venkata Sastri and his collaborator were mesmerized by her knowledge of Hindu religious texts and her admiration for Hinduism. The brief description Venkata Sastri gives of this meeting does not offer enough scope to measure the impact she might have had on the minds of the poets when they were young, but we do know that Theosophy's appreciation of Hinduism did not include the killing of animals at Vedic sacrifices. Furthermore, Western influences on the interpretation of Hinduism and Buddhism were in the air as the Twin Poets began to move among the modern elites. Arnold's *The Light of Asia* clearly added to the new perspective the Twin Poets were developing. The way they blend Buddhist and Hindu concepts in their work seems to result from their understanding of the two religions as partners in peace and spirituality.

In this context it is also noteworthy that the Twin Poets detach themselves from the Hindu representation of Buddha as one of the ten avatars of Viṣṇu. According to this story, Viṣṇu is born as Buddha to willfully misguide the anti-gods to despise the Vedas and the Upanishads and to seduce their wives so as to deprive them of their *pātivratya* (the power of a faithful wife). When the wives lose their chastity, their husbands lose in their battle with the gods. This story, retold in poetry and song, and represented in sculpture for at least six centuries, was already losing its impact on educated minds by the time the Twin Poets wrote their work.[18] The Twin Poets would remember the negative description of Buddha as an avatar of Viṣṇu from the many Telugu *prabandhas* they knew so well that they could recite verses from them from memory. We can only conclude that they avoided any reference to that story, not only because it would be inappropriate in the text they were translating but because it was distasteful to them.

The Twin Poets smoothly pass over difficult areas where Buddhism differs from Hinduism. For instance, when Buddha, in one of his discourses, raises the question of whether there is an *ātman* that survives the body, the Twin Poets do not pay critical attention to the issue. They present the idea as a seamless part of a flowing narrative and make it appear fairly non-controversial.[19] They use words such as *dharma, karma, śānti, and ahimsā* throughout the poem without subjecting the concepts to serious examination which might sharpen the differences between their Brahminic and Buddhist meanings. The poets even describe the Buddhist way as *jñāna mārga*, the path of knowledge, giving the impression that it is similar to one of the many paths available in Brahminic teachings. This gives rise to the impression that what Buddha said was not all that different from what the Brahminic sages taught. This may appear like interpretive fuzziness, but I suggest that the Twin Poets deliberately adopt this new hermeneutics. Equating concepts represented by a terminology shared by Brahminism and Buddhism allows for a new Brahminism which accepts Buddha's teaching and a new Buddhism that finds Brahminism not too alien. The fact that such representation of Buddha's teachings was not found objectionable by scholars of the time suggests that the Twin Poets were not seen as too radical. At the end of the poem the Twin Poets have a confession to make:

> Śankara was angry with this religion and crushed it, but still Buddhism flourishes in the world at large. If you put all the people in the world who follow other religions on one side of the scales and the Buddhists on the other side, the needle will tilt toward the Buddhists. Among all the religions in the world, Buddhism stands superior even today. The reason is because this religion teaches compassion to all living beings, and that's why it wins.[20]

This is an extraordinary statement from Brahmin scholar-poets who grew up in traditional Brahmin families. If we recall that "Buddhist" was a curse in their community during their childhood, they have traveled far indeed, as has the society around them.

Gandhian Buddhism: *Saundaranandamu* by Katuri and Pingali

The next generation of poets came under the influence of Gandhi and were sympathetic to the national movement that he was leading against the British. Among them were Katuri Venkateswara Rao (1895–1962) and Pingali Lakshmikantam (1894–1972), who were students of Chellapilla Venkata Sastri. In fact, nearly all major poets who came into the literary field during the 1930s were Venkata Sastri's students. The Twin Poets were an inspiration and a role model for many poets of this generation. Imitating them, a number of young poets paired up in teams of two to compose their works. Following the trend, Katuri Venkateswara Rao and Pingali Lakshmikantam together wrote *Saundaranandamu*,[21] in Telugu, based on Aśvaghoṣa's Sanskrit poem. Both Katuri and Pingali were trained by traditional pandits in Sanskrit and Telugu, and Pingali was educated in English as well. Katuri, who was independently wealthy, did not need a paid job, but Pingali served as Professor of Telugu at Andhra University and later at Sri Venkateswara University.

Although they were students of Chellapilla Venkata Sastri, they were powerfully drawn into the new poetry movement famously known as Bhāvakavitvam (poetry of feeling). The Bhāvakavitvam movement was a response to the pandits' control of grammars and restrictions on poetry by means of an outdated *alamkāraśāstra*—also a protest against the *prabandhas* which described the female anatomy, limb by limb, from head to foot, breasts and pubic hair included. The modern poets felt that an excess of interest in the female body left no room for a woman's feelings. *Prema* (love) in the Bhāvakavitvam vocabulary replaced *kāma* (desire) in the *prabandha* poems. Through Bhāvakavitvam, Katuri and Pingali were exposed to the literary influence of Tagore, whose poetry emphasizes love. Tagore's philosophy of love is that it should be unblemished by desire and sensuousness and find meaning in celebrating beauty. Tagore's God is in the heart of one who loves beauty.[22]

Politically, Katuri was a Gandhian. Gandhi was leading a peaceful satyagraha against the British, and his message of service to the poor and downtrodden appealed to the Telugu poet. Katuri wrote some of the best poems in modern Telugu literature celebrating the entry of untouchables into the famous temple of Venkateswara at Tirupati. Pingali's political sympathies are not so clearly evident, but he was willing to be led by Katuri, who many of his contemporaries thought was the better poet of the two.[23] Two things led Katuri and Pingali to choose the theme of *Saundarananda*: the Gandhian philosophy of service to the poor and the downtrodden, and the Bhāvakavitvam philosophy of love free from eroticism.

Neither of them were particularly Buddhist, and the poets themselves were not interested in the serious Buddhist teachings of the Sanskrit text. It is understandable that they borrowed the theme but none of the details of the narrative of Aśvaghoṣa.

Katuri and Pingali did not even mention Aśvaghoṣa's name in their work. All they needed was the title and the theme. They did not write a *prabandha*, as the Twin Poets had. During the Bhāvakavitvam period, the *prabandha* genre, with its erotic overtones, was out of favor. Instead, they created a new genre that, unlike the *prabandha*, enters the narrative right at the beginning and does not have room to acknowledge any sources, much less to describe the context in which the poets came to compose the work. They dedicated their book to their teacher, Chellapilla Venkata Sastri, on his sixtieth birthday as a tribute to the one "who created a whole world of modern poets." However, it is common knowledge among the literary community that Katuri and Pingali had Aśvaghoṣa as their source.[24]

The theme of *Saundaranandamu* is simple. Nanda, the younger brother of Buddha, is passionately involved with his beautiful wife Sundari, and spends every minute of his life in her presence. Sundari is everything to him. One day, Buddha comes to his door begging for food (*bhikṣa*), and Nanda and Sundari, lost in each other, fail to notice. When Buddha does not get a response, he moves on to another house. Nanda realizes his terrible mistake. He promises his wife that he will be back before the makeup he has applied to her face dries, and runs out to catch up with Buddha and bring him back to his house. Buddha sees his brother and without a word puts his begging bowl in his brother's hands and keeps on walking. Fearing to ask him for permission to leave, Nanda obediently follows, with Buddha's begging bowl in hand, all the time worried about his beloved at home.

Soon he finds himself in Buddha's monastery, where the monks forcibly shave his head, give him ochre robes, and ordain him while he kicks and screams. The next chapter describes how Sundari, so suddenly separated from her lover, becomes intensely distressed by his absence and questions his love for her. The servants tell her that they have seen him in the monastery. Unable to believe that her husband has become a monk of his own volition, she concludes that Buddha has forced him to convert. She accuses Buddha of ruining her life and that of her husband. At the monastery, Nanda is grieving endlessly, missing his loving companion, when Buddha comes to see him. Nanda tells Buddha that his love for Sundari is not infatuation, it is a love that would brighten their world and make it a beautiful place to live in. Buddha insists that this love is rooted in passion and gives Nanda a sermon on celibacy and freedom from desire. After this eloquent speech Nanda appears to be persuaded and asks Buddha if Sundari could also be ordained, if she accepts the principles of celibacy. On Buddha's invitation Sundari is ordained and begins to serve the poor.

The narrative ends with a poignant scene where Sundari and Nanda find themselves at the bedside of a dying poor woman in an untouchable colony. They are about to call each other "my love" but stop before they even complete the first syllable and instead say, "I surrender to Buddha." Before she dies, the poor woman puts her little son's hand in Sundari's and her little daughter's hand in Nanda's, thus entrusting her children to them. Suddenly Buddha appears and says that even though he had separated them from each other, he is now giving a new Nanda to Sundari to raise as her little brother and a new Sundari to Nanda to raise as his little sister. The poem ends with Nanda and Sundari joyfully singing the praises of Buddha.

Compared to Aśvaghoṣa's *Saundarananda*,[25] the Telugu *Saundaranandamu* reads like a romantic tale with a Buddhist flavor. The Sanskrit poem is a serious Buddhist text with relentlessly harsh Buddhist teachings. Following Nanda's forcible induction into the monastery, a monk lectures him about how unreliable, selfish, wicked, and cruel women are. Buddha takes him to heaven and shows him all the beautiful *apsaras*. Nanda falls madly in love with them. But he finally realizes that his desire and the handsomeness of his body are the main obstacles to *nirvāṇa*, he sees that even the enjoyment of pleasures with the *apsaras* in heaven is a part of the cycle of rebirth and death.

Saundaranandamu was considered good poetry in Telugu and received praise soon after its publication. The carefully carved poems and the soft, smooth words that make up each stanza appealed to readers who appreciated its lyricism. A controversy about whether it worked as poetry because it combined *śṛngāra* (eroticism) and *śānta* (peace), two rasas that should never be combined, was limited to a small circle of critics and did not damage the poem's literary standing.

To a more modern taste, the work might sound sentimental and unconvincing, but in the 1930s when it was published it was received as a poem with a noble message. It appealed to the educated middle class who admired Gandhi's vow of celibacy (*brahmacarya*), his philosophy of truth and non-violence, and his call to work for the uplift of the untouchables. In the mind of this new class, Gandhi and Buddha were easily associated and became symbols of modern India. The untouchable colony reminded readers of actual untouchable colonies in Indian villages, with lepers and beggars looking for food on filthy and narrow streets filled with stray dogs and pigs. There is a subtle influence of Christian values in the description of Sundari serving the sick and the poor. Even the image of Buddha depicted in the poem as he preaches to the people on the streets of Kapilavastu is reminiscent of Christian evangelists. However, the shared ethos with Christianity was not noticed by contemporary readers, and the poets themselves were unaware of it, apparently because in their minds it was inseparably mixed with the Gandhian message of service to the poor.[26] Gradually, an image of Buddhism as the religion of peace, and Buddhist monks as selfless servants of the poor and suffering masses, became popular. Buddhism was now accepted as a clean form of Hinduism, free from its caste hierarchies and the blemish of treating some members of the religion as untouchables, as Gandhi himself believed Hinduism should be.

Modernist Critique of Buddhism: Buccibabu

By the mid 1930s a new wave of critical realism became popular in Telugu. Writers and poets rewrote the epics and *purāṇas*, radically reinterpreting them and revising the conventional reading of problematic incidents and negative characters. These writers took tremendous risks by opening gaps in the established meanings of classical texts. They questioned the moral stance of heroes like Rāma in the *Rāmāyaṇa*. Sīta, who suffered hardships in the original *Rāmāyaṇa*, received more sympathetic treatment in their works. The more radical writers among them even had Sīta reject Rāma and declare her love for Rāvaṇa.

In this vein of critical realism, Buccibabu's play, *Tiṣyarakṣita* (1940),[27] is a direct indictment of Buddhism and everything it stood for. The play was broadcast on All India Radio at a time when the euphoria about Buddha as a messenger of peace reverberated in poetry, theater, and film; and images of Buddha appeared in many drawing rooms of modern, educated Indians. Next in popularity was Ashoka, described in history textbooks as an emperor who chose peace, renouncing war after his victory. He was so remorseful for the violence he caused that he turned to Buddhism. He was represented as a popular emperor who ruled over a welfare state. A routine line from school textbooks in those days said that he planted trees on the roadside to provide shade for travelers.

One would think that a play which shattered popular positive images of Buddha and Ashoka would stand out as a good candidate for condemnation. Surprisingly, there was no serious negative reaction to it. Rather, it was received with appreciation. Listeners of the radio play—and readers when a longer version of it was published in 1964[28]—took it as an interesting story that revealed the darker side of a famous emperor known for his good work. It was appreciated as a human drama that depicts some of the complex psychological problems in history.

Buccibabu (1916–67), whose birth name was Sivaraju Venkata Subbarao, was educated in English literature and taught English in college before he worked for All India Radio. He was one of the few modernist writers in Telugu at a time when most of the prominent writers and poets were nationalists, Marxists, or advocates of one social reform movement or the other. Already well known for his novel *Civariki migiledi* (What Lasts, 1946), Buccibabu wrote in a style that created a new language of sensual expressivity in Telugu. His syntax captures the mental movements of his characters and shatters the façade of normalcy that put a lid on sexual desire, especially the sexual desire of women. One may have thought that Buccibabu's style, like that of his predecessor Chalam (1894–1979), would have provoked controversy. However, Chalam had paved the way and had made radical openness about sex less controversial. Moreover, in the minds of a modern educated middle class, legends and stories from Buddhism and even Hinduism were treated as parts of a national culture and not so much as integral aspects of specific religious belief systems. The play thus did not cause an uproar as an attack on anyone's faith.

The theme of this play is based on a story from Buddhist lore, from the *Aśokâvadāna*,[29] and is hardly known in Andhra except among specialists. The parts of the story in the *Aśokâvadāna* that Buccibabu borrows go as follows: First there is the Bodhi tree under which Buddha attained enlightenment. The emperor Ashoka worships this tree with special reverence. He sends the most precious of royal jewels to the tree. His wife Tiṣyarakṣita thinks that Bodhi is a woman and grows very jealous. She asks a sorceress to kill Bodhi, which the sorceress agrees to do for some money. When the tree begins to show signs of distress, the king's messengers inform him. Ashoka collapses at the news and says he will die if Bodhi dies. Tiṣyarakṣita comes to console him and reassures him that she will make him happy if that woman should die. The king tells her that Bodhi is not a woman but a tree. Tiṣyarakṣita realizes her mistake and asks the sorceress to bring the tree back to life. The sorceress undoes her spell and nurtures the tree back to health.

The second set of events relates to Tiṣyarakṣita's falling in love with Ashoka's son Kuṇāla. Kuṇāla was born with extraordinarily beautiful eyes. He was called Kuṇāla because his eyes resembled the eyes of the Himalayan bird Kuṇāl. When Tiṣyarakṣita comes across Kuṇāla meditating alone in the forest, she is so irresistibly attracted to him that she embraces him and expresses her love for him. Kuṇāla rejects her by gently saying:

> You are mother to me!
> Shun this non-*dharmic* path
> For it will lead to a lower rebirth.

Tiṣyarakṣita is wounded by this rejection and threatens his life in anger. Thereafter, Ashoka falls ill with a mysterious disease; excrement begins to emerge from his mouth. When his doctors are not able to cure him, he decides to make his son Kuṇāla the emperor. Tiṣyarakṣita fears that, as king, Kuṇāla will put her to death, so she takes it upon herself to cure her husband. She finds a patient who suffers from the same disease and has him killed so that his body can be cut open. Finding a worm in this patient, she discovers that onions will kill the worm; she then treats her husband with onions and brings him back to health. A grateful emperor offers to give anything as a reward for her services to him. Tiṣyarakṣita asks for the kingship for seven days. When she gets the throne, she orders the blinding of Kuṇāla. She stamps the ordering letter with the emperor's teeth when he is in deep sleep and sends it off. Kuṇāla is duly blinded. When the emperor sees him and discovers that the perfidy has been masterminded by Tiṣyarakṣita, he has her brought to him to be punished. But Kuṇāla pleads for forgiveness on her behalf and says he himself does not feel any pain and has no suffering. He says he only has kind thoughts for his mother. When he says this, his eyesight is miraculously restored. Ashoka, however, does not forgive Tiṣyarakṣita. He has her thrown into a lacquer house to be burned to death.

Buccibabu borrows this storyline very minimally and transforms the character of Tiṣyarakṣita from a jealous, ruthless, and cruel woman into a passionate, dynamic, brilliant, and articulate woman who is the victim of a religion that has destroyed all human emotions. Buccibabu borrows traces of the story from the *Aśokâvadāna*, where Tiṣyarakṣita is at times passionate and intelligent—for instance in the way she takes charge of Ashoka when he falls ill, and the way she ruthlessly but brilliantly conducts her experiments with another patient afflicted with the same disease. The idea of dissecting a body to find out how a disease spreads is original (and modern) in itself, and her determination to save the emperor, while purely motivated by a selfish desire to prevent Kuṇāla from taking over, shows a strong-willed person at work. Buccibabu leaves out the details but picks up on important character traits from the original legend.

The *Aśokâvadāna* as a collection of stories about Ashoka appears to be, as John Strong tells us, based on popular legends orally told among the community. These legends had a life of their own and served as a record of collective memory before they were written up in Sanskrit, thus acquiring an authoritative status among the Buddhists. Now a modern Telugu writer uses this to create an entirely new legend out of one of its stories. That Buccibabu did this in an atmosphere where others were rewriting legends and stories about gods, kings, queens, and ministers reveals a revisionist attempt to reshape the collective memory. The poets and writers of this generation refused to see the ancient past as glorious and golden, as poets during the nationalist movement had. Rather, they represented the ancient heroes as human beings with faults and foibles. The evil characters of the old stories are given a new voice and more complex personalities, whereas characters that were presented as totally good now appear with deadly weaknesses.

In Buccibabu's play the venerated Buddhist theological concept of *śūnyatā* (emptiness) becomes literally empty. One of his characters, a Chinese young man called Li Lov, explains what Truth is to another minor character, Sulabhā-darśini. Li Lov opens his closed fist and shows an empty palm. He says:

> That's what the Truth is. Whoever teaches it, Bodhisattva, the Devānāmpriya, Dharma-mahā-māta, whoever—that's what the Truth is. Once, Ānanda and Kaśyapa made an announcement that they were going to give away the book that contains the sacred teachings of the Buddha, and a certain monkey came all the way from China to get it, just like me. They gave the monkey an unwritten bunch of palm leaves and said that was the Sacred Book.

That is for starters. The play relentlessly demonstrates that the young and energetic Tiṣyarakṣita is surrounded by men with no desires, no feelings, and time after time we see her confronting them, even teasing them to reveal their insensitivity. Tiṣyarakṣita had been in love with Mahendra, Ashoka's brother, before Ashoka married her. Mahendra had rejected her to become a Buddhist. She tries to provoke him in an effort to rekindle a passion in him. In defense of herself she says:

> Tell me which plant grows without sunlight? Which wave of the ocean that did not rise up to reach the moon took the lost sailor safely to shore? Don't reject my love. A flower that has not opened is not fit for worship. A voice does not break until you sing. There's an unknown energy in me, which one day will explode as an earthquake.

Time and again in the play, it is a frustrated and emotionally deprived Tiṣyarakṣita who continues to speak rebelliously, irreverently, and utterly fearlessly. Buccibabu uses the Bodhi tree legend from the

Aśokâvadāna to show that Tiṣyarakṣita defies power, even that of the chief judge and the emperor himself. Near the end of the play, we see Tiṣyarakṣita chopping a branch into small pieces. She tells her maid-servant that she ordered it cut from the Bodhi tree because she was not happy that her husband was paying more attention to it than to her. The legend of Tiṣyarakṣita mistaking Bodhi to be a woman and correcting her mistake is not even mentioned. Buccibabu evidently presents his heroine not as a jealous woman, but as a frustrated one. Neither are her failed advances toward Kuṇāla presented in the play. We come across mention of the incident a little before the last scene and then again when Tiṣyarakṣita is being interrogated by the chief judge, Dharma-mahā-māta. Tiṣyarakṣita admits she is responsible for sending Kuṇāla away from the country. She has been ordered to stay away from him but could not resist touching him as long as he stayed in the palace. She also admits that she is the one who had his eyes plucked out.[30]

In an outburst of emotion at the end of the play, Tiṣyarakṣita declares Ashoka a sham. She says Ashoka married her after his first wife died because he did not want to give up the pleasures of his youth. He played with her and enjoyed himself. She thought he was in love with her and so she respected him, even worshiped him. Ashoka is not young any more, his strength and energy have waned. He has realized he cannot keep his empire through physical power. So he has resorted to Buddhism because he can maintain peace with a message of non-violence. His desire to expand his empire has now become possible through peaceful means on the basis of this religion. While his empire has grown strong in the name of religion, his fame has grown with it. Tiṣyarakṣita says that this is all a game. Now that Ashoka is old and his body has withered he wants to use religion to blame the body, so he imprisons his wives in his palaces. This is his strategy and he is even succeeding in it. Finally she declares:

> Buddhism is the devil that masks all weaknesses and differences. As long as this religion is alive, human beings will not have happiness or freedom. In the end all religions will die. The human being who withstands the prophets, lives fully, enjoys pleasures, and finds freedom right here in this world.

The play ends with Tiṣyarakṣita pulling a huge stone statue of Buddha onto herself; she dies crushed under its weight.

Buccibabu's play destroys the illusion that Buddhism is a peace-loving and humanistic religion. The play's message in the end is that no religion is truly liberating and that all of them are destructive of the spirit of human freedom and life. The play, however interesting it might have appeared to middle-class intellectuals, did not create an anti-Buddhist, or anti-religious atmosphere. Rather, it helped promote a general secular understanding of Buddhism as a part of Indian culture.

Buddhism was not perceived as a religion that people could convert to, but as a part of ancient Indian history and a symbol of national pride. Ashoka was represented as a great emperor of ancient India, unique among emperors, because he opted for peace, not because he was too weak to fight a war, but because he repented for the violence he had caused. This was the atmosphere that led to a proud acceptance of the images of Buddha and Gandhi as messengers of peace while a newly independent India inhabited the minds of middle-class intellectuals as a nation of peace. Nehru, the first prime minister, went around the world as a messenger of peace, refusing to align India with either the Soviets or the Western bloc that were fiercely contesting with each other to dominate the world. This euphoria was rudely disturbed by the Sino-Indian war over a disputed border in the Himalayan region. Many Indian political leaders began to question the wisdom of the Nehru government in following a policy of peace without adequate military preparation.

Brahminic Reaction: *A Jātaka Tale* by Viswanatha Satyanarayana

Satyanarayana (1895–1976) was also a student of Venkata Sastri. Satyanarayana had a phenomenal control of Sanskrit and classical Telugu; he wielded Telugu meters with a command superior even to the traditional writers of the past. His words were arcane, his syntax difficult. In everything he was different from everyone else writing during his time. He was so different that his teacher Venkata Sastri had to say: "He doesn't follow my path, nor the path of my father or grandfather. His way is different, and no one knows what it is. But then that is no reason to think of him as an ordinary poet. This student of mine is called the King of Poets—and he deserves that title. I am happy for him." Satyanarayana's formidable scholarship was matched by his monumental imagination and creative energy. He took Telugu poetry to unsurpassed heights, using mythological themes and writing in a classical style, but with a compelling modern sensibility. Boldly challenging those critics who argued against traditional values and traditional poetry, Satyanarayana took the less popular position, arguing that it was English education that made Telugu poets and intellectuals lose their heritage and their traditional excellence. Defying the fashionable modern position that themes like the *Rāmāyaṇa* were detrimental to the progress of society, he wrote a *Rāmāyaṇa* of his own, in six volumes, and called it *Rāmāyaṇa Kalpavṛkṣamu* (*Rāmāyaṇa, the Wish-Giving Tree*). Satyanarayana is best represented by a poem he wrote in one of his mythological plays expressing rage against the enemies of the Vedic sages in breathtaking Sanskrit words:

atimanobuddhyahaṅkṛtul aupaniṣadul
āttaganduṣitatrayul aurvavahni-
garbhitântaḥtapaskulu ghanulu ṛṣulak
ĕvvaḍu virodhi tad vadhak' ĕttina yadi

They are beyond the mind, intellect or ego.
They personify the Upanishads and hold the three Vedas
in their full-throated voices.
Fierce with the submarine fire in the depths of their inner self—
they are the seers, the wise men, the greats.
Anyone who dares to oppose them,
I'll kill him.

The high-voltage Sanskrit compounds and the energetic combinations of its phonemes create an atmosphere of breathless rage. The opening vowels of the first three phrases /a/ and /au/ and the long /a/ are followed by another diphthong and a compound with the difficult consonantal cluster of /hni/; then a repetition of /ta/, once with a *visarga*, makes you almost breathless—but before you have the chance to catch your breath, the poem relentlessly demands utterance of an aspirate /gh/, and you cannot stop when the clause ends with /ĕvvaḍu virodhi/ but are forced to go on until the sentence ends with *tad vadhak' ĕttina yadi*. This one-sentence poem and its style came to represent Satyanarayana in his battle against the *nāstikas* to protect the Vedas. As a defender of Vedic Brahminism, Satyanarayana was not ready for compromises with Buddhism, as his teacher was. He was not confused about the position of Buddha in Indian religions, and he was well informed of the major difference between Buddha's teaching and that of the Brahminic texts.

Satyanarayana's short poem, entitled "A Jataka Tale," is a good example of his position on Buddhism.[31] Written in conventional meter, this poem tells a story that follows the lines of a Buddhist Jataka tale. Here is a summary of the poem.

> In one of his many lives the Buddha was born as a snake. He was a wise scholar and very peaceful. He became the teacher of the king of snakes. Snakes have poison in their fangs which can be deadly when they bite. So no one touched the snakes. Therefore the snakes lived in comfort.
>
> The Buddha thought it was a sin to bite and kill people, and wanted to uplift the lives of the snakes. He went to the king of snakes and said: "Don't bite anymore. I am the Buddha and I will teach you love." Seeing the Buddha with a halo around his head, the king of snakes said: "Bhagavan, I will not bite anymore, my heart is filled with compassion. I won't commit this sin any longer. My clan is at your feet, make us good."
>
> From that day on the snakes became peace-loving Buddhists. The tigers and lions praised them. But there was a clan of rodents in the neighboring country—a mean group that did not love peace. When the snakes became peaceful, the rats bit the snakes, crushed their throats, and ran all over the land of snakes. The rats dug up the anthills where the snakes lived. The snakes were troubled and said to themselves: this is ridiculous—we are snakes and cannot even stand up to mere rats! They went to ask their king to put an end to this nonsense.
>
> The king said he could not suffer even the sound of the word "violence. Our ancestor is the great First Snake, Ādi Śeṣa, who peacefully serves as the bed of Viṣṇu," he said. "It is not right to give up our cause of peace because of these silly rats. Rats fear cats. The king of cats loves peace, and is a great soul. I will seek his help," said the king of snakes. He went to the king of cats and secured a promise that the cats would come to help. From

then on, the cats stood guard at the snake holes and protected them from the menace of the rats. But the rats were trickier. They lay in wait until the cats left the place, and then they jumped on the snakes. In the course of time the population of snakes grew thinner until they were practically eliminated. When anyone would ask what a snake looked like, people would show a string of twine and say, "They were thin like this."

Satyanarayana clearly does not accept the notion that Buddhism as a non-violent religion is more humane than Brahminism. The deceptively simple new Jataka tale he creates gives a clear message that a nation cannot exist if it follows an altruistic policy of peace at all costs, without a strong military to fight the enemy. The strategy of having your enemy killed by somebody else or, in other words, waging a proxy war, is no less violent, and in principle admits to a failure of the practice of non-violence as a religion. The alternative to fighting your own war could result in the total destruction of your nation.

Theoretically, Satyanarayana's poem (1965) is a response to the general national willingness to adore Gandhi as an apostle of peace. Satyanarayana was not a blind admirer of Gandhi, as were most poets of his time. He wrote subtly hinting at the incongruity of calling Gandhi an avatar of Viṣṇu, *daridra-nārāyaṇa* (Viṣṇu as a poor man), because none of the ten avatars of Viṣṇu are non-violent and Viṣṇu took those avatars expressly to punish the evil-doers on earth. Perhaps Satyanarayana was a little too realistic for his time.

But Satyanarayana presents his Brahminic message with the skill of a poet. The poem begins with a magnificent image of Buddha in a few simple words: *talacuṭṭuṅgala vĕlgu goḷam'agu buddhasvāmi*, Buddha, the lord, with a globe of light encircling his head. This is immediately followed by the unconditional conversion of the king of the snakes to surrender his clan at the feet of Buddha. The power of an arresting personality and the immediate transformation of a venomous creature into a devotee of love are depicted here in a tone of calm honesty and goodness in a short couple of lines.

The poem moves into the realm of reality when thousands of snakes approach their king to present their woes. Here, Satyanarayana begins to ridicule the policy of peace, very subtly, when he describes the snake king's solution to the problem posed by the rats. The rest of the poem and the matter-of-fact but devastating ending completes the disastrous effect of Buddha's message of peace. The entire poem superficially replicates the telling of a Jataka tale, but the underlying movement or the final message of the tale makes it a quiet parody. The low-key nature of the tale serves to enhance the unspoken Brahminic critique of the Buddhist doctrine of peace. However, directly revisiting the ancient opposition between Brahminism and Buddhism would have sounded irrelevant since neither Brahminism nor Buddhism, as Satyanarayana would present them, was alive. However, the poem reinforced the political fact that Gandhi and his message of peace and non-violence had lost their appeal.

Concluding Remarks

The four literary texts I have chosen represent four important phases of Telugu literary and cultural history during the twentieth century. In the first phase poets were comfortable with colonial rule, as their patrons were making a good living under the umbrella of the British Raj. The Twin Poets' representation of Buddhism was received very favorably by the English educated elite. The Telugu poem reinforced their understanding of *The Light of Asia*, and they felt good that Buddhism was a proud part of India's cultural greatness. The Twin Poets also had a deeper impact on the traditional, non-English-educated Brahmin community. The *prabandha* genre they chose and the classical style they adopted achieved what a straight translation of a poem written in a Western language could not have done. The teachings of Buddha couched in a language that sounded similar to Brahminic/Hindu religious texts were so convincing that devout Hindus read the work with reverence. Buddha was accepted as a revered sage who taught compassion toward all living beings. The book was reprinted as many as six times, which suggests that it was hugely popular. I sometimes wonder if not mentioning Arnold in the book had something to do with its popularity among traditional Brahmins, most of whom were still very conventional in their lifestyle. It might be that with all the prestige English had acquired in the secular sphere, it had not yet entered the religious discourse or the *puja* room of Brahmin households. But their resistance to new ideas was slowly growing weaker and the influence and importance of English was surely felt in their lives.

Pingali and Katuri's *Saundaranandamu*, a romantic tale with a Gandhian message of celibacy and service to the poor, reinforced the middle-class understanding of an ideal Indian society. The Buddhism these poets represent is close to what Gandhi talked about as an integral part of Hinduism: a "cleansed Hinduism." Gandhi wrote in his autobiography how he was influenced by Arnold's *The Light of Asia*. Significantly, Gandhi equated Arnold's work with the *Bhagavadgīta*. Acceptance of Buddha's teachings, which Gandhi learned from Arnold, paved the way for the Mahatma to propound a new interpretation of Hinduism, which his followers fervently supported. The Gandhian interpretation toned down the colonial criticism of Hinduism as a religion that supports caste hierarchies and untouchability. Images of Gandhi and Buddha began to appear in middle-class drawing rooms, even as an understanding of Buddhism in conformity with the secularism imagined by India's greatest modern leader and its first prime minister, Nehru, gained ground. Buddhism and Hinduism were now seen as parts of the great Indian culture that could be proudly showcased to the world.

An atmosphere where religion is seen as culture instead of as a scripturally sanctioned belief system was precisely right for writers like Buccibabu. This was the high noon of Nehruvian India, in which writers questioned and critically rewrote religious themes. Rational thought gained hold of the elite, who favored European thinkers and writers such as Sigmund Freud, Bertrand Russell, and Aldous Huxley. Buccibabu's play *Tiṣyarakṣita* was welcomed by a modern, secular middle-class elite, the same elite that was already comfortable with the Nehruvian understanding of Buddhism as a part of the great culture of India. Consequently, the rationalism the play presented did not conflict with the new ideology of modern India.

Satyanarayana's poem, "A Jataka Tale," which defends a Brahminical reading of Buddhism, appeared three years after the Sino-Indian war. By that time the general public opinion in India had shifted away from the Gandhi–Buddha message of peace in favor of a stronger military.

Alongside the images of Gandhi dressed in a loincloth and bent over his walking stick, statues of Subhas Chandra Bose in his military uniform began to appear in public places. Satyanarayana opposed the populist version of Buddhism and its message of peace and clearly supported a stronger Indian nation with the military capability to protect its borders from invaders. His poem was right along the lines of the new Indian ideology with its enhanced military budgets. However, it had a limited appeal, which faded as the border problem with China subsided.

In present-day Andhra, a more relaxed attitude toward Buddhism as a part of India's ancient culture prevails. A few intellectuals seriously engage with Buddhist doctrine and philosophy and make scholarly efforts to make Buddhist texts accessible in Telugu. Their efforts have been received well, even though they have not yet generated much discussion.[32]

When a huge seventeen-meter-tall monolithic statue of Buddha, said to be the tallest in Asia, was erected (after several failed attempts) in the middle of the Hussain Sagar Lake in Hyderabad, the capital city of Andhra, it was welcomed with pride. When the Dalai Lama visited Andhra Pradesh to perform the Kālacakra ceremony in 2006, the state government gave him a red-carpet welcome and paid to renovate the ancient Buddhist stūpa at Amaravati. The press welcomed it as a tribute to the ancient culture of Andhra. Buddhism has apparently been incorporated as part of Telugu nationalism.

Notes

Thanks to David Shulman and Joyce Flueckiger for their close reading of the paper and for their suggestions both stylistic and substantial, and to Laurie Patton for her comments after reading the first draft. Thanks to Paruchuri Sreenivas and V.S.T. Sayee for making inaccessible Telugu sources available to me in record time and to Vasireddi Naveen and Sivaraju Subbalakshmi for helping me with information about Buccibabu's play.

1. Patton 2008: 51.
2. For a discussion of the debates in the Constituent Assembly when it adopted the flag and the seal of the new Republic of India, see Roy 2006: 485–527. Roy writes: "Nehru's resolution was presented

as a *fait accompli* in that there was no debate on the design or the meaning of the flag" (509). For the eloquent speech of Jawaharlal Nehru introducing the resolution to adopt the national flag with the chakra of Ashoka on it, see, Asoka 2300, *Jagajjyoti* 1997: 165–8. In Nehru's words, "The Asokan period in Indian history was essentially an international period of Indian history. It was not a narrowly national period. It was a period when India's ambassadors went abroad to four countries and went abroad not in the way of an empire and imperialism but as ambassadors of peace and culture and goodwill" (168).

3. For the history of early Buddhism in Andhra, see Sarma 2008, and Sekhar 2006.
4. For a brief introduction to the Twin Poets, see Krishnamurthi 1985.
5. For more on the Twin Poets, see "A Historical After-Essay" in Narayana Rao 2003: 277–323.
6. Arnold 1969. For a publishing history of *The Light of Asia*, see Right 1957: 68–75.
7. Venkata Sastri and Tirupati Sastri 1956.
8. Among the admirers of Arnold's *The Light of Asia* was Gandhi himself, who wrote in his autobiography that he read it with even greater interest than the *Bhagavadgīta*.
9. *Buddhacaritramu*, 2.62.
10. *Buddhacaritramu*, 2.63.
11. Also, *Tĕlugu Sāhitya Kośamu: Ādhunika Sāhityamu* 1986, records that the *Buddhacaritramu* of the Twin Poets is based on Arnold's *The Light of Asia*.
12. Venkata Sastri 1956: 519.
13. *Sāstrāniki* is a Telugu word colloquially used to indicate a symbolic gesture to satisfy a sastric prescription.
14. See Knipe 1997: 306–32 and Knipe 2000. Knipe describes in rich detail the actual process of killing goats by suffocation at Vedic sacrifices in Andhra.
15. "Edi ahimsa?" *Andhra Vāṇi*, 1944, reprinted in Venkata Sastri 1958: 15–17.
16. Publications such as Jha 2001 are factually unassailable.
17. Except in a satirical manner in the *Basavapurana*. See *Siva's Warriors: The Basava Purāṇa of Pālkuriki Somanātha*, trans. Velcheru Narayana Rao, assisted by Gene Roghair, Princeton: Princeton University Press, 1990, p. 232.

18. The story of the Buddha as one of the ten incarnations of Viṣṇu is told over and over in Telugu. The earliest reference to the Buddha as an incarnation of Viṣṇu is in Pālkuriki Somanātha's (thirteenth century) *Paṇḍitārādhyacaritramu*, where it is briefly mentioned that Viṣṇu took the avatar of the Buddha in support of Śiva, who went to destroy the three cities of the anti-gods. He teaches the anti-gods to despise the Vedas because they preach violence in sacrifices. Then he seduces their wives. Reference to the Buddha as an avatar of Viṣṇu appears continually in Telugu literary texts through the centuries. The story is told in detail in Rāmayamantri 1926. A twentieth-century reference for the story is in Cinaveṅkaṭaraya (1925).
19. *Buddhacaritramu*, 6.78.
20. *Buddhacaritramu*, 6.101–102.
21. Lakshmikantam and Venkateswara Rao 1932.
22. For more on Bhāvakavitvam, see Velcheru Narayana Rao, "Hibiscus on the Lake," 277–323; and for Tagore's philosophy of love, see Kaviraj 2006: 161–82.
23. As one who knew both of them and many others in the literary circles personally, I knew that such opinion was held by a number of people.
24. *Tĕlugu Sāhitya Kośamu* records that Katuri and Pingali's *Saundaranandamu* is based on Aśvaghoṣa's *Saundarananda*.
25. Covill 2007.
26. For more on the Christian and Gandhian influences on Pingali and Katuri, see Rockwell 2006.
27. Though *Telugu Sāhitya Kośamu* says it was written in 1940, it was apparently not published until 1964. The text I have is from Subbarao 1964: 41–75. Unfortunately, this publication is not properly proof-read. In places, sentences are garbled. A shorter version of the play, apparently abridged for broadcasting on radio, is published in an anthology entitled *Neṭi Uttama Nāṭikalu*.
28. No information is available as to the date when the play was broadcast. It must have been sometime between 1948 and 1956, when Buccibabu worked for All India Radio in Bezawada, now called Vijayawada (Oral communication via telephone from his widow Sivaraju Subbalakshmi, 23 June 2008).
29. Strong 1983. I am indebted to John Strong for all the information I have about this book, including the translation of the passage which I quote.

30. In the text that I use Tiṣyarakṣita says she was responsible for blinding Kuṇāla. The positive and emphatic admission *atani kaḷḷu tīyiñcindi nenenu* (It was I that had his eyes removed) is unequivocally clear, but a conjunction *kāni*, "but," precedes this sentence, which makes no sense. Moving *kāni* to the beginning of the next sentence would make more sense. I had the shorter version of the play (see footnote 27) read to me by a friend from Hyderabad on the telephone, in which Tiṣyarakṣita denies blinding Kuṇāḷa. I am still uncertain as to how to interpret Buccibabu's representation of this event. My interpretation here is tentative. I am preparing a complete translation of the 1964 version of the play where I will discuss the textual problems and possible emendations.
31. Satyanarayana 1972: 136–8.
32. The political arguments of the neo-Buddhist followers of Ambedkar, actively presented in the newspapers, are not relevant to this article and are not discussed here.

References

Arnold, E. 1969. *The Light of Asia* (1879, revised 1885). Adayar, India: The Theosophical Publishing House.

Asoka 2300. *Jagajjyoti, Asoka Commemoration Volume. 1997 AD/2541 BE*. Calcutta: Buddha Dharmankur Sabha, 1997.

Buccibabu. See Subbarao, S.V.

Cinavenkataraya, D. 1925. *Daśâvatatāranutiśatakamu, with Telugu glossary, and translation into Telugu verses by Ramasastri, D.* Madras: Ananda Mudranalayamu.

Covill, L. (trans.). 2007. *Handsome Nanda by Aśvaghoṣa*. NY: New York University Press, JJC Foundation (Clay Sanskrit Library),

Dirks, N. 1988. *The Hollow Crown: Ethnohistory of an Indian Kingdom*. Cambridge: Cambridge University Press.

Jha, D.N. 2001. *Holy Cow: Beef in Indian Dietary Traditions*. New Delhi: Matrix Books.

Kaviraj, S. 2006. "Tagore and the Transformation in the Ideals of Love." In F. Orsini, ed., *Love in South Asia: A Cultural History*. Cambridge: Cambridge University Press.

Knipe, D.M. 1997. "Becoming a Veda in the Godavari delta." In D. van der Meij, ed. *India and Beyond, Aspects of Literature, Meaning, Ritual and Thought. Essays in Honor of Frits Staal*. Leiden: International Institute for Asian Studies.

———. 2000. "Goats are Food Divine: Comparison of Contemporary Vedic God and Hindu Goddess Sacrifices in Coastal Andhra." Paper presented at the 29th Annual Conference on South Asia, University of Wisconsin-Madison, October.

Krishnamurthi, S. 1985. *Tirupati Veṅkaṭa Kavulu*. New Delhi: Sahitya Akademi.

Lakshmikantam, P., and K. Venkateswara Rao. 1932. *Saundaranandamu*. Machilipatnam: Triveni Publishers.

Narayana Rao, V. 2003. *Hibiscus on the Lake: Twentieth Century Telugu Poetry from India*. Madison, WI: University of Wisconsin Press.

Patton, L.L. (trans.). 2008. *The Bhagavad Gita*. Harmondsworth: Penguin Books.

Pingali and Katuri. See Lakshmikantam, P.

Ramayamantri, D. 1926. *Daśâvatāracaritramu*. Madras: Vavilla Ramasvamisastri & Sons.

Right, B. 1957. *Interpreter of Buddhism to the West: Sir Edwin Arnold*. NY: Bookman Associates Inc.

Rockwell, A.V. "Western and Western Buddhist Influences on Telugu Literature in the Late Nineteenth and Early Twentieth Century: A Study of *Saundaranandamu*." Unpublished M.A. Thesis. Madison: University of Wisconsin.

Roy, S. 2006. "A Symbol of Freedom: The Indian Flag and the Transformations of Nationalism, 1906–2002." *Journal of Asian Studies* 65 (3 August), 485–527.

Sarma, I.K. ed. 2008. *Early Historic Andhra Pradesh 500 BC–AD 624. Comprehensive History and Culture of Andhra Pradesh*, vol. II. New Delhi: Tulika Books.

Satyanarayana, V. 1972. *Kedaragauḷa: Khaṇḍa-kāvya-samputi II*. Vijayawada: The Author.

Sekhar, S. 2006. *The Wheel and its Tracks: A History of Buddhism in Early Andhra*. Rajahmundry: Mokkapati Subbarayudu.

Somanāthuḍu, P. 1990. *Paṇḍitārādhyacaritramu*. Hyderabad: Telugu Visvavidyalayam.

Strong, J.S. 1983. *The Legend of King Aśoka: A Study and Translation of Aśokâvadāna*. Princeton: Princeton University Press.

Subbarao, S.V. 1964. *Buccibabu Natikalu*. Vijayawada: Visvavani Publishers.

———. *Neṭi Uttama Nāṭikalu* (*Best Plays of Today*). No publisher, no date.

Tĕlugu Sāhitya Kośamu: Ādhunika Sāhityamu (*Dictionary of Telugu Literature: Modern Period.*) Hyderabad: Telugu Akademi, 1986.

Twin Poets. See Venkata Sastri.

Venkata Sastri, C. 1958. *Kathalu: Gāthalu* (*Stories and Legends*), *Part 1*. Kadiyam: Chellapilla Venkata Sastri and Sons.

Venkata Sastri, C. and D. Tirupati Sastri. 1902. (Tirupati Venkata Kavulu.) *Buddhacaritramu*. Kadiyam: Chellapilla Venkata Sastri and Sons. Sixth reprint 1956.

———. 1934. *Jātakacarya*. Kadiyam: Chellapilla Venkata Sastri and Sons. Second edition 1957.

Venkateswara Rao, K. See Lakshmikantam, Pingali.

12

The Indigenous Modernity of Gurajada Apparao and Fakir Mohan Senapati

There is a broad consensus that India only became "modern" on account of its conquest by the British in the late-eighteenth and early-nineteenth centuries. It is generally agreed that Apparao and Senapati are the first creators of modernity in their respective languages, Telugu and Oriya. Apparao is celebrated as the father of modern literature in Telugu, as Senapati is for Oriya. While the consensus I refer to defines modernity as a specifically *colonial* modernity, one that was produced by the impact of English on Indian literature and society, I suggest here that in the two late-nineteenth-century works under review, *Kanyāśulkam* (*Girls for Sale*) and *Chha Mana Atha Guntha* (*Six Acres and a Third*) Apparao and Senapati present an indigenous modernity, distinct from the colonial variety.

In my study of Gurajada Apparao's *Girls for Sale*,[1] I have argued that his work represents a continuation of a modernity that was flourishing in Telugu literature from the sixteenth century onward. During this period, Telugu literature saw the emergence of a new subjectivity, which included psychologized characters and even characters with split personalities (often falsely assumed to be the gift of the West at a later date). A new sense of time and a new understanding of the individual emerged in this precolonial period; a new sense of history emerged, with history being written in several genres. The courtly tradition of patronizing poets gave way to a public patronage, distributed over a wide range of affluent individuals who aspired to a new social status. A major shift occurred in most parts of India during this period, which my collaborators, Sanjay Subrahmanyam and David Shulman, and I call the emergence of an indigenous modernity.[2] This was not a radical break from the past, but it involved a significant change in social practices, political institutions, and literary sensibilities.

Colonialism in the nineteenth century eclipsed these developments. The familiar story, which I need not repeat here, recounts how the English education system encouraged Indians to devalue most of their literature as immoral or decadent. A cultural amnesia overtook the newly educated middle class, who rejected their immediate past in favor of colonial modernity. English education, with all the opportunities and perspectives it opened for Indians, infused a distinct sense of inferiority in them, which affected their confidence in what Indian society had achieved before the arrival of the British. The new middle class accepted the colonial representation of Indian society as stagnant and decadent, with Indians as a group of people steeped in superstition and immorality. Committed to changing these conditions, social reformers in several areas of India began to lead movements to improve the moral and social conditions of Indians.

Girls for Sale

Apparao wrote *Girls for Sale* against the backdrop of the social-reform activities of Kandukuri Viresalingam in Andhra, who was influenced by Raja Rammohun Roy and Kesabchandra Sen in Bengal. Viresalingam led an attack against the two evils of society: not allowing child widows to remarry and allowing courtesans to practice their profession.

Viresalingam's social reform movement was aimed at the evils that primarily affected the upper castes, particularly Brahmins, and to a lesser extent some of the Brahminized landed castes. The top layer of society that this movement touched was a small minority as compared to the huge population of the lower castes who were beyond the so-called evils the reform movement militated against. Widow remarriage was not a problem for the lower castes, because their women freely married after the death of a husband and sometimes even while he was still alive. The anti-nautch movement aimed against courtesans did not touch them either, because the lower castes had no money to pay for high-class courtesans, nor did the courtesans entertain them even if they paid. This social reform, despite its high-sounding name, was actually upper-caste reform. As a result of this successful movement, the institution of courtesans, so distasteful to the new Victorian moral order, was gradually eliminated. Widow remarriage and the prohibition of child marriages freed the upper castes from the clutches of the ritual order to which they were bound. This, together with the economic benefits resulting from new jobs in the British administration, paved the way for the upper castes to grow into a new middle class, which would be poised to inherit political, cultural, and economic power from the British. This was the social background for the emergence of (colonial) modernity in India, spearheaded by the Bengali and later the Hindi writers and poets of the late-nineteenth and early-twentieth centuries.

On the surface, Apparao's *Girls for Sale* reads like a play in support of social reform. To briefly present a summary of the play:

> A miserly old Brahmin, Lubdha Avadhanlu, makes a deal to buy, as his wife, a very young daughter of another Brahmin, Agnihotra Avadhanlu. The bride's mother is opposed to the marriage. She knows how disastrous such marriages can be from her own experience of seeing the pain of her elder daughter Bucc'amma, who was widowed when her very old husband died. Her brother Karataka Sastri promises to foil the match. In the drama that ensues, Madhura-vani, a courtesan who is now kept by Ramap-pantulu, takes an active role behind the scenes. Ramap-pantulu is a village politician who is unscrupulous in forging documents and telling lies. He has been advising Lubdha Avadhanlu in matters of his marriage. Karataka Sastri is an old customer of Madhura-vani, and she promises him her support to save the little girl from the disastrous marriage. Karataka Sastri's plan is to dress his own disciple, a young boy, as a girl and offer "her" to Lubdha Avadhanlu for a cheaper price. Madhura-vani successfully manipulates Ramap-pantulu to get Lubdha Avadhanlu to accept the pseudo girl.

In a parallel story within the play, Girisam, a young and handsome con artist with a glib tongue, who flaunts his knowledge of English and appears as a supporter of the social-reform movement, secretly keeps

Madhura-vani as his concubine. He enters Agnihotra Avadhanlu's house under the pretext of teaching English to his son and seduces his widowed daughter Bucc'amma even as wedding arrangements for his second daughter are in progress.

Meanwhile the pseudo wedding is successfully performed, after which the bride (the boy) takes off his costume and escapes. When the bride cannot be found, the police accuse Lubdha Avadhanlu of murdering her. The idealist social-reformer lawyer Saujanya Rao defends Lubdha Avadhanlu but does not find evidence to prove his client's innocence. The last scene of the play is the most crucial.

I will present a close reading of the last scene as a point of entry to comprehend the complexity in Apparao's play.[3] Madhura-vani, dressed as a man, enters Saujanya Rao's upstairs bedroom unannounced, since the front door downstairs is open and there is no attendant to ask for permission. (Apparently, there was no fear of crime and people did not lock their doors until late in the night.) Girisam happens to be there because he has taken shelter with Saujanya Rao and is trying to get his help in marrying Bucc'amma with whom he, Girisam, has recently eloped. Girisam continues to pretend he is an honest and enthusiastic supporter of the social-reform movement in order to gain the support of Saujanya Rao. Madhura-vani, who enters in the middle of the conversation, takes Saujanya Rao's permission to remain anonymous and says she knows Girisam, and that she is his follower in the anti-nautch movement. Clearly, Girisam has detected that this stranger is none other than Madhura-vani in a man's clothes, but he is too scared to expose her because that will betray his own shady past.

Tactfully, she says that she has come on private business, forcing Girisam to leave her and Saujanya Rao alone. The gesture Girisam makes to her as he leaves the room shows his desperate appeal to Madhura-vani not to reveal him. Madhura-vani cunningly asks Saujanya Rao what he thinks would happen to reformed courtesans. How would they make a living? How will reformed courtesans find decent husbands? Would Girisam or he himself consider marrying one? Shocked at the audacity of this suggestion, Saujanya Rao states that he would never marry a courtesan and would not even so much as touch one. And if he should touch one by accident, he would cut off that part of his body.

Having allowed Saujanya Rao to dig a hole for himself, Madhura-vani tells Saujanya Rao that she knows someone who would be of great help in his client Lubdha Avadhanlu's case. The trouble is that the woman in question happens to be a courtesan. This is not a problem for Saujanya Rao, for he assumes that all courtesans can be bought. He suggests paying the courtesan for the information. Madhura-vani responds that the woman in question is not interested in money and that her price is of a different order. Saujanya Rao takes the hint and asks if the courtesan wants him to keep her and says that is out of the question. Madhura-vani forces a break in the negotiation and declares that Saujanya Rao's client cannot be saved any other way. Saujanya Rao still presses on in the negotiation, when Madhura-vani, without batting an eyelid, says that if he does not want to keep her as his pleasure woman she would consider marriage.

Offended by this unexpected turn in the conversation, Saujanya Rao now demands to know from the stranger how he has come to know a courtesan if he is a follower of Girisam in his anti-nautch movement. At this point Madhura-vani removes her turban and coat, revealing her true identity. Furious at this audacity, Saujanya Rao asks her to leave, but as she is leaving he calls her back to further explore the possibilities of saving his client. Madhura-vani offers a compromise. Clearly under her spell now, Saujanya Rao says, "If you stand here long enough before me, I am afraid I will accept any compromise you suggest." Madhura-vani gently says, "How about a kiss?" (Apparao 154). Saujanya Rao is surprised that a kiss is more valuable than money for her. He admits that he would not mind kissing a beautiful woman like Madhura-vani, but agonizes over breaking his vow never to touch a nautch girl. Despite all his reservations, Saujanya Rao agrees to Madhura-vani's demand. Having clinched the deal, Madhura-vani tells the lawyer that the "bride" Lubdha Avadhanlu married is not a girl and that Karataka Sastri dressed his boy disciple as a girl and married him to Lubdha Avadhanlu. Therefore, the whole thing is a hoax. There is no murder.

Now Saujanya Rao has to pay up. But just as he is about to kiss her, Madhura-vani stops him. She tells him that she has remembered a vow of her own. Her mother made her vow not to corrupt people who were not already corrupted. So she must not allow him to kiss her. While a relieved Saujanya Rao is still recovering from this double surprise, Madhura-vani's attention turns to a book Saujanya Rao keeps at his bedside. It is the *Bhagavadgīta*. Saujanya Rao tells Madhura-vani that the *Bhagavadgīta* is a book that converts bad people into good, and those who read it will find an invaluable friend in the god Krishna. Madhura-vani mischievously asks, "So Krishna is not anti-nautch!" As Madhura-vani is about to leave, with the *Bhagavadgīta* pressed against her chest, Saujanya Rao asks how she came to know Girisam. Madhura vani initially pretends to be reluctant, but finally reveals that she was his kept woman for some time. Saujanya Rao calls Girisam, makes him confess, and throws him out of his house.

This is a very intriguing scene that can be read at many levels. Crucial junctures in the scene leave room for multiple interpretations, and nearly every line of dialogue has many implications and layers of meaning. The best part of the scene lies in Madhura-vani's skillful use of language in manipulating Saujanya Rao. She assiduously addresses Saujanya Rao with a "Sir" all the way through, stroking his ego while cornering him with her questions. But her tone changes once Saujanya Rao shows signs of being attracted to her. When she stands before him without her disguise, he says that if she stands there long enough he is afraid he will accept any compromise she suggests. This is the point at which she is sure that Saujanya Rao has fallen for her beauty and charm. Once she is certain that she wholly controls his erotic feelings, she drops the "Sir" and addresses him with a confident tone of dominance. From this point on, her answers to his requests are curt and monosyllabic: "I won't," "I don't," and so on. She is so sure of her power that she knows once a man has come into her feminine arena he cannot escape and she can totally humiliate him. Through the rest of the scene, she has a field day deflating Saujanya Rao's large ego and playing games with him, to the point that she even makes him believe she really wants to read the *Bhagavadgīta* with him, when in fact she has almost certainly read it before, since she clearly knows Sanskrit well enough to accurately quote the *Mṛcchakaṭika*, a rather difficult play in that language. One may even suspect that she also knows Saujanya Rao himself has not read the *Bhagavadgīta*, because he has been misquoting it.

So, at the end of the play, does Madhura-vani really change her ways, realize the sinfulness of her profession, and want to read the *Bhagavadgīta* in order to repent and turn a new leaf in her life? Or is she just playing an elaborate game to make a fool of Saujanya Rao, the "modern," Westernized professional who assumes the role of a Catholic missionary, who hears confessions and absolves the confessor of his or her sins and provides moral guidance by giving a sermon from the Good Book! Or is it possible she has realized that times have changed, that no respectable man will come to her door anymore, and that rather than work with low-level village men she has to make her life worthy of the company of "gentlemen" like Saujanya Rao?

Nearly every critic who has read this play is certain that it supports social reform, that Madhura-vani has changed her ways, that Girisam has been punished for his false pretences and immoral practices, and that Saujanya Rao has saved Bucc'amma's life from being ruined by Girisam. The ambiguities of the play, like the irony in Senapati's novel, do not give room for such a one-sided reading.

Let us turn our attention to the other parts of the play, especially the court scenes. Apparao and Senapati share a common perspective in depicting courts and lawyers as sources of lies, deceit, and corruption. Ramap-pantulu, the tout, does not have any problem forging horoscopes and giving false evidence. Lawyers swindle their clients out of their money and leave them destitute. Even Saujanya Rao, the lone honest lawyer, complains that witnesses resort to fiction when they are asked to give evidence. He even compares lawyers to whores because both offer their services to the highest bidder.

English is the new language of power, and members of the upper castes, who can pay for an English education, hanker after it because it leads to jobs where opportunities for corruption are plentiful. A hilarious scene in *Kanyāśulkam* shows how naively attracted the village Brahmins are to the mere sound of English. Venkatesam, Agnihotra Avadhanlu's son, who is learning English in a nearby English school, displays his learning at the request of his illiterate mother. He and his tutor Girisam converse as follows:

Girisam addressing Venkatesam:

My dear Venkatesam,

Twinkle, twinkle, little star!
How I wonder what you are!
Venkatesam: There is a white man in the tent.
Girisam: The Boy stood on the burning deck, Whence all but he had fled.
Venkatesam: Upon the same base and on the same side of it, the sides of a trapezium are equal to one another.
Girisam: Of man's disobedience and the fruit of that mango tree, sing, Venkatesa, my very good boy.
Venkatesam: Nouns ending in "f" or "fe" change their "f" or "fe" into "ves".

Agnihotra Avadhanlu, who does not understand a thing they are saying, innocently asks, "What's the meaning of what you are saying?" and Girisam answers with a straight face, "We are discussing what we should read during this vacation and all that" (Apparao 22–3). As for the illiterate mother, the very sounds of the language are music to her ears and make her proud that her son speaks like a *dora*, the white boss.

Their reaction is entirely different when they test Venkatesam's Telugu learning. His uncle, Karataka Sastri, a good scholar of Telugu and Sanskrit in his own right, asks the boy to read a Telugu verse. Girisam suggests a respectable verse from the Telugu *Mahabharata* by the great poet Nannaya. Venkatesam manages to read the verse:

Nala-damayantul'iddaru manaḥ-prabhavanāla dahyamānulai
salipiri dīrghavasaranisal . . .

Karataka Sastri stops him and asks, "What is the meaning of *manaḥ-prabhavānala?*"

Venkatesam looks up toward the ceiling when Girisam intervenes and says, "How can a young boy know the meaning of such difficult poems?" A surprised Agni asks, "Don't they teach the meanings of poems?" Girisam with his ready wit answers, "For now they make them chant the verses like the Veda. In the white man's school they don't care much for Telugu poems. All the time they bombard the students with *jagarphi, gigraphi, arthametik, alligibra, mathamatiks*, and all that heavy stuff." Agni asks in innocent amazement: "They teach all that?" Girisam solemnly confirms, "Yes, sir, all that and more. A boy who works hard like your son will not have a break even for a minute" (Apparao 23). In short, Apparao quietly portrays without a comment how a shallow culture is replacing a traditional education, and how the upper caste is all for it.

Let us look at the central event of the play—the wedding of a child to an old man. This is the supposedly big evil social reformers loudly condemn, declaring society morally bankrupt because it allows such things to happen. The careful reader of the play easily realizes, unless he or she is brainwashed into thinking that Apparao wrote his play in support of colonialist social reform, that a whole village, across all castes, unites to make sure that the sham wedding goes through without a hitch—thus stopping the real child marriage. From the priest to the policeman, to the servants and the schoolboys, including the bridegroom's own daughter, all join hands to foil the real wedding. They make a fool of the cunning middleman who arranged it and the septuagenarian groom who was foolish enough to agree to the idea. The point becomes clear: this is not a society that normally allows such marriages to take place. The people in the village know that the practice is wrong. But people like Saujanya Rao, the leader of the upcoming urban middle class, make a big issue of reforming society and believe that it is their self-appointed task to lead it to morality.

Six Acres and a Third

Now let's look at Senapati's novel, *Six Acres and a Third*.[4] The most striking thing about this novel is that a narrator, rather than the author, tells the story from beginning to end. This allows the author Senapati to gain a certain distance from the narrator of the story.

Satya Mohanty posits that in creating the narrator Senapati has drawn on the *touter*, a new social type that emerged in the nineteenth century in Oriya society, a "disreputable wit who inhabits the lower rungs of society and is always a bit unreliable," and that he transforms this disreputable character into a "self-conscious satirist, social critic, and a moral philosopher." I want to pursue Mohanty's insightful comment that this narrator "enters the modern Indian novel from the world of oral discourse."[5] In a typical *purāṇa* performance, well known in the oral tradition of India, a *paurāṇika* tells a story with his comments and quotes from several texts. It is his voice we hear in any oral performance of the *purāṇas*—whether it is the *Mahābhārata, Bhāgavatapurāṇa*, or the *Rāmāyaṇa*—and not the voice of the author: Vyāsa, Vālmīki, or their regional language retellers. Occasionally, the narrator who sits in front of the audience might bring in the name of the original author, Vyāsa (or in the case of the Oriya Rāmāyaṇa, Balaram Das, or, for the more popular Oriya Bhāgavatapurāṇa, that of Jagannatha Das). In the mind of the audience, however, the narrator becomes the original author, while they themselves merge with the first listeners who sat in the Naimiṣa forest listening to Saunaka or King Parīkṣit listening to Śuka. The narrator comments on the events of the story in his own voice throughout the narration, even as he reads from the text of the original author. The narrator in Senapati's novel is an intelligent modernized version of the *purāṇa* narrator, who impersonates the role of the author. An innocent reader might mistake the narrator for Senapati himself, but will recognize the literary device if he or she is careful not to be lost in the illusion.

As we silently read Senapati's novel, we feel we are hearing the story rather than reading it, despite the narrator's occasional references to the act of writing his story. In this sense, it is an oral novel, as it were; it does not read like a written text. Senapati's narrator, however, is not exactly like a *purāṇa* performer. The narrator is tricky, funny, and intriguing, even downright false at times. His is not the authoritative, trustworthy, and full-throated voice of the *purāṇa* narrator; he only pretends to be one.

The creation of a pseudo *paurāṇika* distinguishes Senapati as a creator of an indigenous modernity. At first reading, *Six Acres* looks like a realistic novel authentically representing the events taking place and reporting conversations in a modern spoken idiom, faithfully depicting the characters as they move through their lives. But on a closer reading we see that what Senapati creates is not realism that produces a literary image of reality, but a pseudo realism that provokes the reader to question what appears as reality in the world.

To begin with, the narrator does not have a name. Is the narrator a man or a woman, upper caste or lower caste? For some reason we are inclined to assume he is a man. Could it be that somewhere in our minds we identify the narrator with the author? But we realize that the identification does not work; the narrator is unreliable, downright dishonest, and pretentious—not qualities we would like to associate with the author, Senapati. The narrator is clearly educated because he quotes Sanskrit texts; even when he misinterprets them, he does so deliberately. He demonstrates a fairly sophisticated knowledge of history and contemporary politics. That is a strong enough reason to assume that the narrator is an upper-caste man. The lower castes and women had no access to such education in Orissa at the time Senapati was writing.

Senapati's narrator changes his tone and voice in so many ways that the reader may wonder whether he is a single narrator or more than one. The seamless continuity of the story and its development imply a single narrator, who, however, acts like a ventriloquist or a composite person, housing many individuals inside him. Let us take a look at the various voices of the narrator.

Sometimes the narrator adopts a tone that demands an opposite reaction. The opposition is intentionally provoked. The narrator not only does not want to be listened to with approval, but he expects his words to be vehemently opposed and summarily rejected. Every argument the narrator presents, in favor of Mangaraj's fasts on Ekadasi days, for instance, comes with an invitation to laugh the narrator out of court. The narrator comes before us with the words "don't take my words at their face value" writ large on his forehead.

Then there is another voice of the narrator, this time tongue-in-cheek, as when he talks about the drumsticks that Mangaraj never serves to his servants, because they are not good for their health. But Mangaraj gives them plenty of the drumstick leaves instead, which are good for their health. A little later the narrator informs us with a straight face that the drumsticks are sent to the market to be sold for a good price.

When the narrator tells you the story of the auntie from Tangi, we read, or rather listen, to the narration with great interest. The voice of the narrator is quite trustworthy, and the cultural information given is authentic. We listen with attention to the quality of his description which sounds like that of a competent ethnographer. The narrator does not give you a clue to suspect that the auntie visiting is actually Champa in the guise of a rich relative. In the chapter that follows we begin to hear clues that confirm there is no such person as Auntie Tangi and it might be Champa in a different guise. And even after the end of the narration, we are left wondering what exactly she, Champa, might have done to cause the accidental fire in the house immediately after her brief, disguised visit. After carefully sifting through the dense ethnographic details, we find that the place where the fire started was the very place where the auntie from Tangi went to relieve herself.

The narrator uses all his skill in describing Champa to us. The first impression he gives us is that the novel's main character, Mangaraj, a man who grew to be a rich zamindar from his humble birth in an obscure and poor family, is the hero of the novel. It is, after all, his story. As we follow the life and times of Mangaraj, the novel reads like a moral tale of greed and injustice. But on a second and more critical reading details disturb this picture. Slowly Champa gains importance. She stands out as the "hero" of the story. She is the brain behind Mangaraj and the one who masterminds the acquisition of the six acres and a third and the cow from their owners, Bhagia and Saria. She personally brainwashes Saria to mortgage her land in return for the cash to perform rituals for the birth of a son. Right at the beginning of the story we are told that Champa is an artist. She painted a great many varieties of pictures of women and animals on the walls of Mangaraj's palace. She is a talented actress as well, if we consider the skill with which she impersonated a non-existent aunt and managed to have the Baghasingha family home and wealth destroyed by fire.

The narrator doesn't tell us about her caste, but we can suspect that her name Harakala, which she doesn't want to be called by and which

Mangaraj orders never to be uttered, suggests something fishy.[6] She is respected in Mangaraj's household and commands authority over the servants. The narrator devotes a considerable amount of time to describing her, parodying the descriptions of the modern romantic poets and the great Sanskrit poet Kālidāsa. We come to know that the narrator is learned and very clearly wants to give a lot of attention to Champa. No other character in the story receives such attention. As the description progresses we casually hear, along with many other physical details, a humorous description of Champa's teeth. One of her front teeth is crooked; it sits on top of the tooth next to it, protruding forward. The narrator twists the meaning of Kālidāsa's phrase *śikhari daśanā*, one who has a row of teeth each shaped like mountain peaks, describing Yakṣa's beautiful wife in *Meghadūta*, to fit Champa's protruding front tooth, which looks like a small hill in itself. The description makes you laugh as you appreciate the narrator's sense of humor. Later when women in the Baghasingha household comment on the auntie from Tangi after she has left, we hear that the auntie's front tooth is crooked too. Much later, we see the point. This particular feature of Champa's front tooth is what the narrator skillfully marks to give us a clue to identify the auntie from Tangi as none other than Champa in disguise. It takes a while for us to make the connection, and to admire the craft of the narrator in telling the story.

Mangaraj prefers Champa's company during the night to his wife's. We are told that he and Champa confer secretly after dark, and Mangaraj dismisses his wife when Champa shows up. No sexual relationship between Mangaraj and Champa is clearly indicated, but the narrator leaves room to imply it. In any case, sex is not on her mind. She is clearly motivated by an irrepressible urge to move up to a position of power and status.

The narrator often resists telling us anything he has not himself seen or found out from other secret means. One such instance is when the barber who murdered Champa jumped into the river and was unable to swim to the shore. The alligator that swallowed him is intriguingly called *gomuhan* or crocodile. The Sanskrit word *gomukha*, from which the Oriya word is derived, means "cow-faced," a word often used in the

Sanskrit phrase *gomukha-vyāghra*, a tiger with the face of cow, used to describe a dangerously deceptive person.

This raises questions about the accident itself. Was it truly an accident? Was the crocodile a real crocodile? We know that Champa and her accomplice, the low-caste barber, stole a lot of gold from Mangaraj's house. Apparently the gold was in the bag that the barber was carrying on his back when he jumped into the river. We hear nothing about it and are left with nothing but a bunch of palm-leaf records. One of the palm leaves on which an innocuous IOU was inscribed fell out of the bag and was recovered by the boatman. We even get the complete text of the IOU, which gives us one more piece of evidence to show how Mangaraj swindled innocent poor farmers. This piece of evidence is hardly necessary at this stage of the story. Mangaraj's plunder of the peasants is demonstrated many times before. The IOU on the palm leaf is to distract our attention from Champa's murder. The reason the narrator gives us for not telling the full story is clearly a lie in order to put a lid on Champa's murder. The people in power are not interested in Champa. They have nothing to gain by proving that she was murdered, nor in showing that the barber is the murderer. So the case is closed. We are left with a suggestion that makes things even more bizarre. Champa's corpse, without her silk sari and her silver anklets, is thrown into the river and a crocodile pulls her away in exactly the place where her co-conspirator and murderer was carried away earlier. And we are told that the shopkeeper deserted the area, where people claim to see a *pisaci* (spirit) inhabit.

What happened to the gold and silver in the bag, the value of which was so huge that Champa had said that it would be enough for them to live on for the rest of their lives? The shopkeeper does not say and neither does the narrator. The comment that the narrator makes soon after reporting the incident of Champa's murderer's fatal jump into the river is sarcastic on the surface: "You see, dear reader, we are the author, and therefore we are omniscient. We know why this crocodile snatched the man away, where it carried him, whether it treated him well or not; we have answers to all these questions. However, we are unwilling to talk about this openly since Chandia Behera himself kept the story a secret for reasons best known to him" (Senapati 196–7). If this is the commentator that appears before us time and again, right from the beginning of his narration, how are we to take his words when he narrates events of the story without his commentary? As, for example, when he tells us what was going on in the mind of Mangaraj as he lay dying.

Only a few minutes earlier the narrator has been telling us about the village *vaidya*, doctor, Kaviraj, who comes to treat Mangaraj after all the other doctors left him to die. The narrator indicates how pretentious the *vaidya* was, when he quotes from Sanskrit texts hilariously out of context, applying Kālidāsa's love poem to diagnose a disease. But very soon the narrator disappears and we read, *not* hear, the silent thoughts and visions in Mangaraj's delirious mind. This technique of leaving us alone with the dead man's thoughts is deliberately adopted to make us believe that in the end Mangaraj has repented for all his sins, and his *pativrata* wife has received him in heaven. The novel ends with the cries of Hari Bol, saying everything is back to normal.

On reflection, the reader decodes the silence of the narrator. Mangaraj's confession symbolizes the new order of power that has taken over under colonialism. In this order, modern prose, supposedly neutral, represents truth as is. It does not need a commentary because it is supposed to be transparent. The prose declares that the efforts of a Mangaraj or a Champa to acquire power and status have not succeeded.

Let us take a moment to see why they have not succeeded. It is not because they were greedy, unethical, or immoral. The new order that has taken over is not any less unethical or immoral, but Mangaraj and Champa were not modern in the mode of their operation. They did not know how to steal in the new style. Mangaraj wanted to become an old-style landlord, and Champa, even worse, wanted to be treated as a *zamidarini*. She succeeded briefly on two occasions, once when she pretended to be the auntie from Tangi, and a second time just before her death, when the shopkeeper treated her with great respect.

How do we take the silences of the narrator, then? If his silences are strategic, what about the words he speaks—are they not strategic too? We come away with the feeling that the narrator knows everything but is not straightforward with us. We have to suspect every word he says and does not say—every description he gives, every comment he makes, every detail he presents, and every silence—nothing can be taken at face value. This feature makes Senapati's novel, despite its apparently realistic mode, anything but realistic. Realism is too impoverished a label to adequately describe his style.

The structure of the novel alternates between description and narration. After a brief introduction to Mangaraj, we hear about a number of people, including the goddess Mangala, almost as if she were an actual person. We listen with great interest because these introductions are so lively that we begin to feel we practically know these people and want to talk to them the next time we see them. We do not even wonder why we are being introduced to them. They seem to do nothing except appear like people in their own right. But we do not object or become bored by these introductions because the prose is so lively and good-humored. In the process we also hear about a pond with four different shores where a lot of things happen. The description of the pond makes us realize how it is the center of life and death of the village. It is a metaphor of life in the village and the center of the story as well. We know about the irrational beliefs of the villagers in the story of the tunnel to the Ganges from under the lake, which the goddess Mangala's tiger made from her temple. The myth, however, has two sides to it. There are people who believe in it and succumb to it like Saria, and people who use it to make money, like Mangaraj and Champa. The elaborate trick played upon Saria by Mangaraj with the collusion of the village guardsman, Gobara Jena, is evidence that the myth is not universally believed. However, we hear only a hint of it during the first introduction of the lake and the goddess. For the rest of the story we have to wait until the first investigation of Saria's murder and her alleged murderer, Mangaraj.

The story begins right on the bank of this pond. It is here that the seeds of the central event of the novel are planted. Champa brainwashes Saria to mortgage her six acres and a third of land to the zamindar Mangaraj and get some money to build a temple for the goddess. Surely the goddess will give Saria children and lots of money. The loan would easily be repaid to Mangaraj, and she would live happily ever after with Bhagia and her children. The Asura Pond is a metaphor for India, Orissa, and the village during the early nineteenth century. It stands as a metaphor for the colonization of the Indians by the English, of the Oriyas by the Bengalis, and of the decline of the old classes under the influence of an emerging middle-class culture.

The descriptions in the novel keep the reader engaged while constructing a carefully layered picture of two of the major weaknesses that plagued Indian society and paved the way for the English Company to grab power. One was the decadence of the Muslim zamindars and the other was the degeneration of the weaver communities. The story of Sekh Dildar Mian and the story of Bhagia and Saria are representative of these communities. Before the colonial takeover, it was these two communities that kept India on the world map with their wealth and international trade. The novel takes note of them long before the cultural and economic history of the colonial period pays attention to them.

The digressions in the narrator's descriptions are as important as the main story in the novel. It is the digressions that give us a deeper understanding of the social and political changes during the early colonial period. For instance, one such digression tells us of the *panchayat*, which settled disputes. If a person in a caste was found to have committed an offense or a crime, the *pañcāyat* fined him, and the fines thus collected stayed with the caste. The new court system removed such settlements at the local level, transferring funds from the village to lawyers and the newly established British courts in towns. Now justice is available only to those who can pay for it.

Even a comment that looks casual is not really casual, such as this one from Chapter 10: "Do you know how cash contributions are raised? Although you may need no explanation, the new babus do, for they are educated: they have studied and have mastered profundities. Ask a new babu his grandfather's father's name and he will hem and haw but the names of the ancestors of England's Charles the Third will readily roll off his tongue."[7]

The success of colonial education consists of creating a generation of people who are cut off from their own past in favor of a new education in the name of history and science. It is a common feature in the nationalistic novels of the time to decry the loss of indigenous knowledge. But Senapati does this with a sense of irony.

Two characters in the novel—one who speaks very little and inaudibly, and the other who is deaf and dumb and cannot even speak a word—stand as silent witnesses of the deterioration around them. They are Mangaraj's wife (she has no name) and Gobinda, the low-caste servant who came with her from her parents' house and has taken care of her since her birth. We have a long description of both these characters. They do not speak a word but you cannot forget them. They stand as ineffective representatives of a dying culture—good, honest, and kind according to the values of a dying order, but incapable of correcting the injustice they see or unable to imagine the cruel but inexorable dynamics of power unveiling right before them.

Senapati's novel, as Satya Mohanty says, can be read on one level as a "tale of wealth and greed, of property and theft" (Senapati 1). An established social order, whether it is a traditional society based on Brahminic dharma, with its four-*varṇa* order and caste hierarchies, or a modern society based on democracy and rule of law, tries to keep the property and status relations in a tolerable equilibrium. Minor adjustments are allowed where a relatively poor upper-caste individual is allowed to acquire wealth and status, but no really poor and low-class person is allowed that opportunity. If ever such a person should try to become wealthy and aspire for status, he or she has to break a lot of laws, transgress dharma, and be willing to be seen as a criminal or even worse. Marx may have said all property is theft, but after a proletarian revolution property again settles in the hands of a new class of people who come into power. Not only is all property theft, all power is theft as well.

Because of their nature, property and power never shift from one group to the other without some kind of violence, destruction, or transgression of law. If people who act violently end up succeeding, they are called heroes. Heroism is valued in all societies, but only some people are allowed to become heroes. In the *Mahābhārata* society, Arjuna could become a hero, but not Ekalavya. Or in a *Rāmāyaṇa* society, Sītā could be a queen but not Śūrpanakhā. In troubled times, when the law and order situation is weak, when the old order is crumbling and a new one has not yet been established—that is when aspirants who never had a chance to move up in society have an opening. The juncture between two orders of society, the space between two major changes—that is the time for people on the lower level to try to grab power.

Is there a time for Ekalavyas and Śūrpanakhās to assert their superiority? Yes and no. Initially Senapati's novel makes you think that Mangaraj, Champa, and the barber who killed her suffered the consequences of their greed. But an attentive reader will realize that they were merely doing what rich people of the past have done and the rich people of the future will do as well—those who somehow are believed to have a time-honored right to be rich. It turns out that Mangaraj and Champa are revealed to be usurpers, greedy for status and power. A just society punishes them. In the end, an unknown lawyer, a representative of the new middle class that has emerged in the new space for power created by the colonial administration, legally grabs the accumulated riches without a hitch.

A similar transition takes place in Apparao's play as well. The old-fashioned courtesan, who was not considered to be doing anything immoral in society before colonialism, is now called a whore. Saujanya Rao has moral qualms about seeing or touching her, and believes she must be reformed before she becomes respectable. Girisam, who has no property, no job, and no earnings, but has a dazzling brilliance and the ability to turn any difficult situation to his advantage, is punished because he has associated with a courtesan. His irresistible urge to move up in society is dampened and his future left in doubt. What is conveniently overlooked is the fact that he has no money to buy a wife properly and that the only recourse he has is to find one to elope with. In contrast, the new class of lawyers and police officers who are corrupt to the hilt are considered citizens of high class.

It is of course possible to read *Six Acres* as a critique of traditional Indian society, as a demand for social reform. Such an interpretation would be similar to the one provided by the Telugu critics who read Apparao's *Kanyāśulkam* as a work that supports the social reform movement of Viresalingam in Andhra. Other readings of these two literary works are possible, depending on the location of the reader and his or her perspective. I have provided the outlines of an alternative reading of these two important texts.

In the end, the two authors, Apparao and Senapati, do not produce their works in a realistic mode. Neither do we find an authorial intention nor an omniscient author who sees and reports it all for the reader to receive. They do not unequivocally condemn society as decadent and superstitious, nor do they invite the changes introduced by the colonial administration as liberating and uplifting. They do not reject Western influence in a blind patriotic stance, eulogizing everything traditional. Rather, they adopt a critical perspective that liberates the reader to read their works unfettered by an overpowering authorial sermon, while they take inspiration from the traditional oral forms of literature, including the epic performances with their multiple voices and polyphonic characters—their "truth" open to interpretations.

Notes

1. All references to Apparao's *Kanyāśulkam* are from my translation of the play, *Girls for Sale: A Play from Colonial India.*
2. See my *Symbols of Substance: Court and State in Nayaka-Period Tamilnadu* with David Shulman and Sanjay Subrahmanyam; *A Poem at the Right Moment: Remembered Verses from Premodern South India*, with David Shulman; *Textures of Time: Writing History in South India,* with David Shulman and Sanjay Subrahmanyam; *The Sound of the Kiss, or the Story that Must Never be Told: Kalapurnodayamu* by Pingalī Surana, with David Shulman; *God on the Hill: Temple Songs from Tirupati* by Annamayya, with David Shulman; *The Demon's Daughter: A Love Story from South India* by Pingalī Surana, with David Shulman.
3. Adapted from my afterword to the play, "The Play in Context: A Second Look at Apparao's *Kanyāśulkam*," pp. 159–92.
4. Fakir Mohan Senapati, *Six Acres and a Third: The Classic Nineteenth-Century Novel about Colonial India*. Trans. Rabi Shankar Mishra, Satya P. Mohanty, Jatindra K. Nayak, and Paul St Pierre. Berkeley: University of California Press, 2005.
5. Senapati, *Six Acres*, pp. 6–8.

6. No one has discussed the meaning or social connotations of this word in Oriya. Other than the implication that the word indicates something derogatory, we do not know much about it. Siddharth Satpathy (oral communication) says that the word means one who is skilled in all the arts of deception. He says that she could be a *poili*, a common noun meaning a concubine, and that the name Harakala could relate to her skills of manipulating men.
7. Mohanty draws our attention to this in Senapati, 7. The quote from the novel is on Senapati, *Six Acres*, p. 84.

References

Annamayya. *God on the Hill: Temple Poems from Tirupati*. Translated by Velcheru Narayana Rao and David Dean Shulman. New York: Oxford University Press, 2005.

Apparao, Gurajada. *Girls for Sale: A Play from Colonial India* (*Kanyāśulkam*). Translated by Velcheru Narayana Rao. Bloomington: Indiana University Press, 2007.

Narayana Rao, Velcheru, and David Dean Shulman. *A Poem at the Right Moment: Remembered Verses from Premodern South India*. Berkeley: University of California Press, 1998.

Narayana Rao, Velcheru, David Dean Shulman, and Sanjay Subrahmanyam. *Symbols of Substance: Court and State in Nayaka Period Tamilnadu*. Delhi: Oxford University Press, 1992.

———. *Textures of Time: Writing History in South India*. New York: Other Press, 2003.

Senapati, Fakir Mohan. *Six Acres and a Third: The Classic Nineteenth-Century Novel about Colonial India*. Translated by Rabi Shankar Mishra, Satya P. Mohanty, Jatindra K. Nayak, and Paul St Pierre. Berkeley: University of California Press, 2005.

Surana, Pingali. *The Demon's Daughter: A Love Story from South India*. Translated by Velcheru Narayana Rao and David Shulman. Albany: State University of New York Press, 2006.

———. *The Sound of the Kiss, or the Story that Must Never be Told: Kalapurnodayamu*. Translated by Velcheru Narayana Rao and David Dean Shulman. New York: Columbia University Press, 2002.

13

Purāṇa

Purāṇa is a general term used to refer to a large number of religious texts, most of them composed in Sanskrit, which defy ready description, classification, authorship, or dating. Despite this obvious difficulty, efforts to assign authorship, classify, date, and describe them have been made both within the Hindu tradition and outside the tradition by modern scholars. This essay is an effort to present the indigenous concepts of the Purāṇa and to provide a brief overview of modern scholarship on the Purāṇas.

Indigenous Concepts of the Purāṇa

Traditionally, Vyāsa is believed to be the author of all Purāṇas. The son of Parāśara, Vyāsa, also known as Kṛṣṇa Dvaipāyana, was born an adult and had direct access to perfect knowledge of everything past, present, and future. Vyāsa was also the editor of the Veda, which he had divided into four parts: *Ṛg, Yajur, Sāma*, and *Atharva*. Authorship by such a superhuman person elevates the Purāṇas to an infallible status and endows them with a coherent meaning. The disparate texts themselves include a variety of contents, which in fact are not organized coherently. However, the idea that such a powerful personality as Vyāsa is the single author of these many texts encourages the readers and listeners trained in the culture to see a coherent meaning throughout despite apparent inconsistencies. Tradition also speaks of the Purāṇa as a broad genre, including the epic texts. While it is generally stated that there are eighteen Purāṇas and eighteen more Upapurāṇas or minor Purāṇas, the fact is that there are a lot more than thirty-six texts. It is difficult to list all the names under which the various texts are known in different parts of India or to arrive at a firm textual boundary to each text. Such textual flexibility of the Purāṇas was accepted in the tradition with no anxiety. No one seriously concerned themselves with minor variations between one version of a text and the other or for that matter even when the variations were huge, as is well known in the case of *Skanda Purāṇa.*

In contrast, the Vedas, included in the class of *śruti* (revealed texts), are considered fixed, unalterable, and beyond translation. They were rarely put into writing but were memorized with meticulous care to their word order, accent, and stress. The Hindu tradition speaks of the Purāṇas as texts that expand on the Vedas and considers them complements of each other. The Purāṇas renew themselves and adapt to the changing times by including new material and new meanings, while the Vedas keep the religion unified and authorized under their inflexible verbal power. This allowed Hinduism a flexibility unavailable for the religions of the book, such as Christianity or Islam, which depend upon one single source, the Bible or the Qur'ān, for both divine word and meaning.

The interdependence of the Purāṇas and the Veda is best stated in the following frequently quoted verses, which occur in many Purāṇas (for instance, in *Vāyu* 1.200) and the *Mahābhārata* as well: "The Brahmin who learns his four Vedas along with their Upaniṣads and ancillary texts does not become a learned man until he learns the Purāṇas. The Veda has to be expanded with the aid of the epics and the Purāṇas. The Veda itself fears a man of little learning lest he should hurt it."[1]

The complementarity of the Vedas and the Purāṇas is crucial for an understanding of the text culture of Brahminic Hinduism. It is as if the two inseparable components of language—the sound of an utterance and its meaning, the signifier and the signified—have been split apart and located in two separate groups of texts perceived as one unit. The Veda is considered to be *śabdapradhāna*, that which is important for its sound, and therefore untranslatable and unchangeable. The Purāṇa is *arthapradhāna*, that which is important for its meaning. This classification allows the Purāṇas to be told in many different ways as long their meaning is kept unaltered. Their meaning is authorized by Vyāsa, but the actual text in which Purāṇas are written may vary depending on the choice of the *paurāṇika*. Such freedom in reworking the texts gave modern scholars the impression that the Purāṇas are loose and disorganized, where any *paṇḍita* with a modicum of Sanskrit changed and added sections as he pleased. Despite these allegations, the Purāṇas are a genre with well-recognized stylistic features, understood and respected by the *paurāṇikas* and the listening public. The popularity of these texts, as evidenced by a huge number of manuscript copies disseminated all over India and the adaptations and translations into many regional languages, attests to the widespread community approval of these texts. The Purāṇas were also rewritten in many languages with alterations and embellishments appropriate to the language into which they were rewritten. The fifteenth-century rewriting of the *Bhāgavata Purāṇa* by the Telugu poet Bammera Potana illustrates the transformations a Sanskrit Purāṇa could undergo when retold in a regional language.[2]

What the Purāṇas Say about Themselves

As highly intertextual and self-conscious texts, the Purāṇas themselves are a useful source to learn about the Purāṇas. The *Viṣṇu* (3.6.15f.), *Agni* (271.11ff), *Vāyu* (61.55ff), and *Brahmāṇḍa* (2.35.63ff) *Purāṇas* say that Vyāsa composed a *Purāṇa Saṃhitā*.[3] He gave it to his disciple Romaharṣaṇa, who in turn gave it to his six disciples, Sumati Ātreya, Akṛtavraṇa Kāśyapa, Agnivarcas Bhāradvāja, Mitrāyu Vāsiṣṭha, Sāvarṇi Saumadatti, and Suśarman Śāṃśapāyana. The *Matsya Purāṇa* (53.4) says that in the beginning there was only one Purāṇa of one hundred *crore* (ten million) verses, and it still exists in the world of gods. For the benefit of the humans, Viṣṇu assumes the form of Vyāsa in every Dvāpara Yuga and proclaims it in a shorter version of four hundred thousand verses in eighteen texts.[4]

In a culture where the Purāṇas and the Veda are always linked together and the Veda is considered the highest authority, it is interesting to see how the Purāṇas relate themselves to the Veda. In several Purāṇas there is a statement which says that the Purāṇas were created earlier than the Veda (for instance, *Brahmāṇḍa* 1.40-41, *Matsya* 3.3-4, *Vāyu* 1.54).

R.C. Hazra suggests that this blatantly anachronistic statement makes perfect sense if we take the word "*Purāṇa*" not to mean the Purāṇa texts as we know them but in its etymological meaning, that is, ancient stories and legends, for such stories were told during Vedic sacrifices. He brings in evidence for his suggestion from the *Atharva Veda*, the earliest text to mention the word "*Purāṇa*," which says that chants, songs, meters, and *Purāṇa* are leftovers (*ucchiṣṭa*) from the sacrifice along with the sacrificial formulas.[5] However, the *Bhāgavata Purāṇa* (3.12) says that Brahmā uttered the four Vedas first, one after the other, with each of his four mouths and afterwards spoke the Purāṇas with all four of his mouths in unison.[6]

The Purāṇa as a Distinct Genre: Five Distinguishing Marks of a Purāṇa

Amarasimha, the fifth-century lexicographer defined the Purāṇa as one that has five marks (*purāṇam pañcalakṣaṇam*), and his commentators add an explanation as to what constitutes the five marks, *lakṣaṇas*. These are: *sarga*, the story of the creation of the universe; *pratisarga*, the secondary creation or recreation of the universe after its dissolution; *vaṃśa*, genealogies of the gods, the sun, the moon, and other beings; *manvantara*, the period oftime when a particular Manu from among the fourteen Manus in every *kalpa* (see below) is in charge; and *vaṃśānu-carita*, the history of the kings in the ruling dynasty during the particular *manvantara* in question. The significance of the *pañcalakṣaṇa* is generally misunderstood among modern scholars who thought they were the five main topics that a Purāṇa should cover and were puzzled why such important subjects do not occupy much space in some of the Purāṇas and were nowhere to be found in others. Vans Kennedy was the first to observe that these five *lakṣaṇas* are by no means the principal subject of the Purāṇas.[7] P.V. Kane agrees that these five topics occupy less than 3 percent of the extant Mahāpurāṇas, but their significance according to him consists in marking the Purāṇas as distinct from the epics. Apparently the line of demarcation between these two genres was rather thin before the fifth century.[8] An entirely different interpretation is suggested by Stephan Levitt,[9] who says that the standard understanding of the phrase *"pañcalakṣaṇa"* in Amarasiṃha's dictionary was due to a misunderstanding and that it meant "having five different descriptions," *itihasā, ānvīkṣikī, daṇḍantti, ākhyāyikā,* and *purāṇa* itself. I suggest that the five *lakṣaṇas* serve to indicate the time and place within which the events recorded in the Purāṇa texts occur, and so there is no reason why they should occupy a major portion of the Purāṇa text. The significance of the *pañcalakṣaṇa* is that they ideologically transform whatever content is incorporated into the Purāṇas into a Brahminic scheme of time and place.[10]

Purāṇic Time and Space

Events included in a Purāṇa are assumed to have happened at a particular point in a downward spiraling, circular, repetitive time frame. Purāṇic time is divided into four *yugas*, Kṛta, Tretā, Dvāpara, and Kali. Each of these ages is smaller than the preceding until finally the shortest age, Kali, ends in a dissolution (*pralaya*) of the universe, leaving room for a new cycle to begin. Purāṇic time is measured in divine years, where each divine year is equal to 360 human years and each divine day is equal to a human year of 360 days. The four *yugas*, Kṛta, Tretā, Dvāpara, and Kali each last for 4000, 3000, 2000, and 1000 divine years, respectively, and each of these ages have a transition time before the next one begins, lasting respectively for 800, 600, 400, and 200 divine years. Together the cycle of four *yugas*—a *mahāyuga*—lasts for a period of 12,000 divine years. A thousand such *mahāyugas* is a *kalpa*, which is a fabulous total of 4320 million human years. The decreasing number of years of each *yuga* in a *four-yuga* cycle also symbolizes a decrease in the virtues and excellence of human beings. A story from the *Varāha Purāṇa* (32.2-5) popularly retold is that Dharma, in the form of a bull, walks on all four legs in the Kṛta Yuga, on three legs in the Tretā, on two legs in the Dvāpara, and on one leg in the present age of Kali. Kṛta is the best of the ages, when human beings live long lives of honesty and happiness in harmony with divine law, the all-pervasive *dharma*. During the Tretā Yuga human beings need laws prescribing social behavior and a king to maintain the laws. Dvāpara is characterized by a confusion of social and religious conventions. Vyāsa is born to arrange the Vedic hymns into four Vedas and compose the Purāṇas. The Kali Yuga represents the lowest level to which humans deteriorate, where men and women lose their moral standards, Brahmins fall from their level of purity and acquire Shudra habits. Shudras, in turn, attain kingship and pretend to be Kshatriyas. Atheists, such as Buddhists and Jainas, emerge and misdirect people onto wrong paths. The *yuga* ends with Viṣṇu incarnating himself to dissolve all creation, after which a new cycle begins all over. This concept of circular, spiraling, and deteriorating time created by the Purāṇas is their single most important contribution to Hindu civilization. Hindus still calculate their ritual calendar based on Purāṇic time.

The concept of space in the Purāṇas is equally complex. Space is conceived as the egg of Brahmā (*brahmāṇḍa*), made up of seven concentric spheres. Seven successively higher heavens where the gods and immortal beings live are situated above the earth, and seven lower worlds where demons live are below. The earth, on which human beings live, is located in the middle. On earth the central location is Jambūdvīpa, surrounded concentrically by six other circular lands separated by seven seas: one each of salt water, milk, *ghi*, curds, liquor, sugarcane juice, and fresh water. Holy Mount Meru rises in the center of Jambūdvīpa. Four lesser mountains support Meru from the four directions: Mandara from the east, Gandhamādana from the south, Vipula from the west, and Supārśva from the north. A godly city sits on top of Meru where Brahmā, Viṣṇu, and Śiva dwell, worshiped by mortals and lesser gods. On the sides of the great mountain in the four major and the four intermediate directions lie the cities of the lesser gods. The chiefs of those directions are: Indra in the east, Agni in the southeast, Yama in the south, Nirṛti in the southwest, Varuṇa in the west, Vāyu in the northwest, Soma in the north, and Īśāna in the northeast. The river Gaṅgā falls from the heavens and passes through the lands of Jambūdvīpa. One of these lands is Bhāratavarṣa, the ancient name for the land of India, home of the Bharatas, named for the legendary progenitor of the Indian people. Bhāratavarṣa is where proper rituals are performed, and therefore it is called *karmabhūmi*, the land of ritual. Apparently this is where Purāṇic time of the four *yugas*, dissolution and recreation, operates. "The

Purāṇic picture of space is complex, highly organized and symmetrical. Envisioned is a three-dimensional *maṇḍala* with the land of Bharata near the center . . . The whole is an imaginative vision of the shape of the cosmos which clearly locates the land of India in the center of the universe."[11]

Hindu ritual performance is oriented to time and space based on the Purāṇic concepts. For instance, a Brahmin householder performing a ritual in India is likely to say that he is performing the ritual in the first quarter of the *yuga* of Kali, during the reign of Manu Vaivasvata. He will mention the particular name of the year in the sixty-year cycle and the fortnight, light (when the moon is waxing) or dark (when the moon is waning) as the case may be, and mention the name of the day according to the Purāṇic calendar. He will then continue by mentioning his location in terms of Purāṇic space in the land of Jambūdvīpa, in the area called Bhāratavarṣa, and in the country called Bharatakhaṇḍa (if he is in the south, he will orient himself as being south of Mount Meru), and finally he will conclude the chant by saying that he is performing the ritual in his own house with his wife and children.

The Number of Purāṇas and Their Classification

As mentioned earlier, tradition accepts that there are eighteen Purāṇas. The fact, however, is that there are many more, so many that the number one comes up with depends on how one counts. A verse in the oral tradition about the Purāṇas serves as a mnemonic device to list the eighteen Purāṇas.

bha-dvayam ma-dvayam caiva
bra-trayam va-catuṣṭayam
a-nā-pa-liṅ-ga-kū-skāni
Purāṇāni pracaksyate

Two begin with a "bha," and two more with a "ma."
Three begin with a "bra," four with a "va,"
and one each with "a" "na," "pa', "lin," "ga," "ku," and "ska."
That's how the names of the Purāṇas go, they say.

The Purāṇas listed in this verse with their first syllable are: *Bhāgavata, Bhaviṣya, Matsya, Mārkaṇḍeya, Brahmā, Brahmavaivarta, Brāhmaṇḍa, Viṣṇu, Varāha, Vāmana, Vāyu, Agni, Nārada, Padma, Liṅga, Garuḍa, Kūrma*, and *Skanda.*

These eighteen are considered *mahā-* or great Purāṇas, and a further list of eighteen are called *upa-* or minor Purāṇas. The convention of listing eighteen Purāṇas in each group is well established, even though there are discrepancies as to which Purāṇas are included. Some Purā nas themselves include such a list, and Ludo Rocher observes that *Vāyu Purāṇa* begins a list of eighteen but enumerates only sixteen; it introduces *Ādi Purāṇa* to the list but omits *Liṅga Purāṇa* and, according to one reading, also *Agni.* The *Bṛhaddharma Purāṇa* announces eighteen but only lists seventeen and, furthermore, considers *Nārada* and *Vāmana Purāṇas*, which are normally onsidered Mahāpurāṇas, as Upapurāṇas.[12] As may be expected, we find no uniformly accepted list of eighteen Upapurāṇas either.

Classifying texts into *mahā* and *upa* appears to be a convenient device to organize the texts in a schematic order. The prefix *mahā*—does not necessarily give the text a greater authority, nor the prefix *upa-* relegate the text to a lower order. Since the name Purāṇa itself elevates the text to a level of infallibility, the question whether a particular text is called a Mahāpurāṇa or an Upapurāṇa does not appear to be relevant to determine its status. The relative status of these texts, actually, seems to be highly contextual, depending on the area and community in which the text is presented. For instance, James Nye notes vastly divergent opinions in the Purāṇa texts: we find statements saying that the Upapurāṇas are only appendixes (*khila*) or a subvariety (*upabheda*) of the Mahāpurāṇas, while the *Parāśara Purāṇa* goes to the other extreme to state that the Upapurāṇas are greater than the Mahāpurāṇas.[13] Furthermore, there are many highly respected texts called Māhātmyas such as *Gayā Māhātmya* which describe the religious power of a location, temple, or a river. Some of these texts are found as independent Purāṇa texts, and some as parts of a Purāṇa such as *Skanda Purāṇa.* Finally, one finds some Upapurāṇas claiming the status of Mahāpurāṇas. *Narasimha Purāṇa* appears in the list of Mahāpurāṇas in *Padma* and *Bhaviṣya*

Purāṇas, while *Devibhāgavata Purāṇa* asserts that it is the real *Bhāgavata Purāṇa* and the other *Bhāgavata Purāṇa* is merely an Upapurāṇa. V.R. Ramachandra Dikshitar considers that the classification of *mahā* and *upa* a later development,[14] and Rocher suggests that "the distinction between mahāpurāṇas and upapurāṇas is not as historically important as it is generally made to be."[15]

Dialogical Structure of the Purāṇas: The Purāṇa Ethos

The Purāṇas are framed in a dialogical structure. They are invariably set as a conversation between an interlocutor and a respondent. For instance, in the *Nārada Purāṇa*, Romaharṣaṇa tells Śaunaka and other *ṛṣis* the story that was originally told to Nārada by Sanaka. In the *Brahmā Purāṇa*, many *ṛṣis* attend a twelve-year *sattra yāga*, where *sūta* Romaharṣaṇa arrives. The *ṛṣis* ask him: "How did this world come to happen, the moving and the stable beings, the gods, the antigods, the *gandharvas*, the *yaksas*, the snakes, and the demons?" (*Brahmā Purāṇa* 1.18). In answer to that question, the *sūta* narrates the *Brahmā Purāṇa.* Similarly, in the *Varāha Purāṇa, sūta* is the narrator of an original story narrated by Viṣṇu to Pṛthvī, the goddess of the earth, when she asks Visnu to tell her how he, in the form of a boar, *Varāha*, saved her from the demon. Again in the *Viṣṇu Purāṇa, sūta* narrates what Parāśara (Vyāsa) said when Maitreya asks him: "I am interested in knowing from you how the world has come into existence and how it will be in the future" (104). The atmosphere of a Purāṇa narrative is set in such questions, which are answered by an all-knowing sage. The readers/listeners perceive the answers as being given for the benefit of the world. In this framework, which creates an elevated tone and authenticity, the topics discussed acquire an aura of infallibility.

The topics covered in the Purāṇas, as described by Hazra, include:

> glorifications of one or more of the sectarian deities like Brahmā, Viṣṇu, Śiva . . . numerous chapters on new myths, and legends, and multifarious topics concerning religion and society, for instance, duties of the different castes and orders of life, sacraments, customs in general, eatables and

non-eatables, duties of women, funeral rites and ceremonies, impurity on birth and death, sins, penances and expiations, purification of things, names and descriptions of hells, results of good and bad deeds . . . pacification of unfavourable planets, donations of various types, dedication of wells, tanks, and gardens, worship, devotional vows . . . places of pilgrimage, consecration of temples and images of gods, initiation, and various mystic rites and practices.[16]

Sūta: The Teller of Stories

Sūta is ubiquitous as the teller of the Purāṇa stories. He is called Romaharṣaṇa because he made his listeners' hair (*roman/loman*) stand on end with his engaging narrative skill. *Skanda Purāṇa* says that Romaharṣaṇa's own hair stood on its end when he heard the stories from Vyāsa.[17] It is well known that *sūta* Ugraśravas, the son of Romaharṣaṇa (or Lomaharṣaṇa), narrated the story of the *Mahābhārata* to Śaunaka and other sages in the forest. Other references to *sūta* seem to relate to a caste of people who have a high position as senior confidants of the king and are very learned even though they do not have the right to study the Veda. Manu (*Manusmṛti* 10.11.17) clearly states that *sūta* is of a mixed-caste origin from a Kshatriya father and Brahmin mother. Amarasimha's dictionary lists the word "*sūta*" twice. It is defined, first, as a charioteer *(Nāmaliṅgānuśāsana* 517), and the second time as a son born of a Brahmin woman by a Kshatriya father (662). The appearance of *sūta* in the *Mahābhārata* and the Purāṇas has given rise to a speculation among modern scholars whether the Purāṇas were originally non-Brahmin oral texts later appropriated by Brahmins. But Kane quotes Kautilya's *Arthaśāstra* (3.7.29) to distinguish *sūta* of the Purāṇas from the mixed-caste *sūta.*[18] R.N. Dandekar states that the narrator Sūta of the Purāṇas and the *Mahābhārata* is the name of a person and should not be confused with the word that indicates a caste of charioteers.[19] Rocher quotes two parallel passages from the *Vāyu* and the *Padma Purāṇas* which state that *sūta*'s special duty is to preserve the genealogies of gods, sages, and glorious kings displayed in the epics and the Purāṇas and, after some discussion, concludes that the status of *sūta* cannot be ascertained definitively. "Either one tries the synchronic approach: the mixed caste element explains how the *sūta* could simultaneously fulfill a kṣatriya function, that of a charioteer and equerry, and a purely Brahminic role, that of bard and singer. Or one looks for a diachronic explanation: the *sūta* as the son of a kṣatriya father and a Brahmin mother is a later application of the term only, and it was not that of the Vāyu and Padma texts . . ."[20]

Purāṇas in the Popular Understanding of the Hindus

It is generally stated that the Purāṇas are meant for the benefit of women and Shudras who are not eligible to receive instruction from the Vedas. However, the popularity of the Purāṇas suggests that these texts were read/listened to by all Hindus, including the highest caste, Brahmins. Scholars prided themselves on having mastered all the Purāṇas, and poets listed the Purāṇas as an important item in their education. The Purāṇas were read/performed in temples and other religious locations. A class of *paurāṇika* performers made it their profession to perform these texts, and they were patronized by kings, local chiefs, elders of society, and temple authorities. For the average listener, the Purāṇas tell the stories of gods, goddesses, demons, and devotees and the stories of why sacred places became sacred. They also contain instructions for various rituals and pilgrimages to holy places. As a repertoire of stories, the Purāṇas are unrivalled. The worldviews most characteristic of Hindus are almost completely derived from the teachings of the Purāṇas. Their views of the creation, protection, and dissolution of the universe, the gods who are responsible for these activities, their views of time and space, cosmological perceptions, ideas of good and evil, *karma* and rebirth, the sacred and profane, are all derived from the Purāṇas. The most popular stories known to every Hindu about gods and demons are from the Purāṇas, even though no one, other than Purāṇa scholars, cares to remember which Purāṇas tell what story. All the Purāṇas merge in the memory of the average Hindu into one single group of texts. It is from the Purāṇas that Hindus know that Lord Nārāyaṇa sleeps on the milky ocean, on the thousand-hooded snake, Ādiśeṣa, and that his consort

Laksmī, the goddess of prosperity, sits by his side serving him. From Viṣṇu's navel rises a lotus out of which emanates the four-faced god, Brahmā, who creates the world. The Vedas come out of his four mouths, and his consort, Sarasvatī, is the goddess of speech. Nārāyaṇa as Viṣṇu takes *avatāras*, which include the fish, tortoise, boar, man-lion, dwarf, Rāma, Kṛṣṇa, and Buddha, with a final *avatāra* of Kalkin yet to come. Again, it is from the Purāṇas that the Hindus know all the stories about Śiva, who lives in the cremation ground or alternatively on the peaks of the Himālayas, wears snakes as ornaments, and is naked except for the skin of an elephant around his loins. His vehicle is a bull and his consort is Pārvatī, the daughter of the Himālayas. The Purāṇas also tell the stories of the great goddess Devi, mother of the universe, fierce to her enemies and compassionate to her devotees. Essentially, all Hindu religious, political, social, cultural, and even literary education is derived from the Purāṇas.

Internal contradictions among the Purāṇas, however, do not seem to be an issue in the popular mind. During their performances, *paurāṇikas* interpret the apparent contradictions to the satisfaction of their listeners. To quote Janamanci Seshadrisarma, a famous *paurāṇika* of the early twentieth century: "The intentions of the Purāṇas are deep and not easily available on the surface. Every action is properly directed in them with appropriate results. The deities described in them are made to suit the specific eligibility of each person, but not every Purāṇa is meant for everybody. The path for liberation for each person is different, and therefore the teaching of the Purāṇas appears self contradictory."[21]

Three Kinds of Purāṇas

According to the Hindu worldview, all things in creation are made up of three qualities or *guṇas: sattva*, a light, gentle, and enlightening quality; *rajas*, a fierce, dynamic and aggressive quality; and *tamas*, a dark, dull, and vegetative quality. Even the Purāṇa texts have not escaped this classification. According to the *Padma Purāṇa*, the classification is as follows: The *sāttvika* Purāṇas are *Viṣṇu, Nārada, Bhāgavata, Garuḍa, Padma*, and *Varāha.* The *rājasika* Purāṇas are *Matsya, Kūrma, Liṅga, Brahmāṇḍa,*

Brahmavaivarta, Bhaviṣya, Mārkaṇḍeya, Vāmana, and *Brahma*. The *tāmasika* Purāṇas are *Matsya, Kūrma, Liṅga, Śiva, Skanda*, and *Agni*. The *sāttvika* Purāṇas are supposed to lead to liberation, the *rajasika* ones to heaven, and the *tāmasika* ones to hell. It is interesting indeed to note that texts supposed to be authored by such a great sage as Vyāsa could lead one to hell. The division of the Purāṇas into these three classes is apparently based on the gods favored in each Purāṇa and motivated by sectarian passions of the Vaiṣṇavas. It is well known that Hinduism passed through some rather rough periods of sectarian conflict, and obviously the Purāṇas reflect that situation. It would, however, be risky to interpret the sectarian statements of the Purāṇas as their essential meaning because such statements represent highly contextualized connotations. Rocher has aptly stated that the sectarianism of the Purāṇas should not be interpreted "as exclusivism in favor of one god to the detriment of Others."[22] The same Purāṇa may make a passionately sectarian statement in favor of one god on one page and a few pages later may make an equally passionate statement in favor of another god.[23] Such apparent contradictions, however, become irrelevant when one realizes that no Purāṇa text is ever read from cover to cover and that a Purāṇa performer chooses sections and interprets them appropriately to the occasion and the audience. This also underscores the fact that part of the problem modern readers face in interpreting the Purāṇas is that protocols of reading have changed, and we read every page and every line subjecting them to a uniform valence based on one-dimensional textual linearity. More on this later.

The Purāṇas and the Bhakti Tradition

Bhakti marked a significant shift in the religious traditions of India, and the Purāṇas reflect this change. As a term, "*bhakti*" is more a cover word for a variety of personal relationships to a deity rather than a single definitive theological concept. Broadly speaking, the *Bhagavad Gītā*'s concept of *bhakti*, which is also stated in the *Viṣṇu Purāṇa*, presents god as accessible to living beings through a discipline of personal worship and surrender. In contrast to this, the seventh-century Āḷvārs of

Tamilnadu sang and preached a different mode of *bhakti* where human emotions of passionate erotic love and affection are accepted as modes of worship. Experiencing god through such a passionate personal relationship is superior to the knowledge one can gain through the study of philosophical texts, the performance of ritual practices, and the chanting of the Veda. Furthermore, people of all classes and stations in life, from kings to commoners, from learned Brahmins to illiterate outcastes, men and women, all have equal access to god through this *bhakti.* In fact, the lower the station of a person in life, the easier it is for him or her to reach god. This is clearly a subversive concept in a society based on Brahminic ritual superiority and social hierarchies. The *bhakti* of the Āḷvārs gradually undergoes a Brahminic reformation when it is incorporated into the *Bhāgavata Purāṇa* and becomes a part of the Purāṇic religious complex.

The *Bhāgavata Purāṇa*

The bulk of the *Bhāgavata Purāṇa* represents what was first told by Vyāsa's son, Śuka, to King Parīkṣit, son of Abhimanyu of the Pāṇḍava line. The context of narration is especially poignant. King Parikṣit was cursed by Sage Śṛṅgi to die within seven days from the bite of the deadly snake, Taksaka. The reason for the curse was that the king playfully hung a dead snake around the neck of Śṛṅgi's father, when the latter was deeply lost in meditation and did not respond to the king's inquiries. King Parikṣit, realizing that the end is near, asks Sage Śuka what a man nearing his death should do. Basically, Śuka's answer to this question is the core of the *Bhāgavata Purāṇa.* Stories from the *Bhāgavata Purāṇa* have become independently popular and have been retold in many languages and genres.

To get acquainted with the message ofthe *Bhāgavata Purāṇa,* let us visit a few of these stories beginning with the story of Prahlāda Prahlāda, anti-god Hiraṇyakaśipu's son, rejects his father's beliefs and sings of God Viṣṇu, until his father angrily demands that he show him where Viṣṇu lives. Prahlāda replies that Viṣṇu is everywhere, he is omnipresent. Hiraṇyakaśipu points to a pillar in the assembly hall and sarcastically asks if Viṣṇu is also present in the pillar and then furiously kicks it. Viṣṇu emerges from the pillar as a half-man, half-lion and claws Hiraṇyakaśipu to death. Another story relates how the elephant-king Gajendra, who is caught by a mighty crocodile, cries to Viṣṇu for help. Viṣṇu appears and kills the crocodile with his discus. The story of Rukmi tells of how she fell in love with Kṛṣṇa, whom her elder brother Rukmīṇi hated. When Rukmi arranges a marriage for Rukmīṇi with another man, the distressed Rukmīṇi sends word to Kṛṣṇa to come and take her away. Kṛṣṇa appears on the wedding day and takes Rukmīṇi away on his chariot, defeating her brother's army, which chases after him. All these stories celebrate the superiority of personal devotion to god even at the expense of social status and normal family relations between father and son, brother and sister, husband and wife.

The narratives of the *Bhāgavata Purāṇa* create an opportunity to celebrate god. The style in which the stories are told is aimed not so much at informing the readers, as is the case with the other Purāṇas, but of reminding them of what they already know, thus creating an atmosphere in which they can remember god's name. At the beginning of each of these stories King Parīkṣit asks Sage Śuka to tell him of a particular event in Kṛṣṇa's life, such as his birth or wedding, and then immediately says how wonderful it would be to hear these stories one more time. Listeners/readers of the *Bhāgavata Purāṇa* feel exactly like the king. They already know these stories but want to adore god one more time.

Acceptance of the *bhakti* stories, so different from what the earlier texts preach, left their mark on the Purāṇa itself. The emotional/devotional nature of the stories gives the Purāṇa a lyrical quality. The *Bhāgavata Purāṇa* is written in a language both more beautiful and at the same more archaic than the other Purāṇas. The archaism of this Purāṇa, as J.A.B. van Buitenen notes,[24] serves to legitimize the late text and gain for it a degree of ancientness. In fact, the *Bhāgavata Purāṇa* itself makes us aware that it is a different kind of Purāṇa in that it lists ten *lakṣaṇas* instead of the usual five that are supposed to mark a Purāṇa.[25]

The most popular part of the *Bhāgavata Purāṇa* is the tenth chapter, which narrates the love-games Kṛṣṇa plays in Vṛndāvana with his cowherd girls. Kṛṣṇa's love-games inspired a number of poems in many regions of India, among which the *Gītā Govinda* is the best known. Scholars have noted that Rādhā, the most important of Kṛṣṇa's cowherd girls, does not have a place in the *Bhāgavata Purāṇa* stories. Scholars attribute this absence to the South Indian origin of the text, whereas Rādhā stories originate from North India. In addition to being South Indian in origin, it is also claimed that the *Bhāgavata Purāṇa* was a late composition attributed to a certain Vopadeva.

The *Skanda Purāṇa*

The *Skanda Purāṇa* is in sharp contrast with the *Bhāgavata Purāṇa.* If the *Bhāgavata* expounds the value of *bhakti* as an experience of total devotion to the deity and rejects the value of ritual practice, *Skanda* emphasizes rituals and the power of sacred places. This Purāṇa is largely a collection of stories describing the power of holy places and temples (Sthalapurāṇas). As such, this Purāṇa apparently continued to grow as new temples and holy sites came under the influence of Brahminic Hinduism. This also explains the popularity of the *Skanda Purāṇa* as well as its segmentary nature because each holy place promoted its own story under the rubric of this Purāṇa. Additions to the *Skanda Purāṇa* are so numerous, with some as recent as the sixteenth century, that even the native tradition regards this Purāṇa as a "scrap-bag."[26] The expansive *Skanda Purāṇa* is available in two versions, one made up of *khaṇḍas* and the other made up of *saṃhitās*—each of which contains a number of sub-*khaṇḍas.* The stories in the *Skanda Purāṇa* cover the major Brahminic holy places in virtually the entire subcontinent. For instance, *Kedārakhaṇḍa* and *Badri Māhātmya* cover the Himālayan region, *Kāśi-khaṇḍa* and *Ayodhyā Māhātmya* describe the holy places in Uttar Pradesh, *Āvantyakhaṇḍa* tells of the holy places in Malva, Rajasthan, and parts of Gujarat, *Revakhaṇḍa* relates to the holy places in the Narmadā Valley, *Nāgarakhaṇḍa* and *Prabhasakhaṇḍa* cover the sacred places in Gujarat and other parts of western India, *Puruṣottamakṣetra Māhātmya* tells the story of Puri in Orissa, *Veṅkaṭācala Māhātmya* and *Setu Māhātmya* describe Tirupati in Andhra Pradesh and Ramesvaram in Tamilnadu.

One of the notable sections of the *Skanda Purāṇa* is the *Kāśīkhaṇḍa,* which tells the story of Kāśī (Banaras). Once, the Vindhya Mountain grew higher and higher in competition with the Himālayas, and it obstructed the sun and the moon from traveling across the sky. Time stopped since the sun and the moon stood still. Śiva intervened and asked Agastya to take care of the problem. The sage and his wife, Lopāmudrā, travelled south towards the mountain. Seeing the great sage and his wife, the mighty Vindhya bowed to them in respect. Agastya walked across and asked the mountain to stay bent until his return, which he never did. This was how the power of the mighty Vindhya Mountain was subdued. However, Agastya, a long-time resident of Kāśī, missed his city and remembered it by describing its beauty in detail to his wife. It is in this context that the *Kāśīkhaṇḍa* lists all the sacred places along the Gaṅgā and serves like a guide to the city, including stories and descriptions for each of its shrines.

The Other Purāṇas: *Agni* and *Bhaviṣya*

Each Purāṇa is interesting in its own way,[27] but I will briefly focus on two because they are very different from the rest. The *Agni Purāṇa* is extraordinary in that it includes discourses on the science of politics and statecraft, administrative branches of the state, qualifications of the king, his duties, the role of his ministers and other officers, the army, and so on. It includes information on trees and water resources, medicine, and anatomy. Furthermore, it has elaborate chapters on metrics, poetics, and lexicography. In a way this is an encyclopedic Purāṇa.

The name *Bhaviṣya Purāṇa* is a contradiction in terms, since *Purāṇa* means "old" and *bhaviṣya* "future." Cast in a frame of telling events that will take place, this Purāṇa, to summarize Hazra, tells the stories of Adam, Noah, Nādir Shāh, and Jalaluddin Akbar.[28] It tells the story of Pṛthvīrāja and Jayacandra and goes on to include information about Varahamihira, Śaṃkarācārya, Rāmānuja, Nimbārka, Madhva, and Jayadeva. It includes the grammarian Bhaṭṭojidīkṣita, Kabīr, and Nānak. It even describes British rule in India and mentions Calcutta and the parliament. Evidently, the text was composed after all the events that it purports to predict took place, which makes it a new and innovative mode of writing history.

Counter-Purāṇas

Prominent opposition to the Purāṇic worldview came from the Jainas. The Jainas were great storytellers and competed with the Brahmins in precisely the same narratives, which the Brahminic religion used for spreading its message. In contrast to the Brahminic Purāṇas, which are composed by anonymous authors under the cover name of Vyāsa and run into many redactions, the Jaina Purāṇas are all written by historically identifiable authors, and their texts are relatively more fixed and datable. The Jainas used Maharashtri, Prakrit, Apabhramsa, and Kannada, in addition to Sanskrit, and apparently succeeded in bringing their versions to the people more successfully than the Brahmins. It is possible that the medieval retellings of the Brahminic Purāṇas by Brahminic poets in regional languages was motivated by the desire of the Brahmins to counter the popular reach of the Jaina versions. To the Jainas goes the credit of questioning the truth-value of the Brahminic Purāṇa stories, continuously offering critical and rational alternatives to them.

The Jaina Purāṇas essentially narrate the lives of the sixty-three great men (*triṣaṣtiśalākāpuruṣa*) of the Jaina tradition through which the Jainas will learn the work of *karma* according to the Jaina worldview. While this is the larger goal, there is also an unmistakable interest on the part of the Jainas to create a counter-Purāṇa to the major Brahminic epic narratives. The Jaina *Rāmāyaṇa* and the Jaina *Harivaṃśa* are important among such attempts. The Jaina narrative of the *Rāmāyaṇa* is told in Vimalasūri's *Paumacariya.* These texts were not always called Purāṇas. They were also called Caritras, life stories. According to John Cort, the Digambara Jainas called their texts Purāṇas, while the Svetambara Jainas called their texts Caritras, although in some cases both terms were applied to the same work.[29]

Purāṇas from Below

Following the established convention of calling narratives that are not fixed in writing or not written in a standard language folk narratives, A.K. Ramanujan identified several folk mythologies and folk Purāṇas.[30] However, there is also a genre of Purāṇa texts relating the origin myths of non-Brahmin castes, which are often, if not always, written in Sanskrit. We can call these Purāṇas of the lower castes who have moved up in society or had attempted to do so. It is well known in Indian social history that one of the strategies of upward mobility for a low caste is to create a Sanskrit text and invent a mythology associating itself with Vyāsa. Rocher reports a number of caste Purāṇas from Gujarat. In addition, there is a text called the *Bhāvanarṣi Purāṇa* which relates the origin of weavers, and another called the *Viśvakarma Purāṇa* which tells the story of the goldsmiths.[31] The *Kanyakā Purāṇa* tells the origin myth of the unity of trading castes, and the *Jāmba Purāṇa* conveys the caste story of leatherworkers. All these Purāṇas are known in the Telugu-speaking area of Andhra Pradesh, and, except for the *Jāmba Purāṇa*, all these texts are written in Sanskrit. The *Jāmba Purāṇa*, sung among the Madiga caste of leatherworkers, is interesting because it borrows the name Purāṇa but is actually a Telugu oral narrative, a genre often studied by anthropologists and folklorists rather than by Purāṇa scholars. The regional nature of these Purāṇas is both an asset and a problem in coming to a comprehensive understanding of the nature of these texts. An asset because the texts of these Purāṇas are relatively few and do not create major problems in determining their path of transmission, and a hardship because of the vast areas one has to cover to collect these regional texts.

Unlike the Brahminic Purāṇas, which are written with a view to establishing a Brahminic ideology, these Purāṇas question Brahminic superiority and attempt to upset it. The lower-caste Purāṇas, if written in Sanskrit, closely follow the general style of the Brahminic Purāṇas. The differences are ideological and political rather than textual. Among these Purāṇas, the Purāṇa of the goldsmiths, the *Viśvakarma Purāṇa*, attacks the Brahmins for usurping a ritual superiority assigned by god to the Viśvabrāhmaṇs, the goldsmiths. The *Kanyakā Purāṇa*, the Purāṇa of the Komatis (merchant caste), does not oppose the Brahmins but shows that the Komati caste is as pure as the Brahmins. The well-known *Basava Purāṇa* may be studied in this context, even though it is not strictly a caste Purāṇa but a Purāṇa of Vīraśaivites who were virulently anti-Brahminic. The *Basava Purāṇa*, written in Telugu and Kannada, tells the stories of the militant followers of Basaveśvara, the twelfth-century leader of the Śaivite movement in Karnataka. It also narrates a number of stories of Śaiva devotees from the earlier *Pĕriya Purāṇa*, written by Cĕkkiḷār in Tamil.[32]

Colonial Scholarship of the Purāṇas

Early Western scholars of the colonial period, eager to gather religious and cultural information and knowledge about the Hindus, encountered the Purāṇa texts and were bewildered by their variety, complexity, and multiplicity. As early as 1784, Warren Hastings commissioned Radhakanta Sarma to prepare a summary of the Purāṇas.[33] Vans Kennedy, an Englishman in the military service, and Horace Hayman Wilson spent most of their lives studying this vast body of texts. Wilson employed a small army of native Sanskrit *paṇḍitas* to produce detailed indices of the contents of all the Purāṇas. He trained native young men to translate these indices into English and then examined the original and the translation "and corrected them wherever necessary."[34] In 1840, Wilson published a translation of the *Viṣṇu Purāṇa* with a scholarly introduction. However, Purāṇa studies did not hold a sustained interest for him because they were not, in their present form, ancient texts such as the Vedas. "They preserve, no doubt, many ancient notions and traditions; but they have been so mixed-up with foreign matter, intended to favour the popularity of particular forms of worship or articles of faith, that they cannot be unreservedly recognised as genuine representations of what we have reason to believe the Purāṇas originally were."[35] Attention to the Purāṇas was revived when Vincent A. Smith demonstrated that the *Vaṃśānucarita* of the *Matsya Purāṇa* was basically an accurate record of the ancient Andhra dynasty. Frederick Eden Pargiter energetically established the historical validity of the Purāṇas, followed by R. Morton Smith.[36] Only then did the Purāṇas become valuable because they were believed to be useful in reconstructing the ancient history of India.

However, the general attitude of suspecting the Purāṇa texts as reliable records continued. More bewildering than anything to the colonial scholar was the very nature of their existence as texts. As serious classical students trained in Latin and Greek, colonial scholars expected the

Purāṇas to be concrete written texts with the usual corruptions that result from centuries of use. Little were they prepared to encounter a tradition whose concept of text is very different from their own, where texts interact with their oral discourses and where *paurāṇikas* move through these texts with unfathomable conventions, and whose practices appeared to Western eyes to be verging on forgery, interpolation, and textual manipulation. Lack of communication between the two groups of scholars—the Western Indologists and the native *paṇḍitas*—developed into irresolvable suspicion of each others' methods. As for the colonial scholar, ancient India was great; it was only contemporary India that was rotten. This belief led to their perception that the texts deteriorated in the hands of ignorant transmitters. The ancient texts were magnificent, but the Purāṇas we have at hand are corrupted.

The Austrian scholar Maurice Winternitz carries this line of thinking and reports the general view of colonial scholarship. According to his survey, the language of the Purāṇas was sloppy and grammatically flawed, and their content was wildly confusing and full of meaningless exaggerations. For him the extant texts represent an inferior class of literature, belonging to the "lower, uneducated priesthood," who transmitted the Purāṇas.

> Still many old sagas of kings and many very late genealogical verses (*anuvaṃśaślokas*) and song stanzas (*gāthās*) of the original bard-poetry have been preserved to us in the later texts which we have received. And fortunately the compilers of the Purāṇas who worked haphazardly did not disdain what was good and have included in their texts some dialogues reminiscent of the Upaniṣads in form and content as well as individual legends and texts of profound thought-content taken from the ancient ascetic poetry . . . Even in the desert of the Purāṇa-literature there is no lack of oases.[37]

However, prejudices of this nature did not last for long as a more sophisticated and nuanced modern scholarship developed.

Modern Scholarship on the Purāṇas

After two hundred years of active and persistent application of Western methods and progressive training of Indian scholars in Western text-criticism, a highly sophisticated field of Purāṇa study has emerged which should be called modern rather than Western or Indian, since it includes Indian as well as European scholars. An international group of philological scholars has rigorously applied principles of text-criticism to a number of manuscripts and made strenuous and laudable efforts to refine the methods of producing critical editions of the Purāṇas, including the *Mahābhārata* and the *Rāmāyaṇa.* Scholars from different countries—Australia, England, France, Germany, India, Italy, and the Netherlands, to name some—participate in active debate and discussion in this enterprise.

The idea of producing critical editions has exercised the minds of Indologists for a long time. Winternitz first expressed the need for a critical edition of the *Mahābhārata* at the 11th International Congress of Orientalists in Paris in 1897. In 1908, Heinrich Lüders submitted an eighteen-page prospectus of the *Mahābhārata*, drawing upon twenty-nine manuscripts. However, nothing came of this until 1920, when Ramakrishna Gopal Bhandarkar began to work on a critical edition of the *Mahābhārata* in Pune. At the completion of this renowned critical edition, Haraprasad Shastri expressed a fervent hope that similar editions should be produced for all the Purāṇas. Serious work on the Purāṇas began when the All-India Kashiraj Trust was formed under the patronage and guidance of Vibhuti Narayan Singh, the Mahārājā of Kāśī, which, in addition to producing critical editions of the Purāṇas, also published the journal *Purāṇam.*

The standards of philological method require that all the available manuscripts of a particular Purāṇa be gathered together and closely examined for variations. Following strictly established practices of text-criticism, the Ur-text of a Purāṇa is theoretically possible to reconstruct. This model assumes that there was a single author for each of the Purāṇas who produced a single text which was then transmitted throughout a wide area over a long period of time during which the text acquired scribal errors, textual attritions, not to mention deliberate interpolations by motivated anonymous authors.

Controversies regarding critical editions led to a range of opinions regarding the feasibility and usefulness of such editions. On one end were scholars who wanted to adopt Western methods to reconstruct as pristine a text as possible, if not exactly the Ur-text of the Purāṇa from which all the other texts of the Purāṇa in question took off. On the other end were scholars who argued that the very idea of a critical edition was wrong and that texts should be read as they are, in their localities and communities.

Madeleine Biardeau opposes the methods of producing critical editions of the Purāṇas and the methods adopted by V.S. Sukthankar in his critical edition of the *Mahābhārata* as well.[38] Following her teacher Sylvain Lévi, Biardeau questions the validity of making critical editions of texts which are primarily oral and local. She draws a sharp distinction between the connotations of an oral tradition in the West and in India and observes that in the West the written word is valued more highly than the oral tradition, whereas in India it is the oral word (*śruti*) that is respected as the highest authority. Furthermore, she asserts that the Purāṇas derive their acceptance from the local Brahmin communities who use the texts. To erase the pivotal importance of the locally authorized text in favor of a constructed text because the latter is perceived to be closer to the oldest possible version is to distort the reality. She points to her experience with the Śrīvaiṣṇavite Brahmins of Simhachalam temple in Andhra Pradesh, who insisted that a certain version of the Narasimha and Prahlāda story they tell was, for them, authoritative. They claimed that their version was from the *Skanda Purāṇa*, while at the same time they had no difficulty admitting that it differed from what appears in the extant version of this Purāṇa. Biardeau maintains that "any locally accepted version is authoritative in its own right" and should prevail over the version of the so-called critical editions which are assumed to be older and therefore closer to Vyāsa's text.[39] Biardeau's method raises a different problem in that it leads to a plethora of texts from different regions under one name with no unity. To resolve this problem, she suggests that their unity is to be found in the meaning of the stories and "not in their particular contents or historical bearing."[40] She also suggests "the manuscript evidence be checked and strengthened through consultations with the people who, even now, have a first hand knowledge of the . . . Purāṇas."[41]

V.M. Bedekar of the All-India Kashiraj Trust responds to Biardeau's critique by defending Sukthankar's methods, strongly insisting that once a tradition is committed to writing it is open to textual criticism irrespective of whether it is originally oral or written. He does not deny that local Brahmins hold the power of authorizing their version, but that in itself does not cause a problem for the editors of critical editions, since the latter are not competing for authority; rather they are only producing an edition which presents the text—in Sukthankar's words (1933: ca), which Bedekar quotes "in all its variety, all its fullness."[42]

Anand Swarup Gupta, also of the All-India Kashiraj Trust, who undertook the preparation of critical editions of the *Vāmana, Kūrma*, and *Varāha Purāṇas*, steers clear of most of the debate but firmly rejects the Western methods, including those adopted by Sukthankar. Gupta questions the assertion that additions made to the Purāṇas over time should be considered "spurious." Gupta prefers to view them as a natural growth of the texts and wanted to "keep them in line with the current religious and social ideas of their times in order to preserve the encyclopaedic nature of the Purāṇas and keep them up-to-date."[43] His project was to reconstruct a single text of a Purāṇa based on all the available manuscripts collected from different regions of the country. "Such a single critical text must be a conflated text by its very nature, but this defect is more than compensated by giving the readings and variants ofall the available versions in the critical apparatus (in the form of the critical footnotes of a critical edition)."[44]

Rocher, too, rejects critical editions, saying that in so far as the Purāṇa tradition is purely oral, of which only parts were accidentally committed to writing, producing critical editions based on the standard rules of textual criticism makes little sense.[45] Elsewhere, he says: "I too have been trained in classical philology in Europe. I too have learned how to prepare critical editions, comparing manuscripts and reconstructing *the* original text—the archetype. But I am prepared to forget all that when it comes to the Purāṇas."[46]

In contrast to Rocher, however, R. Adriaensen, H. Bakker, and H. Isaacson strongly believe in the written text of the Purāṇas.[47] In their view there is "no reason to assume any but a written transmission of the Purāṇa, although it is certainly the case that at times a transmitter's memory of other similar texts may have had some influence."[48]

They categorically state that the oral character of the Purāṇas was exaggerated. They follow the strict philological approach of starting with the oldest available text of the *Skanda Purāṇa* from which they aim to produce an edition that accurately presents the readings of available manuscripts and a constituted text that is superior, as a whole, to that found in any of the individual manuscripts.[49] They published their first volume of *Skanda Purāṇa* in 1998, and their work is still in progress. Earlier, in 1995, Greg Bailey had articulated a wholly different approach of working with Purāṇa texts in his *Gaṇeśapurāṇa.*[50] Adopting a structuralist methodology, Bailey argued that every single Purāṇa text is a coherent whole and every redaction of it is equally systematic. In response, Adriaensen, Bakker, and Isaacson affirm that "It is through philological research based on manuscripts that this selection on the one hand and substitution on the other, as well as the intrinsic criteria by which they operated—i.e. the general generic principles of Purāṇa literature—can be brought to light. No structuralistic analysis, taking printed texts for granted, will ever delve so deep."[51] Apparently, the debate concerning the production of critical editions of the Purāṇas is not over yet.

Dating the Purāṇas

Modernity is inseparably connected with historicity, and as such, there is no wonder that a text without a date causes anxiety to a modern mind. Traditional ideas that connect the Purāṇa with the Veda and therefore consider them dating from the beginning of time while also presenting a gradual development of the texts in the hands of Vyāsa, his disciples, and other *paurāṇikas* sharply clash with the modern positivistic need for a date on a linear time line. Purāṇas as religious texts created by a superior authority in a cyclic time and Purāṇas as empirically verifiable, man-made texts in historical time belong to two different worldviews, and a reconciliation of the two is impossible. Still, scholars made valiant efforts to fix a date for each of the Purāṇas. The early colonial scholars tended to give the Purāṇas a relatively late date, while Indian scholars tried to push them as far back as possible. For Wilson, the Purāṇas belong to the late period when Hinduism was developing a sectarian character, worshiping Śiva or Viṣṇu, and therefore cannot be older than Samkara, Ramanuja, Madhva, and Vallabha. Gradually, a consensus seems to have emerged that there is a great deal of ancient material in the Purāṇas along with very modern material and that composite, ever-changing texts such as these are impossible to date as whole texts.[52] Cornelia Dimmitt and J.A.B. van Buitenen suggest an innovative idea of dating the Purāṇa material by correlating different sections of the Purāṇas with phases of Hindu tradition as known from other literature.[53] They speculate that

> the oldest material in the Purāṇas is contemporaneous with the Vedas, but was recited either in a different milieu than the brahminic ritual or by persons other than the brahmin priests. This alternate milieu would be the source of the *smṛti* tradition that gave rise eventually to both epic and Purāṇic collections. Thus the Purāṇas, which share many stories from the epics, the *Mahābhārata* in particular, do not derive from that epic, but from the same body of oral tradition, or *smṛti,* whose origins may be as old as the period of the Vedas.[54]

Dimmitt and van Buitenen go on to suggest that some of the Purāṇa material was collected about 1000 BCE, the period after the *Mahābhārata* war, and again during the Gupta period, that is, fourth to sixth century. More new material continued to be added to the Purāṇas well after the sixth century, and there is no final closing date for the Purāṇas.[55] Rocher says that despite insurmountable difficulties in dating individual Purāṇas, scholars still assign specific dates to them. He reports dates set by others in his very erudite and informative book, *The Purāṇas*,[56] stating at the same time that it is not possible to set a specific date for any Purāṇa as a whole.

The Absent Paurāṇika

Prevailing ideas about critical editions fall on one or the other side of the oral/written divide. For Rocher, the Purāṇas were oral texts that were accidentally written down. For Adriaensen, Bakker, and Isaacson they were basically written texts. The fact, however, is that they were both.

The orality of Indian languages, unlike that of Western languages, allows for what I call oral literacy. The *paurāṇika* performer prided himself in his scholarship and distinguished himself from the nonliterate performer who sang oral narratives which have no written authority. Every Purāṇa says in writing that it was orally told by *sūta* who himself heard it from an earlier telling by Vyāsa or some such authority. Nowhere in the long line of transmission of the Purāṇa recorded in writing in each Purāṇa text is the act of writing mentioned (except in the case of the *Mahābhārata* where Ganesa serves as the scribe for Vyāsa). Curiously, then, an authentic Purāṇa happens to be a written text, which claims in that very writing that it is not a written text. Scholars agree that no Purāṇa is ever performed in its entirety as it is written. A typical *paurāṇika*, a *paṇḍita* who is well versed in the Purāṇa tradition and would be known by different regional language names throughout India, chooses a section of a Purāṇa for a discourse, reads out a portion of the text in Sanskrit or the regional language, and comments on it, incorporating material from other similar texts and expanding on their relevance to that specific place and point in time. The erudition of the *paurāṇika* allows him to move across many Purāṇas with his memory as the only authority to determine which text he has borrowed from. When such a *paurāṇika* serves also as a producer of Purāṇa texts, he feels justified in incorporating material that he has quoted from other texts into the one he is producing. The style in which Purāṇas were composed, a simple Sanskrit meter called *anuṣṭubh*, easily allows for moving substantial portions of one Purāṇa text to another Purāṇa text. Vyāsa was the author of all the Purāṇas, but the actual producers of the texts were the *paurāṇikas* who made these texts and renewed them as context required. Literally thousands of such producers of texts over a period of hundreds of years worked quietly without seeking any individual recognition under the imagined direction of the legendary sage Vyāsa. The creativity that went into the making and remaking of the Purāṇas is quite remarkable.

Elsewhere I draw a distinction between the recorded text and the received text in India.[57] What is recorded on palm leaf, and later on paper, is not the entire text, it is only a part of it. It acquires its fullness in performance, at which time it is appropriately recreated by the *paurāṇika*, who is trained in reading the Purāṇas and interpreting them. His knowledge, which was not written down, would be crucial in determining the received text. The recorded Purāṇa text tells only part of the story. When the *paurāṇikas* who knew the received text disappeared, scholars were left with only the recorded text, which has become our sole text. Simply reading the recorded text in a linear order, without the training in performing it, scholars found a number of irresolvable contradictions and discontinuities, not to mention a plethora of scribal errors. But if the early scholars had actually studied the Purāṇa in performance and learned how the trained performer constructed and presented a Purāṇa in each performance, we would have an entirely different kind of Purāṇa scholarship today. Instead of suspecting the *paṇḍitas*, the agents of transmission of this tradition from generation to generation, if the early scholars had striven to understand the nature of this text culture, a whole different way of asking questions would have emerged.

The *paurāṇikas* who knew this text culture had been initially marginalized and eventually disappeared from the scholarly scene. So much so that the entire scholarship of the Purāṇas has been conducted viewing these texts as artifacts with little direct interaction with the users of these texts and their textual practices. The textual activities of this culture—production, transmission, performance, and reproduction, which includes the training of the *paurāṇikas*, the principles and methods of text creation they employed, and the rules governing such activities—need to be properly understood. In the absence of such an understanding, texts collected from their original locations and stacked in the air-conditioned rooms of libraries and studied in isolation could only give a distorted picture. The Purāṇa culture where hundreds and even thousands *paurāṇikas* served as silent authors without claiming individual recognition—all speaking in the voice of the revered Vyāsa over such a long period of time in the history of India—waits to be properly understood.

Notes

1. Rocher 1986: 15, 15n10.
2. Shulman 1993.
3. Rocher 1986: 45–6.
4. Ibid.: 47.

5. Hazra 1962: 241.
6. Anantaramayya 1984: 17.
7. Kennedy 1831: 153n.
8. Kane 1930–62, 5.2: 840–1.
9. Levitt 1976.
10. Narayana Rao 1993: 87–9; see also Bailey 1995: 12–14.
11. Dimmitt and van Buitenen 1978: 28–9.
12. Rocher 1986: 32.
13. Nye 1985.
14. Dikshitar 1951: xiv.
15. Rocher 1986: 68.
16. Hazra 1962: 246–7.
17. Kane 1930–62, 5.2: 862.
18. Ibid. However, according to Kangle (1960–65, 2: 2, 5n), the text of the *Arthaśāstra* is difficult to construe.
19. Dandekar 1985.
20. Rocher 1986: 56.
21. Janamanci Seshadrisarma 1931: 15.
22. Rocher 1986: 23.
23. Ibid.: 21–2.
24. van Buitenen 1966: 38.
25. Rocher 1986: 27.
26. Doniger 1993: 59.
27. See Rocher 1986: 133–254 for a full survey of the Purāṇas.
28. Hazra 1975: 169.
29. Cort 1993: 187.
30. A.K. Ramanujan 1993b: 101–20.
31. Rocher 1986: 72.
32. Narayana Rao 1990.
33. Rocher 1986: 2.
34. Wilson 1839: 64.
35. Wilson 1961: lvi.
36. Rocher 1986: 115–25.
37. Winternitz 1963–83, I: 507.
38. Biardeau 1968.
39. Ibid.: 122–3.
40. Ibid.: 123.
41. Ibid.
42. Bedekar 1969: 225. For a survey of the debate, see Coburn 1980.

43. Gupta 1971: xxxi.
44. Ibid.: xxxa.
45. Rocher 1986: 99.
46. Rocher 1983: 72; emphasis in original.
47. Adriaensen, Bakker, and Isaacson 1998.
48. Ibid.: 38.
49. Ibid.: 40.
50. Bailey 1995: 3–73.
51. Adriaensen, Bakker, and Isaacson 1998: 17; see also the Preface by Heinrich von Stietencron of the Tubingen Purāṇa Project in Bailey 1995: ix–xi.
52. Rocher 1986: 100–3.
53. Dimmitt and van Buitenen 1978.
54. Ibid.: 5–6.
55. Ibid.
56. Rocher 1986.
57. Narayana Rao 1995.

References

Adriaensen, R., H.T. Bakker, and H. Isaacson. 1998. *The Skandapurāṇa*, Volume I. Groningen: Egbert Forsten.

Anantaramayya, Eluripati. 1984. *Sri Vāmana Purāṇam*. Tirupati: Tirumala-Tirupati Devasthanamulu.

Bailey, Greg. 1995. *Gaṇeśapurāṇa*. Part 1: *Upāsanākhaṇḍa*. Weisbaden: Otto Harrassowitz.

Bedekar, V.M. 1969. "Principles of Mahābhārata Textual Criticism: The Need for a Restatement." *Purāṇam* 11, 2: 210–28.

Biardeau, Madeline. 1968. "Some More Considerations about Textual Criticism." *Purāṇam* 10, 2; 115–23.

Coburn, Thomas B. 1980. "The Study of Purāṇas and the Study of Religion." *Religious Studies* 16, 3: 341–52.

Cort, John E. 1993. "An Overview of the Jaina Purāṇas." In Wendy Doniger, ed., *Purāṇa Perennis*: *Reciprocity and Transformation in Hindu and Jaina Texts*, 185–206, 279–84, 308–15. Albany, N.Y.: State University of New York Press.

Dandekar, R.N. 1985. "Gleanings from the Śiva Purāṇa." Paper Presented at Conference on the Purāṇas at University of Wisconsin, Madison, August.

Dimmitt, Cornelia, and J.A.B. van Buitenen, ed. and trans. 1978. *Classical Hindu Mythology: A Reader in the Sanskrit Purāṇas*. Philadelphia: Temple University Press.

Doniger, Wendy, ed. 1993. *Purāṇa Perennis: Reciprocity and Transformation in Hindu and Jaina Texts.* Albany, N.Y.: State University of New York Press.

Gupta, Anand Swarup, ed. 1971. *The Kūrma Purāṇa.* Varanasi: All-India Kashiraj Trust.

Hazra, R.C. 1940. *Studies in the Purāṇic Records on Hindu Rites and Customs.* Dacca: The University of Dacca.

———. 1962. [1937] "The Purāṇas." In S.K. Dube, U.N. Ghoshal, A.D. Pusalkar, and R.C. Hazra, ed., *The Cultural Heritage of India.* Volume 2 of 6: *Itihāsas, Purāṇas, Dharma and other Śāstras*, 240–70. Calcutta: Ramakrishna Mission Institute of Culture.

———. 1963. *Studies in the Upapurāṇas*, Vol. A. Calcutta: Sanskrit College.

Kane, Pandurang Vamana, 1930–62. *History of Dharmaśāstra (Ancient and Mediyal Religious and Civil Law*). 5 volumes in 7 books. Poona: Bhandarkar Oriental Research Institute.

Kangle, R.P. 1960–5. *The Kauṭilīya Arthaśāstra.* 3 parts. Bombay: University of Bombay.

Kennedy, Vans. 1831. *Researches into the Nature and Affinity of Ancient and Hindu Mythology.* London: Longman, Rees, Orme, Brown, and Green.

Levitt, Stephen Hillyer. 1976. "A Note on the Compound Pañcalakṣaṇa in Amarasimha's Nāmaliṅgānuśāsana." *Purāṇam* 18, 1: 5–38.

Narayana Rao, Velcheru. 1993. "Purāṇa as Brahminic Ideology." In Wendy Doniger, ed., *Purāṇa Perennis: Reciprocity and Transformation in Hindu and Jaina Texts*, 85–100, 265–6. Albany: State University of New York Press. Also Chapter 3 in this volume.

———. (assisted by Gene H. Roghair). 1990. *Śiva's Warriors: The Basava Purāṇa of Palkuriki Somanatha.* Princeton, New Jersey: Princeton University Press.

———. 1995. "Review of Philip Lutgendorf's *The Life of a Text: Performing the Ramcaritmanas of Tulsidas.*" *Journal of Asian Studies* 54, 2: 600–3.

Nye, James. 1985. "Upapurāṇa and Mahāpurāṇa: Appendix and Appendee?" Paper Presented at Conference on the Purāṇas at University of Wisconsin, Madison, August.

Ramachandra Dikshitar. 1951. *The Purāṇa Index.* Volume 1 of 3. Madras: Madras University.

Ramanujan, A.K. 1993. "On Folk Mythologies and Folk Purāṇas." In Wendy Doniger, ed., *Purāṇa Perennis: Reciprocity and Transformation in Hindu and Jaina Texts*, 101–20. Albany, N.Y.: State University of New York Press.

Rocher, Ludo. 1986. *The Purāṇas.* Wiesbaden: Otto Harrassowitz.

Seshadrisarma, Janamanci. 1931. *Sri Rāmavatāra Tattvamu.* 11 volumes, Madras: V. Ramaswamy Sastrulu & Sons.

Shulman, David. 1993. "Remaking a Purāṇa: The Rescue of Gajendra in Potana's Telugu Mahābhāgavatamu." In Wendy Doniger, ed., *Purāṇa Perennis: Reciprocity and Transformation in Hindu and Jaina Texts.* Albany, N.Y.: State University of New York Press.

Sukthankar, V.S. 1933. "Prolegomena." In V.S. Sukthankar, S.K. Belvalkar, and P.L. Vaidya, general editors, *The Mahābhārata for the First Time Critically Edited.* Volume 1 of 19. The Adiparvan, i–cx. Poona: Bhandarkar Oriental Research Institute.

van Buitenen, J.A.B. 1966. "On the Archaism of the Bhāgavata Purāṇa." In Milton Singer, ed., *Krishna: Myths, Rites, and Attitudes*, 23–40, 215–17. Honolulu: East-West Center Press.

Wilson, Horace Hayman. 1839. "Essays on the Purāṇas." *The Journal of the Royal Asiatic Society of Great Britain and Ireland* (n.s.) 5: 61–72.

Wilson, Horace H. 1961 [1840]. *The Vishṇu Purāṇa: A System of Hindu Mythology and Tradition.* Calcutta: Punthi Pustak.

Winternitz, Maurice. 1963–83 [1904–20]. *A History of Indian Literature.* Trans. V. Srinivasa Sarma (volumes 1 and 2) and Subhadra Jha (volume 3). 3 volumes in 4 books. Delhi: Motilal Banarsidass.

14

A Day in the Life of a Housewife

"Sīta Locked Out"

Translated from the Telugu

She is born of Earth, and raised by Janaka.
She serves her in-laws with devotion.

Her loving husband calls her, but she doesn't go.
Flowers in his hair, perfume on his body, her husband is in a joyous mood.
Looking for her, he waits, and waits.
He is impatient about the time she takes.
"Why doesn't she come, what's taking so long?"
The solar hero[1] is upset with her.

He closes the door and bolts it.
"You and your chores, Daughter of Earth!
You've grown too proud," he says shaking his head,
and totally deluded, lies down on his bed.

Sīta comes rushing.
She quickly presses her mother-in-law Kausalya's feet.
Gives betel leaves to her father-in-law. Fans Kaika and Sumitra too,[2]
and makes the bed for Kausalya.

*

Then she takes her turmeric bath,
chooses a sari with golden flowers,
combs her hair and ties it into a bun.

She puts on her jewels—
a tamarind-leaf of gold in the part of her hair;
a drop of pearls crowning her forehead;
a spread of gems around her bun;
earrings worth a thousand,
a gold chain worth two thousand,
a nose ring worth three thousand,
a choker worth some four thousand,
and a pendant worth ten thousand,
a belt of gold with bells on it,
and bracelets with sapphires inlaid,
and a necklace of precious stones.

She brushes kohl along her lashes
and looks at herself in the life-size mirror.
Pleased with herself, the woman smiles.

She eats her dinner, five different courses,
sweets and all, then washes her hands.
She covers herself with a golden shawl.
Takes water to drink in a jug of gold,
betel leaves, areca nuts, fragrances, sandal paste,
jasmine water, fruits and snacks on a platter of gold.
She wears jasmine and *jāji* flowers in her hair
and arrives with joy to meet her husband.

"Lord, my hero, I brought you flowers.
You never bend before any rival.
You're the one that humiliated
the other Rāma that challenged you.
You are my lord, my Kakutsa.[3]

"Can I bear your anger? You closed the door.
My feet are aching, my hands are tired.
Open the ivory door, my lord,
it's beginning to rain. I am getting wet.
Open that golden bolt, My Handsome!
It's raining hard, my sari is soaked.
My Emerald Young Man, open the door.
It is the fourth phase of the night, Lord of My Life.

I'll give you my necklace of precious gems.
Let me lie at your feet, to get a little sleep."

Rāma says,
"If you lose sleep, what do I care!
The lampstand here keeps me company.
If you stand out there, what do I care!
Flowers and *bukkā* scents keep me company.
If you stand out there, what do I care!
Sandal and musk keep me company.
If you stand out there, what do I care!
The mattress and pillows keep me company."

*

Upset at Rāma's words, Sīta quickly runs to mother-in-law's house. When she hears it all, Kausalya comes to Rāma's door.

"You're the son of King Daśaratha,
married into the house of great Janaka.
Earth give her daughter to you.
Have you lost your senses?
What did Sīta do?
Tell me, my little boy, if something's wrong."

"Mother, if you pamper your daughter-in-law,
will she ever care for me?" says the hero of the house
as he opens the door, with a big smile.

"Mother, my father-in-law is waiting. You go to him, he is all alone," says Sīta to Kausalya, and Kausalya leaves.

When Sīta goes shyly to her husband, the lamp laughs with joy.

Fragrance of betel leaves all over the bed.
Fragrance of betel nuts all over the bed.
Fragrance of flowers all over the bed.
Fragrance of musk all over the bed.
Fragrance of *bukkā* all over the bed.

Who knows how angry Sīta is?
Rāma turns to the other side.

"Just how long it takes for butter to melt
when it is near fire,

is how long a woman's anger lasts,"
says Sīta and moves swiftly to Rāma.
to make love.
Rāma enjoys the games of pleasure,
and lives in glory and honor.

*

Women who sing this song on earth or listen to it, will live in riches.

A Day in the Life of a Housewife: A Second Look at "Sīta Locked Out"

The title of a song that my mother used to sing intrigued me, *Sīta Gaḍiya*, which I translate as "Sīta Locked Out," has haunted me ever since I heard the song as a young boy. Literally *gaḍiya* in Telugu is a bolt or a crossbar that locks the door inside. The song talks about Sīta locked out, when Rāma bolts the door inside their room. If it is actually Rāma that bolts the *gaḍiya*, the phrase should be *Rāmuni gaḍiya* and not *Sīta gaḍiya*. Significantly, the composer defines the *gaḍiya* as the one that Sīta caused to be opened, rather than the one that Rāma bolted, and even deviates from the conventions of Telugu grammar to make the striking title—quietly foregrounding the unusual events that the song sings of.

Telugu women sing melodious songs on Rāmāyaṇa and other mythological themes.[4] For a long time, perhaps for more than a couple of hundred years, literary scholars treated them as simple women's songs not worthy of a second look.[5]

Songs sung at the door are a popular genre in weddings. Pandit S.M. Natesa Sastry reports one such song in *Indian Antiquary* (September 1888). He classifies the songs under "Epithalamia," where the wife, in this instance Lakṣmi, locks her husband Viṣṇu out. Viṣṇu keeps begging her to open the door, as Lakṣmi accuses him of being unfaithful to her by taking another wife, a low-caste *cĕñcu* girl. Viṣṇu admits his fault and tries to appease Lakṣmi by offering gifts to her. Lakṣmi, however, refuses to open the door, and asks Viṣṇu to give his gifts to that *cĕñcu* woman and go make love to her instead. Similar songs are also sung in dance performances by Kuchipudi dancers where Viṣṇu, who is locked out, answers with his name when Lakṣmi from inside asks him for his identity. Lakṣmi playfully takes the name "Viṣṇu" as something else by reading it literally, and tells him off. Viṣṇu then tries another of his names—after all he has a thousand names to choose from—which again is subjected to another deviant interpretation, leading to one more rejection of entry. For example, Viṣṇu says he is Cakri, and surely that is one of his names, because he wears a *cakra*, the wheel, as his weapon. But then Lakṣmi applies this name to a potter, since a potter is also a *cakri*, one who turns the wheel to make pots. She then says that if he is a *cakri* the potter, he should go to potters' quarters and has no business to knock on the door here. Such punning frustrates Viṣṇu, who never gets admission into his house.

The genre of open-the-door songs (*Talupu daggira pāṭalu*) regularly has the husband locked out by the wife, whereas the roles are reversed in "Sīta Locked Out," a song I would like to discuss in some detail. My close reading shows how surprisingly nuanced it is with its subtleties of diction and ironies of meaning, the things we expect from a well-written poem.

On the surface, "Sīta Locked Out" looks not only simple, but also defective. The meter does not run smoothly and some of the words appear to be wrongly placed, or meaninglessly repeated. It is easy to assume that this defect is due to the composer's lack of sophistication in the use of language—an all-too-common assumption of learned critics. But a careful reading proves otherwise.

Let's talk about the meter first. The meter is quantitative—Telugu metrical texts call it *mātra chandassu*, in which a short syllable counts for one *mātra* and a long syllable counts for two. Each line has sixteen *mātras* broken into two halves of eight *mātra*s each. However, the syllables in the text as it is printed do not uniformly conform to this number. Some lines are shorter, and some longer—so it looks like the meter is off. But, in singing, what looks like a short line is made longer by extending the length of some syllables, and vice versa. When we realize that this is not originally a written text, nor is it meant to be read as a written text, the problem of meter is instantly resolved.[6]

In fact if all the space on the line is packed with syllables, the singer feels suffocated, for lack of room for musical flourishes. The editor,

Sripada Gopala Krishnamurty (1955), makes note of this feature in his introduction, but apparently the publishers did not have the technical facility to indicate musical notations on the printed page.

Structurally, the text itself is tightly organized with no padding or uninteresting repetitions. The language is exquisitely layered and the diction is subtle and nuanced. The first line begins with the customary auspicious syllable *śrī*, to ward off bad luck. However, the word that begins the song, *Śrīrāma*, is syntactically unconnected to the rest of the lines while it is metrically integrated all the same. It hangs there independently, unrelated to anything that follows, as if uttered just to take care of the requirement of the first syllable and also to pay respect to Rāma's name. Many of the women's songs in this genre begin by paying homage to Rāma but as they proceed they tend to be very critical of Rāma and give Sīta and other women in the narrative far more agency and initiative than the Vālmīki text allows.[7]

The song is built around several strategically orchestrated moves. The first two lines show how devoted Sīta is in serving her mother-in-law and father-in-law and how attentive she is to the needs of the elders. A good daughter-in-law should give priority to the service of her parents-in-law over her love for her husband. The next few lines describe the problem. Rāma calls her to bed, but she doesn't show up. All dressed up, and eager to have his wife in bed with him, Rāma is angry for the attention she gives to her chores around the house, neglecting him, and bolts the door. He determines to teach her a lesson and pretends to be asleep. The song clearly says he misunderstood her intentions, but the word used to indicate this misunderstanding is *bhrama*, which has a range of meanings from a simple misunderstanding to total delusion. Does the author wish to indicate that Rāma is deluded with his oversized ego and could not stand Sīta being late when he summoned her? Sīta on her part is described as rushing to complete her chores so she can join him without delay. She quickly attends to her parents-in-law. Description of her duties takes just two lines, which conclude this short section. So far, the song describes a dutiful daughter-in-law, obedient and devoted to her parents-in-law, putting service to them above her own pleasures, but at the same time very eager to please her husband, too.

Now begins the next section where Sīta takes her time to bathe, comb her hair, and dress herself with all her finery. This section of the song takes its time describing each ornament in detail, even telling us how much each item costs. Then follows the leisurely dinner of five courses and sweets, and the long look in the life-size mirror. Clearly, Sīta is in no rush to go to her husband. She is in charge and will go to meet him in her own time. The pace of the song in this section is relaxed and comfortable, switching to a descriptive mode from the fast-paced narrative that precedes and follows. The words chosen and the time taken (24 lines in a song of 102 lines) indicate in no uncertain terms that Sīta is in full control of the situation.

When she finally goes to Rāma, she calls out saying she has brought him flowers, and boosts Rāma's male ego by recalling that he never bent his head to another warrior. When Paraśurāma, an equally powerful warrior, challenged him, Rāma deflated his pride. References to Rāma's past heroic deeds are carefully placed here to make Rāma feel good about his manhood, to create a helpful environment for the role of lover Sīta wants him to play soon. Elite *Alaṃkaraśāstra* texts in Sanskrit inform poets to combine *vīra*, the heroic mood, with *śṛṅgāra*, the erotic, to enhance the latter. The author(s) of this song utilize the heroic suggestion not only to enhance the aesthetics of the poem, but also to assure the success of the heroine in achieving her goal. *Alaṃkarasastra* scholars would love to see this level of sophistication in the craftsmanship of a poem.

Now we enter a more difficult stage in the narrative. Rāma bars the entry door. The song does not include any suggestion that Sīta was surprised at this or was not prepared for it. On the other hand, Sīta takes this in her stride, and the lines that deal with Rāma locking her out flow seamlessly after her praise for Rāma's heroism. Very skillfully, Sīta begins her plan of action, trying to talk him into opening the door. She pleads with him that she is no match for his anger, that her feet and hands are aching, and that it is raining and she is getting soaked. (Clearly, the claim of rain is a lie since there is no mention of it after the door is opened.) She praises him, cajoles him, and even tries to bribe him. Trying to bribe a husband with the gift of a gold ornament is fascinating indeed. That is what men do in this society. Sīta seems to have taken a rather aggressive role in this negotiation.

Rāma, in the act of locking Sīta out, has actually locked himself in. The next few lines show that while Rāma protests he is not alone, and he does not need Sīta, he is actually desperately lonely. Rāma has the lampstand, the sandal paste and musk, and even the mattress and pillows to keep him company. The list is pathetic. If Rāma thinks he is humiliating Sīta by equating her with these inanimate items, he hasn't succeeded.

Sīta's next weapon is her mother-in-law. She knows that Rāma cannot disobey his mother. She quickly brings Kausalya, who roundly scolds Rāma. The words that Kausalya uses to admonish Rāma express both the mother's power as well as her affection. Only a mother can simultaneously scold her son with words such as *buddhi ledaṭarā*? (lit. have you lost your senses?) and then show affection in the next sentence by addressing him as *nanu ganna taṇḍri* (my little boy). Rāma opens the door with a big smile, intended, of course, to show his mother that he is not really angry. He sheepishly complains, however, that if she keeps pampering her daughter-in-law, he, as a husband, will lose control of her. In effect he is asking his mother not to support Sīta and to join him in his efforts to discipline her—a reversal from the usual story we hear in traditional joint families where the mother asks her son to join her and not take sides with his wife. The song imagines a different alignment in family politics—where the mother supports the daughter-in-law as opposed to her own son.

As soon as Rāma opens the door, Sīta adopts a delicate strategy to send her mother-in-law on her way. Daśaratha (Sīta's father-in-law) is alone, and Kausalya (his wife) should go to him. It is significant that Daśaratha is referred to here as *mā mama*, my father-in-law, stressing the affection Sīta has for him. These carefully chosen words hint at the active sexual life of her in-laws, and that Daśaratha prefers Kausalya to his other wives—a hint that enhances the self-image of Kausalya—and something only an affectionate daughter-in-law could speak of in a joint family. These words actually carry a suggested meaning, distinct from the surface, verbal meaning. They mean: your son wants to be alone with me, you should leave me free to attend to him—a subtle way of saying: leave us alone.

Now Sīta is with her husband. The song describes in five lines fragrances of various items emanating from the bed. These lines appear unconnected to the text which precedes it and are intriguing, especially when read with the line that follows: "Who knows how angry Sīta is?" This line puzzles the reader. Is it possible the author of the text is sloppy or artless and didn't pay attention to the smooth flow of the text of the song? But a closer examination indicates that the gap in the text is deliberate. The fragrances listed match the items Sīta brought in with her on the golden platter. The only additional fragrance is from *bukka*, a substance used to perfume clothes, apparently wafting from Sīta's sari as well as Rāma's clothes. Sīta must have placed the platter somewhere near the bed—without offering it lovingly to Rāma. We can see that Sīta was not too pleased by the treatment meted out to her by her loving husband. We can also imagine that Rāma is still angry, despite his smile for his mother. We can imagine him returning to his sullen mood—as soon as his mother has left and he is alone with Sīta in the bedroom, turning to the other side on the bed—but wondering how angry Sīta is.

Placed in this situation, it is Rāma who has to figure out the next move; clearly Sīta has succeeded in making him feel it was his fault to lock her out. She makes this clear by showing to him that she was in no mood to offer the items she brought, but she gives no hint to him to gauge how angry she is. The fragrances are maddening, as well as her closeness to him, but he is not sure if he could turn toward Sīta to make the first move, as if nothing has happened. He is too proud to admit that what he has done is wrong. He turns facing the other side of the bed, away from Sīta.

Sīta knows what to do next. She comes out with a confession—that a woman's anger does not last any longer than butter near fire. This gives her enough excuse to turn to Rāma and, without losing time (*śīghrāna*), to engage in lovemaking. Rāma's anger is gone like fog in sunlight. He happily turns to her, playing along in the games of love (*keḷi-vilāsamulu*). One wonders who exactly is the butter and who the fire. What is in fact interesting here is that Sīta's statement reverses the well-known analogy stated in many religious texts, which compares woman to fire and man to a pot of butter, to underscore the sexual vulnerability of man.[8]

Describing Sīta's move towards Rāma, the song uses an intriguing verb: *kalisĕnu*, meaning literally "met." This is a euphemism in Telugu for having sex, but is usually used for a man making love to a woman, or in the plural for a man and woman making love together. It is never used in the singular with a woman as the subject. It clearly indicates that in this situation Sīta is the one who takes the initiative, a very bold usage, considering the conventions of shyness under which women live in this traditional society.

The poem concludes that Rāma lives a life of power and luxury, *vaibhoga padavulu.* This information takes the listener out of the bedroom, into Rāma's public life, in effect, telling the listeners that a husband who lives happily with his wife has a successful career too. As a customary benefit (*phalaśruti*) to singers and listeners, who happen to be all women in this case, the song offers a life of riches. It is very interesting that women place such a heavy emphasis on wealth and not as one would expect on love. The description in the song of the ornaments with their price-tags, the expensive clothing, and the sumptuous and luxurious dinner is indication of the priorities of women in this society.

As we reflect on the song it becomes clear that the song is not about Rāma and Sīta as such, but about women in premodern Andhra upper-caste families: women who do not have property rights, no assurance of love in an arranged marriage, and who have to live in a joint family soon after marriage. A woman's only personal security in this situation is the gold she owns in the form of jewelry. Considered bride's wealth or *strī-dhanam*, this property is sacred and cannot be appropriated by the husband's family. It gives a woman far better security than the love of her husband, who after all, could take another wife any time.

Another significant underlying meaning of the song is that the women of the household stand by each other. Contrary to the customary rivalry between a daughter-in-law and a mother-in-law, and the ill-treatment a daughter-in-law is subjected to at the hands of the mother-in-law, this song portrays a very affectionate and gently supportive relationship between them. Normally we hear of the mother-in-law pleading for the support and collusion of her son in disciplining the daughter-in-law, because as his mother she has the higher claim to her son's loyalty. The song imagines a reversal of the situation: a mother-in-law supports her daughter-in-law against her son. A woman knows how a woman feels, and together they know how to handle their men. And that's what the song seems to suggest.

Does the song present a fantasy of harmony in a joint family where a wife has to live as a daughter-in-law? Perhaps it does, because the reality could often be just the opposite. But perhaps, using the Rāmāyaṇa as the theme to sustain this fantasy, it also transforms the reality. Telugu women make a world for themselves in a creatively reworked Rāmāyaṇa.

Notes

During the last century women's songs received scholarly attention as a result of the efforts of savants such as Nandiraju Chelapthi Rao who published them in 1899, and Mangu Jaganandha Rao, who published *Nūru Hindū Strīla Pāṭalu* (One Hundred Hindu Women's Songs) in 1905. In 1955 Sripada Gopala Krishnamurty wrote an introduction to a collection, *Strīla Ramayanapu Pāṭalu* (Women's Rāmāyaṇa Songs), published by Andhra Sarasvata Parishattu, Hyderabad, making a passionate plea to treat them as poetry. These translations are an attempt to present one of the songs from that book. This is in continuation of my study of women's Rāmāyaṇa songs which I began with my "A Rāmāyaṇa of Their Own: Women's Oral Tradition in Telugu," in Paula Richman, *Many Rāmāyaṇas: The Diversity of Narrative Tradition in South Asia* (Berkeley: University of California Press, 1991, pp. 114–36), in which I made a reference to this song. See chapter 7 herein. The text of the translation is published in Paula Richman, ed., *Rāmāyaṇa Stories in Modern South India: An Anthology* (Bloomington: Indiana University Press, 2008). My thanks are due to Professor K. Malayavasini, and Dr Bhavaraju Lalitha Devi, who discussed these songs with me and clarified the meaning of several words related to women's ornaments.

1. Rāma is born in the Solar dynasty, one of the two dynasties of Kshatriyas in Hindu mythology.
2. Kaika (also Kaikeyi) and Sumitra are the other wives of Daśaratha, therefore they are mothers-in-law for Sīta.

3. Name of Rāma's family.
4. The songs published as well as the ones I collected are sung only among upper-caste families of Andhra.
5. There is no definite evidence to date these songs. But Sripada Gopalakrishnamurty cites a line from Tyāgarāja's song which refers to the game of *Vāmanaguṇṭalu* Rāma plays with Sīta. The game is described in one of the women's songs, "Sīta Vāmanaguṇṭalu," and Gopalakrishnamurty persuasively argues that Tyāgarāja (1767–1847) refers to the women's song when he mentions the game in his song. This indicates that at least some of the songs that women have been singing for some generations now date at least to as early as late eighteenth-early nineteenth century.
6. The meter here is 8 + 8
   To illustrate this with an example, here are two lines that begin the song.

   śrī rā ma bhū sa ti ki—ce ḍe yai bu ṭṭi
   kū rmi to ja na ku ni—kū tu rai pĕ ri gi

   Each line has eight plus eight *matras*, and the first syllables of each half *śrī* and *ce*, and *kū* and *kū,* respectively, are phonetically harmonious. This feature of the harmony of first syllables is called *yati* in scholarly metrical literature, and is strictly adhered to by all poets. Here, the composer/author follows the convention when it flows naturally, but does not mind when the harmony does not work smoothly.
7. See my "A Rāmāyaṇa of Their Own," in Paula Richman, op. cit.
8. For instance, the *Varāha Purāṇa* says:

   agni-kuṇḍa-samā nārī ghṛta-kumbha-samaḥ pumān/ ghṛta-kumbho'agni-yogena dravate natu darśanāt/ pumān strī-darśanād eva dravate yad vimohitaḥ, Woman is like the fire-pit and man is like a pot of clarified butter. The only difference is that clarified butter melts when it is placed near the fire, not by its sight alone, whereas a man gets excited and melts by the mere sight of a woman. See *Varāha Purāṇa,* ed. Hrishikesh Sastri (Calcutta, 1893), pp. 146, and 38–9. This verse is popularly quoted among Sanskrit pandits in Andhra, but I don't find this in the critical edition published by the All India Kashi Raj Trust.

15

Urmila Sleeps

A Rāmāyaṇa Song that Women in Andhra Sing

Translated from the Telugu

King Rāma on the throne, the court is held in glory.
Bharata, Śatrughna and Lakṣmaṇa were in attendance to serve him.
Hanumān pressed Rāma's feet. Sugrīva stood by humbly.
Tumbura and Nārada sang and Rambha and her troop danced.
Śaunaka and other great sages discoursed high disciplines.
All the gods were pleased and flowers rained from the sky.

Sīta took a look at all the people present.
She looked at her husband and joined her hands in prayer.
"God of gods, listen, I have an appeal to make to you.
When we were going to the forest, when your brother Lakṣmaṇa followed us,
Urmila was ready to go with him, but he said she should not go.
The woman went to sleep beginning from that very day.
Now Lakṣmana should go to her. You should ask him to go to her."

When Rāma heard what Sīta said, he felt sad for Urmila.
He called Lakṣmaṇa close, and said: "Is it proper to leave
your wife alone? Go to your dear wife. And talk
lovingly to her, and make her forget her grief."

Lakṣmaṇa was pleased and quickly left the court.
He went past many doors and many a wide courtyard.

He went to his own palace, where Urmila was sleeping.
He entered his room and saw the woman in deep sleep.
He bent over the bed and fixed her sari and sash.
He sat by her side and talked to her, she was
dearer to him than his own life: "Woman," he said
"The moon is nothing before your face, and betel misses your lips,
Speak your words, sweet like nectar, and cool my parched soul.
Your feet are soft like lotuses, wake up and wear gold on them."

Urmila shivered in her sleep and said, "Who are you, sir? And why are you here?
"You dared to be so brash, you dared to commit a wrong.
Prowling through alleys and lanes, you came to grab me alone.

"If my father Janaka hears of this, he will punish you, count on it.
If King Rāma hears of this, your life will be in severe danger.
If my sister's brother-in-law hears of this, he will not let you live.

"My great family's name is tarnished now, helpless me, what can I do?
The family of my birth is blemished now, helpless me, what can I do?

"Because he went after another man's wife, Indra has an ugly body.
Because he went after another man's wife, Rāvaṇa was killed and his kingdom was lost.
You know these well-known stories, and still you are intent on this.
Don't you have a sister like me, and aren't you born of a mother?"

As Urmila went on talking, Lakṣmaṇa said to her in grief.

"I am Rāma's brother."
"Never heard of that name."
"I am Janaka's son-in-law,"
"Who on earth is he?"
"You are like my goddess of wealth, I am Sīta's brother-in-law."
"What are you talking about, and who is Sīta, anyway?"
"You are Urmila, aren't you? Don't you tell me a lie.

"Aren't I Sīta's brother-in-law? Kindly wake up from sleep.
And you know something else, Sīta was taken away.
She was separated from us; we had to fight a battle for her
We had to kill Rāvaṇa to bring the woman back.

"If you don't accept me, my beauty, people will speak badly of me.
From the day I left you in the city, I have neither eaten nor slept.
If you do not accept me, I will not live any longer."

Lakṣmaṇa took the sword from his sheath. He was ready to kill himself.
As he spoke with tears in his eyes,
Urmila was startled and woke up scared.
She saw it was her husband, and her mind became clear.
She fell on his feet and bowed to him. He picked her up in love,
and wiped the tears from her face.

"My father was naive in giving me to you," she said,
"He didn't know the truth. He thought you were a proud man
and was blissfully happy for you. But in fact,
you have your mind elsewhere, you belittle your own wife."

Lakṣmaṇa knew her mind and felt sad for how she felt.
"I've barely survived without you all these fourteen years.
I neither ate nor slept, it's true, I'll take an oath on you.
We probably separated a good couple, in some past life,
and we have suffered for that now. No point in worrying.
What we did in the past has to be paid for in this life."
Kausalya saw the distressed couple and gave them a warm bath.
She dressed Urmila in a soft silk sari and a shining golden blouse.
She gave her jewels and ornaments and dressed Lakṣmaṇa too.
She made a white and orange mark on Lakṣmaṇa's handsome face.
When they saw themselves in a mirror, Urmila bent her head and smiled.

Prince Lakṣmaṇa sat like the king of gods on a seat of pearls.
Śānta led Urmila to his side and she came walking gently.
Her face was bent in shyness, while the bells on her feet jingled,
Sumitra made her sit next to Lakṣmaṇa and she served them on golden plateṡ
five delicious dishes and gave them ghee from silver bowls.
Śānta said to Lakṣmaṇa, "Eat well, my brother, in the company of your wife,
free from the fatigue of the forest, where you neither ate nor slept.
Enjoy the delicious dishes specially made for you,
and curds and buttermilk, as much as you would want."

They ate their fill, and washed their hands, and sat chewing betel.

"Someone here has slept for fourteen years in a row,"
Śānta teased Urmila, calling on Sīta to listen.
"We don't know where she has stashed away
this golden glow of her face.
We should make an offering to the gods to ward off the evil eye."

"It's your handsome brothers," said Sīta, "that need such an offering, not us."
"They rule the whole world, and their moon-like faces
make the world fall in love with them."

"No," said Śānta, "It's you four sisters who made my brothers
fall in love with them. You are skilled at such things, so we need
to ward off the evil eye from affecting your lovely faces."

Now Sīta said in return,
"You made my brother Ṛṣyaśṛṅga fall for your charms and games.
He was a totally innocent man doing his austerities in the forest."

Śānta quickly retorted,
"You were the goddess of wealth born on the lotus in heaven
but you didn't want to stay there and came to live in our house.
We are lucky you are here."

"We are lucky you are here too," Sīta said to Śānta,

Sumitra made a bed of down for her son who returned from the forest.
She made soft silk pillows and sprinkled rose water on them.
A maid set up fans made of cool *vaṭṭi* straw,
sandal paste and musk, *punugu* and *javvādi* in cups.
There were betel leaves, areca nuts and pearl-lime as well.
As the breeze gently blew over the sweet *campaka* flowers
they closed the doors of the bedroom.

As the breeze from the jasmine bushes blew in through the window,
the couple sat on their bed.
Lakṣmaṇa loosened Urmila's hair, which was tightly made into a bun
and skillfully braided it, and put *jāji* flowers in it.
Chewing betel leaves, the couple sat talking to each other.

"How did that happen?" asked Urmila. "How was my sister taken away?
When you were there, stronger than a lion,
how was my sister taken away?"

Kausalya, Sumitra, and Kaika sat on raised seats.
Śānta was with them too, and they didn't make a sound.

"When Rāma and you were there, how was my sister taken away?"
"Fate is impossible to avoid, even for the creator god.
We left Ayodhya and lived in the forest in a hut of leaves we built.
A golden magic deer came near the doorstep of our hut.
Your sister wanted that deer and begged Rāma to bring it to her.
Rāma with his bow and arrows went out to hunt the deer.
He hit the animal with his bow when it made a strange cry.
It cried, 'Haa, Sīta, haa, Lakṣmaṇa!,' Sīta was frightened and said:
"Go to help Rāma," and I said "Mother, I should not go."
She spoke words sharp as arrows that pierced my ears and hurt me.
I drew a line around her, a command that none should cross.
I left to help my brother when Rāvaṇa came in disguise
and stood in front of the hut calling out god's name.
Thinking he a was a servant of god, Sīta came out to give him food.
She saw his ten heads, and fell down unconscious.
Rāvaṇa took her away lifting her with the earth on which she stood.
When Rāma returned to the hut holding the golden deer,
We searched for her all over, in the hut and the entire forest.
But we didn't find a trace and we were very tired.
We went over to Kiṣkindha, and Sugrīva gave gifts to Rāma,
because he was Kausalya's son, he had such respect for him.
Rāma opened the gifts and saw Sīta's jewels among them.

"Brother Lakṣmaṇa, come," he said and showed the jewels to me.
I never saw those jewels, but I recognized her anklets.
I saw them every day when I bowed to her at sunrise.

Rāma called Hanumān and gave his ring to him.
He told him how Sīta looks and sent him to search for her.
Hanumān crossed the ocean, searched the Asoka garden.
He gave Sīta the ring,
he talked to her.
He took her crest-jewel
and came back fast and stood before Rāma.

"How could I bring your wife? Tell me.
Her hair is all matted and a bamboo grows in her belly.[1]
I couldn't bear to see her, nor think of her condition now."

When Hanumān said this, grieving, Rāma fell unconscious.

"Rāma invaded Lanka and destroyed Rāvaṇa and his army.
He asked Sīta to be brought to his presence,
beautifully dressed.
When she was brought to him, he said,
"She lived in captivity for ten months, I cannot talk to her."

"What good are words of truth, make a fire for me," said Sīta.
From a fire blazing high as the sky, my sister-in-law talked.
The fire was cool to her, like she was bathing in a lake.
Because she was chaste, my sister-in-law came back.
Sīta and Rāma are now on the throne of Ayodhya."
Thus, Lakṣmaṇa told the story of all the troubles they suffered.

Then the sisters talked of Sīta's hardships in captivity.
"Now you have heard what kind of a mind our Man with the Wheel has?"
Look, they said to each other, "Our sister had to live
away from her handsome husband in that horrible forest
imprisoned by that sinful demon
for ten months in Lanka."
They all agreed that there is no point
in regretting what had happened,
They praised Rāma and Sīta,
who were installed on the throne.

This is the song of Urmila's separation.
Anyone who sings or hears it
Lakṣmaṇa gives them the word of God.

*

Perhaps the most neglected character in the Rāmāyaṇa is Urmila. Vālmīki's text mentions her only once, in two lines to tell us that she was married to Lakṣmaṇa. We don't hear of her again. Neither does she have a role in any of the Sanskrit tellings of the Rāmāyaṇa by poets such as Kalidasa, Bhavabhuti, and a number of others that follow all the way up to the nineteenth century.

Two Telugu women's Rāmayaṇa songs make Urmila prominent in the narrative, particularly the one usually titled *Urmilādevi nidra*

(Urmila's sleep). Poets of this Rāmāyaṇa invent an ingenious event: when Lakṣmaṇa follows Rāma and Sīta to the forest, Urmila wants to go with them too. But there is a problem. Family conventions do not allow a sister-in-law to walk in the company of her elder brother-in-law. Lakṣmaṇa therefore has to advise Urmila to stay home. They make a pact to exchange their sleeping and waking hours. This way Urmila will sleep all fourteen years, thus avoiding the pain of separation from her husband. Lakṣmaṇa will remain awake during that whole time, all the better for him to serve his brother day and night.

The central theme of the song is how Lakṣmaṇa is reunited with Urmila. In the following pages I will present a close reading of the song.

As is usual with the women's songs on the Rāmāyaṇa, the song begins with a description of the glory of Rāma. The first six lines of the song describe how at the end of the period of exile, Rāma returns triumphantly to his capital, and holds court in glory. Everything is in order, when Sīta reminds Rāma that his brother should go and visit his wife who has been sleeping ever since they left for the forest. Lakṣmaṇa dutifully takes orders from Rāma, leaves the court, and goes to where Urmila is sleeping. This is where the song begins to deepen. To bring an analogy with the structure of the upper-caste household, the beginning of the song is like the front of the house where men rule, from where we move gradually into the interior of the house where women control the space.

> "If my father Janaka hears of this, he will punish you, count on it.
> If King Rāma hears of this, your life will be in severe danger.
> If my sister's brother-in-law hears of this, he will not let you live.
>
> "Because he went after another man's wife, Indra has an ugly body.
> Because he went after another man's wife, Rāvaṇa was killed and his kingdom was lost.
> You know these well-known stories, and still you are intent on this.
> Don't you have a sister like me, and aren't you born of a mother?"

Urmila senses even in her sleep that a man has entered her room and begins to admonish the stranger of the consequences of entering her bedroom. The gradual progression of her words to the intruding man are carefully organized, poignantly describing the helpless state in which a woman is placed in a society where rape is not a recognized crime and where the victim is blamed for the offense, and where fathers, brothers, and husbands cannot be counted on for help. She begins with respectful words addressing him as sir, and tries to put on a show of strength by listing her men and their power. The order in which they are invoked is itself interesting in that it follows the order of their status in the family. First, King Janaka (it would have been the father-in-law Dasaratha had he been alive), and then Rāma, and then her husband. It is very significant that she refers to her husband not directly, but in a roundabout way—"my older sister's younger brother-in-law." (But in my translation I preferred a less roundabout form, "my sister's brother-in-law.") Of course, her husband Lakṣmaṇa is Sīta's younger brother-in-law. In upper-caste families, women do not refer to their husbands directly and even at a time of grave danger Urmila follows propriety. She knows very well that neither Rāma nor Lakṣmaṇa are at hand to save her, and as far as she knows they are still in the forest. There is no way a sleeping Urmila could know the recent events in the palace. Apparently nobody has cared to wake her up and give her the good news of her husband's return. They have practically left her to her fate. What follows is a mood of helplessness and despair.

> "My great family's name is tarnished now, helpless me, what can I do?
> The famous family of my birth is blemished, helpless me, what can I do?"

It is a familiar story: the family is scandalized when a woman is raped. The victim does not even have the freedom to suffer for herself; she has to bear the guilt of bringing her families—the one into which is married, and the one in which she is born—into disrepute.

Urmila takes a different tack, that of intimidating the attacker by reminding him of the horrible fate men who have desired other people's wives have suffered. First is the story of Indra. He desired sage Gautama's wife Ahalya, and went to bed with her by taking on the appearance of her husband. The sage catches him red-handed and curses him to wear a thousand vaginas on his body. Then comes, very interestingly, the story of Rāvaṇa who kidnapped Sīta in the forest and in the end lost his kingdom and his life in a battle with Rāma. One would of course wonder how Urmila came to know of this. She is fast asleep when these events are taking place in the forest. This extreme anachronism does not seem to bother the poet. It is a good story, and a powerful weapon in the hands of a woman to ward off a rapist, too good to be left out for reasons of linear chronology. Then follow the usual pleas for sympathy. Doesn't the rapist have a mother and a sister? Would he wish that they suffer a similar tragedy?

Let us remember that Urmila is still sleeping. Even in her sleep, she knows that she is vulnerable, an existential condition of women in general in this society. One may imagine that all her words are well rehearsed in her subconscious many times before she could reel them off, even in her sleep.

Now comes an even deeper layer of her subconscious. Lakṣmaṇa tries to tell her that he is her husband. But note, he never uses the word "husband"; this culture does not allow him to do so. He finds a circuitous route to identify himself, as his wife did when she had to refer to him earlier in the song. He is Rāma's brother, Sīta's brother-in-law, Janaka's son-in-law, and so on. What is totally mind boggling is how Urmila responds. A devoted wife and a properly behaved daughter-in-law of a noble family totally trashes every family relationship. She has never heard of Rāma, she does not know who on earth Janaka (her father) is nor does she know Sīta.

How to interpret this bizarre conversation? Let's remind ourselves again that Urmila is talking in her sleep. Is this the real Urmila, who is free from the burdens of life as a wife, and the shackles of family, free to speak for herself? Has she harbored deep resentment against all the folks who have kept her under proper family rules of behavior expected from a good daughter-in-law, depriving her of freedom and joy, and making her utterly helpless? She is the lowest on the totem pole; her father has abandoned her, giving her in marriage to a young man who has no backbone to stand up for his or his wife's interests. The big man Rāma did not even care to know if she exists or not. Sīta, her senior in the hierarchy of palace women, who has negotiated and won her own freedom to follow her husband to the forest, did not give a second thought to Urmila, her own sister. She could have advised Rāma not to stop Urmila from following her husband to the forest. Clearly, everyone in the family left her as dead. Urmila is painfully aware of the cruel politics of a family which pretends that all is well. She has every reason to be resentful of these folks. It is only under the freedom of deep sleep that she is able to give expression to her repressed anger, which she would never be able to do when she is awake and obliged to behave properly. It is common knowledge in India that women give vent to their anger against the senior and respected members of the family in states of hysteria, when they are possessed, or when they are otherwise sick. This altered state gives them the alibi of a different persona, which allows them the perfect mask to speak their mind.

Lakṣmaṇa tries shock treatment: He breaks the news that Sīta was kidnapped in the forest and that they had to fight a battle with Rāvaṇa to bring her back. The strategy does not work, and Urmila does not move. Lakṣmaṇa makes a pathetic appeal. You are the woman I married, and if you don't accept me I lose my good name in the world. Totally counterfactual, this statement attracts our notice. It is common knowledge that women who are left by their husbands get a bad name in this culture, but never the other way around. Apparently, women want a world in which men get a bad name (*apa-kīrti*) as well, when they are rejected by their wives, and they represent their wish in this song. But let us hear Lakṣmaṇa some more.

Lakṣmaṇa repeats his identity as Sīta's younger brother-in-law and urges her to kindly wake up from sleep. This is a message that he has understood her anger and that he does not mind the words spoken in sleep, and he does not hold them against her.

Lakṣmaṇa keeps on talking to his wife to convince her of his love. He could not live any longer if she does not accept him; he has not eaten or slept since he left her (which is true)—the kind of words women love to hear from their husbands.

Finally, when a crying Lakṣmaṇa takes his sword and is ready to kill himself, Urmila wakes with a start and sees Lakṣmaṇa for who he is—and falls at his feet, as a proper wife should. He picks her up and wipes her tears. Urmila still voices her grievance, this time politely, like a proper wife, but in an accusing tone all the same:

> "My father was naive in giving me to you," she said.
> "He didn't know the truth. He thought you were a proud man
> and was blissfully happy for you. But in fact,
> you have your mind elsewhere, you belittle your own wife."

A strong indictment indeed. Lakṣmaṇa is a weak husband, incapable of protecting his honor, and furthermore he does not even love his wife. He cares more for his elder brother and his wife and has no qualms humiliating his own wife.

Lakṣmaṇa understands the gravity of Urmila's feelings and feels sincerely sad for her. He reiterates his love for his wife and repeats the things he has said to her while she was asleep. He wants to make sure she hears him fully awake. He swears he did not sleep or eat and stayed alive all these fourteen years only for her. He resorts to the idea of fate to explain what had happened—they must have caused the separation of some innocent couple in a previous life, and they have paid for it now in this life; the result of past karma is inescapable, and anyway he is not the only one to blame.

The rest of the song is all a happy story of family reunion, a delightful picture of harmony, fun, and joy—things women love.

Urmila for once is the center of attention, the heroine of the day. She and her husband are bathed and dined in a celestially beautiful dining room and the sisters-in-law tease her lovingly. The family humor of women, particularly familiar in Telugu families, adds a gentle touch of love and affection to the song. Sīta (and we can imagine, also Māṇḍavi, and Srutakīrti as silent partners, even though they are not mentioned in the text) takes Urmila's side and Śānta is on the opposite side as the joking parties are formed.

Śānta is a relatively unknown character in Vālmīki's text, but as Rāma's sister she has a fully developed role in women's Rāmāyaṇas. A husband's sister, called *āḍapaḍucu* in Telugu kinship terms, has a role that could smoothen the transition of a bride from her parents' family to the parents in-law's family. As a woman she can be closer to the bride than her own husband, and almost always belongs to the same age group as the bride. She can also be a mild authority figure since she is closer to the husband; she is his sister, she grew up in the same family as he did while the new bride is from a different family. A Telugu proverb says that a sister-in-law is half a husband (*āḍapaḍucu ardha mŏguḍu*). She is potentially capable of making or breaking the relationship of the new bride and her husband. The new bride fears her more than the husband and worries if she is on her right side or not. She dreams of a sweet sister-in-law as much as she fantasizes about a loving husband, because a difficult sister-in-law can cause trouble for her while a friendly sister-in-law can be a source of great comfort. In this context, an affectionate and friendly role for Śānta in the women's songs is easy to imagine.

Also, in the joint family culture, a wife never accepts that she has attracted her husband by her beauty, and often rejects being described as attractive. If we follow the course of the banter, we see that the first remark Śānta makes is about Urmila's beauty. It is so seductive that jealous people could cast an evil eye on her. Śānta proposes an offering to cast off the evil eye and protect Urmila's beauty.[2] Sīta quickly but politely (*vinayamuto*) retorts that the honor should belong to Rāma and his brothers who make the whole world fall in love them. They are ruling kings, they are handsome like Indra the king of gods, and Candra, the moon—the most handsome among gods—the ritual of casting off the evil eye should done for them. But Śānta is not done yet. Haven't the four sisters—Sīta, Urmila, Māṇḍavi, and Srutakīrti—cast a spell of beauty on her four brothers? Sīta again has a quick response. Śānta is no less skilled at the game of love. She has charmed a virgin sage Rṣyaśṛṅga, living in the forest innocent of a woman's touch. (It may be recalled that Rṣyaśṛṅga, a unicorn figure in the Rāmāyaṇa, grew up in the forest knowing only his father and had never seen a woman.) Note that Sīta refers to Rṣyaśṛṅga as her brother, that being how it works in the Telugu kinship chart of an extended family: A sister-in-law's husband is a brother.

Now comes the bedroom scene. The description is again very familiar to Telugu listeners and a staple in older Telugu movies—the soft and inviting bed, the bedside items of fragrances, aphrodisiacs, and mild narcotics such as betel leaves and areca nuts.

A fan made of *vaṭṭivellu* (dried fibrous roots of a plant which are used to make fans and which emit a pleasant fragrance when they are sprinkled with water) is put in place for the couple to fan each other.

The doors are closed and the couple are alone with each other. The song moves to describe some of the most delicate moments of the couple's love life. The wind brings the fragrance of *campaka* flowers and jasmine. The couple is sitting on the bed. Lakṣmaṇa loosens Urmila's long hair tied into a bun, and skillfully braids it. He decorates the braids with jasmine and *jāji* flowers, something he is very good at. A very gentle touch indeed, and perhaps one of the rare fantasies of women who hardly have their husbands doing such womanly things for them. As they sit chewing betel, Urmila asks about Sīta's capture by Rāvaṇa. Apparently she did hear when Lakṣmaṇa broke the news to her while she was sleeping.

Now she wants to know the complete story, a blow-by-blow report of the events as they happened. The most important thing she wants to know is how it is that when Lakṣmaṇa, who was a warrior like a lion, was present, Sīta could be abducted. Right at this moment the poet informs us that Kausalya, Sumitra, Kaika, and Śānta—all the senior members of the family—are seated, on raised seats, very silent. They are listening in and keeping an eye on the goings-on in the bedroom. So much for the privacy of the new couple in joint-family households. But, unaware of the spying elders, Urmila continues her line of questioning, repeatedly asking how, when great warriors such as Lakṣmaṇa and Rāma were around, Sīta was carted off by the demon Rāvaṇa.

What follows is a short retelling of the central story of the Rāmāyaṇa, one from Lakṣmaṇa's point of view. The nuances of what is included and what is left out make the retelling very significant and make you want to listen to it, even though it is a story everyone knows. The narrative begins with a rationalization that it was all fated to happen the way it happened. No one is to blame, except Time, the ultimate maker of events. Lakṣmaṇa gently reiterates the point that he entreated "mother Sīta" not to ask him to go when the magic deer cried out Sīta's and Lakṣmaṇa's names. (A subtle touch here is that Sīta's name is also included. The standard Rāmāyaṇas tell us that Marīca, who came in the form of a magic deer, cried out only Lakṣmaṇa's name.) Just as gently he includes the point that Sīta said words sharp as arrows, without going into the details. He relates that he had drawn a line around Sīta and commanded that no one should cross it, and that Rāvaṇa took Sīta away by breaking the very earth on which she stood. (This is what the southern Rāmāyaṇas tell, as opposed to Vālmīki's version, which describes Rāvaṇa taking Sīta away by lifting her up with his hands under her buttocks.) Lakṣmaṇa takes care to tell that he recognized only the anklets among Sīta's jewels.[3] He is implying that, as a good brother-in-law, he has only looked at her feet, not upon the rest of her body. And it was he who made the fire for Sīta to enter. He rejoiced that the fire was cool like a lake to the supremely chaste Sīta. Sīta was pure and therefore came back to Rāma. And then the poet tells us that Lakṣmaṇa told Urmila "all the troubles they had suffered in the forest."

As we come to the end of the song, we move out of the bedroom, into the women's circle of Urmila's sisters. They talk among themselves about what Rāma did to Sīta, "Now you have heard what kind of a mind our Man with the Wheel has." The word used "*buddhulu*" is a gentle reproach. They know that's where they have to stop. No severe protests, only a general word resignation: "What's the point in worrying about the past." They are happy now, Rāma is on the throne.

The title the singers give to the song is "Urmila's agony in separation." And the text says at the end that Lakṣmaṇa bestows the world of Viṣṇu to whoever sings or listens to this song.

This is a song of Urmila and Lakṣmaṇa, but more significantly, this is song of about women, about how they feel and think. Rarely do we have, if ever, a Rāmāyaṇa where female subjectivity is presented with the sensitivity and empathy that we find here. The sensibilities, the interiority of the characters, the representation of a subconscious, and the attention given to the neglected "subaltern" characters of the mainstream Rāmāyaṇas makes the song very much a modern song. It makes you wonder if modernity in India began only in the late-nineteenth and early-twentieth century, as is commonly claimed, or much earlier, like in the late fifteenth century—as my collaborators, David Shulman and Sanjay Subrahmanyam and I, have been arguing for some time.

Notes

1. The meaning is unclear. Singers whom I could consult were not able to decipher the meaning.
2. Evil eye, *diṣṭi*, derived from skt. *dṛṣṭi*, A ritual to cast off the evil eye is to take a pungent substance, such as red chilies, or water in which calcium and turmeric are mixed to make it dark

red, and turn it round the face in an anti-clockwise direction. The term used in the text is *nilāla nivvāḷulu*, meaning an offering of water which is turned around the face, in the anti-clockwise direction to ward off the effects of the evil eye.

3. A detail that deserves our attention here is that Sugrīva gave the jewels to Rāma as a gift "because he was Kausalaya's son,"—a touch attributable to the woman poet who composed this song.